# ONE WEEK
## LOAN

This book is due for return on or before the last date shown below.

*Also by Chris Ryder*

THE ULSTER DEFENCE REGIMENT: AN INSTRUMENT
OF PEACE?

CHRIS RYDER

# The RUC 1922–2000

## *A Force under Fire*

ARROW

Published in the United Kingdom in 2000 by
Arrow Books

1 3 5 7 9 10 8 6 4 2

First published in the United Kingdom in 1989 by Methuen London
First paperback edition published 1990
Revised 1992, 1997
This revised edition published 2000 by Arrow Books Limited
The Random House Group Ltd
20 Vauxhall Bridge Road, London, SW1V 2SA

Random House Australia (Pty) Limited
20 Alfred Street, Milsons Point, Sydney,
New South Wales 2061, Australia

Random House New Zealand Limited
18 Poland Road, Glenfield
Auckland 10, New Zealand

Random House (Pty) Limited
Endulini, 5a Jubilee Road, Parktown 2193, South Africa

The Random House Group Limited Reg. No. 954009
www.randomhouse.co.uk

A CIP catalogue record for this book is available from the British Library

Papers used by Random House UK Limited are natural, recyclable
products made from wood grown in sustainable forests. The
manufacturing processes conform to the environmental regulation
of the country of origin.

Printed and bound in Great Britain by Cox & Wyman Ltd, Reading, Berkshire

ISBN 0 0994 1099 0

# Contents

List of Illustrations                                      vii
List of Abbreviations                                      ix
Introduction                                              xiii
Preface to Previous Edition                                xv

 1 'Extraordinary People'                               1
 2 Barneys, Peelers and Specials                       13
 3 War and Peace                                       50
 4 Descent into Disorder                               96
 5 The Wee Man                                        136
 6 'Wall-to-Wall Interrogation'                       187
 7 Drinks, Dames and Debts                            226
 8 'Popularity Is Not My Business'                    273
 9 In the Eye of the Storm                            309
10 A Most Damaging Episode                                 344
11 'A Bright Future'                                       373
12 'The Silence of the Guns'                               411
13 Days like This                                          439
14 Waiting for Patten                                      479
15 A New Beginning                                         499

Index                                                      527

# Illustrations

1 Sergeant Instructor Tom Ashfield, 1940s
2 RUC constable in Londonderry, 1980s (Pacemaker)
3 Examining a lorry at Balmoral, 1922 (*Belfast Telegraph*)
4 Road barrier on the Fermanagh-Monaghan border, 1922 (*Belfast Telegraph*)
5 Newtownbutler Specials, 1922 (*Belfast Telegraph*)
6 C Specials, Belfast, 1922 (*Belfast Telegraph*)
7 Sir Charles Wickham
8 Sir Richard Pim
9 Funeral of Constable Henry Ross, 1958 (*Belfast Telegraph*)
10 Digging a road barrier on the Derry–Letterkenney road, 1958 (*Belfast Telegraph*)
11 Brookeborough RUC station, 1958 (*Belfast Telegraph*)
12 Sir Albert Kennedy
13 Anthony Peacocke
14 Sir Arthur Young
15 Sir Graham Shillington
16 Petrol bomb attack, Londonderry, 1969 (*Belfast Telegraph*)
17 RUC in riot gear, Londonderry, 1969 (Pacemaker)
18 Inspector Devlin's body being removed from the bombed police station at Chichester Road, Belfast, 1971 (Pacemaker)
19 Constables William Forster and Samuel Cairns, awarded Queens Medals for Gallantry, 1976
20 Sir Kenneth Newman with senior RUC officials and army officers at the funeral of Constable Hugh McConnell, 1978 (Pacemaker)
21 Sir Jamie Flanagan
22 RUC policewomen searching shoppers in Belfast (Pacemaker)
23 RUC casualty of the Londonderry Civil Rights disturbances, 1978 (Pacemaker)

24 Victim of rocket attack Constable Michael Paterson, 1981 (Pacemaker)

25 RUC Birches station, Armagh, after the bomb attack in 1985 (Pacemaker)

26 The RUC using plastic bullets during rioting in Londonderry, 1981 (Pacemaker)

27 Rioting in Belfast when Sean Downes was killed by a plastic bullet, 1984 (Pacemaker)

28 RUC search around Dunloy, County Armagh, 1984 (Pacemaker)

29 RUC officer on border guard duty (Pacemaker)

30 The RUC removing barricades on the Loyalist Day of Action, Shankill Road, 1985 (Pacemaker)

31 The RUC and the army on the streets after rioting in Belfast, 1986 (Pacemaker)

32 The smouldering wreckage of Lisburn Road RUC station, Belfast, 1986 (Pacemaker)

33 Andersonstown RUC station, West Belfast (Pacemaker)

34 The RUC in riot gear at the funeral of Laurence Marley, Belfast, 1987 (Pacemaker)

35 The funeral of Constable Clive Graham, 1988 (Pacemaker)

36 Sir John Hermon with GOC Lt-Gen. Lawson at RUC headquarters (Peter Dunne)

37 Ronnie Flanagan, appointed Chief Constable in 1996 (Kelvin Boyes)

# Abbreviations

| | |
|---|---|
| CID | Criminal Investigation Department |
| DMSU | Divisional Mobile Support Units |
| DPP | Department of Public Prosecutions |
| DUP | Democratic Unionist Party |
| GOC | General Officer Commanding |
| INLA | Irish National Liberation Army |
| IRA | Irish Republican Army |
| IRB | Irish Republican Brotherhood |
| IRSP | Irish Republican Socialist Party |
| PIRA | Provisional Irish Republican Army |
| RIC | Royal Irish Constabulary |
| RUC | Royal Ulster Constabulary |
| RUCR | Royal Ulster Constabulary Reserve |
| SDLP | Social Democratic and Labour Party |
| SPG | Special Patrol Group |
| UDR | Ulster Defence Regiment |
| UFF | Ulster Freedom Fighters |
| UUAC | United Ulster Action Council |
| UVF | Ulster Volunteer Force |
| UWC | Ulster Workers' Council |

*For Ciara*

# Introduction

This is the fourth edition of *The Royal Ulster Constabulary: A Force under Fire* and it has been updated to take account of the Belfast Agreement of April 1998 and the comprehensive report of the subsequent Independent Commission on Policing in Northern Ireland, which was chaired by Chris Patten, and published in September 1999.

If the agreement can, at last, be fully implemented and the threat of terrorism convincingly lifted, the way will be clear for a new beginning to policing with a routinely unarmed, high-technology, close-contact, non-aggressive, community-based Northern Ireland Police Service replacing the RUC.

After nearly eight decades, the RUC is not being dismantled or disbanded. Instead it is to be reorganized and restructured, welding its unique courage and expertise into a new framework more closely designed to meet the demands of policing the deeply divided society that is Northern Ireland.

Even if the fragile peace and the uneasy Republican and Loyalist ceasefires fail to consolidate, and the RUC is once more faced with policing conflict, much progress can still, and must, be made in redefining the relationship between the police and the policed, putting the divisive controversies of history into the past and creating a new era of co-operation with the police from all sections of the community.

Above all, Unionist and Loyalist politicians must finally understand that while they have a right and a duty to oversee the conduct of the police, and call them effectively to account, they do not enjoy an exclusive or proprietorial relationship with them. Similarly, Republicans and Nationalists must come off the fence and change their traditional anti-police mindset, work actively with them to deliver an effective service and encourage young people to come forward and serve in the police so that it is truly representative of the entire community.

However events unfold, the year 2000 promises to be significant, demanding and uncertain for the courageous men and women of the Royal Ulster Constabulary as their future role is ultimately decided by parliament. My limitless admiration for the professionalism of the RUC is undiminished and I am confident that, as they have done in the past, they will meet these new challenges, innovatively and effectively, for the benefit of all the people of Northern Ireland. The alternative 'policing' offered by those who resort to violence and intimidation is still entirely unacceptable.

My thanks for their unstinting help and frankness in understanding the RUC are due to the Chief Constable Sir Ronnie Flanagan, Assistant Chief Constable Alan McQuillan, Detective Chief Superintendent Eric Anderson, Chief Superintendent Roy McCune, Superintendent Kevin Sheehy and, particularly, Chief Information Officer Dave Hanna. Other members of the RUC, and Alan Burnside, the public relations adviser to the Police Federation, are also due my gratitude for their co-operation with my additional research. As before, however, the views expressed in the book are mine entirely.

Chris Ryder
Portavogie, Co. Down
October 1999

# Preface to Previous Edition

In advance of the Royal Ulster Constabulary's sixtieth birthday in 1982 there was an official attempt by some of its members to write its history. However, the more people who saw the draft, the more alterations were made to it. It seemed a classic example of the old saying that a camel is a horse designed by a committee. In the end the attempt was abandoned.

Since then the force and the RUC historical society have been collecting relics of RUC and Royal Irish Constabulary history, and the Northern Ireland Police Authority has appointed an archivist, all with the aim of preserving material to produce a definitive history some time in the future. The objective cannot be achieved in the short-term, for many of the official records concerning the early days of the RUC have been closed for seventy-five or a hundred years and their release will have to be awaited before the RUC itself or independent academics and historians can fully analyse the birth or role of the police in Northern Ireland's troubled history.

Journalists, like myself, accustomed to providing the immediate, rough draft of history, can, however, offer an interim version, based on the available material. And that is what I have tried to do. Having first-hand acquaintance with many of the most recent figures and events enhances the importance of recording the material for future reference. I know that when dealing with such a controversial subject, my conclusions will provoke some people and please others. I accept that as a professional hazard and I especially hope that those who helped me in various ways will accept my sincerity, even if they disagree with me.

In writing this book I have been motivated by a limitless admiration for the valiant men and women of the modern RUC. They represent all that is best about the good people of Northern Ireland and they are truly the cement that holds the divided community together. In saying that, however, I believe that no mature society should give its police a blank cheque, and that proper accountability and safeguards are essential for both the police and the community. In the particular circumstances of Ulster this is crucially important.

In recent years I think the RUC has increasingly proved itself to be an impartial police force, tackling terrorists and criminals without fear or favour and, when necessary, plucking the bad apples from its own ranks. The lack of reprisals by the RUC, despite all it has suffered, is a remarkable testimony to its integrity. In these circumstances those in the minority community must reassess their attitude to the force. Catholics cannot for ever call on the RUC to protect them without sharing the attendant risks. Whatever shortcomings they perceive in the RUC, whatever inadequacies it contains, can be more effectively addressed and changed from within by minority participation in both the police and the Police Authority, which needs to do far more to abandon its anonymity and secrecy to act more effectively as a bridge between the police and the community. There is much to do. The risk of threat and intimidation must be confronted, particularly by the minority community. Setbacks, no matter how tragic, must not be allowed to stop the process.

For all the people of Ulster, the alternative to the RUC is quite clear – the reign of terror imposed by the IRA and the UVF, and like-minded pseudo-military organizations, who masquerade as protectors of the community when, in reality, they corrupt and exploit it. Their kangaroo courts, self-appointed thuggery, kneecappings, racketeering and other brutalities are a grim advertisement for the sort of society and values they would impose and tolerate if they ever gained political power.

Those who have been prepared to kill and die for Ireland or Ulster have left a terrible legacy. Yet the situation in Ulster is not without hope of bequeathing one infinitely more worthwhile. Although it may be of little or no consolation to present generations whose lives have been blighted, there will be a better tomorrow. By the long yardstick of Irish history, progress towards a more stable society is being made, albeit slowly and at a terrible price.

There are many people whose assistance was vital in researching and writing this book, and in listing those who follow I apologize for any inadvertent omissions. Because this is not an official account of the RUC's work and history, and I received neither help nor encouragement from the force, many of my sources in the RUC would not thank me for publicly acknowledging their advice and information, especially one detective sergeant who was unjustly disciplined for providing me with information, which he did not. Nevertheless, I owe substantial gratitude to Sir Jamie Flanagan, Sir Kenneth Newman and Sir John Hermon for their background briefing over the years. Alan Wright of the Northern Ireland Police Federation, a man of whose quality the RUC and Northern Ireland is fortunate to have, is also owed much for his help. Dave Hanna, Bertie McCaffrey, Herbie Norris and others at the FCIC over the years have also helped me within the bounds, with good grace, honesty and frequent conviviality.

Jim Hamilton among others at the Northern Ireland Office, and members of staff at the army headquarters in Lisburn, have found no request for help too trivial to ignore.

Richard Ford and Paddy Devlin have not only been good friends but wise sounding-boards. So too were ex-Chief Superintendents Bill Mooney and the late Bill Wilson, who gave me much appreciated advice – although I did not always heed it. I must also mention the admirable Joe Mounsey, who proved what a great detective he was by getting so much right.

Bob Colhoun, Paddy McAndrew, the late Mick Slevin and others too numerous to mention gave much of their time and, frequently, their gin, to teach me a lot about the intricacies of policing, while Michelle Slack of *Police Beat*, Bruce Hill, David Gilliland, Alan Burnside and Tom Rainey all helped in many different ways. Walter Macauley, the unbeatable librarian at the *Belfast Telegraph*, and Edward Ryder assisted considerably with the research. John Kennedy and George Woodman, at the library in Stormont, also extended their facilities, which I found useful.

I must also thank the staff at the Public Records Office in Belfast for their help and permission to refer to public documents and include extracts from the Regan manuscript.

Anne Tannahill at Blackstaff Press was most obliging in giving permission to quote from 'Voices and the Sound of Drums' by Paddy Shea and to draw on Paddy Devlin's 'Yes we have no bananas'.

I also want to record my appreciation of past encouragement by Harry Evans, John Whale and Del Mercer when at the *Sunday Times* and now to Max Hastings and Jim Allan at the *Daily Telegraph*.

Finally I must thank my agent, Anthony Goff, the editor of the manuscript, Ann Wilson, and the staff at Methuen, most of all Ann Mansbridge, who kindly tolerated an overlong gestation period and then masterminded a speedy schedule to produce the book in record time.

Chris Ryder
Belfast, 1988

Whence does this mysterious power of Ireland come? It is a small, poor, sparsely populated island, lapped about by British sea power, accessible on every side, without iron or coal. How is it that she sways our councils, shakes our parties and infects us with her bitterness, convulses our passions and deranges our action? How is it that she has forced generation after generation to stop the whole traffic of the British Empire in order to debate her domestic affairs?

**Winston Churchill**
House of Commons, 15 December 1921

# 1

# 'Extraordinary People'

On the afternoon of 14 February 1988 more than 1,000 people crowded into St Anne's Church of Ireland Cathedral in central Belfast. Common threads of grief and loss bound them together, for they were the fathers, mothers, widows, children and former colleagues of the 252 members of the Royal Ulster Constabulary who had lost their lives in the political violence that has disfigured Northern Ireland since it was established in the early 1920s. (Before the year was out another six RUC officers had become victims of the terrorists.)

They were there on that sombre winter Sunday to remember their loved ones and to see the Duke and Duchess of York dedicate a stained-glass memorial window. It now stands at the head of the stairs in the Northern Ireland Police Federation building at RUC Garnerville in Belfast and depicts the figure of a uniformed constable superimposed on the outline of the Northern Ireland coast and boundary, with a montage of landmarks from each of the six counties. There is the façade of the Londonderry Guildhall; the Giants Causeway; the crest of the city of Belfast; the Bessbrook viaduct with the silhouette of the Mourne Mountains; a Fermanagh lakeland scene at Devenish Island and the distinctive old Dungannon police barracks, which is popularly believed to have been constructed to a Khyber Pass design after a mix-up over plans. The coats of arms of the Royal Ulster Constabulary and the Police Federation complete the illustration.

At the service of dedication the Archbishop of Armagh, Robin Eames, said that for those left behind to grieve, the memorial window, a photograph on the mantelpiece or a service certificate on the wall would never be a real substitute for a voice, a face or the grip of a hand. His words were a poignant reminder of the human sacrifice made by the members of the RUC, and their families, in the task of policing Northern Ireland's perplexed and divided community. They are indeed, in the words of chief constable Sir John Hermon, 'extraordinary men and women doing an extraordinary job'.

Interpol figures, published in the *International Criminal Police Review* in 1983, showed that Northern Ireland was the most dangerous place in the world to be a policeman. The risk factor was twice as high as in El Salvador, the second most dangerous. The policeman's lot in Northern Ireland is exacerbated by the fact that the murder of a policeman is rarely incidental to the crime – as it is in nearly every other country; hatred of the police is all too often the primary purpose of the crime itself.

Nevertheless, night and day, 365 days a year, the 12,800 men and women of the Royal Ulster Constabulary perform their duty. They never know what danger there may be at the other end of a 999 call; where a landmine may be planted in the path of a mobile patrol or if a sniper might have his sights trained on an officer walking the beat. They have to be as much on alert at home as on duty, for many have been ambushed at or forced from their homes by the terrorists.

In running the risks of policing Ulster not all the RUC victims have paid with their lives. Over the last twenty years some 8,000 members of the RUC have suffered injury. There are few that have not received cuts, bruises and fractures in the disturbances that are an everyday hazard. For the majority the wounds have healed but others have paid a more permanent price, some just short of death. Today throughout Northern Ireland there are many ex-members of the RUC coping with the hardships of losing limbs or sight or hearing. Their plight is inevitably shared by their families.

On 4 May 1973 Constable Jim Seymour, from Bristol, an ex-Royal Navy man who had married an Ulster girl and joined the RUC two years earlier, was on duty at Coalisland police station. That evening, as he was opening the gate to admit a police Landrover, an IRA sniper, under cover of darkness, fired a number of shots. One of the bullets embedded itself in Jim's head. He was taken to a local hospital where he remained for twenty-two years, completely paralysed, slipping in and out of consciousness. Nobody knew if he could understand or even see the television that the nurses put on when he was what they called awake. When his wife called, as she did every day, he could not talk or communicate. His children, a son and daughter, were aged fourteen and nine at the time of the shooting. They grew up with the aching burden of his twilight existence constantly hanging over them until he died in March 1995.

Ex-Sergeant Noel McConkey is another man who has paid a terrible price for his nine years' service in the RUC. On 19 December 1978, forty-five minutes before his shift was due to end and he planned to go off to organize a children's Christmas party, he spotted a suspicious looking Vauxhall Viva car in a side street in West Belfast. He described what happened next to the Northern Ireland police magazine, *Police Beat.*

I did all the usual checks. It wasn't a stolen car. We positioned the crew around the car and I proceeded to check the car myself. There was nothing strange about it apart from the fact that it wasn't taxed, no wires, nothing. One of the wheels was parked on a [drainage] grid and at that stage bombs under manhole covers were fairly common so we checked that but there was nothing there.

As I came round the car the second time I noticed on the back of the wall beside it a downspout and saw that a hole had been cut in it. As I saw it the penny sort of dropped with me and I thought – this is it, time to get out of the road. So I backed away from the wall. The boot of the car was about two feet from my left-hand side. I was just backing off and telling everyone to get out of the way when someone detonated the bomb, knowing that if they didn't do it then they were going to get nobody.

It was all in slow motion, just like it shows in reconstructions on television. I can remember the process of falling in slow motion, not the actual hitting the ground. Obviously it doesn't happen in slow motion but seems to inside your head. I remember thinking, this is what it feels like to be dead.

Then I bounced off the ground and I knew I was in big trouble. It was like getting run over by an invisible train. It just rolls over the top of you starting at your feet and knocks you down. I was lying there roaring, screaming, effing and blinding. I felt like I was doing that but don't really know if I was or not.

I knew my arm was very, very sore and knew that I was in big trouble with it but I couldn't actually get my head off the ground to see what was going on. The blast came out of the boot of the car and went back over the top of the car up the street again. A guy standing at the door of the Landrover up the street saw my arm fly past him.

I thought to myself, thank Christ my feet are still there, because I was able to see the cap of my boot. My foot was there at that stage but the leg had been blown away. My left foot was in such a mangle that they had to cut it off the next day.

Immediately after the thing went off one of my crew came and started beating me around the head with the big coat we used to have. I lay there thinking, 'What the hell are you hitting me over the head for? Am I not bad enough lying here?' He was putting out the flames. I was burning and didn't know it. The blast took all of my hair, eyelashes, eyebrows, nothing left.

People were shouting, 'He's dead, he's dead,' and I'm lying there thinking 'Who?'

I remember seeing a red blanket and a grey blanket on the stretcher and thinking I was in trouble. The grey blankets only come out when they are scraping you up. I didn't feel any great pain and didn't know that my legs weren't there. I was still conscious when I arrived at hospital. As far as I'm concerned when they closed the doors on the ambulance, I thought I'll close my eyes here and go for a wee snooze until I get to the Royal [Victoria Hospital].

I knew that I was in trouble but I wasn't panicking and couldn't move anyway. When the doors were shut the daylight went out and I went out.

At the hospital a team of surgeons and nurses worked for nine hours to save his life:

My wife was told the only thing she could do for me was to pray. They didn't think that I would survive coming out of the recovery ward. I was then put into intensive care where they didn't think I could get through the night, but I did and after that it was a case of keeping me alive until after Christmas – for the sake of the youngsters. The biggest one was seven and the other five at the time.

It's a question of fighting to stay alive. There's this feeling that you're being sucked towards a big black hole and what you're doing is fighting to stay away from it.

He was unconscious for four weeks but then as the slow recovery process went on, the time to confront the extent of his injuries arrived.

It didn't really hit me for a while. When you start to come round they start to pump you with morphine to keep you calmed down and whilst on the morphine you maybe only have lucid half-hours. The more they take you off, the more lucid you become. They don't actually tell you about your injuries. You have to ask. The theory of it is that whenever you ask, you are ready to hear the answers.

When I asked and was told the extent of my injuries, I asked 'Does my wife know?' I was told 'yes' and I said 'Well, that's alright.' That was it. There was no great shock horror, my legs have gone. I don't know if there's any great coming to terms with your injuries – you've no choice.

Altogether he spent a year in hospital, having operations on his injured ear drums and throat, and learning to walk again on artificial legs. Two years after the incident he was medically discharged from the RUC and accepted a job as a communications assistant at a police station. It was a very reluctant option.

I was well aware when I joined the police of what could happen and often thought that it would eventually. I served for nine years before the explosion. Even though I'm now out of the police longer than I was in it, it has taken a long time to get the police out of my system. It's very, very hard to shake off. Probably harder for me because I went back to work in a police station.

By the end of my two years on the sick [leave] everybody was fairly well aware that had I been allowed to stay in the police, my next move would've been to sit the inspector's exam, and what would they do with you then? The fact that I feel I can do a station sergeant's job is getting more frustrating and the further I get away from the police, the more frustrating that becomes.

If I was put face to face with the people who did it I would shoot them. Because someone watched from a distance and detonated the device. I have no individual to direct my feelings towards. Some of those involved are undoubtedly dead now. I'm sort of disappointed that they didn't have twenty years in jail first. I'm not religious and can't forgive. I want to be in court when those involved in my case are brought in. I don't think my feelings will diminish with time. In fact the older I get the worse I'll get, which is maybe not a good thing.

Frank Murray is another man who illustrates the unique qualities of the RUC to overcome even the most dreadful injuries. On 7 July 1975 he was given information about a weapons hide in the countryside near Portadown. In fact he was lured to where a booby-trapped gun exploded when he lifted it. As Murray lay bleeding, critically injured from the loss of an eye, an arm and a leg, his partner, Detective Sergeant David Davidson, himself suffering from severe stomach injuries, stumbled and crawled three-quarters of a mile in darkness to get help. It was not an easy task. A frightened motorist drove on at the sight of him in torn clothes and bleeding. Several houses he knocked at refused to help and when he finally got through to the police they were reluctant to come to his assistance, fearing an elaborate lure.

Eventually help turned up and Murray, still conscious, was removed to hospital. He recalls part of the ambulance journey, saying that when he rolled over going round the corners he knew he had lost his limbs. Nobody gave him much chance of survival but Murray, with the encouragement of his wife, fought back and survived. When he left hospital seven months later he had come to terms with his false eye, arm and leg, and his first action was to order a specially adapted automatic car to give him back independent mobility.

He had wanted to be a policeman since he was ten years old and all through his spell in hospital he was determined to resume police duty. Not only did he do so, but he has since won promotion twice, first from detective chief inspector to superintendent and then to chief superintendent. The promotion was genuinely earned, not in a token inside desk job, but in a demanding post, commanding operations in one of the most dangerous patches in Northern Ireland.

There are many equally inspiring stories of courage and commitment to be found inside the RUC. On 25 April 1974 an 800 lb proxy car bomb was abandoned in Newtownbutler, County Fermanagh. Police officers trying to clear the area met considerable opposition from a group of people under the influence of drink. One of them walked towards the bomb for the third time and was pursued by two members of the RUC. As they were forcibly removing him from the vicinity, the bomb went off. The drunken civilian lost part of one leg, above the knee. One of the policemen also lost a leg and suffered severe injuries to his other leg and head. The second policeman was also seriously hurt. Both were later decorated for their devotion to duty and disregard for their own safety.

Clearing people from the path of bombs is a common source of both the maiming and bravery of police officers. In Lisburn a constable suffered multiple injuries, including the loss of an arm, in May 1974 when a bomb exploded while he was trying to clear part of the town. Thirty-nine other people were injured in the blast. In September 1986 a police constable in Downpatrick lifted a bomb from outside a crowded pub and carried it 80 yards to a field where it exploded harmlessly. Two constables carried two elderly ladies from their first-floor flat in February 1976, moments before a bomb, which had been planted directly underneath, exploded.

At the height of the morning rush hour on 31 January 1972 police identified a large van, containing a bomb, which had been abandoned outside a department store in a narrow street in Belfast city centre. As the confined area was being cleared, a sergeant was informed that a person was still in an office near the bomb. Without hesitation he ran past the van and into the building. As he ushered the man out, there was a huge explosion. Regardless of his own safety the sergeant threw himself on top of the man, protecting him from the force of the blast and shrapnel. The man was uninjured but the sergeant received a serious head wound. The constable who had discovered the bomb was also gravely hurt but despite receiving injuries that necessitated the later amputation of his leg, he continued to use his radio to relay information from the scene and alert the emergency services. For their disregard for their own safety both officers were awarded the BEM. (The sergeant, James Hazlett, was later murdered outside his home by terrorist gunmen.)

On 23 March 1972 after calls of a bomb warning and a fruitless search of several locations in Carrickfergus, police identified a suspicious Mini car parked in a narrow street with homes and shops. At great risk to his life a sergeant established that there was a bomb in the car and together with five constables made urgent efforts to clear the immediate area. As they were doing so the device went off, injuring seventeen civilians as well as the police officers. Despite their own condition the officers remained at the scene and searched all the wrecked buildings until every person had been accounted for. The sergeant was awarded the BEM for gallantry, the five constables were given the Queen's Commendation for brave conduct.

Many more officers have acted equally selflessly during bomb scares or shooting incidents, disregarding the dangers in order to clear people from risk areas or pull the injured to safety, frequently under continued gunfire or defying the risk of further explosions. There are countless other examples of officers coming to the aid of more seriously wounded colleagues. In Tyrone in 1974 one police-man risked his life further to reach a police car and radio for assistance after two colleagues had been shot dead and a third gravely wounded in a terrorist ambush. In another case in South Armagh in 1972, two undercover officers were seriously wounded in an ambush by gunmen. Despite his severe pain and serious wounds the driver managed to reach the police station two miles away before collapsing, undoubtedly saving his own life and that of his colleague. Both were given the BEM for gallantry.

Indeed officers on duty in Northern Ireland never know what they will encounter every time they are tasked to answer a call and what demands it will place on their skills and nerves. In February 1973 a sergeant was taken hostage in a strong-room by four armed terrorists during a bank raid in Belfast, but he persuaded them to surrender without a struggle.

Many RUC bravery stories cannot be told for security reasons. Disclosing details, senior officers fear, could help terrorists pinpoint informers in their own ranks or, from gaining knowledge of police methods, evade detection or capture in the future. Many plainclothes officers on surveillance duties or in the Special Branch, handling sources and informers, have acted with such resourcefulness and skill that major terrorist operations have been blown, stocks of terrorist arms and explosives captured and dangerous individuals apprehended. Countless terrorist attacks have been foiled and lives saved, not only in Ulster but in other theatres for Irish terrorists like the Irish Republic and Great Britain, by the RUC's professional skills.

The record of awards to the RUC for bravery and gallantry, unequalled in war or peace by any other police force, reflects the unique and selfless courage of the force. In the last eighteen years members have been awarded: 15 George Medals, the highest award for courage possible in peacetime; 85 Queen's Gallantry Medals; 86 Queen's Commendations for brave conduct; 48 Queen's Police Medals; and 145 British Empire Medals. In addition a substantial number of members have been awarded the MVO (2), CBE (3), OBE (17) and MBE (67) in both the Birthday and New Year Honours Lists. In a unique achievement in February 1979, sixteen officers were decorated in a single list of gallantry awards, six receiving the George Medal, five Queen's Gallantry Medals and five Queen's Commendations for brave conduct.

In August 1988 Woman Police Constable Alison Johnston lost an eye and received limb and facial injuries when terrorists exploded a radio-controlled bomb at a petrol station where her police patrol was checking what was clearly a bogus report of a burglary. She had only been in the police force for eight months, having spent several years previously as a resident social worker dealing with deprived and disturbed children. For Alison, and many public-spirited young men and women like her, the continued violence is no deterrent to joining the RUC. Even after twenty years of trouble there is no shortage of potential members. In 1987 alone there were 4,872 applications for 246 vacancies in the Regular Force and more than 6,600 people tried to get one of the 600 posts in the RUC Reserve.

With such demand for posts in the RUC, the force can impose the most rigorous selection standards to ensure that only young people of the highest integrity, public spiritedness and potential are admitted. This is important, for with no signs of an emerging consensus in Ulster about how the community is to be governed the RUC seems destined to have to continue impartially to hold the ring between the two sides well into the foreseeable future.

The RUC, the second largest police force in the British Isles, costs £1 million a day to operate and is organized and run to the standards laid down by the British government for every other police force in the United Kingdom. The only concession that is made to the abnormal situation it faces is that all members of the RUC are paid a special Northern Ireland allowance, presently £1,211 per year before income tax, and carry arms, on and off duty.

At the 1988 dedication service, Dr Eames summed up the RUC's contribution to ensuring public tranquillity in Ulster. 'Do not let us ever forget that so many duties taken for granted in any other community must be performed here under the constant threat of terrorist action. Society asks of its police so much without always recognizing the cost of what it is asking.'

Although the Catholic Church was represented at the service, by the lone figure of the notably ecumenically minded Canon Hugh Murphy, the absence of higher powered Catholic delegates reflected a historical hostility to the RUC. This went back to the RUC's birth, out of the turmoil and excesses of the Irish war of independence when the six counties of Northern Ireland were partitioned from the rest of the island.

The legitimacy of the Northern Ireland state that was founded in 1922 was disputed, then and since, by nationalists of the minority Catholic community, who increasingly felt themselves to be second-class citizens under the heel of an unfair Unionist ascendancy. The Unionist majority, always distrustful that Britain would ultimately protect it from being swamped in a Roman Catholic-dominated Irish state, tried to secure peace of mind by adopting measures to dominate the minority and prevent it from getting any grip on the levers of power. The RUC was thus given a dual role: to protect the new state from armed subversion, internally and externally; and to provide a service of more routine law enforcement. So, although many Catholics served in the force, some with distinction, the RUC was never a conventional, community-based police force in the mould of the friendly British 'bobby'.

Memories of the violence surrounding the formation of the state and its responsibilities as a state defence caused Catholics to see the RUC more vividly as the armed wing of Unionism and from the outset this damaged its relationship with the minority community. In practice there was little hostility to the police as individuals when they were carrying out their other role as law enforcers but the lack of consent, so vital for a police service in a free society, was a corrosive factor. By contrast the majority community, Unionist and Protestant, regarded the RUC as 'our' police and cherished them as its defence against the IRA and any drift to a united Ireland. The fact that the police operated emergency legislation almost exclusively against the minority and sided with the Protestants in any confrontation endeared them further to the majority community as strong defenders.

Nevertheless for forty-five years the politically directed and supervised RUC, obsessively concerned with subversion of the Unionist government, subdued the festering rivalry between the two sides and any challenges to the uneasy peace were quickly extinguished. But the inevitable crunch came in 1968, when the Catholic minority, fortified by education and fired by the civil rights movement in the United States, demanded equal treatment between majority and minority. The Unionists at first tried to crush the gathering revolt, using the RUC as its sledgehammer, but in barely eight months the force was exhausted and overwhelmed by the scale of the disorder.

In August 1969, after the 'Battle of the Bogside' – three days and nights of furious street rioting and petrol bomb attacks in Londonderry – the RUC was forced to withdraw to barracks and British soldiers had to be deployed to restore order. It was the same story in Belfast, where entire streets had been burned down in vicious sectarian clashes which intensified after indiscriminate machine-gun fire from RUC armoured vehicles had killed several people. There too soldiers had to go in to contain the situation.

The 1969 collapse marked the end of the first phase of policing history in the province. With troops on the streets, aiding the civil power, the British government, which had turned a blind eye to Ulster for almost half a century, was reluctantly forced into direct action. An English police chief was drafted in to implement a series of reforms designed to disarm the RUC, divorce it from political direction and bring its outdated training and practices into line with the more enlightened police forces on the British mainland. But before these second phase reforms could be fully implemented, the Provisional IRA emerged from the mists of history, hijacked the civil rights cause and through a terrorist campaign of unprecedented viciousness re-opened the whole Irish problem and plunged the RUC once more into the front line.

The future of the RUC became a major political issue in the early 1970s and remains so now, twenty years after the start of the conflict that has become Britain's unending and thankless Vietnam. Now in the third phase of Ulster's policing history, a modernized and greatly expanded RUC, with the continued help of the British army, has reduced the level of violence to a tenth of what it was a decade earlier. But as the province rests on what security chiefs are now calling the 'plateau of violence' there is no sign of permanent peace or political stability in Northern Ireland. The IRA still plants bombs, shoots its opponents, murders members of the security forces on and off duty and causes economic and social disruption and terror. Extreme Ulster Loyalists still carry out sectarian murders and prepare for what they call 'doomsday' – the day they believe Britain will withdraw from Ireland and leave them at the mercy of the IRA.

The effects of this turmoil are by no means confined to Northern Ireland. Irish terrorists have killed an MP within the precincts of the parliament at Westminster, and by bombing the Grand Hotel at Brighton in 1984 have come within an ace of assassinating virtually the entire British cabinet, the most serious attack since Guy Fawkes's gunpowder plot. British soldiers and diplomats abroad in Europe have also been assassinated, while Ulster Loyalist terrorists have carried out atrocities in the Irish Republic.

The entire concept of an open society in Britain has been redefined, initially because of the Irish threat, later because of the growth of international terrorism. The British royal family and government members now live behind a screen of smart-suited, discreetly armed bodyguards. They travel in bomb- and bullet-proofed limousines.

Their palaces and residences, like parliament, have become armed fortresses bristling with electronic and other protective devices. A new genre of anti-terrorist architecture, to make fortifications aesthetic, has been born. The unarmed British 'bobby' has become a thing of the past.

In the process of pacifying Ulster and heading off the effect of the IRA campaign, the RUC became the most skilled anti-terrorist and innovative police force in the world, and their techniques and expertise, which have been studied and copied by police forces internationally, made them the model for the rapidly changing style of tougher conflict policing throughout the rest of the United Kingdom.

Today, a new, professional RUC stands, impartially and politically independent, between the two communities in Ulster. The following chapters tell the remarkable story of a force under fire, tracing its origins from the Royal Irish Constabulary to the controversies and tragedies of the present day.

# 2

# Barneys, Peelers and Specials

The foundations on which the Royal Ulster Constabulary was built in 1922 and some of the traditions that it inherited can be traced back more than a hundred years to Sir Robert Peel, the scholarly son of a wealthy Lancashire mill-owner, who was later to become a reforming prime minister and one of Britain's most important statesmen. When he arrived in Dublin in 1812 as the new Chief Secretary of Ireland, the country was in a state of rampant lawlessness. How Peel tackled the problem was to create the model for modern policing systems not only in Ireland but in Britain too. To this day his crucial role is commemorated in the largely affectionate nicknames 'Bobbies' and 'Peelers' which are widely applied to the police.

For most of the hundred years before his arrival a plague of rival oath-bound secret societies had imposed a reign of terror on rural Ireland. One of the most feared of these mainly peasant-based groups was the Whiteboys, who waged war on the landlords and tax collectors and who took dreadful reprisals on anyone who attacked its members. Other groups had names like the Rightboys, Ribbonmen, Thrashers, Peep O'Day Boys and Levellers. One was called the Carders from its habit of slashing the backs of its victims with wire brushes used to card wool.

Although most of them were motivated by agrarian grievances some, especially from the north of Ireland, had a sectarian tinge. Whatever their motivation, however, their crimes were remarkable for their brutality. They would descend on property and plunder food, arms and money before burning it and either killing or stealing the livestock. Anyone who got in their way was mutilated, raped, abducted or shot. Those who dared give evidence against the attackers were singled out for special treatment. A man who had testified against the organizers of one secret society was later taken from his home, beaten to a pulp with stones and then pitchforked on to a dungheap. His wife was shot through the temple with a pistol.

Peel, whose aim was to 'enforce the common law of England in Ireland', was so disturbed by one case that he took a personal interest in it for many years. It concerned a man called Dillon, whose evidence against some Whiteboys had led to their execution. To avoid the inevitable reprisal he stayed away from his County Limerick home for some time but one night, soon after his return, about a dozen men with pitchforks turned up and dragged him from his bed. As they speared him to death outside, his wife threw turf on the fire and urged her fourteen-year-old daughter to study and remember the faces of the men when they came in again for her. The young girl then watched by the firelight as her mother fought until the men overwhelmed her and dragged her outside, where they killed her beside the body of her husband.

Although the neighbours ostracized the girl, the killers were brought to justice through the diligence of a local clergyman and the girl's evidence of identification. Nine were hanged, the other four transported for life. When the case was brought to Peel's attention he interested himself in protecting the clergyman and the girl from reprisal. Through his good offices a living was found for the son of the brave clergyman, who had also joined the Church, and the girl was apprenticed to a milliner, received a £50 dowry from the government on her marriage and emigrated to make a new life in India.

Responsibility for law and order at this time rested principally with the baronial constables, appointed under a 1787 Act which stipulated they must be Protestants. For the 'Old Barneys', as they were better known, taking their name from a noted wag, Constable Barney McKeown, 'old' was indeed the operative word. They consisted mainly of pensioners appointed by the magistrates and, while they were capable of serving writs or officiating around the courthouses when the courts were in session, whenever there was any real trouble the military had to be called on to contain it.

Peel, however, had few military to call on. Since his arrival in the country most of the Irish garrison had been withdrawn to fight in the Napoleonic campaign. Peel was anyway opposed to the idea of using soldiers to enforce the public peace. Their frequent use in that manner, he told parliament, made the people look upon them as their adversaries rather than their protectors. So, with the full support of the Lord Lieutenant, the senior British representative in Ireland, Peel proposed to set up a country-wide police force which could move into disturbed areas and provide some effective muscle to restore public tranquillity, as it was described.

The cabinet in London baulked at what was then the highly radical concept of a police force. There were fears that it would interfere with accepted standards of personal liberty. It was not the first time essentially English values were wrongly applied to an Irish problem. Nevertheless, Peel used his considerable tact and succeeded in getting the bones of his proposals passed by parliament. In the process his original Police Bill had tactically become the Peace Preservation Act 1814.

Peel's philosophy, enacted in the new law, was to create a new breed of salaried magistrate who would serve as a stranger in a district, thus breaking the cycle of patronage. He would have a body of salaried constables under his control and when a troubled area was 'proclaimed', they would move in to restore the peace. The cost of their operations was to be borne locally by a levy – but for deterrent as well as economic reasons. To bypass the conduits of patronage Peel sought his magistrates among the officers of the army and his constables from the non-commissioned ranks.

The first Peace Preservation force was deployed in the barony of Middlethird in County Tipperary on 6 September 1814, when a superintending magistrate and a force of twenty constables, all discharged cavalry sergeants, were sent in. In no time it had a marked effect on the level of disorder.

Over the next few years the forces enjoyed much success on the ground where they were brought in. However, some local magistrates refused to proclaim areas in order to save the expense and in other cases the force was expected to get quick results for the same reason. To take account of this, especially to benefit the poorer areas of the country, Peel persuaded parliament in 1817 to change the financial arrangements so that at least some of the policing cost could be defrayed by central government in appropriate cases.

Peel wanted to extend the role of the peace forces by establishing a permanent barracks and detachment in every county and by setting up a corps of magistrates to command them. None would serve in their home areas and the men would be moved round the country periodically in a conscious move to circumvent patronage. But opposition from politicians and magistrates, who rightly saw it as removing their powers, together with inability to find sufficient numbers of suitable candidates to become magistrates and constables, forced him to shelve the plan. Nevertheless, by the time Peel left Ireland in 1818, taking his ideas and the lessons he had learned about their practicality to influence the setting up of the London Metropolitan Police in 1829, it was established as policy that there should be a unified, non-military Irish Constabulary.

This step was taken in 1822 but the fierce opposition of the Irish MPs at Westminster caused the government to drop plans for central control. Under the Irish Constables Act, each barony was to have a force of sixteen constables commanded by a chief constable. There would also be four inspector-generals, one for each of the four provinces, Ulster, Leinster, Munster and Connaught. It was envisaged under the Act that the force would grow to an establishment of 313 chief constables and 5,008 constables. The lack of central control constituted the main weakness in the new policing system and the standards of application of the law were not universal owing to the autonomy vested in each of the chief constables.

Despite its notable efficiency this overwhelmingly Protestant County Constabulary was identified with the landowners and gentry, and thus failed to win the consent of the predominantly Catholic peasantry. The ongoing campaign for Catholic Emancipation and against payment of tithes to the Established Church aggravated this division and led to such trouble in some places that Peace Preservation forces had to be sent in. Seventeen policemen, including the chief constable, were killed in one vicious encounter in Carrickshock, County Kilkenny, in 1831.

Thomas Drummond, Under-Secretary of Ireland, with an informed and sympathetic insight into the problems of Ireland, was charged with further reforming the policing arrangements. Under his 1835 Constabulary Act, a single force for the area outside the cities of Dublin, Belfast and Londonderry was set up. (In 1864 Belfast was included in the national police net after its local watch, known as the 'Bulkies', had been unable to cope with serious sectarian rioting, and six years later Londonderry followed suit. Dublin, however, retained its own metropolitan force until 1921.)

Commanded by an inspector-general, directly responsible to the Chief Secretary and the Lord Lieutenant, the Irish Constabulary was charged with consistent law enforcement throughout the country. By 1867, when Queen Victoria granted the 'Royal' prefix to the Irish

Constabulary and its harp and shamrock crest, for putting down an organized rebellion by the Irish Republican Brotherhood, it had become established as a major feature of Irish life, with some 1,600 barracks dotted strategically about the countryside and some 11,000 constables.

Command was exercised from Dublin Castle, the seat of British power in Ireland, by the inspector-general, who had a deputy and several assistants. The basic division was the county and each was supervised by a county inspector. Each county was subdivided into a number of districts, each headed by a district inspector, who was assisted by a head constable. Depending on the local circumstances, there were a number of stations in the district, usually with a sergeant and four constables, but sometimes more.

The non-commissioned personnel, mainly recruited from the Catholic tenant-farming class, were not allowed to be posted to their home areas or anywhere with which they had an association such as relatives, and they were rotated regularly, consistent with continuity of local knowledge. This was designed to keep them immune from local patronage or influence and indeed the RIC jealously guarded its independence from local authorities of all kinds, including the magistrates who once had such influence over the police. It was said at the time that it was the ambition of every farmer to have a son to carry on the farm, with another in the clergy or in the police or sometimes both.

It was a rigidly disciplined force. There was no official system of duty, rest days or annual leave. Constables were required to remain in the barracks at night. Marriage was out of the question unless the man had at least seven years' service and his bride passed the vetting of the RIC authorities. Even then, the force manual prevented her from moving in unauthorized social sets, keeping fowls or entering the greengrocery trade. Members of the force were even banned from voting at elections in case of the slightest whiff of political favouritism. Officers were also ordered to maintain a horse, although it was laid down that keeping racehorses was an offence meriting instant dismissal.

This regime was strictly enforced by an officer class, district inspector and above, which remained overwhelmingly Protestant. Vacancies were filled equally by promoting head constables who had progressed through the ranks and by cadet officers, who were commissioned as district inspectors. There was some discontent at the latter among the men, who believed it narrowed the opportunities for promotion, although the cadet officers, usually well educated young men who had been unable to make a military career, were generally more popular and respected.

The RIC, through the constables, soon ingratiated itself into the fabric of a rapidly developing and gradually less turbulent society. By the end of the nineteenth century sectarian passions had cooled and reform had enabled many tenant farmers to buy land. In rural areas especially, where there were few people with any education, the help of the local constable was frequently enlisted to write or read a letter or fill out a form. This enabled them to get to know the community and virtually everything about the affairs and history of every family on their patch.

Other official duties superimposed on their responsibility to maintain law and order required them to act as Inspectors of Weights and Measures, Food and Drugs, and to compile agricultural statistics, which was a time-consuming task for the officers assigned to it. All of these additional duties gave further access to the workings of the community and increased the intimacy of the RIC's knowledge. It was this access that provided the flow of detailed intelligence to the Castle about the state of the country.

In a few disturbed counties in the west the force also acted as a gendarmerie, protecting landlords and their agents, and persons taking over evicted farms, from outrage by the peasantry. In an unpublished memoir, lodged at the Public Record Office in Belfast, John Regan, who served in both the RIC and RUC, where he attained the rank of county inspector, recalled the heyday of the force:

The force, as a force, was not popular, more especially in the west and south. It was, with perhaps some reason, regarded as a landlord's force. Parties of police lived in the houses or out-houses of landlords and their agents to protect their lives and property. They lived in the houses of emergency men, men who had taken the post of caretakers of evicted farms, and farmers who had rented such farms, for the same purpose.

Large bodies of police had attended at evictions in the days before land purchase came into being and it was no unusual sight to see a couple of police, armed with rifles, cycling after obnoxious persons when they journeyed away from home.

While these duties inevitably made the force unpopular and it was regarded as being the eyes and ears of Dublin Castle, the individual members of the force were respected figures of substance in their local areas. Throughout its lifetime this was the case, although its unpopularity clearly soared and subsided when times were troubled or more tranquil. Regan recalled:

Poorly paid as they were, graft was unknown. He would be a brave man who dared to offer a member of the force a tip for some service rendered – a thing I saw happen in police forces on many occasions elsewhere. They were proud and had a standing in the community.

I have never seen an RIC man depicted on the stage, even in plays produced by those with little regard for them, as waiting at back doors, or in the kitchen, to be handed a piece of pie or a sandwich by a servant girl, a scene not unknown in plays embracing members of other forces. They invariably married good class girls – school mistresses, farmers' daughters, etc, and although poor, held their heads high.

Law enforcers are by implication never going to be popular anyway, but Regan thought that there existed in the Irish of every class an aversion to complying with the law.

Irish people seemed to lack the civic spirit of the Englishman, and whether from moral cowardice or good nature never would, if possible, incur the ill will of their neighbours or friends by assisting the officers of the law against them. It was not only a matter of dislike for the law in general. In the case of ordinary crimes like larceny, housebreaking, etc. (which were few in number) there was some chance of getting evidence, but in that of crime connected with land disputes, or indeed family disputes, it was practically impossible. The people had their own way of dealing with them and vendettas were not by any means unknown.

I always pitied the unfortunate tramp. He never had any friends in the place, and the public often became most helpful in assisting the police in such a case, while local magistrates, who would never convict anyone they knew, would show their high regard for law and order in sending the unfortunate tramp to gaol for a couple of months for something quite petty.

The RIC ethos was first laid down in 1837 when Drummond published the Constabulary Code of Regulations. One of its most significant decrees was that the force should wear a uniform of rifle-green, a tradition maintained by the RUC. The standards set by the Code and the rigid disciplinary structures that were the hallmark of the force were drilled into recruits at the central depot at Phoenix Park in Dublin, first established in 1839.

Run on military lines by the commandant and his staff, the training laid much emphasis on drill, weapon handling and learning chunks of the law by rote. In 1822 the RIC had adopted the Light Infantry fast march – 140 steps to the minute – and as regimental march, 'The Young May Moon', an appropriately paced Irish jig. The depot contained an officers' mess whose grand furnishings and fine silver inspired awe in many of the officer cadets from modest backgrounds and abroad. Over the years the depot also trained several hundred officers for police forces in other parts of the British Empire.

Such was the reputation of the RIC depot that in 1907 the Colonial Office decreed that henceforth all commissioned rank police officers for the colonial forces would be trained in Dublin. The RIC had already become the model for policing in several parts of the empire. Its position in the mainstream of Irish life seemed invincible but sinister forces were already at work, plotting in the background.

All through the 1800s the British administration constantly feared an uprising to secure Home Rule in Ireland. The fear dated from the 1790s when Wolfe Tone tried to unite 'Protestant, Catholic and Dissenter' to break the connection with England. Tone had vested much hope in a French invasion to help drive the British out but in 1796 the plot was aborted when gales stopped the French ships putting the invasion force ashore. Another rebellion in 1798 was brutally suppressed. But the fear of outside help lingered on and during Peel's time in Ireland there were anxieties that the French would once again aid the Irish rebels in fomenting revolt.

The fears turned out to be groundless but in the latter half of the century a new source of potential foreign assistance emerged. Many of those who had survived the devastating Irish famines in the early 1800s, when one million died, had emigrated to the United States, where they continued to blame British exploitation for the disaster and nurture hopes of an Ireland freed from Britain. A number of groups, notably the Irish Republican Brotherhood, sprang up to pursue this aim. Fenian bombers, with the help from Irish-American sympathizers, carried the fight for Home Rule to Britain itself and between 1867 and 1885 there were a number of explosions throughout the country. In March 1883, after devices went off at *The Times* newspaper office and outside a government building in Whitehall, the Royal Irish Constabulary was asked to provide a detachment of officers to guard the nerve centre of government in central London. Before long, armed constables, in their distinctive, rifle-green uniforms, were posted throughout Whitehall. About the same time the government ordered the Metropolitan Police to set up a team of detectives to track down the Fenian dynamiters. So the Special Irish Branch, later the Special Branch, was born.

Back in Ireland, the Fenians and others in favour of Home Rule were just as active. One group, the Invincibles, gained much notoriety in 1882 when they murdered Lord Frederick Cavendish, the Chief Secretary for Irish affairs, and the Under-Secretary, Thomas Burke, in Dublin's Phoenix Park. They had been hacked to death with surgical knives. In 1867 a Fenian uprising was thwarted when the RIC infiltrated the rebels and arrested the ringleaders.

The Home Rule cause, promoted by Charles Stuart Parnell, continued to gather steady support and in a general election in 1885 Home Rule candidates won 85 of the 103 seats in the Westminster parliament. The Conservatives had 249 seats and the Liberals 335 so the Irish members had the balance of power and therefore a strong bargaining position to achieve their demand. A convinced Home Ruler by conscience, William Ewart Gladstone, adroitly balancing statesmanship and the Liberals' political interest, conceded the case for Home Rule and became prime minister. But the Bill was lost by 32 votes the following year when some members of his own party rebelled.

In Ulster the prospect of Home Rule had triggered off a fierce reaction among the largely Protestant population and the most serious of a series of sectarian riots in Belfast, which lasted all summer, from June to September. After one previous bout of disturbances in 1864 the Belfast police force, the 'Bulkies', was disbanded and responsibility for policing the city was vested in the Irish Constabulary.

The terms of the Bill granted Dublin only a limited degree of autonomy. As far as policing was concerned, the RIC would have remained answerable to the London government, although it was envisaged that, after two years, control of the affairs of the Dublin Metropolitan Police would pass to the new two-tier Irish legislature. For the longer term a new system of police forces accountable to the Irish authorities had been discussed.

Gladstone eventually got his revived Home Rule Bill (with similar policing provisions) through the House of Commons in 1893 after an acrimonious struggle but it was defeated in the House of Lords. Home Rule remained on the political agenda as the century turned but when the 1905 Liberal government did not need to rely on the Irish vote in parliament there was no immediate pressure to concede the demands of the Irish members.

In Belfast, where Home Rule was regarded as inevitable, the Protestant majority, largely descended from the Scots settlers who had first planted Ulster, were bitterly opposed. They feared it was the first step to independence and poverty, after which they, as only a quarter of the population, would be an oppressed minority submerged in a Catholic-dominated state. 'Home Rule means Rome Rule,' a popular slogan at the time, summed up their feelings. In March 1905, the cause of Irish Unionism effectively became Ulster Unionism, with the formation of the Ulster Unionist Council, which was to lead the anti-Home Rule campaign. If they could not stop it, they would at least limit it, by keeping north-east Ulster, where they were in a majority, ruled from London.

In 1910, after a general election, the parliamentary arithmetic once more left the Liberals dependent on the votes of the Irish members to form a government. The Home Rulers predictably pressed the claim for a new Bill as the price of their support for keeping the Liberals in power. Most notably, they voted with the government in pushing through an Act, passed in 1911, removing the House of Lords' ability to veto Commons' legislation.

They got their Bill in 1912 when, for the third time in just over twenty-five years, the House of Commons was asked to grant a measure of independence to Ireland to run its own affairs. After a protracted debate in the Commons the Bill was passed in 1913. When the lords considered it they exercised their right, under the new 1911 Act, to delay it coming into force. However, the outbreak of the First World War intervened and although King George V signed the Bill into law in September 1914, it was agreed that the Act would not be implemented until the end of the war.

By then, in Belfast, there had been militant stirrings of discontent against Home Rule. The distinguished Dublin-born lawyer, Sir Edward Carson KC, who was renowned for his withering skills at cross-examination, had become leader of the Unionist Party in 1910. Soon afterwards, at a mass rally of 100,000 people, Carson said that if the Home Rule Bill was passed, Ulster would ignore it and form its own provisional government.

In 1911 the Ulster Unionist Council had expanded to 370 members and had become the umbrella organization to oppose Home Rule. In September 1912, in another impressive demonstration against the Bill, a Solemn League and Covenant was signed by 218,206 men throughout Ulster. Some signed in their own blood rather than ink. At the same time women were invited to sign a Declaration of Support and 228,991 did so. Four months later, as a further sign of intent, the wealthy landed gentry and the business community, working through the Ulster Unionist Council, financed the raising of an armed militia from among the signatories to the Covenant. They called it the Ulster Volunteer Force, which soon reached its target of 100,000 men.

Within a short time the UVF was openly drilling throughout the province although at first its men had only brush shafts or wooden replica arms. Training camps were set up by some of the gentry on their estates and cavalry units were even formed in a few areas. Some more enterprising members began to acquire and smuggle in real arms; cars and vans were commandeered to increase the effectiveness of the force, and women and others were mustered as first-aiders and stretcher bearers. Before long they were effectively armed with 30,000 rifles and 3 million rounds, run from Germany into Larne Harbour by Lt-Col. Fred Crawford in April 1914, with the active approval of Carson and the other Unionist leaders.

The London government could only look on powerlessly as the scale of the Ulster defiance increased. A month earlier, in March 1914, a group of British army officers based at the Curragh, near Dublin, had jointly pledged that they would resign rather than act against the Ulster Unionists. Many senior army officers in London supported them, including General Sir Henry Wilson, an Ulsterman who opposed Home Rule and supported the formation of the UVF. Ulster would fight and Ulster would be right, Carson had said, and it seemed nobody in London was prepared to challenge him.

In July, King George V called a conference at Buckingham Palace to try to resolve the crisis. Partition dominated the proceedings, with proposals for four of the nine Ulster counties to be excluded from Home Rule and possibly Tyrone and Fermanagh as well, but the conference reached no consensus and ended after three days.

With the outbreak of the war, the Home Rulers as well as Carson and the other Unionist leaders willingly accepted that the Home Rule Bill be postponed from taking effect until the war was over. The Unionists in fact urged the UVF to show national solidarity with Britain and the Empire by taking up arms. The Ulstermen, reinforced by thousands of volunteers from the south of Ireland, willingly went off to war. Their finest hour came on 1 July 1916 at the Somme in France when the 36th Ulster Division bore the terrible brunt of an offensive against the Germans, suffering 5,000 casualties and winning four Victoria Crosses in a single day. Unionists regarded the sacrifice as a demonstration of the loyalty of Ulster to the Crown and Empire.

Despite the willingness of a large number from the south to fight and die for the Empire, there had been growing dissent about the scope of Home Rule on offer. In November 1905, a grouping had been formed by Arthur Griffith, a Dublin journalist and printer, who advanced his ideas in a small political paper called *The United Irishman*. For them Home Rule did not go far enough. They wanted nothing less than full Irish independence from Britain. Griffith called them Sinn Fein – 'ourselves alone'.

About the same time, some of Griffith's supporters were involved in reviving the Irish Republican Brotherhood, first formed in 1858. It soon reached a membership of about 1,600 in Ireland with support groups in both Britain and America. In 1913, concerned by the raising of the UVF and the Larne gun-running, members of the Brotherhood played a key role in forming the Irish Volunteers and in April 1914 partly emulated the Larne operation by smuggling 900 rifles and 29,000 rounds of ammunition bought in Germany through Howth near Dublin.

Working on the basis that England's difficulties with Germany were Ireland's opportunity, a number of members of the Brotherhood were the prime movers in forming a secret military council towards the end of 1915. It had one objective, to plan a nationwide uprising. Over the final months of that year and early in 1916 they sought German support through Sir Roger Casement, planned to raise an Irish Brigade from prisoners of war captured by the Germans and drew other sympathetic groups into their plan. Among the tactics they adopted was the forging of orders from Dublin Castle ordering the suppression of the Irish Volunteers, a ruse to anger them into unequivocal support.

The Rising was set for Easter Sunday, 23 April 1916, but had to be postponed for twenty-four hours when several crucial elements of the plan went wrong. Casement was captured after being put ashore in Ireland from a German submarine and a British navy patrol intercepted the ship carrying the arms for the rebellion from Germany, causing the German captain to scuttle. Nevertheless, at noon, a day late, a bunch of armed men mostly in civilian dress chased people out of the General Post Office in Sackville (now O'Connell) Street, Dublin, where they took over the building and posted a proclamation declaring the creation of an Irish Republic.

After a week of violence, virtually limited to central Dublin, in which some 500 people died and 2,500 were wounded, the rebels were rounded up in an operation commanded by General Sir John Maxwell, who had rushed to Dublin to take command of the situation. As they were led away to prison, they were jeered by many of the population. But as the government inquest into how the intelligence system failed and Dublin Castle was caught napping got under way, the public mood rapidly changed when fifteen of the rebels were executed in quick succession between 3 and 12 May. One of the prisoners, James Connolly, was so badly wounded that he had to be tied to a chair to face the British firing squad.

Michael Collins, one of those transported to Wales when the rising ended, was released in December 1916 and quickly became a prominent figure in reorganizing the Brotherhood and the Irish Volunteers. Collins had correctly identified British infiltration and foreknowledge as the reason for the failure of previous rebellions and in great secrecy he set about constructing a network of agents in high places sympathetic to the Republican cause. At the same time he created teams of what today we call hit-men to carry out a new type of hit-and-run terrorist warfare against the British forces.

To be effective, Collins realized that he required a flow of hard, accurate, inside information. To provide it he recruited sources in every walk of life. By piecing together scraps of information about the times of special trains, the docking of ships or the booking of hotel rooms, breaches of security could be planned. He even had post office clerks who would intercept mail or leak the contents of coded telegrams. His preparations were so thorough that undercover members of the Brotherhood were either recruited or placed in Dublin Castle itself and other members were delegated to join Sinn Fein and position themselves to fight elections.

Public revulsion at the executions and widely condemned British proposals to extend military conscription to Ireland helped to prepare the ground for a new Republican onslaught. This time it was not going to be a grand frontal rising to drive the militarily superior British into the sea but a relentless effort to finally break their capacity and will to govern.

The political circumstances which created the right conditions for Collins' carefully thought out campaign developed at the end of 1918 when the old Home Rule politicians were routed by a Sinn Fein landslide in a general election; Sinn Fein won 73 of the 103 Irish seats. On 19 January 1919, instead of taking their places in London, those of the newly elected Sinn Fein members who were not imprisoned met in Dublin and declared themselves to be the first Dail Eireann – the parliament of Ireland.

The same day, at a remote place called Soloheadbeg, three miles from Tipperary, one of Collins' new-style 'flying columns' ambushed a two-strong RIC party escorting a load of gelignite to a quarry. The constables were shot dead by the rebels, who escaped with their weapons and the explosives. Collins had identified the RIC as the cement that held the British presence in Ireland together. The ambush at Soloheadbeg was the first declaration that they were to be neutralized as the opening step in the campaign for independence. It was the beginning of the end for the RIC but the decline that allowed them to become so vulnerable had set in some time before.

By the early 1900s the RIC had become an Irish institution and a policing inspiration for further afield. Where Britain formed police forces in the colonies worldwide, the RIC was always used as the model. But the advent of Home Rule had punched a hole in the motivation of the British administration in Ireland. The will to govern had been replaced by an attitude of holding on.

When the RIC reported that the IRB was re-grouping, the normally sensitive intelligence analysts at the Castle failed to heed the warning signs. Their reaction was a symptom of the malaise that had set in. The official report into the Rising also criticized the police, especially the urban-rural division between the RIC and Dublin Metropolitan Police. The new Chief Secretary, Henry Duke, remarked on the failure of the authorities to detect what was being planned and said that having seven independent agencies involved in gathering intelligence was not efficient.

As the arrangements for Home Rule envisaged the Irish raising tax revenues locally, London tightened the purse strings on the Irish vote and the RIC inevitably suffered. It was a measure of the grudging financial priority the force was given when in 1908 a proposal for six new baths to supplement the three baths then serving 500 men at the RIC depot had to be debated by parliament at Westminster.

RIC efficiency and morale was an early casualty. The strength of the force had been allowed to fall steadily from a peak of 14,500 in 1883 to just under 9,500 at the time of the Rising. The roots of the decline of the RIC can therefore safely be traced back to Gladstone's concession of the principle of Home Rule. As the administration in the Castle atrophied, there developed a perception inside the force that it had no long-term future under Home Rule despite what the various Acts envisaged.

Further debilitating factors were the low pay, which had been stagnant for years, and slow promotion, which was influenced in many cases more by freemasonry than merit. No wonder that by the early years of the century recruitment had fallen away and resignations were soaring. In 1915, soon after the start of the war, things were so bad that the government was forced to bring in a Bill to stop the exodus from the force. The only way to leave was to join the military. For the duration of the war resignations and retirements were outlawed.

Individually, the men had always been treated shabbily, taken for granted indeed. Half of them were from farming stock or labourers. One senior officer had said arrogantly that they liked to take men 'right from the plough, they are slow but steady'. They were subjected to relentless, frequently petty, discipline and bureaucracy. Every morning there was drill at each barracks, with a formal inspection at least monthly. Once a year each man had to fire twenty-one shots, seven from each of three prescribed positions, as a certification of his continued marksmanship. The completed target, with the required accurate bullet marks, was enclosed in his personal file. In 1918 the *Constabulary Gazette* summed up the policy as 'using two men for one man's work and underpaying both'.

Earlier in 1916 the *Gazette* had reflected the growing disillusionment in the force by likening the RIC 'to a noble mansion of the early Victorian era, still occupied but showing visible signs of decay'. The situation stimulated a serious debate within the force about its future role. The contradiction between its military style and the need for a civil police more in tune with the changing times was realized by many. Some of the more far-seeing members feared the political situation that was fast developing as the momentum towards independence built up and the consequences for the RIC of the inevitable conflict of loyalties that would ensue.

It is not surprising that there was a move in 1918 to form a representative body to fight for better conditions. But Sergeant Thomas McElligott, the founder, was forced out of the RIC a year later for his active promotion of Sinn Fein views. He then became a valuable source of information to Collins' burgeoning army of sources.

As the divisions in the country between north and south and Catholic and Protestant deepened after the Rising, it became ever more uncomfortable to be a member of the RIC in the middle of the shifting ground. The Soloheadbag attack in fact marked the beginning of what is called the War of Independence. Dan Breen, the man who led the attack, said later: 'Our only regret was that the police escort had consisted of only two peelers instead of six. If there had to be dead peelers at all, six would have created a better impression than a mere two.'

At this point the emphasis was on concerted murder bids on the force and there were regular raids by armed men on the isolated barracks dotted around the Irish countryside, in an effort to break the grip of the Castle on the country as primarily exercised through the RIC. Throughout 1919 and 1920 the campaign, chiefly against the RIC, continued with ruthless efficiency.

The IRA did not have it all its own way, however. In May 1920, in a notable incident at Kilmallock Barracks, in County Limerick, a sergeant and ten constables held off a five-hour gun and bomb attack by a force of about a hundred men. Then, with the barracks blazing above their heads and two of the police party killed, the eight survivors, led by Sergeant Tobias O'Sullivan, fixed bayonets to their rifles and charged, putting the attackers to flight. O'Sullivan was promoted head constable on the spot and afterwards district inspector, but he died only eight months later in troubled Listowel, where he had been posted after a mutiny. He was shot dead while walking unarmed with his eight-year-old son from the barracks to his nearby residence.

By October 1920, according to Lord Curzon, the Foreign Secretary, addressing the House of Lords, the IRA had murdered 117 policemen, injured 185 and driven the force out of more than 600 of its 1,400 barracks. Another 70 had been destroyed or damaged, as well as 64 courthouses.

A nationwide boycott of the police was begun and in those stations where they remained, marooned behind sandbags and barbed wire, they lived a spartan, overcrowded life in constant fear of attack. The boycott was enforced ruthlessly to isolate the police from the community. In County Sligo fifteen armed men made a woman kneel in front of her husband and swear she would cease working for the police. A turf-seller in Longford defied warnings not to deal with the RIC and his turf was thrown in a ditch by armed men. In Newry three shop girls were abducted in a car and driven outside the town; there, two men armed with revolvers made one of the girls kneel beside the car and her hair was shorn because, the men said, she was keeping company with an RIC man.

Paddy Shea, later to become a distinguished civil servant in the Northern Ireland administration, was the son of an RIC sergeant stationed at Athlone. In his memoir, *Voices and the Sound of Drums*, he recalls:

After the Soloheadbeg ambush people hoped there would be no more shooting, that the killing of the two constables was an isolated act of folly by a few wild men. But their hopes were vain. Soloheadbeg had only drawn the headline. Policemen were shot in the streets, in their homes, going to Mass, doing messages for their wives, having a drink in the pub.

The shots which killed them were fired from behind ditches, from alley-ways, sometimes in busy thoroughfares; those who looked on and were disposed to disapprove were too fearful of the consequences of giving information. In places where there had been shooting, policemen began to carry arms on duty.

Small police barracks in remote southern villages were being attacked at night and we saw photographs in the Dublin newspapers of garrisons who had repelled the raiders. Mother, her Ulster blood roused by the whole sad business, was full of admiration for the men who had refused to be terrorised. Father was silent.

Because of the increasing frequency of attacks on remote barracks, some of those in the smaller villages were closed and the men transferred to the towns.

After what appeared to be an unconscionably long delay the British government decided that the attacks on policemen were more than sporadic acts of local disaffection and that something must be done to help them protect themselves. The obsolete arms were gradually replaced by more recent makes of rifles and revolvers; sandbags were being provided for the protection of barracks which, for the most part, were rented houses hopelessly vulnerable against organised attack.

Ford touring cars and Crossley tenders which could hold ten men sitting back to back were supplied to garrisons in the more troubled counties so that the chance of getting a shot at an unwary man cycling along a country road would, at last, be lessened. The Government could not yet rise to supplying motor transport to places like Athlone where no-one had yet been killed – it seemed that entitlement was measured in dead men – but we were on one of the main roads to the south and west and the new vehicles, driven by dust-covered men wearing goggles, who told us about their journeying, often stopped for a few hours at Fry Place [Athlone].

As the RIC withdrew from many of its barracks, Dail Eireann endorsed the boycott of the police and the ruthlessness continued, with many people shot dead and dumped with placards around them stating they had been informing to the police. In the vacuum left by the RIC there sprang up a series of courts and then a Republican police, orchestrated by the IRA and Dail Eireann. At first their activities were not well organized. Offenders were simply rounded up and paraded before crowds at Sunday Masses throughout the country so that they would be ostracized locally. Later this alternative system of police and courts became more cohesive and a rudimentary system of rough justice enforced at parish level replaced the increasingly absent RIC.

In October 1919, in an effort to get a grip on the deteriorating situation, the British government set up a cabinet committee to handle Irish policy. After due deliberation they decided on a twin policy – repression and partition. There would be a determined campaign to put down the rebellion and then Better Government of Ireland legislation would be introduced, conceding partition to placate the Unionists in Ulster. But the plan only envisaged a measure of devolution to new parliaments in Belfast and Dublin linked in a Council of Ireland. With many key powers reserved by the British, it was far short of the full-blooded independence that Sinn Fein and the Dail were after. Nevertheless, the Bill was introduced at Westminster in February 1920.

By then, tough new security measures to deal with the outrages were becoming apparent. With the RIC in ever increasing disarray and its numbers falling further, the cutting edge of the security effort became the soon to be notorious 'Black and Tans'. They were recruited from all over Britain early in 1920, many being demobbed soldiers, who took their name from the khaki army trousers and dark-green police jackets they were forced to wear because of a shortage of RIC uniforms. At their peak, some 7,000 of them imposed a reign of terror and reprisal, mainly in the south and west of the country. At the same time the Commissioner of the Metropolitan Police, General Sir Nevil Macready, a former Gordon Highlander who had served in the Boer War, was sent to Ireland as General Officer Commanding, to direct the offensive.

Later in the year, to compensate for 600 men who had left the RIC in just three months, another security force, known as the Auxiliaries, was raised from among commissioned ex-officers. It was organized into companies of 100 men, paid the then astronomical sum of £1 per day and sent into the fiercest trouble spots throughout Ireland as shock-troops. It eventually grew to 1,400 men before disbandment.

To enable the forces to act effectively, parliament passed the Restoration of Order in Ireland Act, which came into effect in August 1920. Anyone suspected of IRA or Sinn Fein membership could be arrested on suspicion and held without trial. Coroners courts were suspended and secret court martials introduced where there was no provision for defence counsel.

The new Act regularized the growing wave of reprisals by the Crown forces that had begun in earnest on 19 March 1920 when Thomas MacCurtain, the Lord Mayor of Cork, a senior figure in the IRA, was gunned down at his home by three night-time callers, barely disguised RIC members. A month later one of them was named at a Coroner's court as District-Inspector Oswald Swanzy, who had by then been hastily transferred to Lisburn in Northern Ireland.

The new policies of repression and rough justice were too much for the dwindling core of pure RIC men. The situation came to a head at Listowel in County Kerry on 16 June when a station party led by Jeremiah Mee refused to hand over to the Black and Tans and co-operate with them. The Divisional Commander of the RIC, Lt-Col. Gerald Smyth, a tough Ulsterman who had been wounded six times and lost his left arm in France in the war, had urged the men to go on the attack against the IRA and Sinn Feiners. 'You may make mistakes occasionally and innocent persons may be shot, but that cannot be helped, and you are bound to get the right parties some-time. The more you shoot the better I will like it and I assure you no policeman will get into trouble for shooting any man,' he said. Most of the RIC party at Listowel resigned rather than fight on and the incident brought to a head the tensions between the pure police and the new special forces.

Paddy Shea says that those who flocked to join the Black and Tans were

decent men and scoundrels, adventurers and frightened youths, domesticated family men and fugitives from deserted wives; they were English and Scottish and Welsh, Jew and Gentile. They came in all sizes and for all sorts of reasons, the most unlikely of which was, probably, to do a policeman's job. Once they passed an elementary test in reading and writing they were in without, apparently, much inquiry about character or background or much thought about suitability for police duties.

Irish policemen, by and large, were unsophsticated, untravelled countrymen who said their prayers and did their duty as they saw it. The newcomers, they found, had neither religion nor morals, they used foul language, they had the old soldiers' talent for dodging and scrounging, they spoke in strange accents, called the Irish 'natives', associated with low company, stole from one another, sneered at the customs of the country, drank to excess and put sugar on their porridge. To the men of the RIC they were a revelation and a plague and a Godsend. They brought help but they frightened even those they had come to help.

The uncontrolled fury of events in the second half of 1920 justifies his recollection, which is shared to this day by Irish people and many ex-members of the RIC.

Typical of the tit-for-tat cycle of attack and reprisal was the events in Trim, County Meath, in September. Early one morning the small midlands town of 1,500 people some thirty miles from Dublin was isolated when telephone and telegraph wires were cut. The poles and felled trees were used to block the approach roads. Soon afterwards a 100-strong IRA 'flying column' invaded the town and attacked the solidly built police barracks.

The head constable was wounded before the station party surrendered. Five policemen, who had been attending Mass, were rounded up and marched back to the barracks at gunpoint. There the barracks was set on fire. The attackers made off, having ransacked the armoury for the police rifles and ammunition.

That afternoon eight tenders of Auxiliaries arrived in the town and opened fire on a hurling match, wounding two youths. Priests intervened and there were no further incidents but during the night a party of Black and Tans descended on the town. As some fired their guns indiscriminately to waken and frighten the inhabitants, who fled the town in terror, others looted and then poured petrol in shops and houses before firing them. By dawn forty houses, many shops, the town hall and a factory were in smouldering ruin.

On 21 November Collins' formidable intelligence network pulled off its biggest coup when eleven British intelligence men, known as the Cairo Gang, were singled out and killed at a number of addresses throughout Dublin. That afternoon the Black and Tans opened fire into the crowd at a football match in Croke Park, killing twelve and wounding sixty people before officers from the Auxiliaries ordered them to stop firing. Later at Dublin Castle two prisoners were shot dead by police, apparently while trying to escape, the authorities said, but nobody believed them.

In the autumn, after another sacking at the town of Balbriggan when two local men were killed, the Chief Secretary for Ireland, Sir Hamar Greenwood, had to answer growing concern in the House of Commons about events in Ireland.

> I found that from 100 to 150 men went to Balbriggan determined to avenge the death of a popular comrade shot at and murdered in cold blood. I find that it is impossible out of that 150 to find the men who did the deed, who did the burning. I have had the most searching inquiry made. But I cannot in my heart of hearts condemn in the same way those policemen who lost their heads as I condemn the assassins who provoked this outrage.

The same day in the Lords, Curzon said that what was happening in Ireland was not guerrilla warfare. 'It is the warfare of the red Indian, of the Apache.'

On 23 December 1920 the Government of Ireland Act was passed. In the south of Ireland elections in May 1921 were used by 128 unopposed Sinn Fein candidates to reinforce the mandate of Dail Eireann, which had to meet in secret because it had been banned. The proposed southern parliament was simply ignored. Meanwhile, the violence in some parts became so bad that martial law was declared, triggering off yet another cycle of attack and reprisals, 150 in all, in just five months.

Early in 1921, Brigadier-General Hubert Gough, leader of the 1914 Curragh mutiny, articulated the growing concern in Britain about the situation:

> Law and order have given place to a bloody and brutal anarchy, in which the armed agents of the Crown violate every law in aimless and vindictive and insolent savagery. England has departed further from her own standards even of any nation in the world, not excepting the Turk and Zulu, than has ever been known in history before.

Gough reflected a growing outcry in parliament and the press against the situation in Ireland. Field Marshal Sir Henry Wilson, the Chief of the Imperial General Staff and an Ulsterman of strong Unionist views, deplored the outcry in a letter to Laming Worthington-Evans, the Secretary for War, in June 1921:

> For the last two years I have always thought and openly said that we have only two courses open to us in Ireland. One is to crush out the murder gang with a ruthless hand and restore law and order and the King's writ, and the other is to clear out altogether, i.e., grant independence. Now as regards the grant of independence I am quite clearly of opinion that this will mean that we shall have a hostile Ireland in our rear and right athwart all our trade routes, and this again will mean that we shall have to reconquer Ireland or lose our Empire. I have therefore always been driven to advise the first of the two alternatives . . .
>
> But although I believe this to be the proper, and indeed the only, course to pursue if we want to keep our Empire I have always said that it is an impossible course and one which should never be attempted unless Great Britain is whole-heartedly in favour of it. Now as far as I can judge Great Britain is not whole-heartedly in favour of ruthless suppression of crime in Ireland. I am judging by the way in which the military authorities, even in the Martial Law area, are constantly being interfered with, I am judging by speeches and meetings of the Church of England, of the Labour Party, of the Liberal Party, and even of the House of Lords, but I am judging still more by the Press which appears to be almost unanimously in favour of more concessions and yet more concessions. If I am right in this then to embark on a ruthless campaign against the murderers in Ireland is a hopeless task.

By now Prime Minister David Lloyd George, who had earlier boasted of taking 'murder by the throat', was persuaded of the need to find a peace formula with the IRA and at noon on 11 July 1921 a truce, arranged with some difficulty, came into effect. In the previous thirty-six hours the IRA had killed twenty people. The shooting had only stopped five minutes before the deadline. In all, 418 RIC men as well as 146 British soldiers had lost their lives.

Nine days later the British government offered a limited form of self-government to the south but insisted on partition for the north, which was to remain under British control. Dail Eireann rejected the proposals unanimously but agreed to open talks with the British government. On 6 December, having failed to shift the British position during the talks, the Irish delegation agreed to partition and limited self-government for the south. A boundary commission would settle the extent of the partition.

Back in Ireland, the new Anglo-Irish Treaty provoked bitter controversy, with Republican hardliners arguing that they should not settle for less than the united independent Ireland they had fought for. When the Dail considered it on 7 January 1922, the treaty was accepted by only 64 votes to 57 and within a short time the country was plunged from the war of independence into an equally bloody civil war between those for and against the treaty. Before it ended in 1923 Michael Collins had been killed in circumstances that remain controversial to this day and wounds were opened up in the southern Irish community that are not fully healed even now, nearly seventy years on.

In January 1922, after agreement between the British and the new Irish government to disband the RIC, the Irish set about forming a new unarmed police force. The process began on 8 February when Michael Staines, head of the now disbanded Republican Police, and General Richard Mulcahy, the ex-Chief of Staff of the IRA, met at the Gresham Hotel in Dublin. Two weeks later the first members of the new force, the Guardians of the Peace or 'Civic Guards', were sworn in secretly; the Dail later changed its name to the Irish version, 'Garda Siochana'. In the midst of the civil war turmoil, the 4,000-strong, unarmed Garda struggled into existence, establishing credibility as a community-based police force against a background of lawlessness, unofficial courts and policing, and the virtual breakdown of the tax collection and local administration system.

*

To trace the course of the parallel events in the north which led to the emergence of the Royal Ulster Constabulary, it is necessary to go back to the passing of the Government of Ireland Act of 1920. By early that year most Unionists accepted that some measure of self-government for the larger part of Ireland was unstoppable. They recognized too that it would entail some form of government being set up in Belfast as well as Dublin. The biggest question the Act posed for them was the extent of partition. If it was too much they might not be able to pacify a disgruntled nationalist minority, especially one supported by Dublin. On the other hand, if the majority was not sufficient they could find in time that the precarious balance would be upset and they could be voted into a united Ireland anyway.

Britain regarded partition as a temporary solution. That is why there was provision in the 1920 Act for a joint Council of Ireland, a body which it was hoped would in the end provide a vehicle for an agreed all-Ireland settlement between the Unionists and Sinn Feiners. Therein lay the seeds of Unionist insecurity that were to germinate and grow to dominate Ulster politics for the next fifty years. The implication of compromise with Catholics and nationalists influenced every policy and affected virtually every decision taken by succeeding Unionist governments.

The British originally envisaged dividing the nine counties of the province of Ulster from the rest of Ireland but later, when the Unionists had done their sums, they persuaded them that the new border should only enclose six counties. The predominantly Catholic counties of Monaghan, Cavan and Donegal were to be excluded, giving the Unionists a comfortable, larger than 2 to 1 majority over the nationalists in the six counties of Antrim, Down, Armagh, Fermanagh, Tyrone and Londonderry.

At first the tentacles of the 'Tan War', as it had become known, spread less effectively into the north of Ireland but after council elections in the spring of 1920 sectarian violence erupted in Londonderry and an RIC Special Branch officer was killed. As pitched gun battles developed between the IRA and reformed UVF groups, the RIC, as demoralized in the north as it was in the south, stood aside, forcing the British government to deploy troops to quell the trouble.

Before long the IRA were in full cry against the familiar targets of RIC barracks and British tax offices. The response in the north was the intensification of sectarian attacks in the big engineering factories, linen mills and shipyards, where the Catholics were beaten and driven from their jobs by Loyalist mobs. In many parts of Belfast they were also driven from their homes.

The trouble was not confined to Belfast and Londonderry. On 17 July the murder in Cork County Club of Lt-Col. Gerald Smyth, the RIC Divisional Commissioner, who had figured in the Listowel mutiny, promoted fresh trouble. A few days later, when his body was brought north to his native Banbridge for burial, a fresh wave of sectarian trouble, aggravated by the traditional mid-July Orange passions, took place in several towns.

It had hardly subsided when the IRA threw fresh petrol on the flames. District Inspector Oswald Swanzy, who was involved in the murder of Tomas MacCurtain in Cork in March 1920, had been hastily transferred to Lisburn, County Antrim, at the other end of the country. On Sunday 22 August, as he was coming out of church in the town, he was murdered. The killing triggered off such serious sectarian rioting and arson that a 10.30 pm to 05.30 am curfew, which was to last until 1924, was imposed. Up to 700 were sworn in as special constables under an 1832 Act to help keep the peace but after the RIC prosecuted some of them for looting in Lisburn 300 resigned.

The growing wave of lawlessness in the north created further difficulties for the security commanders at Dublin Castle, who had barely sufficient men to cope with the trouble in the south and west of the country. Thus longstanding proposals to create a Special Constabulary for service in Ulster, lobbied persistently by the Ulster Unionists, fell on ever more receptive British ears.

The Unionists had in fact been calling for tougher security and more forces for at least two years and the idea of an Ulster Special Constabulary had been mooted by them as a way of incorporating the regrouped elements of the irregular UVF into the fabric of the legitimate security forces. In some areas, especially Fermanagh, unofficial vigilante forces on the same lines already existed. Indeed that July a party of armed Loyalists had driven an IRA raiding party from Lisbellaw. The RIC and the British troops generally turned a blind eye to the activities of the vigilantes on the basis that they were on the same side.

There were a number of reasons why the Unionists wanted security in their own hands. Primarily it was the best way of ensuring they got an acceptable measure of self-government. Although it was firm British government and opposition policy that Ulster was not to be 'coerced', the Unionists already feared the IRA and believed, and continued to fear, that they would attack and overwhelm Ulster once they had secured the twenty-six counties or the Free State, as it was increasingly being described. Sir James Craig articulated the fears in October 1921 when he called for 'all watchdogs of Ulster to be ready in case Sinn Fein should sweep over our fair province and attempt to take away our principles and our rights'.

The Unionists also wanted their own police force because they generally lacked confidence in the RIC. The original proposal under the 1920 Act for the RIC to be organizationally divided and account-able to both proposed parliaments was unacceptable. They considered the large proportion of southern Catholics in the RIC as at best 'disloyal' to Ulster and at worst Collins' men. Apart from many of the officer class, who had either indicated their support for Unionism or had turned a blind eye to Unionist drilling, they dismissed the rank and filers as ineffective. This perception was probably reasonably accurate, for the best men still in the force were in the most troubled areas, while others had resigned or defected, leaving not only a demoralized but also frightened rearguard. At a time of such turmoil and uncertainty the average RIC man was astute enough to realize he should steer a middle course to position himself most safely whatever way events turned out.

So, faced with continued Unionist bluster and the grim realities of the summer of 1920, the government finally agreed in September to raise a force of special constables for use in the six counties only. It was a significant decision because it was the first act of British policy to recognize the partition of Ireland, although it did prejudge the imminent Better Government of Ireland Act. As a bonus for the hard-pressed security chiefs, they had less pressure on the manpower available to them.

The plan, approved by the cabinet, closely reflected the Unionist proposals. There were to be some 2,000 A Specials. They would be a full-time force, trained to support the RIC and under its command. They would be aged twenty-one to forty-five, provided with uniform and quarters, and paid £3 17s 6d a week, a generous sum by the wages' rates at the time and considerably more than military wages. There would be no pension but they would get a 10 shillings a week bounty in lieu at the end of their service. Ex-servicemen were to get priority for the force, which was to be organized on a county basis.

The B Specials were to be a voluntary force of part-timers, required to do duty about one night in ten in their home territory. They were to receive a six-month allowance of £5 to cover wear and tear of clothes and tram fares. A hot meal ration of half-a-crown (2s 6d) was payable for each additional duty. Those who used their bicycles qualified for another shilling allowance. They were given caps and armbands for identification and it was envisaged they would be armed on duty and carry out patrols jointly with an RIC officer, although not in nationalist areas. It was intended to recruit 4,000 B men for Belfast alone.

A third force of 6,000 C Specials was also included in the plan. This was envisaged as a general reserve force to be called out only in an emergency. Its members were to receive no uniform or allowance and would be required only for occasional drilling. Like the arms for the B force, it was planned to issue them from police stations if the need arose. The authorities also appealed for those with cars to put them at the disposal of the new force in the event of an emergency and a register of volunteers was drawn up.

All those to be enrolled in the Special Constabulary were to be chosen by a selection committee of specially appointed magistrates, and enrolment forms were to be issued and processed through police stations. The UVF, however, planned to co-ordinate the applications through its local headquarters and submit them in bulk. Although advertisements were placed in the newspapers on 1 November 1920 soliciting recruits, Lt-Col. Wilfred Spender, the Commanding Officer of the UVF, outlined the proposals in a memorandum to the force issued from the Unionist offices at the Old Town Hall in Belfast on 19 October 1920. 'There is no reason why the UVF should not furnish all the numbers required, and I confidently hope that this will prove to be the case, and that they will elect, as far as possible, those leaders who have voluntarily helped in the past to perform the duty which the state is now prepared to take over.'

Spender set the tone for what Unionists now clearly saw as the legitimizing of their defence force.

The Government has clearly recognised that there are two distinct elements among the population: – those who are loyal to the British Crown and Empire and those who are not. The Government is asking the help of all Loyalists in Ulster, and proposes to arm with Firearms all those called on for duty, to confer certain privileges, to recognise them and to indemnify them for injuries incurred by the performance of their duties. The new Ulster parliament will depend for its initial success in a large measure on the efficient way in which the Special Constables perform their duties . . .

The man the government brought in to organize and command the new force was to have a profound influence on not only the evolution of security policy but the foundation of the Northern Ireland state. Charles Wickham, fourth son of an old landed Yorkshire family, was educated at Harrow and joined the army in 1899 at the age of twenty. He saw service with the Norfolk Regiment in the Boer War for two years, when he won the DSO. In the First World War he was mentioned in despatches, then served in France and Vladivostock, Siberia, where he gained the rank of Lieutenant-Colonel. He joined the RIC in 1920 as divisional commissioner.

Wickham, who died in 1971 at Comber, County Down, where he made his home, is remembered as a tall, keen-eyed, fit man with a strong interest in physical sports, especially tug-of-war. He had a firm, courageous, humanitarian nature, high integrity and indulged a passion for the law. In a letter to Field-Marshal Sir Henry Wilson in October 1921, Sir James Craig spoke of Wickham having 'gained the confidence of everybody . . . as much by his tactful administrative ability, as by his refusal to countenance any inteference with his discipline, no matter from what quarter it comes'. Later the same year, after a visit to Ulster, Major-General Sir Percy Radcliffe described Wickham as 'sober, level-headed and practical' in another letter to Wilson.

The first two platoons of Specials were deployed in Belfast in early December 1920, two weeks before the Government of Ireland Act was passed. The first victim died barely a month later when a platoon escorting a postman at Crossmaglen in County Armagh was ambushed.

In February 1921 Carson, whose health had been troubling him for some time, declined the offer of the prime ministership and stood down from the Unionist leadership, clearing the way for Sir James Craig, a businessman and landowner, to become the first prime minister of the new Northern Ireland state. Elections for the new parliament took place on 24 May and on 7 June its inaugural meeting at Belfast City Hall was attended by King George V. Despite the pomp and ceremony, violence was never far away. Two weeks later, near Newry, the IRA ambushed the train carrying the cavalry escort back to the Curragh, killing four troopers and eighty horses. After the incident, the B Specials press-ganged squads of young men from Newry to bury the horses.

Craig, whose Unionist party held forty of the fifty-two seats, had meanwhile acquired for the sum of £20,000 Stormont Castle, the home of a shipbuilding tycoon, as a seat for the new government. It was set in 235 acres of land on the eastern outskirts of Belfast, and Craig announced plans to build a parliament and courts of justice there. He also appointed his cabinet, the key post of Home Affairs minister going to a Belfast solicitor called Sir Dawson Bates.

Sir Dawson, a founder and then secretary of the Ulster Unionist Council, had organized the major anti-Home Rule demonstrations at Craigavon and Balmoral. A member of a prominent Belfast family, he was said to have been born with the quill in his hand, having followed his father and grandfather into both the legal profession and public life. Close to both Craig and Carson, he was heavily involved in Unionist activities at the time. A contemporary, G. C. Duggan, a former Northern Ireland Comptroller and Auditor-General, writing in the *Belfast Telegraph* on 27 October 1959, described him as

> a man who made a point of being unpunctual for appointments on the ground that he declined to be a slave of time; casual in preparing a formal speech for the Commons, though a master of the non-committal in replying to inconvenient questions; unimpressive in physique and bearing the frequent despair of his civil service staff driven to waylay him, even in the street, in order to obtain urgent decisions.

Writing in *The Irish Times* on 4 May 1967, Duggan also revealed that Bates had 'such a prejudice against Catholics that he made it clear to his Permanent Secretary that he did not want his most juvenile clerk or typist, if a Papist, assigned for duty to his ministry'. Later in 1934, in another anti-Catholic episode, Bates wrote to a senior colleague advising him not to use the telephone to his office as he had discovered the telephonist was a Catholic. Bates believed simply that Protestant ascendancy and Unionist dominance were the best ways to preserve Ulster and as a hardline party hack he acted accordingly.

The truce in the south, leading to the Anglo-Irish Treaty in December 1921, had little impact on the sectarian tensions in Belfast and for the first time savage reprisals became commonplace, with the

Specials taking revenge for the murder of their members. Events reached an ugly climax with Belfast's Bloody Sunday on 10 July, when ten Catholics were among fourteen left dead in an overnight wave of atrocity sparked off by a Specials' raid on the Falls Road area of Belfast.

In a week of violence in Belfast before the truce came into force, twenty-three people died – sixteen Catholics and seven Protestants; more than 1,000 Catholics were left homeless, 216 homes having been destroyed. There was more trouble in August and September when the York Street area of Belfast was routinely raked by snipers, making it and the Short Strand across the river the city's most notorious battlegrounds.

It was against this lawless and uncertain background that the Belfast government assumed responsibility for law and order on 22 November. Under Section 60 of the Government of Ireland Act, the RIC in the six counties were placed at their disposal as well as the Specials but the new government was obsessed with fears of what would happen if the treaty talks in London broke down. Clearly they anticipated an IRA onslaught to overthrow their new government and break the last British grip on Ireland. Their insecurity was compounded by doubts about whether Britain would stand by them in such circumstances.

Bates, in particular, as the minister responsible for law and order, was convinced that the IRA had used the period of the truce and the stand-down of the Crown forces to re-arm and reorganize in the north. The Unionist government had therefore requisitioned 26,200 rifles and 5,240,000 rounds of ammunition from the British government and were using their staunch supporter, Field Marshal Sir Henry Wilson, then Chief of the Imperial General Staff, to press the cabinet for the arsenal to be shipped to Carrickfergus.

Wilson and some of his military cronies were angling to have the security of the province put on a 'military footing', with the 16,000 Specials and RIC being disbanded and placed under a new military command. This force would also have included an estimated 20,000 UVF men, who had been mustered by Lt-Col. Fred Crawford, the veteran of the 1912 Larne gun-running, despite the emergence of the Specials. Crawford was indeed talking of raising a force of 150,000 men.

The existence of this irregular UVF force was of serious concern to the British government, who devised a scheme to bring it under official control by recruiting it into the C Specials. The proposal was in a memorandum prepared by Wickham. However, it leaked to Collins and late in November what became known as the Wickham circular was raised at a vital point in the Downing Street treaty talks. The British government was already sensitive about the growing notoriety of the conduct of the Ulster Specials. There had been widespread national reporting of the Belfast violence and influential newspapers like the *Manchester Guardian* (March 1921) had carried critical editorials:

> The Special Constabulary, drawn almost exclusively from the ranks of the Orange Lodges and the Unionist 'Volunteers', was nominally raised to protect life and property and to maintain order, not to become a force of terrorists exercising powers of death over their Catholic neighbours, for in the Ulster Unionist mind Catholic and Sinn Feiner are synonmous. Ulster's case against a single parliament for Ireland has always rested on its alleged fear of persecution. It will be a bad beginning for the Ulster parliament if its establishment coincides with the dragooning of the Catholic minority in the six counties by an armed Protestant force administering a sort of lynch law.

Craig was promptly summoned to London, where the Wickham circular was withdrawn and the idea promptly dropped, although Craig and Bates almost immediately approved the recruiting of another 700 A and 5,000 B Specials.

Despite the uncertainty over the outcome of the treaty talks, the process of devolution to the new Northern Ireland government continued on 21 December, when responsibility for local government was assumed. Twenty-five local councils, controlled by nationalists, had however refused to accept the authority of the Belfast administration and pledged their allegiance to the Free State. Foreseeing this difficulty, a Local Government (Emergency Powers) Act had been passed by the northern parliament earlier in the month, enabling the councils to be dissolved and their affairs to be run by a commissioner.

The RIC had already been ordered in to deal with rebel councils. On 30 November RIC officers had taken control of the Tyrone council offices and books at Omagh, and expelled officials and councillors from the council building after it had voted to pledge allegiance to Dail Eireann. At Enniskillen Court House, on 15 December, the police moved in five minutes after the end of a council meeting at which allegiance to the Dail had been pledged. They took possession of keys to presses containing record books and documents, and occupied the council offices, sending the staff home for 'a few days holidays'.

There were similar acts of defiance throughout nationalist areas. In Newry the Board of Guardians voted to join with the Free State. Catholic teachers in several areas refused to accept salary cheques from the northern administration and were paid, for a time, from Dublin. There was much acrimony in negotiations between Dublin and Belfast over the transfer of civil servants to man the new Northern Ireland departments, with a mounting wave of accusations that the Unionists refused to accept the appointment of Catholics. One Dublin official complained that he had been asked to mark the religion of staff on a transfer list he had compiled.

Events over the Christmas of 1921 were dominated by debate for and against the treaty, which had been signed at Downing Street on 6 December. At first there was some alarm in Belfast that Fermanagh and Tyrone might be included in the Free State but Lloyd George reassured Craig on that point, although the proposal for a Boundary Commission perpetuated the uncertainty over the limits of the border.

Early in 1922, after the Dail had ratified the treaty and the British hand-over to the provisional Irish government had begun, Craig and Collins met in London to discuss north-south issues. On 24 January, at a meeting with Sir Hamar Greenwood in the Colonial Office, Collins won agreement to finally disband the RIC. The men of the eighty-five-year-old force had already asked for disbandment. The previous November there had been a strong outcry when a form had been circulated throughout the force asking the religion of each member and requiring him to declare whether he was prepared to serve the northern government. They were also annoyed because the form required superior officers to comment on their 'suitability' for service in the six counties.

An RIC correspondent to the *Irish News* said that the force regarded the circular 'as a step to get an exclusively Orange or purely sectarian force in the Six Counties and no one resents the plan more than the decent Protestants in the RIC of whom there are many'. But the majority opposition to the circular reflected widely held fears that members of the RIC would be dismissed on paltry terms if they refused to declare their willingness to serve the Ulster authorities. 'Let us be disbanded honestly and then we can rejoin or not,' an officer said at a meeting of the representative body in Dublin.

Within a week of the London meeting the phased disbandment was under way. At that stage there were nearly 13,000 regulars and 3,000 temporary police. By the end of March they had been withdrawn from nineteen counties altogether and concentrated into a number of disbandment centres in the other six counties of the south. One of the disbandment centres was at Gormanston, just north of Dublin, where almost 1,000 vehicles and tons of equipment were gathered for hand-over to the new Irish government. The acquisition by the southern government of the very latest Crossley, Ford and armoured Rolls Royce vehicles with substantial quantities of machine guns, rifles and ammunition caused near apoplexy among the Unionists, who were convinced they would soon be turned against them.

As the men were discharged they were generally escorted in groups to railway stations and ferry ports or to the border, protected from attack by often hostile or, at best, grudging IRA parties. Some were not so fortunate. Contemporary newspaper reports describe how IRA parties intercepted and screened the departing RIC men, searching for those on their 'blacklist'. Several were abducted and reported to be murdered.

Some were given 'deportation orders' issued by local IRA units, who also meted out rough justice to any RIC men who crossed their path. One report told of an ex-RIC Catholic who was dragged off a train by armed men near his home in Tipperary and badly beaten and kicked. Seeing refuge in Dublin, he was again traced by the IRA and told that he would suffer the fate of all 'traitors to their country'. He then went north and joined the police where he lived in terror that he would be victimized as a Catholic.

In Waterford a constable was forced to march barefoot for a considerable distance before being savagely beaten and robbed of his money and gold watch. A revolver blow broke his nose. Disbanded police there were actually given a written IRA ultimatum, delivered to their twenty homes, to leave the town within twenty-four hours. 'Failing to comply with this order you will have to take the consequences,' the note said. Some of the men left for England on the morning train but others, married men with between three and seven children, sought to have the IRA countermand the threat.

Others approached the local bishop but he said he had no control over the men and could not interfere. The IRA then said it would make one exception only to the ultimatum. Accordingly, Sergeant Minogue, who acted as the local inspector, was given three days to hand his standard weights and measures over to the local council.

Elsewhere, an officer received the severed hand of a dead comrade through the post. Another was abducted, kept in a shed for a week and then forced to leave the country. In Kerry, armed men took a constable to his home, supervised as he packed his belongings and then ordered him out of the country. A mother wrote to her exiled RIC son: 'We never forget praying for you, hoping you don't forget it yourself. There is no such persons as magistrates now and, as this place is turned upside down, no law and order . . .' A coffin was dumped in a Limerick church and turned out to contain the body of an RIC constable who had been abducted five months earlier while carrying despatches between stations. One sergeant was escorted to the boat by a parish priest, who kept five armed men at bay until it sailed for England.

According to newspaper reports in April 1922, sixty to seventy ex-RIC members were arriving in England every day from various parts of Ireland. They outlined their plight in a petition to Winston Churchill, then Colonial Secretary:

We appeal to you to give us – 1. Empty camps or barracks, or empty aerodromes. 2. Protection from our disbandment places till we can get on board the steam-boats.

At present we have to go out disarmed and we are set upon and searched; our money is taken and each man is identified by his discharge certificates given to him with his pay on disbandment. The 'wanted' RIC, when found, having been already court-martialled by the IRA, are dragged off and murdered at once and many of them have suffered unmentionable outrages. The reasons for the execution of these men is only that they obeyed most faithfully the orders given by the British government.

We earnestly appeal to you to give us now large, empty quarters for ourselves and our families. We have all been warned out of Ireland. Every county in Munster, Leinster and Connaught is placarded that all the RIC are to be shot at sight, if they return. Our wives and families likewise are being ordered to leave. Some are turned out with no warning and the house and all its contents burnt on the spot. Others get a few hours or longer. A great deal of luggage has been burned and many of our comrades have already been murdered. But not a murder is allowed to be published now in any Irish paper. We know them however, from private sources.

We are seized in the streets or dragged out from our houses or from the boats unless British soldiers happen to be leaving by the boats also. We appeal to you most earnestly to give us the many large quarters standing empty. We want to emigrate but we want time to arrange for this. We have to flee from Ireland but we have nowhere to go and do not know where to turn. You alone can help us ... many men are being disbanded today and a wire from you to Ireland would save many lives and untold misery.

On 4 April, after a farewell parade at the Phoenix Park depot, the RIC was formally disbanded, although the actual process was not finally completed until August. In May the House of Commons in London debated the disbandment of the force and passed an act, mainly dealing with pension aspects.

Sir Hamar Greenwood told the House that accommodation for the ex-policemen, with the prospect of employment for some, had been found in Chester and nearby towns. All had been housed, with the exception of a few large families, for whom arrangements were in hand, he reported. Some members raised their concern that because the courts in Ireland were being disrupted or even broken up by 'ruffians', compensation claims by suffering members of the RIC were being delayed. Sir Hamar assured the House that the situation meant that it was a postponement not a negation of justice and that a government-financed Irish Distress Committee had been set up to deal with cases of hardship.

Many MPs paid tribute to the force. One member calculated that one in twenty of the force had been murdered and one in twelve wounded in the preceding two years. Sir Hamar praised the men of the RIC as 'the pick of the Irish race'.

The 2,000 RIC operating in the north were reprieved until 1 June to enable proper consideration to be given to the question of policing. On 31 January Bates appointed a committee of inquiry on police reorganization in Northern Ireland. It was chaired by Lloyd Campbell MP and consisted of fourteen others, including MPs and JPs as well as Wickham and James Stevenson, the Chief Constable of Glasgow. They were asked to consider the alterations in the existing organization which would be necessary in establishing a police force; recruitment and conditions of service; the extent to which the new force should be comprised of RIC and Specials; the strength of the force and the cost.

In an interim fifteen-page report published on 28 March, which had the distinction of being the first official report of the new parliament, the committee proposed a 3,000-strong single force for the whole of the province and rejected the concept of local forces as in Great Britain. It should be known as the Ulster Constabulary and they recommended permission should be sought to have the 'Royal' prefix. They said that RIC and Specials should be able to join the new force and continue receiving the same rate of remuneration but that new recruits should have a lower pay rate. It suggested the new force should be one-third Catholic, recruited initially from suitable members of the RIC, with new Catholic recruits completing the fraction if not enough men were available. The majority of the new force would be drawn from the RIC and Specials.

Altogether, nine members of the committee signed ten reservations to the main report, recording dissent on a number of matters, including transfer arrangements for the RIC, pensions entitlement and the proportion of Catholics.

The report was accepted by the Northern Ireland government and within a few days a recruiting notice was published in the Irish newspapers. On 29 April the King, in what the *Belfast Telegraph* hailed as a 'gratifying announcement', granted that the new force could be called the Royal Ulster Constabulary. In May the Belfast parliament passed the 1922 Constabulary Act and the RUC officially came into existence on 1 June. The headquarters of the new force was established at Atlantic Buildings, Waring Street, in the centre of Belfast, and Charles Wickham became the first Inspector-General.

In the weeks before his appointment there had been a campaign against Wickham by hardline disgruntled ex-servicemen, which included the circulation of a scurrilous leaflet. He was accused of having no connection with Ulster, failing to protect men under his command and failing to visit the scenes of outrages in Belfast or elsewhere. The final accusation was that he had placed transport under incompetent English officers, who were giving all the fancy jobs to Englishmen while qualified Ulstermen were unable to obtain employment. The leaflet concluded:

These facts prove that he is utterly incompetent and unfit to have charge of Ulster's little force. When the war was on, everyone was upholding the Ulster Division, now when the war is over, the Ulster officers and soldiers are being ignored and placed by our own government under the heel of incompetent bluffers who openly revile and sneer at us. On all sides the suggestion is made that the Ulster Parliament seems to have been constructed for the purpose of making jobs for incompetent strangers who have no connection or association with Ulster. ARISE OH! ULSTER AND ASSERT YOURSELF BEFORE ALL IS LOST.

Among many of the discharged RIC men who made their way north was Regan:

Having decided to serve with the RUC I was transferred in the RIC to County Tyrone in preparation for the take-over by the former body. I was escorted to Amiens Street station by a lorry-load of police, who really only brought me under notice, seeing that I was going by train without an escort. I did not feel at all comfortable. When the train started I left my coat and hat with my baggage in the first class compartment, and wearing a cap and old waterproof coat, got into the third as far away from my belongings as I could get. The train only stopped a couple of times in southern Ireland. At the stop before entering Northern Ireland, I looked out of the window and two men in plain clothes, very like IRA men, walked from one end of the train to the other looking into every carriage. I got hotter and hotter as they approached, but heaved a sigh of relief when they had looked into the carriage I was in and passed on. Still I was on tenterhooks till the train started, but once over the border I felt able to breathe freely again. In due course I reached Belfast and later took over County Tyrone.

Before leaving the south, Regan had approached an IRA contact, after he had been, inaccurately, named in a book as one of the murderers of a cripple in Bantry, County Cork. He declined the offer of a meeting with Collins, in case he would be marked as a traitor by the police side, but did seek an assurance from Collins as to whether 'accepting a post in the RUC was putting another nail in my coffin'. Later, after he arrived in Tyrone, he received a letter from his friend in Dublin who had raised his position with Collins. The message stated that there was nothing against anyone taking service in the RUC and that 'if I carried on as I had done in Limerick I would have nothing to fear from them'.

# 3

# War and Peace

In the early months of 1922, in the new Irish Free State, as the divisions between those for and against the Anglo-Irish Treaty widened, the British handed over power to the provisional government, headed by Michael Collins. The Unionists in Belfast feared an onslaught across the border by the anti-treaty factions of the IRA to take the six counties as a way to avoid the looming civil war. Many firmly believed that a campaign to wipe out the new northern administration was actually being set up. They were also angry at the continued 'Belfast boycott', which had grown steadily in effectiveness since it was first instituted by the Dail in 1919. Its aim was to prevent any Ulster-made goods and services being sold in the south, and an army of 'enforcers', both official and unofficial, checked shops and incoming railway trains for Belfast goods. The boycott was rigidly enforced. Vehicles and their contents were frequently burned and in one notable raid in Dublin half a million gallons of Belfast-distilled whiskey were poured down the drains. Early in 1922 the west of Ireland even suffered a shortage of coffins because the normal supplier from Belfast had his goods burned.

Unionist anger and insecurity were further fuelled by continued uncertainty about where the boundary between north and south would finally be drawn. Despite a pact reached in London in January between Collins and Craig, which excluded any British representative from the planned Boundary Commission and gave an undertaking that the boycott would be lifted if Catholics were allowed back to their jobs, rank and file Unionist insecurity remained acute. This gave a new impetus to the sectarian trouble that had been a constant feature of life in the north for nearly two years.

The sheer horror of what took place can be gleaned from accounts in the newspapers during 1921 and 1922. The *Newsletter* and the

*Irish News* of course tell the story from their opposite viewpoints. So the nationalist *Irish News* highlighted what was called a 'pogrom' in the River Bann valley, near Banbridge, County Down, home of the Irish linen industry, where a Sinn Fein outrage prompted a mob, 'armed with everything from a Webley to a poker' and led by a band, to go from factory to factory expelling about 1,000 Catholic workers.

In Belfast one night during the curfew, three Catholic men, clad in the scantiest attire, as newspapers reported, were dragged from their homes and left, riddled with bullets, on the city's outskirts. In one of the cases a woman, who offered herself as an alternative victim, was pushed aside by the abductors, who even chased the victim's whippet dog when it ran after them. The funerals became a further source of trouble. Police and soldiers had to clear a route for the corteges through angry mobs and the mourners had to run the gauntlet of snipers in some parts of the city.

Another evening, at 6 pm, a bomb was thrown into a tram packed with home-going shipyard workers, outside the General Post Office in central Belfast, killing and injuring a number of the occupants. Soldiers, with fixed bayonets, had to hold an angry crowd at bay after a policeman arrested a suspect from among the crowds. In a three-week period in February 1922 there were 138 killings: 96 Catholics and 42 Protestants. A police report drawn up by District Inspector R. R. Spears in February 1923 sums up the situation in Belfast after July 1921:

> For twelve months after that the city was in a state of turmoil. Sinn Fein was responsible for an enormous number of murders, bombings, shootings and incendiary fires. The work of the police against them was, however, greatly hampered by the fact that the rough element on the Protestant side entered thoroughly into the disturbances, met murder with murder and adopted in many respects the tactics of the rebel gunmen. In the endeavour to cope simultaneously with the warring factions the police efforts were practically nullified. They were quite unable to rely on the restraint of one party while they dealt with the other.

The principal murder grouping on the Unionist side was the Ulster Protestant Association, a 150-strong group, based in a public house in East Belfast, where it held a formal meeting every Thursday night. According to a police report:

Its whole aim and object was simply the extermination of Catholics by any and every means. On becoming a member of the club, an oath of allegiance to the organization was administered. There was another oath also administered which was practically a vow to murder.

Offenders against the rules of the club were brought in, if they were not at the meeting, by armed members told off for the purpose and tried summarily by a nominated jury of the members. On conviction they were stretched naked across a flogging horse, their arms and legs being fasted to the floor with thongs and were then flogged with a cat-o'-nine tails which consisted of a short wooden handle and leather thongs about a foot long.

Funds for the club were obtained at the point of the gun. Collecting sheets and envelopes were issued to members at each meeting. They left these at houses all over the Newtownards Road and even suburban areas. Failure to subscribe entailed receipt of a threatening letter and a subsequent visit and intimidation by armed men. Publicans, shopkeepers, managers of picture houses and householders were alike approached and such was the state of terror to which they were reduced that none ever refused to subscribe or attempted to inform the police except anonymously. Considerable sums of money were gathered by this means, a large proportion of which was used to pay a solicitor for defending various members of the club who were brought to justice by the police for various offences of violence. The remainder of the money was absorbed by the chairman, the leading desperado and murderer, and one or two others.

The security forces' reaction to the sectarian violence was further complicated by differing approaches and split responsibility between the police and the military, who were inhibited about becoming involved in incidents because of a belief that they were bound not to, by the terms of the truce. Throughout 1921, before responsibility for law and order was assumed by the Belfast government, there had been many exchanges and much recrimination between the political authorities in Dublin, London and Belfast, and the military and police commanders. Lines of authority and communication were unclear and although the police had primary responsibility for ensuring the public peace, the chief officers were hampered by at first being unable to deploy the Specials and by the demoralized state of the outgoing RIC.

By 1922, although the RUC had been formed, it was still an ineffective instrument. It lacked an intelligence-gathering system and three months after formation it had only recruited a third of its complement. As it was being built from the top down, with the more senior posts being filled first, the Specials of the various classes – Protestant to a man, largely unsupervised, frequently indisciplined, and distrusted by London and Dublin – were, controversially, bearing the brunt of the situation.

The tension between the police and the military frequently surfaced. Just before curfew hour on New Year's Eve 1921, a speeding car, transporting two Special policemen from what the *Irish News* called 'an entertainment in the city', crashed in Cromac Square, colliding with a gas lamp-post, injuring four soldiers who were on patrol and sustaining considerable damage. The other soldiers then began to remonstrate with the Specials and police officers who arrived at the scene. In the words of the newspaper: 'On the car being stopped, the incident assumed a very ugly complexion and it was feared by those not immediately concerned that it would result in a tragedy.' It finally took the intervention of a military officer to restrain the angry soldiers.

The role of the army in defending Northern Ireland from the feared IRA onslaught was a major preoccupation of the Belfast government. This became apparent when the cross-border tension reached crisis point early in 1922 after a series of events triggered off by the arrest of ten Monaghan footballers in County Tyrone. It was alleged that they were on their way to Londonderry to free prisoners under sentence of death there for killing a prison officer and Special Constable William Lyttle with chloroform during an escape attempt.

The IRA responded soon after, on 10 February, by crossing the border and kidnapping a reported seventy Unionist hostages from the Fermanagh-Tyrone border area. Some were held under heavy guard at the Ballybay barracks in County Monaghan, while others were transferred to Dublin. The Belfast *Newsletter* described the kidnappings as an act of war and called on the British government to fulfil its obligation to protect the lives of its citizens in Northern Ireland.

A day later cross-border relations deteriorated even further after a clash at Clones railway station in the Free State. There were two ways to travel from Belfast to Enniskillen by rail, the quickest being through Clones. Before partition speed was the only criterion but in the tense days of early 1922 it could only be described as foolhardy for a party of eighteen armed Specials to choose the cross-border route. Clones was in fact the last of several stops in the south and by the time their train reached the station, a cadre of armed IRA men had formed up on the platforms and set up machine guns. Their leader, Commandant Matt Fitzpatrick, revolver in hand, approached the carriage where the Specials were travelling and when he called on them to surrender was promptly shot dead. After an intensive firefight for several minutes, a sergeant and three of the Specials lay dead. One escaped the gunfire and the RIC later smuggled him back across the border; the others were taken into custody by the IRA.

The goverment in Belfast was now at boiling point and in an angry telegram to London called on Churchill to order British troops to take effective action. Churchill took the view that the blame for the heightened tension was attributable to those in Belfast insensitive enough to have despatched the Specials across the border and he accepted Dublin's account that the Specials had fired first. The British government had anyway no desire to confront the new Dublin administration in case it collapsed, allowing De Valera and his hardliners to take over, with even more serious consequences for north-south relations and the breakdown of British policy in Ireland.

Nevertheless over succeeding days Craig continued to press for action. He reported alleged information that the IRA was massing considerable forces in Monaghan for a cross-border attack and demanded that the army command in Dublin supply him with a fleet of nearly 250 military vehicles, 150 guns and wireless sets. Churchill was unimpressed by the barrage of telegrams from Belfast and suspected, quite rightly, that the Unionists were thinking of mounting their own expedition across the border to rescue their kidnapped kinsmen. Such an expedition, he warned Belfast, would be illegal.

Churchill, acting in consort with Collins, tried to defuse the situation by urging the northern government to release the footballers in exchange for the kidnapped Unionists, some of whom were already freed. Craig protested that the law in Ulster must take its course, which earned him both private and public rebukes from Churchill. 'I do not for one moment compare prisoners who have been taken lawfully and are being proceeded against at law in the courts with persons who have been kidnapped – but I do ask men of goodwill not to take fine points in matters of such character,' he told the House of Commons. Churchill also chided Craig over the continued outrages in Belfast, which he said were 'worse than anything which has occurred in the south'. In the three days after the Clones incident thirty people had been murdered in the city.

Churchill's remarks about the serious disturbances in Belfast were soon further underlined by one of the worst atrocities. On the night of 24 March five armed men, who have never been identified, smashed their way into the home of Owen McMahon, a Catholic publican, who resided at 8 Kinnaird Terrace, adjacent to the high, grey-stone walls of Belfast prison on the Crumlin Road. His wife and a maid were tied up, then Owen, his six sons and Edward McKinney, a barman who lodged in the house, were taken into the sitting room, lined up against a wall and shot one by one. All died except for the youngest son, John, who survived the massacre by hiding behind the sofa. He later spoke of the killers being in uniform.

The murders chilled the blood of the Catholic community and before long it was widely accepted that the killers were Specials taking reprisal for an IRA attack in Victoria Street, Belfast, the previous day when two patrolling Specials, William Charmside and Thomas Cunningham, had been shot dead.

By now the British government, seriously concerned about the spiralling violence in Belfast, had initiated renewed dialogue between Craig and Collins, who was under severe pressure from the frightened Catholics in the north. This resulted in the second Craig-Collins pact on 30 March 1922. Churchill's aim was to establish a working relationship between the governments in each part of the island, especially with a view to restoring law and order. To succeed, it was necessary to overcome the nationalist minority's hostility to the new northern state by drawing them into both recognition of and participation in its processes.

So, tackling the areas of greatest immediate distrust, there was a plan for an advisory committee to oversee increased Catholic recruitment to the police; detachments in mixed areas would consist equally of Catholic and Protestant police; so would search parties looking for arms. Outrages were to be investigated by a committee with members from both religions and IRA activity in the six counties was to cease. Following the failure to secure re-employment of the 10,000 displaced Catholic workers, as contained in the January pact, the British government allocated £500,000 to fund relief work schemes and to provide for the 23,000 made homeless in the rioting. These potentially far-reaching proposals, had they been fully enacted, would have had a profound and long-term effect on not only north-south relations but those between Protestants and Catholics in Northern Ireland itself.

The Unionists, however, drew no distinction between the factions in the south for and against the treaty; as far as they were concerned, both posed a threat to the very existence of Northern Ireland. De Valera's faction was the mailed fist. Collins' fist was equally menacing but he wore a velvet glove. In the event Craig, confronted by hardliners like Dawson Bates, proved to be both unwilling and unable to implement the agreement.

This became clear within days when Collins, under the terms of the pact, sought urgent information about yet another sectarian atrocity in Belfast. This time a party of Specials from Brown Square barracks had gone on a violent rampage in Arnon Street after an RIC constable had been shot dead nearby. Two men were killed in their houses, while in a third house a sledgehammer was used to murder the occupant. His seven-year-old son was shot in the head and died a day later. Craig ignored several requests from Collins for more information about the Arnon Street killings, effectively aborting the London pact. There was no more political contact between the two governments for forty years.

There was, however, a half-hearted attempt to get the police advisory committee working, partly through pressure from London, where the cabinet was beginning to baulk at the cost of supporting almost 50,000 men at arms and to question Craig's demands for even more, which were based on a chronic insecurity that Britain would withdraw troops from the north, increasing their vulnerability to an IRA invasion. After many delays, the committee met for the first time on 16 May, with only seven of the twelve members present. There was one further meeting that month on 31 May, when the attendance was five. When it met for the third and last time on 7 June, only three members turned up.

The failure of the committee to make any contribution was to have serious consequences for policing in Ulster. It fizzled out because the Belfast government had no desire to make it work and because the Catholic representatives succumbed to intimidation. If both sides had persevered with generosity and courage, a framework might well have emerged which would have created minority confidence in the security forces and consolidated the substantial Catholic presence in the infant RUC, inherited from the RIC. Over the years such rapport might well have taken the politics out of policing and, through accountability to both communities, when crises developed, might have prevented the RUC from being perceived as the armed wing of the Unionist Party, 'ours' in the eyes of the Protestants, 'theirs' by the Catholics.

In the event the Unionists chose repression rather than conciliation with the minority. Even before the pact had been signed, the Civil Authorities (Special Powers) Bill had been introduced to the Belfast parliament. Sir Henry Wilson, by now retired from the army and sitting as a Unionist MP at Westminster, had been given a role as military adviser to the Belfast government but much of his advice was ignored. Sir Henry had urged Bates and his diehard officials to make a determined effort to get Catholics involved in the Special Constabulary by issuing a proclamation affirming that it was open to all, regardless of creed or class. He also cautioned against taking the power to flog offenders in case it would alienate English public opinion.

When it was given the royal assent on 7 April, the Special Powers Act, as it became known, was a truly draconian piece of legislation. Under it the Minister of Home Affairs could arrest without warrant and intern without trial. Prisoners could be flogged or executed. Coroners' inquests could be dispensed with. Land and property could be commandeered for security purposes. Organizations, meetings, publications and gatherings could be prohibited by ministerial order. If any unforeseen crisis developed, the minister was empowered to take all such steps and issue all such orders as might be necessary to preserve the peace.

At the same time Major-General Arthur Solly-Flood, a protégé of Wilson's, was appointed military adviser. Irish-born, with a distinguished military record in the Boer and First World Wars, the General was given control of the developing RUC and the A, B and C forces of Specials. Before long he had formulated a wanted list of IRA activists for internment, using the new act, and submitted a £5 million-plan to the cabinet in London to expand and more heavily arm the Specials. The arms supplies were quickly approved and shipped to Ulster but the question of the money for expansion was left pending.

The new act did little to deter the level of outrages. Throughout May there was a wave of arson aimed against Unionist business property in Belfast. In some parts of the city, notably York Street, relays of snipers kept up almost constant firing at everything that moved on the streets. The mouths of some streets were blocked off by building walls with planks and heavy wooden railway sleepers to prevent the mobs from coming in and burning houses. Over the weekend of 20–22 May the arson campaign was extended to the 'big house' Unionists, and the splendid homes of several of the business class and gentry like the O'Neills and the Londonderrys were put to the torch. The weekend of violence culminated on the Monday morning with the first political assassination of the troubles when IRA gunmen murdered W. J. Twaddell, a member of the northern parliament, who was shot in the centre of Belfast on his way to open up his drapery shop at Lower North Street.

A crisis cabinet meeting in Belfast later in the day decided to issue an order under the Special Powers Act outlawing the IRA and four other Republican organizations. It was further decreed that membership of them, promoting their aims or possession of documents relating to them would be an offence. That night detachments of Specials, backed up by the military, began a series of swoops throughout the six counties. By dawn they had made 300 arrests. Within a short time the number in custody had topped 400 and they were detained without trial. In due course they were held on the prison ship *Argenta*, moored first in Belfast Lough, then off Larne Harbour.

The violence continued, however. In June, after pressure from Craig on Churchill, British troops backed up by artillery went into action and repelled IRA units who had occupied part of Fermanagh near Belleek and Pettigo. In London on 22 June two IRA gunmen, reputedly acting on Collins' orders, assassinated Sir Henry Wilson outside his home at 36 Eaton Place in Belgravia. Back in Northern Ireland the violence had degenerated into a sickening series of tit-for-tat massacres, some of them carried out by Specials. One incident in Cushendall, when a group of youths was fired on, was the subject of an official enquiry but no findings were ever made public.

At the end of that violent month the Lord Mayor of Belfast, reflecting the widespread shock in the city at the continued destruction and death, called for a ten-day truce. The IRA simultaneously became preoccupied with events in the south, where the divisions between them over partition had erupted in violence. The death of Collins in an ambush in County Cork in August removed the major thorn in Craig's side over his conduct of affairs in the north.

The net effect of these events was to restore a sort of peace to Belfast, where the violence became more sporadic as the year drew to a close. Solly-Flood was quietly relieved of his command at the end of the year. His grandiose plans for a 30,000-strong constabulary and a Directorate of Public Security, with an intelligence-gathering responsibility, were too much for the Unionist leadership, who found them a threat to their own authority. He was given a great send-off from the quay, the *Belfast Telegraph* reported a few days before Christmas, but no one was sorry to see him go, especially Wickham, whose position as the commander of the police was now clear.

By contrast with 1922 when there were 295 murders in Northern Ireland, 231 of them in Belfast, the following two years were virtual models of peace, with only four murders. The curfew was lifted and the internees released. In the same time span the prison population fell from 1,062 to just 400.

The RUC was scarcely three weeks old in June 1922 when Dawson Bates received a handwritten note from an official of the Anchor Purple Star Electricians Loyal Orange Lodge 811. 'Dear Sir and Brother,' he wrote on behalf of some members of the RUC, enquiring if they could attend Orange Lodge functions and ceremonies privately and in plain clothes. The letter was referred upwards from Bates to Craig, the prime minister, before Solly-Flood spelled out the agreed policy in a minute on 18 July. RUC members could remain in or join the Orange Order but they should not attend meetings in uniform nor should attendance interfere with their duties.

The decision, like the half-hearted attitude to a Police Committee, was a further sign of an emerging sectarian philosophy in the Ministry of Home Affairs. On 6 December 1920, soon after his arrival in Ulster, Wickham, by background the classic English officer and gentleman, addressing a parade of Specials at the Newtownards Training Camp, had spoken of the need for 'strict discipline, self-restraint and absolute impartiality' on the part of constabulary members. But Wickham's authority and standards had already been compromised by the unchecked series of reprisals and the one-sided application of internment, at a time when about twice as many Catholics as Protestants were being murdered.

Further sensitivity to militant Unionist feelings was shown in June 1922. A British officer working on Solly-Flood's staff questioned the £15,000 a year cost of storing the 35,000 rifles and ammunition that the UVF had landed in 1912. The Finance Minister had also picked up the problem, which involved twenty to thirty men and strong electric arc lights at the Tamer Street barracks where the cache was being stored. When the officer suggested that the lot should be 'taken out to sea and sunk in deep water', Wickham protested that 'if this was done, the whole of Ulster would be up in arms'. Instead the police secured the consent of Colonel Fred Crawford, the original gun-runner, and transferred the arsenal to the RUC stores at Sprucefield, near Hillsborough, where they stayed until the outbreak of the Second World War, when they were sold to the Ministry of Supply in Britain for use by the Home Guard.

The RUC was hardly in existence before Bates and his advisers began to take an almost paranoid interest in the number of Catholic members, reflecting their residual distrust of Catholics in the RIC. In October 1922 it was disclosed in a parliamentary answer that 896 Protestants and 434 Catholics had transferred from the RIC to the RUC against a quota of 1,000 recruits from each religion. The Catholic representation was over twenty-one per cent. Wickham was ordered to make a weekly report on the ebb and flow of Catholic numbers which Bates closely scrutinized. At the same time the officials in the ministry began to push to fill the RUC vacancies from the ranks of the Protestant Specials rather than by recruiting from the Catholic community, and eventually got their way. By the beginning of 1925 the force was 2,990 strong with 2,449 Protestant members and 541 Catholics. Nearly half the force, 1,435, were former Specials.

Although many Catholics were to serve in the RUC, frequently with distinction, this recruitment line effectively abandoned the one-third Catholic target set by the Campbell committee in 1922. Over the years as the RIC intake retired, the Catholic proportion fell from the twenty-one per cent high point to an average seventeen per cent. In recent years it has hovered around ten per cent. Catholic officers did, however, generally receive promotion. In January 1925, for instance, nine of the thirty-eight District Inspectors and two of the eight County Inspectors were Catholics, a proportion of roughly twenty-five per cent. In the 1970s there was a similar proportion of Catholic officers in the four most senior ranks. However, intimidation, nationalist convictions among much of the Catholic community about serving the Crown, the acquiescence of the successive Unionist administrations and heavy political control of the force doomed it to appear as an adjunct of the Unionist party and a defender of its position.

In accordance with the new ruling about the Orange Order, an

Orange Lodge confined to members of the RUC was formed in January 1923. It took the name of the Sir Robert Peel Memorial Loyal Orange Lodge and soon boasted a membership of about 300, a tenth of the RUC. The Worshipful Master was District Inspector John W. Nixon. Born in County Cavan, Nixon had joined the RIC in 1899 and by passing the competitive examinations became the youngest ever District Inspector. When the RUC was set up, he was given command of Belfast's C District, which covered the Shankill Road area. He was already a figure of great controversy because of his hardline Unionist views and reputed involvement in reprisals by the security forces, notably the McMahon murders and the killings in Arnon Street. Despite his reputation he moved in high Unionist circles and was involved in heavy infighting against Catholic officers when the senior RUC jobs were being handed out. Bates himself was the guest speaker at the first annual general meeting of the Peel Lodge in 1923.

At a meeting of the Lodge on 3 January 1924 Nixon made outspoken political remarks which were soon reported back to his police superiors and the government. They were alarmed because it seemed Nixon was clearly spoiling for a fight; they also knew the Dublin government had an embarrassing dossier on Nixon and his past activities which they had been using to stimulate concern in London about what seemed to them incompatible links between the RUC and the Orange Order. With the government's connivance, Wickham moved to limit the potential damage by issuing a circular outlining regulations about the political activity of RUC members on 17 January 1924. In the two-page document, which was ordered to be posted in every barrack and station, Wickham pointed out that RUC members were to be allowed to vote at parliamentary elections and join certain approved secret societies, a right not enjoyed by the RIC:

It will be realized that these privileges are not to be used in any way likely to impair the efficiency of the force generally, or of its individual members, or to weaken the confidence of the public in the impartiality of the force. It would, for instance, be improper for any member of the force to abuse their privileges by expressing or manifesting political or sectarian opinions, though it is, of course, in no way intended to interfere with the private political or religious beliefs of any member of the force.

Members of the Royal Ulster Constabulary should not, therefore, take any part by speaking, or entering into discussions, at meetings where political or sectarian opinions are expressed, or by organizing or assisting in organizing meetings or gatherings at which political or sectarian speeches or discussions are likely to take place.

Members were also warned that if they attended any meeting where such proceedings took place unexpectedly, they should leave forthwith.

Nixon was unmoved by what was in effect an explicit personal warning that he must toe the line. At another Lodge meeting on 29 January 1924, attended by a member of the government and at least two MPs as well as three newspaper reporters, he, according to reports in the Belfast papers the next day, made explicit political remarks. He warned that although the six counties were intact the border was surrounded by the enemy, who had artillery, armoured cars and aeroplanes, and every engine of war supplied to them by the Imperial (British) government. The opinion down in the Free State was that they were going to get a big slice of Ulster but the response of every leader among Protestants and Orangemen that had expressed himself on that matter, so far as he knew, was 'not an inch'. (Nixon prided himself on being the originator of the phrase which became part of the Unionist political vocabulary.)

Apart from its political content, Nixon's speech was highly untimely for Craig, who was in the middle of discussions with London and Dublin to try finally to resolve the border issue. Nixon was accused of breaching the terms of the earlier circular. A few days later, on 4 February, a file containing the newspaper reports and initiating disciplinary charges was sent to Nixon at Brown Square barracks, where he was based. Two days later he was suspended from duty pending the outcome of a disciplinary hearing. 'I have never known an officer or man of the RIC to be suspended except when charged with a criminal offence or gross insubordination,' he complained.

Supporters of the highly popular suspended policeman arranged a demonstration in his support for the night before Nixon was due to appear in front of the formal inquiry into his conduct. It was extensively advertised by bill posters. Provocatively even a wall at Brown Square police barracks was covered. A crowd of some 10,000, led by bands playing lively airs, according to the *Newsletter*, marched from the Shankill Road through the city centre and back again. During speeches at the 'monster demonstration' outside the City Hall, Nixon was lavishly praised.

Next day, 14 February, the Constabulary Court convened at the Musgrave Street barracks in central Belfast. Two County Inspectors, F. S. Britten of Lisburn and W. S. Moore of Armagh, presided but the proceedings were adjourned without making any progress because of legal argument about the way the case had been laid against Nixon and whether or not Bates himself should attend to give evidence. Nixon had summoned him as a relevant witness. Two days later the court adjourned again, at the request of Nixon's solicitor.

When it assembled for the third time on 19 February, after Nixon denied the four charges, it became clear that the case against him was to be outlined by three newspaper reporters who had been present at the meeting. However, when the first of them was called a barrister announced that they would not be giving evidence 'lest it should be submitted that they were informers, detectives or police note-takers'. The hearing adjourned after District-Inspector Dudgeon, who was prosecuting, asked for warrants to arrest the three reluctant witnesses. Next morning a crowded courtroom waited with keen anticipation for the arrested witnesses to appear but after a confused twenty minutes during which several of the principal participants milled about the room it became clear the court would not sit. Later in the day Wickham revealed that he had dissolved the court.

Some days later Nixon was ordered to attend at the Inspector-General's office at one hour's notice. When he arrived he found Wickham, his deputy, J. F. Gelston, and a shorthand writer present. According to Nixon, Wickham said that he had been directed by the government to put a list of queries to him and that he should answer only 'yes' or 'no'. Nixon answered the questions and left after protesting at length about the manner of the interview. On 28 February he was dismissed from the force on full pension. The matter was raised several times after that in the northern parliament. Bates said several times that the agitation got up on behalf of Nixon was 'the greatest bit of cant and humbug he had ever heard in all his life. The speech was made by Mr Nixon in open defiance of the order of the Inspector-General.' The government refused to reinstate him.

Nixon then entered politics and became both a Belfast councillor and Independent Unionist member of the Northern Ireland parliament, where he sat for twenty years, before his death in 1949, aged seventy. He was something of a Unionist rebel, losing no opportunity to tackle the conduct of the police and their authorities. He fought two major libel actions, winning £1,000 from the *Derry Journal* and £1,250 from the London book publishers, Methuen, for alleging that he was involved in reprisal killings, including the McMahon murders. The final verdict on that allegation awaits the release of the official papers from the Public Record Office in Belfast in due course. There is no doubt, however, that the indictment of Nixon was a grubby political episode carried out to forestall any embarrassment to the government. It was not, as it should have been, a symbol of a police discipline and impartiality. Nixon was the victim of political hypocrisy.

Throughout the year after Nixon's dismissal in 1924 the unresolved border question was a major preoccupation of the Belfast government. The RUC Intelligence Branch had been charged to keep an eye on the build-up and activities of the new Irish army in the Free State. They drew up a detailed dossier for the politicians, outlining the dispositions of the estimated 18,000-strong force commanded by 1,000 officers. The associated Air Corps had two fields at Fermoy and Baldonnel, where a Handley Page bomber, two Bristol fighters, a Bristol Scout and two training planes were based. The detail they amassed was impressive. The report even contained the insignia of each unit.

During the same period a document entitled 'An appreciation of the military position in Northern Ireland' was prepared in the Ministry of Home Affairs in Belfast. It outlined various scenarios that might develop if the ongoing talks about the border problem broke down without agreement. 'The most dangerous', the document forecast, would involve unfriendly pressure on the north from Dublin:

Should this occur, the North might expect a series of border raids and the recrudescence of internal trouble. If the Free State were to adopt open military measures of attack against the north there is little doubt that the Ulster people, with better leaders, and the more determined people, could more than hold their own.

However there is little doubt that the South contains men who are skilled in guerrilla tactics and in the execution of secret assassinations. Such irregular hostility would be impossible to deal with effectively if the Northern security forces were obliged to adopt purely defensive measures. A policy must be adopted which would compel the British government to exercise the necessary pressure on Dublin or else oblige the Free State to desist for fear of the consequences.

It is believed that the only way to bring about this result is to have in hand in Ulster a striking force which can be utilized to hit back outside the Ulster boundary. It is probable that if this striking force, say of 8,000 men, were available, and if it were known that, should the provocation continue, it was the fixed determination of the Northern Government to use it offensively, the necessity for its use would never arise.

The memo also stated that if the boundary question were settled satisfactorily the military situation in the six counties would improve, 'enabling the reduction of the swollen police force'.

The deadlock over the exact border between north and south was finally settled on 3 December 1925 after six days of negotiations between the three governments at Chequers, the British prime minister's country residence near London. 'What we have we hold,' Craig had declared all along and the six northern counties were finally delineated from the rest of Ireland, to remain under British rule through a devolved parliament in Belfast.

Although it was not part of the formal settlement, Dublin had been given to understand that the settlement would herald moves to begin dismantling the Specials. The London government were also in favour of this but primarily for financial reasons. The burden of supporting the 'swollen constabulary' had long been a bone of contention between Belfast and London. Over the previous five years, supporting the 24,000 Specials had cost a total of £7,426,000 of which £6,780,000 had been paid by the imperial government. The last time the force had been threatened with cuts the government had avoided manpower losses by reducing pay from ten to seven shillings per day. It was still a good wage at the time, equating with the top trade rates for a skilled manual worker, and the men reluctantly accepted it.

Exactly a week after the border settlement Craig announced the disbandment of the 3,500-section of A Specials and also the standing down of the 199 members of the Cl part-time force. He asked Ulster employers to recognize their moral responsibilities by absorbing the men in civil employment. Four days later, on 14 December, prompted by discontented A Specials in Londonderry, other men in several locations seized their barracks and locked up officers in some places as a protest against the financial terms of the disbandment – two months' pay. In Belfast, where several hundred men took over the Prince's Dock barracks, a written ultimatum outlining their terms was presented to Craig. In it they demanded an additional £200 bounty, free of tax. 'In default we pledge ourselves to hand in no arms, ammunition or equipment or hand over any barrack until the above terms are agreed to.'

The so-called strike was not total. In many rural areas, where the Specials and RUC shared barracks, work went on as normal but the men at Prince's Dock said they had enough food and stores to hold out until the middle of January if necessary. The government blamed ex-service members of the Specials from outside Northern Ireland for fomenting the trouble. The confrontation collapsed on 19 December within hours of a government ultimatum that unless normal duty was resumed, the A Specials would be disbanded forthwith and the men would forfeit all claims for discharge pay and allowances. The government's original terms were then accepted at a meeting hosted by the men in Londonderry who had begun the protest. Bates said he was glad that common sense had prevailed and that the men had not besmirched their good record.

The framework for maintaining law and order in Northern Ireland which was then established lasted until 1969. The RUC, backed up by the mainly part-time B Special force, not only policed the community but was responsible for protecting the borders of the state and guarding against internal subversion. The cost of doing so continued to be a major political fixation. In January 1926, faced with a budget for running the RUC of £840,000, the officials at the Ministry of Home Affairs ruled out salary and manpower cuts for the force as not being 'in the region of practical politics'. Instead it cut pay for recruits from seventy shillings a week to sixty shillings.

Although a destroyer was deployed in Belfast Lough, Northern Ireland was unaffected by the 1926 General Strike in the rest of the United Kingdom. Indeed, the closing years of the decade were so notably peaceful that in January 1928 the most serious issue exercising Dr J. C. Loughridge, the magistrate at Whiteabbey Petty Sessions, was the prevalence of courting couples in the suburbs parking their cars on the wrong side of the road.

By the conventional right-left political yardstick, Ulster Unionism was and is a highly unorthodox political grouping embracing, as it does, under one roof the representatives of the gentry and big business with the working classes. They are bound together by a single, intransigent constitutional position, rather than consensus on the more conventional bread-and-butter issues. At the end of the First World War there was, for instance, a great upsurge of working-class feeling throughout Britain. The war had broken down the rigid class barriers as never before. But in Northern Ireland when the UVF rank and file returned, the rich captains of Unionism cleverly sidetracked them by planting the idea that while they were away fighting loyally for King and Country the 'disloyal' Catholics, inspired by the Bolsheviks, had stolen their jobs and houses. Thus the scene was set for the pogroms of the period.

There was identical Unionist dirty-work in the early 1930s, again designed to thwart any working-class unity which could lead to the emergence of a Labour movement and pose a threat to the political power of the Unionist establishment. At that time the traditionally high rate of Catholic unemployment was increased by the lay-offs of Protestants from the recession-hit shipbuilding yards and linen mills which were Belfast's staple industries. The unemployed were not as well provided for as they are today. Limited statutory benefits, payable by the government, were made for a time after an employed person lost his job but once that eligibility expired the workers were thrown on the mercy of the Poor Law Guardians, who administered payments through the Outdoor Relief work schemes or gave help in kind, usually groceries, to prevent the money being spent in the pubs. Much of their power was discretionary and their behaviour frequently insensitive and autocratic. One of the Guardians, Mrs Lily Coleman, was notorious for humiliating Catholic fathers with large families by declaring that there was 'no poverty under the blankets'.

Because they kept the amounts of relief paid out to the absolute minimum, poverty and distress among the recipients led to a protest movement getting under way in 1932. At that time a Belfast man with a wife and child was getting twelve shillings a week aid, compared with twenty-seven shillings payable in Northampton, twenty-one shillings in Manchester or twenty-three shillings in Liverpool, to a man in the same circumstances. The discontent came to a head on 3 October 1932 when up to 60,000 workers took part in a torchlight procession to the Custom House Steps, then Belfast's equivalent of Speaker's Corner in Hyde Park, London. The occasion was so firmly non-sectarian that the only tune common to bands from both communities, more accustomed to thumping out party anthems, was 'Yes We Have No Bananas', and it was played over and over again throughout the unprecedented rally.

Next day a large crowd, several thousand strong, marched on the Belfast workhouse at Lisburn Road, and many of them lay on the tram lines, bringing the city to a halt. There was another demonstration the next day despite a police show of strength along the route with Crossley tenders and Lancia armoured cars, and serious rioting developed when the police baton-charged the crowds in Bradbury Place. By the end of the week the increasingly worried government had agreed to increase the relief rates by a half and to cease providing help in kind. However, with talk of a general strike growing, the concessions were rejected by the leaders of the demonstrations, who called for a night of bonfires on 10 October followed by a monster demonstration in Belfast the next day, which would converge from four assembly points.

This manifestation of working-class unity had by then caused such consternation among the Unionist government and business establishment that the Special Powers Act was promptly used to prohibit further demonstrations. (The Act, which had been renewed annually until 1928, had now become permanent legislation.) The government was also aware, through Bates, of the serious concern in the upper echelons of the RUC about the force's ability to contain widespread disturbances. Things had been touch and go for a time earlier in the year when trains carrying Catholics to the International Eucharistic Congress in Dublin had been stoned by mobs, triggering off a bout of sectarian rioting in Belfast and Portadown. At that time Wickham had been forced to trawl every country station for all but essential men and rush the remainder to Belfast.

Given these factors it was no surprise that violence erupted and spread like a bushfire through the city on 11 October. The police in their tenders and armoured cars attempted to hold control of the main arterial roads through the city but as they did so they came under sustained assault from the kidney-shaped paving stones lifted from the side streets, where trenches had been dug and barricades thrown up to prevent the RUC entering. After a day of violence, an 11 pm to 5 am curfew was proclaimed but the violence nevertheless continued through the night and into the next day.

By then it had become clear that in the hour of crisis the Unionist government had consciously set out to use the police force as a tool to divide the workers and protect their own position. The police were specifically told to use their guns in the Catholic areas to stop the IRA using the situation to overthrow the state but only to use batons in the Protestant areas to stop looting. An analysis of the officially recorded deaths and injuries arising from the violence confirms the partiality of the police response. The two people who died in the trouble, John Kennan and Samuel Baxter, had both been shot by the police in Catholic areas. Of those injured in the various clashes, fifteen suffered gunshot wounds, all inflicted by the police in Catholic areas. The fifteen men hurt in Protestant areas incurred leg, scalp and head injuries as well as fractures, all consistent with assault by police batons but not gunfire.

The government's strategy worked, for the city's traditional passions were easily rekindled, and ironically worker was turned upon worker. However, the confrontation did have one positive result, for the new rates of relief quickly introduced, at a cost of £300,000 to the Northern Ireland government, were double those originally paid. The episode had seriously shaken the Belfast government and underlined the internal vulnerability of the Northern Ireland state, especially the shortcomings of the police. In his diary, Sir Wilfred Spender, the secretary to the Belfast cabinet, recorded the government's narrow escape from disaster. The agitation had been so serious, he wrote, that the cost of the wilful damage could quite easily have been greater than the cost of doubling the money for the relief schemes. The ultimate irony, however, was that once the violence had subsided and the curfew was lifted the unemployed were put to work in the back streets replacing the street surfaces with solid concrete where the lethal paving stones had been removed to use as missiles against the police.

Not long after the clashes, on 28 February 1933, the RUC suffered its first fatal casualty when Constable John Ryan was killed. A convoy of lorries leaving the railway goods yard in Grosvenor Road, Belfast, was fired on by gunmen. Ryan, who was nearby on the beat with a colleague, challenged the fleeing gunmen and died in the subsequent exchange of fire. Although forty-seven members of the Special Constabulary had been killed between 1921 and 1922, he was the first RUC man to die in service. In the early hours of 9 October the same year, another officer was killed in a shooting incident. Late the previous evening Constable

Charles Anderson was on guard duty with a colleague at a house in the Falls Road area of Belfast when they were attacked by a number of gunmen and he was wounded. He died some hours later in hospital.

The raw wounds opened up after the Outdoor Relief clashes had barely closed when the volatility of community relations in Belfast was shown once again. This time the cause of the trouble was the sectarian enthusiasm with which the Unionists celebrated the May 1935 Silver Jubilee of George V. The violence that the celebrations provoked was so serious that Bates announced a ban on all parades, including the July Orange marches. This provoked such an outcry that he quickly reneged. The inevitable clashes throughout the long hot summer were a less serious rerun of those fifteen years earlier. The Orange marches degenerated into communal rioting and the city, again under curfew, was once more raked with sniper fire from both sides of its rigid sectarian boundaries and trouble flared in workplaces and residential areas. The RUC, with its cage cars and armoured cars, was in the thick of the violence, which subsided in the autumn leaving eleven people dead.

The British government, led by prime minister Stanley Baldwin, did not interfere despite widespread concern about the situation in the press and parliament, although Craig was called to London for consultations. Early in 1936, reflecting the concern among a substantial body of MPs in London, an investigation carried out for the National Council for Civil Liberties by five eminent academics, lawyers and Liberal MPs into the Special Powers Act and the conduct of the RUC reported that the Unionists had created 'under the shadow of the British constitution a permanent machine of dictatorship'. The report cited one example of the way the draconian powers of the act were manipulated:

> In October 1933, shortly prior to the local elections, the Government carried out a 'round-up' in which some forty or fifty persons were arrested. No reasons were given for the arrests and no charges were, or apparently, could be laid against the men.
>
> After they had been detained for some time the Government promulgated Regulation 22B, under the terms of which the men were privately examined. On declining to answer certain questions put to them by the Resident Magistrate conducting the examinations they were charged with 'refusal to answer questions' and the Magistrate's certificate of such refusal sufficed to secure their conviction

and sentence to terms of imprisonment for an offence which was created subsequent to their arrest.

The report also cited the close links maintained between the government and Orange Order, the discrimination against Catholics in judicial appointments, the maintenance of the exclusively Protestant B Specials, the 'frankly sectarian speeches' made by ministers and the gerrymandering of electoral boundaries as 'tendencies' which 'make it difficult to contradict the assertion that the Unionist government's policy has resulted in the inflammation of religious bigotry and the aggravation of sectarian differences amongst the Northern Irish community'. Noting that the status of the RUC, being under the direct control and authority of the Ulster Home Office, was different from the regular police forces in England, it accused the force of partisanship and abusing its powers of search and interrogation:

> ... to some extent this apparent partiality may be due to a feeling of impotence rather than to a desire (particularly on the part of the ordinary rank and file of the RUC) to show favouritism, for there is no doubt that Orange hooliganism often reaches such a pitch as to require the most drastic use of force to suppress it. But even if this feeling does play some part in producing the effects of partiality, it is difficult to escape the conclusion that the attitude of the government renders the police chary of interference with the activities of the Orange Order and its sympathizers.

Despite this damning indictment of the way law and order in Northern Ireland was being administered, no action was taken. The London government's attitude seemed to be that if the Unionists could keep the lid on the troublesome Irish, then let them get on with it. That the RUC, in extreme situations, had been allowed to become such a political tool seemed obviously to be the fault of Wickham, as the chief officer. Whatever impartial instincts and values he had held, and voiced, soon after his arrival in Ulster appeared to have been overwhelmed by the directions of Bates and his advisers. By becoming their puppet, he had allowed the standards of police independence so vigorously established by Peel and Drummond to be seriously compromised. (Evidence of how far he had been subverted came in 1947, shortly after his retirement. Documents in the Public Record Office in Belfast show that Sir Basil Brooke, who became prime minister in 1943, was called before the Grand Orange Lodge of

Ireland to defend an educational reform which substantially increased funding for voluntary, mainly Catholic, schools. As part of his pitch for the bigoted Orangemen he specifically got Wickham to write a letter underlining his contribution to the Unionist cause in the 1920s.)

Almost a year after the rioting, apprehensive about more trouble during the Orange marching season in July, there was another all-party attempt at Westminster to persuade Baldwin to hold a purpose-ful inquiry into the 1935 riots. In June 1936, a steering group of thirteen MPs (three Conservatives, three Liberals, four Labour and three independent Labour) attracted about 180 of their colleagues to a meeting but despite approaches to the prime minister there was no positive response. Matters were the responsibility of the Northern Ireland government, he insisted, and 'for fundamental constitutional reasons' he could not get involved. By now the seat of government in Northern Ireland had moved to Stormont, where an imposing new parliamentary building had been constructed on the side of the eastern hills overlooking Belfast. The construction cost was met by the British government as a gift to the people of Ulster. It was formally opened by the Prince of Wales on 16 November 1932.

In its other role as a conventional police force, the RUC had also developed considerably. Recognizing the growth of motor transport, the Police Traffic Branch was formed on 1 January 1930. Some time later Mr W. Grant, MP, speaking in the new Ulster House of Commons at Stormont, said that he would like to offer a little friendly advice to the mobile police. 'Some of those police driving about in "posh" cars thought they owned the road and all that was on it. They should appreciate that they were the servants of the public and that they should treat the public with civility.'

On 20 November 1936 the new depot at Enniskillen had been brought into use and an £800,000-scheme to create a network of 196 police barracks throughout Ulster by rationalizing or repairing the 224 premises inherited from the RIC was getting under way. On 20 May 1937, after controversy that many stations still bore the RIC crest, a new white glass lamp, with the RUC coat of arms, went up for the first time at four stations in Belfast: Queen Street, Lisburn Road, Strandtown and Willowfield. About the same time the Criminal Investigation Department in Belfast was significantly expanded, with a Detective Head Constable being appointed to head the CID force in each of the five Belfast police districts.

Meanwhile, members of the IRA, those who opposed the treaty creating the governments in Belfast and Dublin, who had lost the resulting civil war in the south, had been largely dormant in Northern Ireland since the 1920s. However, in 1933 there were signs of a resurgence of activity. In raids on a train at Dundalk and various public houses throughout the country, English-brewed ale was poured away. More direct evidence of reorganization came in Belfast on 27 December 1935 when there was a shoot-out with police who discovered an IRA arms' stealing party trying to break into the Officers Training Corps depot at Campbell College, a leading public school. Constable Ian Hay, who was seriously wounded in the clash, had found the caretaker of the college and his wife tied up in the gate lodge.

One Saturday a few months later, in April 1936, a vigilant constable spotted some known IRA men in Belfast. The Crime Special Branch, which was responsible for keeping an eye on the IRA, was quickly tipped off and a surveillance operation was set up. That evening all were gathered at a club in Crown Entry, off High Street in Belfast, when the RUC swooped. They found a 'court-martial' under way, arising out of the public school raid. It was a substantial coup for the police to mop up eleven subversives in one operation. But the discovery of guns, ammunition, sixty-eight sticks of gelignite and IRA documents in a house in Londonderry in July showed that there was no room for complacency about the IRA threat.

In December 1936 and January 1937 two members of the organization in Belfast were murdered for allegedly being police informers. In July, when the King and Queen visited the province, the IRA blew up a number of customs posts. In November they attacked the customs posts again but three members of the organization died in a premature explosion at Clady on the border with Donegal. The RUC advised the government that the IRA violence was likely to continue, so three days before Christmas internment was once more introduced and twenty-three suspects were taken into custody.

A more serious threat materialized on 12 January 1939 when the IRA issued a four-day ultimatum to the British government to withdraw from the six counties. When the deadline was ignored, the so-called 'S Plan' was implemented and bombs began going off throughout Britain. By July, when parliament rushed through legislation to impose controls on Irish residents, there had been two people killed in about 130 explosions. The campaign effectively ended on 25

August, a few days before the outbreak of the Second World War, when a bomb attached to a bicycle exploded in Coventry, killing five people. Although there were some bombs exploded early in 1940, when two men were hanged for causing the Coventry blast, the campaign in Britain was over.

Back in Northern Ireland, however, where it was judged that England's difficulty was once more Ireland's opportunity, the IRA was once more preparing for trouble. Wickham warned the government of plans for outrages and advised that the B Specials should be mobilized and an internment camp at Ballykinler, County Down, be made ready. Before long a prison ship was also brought in to cope with the numbers of internees.

Although there was some IRA activity in 1940, notably a number of bank raids and a raid on a British Army barracks which netted 100 rifles, the main threat to law and order came from an upsurge in smuggling along the border. The rewards were so high on the black market that had sprung into existence almost as soon as war was declared that the smugglers took to defending their contraband with guns and there were several exchanges of fire with the RUC. During the year, on 8 June, Head Constable Thomas Dempsey was shot dead while on duty in a Londonderry street.

But the main fear of the government and police throughout the year was an uprising in the north, inspired or not by the IRA, in the wake of German parachute troops leading an invasion of the Free State, which had stayed neutral in the war. By the end of 1940 the RUC and B Specials, together with the newly created Local Defence Volunteers, at almost 40,000 strong, were back at their 1920s strength. In addition, in excess of 100,000 troops with air support were posted to Northern Ireland in case the south, neutral or not, had to be invaded to hold any German advance. Throughout 1940, too, Belfast's importance to the British war effort increased. The Harland and Wolff shipyard was working at full stretch, aircraft were being turned out from the nearby Short Bros complex and an ordance factory had been established in the city. Elsewhere the textile mills went over to production of cloth and uniforms, while the engineering industry had diversified into producing tanks and guns.

The defences against air-raids for a city as heavily populated as Belfast with such strategically important facilities were, however, almost non-existent. There was a feeling that 'it couldn't happen here', that the haul from airfields, even in occupied France, was too risky for the Luftwaffe both in terms of fuel range and the chances of being intercepted by the RAF during each leg of the journey. So, at the beginning of 1941, although a start had been made, the city had only 200 public and 4,000 household air-raid shelters. There was also a shortage of fire-fighting equipment. Air defence cover was equally inadequate, with no searchlights, only twenty-four heavy and twelve light anti-aircraft guns – half the proper number – limited radar cover and no night fighters. The effectiveness of the black-out was also in question by fears and rumours that IRA sympathizers in the Catholic areas of the city were planning to show lights to attract the German bombers.

Belfast's first experience of the blitz came on the night of 7–8 April 1941 when a small detachment of bombers, probably no more than six, dropped first flares and then a barrage of incendiary and high-explosive bombs on the docks and shipyard area, where serious damage was done. Fifty bombers under construction were destroyed. In the surrounding residential areas damage from the fires was quite widespread but the casualties for the attack were relatively light, thirteen dead and eighty-one injured, twenty-three of them seriously.

Just over a week later the bombers came back again, this time in force. It was Easter Tuesday, 15 April, just before 11 pm when the warning sirens wailed. From then until 5 am waves of bombers, thought to be 200 in all operating from France and Holland, flew in over the city, causing widespread devastation. Bangor, Newtownards and Londonderry also suffered raids in which another twenty people died. The fires that were raging throughout the city were uncontrollable, and appliances and volunteers from Dublin and other Free State cities rushed to the aid of the people of Belfast. When the dead were counted, they numbered 745, 60 of them in one direct hit in an air-raid shelter. Except for London, it was the worst single night's casualty toll suffered by any other city during the war.

Belfast endured two more raids. On 4 May, 150 people died and the next night, in what turned out to be the last air-raid on the city, another 14 were killed. The RUC shared in the toll. A sergeant, six constables and two Specials were killed in the raids. Another sergeant, eleven constables and eighteen Specials were injured. Two police barracks were destroyed and the City headquarters in Belfast was severely damaged. For bravery during the raids, three members of the force were later awarded George Medals, while two other officers got British Empire Medals.

Soon after the blitz, ministers at Stormont, as always anxious to demonstrate the 'loyalty' of Ulster to King and Country, proposed to London that military conscription should be extended to Northern Ireland. Anxious to muster every man for the war effort, the suggestion was received with some enthusiasm in London until a 'Secret' memorandum from Wickham reached the War Office. For a man who had complied with the excesses of the Unionists for about twenty years, Wickham's objection was perhaps surprising, though perceptive and accurate. Recognizing that the RUC would have to be the 'press gang' in answer to the Catholic/nationalist hostility to conscription and that the IRA would probably benefit, with the attendant dangers for internal stability in time of war, Wickham came down firmly against such an imposition. Coupled with representations from De Valera, who was in power in the south, Wickham's reservations had a profound effect on consideration of the subject by the London cabinet and, to the annoyance of ministers in Belfast, Churchill decided against introducing conscription in the north on the grounds that 'it would be more trouble than it was worth'.

Despite the misery caused by the war and the destruction in Belfast, the IRA kept up its activities in the north, including collecting information about the defences around Belfast on orders from Dublin. On 9 February 1942 the police uncovered conclusive evidence of the IRA's interest in defence matters when they arrested a dining-car attendant on the Dublin–Belfast train and found he was carrying letters in his socks. One of them, from the 'Intelligence Department, General Headquarters Dublin' addressed to the 'Director of Intelligence, Northern Command' asked for a count of the British and American forces in the north, a detailed report on the Northern Ireland power system and a list of factories engaged in war production. Such finds fuelled the belief that there was contact between the IRA and the Nazi regime in Germany and that the information was being collected on their behalf.

However, vigorous repression of the IRA in the Free State by the De Valera administration, and the fact that upwards of 800 people were interned in the camp at Ballykinler and in a ship on Strangford Lough, clearly helped to contain the threat. Nevertheless the violence flared again. On 3 April, a police party, following up a report that IRA men had been operating an illegal road check near Dungannon, raided a house in the town. As they did so, a group of men in the house fled, firing at the police as they escaped. Constable Thomas

Forbes engaged the men with gunfire but sustained wounds himself, from which he died three days later.

In the meantime another policeman had lost his life. On Sunday 5 April, Easter Sunday, the IRA in Belfast planned to defy a ban and hold a commemoration of the 1916 Rising. To distract police attention a number of gunmen took up positions behind an air-raid shelter at Kashmir Road in the Falls area and waited for a target. Soon afterwards they opened up on a police patrol car. Constable Patrick Murphy got out of the car and gave chase to the gunmen, pursuing them into the rear of a house at Cawnpore Street. By now they had dropped their weapons into a shopping bag, which was supposed to be whisked away by two girls waiting nearby, but one of them, Tom Williams, retrieved his gun and opened fire. When police colleagues caught up with Murphy he was found dead in the scullery. Williams, a nineteen-year-old house repairer, was lying wounded on a bed in an upstairs room and he and the rest of the gang surrendered. Murphy, who left a wife and nine children, was later awarded the King's Police and Fire Service Medal.

A few months afterwards all six gunmen were sentenced to death for capital murder after a trial in Belfast. (The girls, who were also arrested, were later released.) It was the first time that the death sentence had been passed on IRA prisoners, despite the violent history of Northern Ireland and the repressive nature of the government. Predictably, the IRA 'martyr-making' propaganda machine swung into action and there were widespread moves for a reprieve. Cooler heads joined the campaign, recognizing the boost that the IRA would receive if the executions took place.

The Appeal Court, however, upheld both the conviction and the sentence. The hangings were set for 2 September 1942 but four days beforehand, after renewed representations, five of the men were reprieved. Williams, regarded as the ringleader, was still to hang. 'The condemned man went calmly to his death without a tremor,' Father Alexis, who had been present at the 8 am execution, told a *Belfast Telegraph* reporter. (Williams is, in fact, the only subversive ever executed in Ulster, where the death penalty was abolished in 1972.)

Outside the prison rival crowds had gathered; one set of sympathizers kneeling and praying; the other, Unionists, singing 'God Save the King' and 'Land of Hope and Glory'. The city was tense and there was heavy police patrolling everywhere but only a few incidents were reported. In Wellington Place, Belfast, there were scuffles with police after two women, part of a crowd protesting about the execution, gave the Nazi salute to two US servicemen. Elsewhere a US army car was stoned and a police sergeant wounded by gunfire, near Crossmaglen in South Armagh. This chance encounter caused a heavily armed IRA gang to abort an assault on the police station there, during which they had planned to capture a British officer to hang in reprisal for Williams. In some Catholic areas of Belfast men forced the pubs to close for the day and in Dublin shops in O'Connell Street closed after a brick was thrown through the plate-glass window of Easons, the newsagent.

A few days before the hanging police uncovered three tons of arms, ammunition and explosives at four farms in the Dundrod area. At one of the dumps they shot a man dead. He was carrying false papers. The major haul was intended for a new offensive, aimed very largely at the police, which had been postponed in order not to prejudice the reprieve campaign. IRA documents later captured by the police stated that members of the force 'should be rounded up, be disarmed and then shot'.

In spite of the lost haul, the IRA swung into renewed action and there was a steady level of attacks, principally on police barracks and patrols until the end of the year. In one of the outrages at Clady, shortly before midnight on 5 September 1942, Constable James Laird and Special Constable Samuel Hamilton were hit by gunfire from men who then escaped across the border. Both officers died the next day from their injuries. Scarcely a month later, on 10 October, Special Constable James Lyons, who was on patrol in an adjoining street, gave chase to men running away from the direction of Donegall Pass barracks in the aftermath of a bomb blast. There was an exchange of fire with the two men and Lyons and a colleague, both wounded, continued to fire. However he later died from his wounds.

The police reacted to the violence, in which another thirteen officers sustained injury from both bomb and bullet, by imposing a curfew and renewed detention swoops. Over the period nearly 400 men were lifted. On 10 September they dealt the IRA a significant blow when they uncovered what was described in court as 'the headquarters of the Northern Command' in a 'secret chamber' built into a house at 463 Crumlin Road, Belfast. That evening police raiding the house to search for arms were fired on, narrowly missing injury. The gunmen surrendered and during the subsequent search the police uncovered a radio transmitter, duplicating machine, typewriters, voluminous IRA publications and documents as well as arms and ammunition.

The IRA attacks tailed off after that but 1943 is still remembered for three IRA actions that caused grave embarrassment to the police and government. In January four top IRA men escaped over the wall of Belfast's Crumlin Road prison. One of them, Hugh McAteer, described in the secret chamber documents as the IRA's 'Chief of Staff', had only just begun a sentence of fifteen years' penal servitude. In March twenty-one internees tunnelled their way out of Londonderry jail and escaped across the border, where most of them were promptly recaptured and interned. The resulting recriminations at government level had hardly settled when another act of bravado took place. On Easter Sunday afternoon, armed men took over a cinema in West Belfast and stopped the film long enough to enable McAteer to read the 1916 Proclamation. In a further incident on 1 October 1943 Constable Patrick McCarthy was in the gate lodge of a mill at Clonard when armed IRA raiders tried to snatch the money to pay wages. They shot and wounded him before running off empty-handed. He tried to pursue them but collapsed in the street and died.

The IRA's wartime campaign effectively ended early in 1944. The last episode was the shooting dead of James 'Rocky' Burns, one of the Londonderry escapees, on 12 February. He was stopped in Chapel Lane by police, who were dissatisfied with his identity documents and decided to take him to the nearby barracks at Queen Street. On the way he pulled a gun but he was immediately shot in the stomach by a plainclothes RUC officer who was watching the operation. On 10 March 1945 the IRA announced a ceasefire.

In July 1945 Wickham retired. Together with County Inspector Regan, he set about organizing and supervising an RUC contingent who were being sent to Greece to organize a police force. RUC officers were also involved with the policing activities of the Allied Control Commission which took over direction of affairs in Germany when hostilities ceased.

The new Inspector-General of the RUC was Sir Richard Pim, who had distinguished himself as one of Churchill's closest aides during the war. Ulster-born, he was the son of a linen magnate, educated at Lancing College, Sussex, and Trinity College, Dublin, from where he graduated with a degree in arts and law. His was an old Irish Quaker family which settled in Ireland in the seventeenth century; one of his ancestors, John Pim, had been political adviser to Oliver Cromwell. In the First World War he had served as a midshipman in the RNVR and then joined the RIC as an officer cadet. In 1921, having attained the rank of District Inspector, he served first in Dublin, then Londonderry and Limavady. On the formation of the northern government in 1922 he joined the Ministry of Home Affairs, where he served for a time as private secretary to Sir Dawson Bates.

On the outbreak of the Second World War he was released for naval service and soon joined Churchill's staff, organizing his wartime map rooms, first at the Admiralty and later at 10 Downing Street. Pim remained at Churchill's elbow throughout the war, travelling with him to the important conferences at Washington, Quebec, Casablanca, Cairo, Yalta and Potsdam. Afterwards he used to recall that he had shaken Stalin's hand but was not proud of it. A feature at all these summits, which shaped the political map of the world for the rest of the twentieth century, was Pim's travelling map display. President Roosevelt was so impressed that he enlisted Pim's help in having a similar installation designed for the White House.

Knighted for his wartime services, Pim assumed command of the RUC on 1 August 1945, directing operations from an office at the Waring Street headquarters with a giant one-inch-to-the-mile wall map studded with pins marking each of the RUC stations. Those who remember him say he was a tall man, always immaculately dressed, with good looks and charm, although this was usually masked by initial shyness. He had the brisk, efficient style of a service officer but none of the pomp and ceremony. He was direct, down to earth and frequently good-humoured.

He took over at a time of great change for the RUC. During the war a section of women police had been formed by Woman Sergeant Marion Macmillan, who had come over from the Metropolitan Police in London to lead them, and the first squad of six women recruits had passed out from Enniskillen in 1944. The barrack replacement programme was well under way too: thirty-nine old premises had been reconstructed and eighty-four new ones built.

One of Pim's first decisions was to expand significantly the Traffic Branch by ordering twenty-six new cars and drafting in a hundred officers to man them. His wartime experience was brought to bear on the ever increasing growth of traffic and accidents, and the Branch set up a map room to plot patterns in accidents and identify blackspots. Crime levels had soared to three times those in the immediate post-war period and the RUC mounted a determined campaign in the late forties to tackle the problem. More policemen were assigned to patrol on bicycles and motorcycles, and the public was encouraged to use the '999' telephone system; in 1948 they made fifty red-handed arrests as a result of emergency calls. People were urged to be more crime-conscious. The police complained that on average two instances of insecure premises, homes and businesses were discovered every night. Soon afterwards cars equipped with radio-telephones were introduced. 'The law breaker has been put "on the spot" as never before,' enthused a *Belfast Telegraph* reporter who studied the radio case-book reports of a succession of red-handed arrests. The system was run from the Belfast Commissioner's office at Templemore Avenue and, again reflecting Pim's expertise with maps, the control room wall was covered with an eighteen-inch-to-the-mile map of the city.

In the early 1950s the force had to mount recruiting campaigns for the first time to keep up its strength, which fell as much as 200 short of the 3,000 establishment. The problem was caused by many of the founder members of the force retiring after completing their thirty-years' service. A brightly coloured poster showing the RUC man in a variety of postures – sportsman, motorcyclist, radio operator – was exhibited outside each station. 'Join the RUC – it's a great career,' the poster urged. The shortage of manpower was further aggravated by the representatives of several Canadian police forces who came over to Belfast and poached men away. Two hundred men applied to one force, which recruited thirty-five RUC members. At £1,000 per year the salaries on offer were twice the RUC rate.

In 1955 Bruce and Bruno joined the strength, the first police dogs in the RUC. Bruno made his first arrest a few weeks later when he apprehended a man who had assaulted a young woman. The women police were allowed to break new ground by taking over point duty at busy 'Zebra' crossings in Belfast. It was also announced in the Stormont parliament that in future the RUC would not be visibly armed. 'We shall never allow a policeman to become a defenceless target for a gunman,' said Mr G. B. Hanna, QC, the Minister of Home Affairs. 'I am endeavouring to take steps that our police force will be adequately armed with weapons which will not be visible. Whether they have them with them or not, it will still be in the mind if the gunmen that they probably are armed.'

But while the pace of change and technology was transforming the RUC, traditional community attitudes remained as intransigent as ever. In February 1955 the Minister of Home Affairs ordered an investigation into why the national anthem, 'God Save the Queen', had not been played at the conclusion of a police dance in Lurgan. In the Commons at Stormont, Hanna said that he shared the indignation of the local MP on the matter and that he and the government most certainly did not approve that at any function under the control of the RUC there should be, for any purpose, a refusal to honour the Queen.

The periodic disturbances that occurred were usually connected with marches by one side or the other. In a significant case in August 1950, Tyrone County Court awarded a Catholic band damages after it was attacked and stoned by a Protestant mob at Cookstown under the eyes of police who did not intervene. The court ruled that all citizens were entitled to the protection of the police and fined the attackers, who included the local Commandant of the B Specials.

The government brought in two new pieces of legislation to strengthen its hand in dealing with the sort of situations being encountered. In July 1951 a Public Order Act prohibited all but traditional parades unless the police were given notice. All others could be banned or re-routed by the police without any right or appeal. In 1954, despite doubts expressed by the police about its enforceability, the government pushed through a Flags and Emblems Act which outlawed the display of a flag likely to cause a breach of the peace – clearly the Irish tricolour – and made it an offence to interfere with the display of the Union flag. Hanna considered that police chief Pim was being 'unduly apprehensive' about the legislation. However, once again the net effect of this security legislation was to discriminate against the minority and impose on the police the responsibility for enforcing it.

Events at Longstone Road, Annalong, County Down – at the time a notorious flashpoint – confirmed the resultant hostile Catholic perception of the RUC, for, after initial hesitancy which infuriated the Orangemen, the Orange marches were repeatedly pushed through the Catholic area by the police deployed in strength. Catholics felt that when they wanted to march in the face of protests, the police banned it rather than protect their right. In July 1955 the RUC used water-cannon for the first time to enforce a ban on a nationalist march in Newtownbutler.

In normal times the police were on foot patrol; they were well known and they knew everybody else. If you were seen kicking a ball in the street, they would take your name; they knew it without having to catch you, and you would be summoned. Playing cards on the street was also an offence likely to result in a fine. But you would know their beat and that way you could avoid them. When thus engaged the bigger boys asked the smaller boys to keep watch for them.

I remember this day I was keeping watch for a card-playing group in Granville Street. I saw the police pass at the bottom of the street. That's fine, I thought, they have to come down MacDonald Street, down which I was facing. Next minute I felt two big arms around me; I was helpless. They had crept up from the opposite direction and I was caught. I found myself brought along by the hand to the barracks and charged with gambling. I hadn't been gambling at all; I had only been looking on. I decided to say nothing about it at home; if my dad heard there would be an awful row.

So when the summons came, I was on the look out; I collared it and went to court, where I was lectured by the magistrate and fined half-a-crown. Of course, when the police came to collect the fine, I was not at home; I was at school. I arrived in to find my mother in tears; fined for gambling and the police after me with a warrant for my arrest. She was distraught and upset at the shame of it. She was prepared to pay it, but there were costs on top of it amounting to five shillings. While there was always enough money for food in the house, she hadn't got the five shillings, so she borrowed it from a neighbour and paid it, because, as she said, if my father got to hear about it, he would have killed me.

Of course my friends who had been gambling did not think much of me as a watch dog after that; the looker-out fella, they called me in fun, and for a while the name stuck to me.

That was the nature of policing in the late twenties and early thirties in the north and around Belfast. Petty fines, keeping order, serving summons, collecting statistics, watching that the pubs observed closing, preventing children playing football, pitch and toss, or cards. There was almost nothing political on either side. Even when I returned from Arbour Hill [a former Dublin prison] in late 1935, walking along Leeson Street, I was spoken to by this [RUC] policeman, Lamont, from Ballycastle. The sooner, says he, they get this border fixed up and I am able to leave my gun behind like the Civic Guards, the better I will like it.

Surprising as it might seem, those are the words of Harry White, a prominent IRA activist in Belfast, recorded in his biography *Harry* as told to Uinseann MacEoinn. They illustrate the dual level on which the RUC operated in the Catholic community, even through the turbulence of the thirties, forties and fifties. Despite what could be called the theological objection to the RUC, at street level, there grew between the police and the Catholic community a practical pragmatism within which both sides ignored the high-level contradictions between them and settled for low-level mutual respect and co-operation.

Catholic members of the force were tolerated in their own community but did not enjoy the social standing or status of their Protestant counterparts. The force was very much run on officers and men lines. The 'men' were the constables, sergeants and head constables. The 'officers', district and county inspectors, who often carried blackthorn sticks, were usually forbidding men, of strong military bearing, who mixed professionally and socially with the ruling class. They were entertained in the big houses and kept themselves informed of local gossip and events.

Like their RIC predecessors, the RUC were very close to the communities, and knew the ins and outs and connections of every family, not only in the sparsely populated rural areas but also in the teeming back streets of Belfast. Their subsidiary responsibilities, which they carried out for many years, examining public service vehicles, checking weights and measures, inspecting explosives and even acting as customs officers on the north-south border, brought them into wide contact with the population. In country areas they acted as livestock inspectors and carried out the agricultural census every year, taking the tillage. This was a popular duty, especially during the years when rationing was in force, for it usually meant having a good meal with the farmer before returning to the station with eggs or butter or sometimes even a chicken for the pot. Despite the temptations, especially from the smugglers, who were making fortunes running contraband both ways across the border, the RUC men were not corrupted. But there was a sensible element of leeway, especially in the matter of illegally distilled poteen. To this day many RUC members enjoy a drop and know the finest sources to obtain a bottle.

They developed a shrewdness in doing their job, dealing as they were with canny country folk on the one hand, and street-wise city criminals on the other. One officer's technique for checking dog licences in the dense network of Belfast streets was to walk along the back alleys kicking each door as he passed and when a dog answered he would note the number of the house. That gave him a check-list for the official call at the front door of each house.

Whatever the partiality of the force *en masse* the individual RUC men generally exercised their discretion judiciously. A timely clip on the ear for a young offender was often more effective than the stigma of proceedings in the juvenile court. Driving an intoxicated man home from the pub did more for local police-community relations than charging him. Common sense and shrewdness, it could well be argued, were the hallmarks of the ordinary policeman. If it had not been for the sectarian layer of affairs, the degree of public tranquillity in Ulster would have been unbeatable, thanks to the grass roots effectiveness of the RUC. In reality life for the ordinary RUC man closely resembled that of the RIC and changed little between the late 1920s and the early 1960s. The force, especially in the border areas, remained on a paramilitary footing, whatever the level of threat, and in the rest of the province it operated more or less on the lines of a conventional police force although every man was permanently armed with a .45 Webley, even while carrying out routine tasks like traffic point duty. For many years the men also had a rifle and bayonet, and were trained to use them.

The first introduction most men had to the force was through their local sergeant, who was expected to cast an experienced eye over potential recruits and test their numeracy and literacy. This was done by having the man write down a passage dictated from a book or even the local paper and do a few simple sums. For sergeants, the opening of a recruit file was something of an event and most of them savoured it to the full. Many RUC aspirants, who were later to have distinguished careers, recall being knocked back on their first application and having to press to be recruited. Having convinced the sergeant to open a file and process it, the applicant was thoroughly scrutinized for his family background and character. The initial forms required details to be given of all previous employment, addresses, parents, uncles, aunts and cousins. The force was even prepared to take recruits from the south. Guidelines circulated in 1956 said that 'candidates from Eire who are suitable and of undoubted loyalty will be considered by the force proved that sufficient Northern Ireland candidates are not immediately available for the vacancies'. Recruiting officers were told to make appropriate enquiries 'as to character and loyalty'.

If nothing to their detriment was discovered, RUC applicants were called to the county headquarters where they sat a written examination to test their general knowledge, mathematics, geography and English. Those who passed, and applicants who had passed the public examinations at school, then found themselves summoned to the force headquarters at Atlantic Buildings, Waring Street, in central Belfast. There they paraded before the medical officer and the commandant of the training centre. If they met with their approval they were subjected to a searching twenty-minute interview by the Inspector-General himself before final acceptance as a recruit.

Billy Mooney, who was later to distinguish himself as one of the most tenacious detectives in the history of the RUC, recalls his motives for joining the force being thoroughly questioned by the recruiting sergeant, who told him he was a mug, and Inspector-General Pim. At the time Mooney was a trained shipwright with a wife and young baby, earning the princely wage, for the early 1950s, of £13 10s a week plus overtime. He had always wanted to be a policeman but his mother had insisted he get a trade first. Pim questioned him closely on why he wanted to join the police where he would be paid only £32 a calendar month with no overtime or extras. Mooney explained that although the shipyard was a good job, there was always the possibility of being laid off. He wanted long-term security but most of all he wanted to be a policeman. 'I really had to convince him I had always wanted to be a policeman,' recalls Mooney.

Recruits were instructed to report to the RUC depot for initial training. This took place at Newtownards, County Down, until 1936, when a new depot was opened at Enniskillen, County Fermanagh. In 1986, after several terrorist attacks on the premises and because of the need for a divisional headquarters in the area, the training organization moved temporarily to a former college at Garnerville, on the eastern outskirts of Belfast. The force hopes that before long it will get the go-ahead and the finance to develop a new purpose-built training centre.

An instruction to new recruits dating to the end of the Second World War, advises them to bring two shirts, two pairs of pyjamas, two undervests, two underdrawers, four towels, four pairs of socks, their ID card and ration books, sufficient clothing coupons for regulation pattern boots, not less than £2 money and a return ticket to their home. In Newtownards days, the local shoemaker sent his boy into the camp with a suitcase of boot samples, to take orders from the new recruits. Boots cost £1 4s. He also supplied travelling trunks. When they joined up, men were given their kit, which had to be scrupulously kept. That meant 'spit and polish' to get a shine on the boots and the peak of the cap, and keep the whistle, buttons, belt pouch, rifle sling, bayonet, frog and scabbard in pristine condition. Uniforms were supplied as a length of cloth to each officer and there was a network of tailors who would cut and sew the jacket and trousers. Each man was given an allowance to pay for this.

The men were subjected to tight discipline. Hair had to be cut short, according to the code, but officers were allowed a cut according to their countenance. At Newtownards the barber came in on a Monday night to ensure hair styles were in order for the Tuesday inspection. At Enniskillen the recruits lived in dormitories and had a table, bed and locker for their use. They ate in a communal canteen under the eagle eye of the Head Constable Major, the equivalent of the Regimental Sergeant Major in the army. One is well remembered sitting alone at a table with his tea and ginger-snap biscuits. The day began with drill and inspection, then classroom work followed by an evening of study and cleaning. On Sunday mornings the recruits formed up and marched through Enniskillen, dropping off groups at each of the churches. After worship the parade would, regroup and return to the depot. Recruits were allowed one thirty-two-hour period of leave each month. Sport was a major interest, especially boxing and tug-o'-war, and over the years the RUC produced many prize-winning teams and individuals in both endeavours.

After six months' training those who met the required standards were sworn in as constables and posted to a station to begin their service. Police life out in the stations was equally spartan and austere. Officially a man was always available for work; there was no overtime or fixed hours. Single men usually lived in. They were not allowed to get married unless they had at least five years' service and even then the woman was vetted to see that she was acceptable to the police authorities. Married men lived in quarters adjacent to the stations in most areas. In some stations there was a cook, usually a local woman, employed jointly by the officers to come in and make the midday meal for them. Frequently these women became alternative mothers for the young policemen, helping them to sew buttons, doing laundry and making sure they had regular square meals. At other locations the men ate by permanent arrangement at local cafes.

Life was regulated by a series of books and controls operated by the orderly officer. An officer wanting to pop out to do some shopping or pay his bills had to fill in the 'PB Book' stating he was briefly absent on private business. Another book, the Pass Book, was used to record longer absences on leave. This had to be approved by the sergeant and signed. Every night at 11 pm there was a roll call for the single men, and married men were expected to be in their quarters. Then the orderly or station guard would fill in the 'state of the party' in the 'Occurrence Book', a heavy, bound volume which sat on the counter in the front office of every station and in which every event, major and minor, was faithfully recorded.

The force was run to exacting bureaucratic standards on extremely tight financial limits. Each new force circular contained the instruction that the previous circular should not be scrapped but the reverse of the paper used as writing material. The practice was so well drilled into the men that it is a notable characteristic of many older policemen to write only on old scraps of paper. The finances were so strict that separate electricity meters were installed in the public and private parts of the stations. The men had to share the cost of lighting and heating their quarters. Some strict station sergeants removed bulbs to save electricity. There was little opportunity for recreation but before the advent of television, playing darts and cards were the popular ways to pass time.

The men were also responsible for cleaning and maintaining the station. Most of the stations had red floor tiles or linoleum, which was highly polished. Officers on duty wore 'skids' – improvised cloth overshoes, slipped on top of their boots, which served the dual purpose of not marking the floor and keeping up the shine as they walked about. Many stations had white exterior walls with a two-foot tarred strip at the base and it was a great annual ritual for the men to freshen up the whitewash and tar. The station sergeant was allowed to buy the lime locally and there was a detailed official instruction for mixing it up with water to the required standard. This was then applied to the wall with a stirrup pump contraption and brushes.

Having the station in good shape was an important factor in impressing the district and county inspectors when they made their periodic visits. Once at Aghalee, where a urinating B Special had killed off part of the hedge, the station sergeant made the men paint the offending branches green to improve the appearance. Many of the country stations had gardens, stimulating a wide interest in the subject, and in the summer there was a regular supply of both flowers and vegetables as a result.

Postings to some stations in remote areas with poor facilities known as 'Block stations', were sometimes made for disciplinary reasons. Even in the 1950s there were such stations with water having to be drawn from a well and dry or 'air-conditioned' outdoor toilets, as they were described. One constable found drinking on duty complained loudly when he was posted to one of these stations. 'Sure the animals in the pound get watered every six hours while we have to stay dry for twelve.'

In line with the official parsimony there was a blacklist of car dealers and garages who would not give a sufficient discount on spare parts for police vehicles, so in some cases it was necessary to go to a neighbouring town to obtain, say, a spare windscreen wiper from an approved supplier. Unserviceable tyres had to be returned to the stores at Sprucefield with the record of their date of issue, registered number and the approximate mileage they had covered before a new, numbered tyre was issued. In 1946, the scarcity of linseed oil caused a consequent shortage of linoleum, so the Ministry of Home Affairs, in a police circular, warned that not only would the RUC be ineligible for any of the limited supply but that floor covering already down on police premises might be lifted for more urgent use elsewhere.

The comfort of the RUC was in fact never a high priority for the Ministry. In 1929 they refused to reduce the period of wear for waterproof coats from three years to two and said the cost of providing canopies and covers for the open Lancia tenders would be prohibitive. Small wonder, then, that an officer caught by his head constable under the canopy of a cinema on Belfast's Shankill Road, sheltering from the rain, explained: 'I joined this job for thirty years and if I walked about in that rain I wouldn't last thirty years.'

Although the IRA had largely been in hibernation since the end of the war, they had not been entirely dormant. There had been a flurry of threats and small explosions at the time of the coronation of Queen Elizabeth in 1953, mostly directed at cinemas showing newsreels of the ceremony. The police had said that they were on full alert but there was embarrassment in Banbridge, County Down, when the picture house was blown up while the local sergeant was curled up asleep in the back row. The first sign of more serious IRA preparation for hostilities, however, came on the afternoon of 12 June 1954 when fifteen men in a borrowed cattle lorry entered Gough barracks, then a British army base in Armagh, overpowered the guards at the armoury and escaped with 670 rifles, 27 sten guns and 9 Bren guns.

Later in the year, on the Saturday night of 17 October, the IRA tried to repeat their success. A party of some nineteen young men got off the Londonderry–Belfast train at Omagh. They all had single tickets and no baggage. At 3.15 am the next morning they were part of a large group of armed men who forced their way into the military barracks in the town. The guard force was alerted and in the ensuing gun battle four members of the garrison were wounded by gunfire; a fifth had been beaten about the head with a revolver butt. Many of the attackers fled in a waiting lorry but the police rounded up eight of them before they could get away and they were later sentenced to long terms of imprisonment.

Everything thus pointed to a new IRA offensive but before they left their starting blocks, a breakaway group called Saor Uladh (Free Ulster) attacked a police station on the border and a number of customs posts, losing a member shot dead by the RUC in the process. The IRA offensive, Operation Harvest they called it, was finally launched on 11 December 1956. That night there were ten attacks on targets throughout Northern Ireland, including bombing a BBC transmitter at Londonderry, burning a courthouse at Magherafelt, firing a B Special drill hut in Newry and bombing an army barracks in Enniskillen. Several bridges were also severed. Next night two police stations at Lisnaskea and Derrylin endured gun and bomb attacks. On 30 December the attackers returned to Derrylin, opening fire from across the border and shooting Constable John Scally dead. A colleague continued to fire until a bomb planted at the front of the building exploded, leaving him buried under a pile of rubble.

The Catholic Church had already condemned IRA membership and declared it a mortal sin. After the attacks, the Irish government in Dublin threatened stern action if the campaign continued, although a minister at the Foreign Office in London recorded that the Irish ambassador was 'more voluble than convincing' when called in to discuss the situation. In Belfast, Prime Minister Brookeborough asserted his determination to crush the campaign.

The RUC were well prepared. The spearhead of their fight-back was the Reserve Force, established in 1950, and progressively strengthened and equipped since then. It had the loan of seventy vehicles from the War Office, including armoured half-track personnel carriers, Scout cars and Landrovers. The 150-strong force deployed along the border area, organized into five platoons, commanded by a head constable and four sergeants, was also armed with heavy, automatic weapons. Later they were backed up by British troops. In addition, 200 Specials were mobilized for full-time duty. Sandbags and barbed-wire entanglements were thrown up at RUC stations throughout the province and several unapproved border roads were either spiked or cratered. Internment was again introduced and before long nearly 200 people had been taken into custody. At night, especially in the border areas, there were widespread road checks and the B Specials were deployed to guard vital installations.

The campaign continued sporadically throughout 1957. Twelve months after it began there had been 366 incidents, with seven IRA deaths and three RUC. The two officers who lost their lives besides Constable Scally were Constable Thomas Gregg and Sergeant Arthur Ovens. Constable Gregg, a member of the Reserve Force, was sitting in the rear of a patrol vehicle at 2 am on 4 July 1957 when, only about two hundred yards from the border, gunmen opened fire after a landmine had failed to detonate under the vehicle. He was hit during the incident and fatally wounded. At 11.25 pm on 17 August, Sergeant Ovens led a party of police and soldiers to an empty house near Coalisland to check out an anonymous report that a man was acting suspiciously at the premises. When the party saw a candle burning in the kitchen, the house was surrounded. The Sergeant entered and when he kicked the kitchen door to open it, he set off a booby-trapped bomb and died instantly in the massive explosion. A constable who was standing immediately behind him had a miraculous escape.

The next RUC casualty was Constable Henry Ross, who was cycling along the road near Forkhill, County Armagh, on 16 July 1958 when a landmine buried in the ditch exploded. He was rushed to hospital where he died from his injuries a day later.

There were two other bomb attacks that year, one aimed at Pim, the other at his deputy, Albert Kennedy, but it soon became clear that they had nothing to do with the IRA. The culprit was in fact one of the senior officers in the force, District Inspector Malcolm Crawford.

He was the son of the, to Unionists, legendary Lt-Col. Fred Crawford, the man who had masterminded the 1912 UVF gun-running expedition from Hamburg to Larne. His son, who had served in Malaya and Singapore, returned to Ulster in 1932 and joined the RUC. He married the daughter of John Andrews, who was prime minister of Northern Ireland for three years during the Second World War. Remembering what his father had done for Ulster, Crawford developed an obsession that he was unjustly being denied promotion to county inspector.

Crawford first came under suspicion on 17 December 1955 soon after a Christmas-wrapped parcel containing mince pies was sent to Pim's private residence, Mullagh Cottage at Killyleagh in County Down. That evening a telephone caller, who did not identify himself, expressed relief that Lady Pim had not consumed the pies, which contained poison. Sir Richard, already suspicious of the anonymous gift, sent it for analysis to the government laboratory and next day the scientists discovered that the pies had been laced with cyanide. It was a sophisticated assassination attempt: the box containing the pies had been sealed with sticky tape to make it airtight and prevent the cyanide evaporating.

The police published the label with its handwritten address and appealed for anyone who recognized the handwriting or who knew who 'M.D.', the supposed sender was. They also fingerprinted a phone box at the top of the Falls Road where it was said the call to the Pim home had been made. Although it was never disclosed publicly, the police began checking on the Inspector-General's closest associates because of the detailed inside knowledge exhibited about his circumspect personal life, the location of his private residence, movements and telephone number, and concern for Lady Pim. From information gleaned inside the force about his attitudes, the finger of suspicion soon pointed to Crawford and for a time he was put under surveillance, but without result.

Nothing further happened for more than a year but one Saturday afternoon on 4 May 1957, the Pims, who were keen sailors, and their two dogs went out on Strangford Lough in their cabin cruiser, *Madge*. It was something of a trial run. The boat had been laid up for the winter and only a week earlier had been fitted with a new engine and moved to moorings near their home. About three-quarters of a mile offshore, Sir Richard heard a noise and assuming a gasket on the new engine had blown, went to investigate. The noise was actually the sound of an exploding detonator which had been ignited by the heat from the engine exhaust. It lit an underwater burning fuse connected to a large salad-cream jar packed with gelignite which had been concealed under the engine. With great presence of mind, he severed the burning fuse with a pair of pliers and turned for shore. For twenty-five minutes, without telling Lady Pim of the predicament, he coolly steered the boat, aware that at any time the heat of the engine could still detonate the explosive.

At Stormont the Unionist Chief Whip, Brian Faulkner, condemned the IRA for a 'cowardly and wicked crime ... a devilish piece of planning'. But the handful of RUC involved in the investigation of this highly sophisticated bombing were sworn to secrecy and put on the trail of Crawford, who was now a district inspector based at Donegall Pass police station in Belfast. They concluded that the bomb could only have been planted by someone approaching at night by rowing boat or dinghy and that the plan had been to sink the boat at sea without trace. As the boat had only been at the moorings a few days, it was a further pointer that the assassin had intimate knowledge of the Pims' private lives. Again Crawford was placed under surveillance but without result.

On 25 September, Albert Kennedy was driving a dinner guest into Belfast at 9 pm when a bomb exploded under his Ford Consul car at University Street. The front of the car lifted off the ground and fumes came from it, according to two young eyewitnesses. Neither Kennedy nor his passenger, businessman Robert Ferris, was injured and the car was able to continue on the journey. Later examination showed that the gelignite bomb concealed under the car had only partly exploded. The method of detonation, the detonator being ignited by exhaust heat, was, however, identical to the salad-jar bomb aimed at Pim and once more pointed the finger at Crawford. Kennedy was actually on leave and therefore more likely to use his own car than official police transport.

Crawford was finally confronted and in January 1958 was forced to resign from the force on pension after twenty-five years' service. The episodes and his alleged involvement were firmly hushed up. The Catholic MP, Harry Diamond, raised it mischievously during questions at Stormont a month later. On 3 February he asked if the Minister of Home Affairs was aware that inquiries into the incidents had been discontinued and if this sycnchronized with the premature retirement of District Inspector Crawford. The allegations were stone-walled but significantly not denied by the Unionist administration.

By 16 October 1958 the ongoing IRA campaign was past its peak and Hanna reported that the 229 incidents to date had caused damage worth £700,000. There were only twenty-seven incidents in 1959 and twenty-six in 1960. Pim retired at the end of the year, after fifteen years in the job, and handed over to his deputy, Albert Kennedy. The contrast between the backgrounds of the two men could not have been greater. Kennedy, born in Belfast in 1906, the son of a detective sergeant, had worked his way up the ranks by passing the competitive examinations and by hard toil. He had gained wide and varied experience during his career, having chased poteen makers in the mountains and helped deal with the riots in the early 1930s. He had also travelled, looking at how other police forces worked in Britain, Canada and the United States. Kennedy was best known as the head of the Crime Branch, during which time he successfully investigated several murders. He was described as 'un-temperamental. People knew where they stood with him.' He was unquestionably a 'copper's copper'. In 1965, when he was knighted, he ordered an extra day's leave for each man in the force, because it was 'their loyalty and co-operation which enabled him to be on a position to receive the honour'.

In his first year as chief, the IRA was responsible for fifty incidents, forty-six of them involving explosives. Two more RUC men died. In the early hours of 27 January 1961 Constable Norman Anderson parked his van on the border near Rosslea and escorted his girlfriend to her home a short distance across the border. When he returned twenty minutes later he was murdered by IRA gunmen lying in wait for him. During the afternoon of 12 November 1961 a group of IRA men ambushed a police patrol in the Jonesborough area of County Armagh. After they fired on it, killing Constable William Hunter, they fled over the nearby border.

The campaign was called off on 26 February 1962 when the IRA called a unilateral ceasefire. They had been humiliated that the Catholic population had not risen in support of their lead. Even the sectarian hotbeds in Belfast had remained dormant. In all there had been 605 outrages since 1956, leaving sixteen people dead: six RUC and ten IRA. Another thirty-two were wounded. Also wounded was Beano, one of the police dogs, who disappeared after an attack on his base in County Armagh and turned up again next morning to get treatment for his bullet wound.

Security operations had cost some £3 million, while damage had exceeded £1 million, and 160 people had been interned. In August, when it was clear that the trouble was over, three platoons of the Reserve force were disbanded and ninety men returned to normal duty, station fortifications were removed and fifty of the seventy borrowed military vehicles returned to the army. Many officers were later decorated for bravery. Among them were a sergeant who got the BEM for pursuing three armed men into Armagh Cathedral and arresting them; a policewoman in Londonderry, given a BEM after helping a colleague pull the fuse from a lighted bomb; and her constable colleague who was awarded a George Medal for pulling the fuse. Another sergeant was given the BEM for clearing his station and then removing a 62 lb suitcase bomb from the front step to waste ground; a district inspector and sergeant got the MBE and BEM respectively for lifting a booby-trapped butter-box bomb from a bridge to a field, preventing damage.

The cessation of hostilities meant that the men stationed at the most heavily attacked station, Rosslea, County Fermanagh, could once more concentrate on their gardening. That summer their colourful flowers and tasty vegetables won them the RUC Sports Club prize for the prettiest and best-kept station garden.

# 4

# Descent into Disorder

The early 1960s were heady years of change not only for the RUC but for the Northern Ireland community. The collapse of the IRA campaign had transformed the situation and for the first time since partition there was a whiff of compromise in the air. Some liberal Unionists began to talk of drawing Catholics into the party and the emergence of the Northern Ireland Labour Party, which drew members from both religions, was a serious, if short-lived attempt to stimulate non-sectarian politics.

The sudden retirement of Prime Minister Brookeborough in March 1963, after a duodenal ulcer got the better of his health, seemed to represent a break with the divided, troubled past. His successor, Captain Terence O'Neill, although he had the traditional Unionist 'big house' background of Eton and the Guards, was no slave to Orange excesses and the old shibboleths were not part of his vocabulary. When he received the Irish prime minister, Sean Lemass, at Stormont on 14 January 1965, the first Belfast–Dublin political contact for forty years, it seemed as if a new era was indeed dawning.

There were major changes afoot in the RUC too. At the end of the decade the force adopted a new-style uniform with a green shirt and black tie to replace the tunic that buttoned up to the neck. The rules were also changed to allow for shirtsleeves in fine weather. A big national pay rise for the police in 1961 was also applied to the RUC and the day of the £1,000 a year constable had arrived. In 1962 the force moved into a brand new £180,000 headquarters, not far from Stormont, at Knock in East Belfast. The heart of the complex was a stylish nineteenth-century mansion called 'Brooklyn', which was to be the office of the Inspector-General, and a modern T-shaped, three-storey complex had been added on to accommodate the force's

200 or so administrative staff. Earlier, in February 1960, a new headquarters and control room at Ladas Drive, Castlereagh, had come into use. It handled police operations in the entire Belfast area. Both had new radio links and soon afterwards the police in Belfast began to use new radio 'pocket-phones' which enabled them to keep constantly in touch with their bases.

Another innovation, in 1963, saw the police boat, *Muriel K*, launched into the waters of Upper and Lower Lough Erne. On shore, the Traffic Branch was expanded again, with unmarked 'Q' cars to entrap speeding drivers and to police the first seven-mile section of motorway between Belfast and Lisburn. It was also housed at Castlereagh. But, as a letter-writer to the *Belfast Telegraph* reported, the traffic police were once again victims of Stormont's frugality: travelling late on a night of severe frost, fog and snow, he encountered a police traffic car with no heater and its windows frozen up. 'Heaters, de-misters, and defrosters are surely essential – and not luxurious – pieces of equipment on any motor vehicle and especially a police one,' he wrote.

In 1963 the Stormont parliament passed a new Constabulary Act, which enabled the Minister of Home Affairs to increase the 3,000 force establishment, set in 1922, with the approval of the Finance Minister. Justifying the decision, Brian Faulkner, the Minister of Home Affairs, said that there had been a 14 per cent population increase since 1922 and a considerable change in its distribution throughout the country. 'The police have duties now – including growing traffic and a rising crime rate, especially in urban areas – which they did not have when the limit on the size of the force had been imposed,' he said.

That September, addressing the Belfast Junior Chamber of Commerce, Anthony Peacocke, the Deputy Inspector-General, said that the RUC had the highest detection rate – 61.1 per cent of any police force in Great Britain, although the incidence of crime in Ulster was only a third of the national rate. He looked forward to the day when the policeman of the future 'would be able to throw away his primitive weapons'. The whiff of reform was by now clearly in the air.

Having taken the powers to increase the size of the force, the Ministry of Home Affairs and Inspector-General Kennedy handed County Inspector Thomas Crozier the task of drawing up the blueprint for the modernized RUC. They also brought in an organization and methods team to help him measure police efficiency and make his recommendations. As he became submerged in his task, Crozier soon found, however, that his real task was not simply one of outlining proposals for efficiency and modernization. The real skill would be in balancing the needs against the available resources, for despite all the political talk about the need for a modern RUC, the old penny-pinching still applied. Anything he suggested would have to be achieved within broadly the same force budget – at that time running at about £5 million a year.

In those days, with television building its first mass and impressionable audiences, the public's image and expectation of the police were heavily influenced by two popular television programmes. In one, 'Dixon of Dock Green', the grizzled old sergeant with his friendly 'Evening all' epitomized the very best of the English 'bobby' loved and respected by all. The other, 'Z Cars', set in Merseyside, reflected the new policing by showing the exploits of a team of brash, down-to-earth young policemen cruising the developing urban jungle of post-war housing estates in their state of the art radio-controlled cars. The fact that one of them was clearly a Belfastman, with an undisguised accent which was then a rarity in national broadcasting, unconsciously made the model more relevant to Northern Ireland.

Thus when the Crozier package was unveiled in March 1967, the backbone of the new policing was to be radio-controlled, fast response patrol cars backed up in the urban areas by the man on the beat, but fewer of them. To pay for sufficient of the expensive radio equipment to give adequate coverage throughout the province, within the appropriation he was given, Crozier decided to close twenty-four smaller police stations in the country and amalgamate those in Belfast which were physically close together. Radio coverage, the reasoning went, would plug the gaps. He also came up with the concept of 'limited opening', office hours' stations to provide a police service in some country towns and villages. This way men previously confined to the station for up to eighty hours a week, waiting by the telephone for calls that rarely came, could be released for more productive duties. The package also contained some significant reforms for the members of the force. An official forty-four-hour week was introduced and the restrictions on off-duty activity, together with the evening roll call and other curbs on freedom of movement, were abolished.

By the end of the next year, 1968, the new-look RUC was firmly established. The number of barracks, or stations as they now preferred to call them, had been slimmed down from the 224 inherited from the RIC to 146. For a time that year there was a scare that one of them, RUC Belleek, was actually built on the wrong side of the border due to a mapping error in the 1920s. However, to everyone's relief a potentially embarrassing constitutional crisis was averted when a fresh survey confirmed that it was safely inside the frontier.

By 1968, too, the strength of the RUC had reached 3,031, topping the old establishment for the first time, besides 180 B Specials, mobilized for full-time duty. There were now 7 county headquarters, 27 districts and 112 sub-districts with radio equipment at 96 of them. The vehicle fleet numbered 550, 294 of them having radio sets. In addition there were now nearly 100 of the 'pocket-phones' in use. With an emphasis on public relations for the first time, force policy and priorities in 1968 were summed up by two well-publicized slogans –'Beat the thief' and 'Help the motorist' – but grotesque events, which would eventually bring the RUC to its knees, were already in train.

The fatal political and policing decision was taken in September 1964 during the British general electrion that brought Harold Wilson to power. (Although Northern Ireland had its own Stormont parliament it still returned twelve MPs to Westminster.) When nominations closed, there were four candidates for the seat in West Belfast, a flashpoint constituency that straddles the Catholic Falls and Protestant Shankill areas. One of them was Liam McMillan, standing as a Republican – meaning the IRA, which, having forsaken its traditional militancy, had come under the influence of some Marxists and was getting involved in agitation over social and economic issues. McMillan established his headquarters in a shop at Divis Street, where a tricolour, the green white and orange flag of the Irish Republic, was promptly displayed in the window. Strictly speaking the display was illegal, for it contravened the Flags and Emblems Act, but the police, working on the principle that tricolours on display in Catholic areas offended no one, usually turned a blind eye to the Act. Catholics generally objected to the Act anyway: if the Union flag could fly in Protestant areas, they did not see why they should not enjoy a corresponding right.

At this time a young, fiery, bible-bashing preacher called the Rev. Ian Paisley had set up his own Free Presbyterian Church, styled himself Moderator and steadily began to earn public notoriety for his anti-Catholic activities, both religious and political. A senior British churchman, who had attracted Paisley's anti-ecumenical ire during a recent visit to Belfast, described it as 'a city of religious nightclubs'. Given its sectarian history, it was no surprise that there was such a demand for the 'hellfire and brimstone' brand of religion and politics which Paisley had mastered. Helped by publicity stunts, including one where an 'IRA assassin' who shot up his church was found by the RUC to be one of his most ardent disciples, he soon outgrew his Ravenhill Road premises and began packing hundreds into the Ulster Hall in central Belfast every Sunday night.

One of his central themes was 'O'Neill must go'. He regaled his audiences with tales of the Prime Minister sipping tea with Roman Catholic nuns. O'Neill's dialogue with the Irish Prime Minister also marked him out as a man not to be trusted in Paisley's eyes. He would sell Ulster out. During the election campaign one of his zealots spotted McMillan's tricolour and reported back. As far as Paisley was concerned it was further proof of O'Neill's weakness and the following Sunday night, 27 September, Paisley told his Ulster Hall congregation about the 'outrage' and threatened to remove the flag himself if the authorities did not do so within two days. The threat caused turmoil among the Unionist government at Stormont where a considerable number of hardliners shared Paisley's reservations about their leader. Their knees jerked in unison and the RUC were ordered into action.

Barely twenty-four hours after Paisley's threat, a team of policemen stormed the Republican election premises in Divis Street and removed the offending tricolour. The officer who took possession of it was, ironically, a Catholic. Crowds of Catholics, who had gathered on the Falls Road to wait for Paisley fulfilling his threat, rioted on that and successive nights. When the tricolour was replaced on the fourth night, more police, armed with pickaxe handles and wearing steel helmets, removed it again, provoking the worst trouble in the city since the 1930s. One of the policemen involved in the Divis Street clashes was a young district inspector by the name of Jack Hermon. From them he learnt a lesson about the interface between policing and politics that he would never forget. The whole business greatly angered the Catholics, who had hoped that at last things were changing for the better in Ulster. One of those who watched the police break into the Republican offices was an aspiring young politician called Gerry Fitt. 'My blood was boiling,' he recalled.

This early and fatal exhibition of weakness by the O'Neill government undoubtedly encouraged Paisley's excessive behaviour in the future. By not standing up to his threats, the government stoked up more trouble and rekindled fears that the Unionists were as repressive as ever. After the turmoil, the Unionists won the West Belfast seat and the tricolour was carried at an incident-free Republican march on the following Sunday without police or Paisley interference. Deep down in the Ulster system, however, the sparks of sectarian conflict, still warm from earlier turbulence, had begun to smoulder again.

The fresh tension surfaced in 1966 when the Republicans announced that they would be marking the fiftieth anniversary of the 1916 Rising. The B Specials were mobilized for the month of April because of the tension in the community. In the event the parades throughout Northern Ireland on 17 April passed off peacefully. In Belfast the police packed Castle Street to separate, at their closest point, the Republican march and a counter-demonstration led by Paisley.

That spring, as a wave of attacks against Catholic schools, homes and shops developed, an elderly woman, Mrs Martha Gould, was burned to death when a Catholic-owned public house next to her home was petrol bombed. In May the Ulster Volunteer Force, reformed by a gang of hardliners in the Shankill Road area, 'declared war on the IRA'. A week later a Catholic called John Scullion was wounded by them in a gun attack and died on 11 June. It later transpired he had been mistaken for another man regarded as being a prominent member of the IRA.

At the beginning of June the customary General Assembly of the Presbyterian Church took place in Belfast. Paisley, whose theological differences with them had caused him to set up his own Free Presbyterian body, decided to march his followers through the sensitive Cromac Square area on his way to protest outside. Predictably, there were clashes with Catholics before the demonstrators reached the church meeting in Fisherwick Place. The police, true to form, pushed the Paisleyites through and batoned the Catholics.

Lord Erskine, the Governor of Northern Ireland, and his wife, Scottish Presbyterians themselves, were among the dignitaries and Lady Erskine was so affected by the jeering and heckling that she became ill. O'Neill, who was both offended and embarrassed, referred to the incident in Stormont on 15 June. 'They called themselves Loyalists but to what were they loyal? To the Queen, whose personal representative they revile? To the United Kingdom, in which their fellow citizens view their conduct with a mixture of ridicule and contempt? To their Protestantism, many of whose leaders they have personally abused?'

Tension in Belfast remained high that summer, with sectarian clashes on the streets and the brutal murder of a Catholic barman, drinking after hours in the Shankill, which forced O'Neill to outlaw the newly formed Ulster Volunteer Force to maintain any credibility. When the Queen visited Belfast that July, it was no surprise that a stone was thrown at her car.

It was against this background of looming trouble that O'Neill and Wilson lunched at Downing Street on 5 August. It was a significant meeting, for Wilson was serving notice that the Unionists were no longer being left entirely to their own devices. O'Neill explained his difficulties and persuaded Wilson to let him have a period of consolidation before pressing on with reforms. Barely a month afterwards the extent of the opposition O'Neill faced became evident. Desmond Boal, a Unionist MP and able lawyer, was prominent in an attempted coup with Brian Faulkner and Harry West. O'Neill saw them off by confronting them but it was clear that there was a deepening rift. He said they did not really want a new prime minister, just an end to his policies.

But the shadow of Paisley was the real threat hanging over the province. He spent part of the summer in prison, having chosen to make a martyr of himself rather than pay a fine for disorder outside the Presbyterian Assembly. O'Neill had publicly linked him with the UVF and talked of a drift towards 'Naziism and Fascism'.

As the Catholic confidence in O'Neill waned, a new organization called the Northern Ireland Civil Rights Organisation (NICRA) began to grow in importance. Although Republicans had been active in forming and developing the group, it was certainly not a front or puppet for the IRA, who had largely renounced violence in favour of agitation. When it was formed in 1967, NICRA took over where local councillor Patricia McCluskey, wife of a doctor in the predominantly Catholic town of Dungannon, had left off. In 1963 when the Unionist-controlled council would not rehouse a group of Catholics from overcrowded homes to more modern accommodation, she had formed a Homeless Citizens League and led a successful campaign of demonstrations and sit-ins. Then in 1964, with her husband Con and a group of fellow Catholics, she founded the Campaign for Social Justice. A wide circle of people throughout the British Isles received their thoroughly researched pamphlets, which listed for the first time the whole damning indictment of Unionist misrule.'

This included the practice of 'gerrymandering' – manipulating electoral boundaries for political advantage. Through unfair housing allocation the Catholics were kept in what amounted to a ghetto in each town so that there was always a majority of Unionist areas (wards) to control local affairs through the council. The most outrageous gerrymander was in Londonderry, where the Catholic majority in the city was denied control. It was divided into three wards – North, South and Waterside; South had a Catholic majority of 12,000, while in the other two wards there were small Unionist majorities (1,500 in North; 1,700 in Waterside). Thus the Unionists were able to secure twelve council seats out of twenty, which meant the one-third Unionist minority controlled local government affairs.

The Unionists' appalling record in office was equally well documented by the McCluskeys. Every department head was a Protestant. No Catholic worked in the Guildhall, the council headquarters. In all they employed 145 Protestant workers and only 32 Catholics. Their record of housing allocation and new building was scandalous. In 1963, for instance, they built only 33 houses when there applications for 211 homes, nearly all from Catholics. In 1965, some ninety· families were still living in 'Nissen huts' vacated by the United States Army twenty years earlier, at the end of the Second World War. Needless to say, they were Catholics. Discrimination in the community was so endemic that a Catholic priest was even blackballed by a golf club and a newspaper advertisement seeking a new home for a stray dog specified that it must be a Protestant home.

The situation came to a head in June 1968 when Austin Currie, a young, university-educated, Catholic politician, took over a house at Caledon, County Tyrone, which had been allocated to a nineteen-year-old Protestant girl despite the fact that many Catholic families were homeless and on the waiting list. Currie was unceremoniously evicted a few days later by a party of police, who included the girl's brother.

Those angered by the incident, influenced by Martin Luther King and his 'dream' of civil rights, decided to take to the streets. Currie then organized a civil rights march over the four-mile route from Coalisland to Dungannon for Sunday afternoon, 24 August. But late on the previous Friday evening, the police served notice on Currie that the march was not to be allowed into Market Square in the town centre, where there was to be a rally and speeches. In a manoeuvre to halt Republican/Nationalist, now civil rights, marches of which he did not approve, Paisley tried a proven tactic: he notified a counter-march for the same place at the same time and the police duly obliged him.

On Sunday, when the civil rights march reached the street leading to the Square, it was blocked by a phalanx of police and tenders. Behind them about 1,500 jeering Protestants had gathered. The entire body of police faced the civil rights crowd: there was no mistaking which side they regarded as threatening law and order. The confrontation ended peacefully, by future standards. A girl student was thrashed by a senior RUC officer with his blackthorn stick and a bunch of youths who tried to break through the police cordon were batoned back.

The civil rights marchers decided to repeat their protest, this time in Londonderry on 5 October. They notified the police in advance, in line with the legal requirements, that they would form up at the Waterside railway station, march across the Craigavon Bridge and proceed to the Guildhall Square for a rally. It was the usual route for parades in the city. The civil rights marchers wanted to process from the Protestant side of the city to the Catholic to symbolize their non-sectarian basis. When a counter-march by the Apprentice Boys of Derry, part of the Orange family, was notified for the same route at the same time, William Craig, the Home Affairs minister, stepped in and banned all marches in the city. NICRA decided that it was morally right and said the march would go ahead as planned.

That Saturday afternoon they formed up at the railway station behind a banner inscribed 'We shall overcome' and moved off, heading against the traffic flow in one-way Duke Street because it was not blocked off by police. As they entered Duke Street the police rushed to position a cordon ahead of them, made up of police tenders and men armed with batons. When the head of the march was ten yards from it, the police loudhailer warnings that the march was illegal stopped and a baton charge commenced. One of the first to be hit was Gerry Fitt, the MP for West Belfast. His coat and jacket were pulled off his shoulders, by policemen, pinioning his arms, and he was struck on the head and body with batons before being arrested and taken away in a police tender with a head wound streaming blood. As those at the back of the crowd turned away from the advancing police, they were batoned and sprayed by one of the two water-cannon deployed that day. This detachment of police had moved in at the rear of the marchers, trapping them between both ends of the narrow street. Seventy were injured in the clash, which sparked off a wave of rioting throughout the city that lasted for several days.

The official enquiry into the disturbances, conducted by Lord Cameron, later concluded that while an extremist section of the crowd wished to provoke violence with the police, the baton charge was premature, uncontrolled and unnecessary, and the police handling of the situation ill co-ordinated and ill conducted. One consequence, he reported, was that very damaging pictures of RUC violence were seen throughout the United Kingdom and abroad.

That autumn, a pattern of marching and counter-marching by crowds of up to 15,000 kept the RUC at full stretch. There were also frequent scuffles and outbreaks of street rioting. Although they had steel helmets and short riot shields, the RUC men in the frontline often had to commandeer dustbin lids to give them some protection.

The demand for civil rights also initiated a profound political crisis. Craig said that known IRA men had been photographed in the various civil rights marches but attempts to explain what was happening as an IRA-inspired uprising cut no ice with the national television and newspaper reporters who flooded into Northern Ireland by the score. No Unionist government had ever been forced to operate under the glare of such searching outside scrutiny and the more the traditional remedy of using the RUC to beat the marchers off the streets was tried, the more their one-sidedness was criticized.

The accusations of RUC partiality and timidity, where Unionist supporters were concerned, reached a new peak after the events at Armagh on 30 November. When NICRA announced its intention to hold a march that day, Paisley and some of his supporters protested to the police. They wanted it stopped and promised 'appropriate action' if it was not. Lord Cameron later reported that 'Paisley's attitude to the police was aggressive and threatening'. When it became clear that the Civil Rights march was not going to be banned, the now predictable counter-demonstration was notified by the Paisleyites. They were going to hold a 'trooping the colour' in a Catholic part of the town.

The police plan was to use 350 officers to cordon the nine roads leading into the town and to seal the intended route of the civil rights march at 9.30 am to prevent interference. But at 1 am Paisley and his cohorts forestalled the police plan by taking up position on the march route. By mid-morning Paisley, complete with a blackthorn stick, was conducting a religious service, including hymn singing, while his supporters milled around armed with sticks and large pieces of timber. By then the police operating the cordon outside the town had seized 220 weapons, including scythes, bill-hooks and pipes hammered into sharp points. By early afternoon the crowd of Paisleyites blocking the civil rights route had swollen to about 1,000 and they refused to move when a senior police officer addressed them. Many were carrying cudgels studded with nails. The police then decided to halt the planned march and divert it. The decision was accepted by the civil rights stewards, who kept their own unruly elements in check and prevented disorder. The police succeeded in keeping the two crowds apart and although there was a minor outbreak of trouble at one location, it was quickly brought under control.

While there is no doubt that the management of the event by the senior police officers prevented grave disorder, the unwillingness of the police to tackle the Paisley faction early on before they grew in numbers was seen by their critics as evidence of fear and partiality, and it further fuelled the growing crisis. O'Neill tried to defuse it and buy time for his much vaunted reform programme by sacking Craig, whose hardline outbursts were aggravating the situation, and making a dramatic television address to the province in December. For a time he won a respite but criticism of the RUC and the B Specials, whose disbandment was one of the main civil rights demands, reached a new crescendo in January 1969.

On 1 January a group of civil rights campaigners, led by the radical Peoples Democracy which had sprung up among students of both religions in Queen's University, Belfast, as the campaign gathered force, set out from Belfast to march the seventy-two miles to Londonderry over four days. At first they were disowned by the majority of NICRA supporters but after skirmishes on the way with Protestant counter-demonstrators, feeling swung behind them. The incidents were, however, of no account when compared with events at Burntollet Bridge, ten miles from Londonderry, on the last day of the march. All morning, as the marchers with their RUC escort drew near, a group of Protestant civilians planned a comprehensive ambush for the marchers. They gathered piles of stones and placed them on the hillsides by the road, under the eyes of police, who laughed and joked with them and did not interfere. It was later established that many of the civilians were in fact members of the B Special Constabulary.

The marchers pushed on, unwarned of what lay ahead of them, by both their own police escort and those at the scene of the planned ambush. When they reached the bridge, a hail of stones rained down and other people in the mob, armed with pickaxe handles, cudgels and even iron bars, laid into the marchers as they broke ranks and ran for cover. Despite the attack the marchers re-formed and continued on to Londonderry but as they entered the city more crowds of Protestants threw missiles and petrol bombs at the column. Enraged at the failure of the police to protect the march, civil rights supporters in the city centre then rioted. Well into the night the police were engaged in running battles in the streets leading to the Republican Bogside area. When the violence eventually subsided, some 300 people had been injured. Cameron concluded that the conduct of the police was 'an immediate and contributing cause of the disorders' and condemned 'the breakdown of discipline' that took place.

A week later the marchers switched to Newry and the moderates in the civil rights campaign were fast losing out to the hot-heads. When the Newry march reached a police cordon, civil rights stewards were overpowered and some of the marchers then overturned a number of RUC tenders and pushed them into the nearby canal.

By now the RUC was suffering seriously from the effects of over-stretch. Every weekend and several nights a week they were having to deploy in massed strength all over the province to cope with escalating levels of disorder. One platoon of the Reserve Force had been on continuous duty from 9 am Friday until 3 am Sunday in connection with the march to Londonderry and the subsequent disturbances. Many of the men were on sick leave after being injured in the clashes. Broken joints and limbs caused by paving stone slabs and burns from petrol bombs were the most common ailments. When a clash developed, often without warning, the call for reinforcements often meant rounding up every available man and vehicle, even if it left whole districts without police cover. But force morale was still high and the 'walking wounded' rallied round to help. One man, with a fractured ankle in plaster, voluntarily held the fort alone in a busy suburban Belfast station for one troubled night while the normal station party helped elsewhere.

There had been no co-ordinated public order training, protective equipment like shields and helmets was in short supply, and hastily arranged courses, based on training films borrowed from Scotland Yard, were designed for pushing and shoving good-natured, unarmed demonstrators into line – tactics that were already obsolete for Ulster. A friendly soul at Scotland Yard suggested to a senior friend in Belfast that the RUC could use horses to curb the demonstrators. 'Not at all,' he was told. 'They might eat them.'

Politically, events were moving swiftly. O'Neill called a general election in February to bolster his position. He was in an impossible dilemma. His own people were increasingly calling for an end to weakness and tougher action, while the Catholic community was becoming steadily disillusioned at the lack of reform. The election result was a foregone conclusion. O'Neill's efforts to appeal to ordinary people to back his plans for a reasonable way forward failed, and in April he resigned and handed over to Major James Chichester-Clark.

The day after the general election was called on 4 February, Albert Kennedy suddenly resigned as Inspector-General and was replaced by his deputy, Anthony Peacocke. Born at Bangor, County Down, in 1909, Peacocke was the son of a Church of Ireland bishop and his brother was, at the time, Dean of Belfast. Educated at Sedbergh, Gonville and Caius College, Cambridge, where he graduated with a degree in Natural Science, he had joined the RUC in 1932 as a cadet officer and progressed steadily through the ranks, serving in Ballymoney, Belfast and Enniskillen, where he was for a time commandant of the training depot. An expert on radio, he was a small, dapper man, who smoked Du Maurier cigarettes through a holder. Colleagues remember him as transparently honest and sincere, speaking his mind without becoming lost in police jargon. He had caused a public stir three years earlier when he said that an Esso petrol television commercial urging people to 'Put a tiger in your tank' was an incitement to speeding.

He caused another stir, on assuming his new appointment, when he stated that the IRA was actively involved in the civil rights campaign. He did not think it likely that there would be any outward IRA violence because the campaign was fulfilling its aims. When shots were fired at a police Landrover in South Armagh a few days later, it was announced that police on border duty were to be armed and patrols stepped up. It was the traditional Unionist knee-jerk analysis of the situation and reflected the complete underestimate in both government and police of the serious situation that was developing.

The position continued to deteriorate throughout the spring of 1969 and the pressures on the police stretched almost to breaking point. A scheme was introduced to pay the RUC overtime for the long hours endured coping with the growing disorder, and a generous pay rise was a boost to morale and a comfort to police families. It was not uncommon for a man to leave home and not return for three or four days, having been on almost constant duty in several different parts of Northern Ireland. Despite the new fixed working week, every RUC man and woman continued to work long, unpredictable hours.

When a series of explosions in April damaged water and electricity installations to the north and south of Belfast, the army was asked to guard vital installations. The sabotage was promptly blamed on the IRA. Before long the army deployed helicopters to watch the water and electricity supply lines. A battalion of more than 500 troops was moved to the province and for the first time the possibility of army involvement in the situation began to be discussed. Peacocke, however ruled it out. The civil authorities could cope, he insisted.

On 19/20 April there was yet another serious outbreak of rioting in Londonderry, which resulted in 214 police casualties. Among the many injured civilians taken to hospital were members of the Deven ney family: Samuel, his daughters Ann and Catherine, son Harry and two other male visitors, who were seriously assaulted when a group of eight policemen broke down the door of their home at William Street in the Bogside. The police were giving chase to a group of youths involved in the rioting who were seen entering the house but who had in fact climbed the rear-yard wall and escaped by the time the police broke in. Samuel Devenney, wo received skull, mouth, eye and internal injuries during the police assault, was detained in hospital for several days. The consequences of the incident were to reverberate for some time.

Meanwhile the violence continued on an almost nightly basis. In May, Prime Minister Chichester-Clark had announced an amnesty for those involved in the violence, except for water and electricity saboteurs, but his hopes for a new beginning were quickly dashed. The traditionally tense Twelfth of July period was marked by widespread trouble, especially in Belfast and Londonderry, and some B Specials were called out and equipped with batons although they were not committed to public order duties. They were actually put on duty in Protestant areas, where they were acceptable to the population, in a bid to free more RUC officers for riot control. At Dungiven in County

Londonderry police tried to halt a Catholic crowd storming an Orange Hall and B men fired shots over the heads of a Catholic crowd leaving a dance hall. The death of a man, assaulted during the clashes, was blamed on the police baton charge, and tension and controversy soared.

The seams holding the RUC together were increasingly straining and stretching as the violence continued unabated. Plans to expand the force without delay were announced and even more B Specials were called out. By now the RUC was in the eye of the storm and was under intense criticism for its tactics, misconduct and policies. A group of Labour MPs from Britain hammered these criticisms home in a meeting with the Inspector-General on 29 July. In particular they mentioned the Devenney case. After a heart attack on 17 July, forty-three-year-old Samuel Devenney had died and his death was being attributed to the injuries he sustained at the hands of the police.

At the beginning of August police used a water-cannon to disperse rival crowds at the inappropriately named Unity Flats, on the northern edge of Belfast city centre. With rioting and sectarian confrontations at several locations throughout the city, eighty troops from Palace Barracks, Holywood, were moved up to the Belfast police headquarters at Castlereagh. The deployment was described as an 'exercise' but it was the first tangible sign of fears at command level that the police were nearing breaking point and might lose control of the situation.

On 8 August there was another sign of high-level anxiety about the worsening situation. After a meeting in London between Chichester-Clark and James Callaghan, the British Home Secretary, the government minister responsible for Northern Ireland, it was said there was no question of British police being loaned to Ulster.

All eyes were now focused on the imminent Apprentice Boys march in Londonderry, scheduled for 12 August. The route through the city passed close to the entrances to the Catholic Bogside area which had been the flashpoint for trouble for months past. That morning, 700 police and 15,000 Apprentice Boys converged on the city from all over Northern Ireland. There had been widespread appeals for restraint. The Catholic civil rights leader, John Hume, had said that if the Apprentice Boys march passed off peacefuly, then it would be absolutely impossible for the government to ban an opposition march again.

But that afternoon as the lengthy parade, with its bands and colourful banners, threaded its way through Waterloo Place in the city centre, crowds of Catholic youths began throwing stones at the marchers. The 'Battle of the Bogside' had begun.

*Green Two:* We're getting it fierce tight here but we'll have to win this war.

*Black Five:* We're on fire, tight at the corner of William Street and she's not making much shape at the barrier. We have had four go's at it and we haven't got through yet.

*Green Two to Sierra:* Can you not get all available armour to take this Lecky Road? Get her in, come on, send all available armour . . . and let's have a go here if we break through. Over.

*Green One to all:* Keep fighting, keep going, come on now, keep going. Everything into the Lecky Road and polish them off. Come on now.

*Sierra to Green One:* Take it steady now because there might be some trenches there. You may get cut off. Over.

This was just one of the frenzied radio exchanges between RUC vehicles at the height of the 'Battle of the Bogside', the unprecedented rioting which followed the Apprentice Boys march. After dark that evening Graham Shillington, the Deputy Inspector-General, arrived in Londonderry from Belfast to make a first-hand assessment of the situation. Late in the evening, after conferring with senior officers at the Victoria police station, he went to the Little James Street/Sackville Street junction, which he was told was the main trouble spot at that time. There he found several buildings burning and a party of what he described later as 'very tired policemen who were doing their best to keep two opposing groups apart'. The policemen had been on their feet for nearly sixteen hours and some were so exhausted they were resting on the footpath. The crowds on both sides of them, each several hundred strong, were throwing stones and petrol bombs. Shillington concluded that the police could not hold the position much longer without help and made up his mind to let them use tear-gas.

A short time later, when he returned to the police station, he took a telephone call from the Minister of Home Affairs, Robert Porter, QC. After hearing the gravity of the situation, Porter agreed that the tear-smoke should be used provided a loudspeaker warning was given first. About midnight, several cartridges of the gas were fired at the crowd. It had the desired effect and they began to disperse. So too did the remaining police, their eyes streaming tears, and mouths and noses burning from the pungent fumes. The few who were lucky enough to have respirators were almost suffocating too. The soldier who had only hours earlier demonstrated the firing of the gas and the use of the brand-new respirators had not told them to remove the cardboard packing from the filter.

Shillington remained in Londonderry that night, listening in as the violence intensified. Rioters on top of the Rossville flats in the Bogside had rigged up a catapult on the roof. On the ground the area had been ringed with barricades. 'Free Derry', they called it, and they were fighting ferociously, as they thought, to hold back the marauding RUC. Little did they know that Shillington was only concerned with holding the interfaces adjoining the city centre business and shopping area in case it was petrol-bombed, looted or even burned to the ground.

At dawn Shillington went out again. He had hoped that the trouble would have died down or even ceased by then but his hopes were dashed. As he toured the perimeter of the barricaded area and realized the intensity of the continued rioting, he permitted several of the beleagured police teams to prepare to use gas in self-defence to prevent their positions being overrun. Back in Victoria at breakfast time he telephoned the duty officer at the force headquarters in Belfast to let the Inspector-General know that troops would be needed in Londonderry within twenty-four hours. A short time later Peacocke came through on the telephone and Shillington advised him the time had come to 'put the machinery in motion'.

But, with petrol bombs, stones and broken paving slabs raining down on them at every point, the RUC had to hold out for another thirty hours before the soldiers came to their aid in the late afternoon of 14 August. Soon after 5 pm detachments of the Prince of Wales Own Regiment formed up in the city centre and one by one took over the police positions. At Waterloo Place, Major David Hanson threw barbed-wire chicanes three-quarters of the way across the William Street entrance, leaving just enough room for the police vehicles holding position further up the street to reverse out. He then walked up to a policeman and asked him to advise his superior officer that they could now withdraw. Two or three minutes later the police pulled back.

About the same time, the situation in Belfast was beginning to get out of control. The night before, following a call from NICRA among others to take the pressure off the Bogside rioters, trouble had flared in Dungannon, Dungiven, Newry and Armagh as well as Belfast. The city had been tense all day and the police commanders were deeply apprehensive about what the night would bring. With so many of their armoured and protected vehicles committed in Londonderry, they were finding it hard to muster a fleet sufficient to meet any problems in Belfast. Things were actually so bad that men at Musgrave Street spent much of the day trying in vain to get the old, 1920s vintage 'Lancia cage cars' ready for action.

At the Belfast police headquarters at Castlereagh, a serious loss of nerve had set in. The commissioner for Belfast, Harold Wolseley, and his deputy, Sam Bradley, were of the opinion that troops should have been brought into the city at the beginning of the month. Now they thought that they were facing an armed IRA uprising and a plot to overthrow the government. That night, with the approval of Peacocke, they authorized Browning machine guns to be fitted to some of the Shorland armoured cars they had at their disposal. Before morning the police had killed four Catholics; a Protestant was shot dead by an armed rioter; and the RUC had lost control of Belfast.

The orgy of burning, looting and intimidation continued throughout the day as a stream of RAF transport aircraft, including, ironically, the locally built 'Belfasts', droned in over the city, rushing troops to its rescue. At tea-time the troops began their progressive occupation of the troubled areas in the west of the city but some parts of North Belfast had to endure another night of destruction and death – one Catholic and one Protestant were shot dead – before there were sufficient soldiers to protect them and separate the mobs.

The social cost of the disturbances during July and August was appalling. In addition to the ten deaths – eight Catholics and two Protestants – many were injured, 154 by gunshots and 745 by other causes. The RUC sustained 366 injuries. In addition first-aid posts in Londonderry treated some 300 people for the temporary effects of CS gas. During the clashes a large amount of property, both residential and commercial, was damaged. When the full extent was totted up it was found that 179 premises had to be demolished, another 94 required major repair and 323 minor restoration. Catholic-owned or occupied premises, 83.5 per cent of the total, suffered the overwhelming majority of the damage. Public houses were a particular target,

60 being attacked, including 24 destroyed. All were Catholic-owned premises.

Fear had spread through the province like a virus and people in mixed housing areas were either driven out by the majority or fled to a safe area among their co-religionists. As the military convoys poured into Belfast from the docks and airport, civilian lorries and vans, piled with furniture, criss-crossed the city. When a study was made by the Community Relations Commission it was found that 40,000 people were involved, the largest movement of civilian refugees ever seen in Ireland and the worst forced movement of population in Europe since the end of the Second World War. Within days, save for the leafy suburbs mainly in the south, the city had become a series of religious ghettoes, their rigid sectarian geography delineated by barbed-wire chicanes guarded by steel-helmeted soldiers with fixed bayonets. Within four days 4,000 troops had arrived in the city. By a week later another 2,000 had been deployed. Behind the chicanes there were barricades of vehicles, planks and oil drums, and 'no-go areas' for the police, increasingly patrolled by vigilantes.

Meanwhile, the exhausted police, half of whose number had been injured since the first civil rights march, were nowhere to be seen. The ten months of escalating disorder had so comprehensively overwhelmed the RUC that Sam Bradley said later that it was not a question of the military coming to the aid of the civil power; the military took over and for eight years thereafter the police did what the army asked them to do.

The authoritative final verdict on the RUC's conduct was given by the distinguished English judge, Lord Scarman, who was appointed to head the exhaustive official inquiry into the disturbances:

Undoubtedly mistakes were made and certain individual officers acted wrongly on occasions. But the general case of a partisan force co-operating with Protestant mobs to attack Catholic people is devoid of substance, and we reject it utterly. In fact the RUC faced and, if necessary, charged those who appeared to them to be challenging, defying or attacking them.

But it is painfully clear from the evidence adduced before us that by July the Catholic minority no longer believed that the RUC was impartial and that Catholic and Civil Rights activists were publicly asserting this loss of confidence. Understandably these resentments affected the thinking and feeling of the young and the irresponsible, and induced the jeering and throwing of stones which were the small beginnings of most of the disturbances. The effect of this hostility on the RUC was unfortunate. They came to treat as their enemies ... those who persisted in displaying hostility and distrust towards them. Thus there developed the fateful split between the Catholic community and the police.

Scarman concluded that overall the RUC 'struggled manfully to do their duty in a situation which they could not control. Their courage, as casualties and long hours of stress and strain took their toll, was beyond praise; their ultimate failure to maintain order arose not from their mistakes, nor from any lack of professional skill, but from exhaustion and shortage of numbers.'

The problem of reshaping and expanding the RUC was one of the most urgent issues addressed by James Callaghan, the Home Secretary, who plunged himself into the Ulster maelstrom in the aftermath of the crisis. Now that British troops were embroiled, political accountability for events, especially in the law and order sphere, was shifted very heavily from Stormont to Westminster. That the RUC had been sidelined was pointedly clear. Callaghan brought with him from London a Scotland Yard bodyguard and when he was out on the streets it was the army who provided his close protection. On 19 August the emasculation of the RUC was further emphasized when the army GOC, Lt-Gen. Sir Ian Freeland, was appointed Director of Operations and given supreme responsibility for ensuring law and order.

Callaghan called in Lord Hunt, leader of the 1953 expedition that first conquered Mount Everest, the world's highest mountain, to assess and advise on the policing problem. With him were Robert Mark, later to become a celebrated commissioner of the Metropolitan Police and Sir James Robertson, then chief constable of Glasgow. Hunt and his colleagues took only six weeks to produce their report. Among its forty-seven recommendations were the abolition of the B Specials; the creation of a Police Authority; the end of military-style duties by the RUC; the setting up of an RUC Reserve; the disarming of the force; an increase in numbers; the establishing of a central recruiting system; and closer links and interchanges with the rest of the British police service, which included adopting the British rank and promotion structure and changing the colour of the RUC uniform to blue.

A few days before the report was published, Peacocke was called in to Stormont and asked for his resignation. Gentlemanly as he was, he wrote it out immediately. His eight months in command had been a rough ride and as events worsened he had found himself out of his depth. Scarman later spelled out Peacocke's flawed record. Throughout August, the report stated, 'police strength was not sufficient to maintain the public peace but the Inspector-General acted as though it was.' Scarman concluded that if Peacocke had correctly appreciated the hopelessness of the police position, like Wolseley and Bradley in Belfast, and not been so sensitive to the political pressures against calling in the army, then Londonderry and Belfast might have been spared much of the ensuing tragedy. Peacocke, who retired in October 1969, was the last Inspector-General.

In line with the Hunt recommendations he was replaced by the RUC's first chief constable, Sir Arthur Young, then commissioner of the City of London police. The new man, who was Callaghan's nominee 'to drag the RUC into the latter half of the twentieth century' as one officer put it, was the very model of the modern British 'bobby'. Outgoing, authoritative, 6ft 4in tall, with a taste for weak China tea and Nat King Cole, he had been a policeman for forty-four of his sixty-two years, having joined up in his native Portsmouth. He had wide experience of policing in Britain and abroad, having served during the emergencies in the Gold Coast, Malaya and Kenya, where he had been concerned in fighting the Mau-Mau.

Hopes that the violence had subsided were, however, quickly dashed. On 11 October, the day after the Hunt report had recommended the disbandment of the B Specials, the police were unable to contain protest rioting in the Protestant Shankill Road area, which soon developed into a full-scale gun battle with the army. Hundreds of shots were exchanged that night and Constable Victor Arbuckle was killed by a volley of shots aimed at his police party. He was the first police fatality for eight years but, regrettably, not the last.

Young refused to be cowed by the tragic setback and, clad in his London police uniform, with RUC epaulettes attached, and peaked RUC cap and crest commandeered from Peacocke, he set about his new task with urgent vigour. He was soon known as 'Softly, Softly' Young, the phrase he coined to describe how the RUC was to be re-established in the Catholic 'no-go' areas.

After weeks of patient negotiation with the defence committees – a grand name for the vigilantes that had sprung up manning every barricade – the Royal Military Police, with their distinctive, bright red berets, were inserted as stop-gap policemen into the Catholic areas of Belfast and Londonderry. A much publicized disarming of the RUC had begun and the continued negotiations with the committees were aimed at getting the 'reformed' RUC in behind the barricades.

Restoring a police presence in Catholic West Belfast was perhaps the most symbolic achievement both the government and the army wanted and a Catholic officer, District Inspector Frank Lagan, was drafted in to pursue it. At a meeting with representatives of the Central Citizens Defence Committee on 22 October, a twelve-point, first phase, written agreement was reached. From 8 am the next morning till dusk, an unlimited number of unarmed foot patrols composed equally of RUC and RMP officers would operate. In a stark characterization of how impotent the force had become, the agreement stipulated that there would be no plainclothes personnel (CID or Special Branch), no use of the Special Powers Act (which was soon to be abolished anyway), no execution of warrants, no serving of summonses, no enquiries, and no RUC vehicles. The whole thing was to be limited to a public relations exercise, the twelfth point explicitly stated.

The new relationship, cultivated through this fragile honeymoon, was never fully consummated. Recriminations about past RUC conduct were used as justification and the ripples from the Devenney case, in particular, were extremely damaging to the process. In his contacts with Catholic politicians, Young was pressed repeatedly about the outcome of an investigation into police misconduct in Londonderry by County Inspector Harry Baille. In March 1970, after Baillie presented the results of his inconclusive investigation, Young sent for two men from Scotland Yard, as a confidence-building measure with the Catholic community. The two officers, Chief Superintendent Kenneth Drury (who was later imprisoned for corrupt dealings with London pornographers) and Detective Sergeant Kenneth Coleman, spent nearly six months trying unsuccessfully to trace the eight policemen who had stormed the Devenney home from among the 500 on duty in the city that day.

In November 1970 Young accused certain members of the RUC of being involved in a 'conspiracy of silence' about the case and at Stormont Chichester-Clark asked for those men acting under a 'misguided sense of loyalty' to speak out and remove the stigma of suspicion from the vast majority of innocent comrades. No one ever did and the officers concerned have never been identified. At the inquest into the death of Mr Devenney, held in December 1969, one of his daughters described how she had twice lain on top of her father to protect him from police blows, but had been pulled away herself and beaten. It is important to record, however, that he died, not from the police blows but from a coronary thrombosis, and that he had a history of such attacks, the first having taken place before the incident. Nevertheless, the family, and critics of the police, argued that the attack had been a major contributory factor in his death.

Another factor that foiled the forging of a historic new intimacy between the police and the Catholics was the formation of the Provisional IRA. Towards the end of 1969 newly painted 'IRA' slogans appeared on the gables in the Catholic ghettoes but where the initials were spelled out, they read 'I Ran Away' not the customary 'Irish Republican Army'. They expressed a sentiment in the areas that the IRA was to blame for failing to stop the Protestant attacks. It was an insult that was to have important consequences.

That December, a group of IRA old-timers in Belfast staged an armed coup and ousted the IRA leadership. The organization split into 'Officials' and 'Provisionals'. By Easter 1970 the Provisionals were strong enough to end the honeymoon between the British army and the Catholics when they provoked a weekend of trouble, luring the army into tough action that caused their 'brutality' to be criticized. Before much longer, financed by Republicans in the south of Ireland and the United States, they were shipping guns and explosives into Ireland.

Their first outrage was carried out on 31 January, when they planted a bomb which blew a large hole in the wall of the police barracks at Brown Square, Belfast. At the beginning of July the army imposed a two-day curfew on the Lower Falls, after rioting, in a bid to hunt down arms. On 16 July the first no-warning bombing at a bank in High Street, Belfast, injured thirty people, two of them seriously. On 12 August the IRA placed a booby-trapped car bomb in the countryside near Crossmaglen, which exploded when two RUC men were examining it. Constables Samuel Donaldson and Robert Millar became the first police fatalities of the Provisional IRA campaign.

The job of bringing people to justice was becoming progressively more difficult. As the trial of five UVF members, accused of blowing up the water and electricity installations in 1969, was drawing to a close on 18 February 1970, a bomb exploded in the corridor of the courthouse. This incident, and the later murder of a bus driver the night before he was to give evidence in a hijacking case, led directly to the abolition of juries for terrorist-type offences and the introduction of single judge courts.

After a series of attacks on police homes, by bomb and petrol bomb, and further incidents at police stations, there was growing apprehension in the force about their vulnerability. Two constables sent on plainclothes duty to watch for bombers among the city centre shoppers were both unarmed and felt totally useless. In mid-August representatives from Belfast stations voted 54–6 in favour of rearming and the government announced that it was making arms available at police stations for their protection. At the end of the month Young set up an internal police working group to monitor the problem and make recommendations. A force-wide referendum a few weeks later narrowly voted against rearming by 1,196 to 1,085.

In November 1970, Young, who had married again for the third time during his stint in Ulster, returned to the City Police after a tenure of only thirteen months in Belfast. He was a hard worker and he had pushed through all the Hunt proposals. There had, however, been trouble over the uniform colour with the rank and file and after some stiff talking the authorities compromised on a distinctive shade of mid-green rather than British police blue. The old RIC/RUC ranks were abolished and replaced by the British structure: constable; sergeant; inspector; chief inspector; superintendent; chief superintendent; assistant constable and chief constable.

The B Specials had been finally disbanded on 30 April 1970 and already the new RUC Reserve had recruited 615 personnel, reaching towards its establishment of 1,500. These part-timers were expected to do duty in the calmer areas, releasing regular police for the more tense locations. Recruiting steadily to increase the size of the main force to a new establishment of over 4,000 was also going well. Increasingly the age profile of the force was getting younger, with more than a quarter of the strength being post-1969 recruits. One of Young's last decisions, announced on 11 November, was that henceforth all RUC officers would be unarmed, except for those on protection duty. By then too Lagan had achieved a breakthrough and a police presence was re-established in Belfast as well as London-derry.

Nobody likes a hatchet man and, not surprisingly, the RUC had not taken Young to its heart. But Young did what was expected of him, and in the long run it paid dividends for the force.

The new chief constable was Graham Shillington, promoted from deputy. Born in Portadown, the son of Major David Shillington, a Unionist MP and one-time Minister of Labour, he was educated in Dublin and then Sedbergh before he graduated from Cambridge and joined the RUC as an officer cadet in 1933. His planned honeymoon in France in 1935 was abandoned when the riots broke out and he had to remain on duty. He rose steadily through the ranks after that, serving in both Londonderry and Belfast. The appointment caused some controversy, being hailed by right-wing Unionists and criticized by some Catholic politicians because of the chief's Unionist back-ground. But, avoiding extremes, Shillington set a moderate, reforming course through an opening policy statement: 'My job is to consolidate the considerable achievements which have already taken place and to see to it that the Force which I command is one which constantly becomes more effective and efficient in its work and one which its members and the population at large can respect and admire.' He in fact turned out to have a cool head and a safe pair of hands in ever more trying times as the Provisional IRA campaign of violence steadily intensified throughout 1971 and the army became increas-ingly frustrated at their inability to get to grips with them.

The tone of army-police relations had been set during a study day organized by General Freeland at his Lisburn headquarters towards the end of 1969. During the lunch break an army officer who was present told a colleague who was not that the army did not like the RUC and vice-versa. This state of mutual hostility was to rise and fall over the years, depending on the personalities of the persons in post at various times. At this point in their enforced relationship the army distrusted the police as being pro-Unionist, resented the fact that the police would not hand over 'intelligence' and in turn would not tell the police what they were doing. The rivalry was so intense that one professional Republican informer could not believe his luck when he found that he was able to get money from both his old police contacts and his new military ones, for the same items of information. There were many near disasters as both sides tried to score points off each other. In one case a bank was put under surveillance for potential robbers by both the police and army, who ended up watching and following each other until the mistake was realized.

As 1971 progressed there was a semi-public row between the two sides about whose responsibility it was to guard police stations. After much infighting, Shillington and the Police Authority, who had fought strongly on his side, lost, but the growing threat meant that the RUC's armed capability had to be stepped up a further degree. About the same time the police were issued with bullet-proof flak jackets for the first time.

On 6 February yet another grim milestone was reached when the first soldier was killed. Gunner Robert Curtis was shot while patrolling the New Lodge Road area. By now the suburbs of Belfast – Ardoyne, Falls, Ballymurphy, etc. – with their notorious reputations as armed strongholds, were almost as familiar to a national audience, through television, radio and the press, as their own backyards.

The RUC suffered a bad blow on 26 February with the murder of Detective Inspector Cecil Patterson, who was shot dead with Constable Robert Buckley at Alliance Avenue, Belfast, when terrorists opened fire with automatic weapons during riots. Patterson was in fact a senior figure in the Special Branch and was reputed to be something of a 'walking filing cabinet' for his encyclopaedic knowledge of the IRA organization in the city.

The early months of 1971 were characterized by intensive rioting in both Catholic and Protestant areas of Belfast and the GOC warned again that petrol bombers would be shot dead. Arson and bomb attacks became a regular occurrence, especially in the centre of Belfast, and in March, after three young Scottish soldiers were abducted from a pub and murdered on the outskirts of the city, a team of Scotland Yard detectives was assigned to Belfast to help with the murder investigation. The assassins were never discovered and the team was glad to leave after a few months and hand the unsolved crime over to the RUC.

Despite the growing ferocity of the violence, Chichester-Clark ruled out a general rearming of the RUC because 'armed combat was a military task'. Nevertheless, Police Federation representatives continued to press for adequate protection for the RUC. By the end of March fire had been directed against RUC personnel on thirty-five occasions. Five bomb attacks on police homes, including those of two senior Special Branch men, on 3 May underlined the fears. Steps were taken to fit protective panels in cars and Landrovers.

By the end of July the RUC reported that there had been 287 explosions. The figure did not include a massive attack which gutted the *Daily Mirror* printing plant in Belfast. When armed men, masquerading as doctors, rescued a wounded prisoner from a Belfast hospital, the government, now led by a new prime minister, Brian Faulkner, opted to introduce internment without trial. The swoops were sprung on the morning of 9 August when the security forces set out to arrest 450 people. Despite the activities of the UVF, who had killed the first policeman and caused the utility explosions as well as the concerted disturbances in Protestant areas, there was not one non-Republican suspect on the list. The last pretence of an even-handed security policy had been abandoned and Catholics now linked the British army with the RUC in doing the Unionists' dirty work.

Any hopes that swoops would end or reduce the violence were immediately dashed. By breakfast time the clear summer sky above Belfast was thick with swirling black smoke from the network of burning barricades throughout the city. During the day there were pitched gun battles in several areas and, in the most impertinent act of all, the IRA held a clandestine press conference under the nose of soldiers in West Belfast at which it produced several of its best-known leaders who had escaped the internment operation. Hostility against the army and police was further aggravated when it became clear that many of those arrested had been ill-treated or roughly handled and that a number of them had been subjected to deep interrogation techniques which the European Court of Human Rights later criticized.

Internment was an abysmal failure because it touched off an avalanche of violence. In July there were only 78 explosions; then after internment the number soared – 131 in August, 196 in September and 117 in October. The faulty intelligence on which it was based reflected the poor performance of the police and the absolute ignorance of the army. The lesson that a blunt instrument was unsuitable for intricate tasks like internal security began to dawn on the more far-sighted soldiers.

The frequency and seriousness of attacks on the police in the aftermath of internment left seven officers dead. On 18 September Constable Robert Leslie was gunned down in the middle of Strabane. On 15 October Constable Cecil Cunningham and Constable John Haslett, who were watching banks from a car, died when gunmen opened up from another car. After being lured to a fire at a farm near

Toomebridge on 27 October, Sergeant Ronald Dodd was shot dead by waiting terrorist gunmen. On 29 October Inspector Alfred Devlin died at his desk in a no-warning bomb attack which demolished Chichester Road RUC station, Belfast. Detective Constable Stanley Corry and Detective Constable William Russell were instantly shot dead by gunmen on 1 November while examining a burgled boutique at Andersonstown, Belfast. Ten days later Sergeant Dermot Hurley and Constable Thomas Moore also died instantly when gunmen fired on them inside an off-licence at Oldpark Road, Belfast.

Later that month the chief constable advised the Police Authority of the increasing risks to the safety of the police, and the government agreed to arm them. Walther PPK pistols were issued for personal protection and automatic weapons for the protection of stations. The principle of an unarmed RUC remains on the record and is a prime policy objective of the Police Federation for Northern Ireland, which represents the force up to and including the rank of chief inspector. However, the continued armed threat renders it only an objective, generally recognized as unattainable well into the forseeable future.

By the end of 1971 the death toll for the year had reached 173; at the time when internment was introduced, only thirty had died. 1972 was an even more violent year, with the death toll reaching 467 for the twelve months, including another thirteen police. This was the year of Bloody Sunday, when the army ignored the police advice not to interfere with a civil rights march, and shot thirteen civilians dead. The Stormont parliament was prorogued and direct rule for the province from London was introduced. William Whitelaw became the first Secretary of State for Northern Ireland and tried to tackle what had become an unprecedented terrorist campaign tying down 22,000 soldiers. When an attempt to secure an IRA ceasefire foundered, he mounted the largest army operation since the Korean War to open up the no-go areas in Belfast and Londonderry and dominate them with military muscle.

Although the RUC was reintroduced, the level of threat was such that the police could only move with heavy military cover. Troops sealed off many town centres to prevent car bombings, which were claiming many civilian lives. In Belfast they constructed steel gates across forty-one streets to create a pedestrian segment where all incoming pedestrians going to shop or work were searched. The RUC played a secondary role in events. Although it was still nominally responsible for maintaining law and order, the burden was being shouldered by the army. The strategy was to use the breathing space created by the army to build up the RUC to once more take the lead. But the timescale necessary to train policemen and build up their experience, together with the level and ferocity of the violence, meant in practice that the RUC had little to contribute.

The year of 1972 also marked the emergence of yet another brutal phenomenon – the sectarian murder. Altogether 106 of the year's deaths came into this category – 70 Catholics, 36 Protestants. Towards the end of the year, the military police and RUC set up a joint patrolling and detective task force to tackle the problem but they were hampered by the lack of clear intelligence and the fear of any witness or accomplice to give information to the police. To overcome this reluctance the 'Confidential Telephone' was set up so that people could pass information anonymously. Although it produced some useful information – the RUC said that 500 calls had been of value – it was also used by the terrorists to lure the security forces into ambushes or booby-traps.

The first police officer who died in 1972, on 12 January, was Reserve Constable Raymond Denham, murdered in his workplace at Waterford Street, Belfast, by two gunmen; he was the first RUCR fatality. Afterwards many reservists deemed to be at risk were given firearms certificates for personal protection weapons. Many of them were civil servants and at several government offices, including Stormont, firearms cabinets were provided so that the guns would be kept safely during working hours.

On 27 January Sergeant Peter Gilgunn and Constable David Montgomery were shot dead when their vehicle was ambushed at Creggan Hill, Londonderry. The next day in Belfast, Constable Raymond Carroll was shot dead while off-duty and working on his car in a garage at Oldpark Road, Belfast. Later, during a trial in Belfast, three accomplices of the gunman were imprisoned. The killer, Sean Meehan, who had taken refuge in the Irish Republic was described in court as a ruthless man who thought no more of despatching the constable than of crushing a fly on a window-sill.

A month later on 29 February, Sergeant Thomas Morrow was shot and wounded outside a factory at Camlough and died on 2 March. Twelve days later Constable William Logan, the driver of a police/military patrol, was shot and wounded at Coalisland and died the next day. On 20 March Constables Ernest McAllister and Bernard O'Neill died in an explosion while trying to clear people from outside the *Belfast Newsletter* office in the city centre during a bomb alert. Six others also died and 146 were injured in the no-warning explosion, which took place when a driver carrying a primed bomb got held up in traffic and abandoned the car.

The day before the IRA ceasefire, 26 June, twenty-two-year-old Constable Samuel Houston was shot dead when he challenged terrorists planting a bomb at Water Street, Newry. He spotted a car with its number plates masked by brown paper and while grappling with the driver was shot three times at point-blank range by men who had planted a bomb in a nearby bar. Posthumously awarded the Queen's Police Medal for Gallantry, the citation stated that he had acted with courage and devotion to duty in the highest traditions of the police service. He left a nineteen-year-old widow, his wife of only a year.

On 16 July Constable Robert Laverty died when his mobile patrol was fired on in the Antrim Road, Belfast. Five days later, on 21 July – 'Bloody Friday' – twenty-two bombs exploded throughout Belfast in forty-five minutes leaving nine dead and 130 injured. Robert Gibson, an Ulster bus driver who was also a Reserve Constable, died in the car bomb explosion at Belfast's Oxford Street bus station.

Detective Constable Robert Nicholl died in a shooting incident on 13 October at Castle Street, Belfast, when he was shot by the army after failing to stop at a checkpoint. Four days later one of the occupants of a stolen car stopped by police on the M2 motorway near Belfast opened fire, wounding Constable Andrew Harron, who died on 21 December. A man was later sentenced to death for the murder but he was reprieved and soon afterwards the death penalty was abolished.

At Enniskillen on 17 November Reserve Constable Joseph Calvin, who was coming off duty, died instantly when his booby-trapped car exploded. Eleven days afterwards Constable Robert Keys died in a rocket attack on Belleek RUC station. On 13 December Constable James Nixon was ambushed and shot dead off duty while leaving a social function at a hotel in the Antrim Road area of Belfast. Two days later Constable George Chambers was helping to evacuate the Kilwilkie housing estate, Lurgan, because of a suspect car bomb when he was fired on and killed. Before the end of the year, on 18 December, Councillor William Johnston, a member of the Police Authority, was kidnapped and shot dead in Armagh.

When the chief constable's annual report for the year was

published, it provided a graphic measurement of the decrease in RUC effectiveness. The detection rate had fallen from its pre-troubles level of 61.9 per cent to just 21 per cent.

The RUC's fiftieth birthday in June 1972 had passed unnoticed, although Graham Shillington had been knighted in the Queen's Birthday Honours. During the early months of 1973 calls for the disbandment of the RUC became a serious political issue. One Catholic group published a 'Black Paper' on the behaviour of the force and Father Denis Faul, a Catholic priest with a fine-tuned sense of justice, put out a number of pamphlets and books, cataloguing what he described as police and army 'brutalities'. For the first time the question of the very future existence of the RUC came into play.

Catholic church and political leaders, who at first said that they could not support a force which shielded the Devenney 'killers', soon found further justification for their hostility to the RUC, such as the ill-treatment of prisoners and the one-sided application of internment (although some Loyalists were rounded up after the introduction of direct rule). In reality there was little hope of any reconciliation between the force and the minority community for historic as well as more recent reasons.

On the Protestant/Unionist side, where there had developed a feeling of helpless vulnerability to the IRA, after the disbandment of the B Specials there was a drift to organize on psuedo-military lines and the Ulster Defence Association emerged. The pervading military presence and the political authority now being exercised by vigorously even-handed British ministers, without Unionist control or even influence, led to real fears that the RUC were being set up for the same fate as the B men.

The army had stamped out the vigilante presence patrolling the streets, but it was still there in the background in each community. Its power base had shifted indoors to the network of shebeens – the illegal drinking clubs that had flourished in place of the pubs destroyed in 1969. On both sides of the sectarian divide, the clubs became the foundation for protection rackets and Mafia-style organized crime, and centres for covert alternative policing. Offenders were kneecapped, tarred or feathered, or even shot dead. Police informers as well as local offenders who breached the unwritten rules set by the gang leaders were hauled before kangaroo courts, frequently held in the clubs, and then punished. The RUC, and army, were too preoccupied by daily security matters to deal with the situation and both the malignant symptoms of racketeering and alternative justice were allowed to grip and grow without interference. Only a handful of more far-sighted RUC men recognized that they were the problems for the future and should be ruthlessly cut out at the start.

Although 1973 was the year the security tide turned to Ulster – deaths at 250 were about half the previous year and the detection rate climbed to 27.6 per cent – Shillington had to begin the fight to secure the future of the force. There was a widespread belief that with Stormont gone, everything else was on the agenda. Uncertainty about the future affected morale in the RUC, especially in the detective branches, which were being dramatically expanded to consolidate the turning tide against the terrorism. Understandably, therefore, advertisements in the *Police Review* to attract British detectives into temporary secondments with the overworked 250-strong RUC CID, and moves to draft in more men from the army's Special Investigation Branch and the Royal Military Police, caused local resentment.

Shillington moved to calm the fears and dispel the rumours, on several occasions writing letters to the force or issuing public statements. Behind the scenes he asserted a calming influence and lobbied as hard as he could for the force to remain in strength and style. Despite all the uncertainty, in one two-week period 999 people applied to join the regular force, with another 273 potential Reservists. By now the force levels in the province were 4,300 RUC, 2,300 RUC Reserve and 17,500 troops.

Whitelaw assured everyone that the future of the RUC was secure, but Paisley and others kept insisting it was not. Given previous public assurances about controversial subjects that turned out to be groundless, Shillington coped excellently in maintaining the morale and commitment of the force, and perhaps this was his major contribution to it.

Despite the improving security situation, more RUC officers lost their lives in 1973. On 14 January Sergeant David Dorsett and Constable Mervyn Wilson died when a booby-trapped bomb exploded in Wilson's car in Londonderry. It was a bad day for the RUC on 14 January, for Reserve Constable Henry Sandford also died when his Landrover was caught in a landmine explosion between Ballygawley and Cappagh, County Tyrone. On 8 February Constable Charles Morrison died when he was fired on while tending to a woman injured in a traffic accident in Dungannon. At the end of the month,

27 February, while Constable Wylie and Constable Ronald Macauley were investigating a suspect car at Aghagallon, County Antrim, they were fired on, Wylie died instantly. Macauley died on 25 March.

Some weeks later, about 10 pm on a Saturday night, an army patrol stopped a car as it was heading for the border in County Armagh. Inside they found an elderly couple and two younger men. An astute army major became suspicious and arrested all four. It was not long before he discovered that the two men were suspected terrorists forcing the couple to take them into the Irish Republic. When they were identified, the detective investigating these most recent police murders was alerted. One of the suspects, known as 'Tipperary Tim', had been seen after the shooting.

The detective spent most of a Sunday questioning him, trying to build up a rapport, inducing him to confess and make a statement. Hour after hour he was getting nowhere. He went out into the corridor for a smoke and walked up and down for a while. As soon as he went into the suspect again, he taxed him with being recognized near the murder scene. The man would not 'cough'. The detective said that although two weapons had been fired, only one of them had killed the policemen. Was it his? Which gun had he fired? The suspect was intrigued. The detective had his breakthrough. Which gun killed them, the suspect wanted to know. 'Tell me which gun you had and I'll tell you,' replied the detective. The suspect answered. 'You didn't kill them.' Some hours later, just after the suspect signed his typed statement, he said to the detective: 'You're a great soldier. It's a pity you and I aren't on the same side. We could have made some trouble for them.'

On 5 June Constable David Purvis was shot and killed from a passing car while on beat duty in Enniskillen. Reserve Constable William McElveen was shot dead on 13 August at the furniture factory in Armagh where he was employed. Another Reserve Constable, William Campbell, lost his life when he was shot while on the beat at Antrim Road, Belfast, on 16 October. Twelve days later Detective Constable John Doherty, who came from Lifford, County Donegal, was shot dead while visiting his family home. Shillington bravely crossed the border to attend his funeral.

On 1 December Constable Robert Megaw was shot dead when his mobile patrol was ambushed at Edward Street, Lurgan. He was on his way to deliver a present to a child injured in an accident with a police vehicle. Eleven days later Detective Constable George Rolston died outside his home at Newcastle, County Down, when a booby-trap bomb exploded under his car. Two days after that a former RUC Special Branch member, Ivan Johnston, was kidnapped at gunpoint from the cab of his lorry on the Armagh/Monaghan border. His body, with gunshot wounds and evidence of torture, was found on 15 October near Keady. Detectives later discovered that he had been repeatedly immersed in a bath of scalding water by his kidnappers. Four days after Christmas Constable Michael Logue died when Loyalist robbers fired on pursuing police after an armed shop robbery at Forthriver Road, Belfast. As he lay dying on the footpath his gun was stolen.

In July 1973 Shillington announced his retirement, to take effect the following October. It was a deliberate ploy to ensure that nobody could say he had been pushed. Indeed he had been pressured to stay on from spring to autumn to ensure continuity. For the first time the vacancy for a chief constable was advertised and for the first time a Catholic chief constable was appointed. Jamie Flanagan, Shillington's deputy, took over on 1 November.

Flanagan, a tall, punctilious man; who had risen through the ranks, was regarded as a 'copper's copper'. He was highly sociable, popular with the men and deeply involved in police sporting activities. He felt that the chief constable of the RUC should get out and about, so he would turn up at golf clubs, sporting functions and the like to 'show the flag'. Both the Police Authority, who had appointed him, and the Northern Ireland Office, who had approved, thought that Flanagan's tenure would be a holding operation. His elevation would be a signal to the Catholics that things were indeed changing in the RUC. While he held the reins of office, their scenario ran, his deputy, Kenneth Newman, newly arrived from the Metropolitan Police, would have time to read himself in and the major security review that was planned would have time to get on with its work. A major item on its agenda was the future of the RUC, if they decided it should even have one.

The scenario did not turn out quite as expected. Proud of the force he had served and its traditions, Flanagan took over the fight for the RUC's survival and quickly made himself unpopular with both the Northern Ireland Office and Police Authority, notably for asserting his independence from operational direction. Flanagan was no tame puppet. During one period of tension, he went off to Stormont to see

Merlyn Rees, the Secretary of State, armed with a pile of dusty legal volumes to argue his case.

In 1974 Flanagan was impervious to criticism that the RUC had not been active enough in confronting Loyalist vigilantes and road blocks during the Ulster Workers' Council strike, which led to the downfall of the power-sharing government so patiently constructed by Whitelaw to give Ulster another chance at self-government. With the community so totally polarized by the issue, Flanagan thought it was to the RUC's eternal credit that not one man mutinied and joined the strikers. If that had happened, it would indeed have spelled out the end of the RUC.

Later that year, after the Provisionals called a ceasefire, Flanagan was one of the first to recognize the inherent dangers. He ignored hints to soft-pedal and not endanger it by police action. Checks were actually stepped up in West Belfast to see that cars were taxed and insured – the chief constable's way of emphasizing that police operations could not be turned off and on like a tap, by political direction. He also opposed so-called 'Incident Centres' set up by the IRA and government to 'monitor' the ceasefire and prevent misunderstandings over incidents causing it to break down. Flanagan correctly realized that the IRA would use them as a foothold to step up the degree of community control that it was exercising through fear and intimidation.

At this time the government were indeed tinkering with various ideas to replace the RUC or create acceptable mechanisms for community policing to work alongside it. RUC chiefs in West Belfast were very angry to discover that army officers, working for the Northern Ireland Office, had even gone as far as compiling lists of potential worthy citizens to lead the embryonic militias without even consulting the RUC. Another factor aggravating the situation was the pressure from the Unionists for 'Third Forces' and the like to assist the security forces. Rees and his security advisers were fearful that if they did not take some action there would be a problem.

Rees finally ended the uncertainty about the future of the RUC in July and August. On 24 July he first scotched the talk about there being any form of voluntary community policing. Recognizing the desire by many people to make a contribution, he said that any such action had to be under RUC control: developing the RUC was the only way to enable a planned, orderly and progressive reduction of the army commitment. On 13 August, with Loyalist belligerents claiming they had 33,000 men available to form a Home Guard, Rees said that his advisers were still examining the policing question but, addressing recruits at a passing-out ceremony in Enniskillen a few days later, he gave further assurances about the RUC's future. The policy was to build up its role and reduce but not withdraw the army involvement. He put the flesh on the bones early in September when he increased the establishment of the RUC to 6,500 and doubled that of the Reserve from 2,000 to 4,000. At the same time he announced that 1,000 troops would be pulled out of the province.

Meanwhile, the regular killing of RUC members continued. Reserve Constable John Rodgers died on beat patrol on 26 January in Glengormley when gunmen opened fire. Three days later another Reserve Constable, William Baggley, was shot dead by terrorists while on the beat, this time in Londonderry. On 2 March Constable Thomas McClinton was shot at point-blank range by two youths while on beat patrol at Upper Donegall Street, Belfast. One of them was aged fourteen.

Constable Cyril Wilson was wounded by gunfire when driving a Landrover at Craigavon on 16 March and died early the next day. Forty-eight hours later Sergeant Frederick Robinson was killed when his booby-trapped car exploded outside his home at Greenisland, County Antrim. On 16 April Constable Thomas McCall was murdered at a security barrier in Newtownhamilton, County Armagh, when terrorists opened fire from a passing car. On 10 May Constable John Ross and Brian Bell were shot dead at point-blank range by two gunmen while on beat duty at Finaghy, Belfast. Ross's policeman brother had also died at the hands of the IRA on 17 July 58.

Constable John Forsyth was killed in an explosion at Market Street, Lurgan, on 18 June 1974 when he was looking for a bomb after a warning call by telephone. Four days afterwards Sergeant Daniel O'Connor was shot dead by gunmen in a car during a parade at Crumlin Road, Belfast.

On 23 August a key figure in the Special Branch, Detective Inspector Peter Flanagan, was singled out and shot dead by two gunmen in a crowded pub in Georges Street, Omagh. Another senior officer was killed on 6 September: Inspector William Elliott was shot dead after challenging armed bank raiders at Rathcoole, County Antrim. He was posthumously awarded the Queen's Police Medal. Reserve Constable Arthur Henderson was among police lured by a telephone call on 8 October to a booby-trapped car at Stewartstown and died when it exploded. On 20 November Constable Robert Forde died in a terrorist booby trap at Craigavon, while on 14 December Constable David McNeice and a soldier died at the scene of a burglary at Killeavey, County Armagh, when terrorists opened fire.

Deaths for the year were, however, down again at 216, a sufficient encouragement to the security forces that their hard work was paying off. Detention without trial was being ended and a new emphasis placed on bringing the terrorists to justice by having the police charge them and bring them before the courts. In a recent twelve-month period they had charged 1,292 people with terrorist-type offences. During the same period they had searched four million vehicles, apprehending upwards of fifty 'travelling gunmen' or potential murderers. They also seized 1,600 assorted weapons and thirty tons of explosives, sixteen tons of it already made up in bombs. Among the people they had seen convicted in court was a twenty-two-year-old man from Londonderry, one of the IRA's top bomb-makers, who was estimated to have constructed almost 200 big bombs.

There were other encouraging signs that the tide was indeed turning. Police called to an armed robbery at a drinking club found the staff had beaten and apprehended the robbers before they got there, and the first poteen-making case for years had been heard in the courts. The magistrate refused to believe that it was 'cattle rub' and fined the moonshiner £125.

The year 1975 began auspiciously with a Provisional IRA ceasefire but before long it fizzled out and the killing continued. Sergeant George Coulter was shot dead in an ambush between Dungannon and Donaghmore on 25 January. On 16 March Woman Reserve Constable Mildred Harrison died on the beat in Bangor when a canister bomb exploded on a pub window-sill. She was the first female RUC casualty and her death by the hand of Loyalists meant that they had killed not only the first policeman of the troubles but also the first woman police officer.

Constable Paul Gray was shot dead by a sniper on 10 May when walking on the old walls in Londonderry. Two weeks later Constable Noel Davies was killed in a booby-trap blast when a stolen vehicle he was recovering exploded as he drove off. On 7 July Detective Constable Andrew Johnston died instantly when examining a booby-trapped desk in a burgled school at Lurgan. Nineteen days afterwards Constable Robert McPherson was shot dead after challenging suspicious men at Dungiven Post Office, County Londonderry. On 22 September Reserve Constable Andrew Baird was in a security hut at Church Street, Portadown, when a bomb exploded underneath. He died on 18 October. Before then, on 6 October, Detective Constable David Love died investigating an armed robbery at a pub near Limavady when a bomb left by the robbers exploded. On 15 November terrorists caused a hayshed fire at Cloghfin, near Sixmilecross in County Tyrone, and exploded a landmine in the path of a police Landrover coming to the scene. Reserve Constable Joseph Clements was injured in the blast and died the next day. Ten days later police delivering a death message at Clonavaddy near Dungannon were ambushed and fired on. Sergeant Patrick Maxwell and Reserve Constable Samuel Clark lost their lives.

As the casulaty list slowly lengthened, Flanagan made another lasting contribution to policing by opening up relations with the Garda Siochana, the police in the Irish Republic. Early in 1974 he had received the commissioner, Patrick Malone, in Belfast. The only previous contact at that level had been in 1964 when Kennedy had visited Dublin to discuss the workings of new extradition arrangements between north and south. Cross-border police and security co-operation was one of the most vital ingredients in stabilizing the northern situation and the fact that the violence could easily spread and engulf the south had been underlined during the UWC strike when car bombs in Dublin and Monaghan had claimed twenty-eight lives and a hundred injuries.

The contact developed slowly, with Flanagan visiting Dublin, paving the way for wider and more intimate inter-force contacts between specialists. After political agreement, a series of study groups, known as the Baldonnel panels after the Irish airfield where the agreement was made, were set up to identify and push forward better exchanges of intelligence and more co-ordinated ground patrolling on each side of the frontier. It was a solid start but when Flanagan, who was knighted in the 1975 Birthday Honours, left office in 1976, much remained to be done.

Before he retired, however, he had five more RUC funerals to attend. On 5 January, the day of the Kingsmills massacre, when ten Protestant workers were assassinated by the Provisional IRA, Reserve Constable William Evans died when a police vehicle he was driving was fired on between Toomebridge and Castledawson. Six officers were examining a captured shotgun in a room at Donegall Pass police station on 22 January. Inspector George Bell had just broken it open when it exploded, killing him and Detective Constable Neville Cummings. The other four were injured. The booby-trapped gun had been taken earlier from a vacant house.

On 6 February two officers walking at Cliftonville Road were approached by two youths and shot in the back and head at point-blank range. Sergeant James Blakely died instantly. The second, Inspector William Murtagh, died from his head injuries the next day. Six days later Constable William Hamer was ambushed and killed by gunmen near Claudy, County Londonderry. On 23 April Reserve Constable William Crooks was shot by terrorist gunmen near Coalisland and died the next day from his wounds.

If the IRA had been successful on two occasions, Flanagan himself and many others might well have become casualties. The first attempt on his life was foiled by his sharp-eyed driver. On Sunday mornings, partly for security reasons and partly in line with his showing the flag policy, Flanagan would attend Mass at various Catholic churches. However, he most frequently attended St Bernadette's at Rosetta, the church closest to the RUC headquarters. When he did, his driver would wait outside. During several of these vigils he became progressively suspicious about movements at he window of a house overlooking the church car park. The police raided the house one morning, when the chief was attending Mass, and found from notes and documents on him that a young man was indeed keeping observation on the chief constable's church attendances. The suspicions of his driver had foiled an IRA assassination plot against the chief in its early stages.

His second escape was a sensationally closer one. On 23 July 1974, Sir Jamie and his wife were on board the late morning Belfast–London flight. Also on board, among the eighty-three passengers and crew, were several MPs and two RUC detective constables, Sean O'Grady and Joe Thompson, who were on their way to receive British Empire Medals for Gallantry at a Buckingham Palace investiture. The British Airways Trident jet left Aldergrove Airport at 12.38 pm bound for Heathrow and as it crossed the Irish coast, high over Portaferry, a girl telephoned the *Irish News* in Belfast and said there were four bombs on board which would go off in fifteen minutes. The plane quickly diverted to Manchester, where it put down at Ringway at 1.18 pm. At a remote corner of the field the passengers were rushed off and police began a search. Concealed under a seat, they found a 2 lb high explosive device, which had failed to explode.

When explosives experts later examined it, they discovered that it had worked as planned but failed to detonate because of one simple but vital oversight on the part of the bomb-maker. A drawing pin had been pushed into the face of the watch being used as a timing device; when the timer ran out, the hand of the watch was designed to connect with the drawing pin, completing the curcuit and detonating the high explosive which would have blown the plane apart in the sky. The timer had indeed made contact with the drawing pin. However, it had failed to explode because the bomber had neglected to scrape the paint on the drawing pin; the paint had acted as an insulator and frustrated the electrical contact. Thus eighty-three lives were saved by the almost immeasurable thickness of a coat of paint on the metal drawing pin.

# 5

# The Wee Man

When Kenneth Newman, then aged forty-nine, took over as chief constable on 1 May 1976, he described it as 'the greatest privilege of my life'. Pipe-smoking, slightly built and dapper, he was widely known as the 'Wee Man' within the RUC, for he had already spent three years in Northern Ireland as one of the two deputy chief constables. 'What kind of nut would take that job?' his wife had asked when she spotted it advertised in *Police Review*. 'I might,' he had replied somewhat sheepishly, not having told her that his application for a move to Belfast was already in the post.

At that time Newman was a commander with the Metropolitan Police, based at New Scotland Yard, in London. What most policemen were studying at college or reading about in books was happening daily on the violent streets of Ulster. As the officer in charge of the pioneering community relations branch, he was fascinated by the situation in Northern Ireland, which he saw as a laboratory for many of the world's contemporary policing problems. He was among a small number who foresaw that the British police service would have to change to meet the demands of an increasingly turbulent society and that the Royal Ulster Constabulary could well provide the model. Taking part in that experiment at the frontiers of police thinking excited him.

Newman's career as a policeman had actually begun fighting terrorists. After three years as a wartime RAF wireless operator in the Far East, he returned to his native Sussex in 1946. How he came to join the police service was more for mundane reasons than any burning sense of vocation. Bored with the wet and cold dullness of post-war Britain, he was attracted by a poster showing a policeman in shorts standing in the sun under a palm tree. So he applied and was accepted for the Palestine police.

He ended up a detective constable, having seen police action at the height of the terrorist campaign against the British policy of excluding the Jews from Palestine. In his wallet he carried the picture of future Israeli prime minister, Menachem Begin, then a most wanted terrorist. Palestine gave the young Newman a grim foretaste of what he was later to experience again in Ulster. He dealt at close quarters with violent death and injury – doctors, nurses and patients massacred in a hospital convoy; the male occupants of a village crucified to the doors of their houses.

He remembers being called to deal with a brawl at the Church of the Holy Sepulchre in Jerusalem. The combatants were the priests from the various sects, who could not agree on the rota for worship. The experience taught the raw twenty-one-year-old much about maintaining police impartiality in a society divided between equally fanatical religious groups. It was the first step in a career that seemed deliberately at every stage to prepare Newman for the challenges of reforming the Ulster police and later the Metropolitan force itself.

The next step was joining 'the Met'. They had sent a recruiting team to the Palestine force before its disbandment in 1948 with the ending of the British mandate and Newman, by then set on the police as a career, had signed on. His first station was Bow Street, in the heart of London's West End, where, following in the footsteps of the famous Bow Street runners, he learnt his profession in the time-honoured way – walking the beat, untangling traffic, rounding up prostitutes and holding his own with large drunken Irishmen in Charing Cross and the Strand, who saw the scarcity of his height as a challenge.

He had a flair for organization and climbed rapidly through the police ranks, with spells in various London 'nicks' as charge room officer, station sergeant and even an undercover member of the vice squad. As an inspector he set up a divisional traffic warden scheme. Any job needing study or method was passed to him, a sure sign to his colleagues that he was destined for the top.

It was in 1968, however, that he was first able to demonstrate his innovative skills and original thinking to the top men in the force. As the wave of international protests about the United States military involvement in Vietnam reached London, the traditional police technique of simply surrounding the US Embassy in Grosvenor Square with a wall of men to hold back the increasingly aggressive demonstrators was soon found to be inadequate. Frequently the wall was breached and running fist fights broke out between police and protestors.

In Paris and Berlin, where similar demonstrations were held, the police had been forced to resort to water-cannon, tear-gas and baton charges to break the protesters up but, in a closely reasoned study, Newman, then a chief superintendent at London's Gerald Road police station, rejected these methods and opted instead for a policy of close physical contact by large numbers of police. Adapting techniques he had learned in Palestine, Newman's paper laid down an organizational strategy for public order operations. Officers would be deployed in 'serials', groups of twenty, controlled by three sergeants and an inspector. A drill was perfected to get them into and out of their buses in a disciplined manner. Crowds were to be controlled by outnumbering them with co-ordinated 'serials' who would use cordons and wedges in close physical contact with demonstrators to prevent disorder. There would be no batons or gas.

The Newman plan was accepted and training began. It was first put to the test in October 1968 when students who had led the angry anti-Vietnam demonstrations on the continent converged on London. More than 4,000 police officers were on duty and there was minimum violence. Scotland Yard and Newman received world-wide acclaim for their riot-handling techniques, which were put on film for training purposes. It was these same films that were hastily shown to the RUC in the desperate days of 1968 and 1969 as they were steadily outflanked by the escalating disorder. (The techniques lasted in Britain as the standard until the early 1980s when they were replaced by tougher tactics, again perfected by Newman, this time drawing on the accumulated expertise of the RUC.)

Newman's growing reputation was enhanced when he was put in charge of the A6 and A7 branches at New Scotland Yard, on promotion to commander. This made him responsible for the Special Constabulary (unpaid citizens who performed part-time uniformed duties with the police); matters relating to juvenile abuse and involvement in crime; road safety; and operating the Missing Persons Bureau. But his most important function was directing the community relations between London's 21,000 police and its eight million citizens, about one in eight of them being an immigrant. At a time of growing racial tension in Britain, it was an eye of the storm posting and Newman is remembered for the innovative, sympathetic sensitivity he introduced. Under his direction the concept of cultivating and establishing constructive police-community relationships was elevated to a new importance. One lasting innovation was to ensure greater selectivity in the appointment of police officers posted to black areas as community liaison officers. In the past such jobs had often been used as a way of side-lining officers who did not fit in elsewhere.

It was at this time that Newman gained an honours law degree at London University, which entailed years of part-time work, often getting up at 4 am to study before going on shifts starting at 6 am or settling down to his books after a spell on night turn.

His arrival in Belfast, in November 1973, was hardly noticed outside the confines of the RUC. 'I thought he was just another smart-assed Brit sent over to try out his ideas on us,' remembers one senior RUC man. But he soon began to make an impact inside the force. 'Hallo, I'm Ken Newman,' he said, introducing himself to a member of the Police Federation for the first time. When the meeting was over, the Federation official remarked: 'He's the first senior officer with a first name I've ever met.'

Newman's initial task was to carry out a reorganization of the way the RUC headquarters worked and he was later responsible for handling complaints and discipline matters. Not surprisingly, he also took an early interest in the work of the community relations branch. At that time the branch was only ten-strong and operating in extremely dangerous circumstances trying to keep lines of contact open to community leaders in the troubled areas. Newman asked to sit in at orfe of their monthly discussions. During the meeting he listened silently and at the end asked what help he could give. The RUC men were sceptical. Senior officers had paid such lip-service to them before but in the heat of the crisis more urgent matters always assumed priority. Within a few months, however, Newman had obtained increased manpower and back-up for the branch. 'He was completely down to earth, oozing with common sense,' recalls one of the officers. 'In no time respect for his ability was sky-high.'

He used the same approach in other areas to familiarize himself with the force and the situation it faced. When he eventually moved into the job as chief, he had already worked out the priorities on which he would have to focus.

Although the controversial Provisional IRA 1974/75 ceasefire had never formally been called off, it was clear from events that it was effectively over. The Constitutional Convention had failed to reach any cross-community consensus on how Northern Ireland should be governed and there were real fears that in this political vacuum the rising tide of tit-for-tat sectarian violence would stimulate even more serious clashes. Mob rule, gun law, 'kangaroo courts' and racketeering had all flourished in the wake of the terrorist violence and only the superior force of the army prevented outright anarchy in many areas.

Newman's immediate priority was therefore to deal with the terrorist violence but his main task was to rebuild the RUC's shattered confidence and morale. He found that many of his senior colleagues had suffered a lot of pyschological damage and were handicapped by serious doubts about the capability of the force. They had no clear idea of their role. Many were happy to let the army carry on patrolling indefinitely without reclaiming their responsibility.

It was necessary to re-bed the RUC's foundations for it to expand progressively and ultimately relieve the army of its peace-keeping duties. Newman privately estimated that it could take as long as twenty years. It was a job that would require all of his organizational skills and draw on the entire range of his policing experience. It also required exemplary communication skills and a great deal of sophisticated man-management. Many RUC men throughout the ranks opposed any return to what they saw as a paramilitary role. The Police Federation articulated these fears in a series of letters and encounters with ministers and officials. They feared the repeat of another backlash against the force of 1969 proportions.

Newman's agenda had largely been set for him in a document called 'The Way Ahead', which was the report of a ministerial working party headed by John Bourne, a civil servant seconded from the Home Office. Before Bourne's working group was set up in January 1976, security policy had for years been one of reaction to the latest atrocity. Reassurance and deterrence were the words used by army commanders to describe their tactics. The police were still widely distrusted by the army or regarded as incompetent and much of the time they were scarcely consulted. The working party therefore took a long-term view and decided that a conscious process of replacing the army with the police should begin. The bureaucrats coined the phrase 'police primacy' to describe the new policy. Senior soldiers and policemen called it 'Ulsterization'.

There would be no time limit. Clearly in the hardest areas the army would have to remain in strength for a considerable time to come. Elsewhere, however, the police could quickly take the lead in maintaining law and order, with military back-up where necessary, which was increasingly to come from an expanded Ulster Defence Regiment. Military support in some intermediate areas would temporarily be provided by members of the Royal Military Police, while the strength and capability of the civilian police was developed. The RUC establishment was to be doubled from 5,000 at the rate of about 500 new officers a year, a number governed by the rate at which they could be trained. The RUCR (4,790 at this time) was to get more manpower, principally to free more highly trained officers from routine work like guard duty. The annual budget, which had reached £49 million, was to be increased to £60 million and beyond.

This new policy was a decisive change of direction for the RUC. Since the dark days of 1969 it had stumbled along, heavily demoralized, overwhelmed by events and the mounting toll of violence. For a time its very existence was under threat while the officials struggled with ideas for a non-aggressive, non-retaliatory civilian force to meet steady Catholic hostility. Nevertheless, recruitment had continued and at this point more than sixty per cent of the strength had joined since 1970, the proper foundation, one member of the Police Authority remarked, for a modern, forward-looking RUC.

Now the uncertainty was gone and the force was to have not only a secure future but also a full-blooded role in impartially enforcing law and order in the uniquely difficult circumstances of Northern Ireland. While the concept of an unarmed, civilian police force would remain a goal, the grim realities of the situation dictated that it would have to meet a serious armed threat for some time to come. So, for their protection, RUC officers would be armed with the standard NATO 7.62 mm rifle, M1 carbines and handguns. The RUC would also be provided with a fleet of new Hotspur armoured Landrovers and armoured civilian patrol cars. The committee described the RUC role in this context as a 'High risk profile'.

More controversially, it would undergo a training programme in public order and riot control techniques, using the equipment and tactics then perfected by the army. In an early skirmish with nervous politicians and officials, Newman insisted that the police should be equipped with shields, batons and Federal riot guns to fire the controversial plastic baton rounds. At first ministers and officials, together with sections of the army, baulked but Newman quietly persisted and in the end won his case. The resistance inside the force was even greater. Some police feared the political consequences of the development, others frankly doubted that the force could cope. The new chief persevered and formed an internal RUC working party to consider tactics, the needs for equipment and to write a public order manual. Further studies were commissioned to estimate future training and manpower needs, and to draw up building and equipment programmes. The Police Authority had already earmarked £25 million for refurbishing old stations and building new ones.

Speaking at a passing out parade in the RUC depot on 5 May, his first public engagement, Newman said he looked forward to the day when every soldier was returned to barracks. Only twenty-four hours earlier Secretary of State Merlyn Rees had announced that 500 soldiers were being withdrawn from Ulster, underlining the government's new political drive to get the army off the streets and out of the Ulster firing line. There was continued dismay within the RUC about being once again pushed into a paramilitary role but at a day-long conference in the Governor's House at Hillsborough on 13 May the new thinking was outlined to senior officers by Newman as well as by senior government officials and army officers. 'The RUC would be hard but sensitive,' Newman said. There was no other way, he told them, otherwise the army would be there for ever.

Newman's philosophy, as articulated in his Enniskillen speech and at the Hillsborough seminar, was given wider currency when it was distributed as a poster and printed as a full-page advertisment in the main newspapers. He outlined three principles for the RUC: equal protection under the law for all citizens and respect for their rights as persons; fair and impartial law enforcement regardless of personal opinion, prejudices or other irrelevant considerations; and enforcement of the law within the law.

There were two objectives he defined for the force: to bring an end to the criminal reign of terror by the most professional means and in the shortest possible time; and to identify as closely and fully as possible with the community and to be sensitive to its needs and feelings. 'Maintaining law and order simply means giving people the freedom to conduct their own lives,' Newman said.

As the details spread throughout the force, there was a new sense of purpose evident and a visible raising of morale. The appointment of Jack Hermon as deputy chief constable at the age of only forty-seven was a further sign to the force of irrevocable change and a new era. Sam Bradley, a prominent member of the old guard with thirty-nine years' service, resigned because he had been given 'a kick in the teeth' by the Police Authority. 'They chose to appoint a man with much less experience than me to a senior position.' He did not think it possible for an officer of his experience and seniority to take instructions from a younger man. There was much sympathy for him but no support and he retired an embittered man.

Meanwhile, the Provisional IRA were taking careful note of the new security policy and in the *Republican News* on 13 May they threatened the RUC with 'a long hot summer'. They were not long in fulfilling their threat and justifying the chilling reality of the mandarins' 'high risk profile'. Overnight on 14/15 May the RUC station at Belcoo in County Fermanagh came under fire. During the follow-up operation about 06.30 the next morning, three RUC officers were examining the location thought to have been used by the gunman. One of them picked up an object, triggering a large explosion. Sergeant Henry Keys, Reserve Constable Francis Kettles and Reserve Constable Thomas Evans were killed instantly. Later the same day, about 11.40 pm, an RUC mobile patrol came under fire in an industrial estate at Warrenpoint. Sergeant James Hunter was fatally wounded in the ambush.

Almost exactly twenty-four hours later Reserve Constable Kenneth Nelson was letting his dog out at his home near Dungannon when gunmen struck and killed him. On 22 May, again near Dungannon, gunmen killed another police officer, Constable John McCambridge. He had just driven up to his lodgings and they opened fire as he stepped from his car.

Next day in Londonderry Woman Reserve Constable Linda Baggley was on beat patrol at Chapel Road, Londonderry, when she was shot at point-blank range by two youths. She died from her wounds on 2 June. (It was a second tragedy for the family. Her father, Reserve Constable William Baggley, had been killed in almost identical circumstances in the same area in January 1974.) Also on 2 June Detective Constable Ronald McAdam was shot dead outside the Royal Victoria Hospital in Belfast as he waited to pick up a relative.

Newman thus found himself attending the funerals of seven murdered officers in his first month in office. No wonder he often remarked that as chief constable of the RUC 'the funeral dirge gets ground into your soul'. Attending funerals was one of the most harrowing and routine duties for any RUC chief but it was an important factor, especially for an outsider to the close-knit RUC circle, in removing the remoteness between the officers at the top and those on the ground. Soon after taking over Newman insisted that all senior officers should wear uniforms on duty to emphasize that they were no different from the men under them. He had in fact a particular skill at removing these barriers and communicating with the junior ranks. Without notice he would turn up at stations in the most difficult areas and go out with patrols, frequently at night, sharing the dangers and listening sympathetically to their problems. Action invariably followed, consolidating the favourable impression.

Once, after a particularly brutal incident in which four policemen died, a group of detectives manoeuvred him into the mortuary where the severed sections of the victims' bodies were being assembled on the slabs. He walked around without flinching, passing the unspoken test they had set him. The way he was prepared to share, and clearly understand, the danger and the distaste endeared him to those in the front line and when they spoke of the 'wee man' it was out of a sense of admiration and respect.

There had been initial ripples of resentment at the 'Brit' getting the top job. Many had pondered the wisdom of his appointment at a time when Merlyn Rees had talked of the rise of Ulster nationalism and the politicians were beginning to think in terms of finding a political solution in Belfast rather than London or Dublin. Putting Newman in charge seemed to reinforce the fear of undue British interference and long-term direct rule from London. However, as Newman went into action the doubts quickly evaporated and before long he was not only a respected chief, but a popular one throughout the ranks. He had no cronies; his relationship with all his men, whatever their rank, was strictly professional and impartial.

There were also, of course, the usual begrudging complaints from the parochially minded Ulster politicians, who really yearned for a return to the days when they could order the police about. At heart they felt that the way to restore peace was to indulge in old-fashioned simple anti-Catholic repression. By then nobody in the RUC saw that as their role, nor did they want it. The more far-sighted of them realized that the RUC's best interests lay in the apolitical road being mapped out for them by Newman.

Eventually the only serious doubts harboured about Newman in hard-drinking Ulster concerned his fondness for tonic rather than gin. 'Just wet the bottom of the glass with gin,' he would tell his hosts. But as they got to know him better, and saw he had a convivial side too, he more than lived even these doubts down. Rarely has the leader of a disciplined service generated such genuine popularity.

When Newman became chief constable there were 500 unsolved murders on the RUC's books, one for every detective in the force. The wanted list had 582 names. During the previous year the terrorists on both sides had increasingly plumbed new depths of brutality by turning to mass shootings. Among the crimes recorded were eight triple killings: three in which four people died; one in which there were six victims; and, worst of all, the shooting of ten workers in South Armagh in January 1976.

The horror seemed to know no bounds. In the early weeks of Newman's incumbency there were forty-nine sectarian murders. In an especially depraved incident on 10 July, a man and woman, both armed, shot dead a young Catholic married couple in front of their children, aged six months and eighteen months. Neither side had a monopoly of brutality. Protestant gunmen on a separate revenge mission eight days earlier burst into the Catholic-owned Ramble Inn pub between Antrim and Ballymena, and shot six people dead. Most of the victims were, in fact, Protestant building workers who had called in for a drink and to cash their pay cheques.

An advertisement placed in the Ulster papers in early August by the Northern Ireland Office summed up the case-load. In the last three months, it said, the men and women of the security forces had worked up to sixteen hours seven days a week; come under attack on 230 occasions; had 13 members murdered and 111 injured; dealt with 181 explosions; searched for the murderers of 69 civilians; made safe 81 bombs; uncovered 4,864 lb of explosives; and charged 264 suspected terrorists with serious crimes. Merlyn Rees, in his final weeks as Secretary of State, had told the House of Commons that the security situation was at its worst since 1972.

Apart from the scourge of terrorism, the cities of Belfast and Londonderry were under gang rule, with respect for law and order virtually vanished. 'The price of a human life was so cheap that there were bars where you could arrange to have someone killed for the price of a few bottles of Guinness,' a detective remarked at the time. Milkmen, bread roundsmen and rent collectors were routinely robbed on their Friday night collection rounds, often for sums as paltry as £10. Bars were frequently held up Wild West style before closing time and the takings removed at gun-point.

Bookmakers were similarly raided on Saturday afternoons at the height of the races. They had become a particularly favourite target on Grand National day each year when they were bulging with the proceeds of the community's annual flutter. Once there was a clash when a gang arriving to rob a bookmaker found another already escaping with his takings.

Small shops, sub-post offices and factories were constantly plundered. One Londonderry post office suffered twenty armed robberies in eight years. Nobody was safe from the lawlessness. On Sunday nights an American-style evangelist with a penchant for parting his followers from large sums of their money was given a police escort to lodge his collection in the bank night safe.

Altogether the RUC estimated there had been some 6,500 robberies in the eight years since 1969, netting an estimated £4 million. The figure is almost certainly a gross underestimate. Fraud, robbery and extortion were so widespread that the authorities dared not disclose the real cost. In just one area, social security, many millions were swindled in a short time in an astonishingly simple operation. On the morning that the local postman was delivering Girocheques for social security payments he was apprehended and held until the cheques were cashed before they had even been reported stolen. Once abductors made the postman sit through Mass in the local church while the cheques were swiftly exchanged for cash at banks and post offices.

The wave of crime soon became an organized web of racketeering and extortion in the style of the Mafia. Organized drug pushing became a problem for the first time. Drinking clubs, taxi services, control of building sites and other employment outlets gave the terrorists total control in their own communities as well as a lucrative and growing source of cash. Big business, the banks and other institutions as well as the government lacked both the foresight and the will to curb the economic takeover in virtually all the working-class areas of Belfast. The only traditional Mafia-style rackets that did not flourish were those associated with pornography and vice. The Loyalists tried for a time to run massage parlours as fronts for prostitution but they were driven out of business by thugs with a twisted sense of morality who would cheerfully rob or even kill but who subscribed to an extraordinarily puritan ethic where sexual activity was concerned.

The temptation arising from such vast sums of easy money soon undermined the traditional purity of both the Republican and Loyalist causes. 'There turned out to be more hoods than patriots,' recalls one experienced detective. After some big bank or post office hold-ups the police mischievously created distrust among the robbers by overstating the amount stolen. Then the 'godfathers' would come after the robbers looking for an even bigger share. When one leading Provisional with a reputation for making money arrived in the internment compounds at the Maze prison, his fellow prisoners greeted him with a chorus of 'Who wants to be a millionaire'. Others were more seriously treated and the gruesome practice of kneecapping or even death was meted out to those who practised freelance crime, 'homers', in the Belfast jargon.

Newman decided that the principal thrust of police activity must be directed against Provisional IRA terrorists as they were primarily responsible for the continuing violence. Efforts to tackle the Loyalists would be next, for much of their violence was reactive, and then, as resources permitted, other crime categories would be attacked.

The phasing out of internment without trial and the abolition of special category prison status had put renewed emphasis on obtaining convictions through the courts. However, there were very serious difficulties for the police in enforcing the rule of law. Although the problem of juries being intimated had largely been solved by the introduction of the Diplock courts, where a single judge tried offenders and decided both matters of fact and law, there were still difficulties with witnesses. All too often the police knew the culprits they were after but found it impossible to turn their intelligence into evidence. The identity of informers, often paid agents, had to be protected from terrorist vengeance. This was especially true in the Catholic community where 'touting', as it was called, was a stigma on a par with that suffered by the French who collaborated with the Nazis in the Second World War.

The climate of fear was so strong that the terrorists rarely needed to resort to threats. All but the most courageous bystanders looked or ran the other way when caught up in an incident. Some of the more public-spirited would make use of the confidential telephones, whose numbers were extensively advertised, to pass information to the police. Many even talked to them informally but when it came to the crunch, they well knew the consequences and refused to go into the witness box.

The obvious physical dangers in hostile areas prevented the police from making the sort of door-to-door enquiries that would have been a reflex action elsewhere, further inhibiting the flow of information. Even getting witnesses to take part in identification parades was unrewarding since the same deterrents applied. By frustrating contrast, a visiting American photographer, who had witnessed an abduction by the Provisionals which led to murder, rendered his testimony invalid by over-enthusiasm. When he was shown into the room he walked directly to the suspect, standing in an identity parade, and floored him with a punch on the jaw.

Similarly, prolonged and minute examination of crime scenes by experts was often difficult. Evidence about the origin of explosions was often buried in tons of debris; angry crowds frequently gathered at the scenes of incidents, causing further trouble; and there was the ever present danger of a sniper attack or a secondary booby-trapped device aimed at the security forces. Some days they were actually overwhelmed by the scale of the violence and they had to settle by necessity for less than the usual professional forensic standards.

The risk or the volume did not, however, deter the experts, pathologists or scientists from doing their jobs and the Northern Ireland Forensic Science Laboratory rapidly expanded to handle a peak workload in excess of 11,000 cases a year, five times the pre-troubles level. Its staff soon became world authorities on many aspects of explosives and ballistic evaluation, and pioneered the use of the very latest scientific techniques and equipment, which often put the RUC on the track of their quarry.

The RUC fingerprint officers were similarly another vital agency overwhelmed by the sheer scale of casework. In 1976 alone they processed 11,206 searches and received 5,551 prints from scenes of crimes but they had a crippling backlog of almost 20,000 sets of prints waiting to be processed against the fingerprint collection. There was no quick solution at the time, for computer techniques that are now in use to compare fingerprints were then still in their infancy. Every impression detected at a crime scene had therefore to be visually identified by a highly skilled fingerprint officer to establish sufficient points of similarity for the courts to accept the evidence as conclusive proof.

Newman turned to New Scotland Yard for help. A special team was established there, reinforced by experts loaned by other British police forces, and 16,000 of the outstanding sets were sent to them on a specially organized RAF flight. Over the next year they made

139 identifications, in addition to the 468 achieved by the RUC team, which resulted in many highly dangerous terrorists being convicted and sentenced to lengthy terms of imprisonment.

However, despite the vital contribution of the forensic and finger-print disciplines, in a majority of cases the RUC was unable to provide conclusive evidence to put terrorists behind bars. One man escaped convinction because his fingerprints in a stolen car used in a murder were not in themselves evidence of his actual participation in the killing. What was needed was either the evidence of a witness or alternatively a confession from the killer himself to copper-bottom the case.

It was this latter area that promised most and within days of taking office Newman moved to reorganize the RUC criminal investiga-tion capacity to exploit it. The strategy was to form teams of experi-enced detectives, briefed by detailed intelligence dossiers, to interrog-ate terrorist suspects in depth to the point where the guilty would make self-incriminating statements.

The concept had first been graphically outlined in 1972 by Lord Diplock, who headed the commission to consider legal procedures to deal with terrorism in Northern Ireland:

If human lives are to be saved and destruction of property prevented, it is inescapable that the security authorities must have power to question suspected members of terrorist organizations. Only the innocent will wish to speak at the start. The whole technique of skilled interrogation is to build up an atmosphere in which the initial desire to remain silent is replaced by an urge to confide in the questioner. This does not involve cruel or degrading treatment. Such treatment is regarded by those responsible for gathering intelligence as counter-productive at any rate in Northern Ireland, in that it hinders the creation of the rapport between the person questioned and his questioner which makes him feel the need to unburden himself.

Diplock defined the criterion on which such confessions should be acceptable to the courts in the words of Article 3 of the European Convention for the Protection of Human Rights and Fundamental Freedoms – that it should be obtained without subjecting the accused to torture or inhuman or degrading treatment. His recommendation was accepted by the Heath government and given legal effect in the Emergency Provisions Act passed through Parliament in London in

1973. A cynical lawyer remarked that henceforth confessions would be in order provided there was no mark on the accused.

While detention without trial remained in force, it had been the softer option for the police but its phasing out and the formation of 'A Squad' in June 1975 to tackle sectarian assassinations had been the first cautious step along the new road through the courts. Newman expanded and renamed 'A Squad' the Headquarters Crime Squad and, together with three similar regional crime squads, based in Belfast and the north and south regions, its task was to concentrate on breaking the terrorist organizations. The membership was drawn from the Special Branch and the CID, the first time these two rival arms of the RUC family had worked side by side in a single unit. One newly posted CID man, who met his previous colleagues in a pub, was given a teasing. 'You've been working with the Special Branch for a week and you're talking out of the side of your mouth already.'

To provide the new units with an effective research and back-up service, a new criminal intelligence system was formed. The first section was established at force headquarters but within a few months there were sections at each of the three regional headquarters and soon after that in each divisional headquarters. Every single piece of information reaching the RUC from any source was now systematically collated. The ballistic and forensic reports on every incident were married with even the most inconsequential scraps of intelligence.

The new arrangements represented the first conscious attempt in the history of the RUC to break open the Special Branch, which had long been an exclusive and secretive sect, and process its information into shape for CID action. Newman well understood the delicacy of Special Branch activity but thought that it advanced the principle of 'need to know' to such lengths that the operational arms were frequently denied valuable information. The aim was to create a system whereby Special Branch intelligence could be 'sanitized' to protect sources and then be given to the front-line teams to get on with their work.

The concept of the 'target criminal' was imported from Scotland Yard and a small group of the most senior and active suspected terrorists were subjected to detailed investigation and surveillance. The aim was to lift a suspected terrorist for interrogation, shock him with the extent and detail that had been acquired about his criminal activities and induce him into making self-incriminating statements.

Working side by side with the new crime squads were the 'Ants', an elite undercover anti-terrorist squad, skilled in surveillance. They undertook much of the work observing the activities of the target terrorists but they had another more immediate role. Briefed by a new incident analysis team, they also carried out preventive patrolling along the routes travelled by terrorists from their heartlands to their intended targets. This tactic gave rise to a new category of criminal – the 'travelling gunman'. Many lives were saved by this tactic of intercepting potential killers.

A typical successful operation took place on 25 August at Finaghy Road North, one of the main funnels from the West Belfast area. An undercover surveillance patrol became suspicious of two vehicles heading out of the area and kept them under observation as they called for support from uniform patrols to intercept them. A chase developed and after the vehicles were cornered a couple of miles away in Cranmore Gardens, the occupants scattered. After a bomb in one of the vehicles exploded, five men were quickly rounded up by pursuing police but three more kidnapped an elderly gardener and took refuge at a house in nearby Osborne Gardens, where a siege developed. Three hours later they surrendered after obtaining assurances from a priest that they would not be shot. (One of the terrorists was Kieran Doherty, who later died on hunger strike while serving a twenty-two-year sentence at the Maze prison.)

By the end of 1976 Newman could point to encouraging early results from his strategy. Deaths in the final quarter were down 30 per cent; explosions by 11.5 per cent. Weapon seizures were up 50 per cent; ammunition hauls by 30 per cent and the capture of explosives had nearly tripled to 20,500 lb. Most importantly in view of the new thrust of security policy, the number of charges brought against suspected members of the IRA more than doubled from 320 in 1975 to 708 in the whole of 1976.

On 18 October 1976 the first major court case arising from the new law and order strategy began when twenty-eight members of the outlawed Loyalist terrorist group, the Ulster Volunteer Force, went on trial in Belfast before Mr Justice MacDermott, son of a former Lord Chief Justice. There was no jury. The fifty-five indictments covered four murders, three attempted murders and a plethora of charges relating to robberies, explosions, shootings and the illegal possession of firearms and explosives.

It was a significant and crucial test of the new government and police policies. If it was not a success they would have to go back to the drawing board with unthinkably serious consequences. If the case succeeded, especially against hardline Loyalists, the police would gain confidence and bolster their efforts to be seen and accepted as an effective, impartial, law enforcement organization able to pursue and convict terrorists through the courts. In particular, it would be a tangible achievement to point out when Catholic politicians accused the force of still being one-sided.

The men in the dock comprised virtually the entire membership of the so-called East Antrim Brigade of the UVF who had terrorized the Carrickfergus-Larne area for much of the previous five years. The local RUC knew the accused men well and, reflecting the close relationship between the police and the Protestant community, had obtained much useful information about their activities. However, the usual wall of fear prevented them from converting it into evidence. One detective who tried had wreaths and then, after further persistence, a coffin sent to his home as a pointed reminder of the realities. The deployment of A-Squad officers to reinforce the local police was no more successful in exposing them.

The first real break in the intensive investigation came on the afternoon of Sunday 31 August 1975 when some armed members of the gang abducted another member from his Carrickfergus home. The twenty-seven-year-old man was taken to a local drinking club which served as a headquarters. While he was held downstairs, a mock trial was conducted upstairs. Eventually he was summoned there to face the adjudicators, who were seated at a table with a gun lying in front of them. Fearing for at least his kneecaps, more probably his life, the man quickly asked to go downstairs again to retrieve his cigarettes. Surprisingly, the guards agreed.

But when he reached the bottom of the steps he made a sudden dash for the front door and escaped. He ran a short distance to a police checkpoint in the town centre and gave himself up. From there the panic-stricken fugitive was taken to the police station. There, soon afterwards, he confessed to being second-in-command of the UVF unit and began to tell detectives a sordid, far from patriotic, story, including the details of a double murder and a secret grave.

Next afternoon, to back it up, he led a squad of detectives, scenes of crime officers and members of the Special Patrol Group, with spades, to an isolated spot on the cliffs at Gobbins Road, Islandmagee, overlooking Belfast Lough. There, in undergrowth, a short distance off a narrow lane, the officers, wearing protective face masks, dug up a plot of new grown grass. Two feet down they uncovered part of a human leg and over the next few hours recovered two badly decomposed bodies with holes in the skulls where they had been shot. 'It was a sickening sight even for men hardened to dealing with the results of violence,' remembers one detective.

The bodies were those of Hugh McVeigh and David Douglas, members of the rival Ulster Defence Association, who had gone missing without trace nearly five months earlier on 7 April while delivering furniture. At the time there was tension between members of the two groups and the victims had been shot by a UVF man wearing a black leather jacket, then bundled into the freshly dug grave. To prevent it being discovered, the police were told, one of the gang had been assigned to visit the scene regularly to plant grass seed and watch for signs of subsidence.

With their informant's credibility now established and with the details he was able to provide about the inner workings of the gang, the police began a major secret operation to round up the previously elusive East Antrim terrorists. It was codenamed 'Operation Jigsaw'. For the next five weeks, upwards of fifty detectives worked night and day drawing together a blueprint to put the terrorists behind bars. It was the largest detective operation ever mounted by the force.

The suspects and their homes and haunts were put under surveillance. Interrogation files were prepared, collating every scrap of material that had ever been gathered about each of them. The reports on every crime listed by the informer, who was given immunity from prosecution and became known as 'Witness A', were re-examined. In what was certain to be a landmark test of the legal limits of the new interrogation process as outlined by Diplock, officers were delegated to monitor and record every salient fact about each suspect while he was in custody. Nothing was left to chance in the pre-planning. Even the number of times the bed linen in the cells was changed would be officially counted.

The swoop on the gang was planned for the early hours of 6 October. Four days earlier the UVF had once more been outlawed by Merlyn Rees after a day-long series of sectarian shootings and bombings which claimed eleven lives, including four members of the organization who died in a premature explosion. At 2 am more than 500 police, backed up by 1,000 soldiers, gathered in Belfast for the pre-swoop briefing by Chief Superintendent Billy Mooney, the newly appointed head of the CID, leading his first major case. By 5.15 am Carrickfergus, Greenisland, Whitehead and Islandmagee had been surrounded and sealed off by the security forces. On the dot of 6 am the arrest teams, working from synchronized watches so that there would be no time for any of the suspects to alert or talk to anyone else, pulled the sixteen men from their beds and brought them to RUC Castlereagh, in East Belfast, for detailed questioning.

The same exactness had been planned into this phase of the operation. Each of the vehicles bringing the suspects in had been given a precise but different arrival time. There was to be no opportunity for any of the men to see or speak to each other. As they arrived they were photographed, fingerprinted, medically examined and lodged in a cell, where they were denied contact with everyone but their interrogators; cigarettes, food from outside and access to solicitors were forbidden.

When the trial eventually got under way, twenty-eight men stood in the dock. Five of them were charged with the double murder of McVeigh and Douglas. Three were accused of murdering Robert McCreight in August 1975. McCreight was another member of the gang who was said to be talking too much but because they feared he would talk to the police if he was kneecapped as a punishment they decided instead to silence him by killing him. One of the gang, with whom he was friendly, was therefore ordered to lure him to a lonely farmhouse in Templepatrick, where guns were produced and he was shot dead.

Two members of the gang were charged with murdering Leslie Shepherd, a young Protestant, who got in the way of a murder bid on two Catholic brothers who operated a scrapyard, at Ballyclare, on 1 September 1975. The other charges related to a number of bungled murder bids on Catholics, a series of bomb attacks on hotels, pubs and a disused cinema, and robberies on banks and power stations.

Over most of the next seventy-three days of the hearing, some 300 witnesses, policemen, doctors and the accused themselves participated in a 'trial within a trial' about the admissability of statements made by the accused while under the interrogation regime. The police faced a barrage of accusations from twenty-six of the prisoners that a 'heavy gang' of detectives had systematically ill-treated them. They claimed to have been slapped, punched, squeezed and dragged around the interview room. One claimed that detectives had made him drop his trousers and underpants and then laughed at him.

The trial judge also heard extensive legal submissions about the situation – one barrister was on his feet for two and a half days – before deciding that in all but one case, where there was medical evidence of bruising, he would admit both the statements made under interrogation and the testimony of 'Witness A'. He had started giving evidence with a mask on but it was removed after debate between the lawyers, on the grounds that all the accused knew who he was anyway.

When the trial concluded on 11 March it had cost in excess of £2 million and lasted seventy-seven days, the most expensive and longest criminal trial ever held in Ulster. As Mr Justice MacDermott handed down sentences totalling some 700 years, fists flew in the dock. One man shouted that he would see the judge in hell, others yelled 'Up the UVF'. In a speech threatening reprisals, another accused 'Witness A' of 'grovelling before God and Ulster for self-preservation'.

Two men walked free – one because the judge ruled there was a reasonable doubt about his role in the McVeigh/Douglas killing; the other because the prosecution failed to convince the judge he had not acted under duress in luring McCreight to his death.

The police were well satisfied at the outcome of the case. The judiciary had minutely scrutinized their handling of the prisoners and accepted its legality, and the new criminal investigation systems had proved their potential in dealing with a major terrorist conspiracy. But behind the scenes there were still major tensions and differences of opinion between the police and army and between the military and the government.

On 18 June 1976, police backed up by troops, acting on a tip-off from an informer, raided an elderly woman's house at Springfield Avenue in West Belfast and captured five of the most wanted Provisional IRA terrorists. There was little doubt they had interrupted an important terrorist planning session. In the past the men would have been questioned and then despatched to the Maze for an indefinite period of detention without trial. This time they were held for a mere three days and released without charge. (One of the six was Patrick Magee, later to earn notoriety as the man who planted the bomb at the Grand Hotel in Brighton which came close to assassinating the Prime Minister and several senior members of the government.)

At the very least, argued some of the military, the courts should be given the power to imprison IRA activists for a minimum of twelve months for membership of an illegal organization. They advocated copying the practice in the Irish Republic where the sworn testimony of a police officer above the rank of chief superintendent was accepted as sufficient evidence for the court to convict.

There were constant ripples of discontent about the wisdom of the police primacy policy in high places throughout that summer of 1976. 'You can't box under Queensberry rules,' grumbled one senior soldier. 'The terrorists don't.' Rees was suspect in many military eyes as being soft on terrorism. The senior military men, who had not forgiven him for flirting with the Provisionals two years earlier, really wanted a return to detention without trial. They thought the new conditional release scheme for prisoners who had served half their sentences was far too lenient, even though the government had increased the terms of imprisonment that the courts could impose. For instance, 'travelling gunmen', as potential murderers were called, were now subject to a ten-year maximum sentence instead of five.

Much of the trouble arose from army resentment at being given what they saw as the back seat to the police. At a time of widespread defence cuts the army was also keen to avoid any retrenchment and Ulster was by far its most powerful *raison d'être*. Any ambitious officer needed a couple of impressive tours in Ulster on his record to stand any chance of promotion.

'The real lesson every soldier has to learn is that he is only in Northern Ireland to help the police while the current level of violence is beyond their capability,' summed up one RUC officer at the time. 'After all, a soldier is only here for a few months at a time and has no stake. The police believe they are creating the climate for a better society which they will live in too.'

Another factor was the inherent difference between the professional skills of the army and the police. The constable was taught to act on his own initiative and use discretion in handling the situations he encountered. By contrast soldiers traditionally worked on blind obedience to orders handed down the chain of command, although army procedures had been significantly modified as a result of experience in Ulster where much more initiative was demanded from junior officers. Many senior officers described Ulster as a 'corporals' war' because of the quick-thinking and sensitivity demanded from the basic fighting unit, the four man 'brick'. It was the patrol leaders, the corporals, who had to make snap decisions in the light of the problems they encountered. Rarely had they time or the opportunity to refer upwards for instructions. The individual discretion about when it was legal to open fire, as laid out in the 'Yellow Card', was the most important example of this.

Nevertheless, through its inherent competitiveness, the army, preoccupied with the attrition rate and riddled with inter-unit rivalry, with each regiment trying to find more guns, search more houses and make more arrests than the one before, continued to create problems for the police. 'Given their philosophy it was difficult to get the required subtlety from the army,' recalls one RUC man. 'They had an over-enthusiastic tendency to clatter into situations and cause complications. We could not find a way to replace their boots with plimsolls.'

This attitude fuelled the old friction between police and soldiers, which flared up again. In the areas where they were still operating together, military police took to eavesdropping on police radio channels, then racing to incidents to prove their superior reaction time. One police patrol beaten to the scene of a robbery by military police was annoyed to find the 'Redcaps' had handed out calling cards to all the eye-witnesses they could find, inviting them to pass information to the military. They retorted by describing their military counterparts as the 'Royal Meddling Police', only to be called the 'Royal Useless Constabulary' in return.

There was further friction between the two sides over access to intelligence data about suspects held on a computer operated by the army. While every military unit had access to the computer through a chain of terminals, there was only one police link with direct access. Further hostility was caused when the army frequently classified material 'For UK eyes only', which denied the RUC sight of it.

The army also maintained an alarming capacity for shooting itself in the foot. At the height of the friction with the police, the army vehemently denied claims that soldiers had burned down a social club in West Belfast. It was merely IRA propaganda, they insisted. The local residents, vociferously led by the then SDLP politician, Paddy Devlin, stuck to their claims and after a rapid police investigation eight soldiers were charged with maliciously setting fire to the club, prompting fulsome apologies from the army headquarters at Lisburn.

Throughout the controversy and in-fighting Newman remained unshaken that the policy of police primacy was the right one and he maintained a lofty scorn at meetings with Rees when the senior soldiers voiced their doubts. In an August speech he said that it was only through an 'unspectacular process – the persistent, impartial, professional application of the law – that terrorism will be defeated'.

On 10 September 1976, Roy Mason, a former Barnsley coal miner, replaced Merlyn Rees at the Northern Ireland Office. As a former minister of defence he had visited Northern Ireland often and knew the situation well but any hopes the soldiers harboured that he would take his cue from them rather than the police were hastily dispelled. Mason decisively backed the security policy laid down by his predecessor. He was firmly of the opinion that this was by far the best way to improve the Ulster situation. By his estimate there was no prospect of any agreement between the deadlocked political parties so he made a conscious decision to pay only lip service to finding a way forward. The priority was to be security and an improvement in the economy. That way the IRA, and the other terrorist groups, could be rendered obsolete, he believed.

Mason made no secret of his hatred for the IRA and all it stood for. At an after-dinner speech soon after his arrival, he criticized his hosts, the BBC, and other news organizations for their neutrality between the terrorists and the security forces. A similarly un-compromising message with constant claims that the IRA was 'reel-ing' became a feature of his regular pronouncements. Their tone was invariably set at what became known as the Monday security meet-ings. After a weekend back home in Barnsley, Mason would arrive in Belfast on Monday mornings refreshed for the priority business at a meeting with the police, army, prison and intelligence services. Afterwards there would be a gung-ho statement about the security successes of the previous week, the number of dangerous terrorists arrested and the brightening prospects for a return to normality.

The message was further hammered home in a £45,000 local advertising campaign that autumn, with newspaper advertisements and posters backing up a ninety-second television commercial. After scenes of bombing and shooting with casualties being rushed to ambulances, the commentary said that in seven years violence had bred nothing but more violence. There followed scenes of dole queues, burning factories and children being escorted by soldiers. The com-mentary said that if the violence ended people would have more freedom of movement and enjoy a better life. The film ended with a picture of a little girl, sitting wistfully on a pile of rubble. Scrawled on the wall behind her was the campaign slogan – '7 years is enough – OK'. The IRA, which was then undergoing some internal policy turmoil, responded with graffiti, 'Stone Mason won't break us'.

Despite their satisfaction with his support, the police did not entirely share Mason's public bravado. Newman still preferred the 'unspectacular process'. At Lisburn, predictably, there was even more scepticism. In private the army called Mason 'Pitprop' – because his policies were liable to sudden collapse.

But all these doubts and the differences were temporarily submerged on 1 January 1977 when the policy of police primacy was firmly re-established under a joint directive signed by the new GOC, Lt-Gen. Sir Timothy Creasey, who had taken over two months earlier, and Newman. For the first time since 1969, the chief constable was back in the driving seat as director of operations and the Thursday morning security planning meetings, which had alternated 'home and away' between Lisburn and Knock for almost a year, moved permanently to Knock. As events were to show the army never completely accepted the situation and when things were tense never lost a chance to advocate tougher measures. Newman and his closest police officers shared many a private joke about what they called the General's 'Malayan view'.

Although during 1976 the tide had clearly turned against the terrorists, RUC officers continued to lose their lives. On 31 July Constable Thomas Cush was killed by a single shot from a sniper while he was on duty at the security gates in Lurgan. Constable James Heaney, who was stationed at RUC Waterside in Londonderry, was shot dead while working on his car outside his widowed mother's home at Andersonstown in Belfast on 26 August. His death was a particular blow for the RUC because he was a young Catholic from a troubled area who had joined the force. When Newman announced his intention to attend the funeral at Milltown Cemetery in the heart of West Belfast, his security team protested. 'He gave his life for the RUC. The least I can do is go to his funeral,' he replied.

Sergeant Albert Craig was on duty outside a stock car racing meeting at Shamrock Park, Portadown, on 18 September. Gunmen, firing from a car, pulled up and killed him. Reserve Constable Arthur McKay was helping to recover a stolen car at Kilrea on 8 October when he died after a booby-trapped bomb left underneath the vehicle exploded.

Detective Constable Noel McCabe was on duty in the Lower Falls area of Belfast in the late morning of 2 November 1976 when a number of youths forced his car to halt. Gunmen then fired through the passenger window and murdered him. A month later, on 3

December, in Dungannon a gunman killed traffic warden Joseph Scott by shooting him in the back at close range as he assisted a school crossing patrolman to escort children across a busy road. The dead man was also a part-time Reserve Constable.

Two weeks later on 15 December, as Constable Norman Campbell was closing the security barrier at High Street, Portadown, terrorists fired from a car, fatally wounding him. Three days before Christmas, Reserve Constable Samuel Armour was killed when a booby-trapped bomb under his car exploded outside his home at Maghera.

Mason's tough policies and pugnacious attitude did not endear him to the hardline Loyalists. The indefinite shelving of the report from Rees's Constitutional Convention and his refusal to tackle the political issues infuriated them. They believed he was implementing an unspoken British government plan to withdraw from Northern Ireland and the lack of a response to IRA violence, they claimed, showed he was going to leave the Loyalists at their mercy.

Despite the improving attrition rate – more than 300 people were charged with serious terrorist offences in the first three months of 1977 – the level of violence remained disturbingly high. In the same period forty victims died. They included a fifteen-month-old boy killed in an explosion outside his home in north Belfast. The Provisionals gave the spiral a new twist by embarking on a murder campaign against prominent businessmen, the 'rich and ruling class'. Three Englishmen died: Geoffrey Agate, head of the Du Pont company in Londonderry; Donald Robinson, a ceiling contractor in Belfast; and James Nicholson, a London-based public relations consultant who was ambushed as he left a government-backed factory in West Belfast to catch a flight at Belfast airport. Of the twenty-three sectarian killings, nine were attributed to Catholic killers, fourteen to Protestant.

On 22 April, hardline Loyalist impatience came to a head when the United Unionist Action Council (UUAC) issued a seven-day ultimatum to the British government in the shape of a strident advertisement placed in the Belfast morning newspaper, *The Newsletter*. 'In the name of the Ulster Loyalist people we give notice to Mr Roy Mason that he has seven days to begin a powerful and effective offensive against the IRA and announce steps to implement the Convention Report.'

The UUAC, which had been set up about a year earlier, took the decision to mount a strike in March at a meeting attended by some seventy people from all over Northern Ireland. The thirty-man council embraced a wide spectrum of Protestant opinion, from Ian Paisley to the outlawed UVF. Significantly, however, the Official Unionist Party distanced itself from the Council, whose main muscle consisted of the Ulster Defence Association and some of those who had been involved in the 1974 UWC strike.

Many of them were convinced that Loyalists had settled for too little with only the fall of the Executive. They believed that if the pressure on the British government had been maintained, with the electricity system on the point of collapse and sewage set to bubble back up through the drains of Belfast, they could have secured virtually any demands, including a new Stormont parliament. This time, the UUAC calculated, it could not fail to win its demands by putting a throttle on normal life through control of the power station workers and bringing the province to the point of no return as in 1974.

Mason predictably refused to meet the terms of the UUAC ultimatum and a week later at a new conference, fronted by Paisley, the Council called for what it described as a 'constitutional stoppage' to begin at midnight on 2 May. 'Although the earth may move, we will not be afraid,' prayed one of Paisley's ministers at the opening of the conference. Paisley himself said: 'Mr Mason will not change his disastrous policies which are bringing ruin to this country. No amount of engaging in parliamentary work is going to change this situation. We only care for one thing, to save our country.' Andy Tyrie, supreme commander of the UDA, said: 'It is important that this strike achieves what it sets out to achieve, that is a government back.'

Mason regarded the whole enterprise as a naked challenge to the authority of the British parliament and government. Although he did not use the words 'coup' or 'putsch' in public, they liberally peppered his private conversation as he moved to forestall the strike threat. His first move was to enlist the support of the trades union movement. It had been stung by its serious failure to control its members during the UWC stoppage. Since then it had worked hard to restore its authority and stamp out sectarianism in the workplace through a 'Better life for all' campaign. The entire movement threw its weight behind Mason in opposing the stoppage and pledging it would stand up against the expected intimidation and strong-arm tactics to enforce the strike.

That Friday there were other encouraging signs, including a vote by 8,000 Belfast shipyard workers not to support the stoppage. This was no doubt influenced by a timely government reminder of the shipyard's precarious viability when the first new orders for two years were announced. The potential strikers realized that the £7 million orders, for two tankers, would preserve many of their jobs. Elsewhere 200 workers on strike over a pay dispute promptly voted to return to work in case their position was misrepresented as support for the Loyalist strike.

Nevertheless, the government preparations for the worst continued. Plans, written when the lessons of 1974 had been analysed, were put into immediate effect. Stand-by generators, installed at all government buildings, were topped up with fuel. The new, secure government telephone network, recently installed, was brought into action. Preparations were made to declare a state of emergency under the 1924 Special Powers Act and the publicity machine at Stormont Castle took control of all official announcements. There was to be no repetition of the confusing policy statements last time.

Over the weekend the emergency Spearhead battalion, 600 men of the Royal Welsh Fusiliers, arrived to reinforce the 14,000 army garrison. In addition, 200 specialists, including Royal Engineers and naval power station technicians, with vehicles and equipment, were deployed. However, despite the post-UWC inquests and studies, there was not much optimism at Stormont Castle that electricity supplies could be maintained by the servicemen if the power station workers walked out. Mason and his officials were highly conscious of the still valid 1974 assessment by General Sir Frank King that even if the army could maintain the generating capacity, there were not enough soldiers in the entire British army effectively to protect every pole and pylon of the distribution grid from sabotage.

In keeping with the policy of police primacy, planning to handle the strike was concentrated at the police headquarters in Knock, where the Civil Emergencies plan was invoked. All leave and rest days were cancelled and personnel were placed on daily twelve-hour duty shifts to make the maximum manpower available. The strike came as no surprise to the RUC. Special Branch had closely monitored the activities of the UUAC and was well aware of its intention to strike. When this had first been reported to Stormont Castle it attracted little attention but after the threat had been made there were demands for more detailed information.

The general police strategy was that everything should be nipped in the bud. Where possible road blocks and barricades should be talked away, vigilantes should be discouraged and crowds persuaded to move. Those fearing intimidation were to be reassured by a widespread visible presence of police and troops. There was great concern that there should be no over-reaction which would drive waverers into the arms of the strikers but if force proved necessary, the orders said, then it would be applied.

The strike began at midnight on Monday with gangs in many rural areas felling trees and telegraph poles to block roads. Throughout the night police and army patrols, many issued with chain-saws, were deployed throughout Northern Ireland to keep the roads open. The police knew exactly where to concentrate their forces: over the weekend, documents had been seized from a prominent UDA member, stopped at a security check, which listed the road junctions the strikers planned to block.

The battle for the hearts and minds of the workforce began in earnest at dawn on Tuesday morning. By then the security forces had cleared ninety road blocks and every main route was open save the Bangor–Belfast railway line, which had been severed by an explosion. At first light Paisley, travelling in his usual armoured police car, was on the streets near his home in East Belfast where crowds of pickets had gathered to meet workers heading for the shipyard and aircraft factories. Altogether half the exclusively Protestant workforce in these two major industries braved the pickets and turned up for work, a major rebuff for Paisley and Tyrie.

Trades union leaders played an important role in encouraging their members to defy threats and pickets. John Freeman, secretary of the Transport and General Workers Union, arrived at Transport House in the city centre at 6 am and went from floor to floor switching on every light as a defiant sign of business as usual.

Support for the strike both in Belfast and beyond was patchy. Pickets did succeed in closing the port of Larne, to the chagrin of mushroom-growers and poultry-processors who rely on ferries from there to supply their customers in Britain. One shopkeeper was asked to close down by a man who came into his premises. He reluctantly complied. Up to a dozen more were leaning on his plate-glass window outside.

Although the power stayed on, rumours more than direct intimidation led to many people going home early. Nevertheless, there was a marked lack of tension and Chuck Berry, the veteran rock'n'roll star, was able to go ahead with a planned concert in Belfast that night. Day one had been a good day for the security forces, with only minority support for the strike and no serious violence.

Early next morning, day two, the main focus was once again East Belfast, where closing the province's two major industrial plants had assumed enormous symbolic significance for the strike leaders. Outside the former doctors' surgery on nearby Newtownards Road, which served as a headquarters for the UDA, Andy Tyrie himself, mug of tea in hand, directed the crowd of burly pickets and made belligerent but good-humoured remarks to newsmen. But his mood swiftly changed when police Landrovers began driving backwards and forwards through the men in an effort to disperse them. At one point there were angry exchanges between Tyrie and a senior police officer who told him to clear the road.

Tyrie responded by ordering his men to put on masks and close the road. Beer barrels from a nearby pub were rolled in front of the police vehicles to halt them and then stones and other missiles began to fly. The police withdrew and regrouped further down the road. Then with support from troops in riot gear, who deliberately remained about 300 yards behind, the police, batons in hand, charged the crowd.

The confrontation between the police and strikers was no accident. Newman judged that the police needed a strong visual image of their determination to break the strike, so he tipped off the local television stations about the planned operation. Those RUC officers who had doubts received a major morale booster when they saw the later news bulletins. More importantly, it demonstrated to the community at large that the police were not taking the soft option of turning a blind eye to road blocks and intimidation as they did in 1974. It was a decisive turning point.

For the rest of the week the strike leaders fought an increasingly ineffective campaign to enforce the stoppage as more and more people turned up at their workplaces. The strike leaders then turned on the power workers, on the basis that if they could be stopped then the lack of power would halt everybody else. Both sides invested much energy in winning the allegiance of the power station workers. Mason even brought a delegation from Ballylumford to Stormont Castle, where he provided drinks and a buffet, mingled with them individually and won them over with his blunt persuasiveness.

Afterwards, in an extraordinary statement issued from the Castle, Mason outlined the 'categorical assurances' the workers had been given about security measures, which 'had been stepped up and would continue to be stepped up further in future'. In particular, Mason said that the RUC would be built up to a strength of 6,500 and provided with more modern weapons, equipment and vehicles, and that ten DMSUs were to be established in the near future. The laws dealing with terrorism were being reviewed, he said, and increased emphasis was being placed on covert techniques which had proved especially effective in combating terrorism. There was nothing new in the promises; every item was already on Newman's active agenda but the fact that such a statement was issued under the circumstances reflected the heat of the battle being fought for their support.

An unpublicized development from the meeting was the posting of a large force of police into the East Antrim area to protect the power workers. Those who had received direct threats were given police bodyguards of as many as six men; some even had armed police temporarily living in their homes. Every time the shifts changed over at the power station, there was a heavy police presence to prevent intimidation.

By the end of the week the 500,000 working population was voting with its feet against the strike. Three out of every four men had drifted back to the shipyard. Higher turnouts were reported elsewhere. Paisley and his dwindling band of activists made further efforts over the weekend to increase the effectiveness of their protest. Long cavalcades of slow-moving farm vehicles took to the roads but after one convoy was pushed into a river at Toomebridge by IRA supporters, many farmers withdrew rather than risk their expensive equipment at one of the busiest times of the year with fields to plough and crops to sow. The UDA threatened renewed road-blocking activity on Monday 9 May in a final try at bringing the province to a halt. Public transport became a specific target and buses were immobilized at several locations by having sugar or water poured into their fuel tanks.

The evening before, Paisley had retreated behind the barricades at his Ballymena stronghold, which had been sealed off by farm tractors and machinery. During the night he had a long meeting with senior police officers at the local police station but he refused to lift the blockade of the town.

Throughout the morning, as Paisley helped man the barricades, a large force of police, backed up by troops with armoured bulldozers, was mustered and deployed on every blocked road leading into Ballymena. There were further troops circling above the town in helicopters. At 11 am, when the encirclement was complete, a police van was driven to the point where Paisley was making his stand. Police officers then bluntly ordered him to call off the blockade or the town would be retaken with whatever force was necessary. The sight of the huge bulldozers and armoured vehicles lined up as far as the eye could see was designed as evidence of the security forces' intent. As the first of the farm tractors, trailers, tankers and other machinery vehicles was moved, Paisley and a dozen of his closest supporters were arrested and taken away in the police van. The strike had reached its final stages.

Next day it was dealt a final blow with the shooting of a busman in Belfast when he stopped to pick up passengers and the death of an off-duty UDR soldier in an explosion at a filling station. Two men making petrol bombs also died, one instantly, the second a few days later. The killings were widely condemned as virtually every sector of business and commercial life reported near-normal operations. After ten days of increasingly futile action the stoppage was finally called off by the humiliated strike leaders. Mason attributed its defeat to the people who were prepared to stand out against the intimidation and physical violence.

The strike had important and long-lasting implications for the RUC. Its vigorous action against Loyalist law breakers, removing 900 road blocks and making 124 arrests, was regarded by Newman as a clear demonstration of the RUC's robust impartiality. The operation against the UDA on the Newtownards Road was, in his view, a model of the law being enforced in a resolute and proper manner. It was also the RUC's answer to continued accusations from the Catholic community that they were partial.

The episode had important internal consequences. Many of the senior, longer-serving officers who had been demoralized by the events of the previous few years regained their confidence. Newman had been required to engage in tough talking with some senior commanders in the build-up to the strike. Now, in the glow of success, criticism and doubts about the wisdom of the 'Way Ahead' were very largely dispelled.

There was particular pleasure that the police themselves had managed to handle the situations they encountered without more than army back-up. 'By God, we did it,' beamed one of the original doubters. Newman was especially pleased that the force had passed such a major test, for it was still far from the state of effectiveness he envisaged. The public order training programme, for instance, was only one-fifth complete.

The Loyalist stoppage was not the only major test the RUC faced in 1977. The year marked the Silver Jubilee of Queen Elizabeth II's accession to the throne and during the twelve-month programme of celebrations she planned to visit every region of the United Kingdom. The force had already participated in one of the year's special events: at Hendon on 6 May, the seventy-two-strong RUC contingent had been given pride of place at the head of the Jubilee review when the Queen inspected British police organizations. Despite the obvious security risks, the Queen herself determined that she would travel to Northern Ireland, however limited the scope of the engagements that would be possible. The bulk of the necessarily complex planning for what became known as 'Operation Monarch' fell on the RUC's newly formed Operational Planning branch.

Buckingham Palace had offered the Northern Ireland Office a number of potential dates for the visit in mid-1975, when a draft of the Jubilee celebrations programme was being drawn up. Merlyn Rees is now said by some of those involved in the decision to have opted for 10 and 11 August as the dates most certain to be cancellable, sandwiched as they were between two of the most predictably volatile summer flashpoints; the anniversary of the introduction of internment on the ninth and the Apprentice Boys of Derry parade on the twelfth.

There were raised eyebrows in the senior echelons of the RUC when they were informed of the plan, especially the nominated dates. Some senior men concluded that the inclusion of Northern Ireland in the Jubilee programme was a formal political necessity and that the visit would be quietly cancelled for security reasons in due course. The older hands remembered that a concrete block had been dropped on the royal car the last time the Queen visited the city in the relative public tranquillity of 1966. It was tempting providence to think that a high-profile royal visit could take place after eight years of unprecedented civil disorder.

Such calculations, however, ignored the Queen's personal courage and determination to make the visit, whatever the risks. As the level of international terrorism increased through the late 1960s and early 1970s, the Queen had steadfastly rejected security advice to increase the level of protection around the royal family. Even after the shooting incident in The Mall in London, when Princess Anne and her husband, Captain Mark Philips, narrowly avoided assassination, she decided it was necessary to preserve the open nature of the monarchy and live with the threat. When the British motor industry offered a £60,000 Rolls Royce as a jubilee present she insisted on a standard model without the discreet bomb and bullet proofing her security advisers would have preferred.

As the Queen's programme was refined during 1976, the Ulster engagements, largely at her own insistence, became a firm fixture. The Provisional IRA reacted as anticipated, with threats to disrupt the visit. 'Elizabrit', as they called her, would not be welcome. The Queen's own determined attitude to the visit forced her advisers to think again. There had been a marked improvement in the security situation since the visit was first mooted nearly two years earlier. To cancel it, especially at a late stage, would, they recognized, give the Provisionals a world-wide propaganda coup. Britain could not govern Ulster, they would crow. Despite the proximity to the inevitably violent anniversaries, the police became increasingly confident that they could protect the Queen and, particularly after the strike, the regular Special Branch threat assessments submitted to Stormont Castle reflected this growing feeling.

Mason, who would play host to the Queen, was equally keen on the visit. Whatever the provocation to the Provisionals, it would effectively demonstrate the British government's commitment to Northern Ireland to sceptical Unionists and be a welcome morale booster for the battered Protestant community. Mason also reckoned that a trouble-free visit would be a powerful advertisement to potential investors in the job-starved region that terrorism was indeed on the decline and life getting back to normal.

Preparations went ahead. It was planned that about 7,000 people would meet the Queen and Duke of Edinburgh at six major functions during the two-day visit. Several months in advance a major security operation got under way at Government House, Hillsborough, and on the campus of the university at Coleraine, the two centres for the visit. Army bomb disposal teams, working with sniffer dogs and the latest explosive detection technology, checked every inch of the grounds and buildings. It was an exacting task. There were 170,000 books in the university library alone, each of which was searched more than once. The area declared sterile was then put under heavy guard and rechecked with increasing frequency as the dates for the visit drew near.

Such long-term precautions had become mandatory because of advances in the technology being used by the Provisional IRA to initiate their improvised explosive devices. Bomb-making activity had been centralized in the hands of a small number of experts, whose 'signature' was readily identifiable to army experts. The timers and detonators were being supplied in kit form to the activists who would plant the devices. The aim was to cut out the risk of premature explosion through faulty assembly. Advances in micro-electronics and circuitry were being harnessed by these 'experts' to make ever more effective bombs. They had, for instance, adapted radio-controlled techniques for flying model aircraft to detonate landmines under passing security forces' vehicles, causing almost total reliance on helicopters for transport in some areas. The roads leading to Crossmaglen in South Armagh were considered so vulnerable that even the rubbish from the army base had to be flown out for disposal.

New and more sophisticated electronic timing divices were constantly being discovered in defused bombs. These utilized components that were readily available for legitimate domestic use. Of particular concern was the terrorists' ability to plant bombs as long as three months in advance of a precisely planned detonation time, which involved a misuse of the sort of timing mechanisms found in video recorders. As events turned out, these fears were not groundless.

Built-in minute-by-minute abort facilities were prepared for every stage of the visit so that alternative accommodation would be available, if there was any disruption or incident. These ranged from renovating a wartime hut and installing a new toilet suite for the Queen's possible use at RAF Ballykelly to putting on stand-by a car ferry with a large through-deck in which receptions could be held at sea if the Queen was unable to come ashore at either Hillsborough or Coleraine. The army garrison was temporarily reinforced by 600 men of the Scots Guards, wearing khaki for this royal protection duty rather than their customary black bearskin busbies and distinctive scarlet tunics. The biggest combined security operation since Motorman five years earlier involved 32,000 police and soldiers at its peak, as well as the searching of some 14,000 vehicles a day.

There was the almost predictable last-minute scare. On the eve of the visit a small bomb, triggered by a ten-day delayed timer, went off just outside the twenty-five-mile-long security perimeter area around the university at Coleraine. No damage was caused but there was a hasty review of security overnight as the royal yacht *Britannia* sailed towards the Ulster coast. Those involved affirmed their confidence in the work that had gone on for several months and the plans were allowed to stand.

On 10 August at 8 am, on the first day of the visit, the security arrangements moved into top gear as *Britannia*, escorted by the guided missile destroyer, HMS *Fife*, loomed out of the swirling summer mist at the mouth of Belfast Lough. A squadron of Royal Marine Commandos aboard Rigid-Raider assault boats slipped into place, circling around the ships to prevent any small craft approaching. In a bizarre manifestation of police primacy each assault boat bouncing across the swell had a policeman aboard, his cap secured by the elastic chin strap. On shore a twenty-one-gun salute was fired from Bangor. The Queen's advisers had rejected the original plan to fire it from the ramparts of Carrickfergus Castle as being too controversial. It was there that the Protestant King William came ashore on his way to rout the Catholic King James, at the battle of the Boyne in 1690.

In mid-morning the Queen was taken by barge from *Britannia* to *Fife*, where she boarded one of the distinctive scarlet Wessex helicopters of the RAF Queen's Flight. The short hop to Hillsborough merited a minor footnote in the royal archives for it was the first time she had ever flown by helicopter. Although there was a clash between police and IRA protesters at Castle Street in Belfast city centre during the afternoon, as the Queen presided at an investiture and garden party, the day passed off without serious incident.

The only logistical problem came that evening. Among the guests invited to a reception aboard *Britannia*, anchored off Bangor for the night, were a number of policemen and others who had been injured in the troubles. There was a heavy swell as they were being ferried by barge from shore to ship and some disabled guests who found it difficult transferring from the barge to the Royal Yacht's ladder had to be manhandled in an undignified manner to get aboard and later off again. Overnight, shadowed by police and army patrols ashore, the floodlit *Britannia* sailed north along the Antrim coast to be in position next morning for another short helicopter flight to the university of Coleraine.

There was another crisis that morning when the Provos telephoned a coded bomb warning to a Belfast newsroom just about the time the royal helicopter was due to lift off from *Fife*. There were hurried consultations between the anxious Newman and Mason, who was aboard the royal yacht. The decision to cancel or not was complicated by the fact that about the same time an army search team had discovered a .45 pistol in working order and fifty rounds of ammunition, wrapped in oily rags, just one mile from the campus.

Mason advised the Queen that the police were confident of their precautions and that the engagement should go ahead. But as the helicopter carrying her, the Duke of Edinburgh and the two princes, Andrew and Edward, touched down twelve minutes late, a discreet unscheduled search was taking place. Newman, operating from the security control point established on the roof of the main university building, ordered yet another check of likely spots for a bomb, including the flower arrangements and, once again, all the books in the library.

There was another anxious moment late in the afternoon when a convoy of ambulances with blue lights flashing and sirens wailing converged on the site just as the final event, a youth pageant, was drawing to a close and the helicopters were warming up for the Queen's departure. It transpired that a number of people had succumbed to food poisoning and it was the caterers not the Provos who caused the casualties.

The explosion of another small bomb outside the secure campus area that night did not mitigate the humiliation that the success of the visit had been for the Provos and the triumph it was for both Mason and the RUC. Newman, with his innate policeman's caution, refrained from any public comment, but Mason, bombastic even by the usual political standards, almost gloated. As *Britannia* sailed from Northern Ireland waters he telephoned *The Times* correspondent in Belfast to make sure his own role in the affair was thoroughly chronicled.

Before long he was talking in ever more extravagant terms about the terrorists being squeezed out of society and into prison like toothpaste from a tube. That autumn there were indeed strong grounds for believing that even the most deeply ingrained aspects of terrorism were beginning to yield under the police pressure. In the first eight months of the year civilian deaths were down to 97 from 222 in the same period in 1976. Shootings had dropped by 33 per cent; explosions by 52 per cent; and there had been no sectarian murders since the previous May. By the end of the year the chief constable was able to report that it had been the least violent for six years and that the death toll had fallen by 62 per cent.

Despite this encouraging picture, Mason was publicly rebuked for his statements that the IRA was beaten, defeated or on the run when he was guest of honour at the Northern Ireland Police Federation's annual conference at Newcastle on 9 September. Pleading for 'propaganda with circumspection', Alan Wright, the chairman, warned that 'Words can be as lethal as bullets in the unfortunate circumstances in which we work.'

He had good reason to question the Secretary of State's analysis, for throughout 1977 another fourteen members of the RUC lost their lives as a result of the terrorist campaign. Reserve Constable William Greer was killed when a booby-trap device attached to his car exploded as he drove away from his home at Portglenone on 14 January. Detective Constable Patrick McNulty was fatally wounded by a gunman at a garage on Strand Road, Londonderry, as he delivered his car for servicing on 27 January. On 5 February two policemen were leaving a shop at Gilford after checking out a false report that an incendiary device had been planted. As they reached their police car gunmen in another car drew alongside, opening fire and hitting Reserve Constable Robert Harrison, who died from his wounds.

Eight days later gunmen lying in wait for Reserve Constable Samuel McKane opened fire when he drove into the driveway of his home at Cloughmills. He died instantly. On 24 February Inspector James Cobb, a member of a police party opening the security gates at Church Place, Lurgan, was shot dead. The next day Sergeant Joseph Campbell was shot dead at RUC Cushendall while closing the station gates after a colleague had driven out. (Charlie McCormick, another member of the force, was later acquitted of his murder.) On 13 March Constable William Brown was shot and killed when terrorists ambushed a mobile police patrol at Ballagh Crossroads, near Lisnaskea. He was later awarded a posthumous Queen's Gallantry medal.

Two constables, John McCracken and Kenneth Sheehan, died on 8 April when gunmen in a car they tried to halt near Magherafelt opened fire. On 20 May Reserve Constable Robert North was driving a school bus near Benburb when he was ambushed by terrorists and died from gunshot wounds. Three officers, Constables Samuel Davison

**1 & 2** The old and the new: Sergeant Instructor Tom Ashfield in the early 1940s (*below*) and an RUC constable keeping vigil in Londonderry in the 1980s (right).

**3 & 4** 1922: Examining a lorry at Balmoral (*above*)
and a road trench barrier on the Fermanagh–Monagahan border (*below*).

**5 & 6** 1922: Newtownbutler Specials on patrol, with their Lancia cage car (*above*) and C Specials on duty in the Albertbridge Road, Belfast (*right*).

7 Sir Charles Wickham  8 Sir Richard Pim
9 The funeral of Constable Henry Ross, County Armagh, July 1958.

10 Workmen under RUC guard digging a road trench barrier
on the Derry–Letterkenny road, 1958.
11 Brookeborough RUC station, sandbagged and under guard, 1958.

12 Sir Albert Kennedy

13 Anthony Peacocke

14 Sir Arthur Young

15 Sir Graham Shillington

**16 & 17** 'Battle of the Bogside', Londonderry, 1969: under petrol bomb attack (*right*) and, in full riot gear, supporting a colleague injured in the rioting (*below*).

**18** The body of Inspector Devlin being removed from the scene of the bomb explosion that destroyed Chichester Road police station, Belfast, 1971.

**19** Constables William Forster and Samuel Cairns, awarded Queens Medals for Gallantry for saving the life of a man in a bomb explosion at King Street, Belfast, 1976.

and Kenneth Lynch and Reserve Constable Hugh Martin, died while on mobile patrol near Ardboe when terrorist gunmen ambushed their vehicle. Early on 6 July Reserve Constable David Morrow was a member of a patrol placing traffic cones in the main street at Aughnacloy in preparation for market day, when terrorist gunmen opened fire, killing him.

The Provisional IRA were at their lowest ebb in the latter half of 1977. Throughout that year there had been bitter internal wrangling over policy. The younger, street-hardened northerners were highly critical of the tactics of the leadership, mainly old, southerners and Dublin-based – the armchair generals. They accused them of being fooled by the British government into conceding a ceasefire out of which no benefit had accrued for the Republican movement. Instead it had allowed the security forces to regroup and reorganize.

Much of the wrangling had originated among the prisoners interned in the Maze, who had formed a think-tank and produced lengthy political discussion papers and new ideas which were being widely debated throughout the organization now that that they were released. There were three major developments. Power was removed from the old men in Dublin and a Northern Command, run by the young men, was set up to conduct the campaign in the north. The Provos also abandoned any hopes of a quick end to the conflict and the concept of the 'long war' was accepted. There was also to be greater emphasis on the movement's political activity, a decision that gave rise to the slogan going forward to 'take power with an Armalite in one hand and a ballot paper in the other'.

Newman's caution about writing the Provos off prematurely was more than justified, for the terrorists were causing havoc with a series of incendiary attacks, shortly to be made worse by the introduction of a lethal new bomb. Tighter security on the ground and a squeeze on the sources of explosive had made it progressively more difficult for the Provos to carry out car-bomb attacks, so since 1976 the organization had instead been using cassette incendiaries to attack property. They were small, simple to construct from readily available materials and easily concealed from searchers. Female fire-bombers often hid them in the thick platform-soled shoes that were then the height of fashion. The devices, usually four ounces of a highly inflammable mix of everday household chemicals, with a detonator, battery and timing mechanism, packed in a tape cassette, were planted in offices, shops and other premises, usually among combustibles like paper, paint or furniture. When they ignited, an intense fireball, at least nine feet in diameter, sent the resulting blaze quickly out of control. In 1976, the commercial heart of Belfast and most towns in the province, notably the seaside resort of Portrush (which was systematically fire-bombed at the height of the summer holidays), had suffered an estimated £50 million worth of damage.

Around the same time an even more lethal incendiary device, which the army described as a 'blast incendiary', made its destructive debut. A small explosive charge, usually less than 2 lb, detonator and timer were strapped to a gallon can of petrol. Late in 1977 its effect was enhanced by using a butcher's meat hook to hang it to the wire-mesh security grilles protecting most commercial property. To prevent army bomb disposal men from making the device safe, it was also given a time delay of only a few minutes, just enough in fact to enable the bomb planter to get away.

The resulting fireball had the same force as a 300 lb bomb and represented maximum damage from minimum materials for the terrorists. 'With blast you generally get surface damage, windows blown out, that sort of thing,' said one explosives expert. 'But with these blast incendiaries, particularly if they are planted amidst inflammable material, there is such a raging fire that you get major structural damage. I have seen instances of steel beams encased in concrete buckling.'

Throughout the winter months of 1977/78 both type of incendiaries were widely used in some 600 attacks, burning down shops, offices, a bus station, cinemas and hotels and causing damage running into millions of pounds. In a single night sixteen devices went off in nine different towns and nine more were defused.

The La Mon House, with a restaurant, dance hall and hotel, set in rolling countryside in the Castlereagh hills east of Belfast, was the sort of thriving target then in favour with the terrorists. On the evening of 17 February 1978 more than 300 people were packed in at a variety of get-togethers. Two of the largest groups were attending annual prize distributions by the Northern Ireland Collie Club and the Northern Ireland Junior Motor Cycle Club.

Shortly before 9 pm two devices which had been hooked on security grilles outside the function room windows exploded without warning and sent a fireball roaring through the crowded building. Panic-stricken guests and staff ran for the doorways as the lights went out and thick, choking smoke enveloped them. Those caught directly in the path of the flames were instantly incinerated. Others touched by the scalding heat had their clothes and skin scorched off. Some staggered from the building, with their clothes and flesh on fire.

Newman, who later described the incident as the 'ultimate in inhumanity', arrived quickly at the scene from RUC headquarters. There he was confronted by journalists who asked him to explain how the IRA could carry out such an atrocity if it was beaten. 'I never made that claim,' he said through tight lips.

Altogether twelve people died in the blast and a further twenty-three were seriously injured, making it the second worst single incident since McGurk's bar. One of the fatalities was Reserve Constable Gordon Crothers, who was off-duty on a night out. The victims were so badly burned that it took several days to identify them conclusively. Pathologists had to rely on dental records. In one case samples had to be obtained from a hairbrush used by one of the victims before going out to La Mon.

The day after the bombing, backing up their appeal for information about the bombers' movements, the police issued 10,000 posters showing one of the charred corpses. The horrifying image was widely published at home and abroad, underlining the strong condemnation levelled at the Provisional IRA, even among those normally sympathetic to their cause. It had a marked effect within the organization. In the six weeks prior to the attack there had been eighty similar incidents. In the ten weeks afterwards there were only twelve.

Meanwhile Newman's strategy of pursuing terrorists through the courts continued to produce ever more tangible results. More than 1,000 suspects were arrested, interrogated and then charged with a multiplicity of serious offences. Some of them were older crimes, going back to the earlier days of the civil disorder; an increasing number were connected with recent offences. The clearing of a double murder that became known as the 'teeth in the apple case' showed precisely how the various components in the strategy dovetailed to match the evidence to a suspect.

Shortly before midnight on 13 October 1976 William Corrigan, forty-one, turned into a laneway leading to his house at Annaghmore on the outskirts of Portadown. A gunman, lying in wait behind a wooden fence, fired a long burst of more than thirty shots from a high-velocity automatic rifle, killing him. Leslie his nineteen-year-old son, who was working at a car outside the house, was also wounded and died in hospital thirteen days later.

Detectives investigating the incident quickly concluded that as the Corrigans were Protestants it was probably a PIRA reprisal for the killing of Peter Woolsey, a forty-year-old Catholic farmer who lived a short distance away. He had been found· shot dead in his milking parlour two days earlier. The revenge killers may have singled William Corrigan out after a court case two months previously in which he was given a two-year suspended prison sentence for receiving 100 rounds of 9 mm ammunition stolen from the army.

Apart from that the detectives had little else to go on. The gun used in the double killing was a Russian-made AK-47 Kalashnikov rifle – a gun that was later auctioned among IRA sympathizers in the United States to raise funds. Ballistic tests on cartridges recovered from the firing point showed that the same gun had been used in other IRA murders. However, the real breakthrough in the investigation came from a most unlikely source, a partly eaten apple, which was found lying adjacent to the point where the gunman lay in ambush for his victims. When it reached the forensic scientists, one expert with an interest in dentistry and anthropology was able to assemble a likely description of the killer. From the bite marks he was able to calculate the height of the man, describe the shape of his face and mouth as well as his general physical characteristics and build.

When his report reached the detectives it was greeted with general disbelief, even scepticism. But ten months later, in August 1977, Thomas McGrath, a twenty-one-year-old man who had been arrested for questioning about other offences, was found to fit the scientific profile. Confronted with the forensic evidence under interrogation, he made a statement of admission and was charged with the two murders. Although he contested the admissibility of his confession when he came for trial, the judge ruled against him and in January 1979 he was sentenced to life imprisonment.

A more wide-ranging challenge to the police came during the winter of 1975 and 1976, when North and West Belfast were subjected to a reign of terror by a group of fanatical UVF killers who became known as 'The Shankill Butchers' because of the way they usually mutilated and slashed their victims. Their activities caused widespread fear among the Catholic community and the RUC crime squads made determined efforts to apprehend them. The police operation was known as 'Knife Edge'.

Cruising the city's unmarked sectarian boundaries late at night in a yellow Cortina car or sometimes in a London-type black taxi, the killers picked up innocent Catholic victims at random and subjected them to merciless beatings before shooting or bludgeoning them to death with guns, cleavers and axes. Finally one of them cut the victim's throat with a sharp knife or blade. They also used more conventional weapons like rifles and bombs during some of their crimes.

There was little premeditation and virtually no planning behind the murders. Fired up by a night's drinking, one of the gang would say: 'Let's get a Taig' (the slang word for Catholics). Belfast's rigid sectarian geography ensured that victims picked up on particular streets would almost certainly be Catholics but they once shot dead two Protestant workmen. Their brutality, which was unusually bestial even by the depraved standards of contemporary Northern Ireland, was not, however, confined to Catholics. Some of their worst excesses were in fact meted out to other members of their organization.

The first person to fall into their brutal clutches was Frank Crossan, a Catholic from the Lenadoon area of Belfast. On 25 November 1975 he was bundled into the gang's London-type black taxi and driven away. Next morning at 7.10 his body was found in an alleyway off the Shankill Road by a woman on her way to buy newspapers. It was an appalling sight. He had been badly beaten, there were two skull fractures and multiple cuts but most notably his throat had been cut through almost to the spinal cord with a butcher's knife.

One of the gang who participated in the Crossan killing was Archie Waller. Four days later, at 10 pm, he became a victim of the gang himself when he was shot four times and killed as he sat in his car outside the Loyalist drinking club at Downing Street in the Shankill area. Other gang members sentenced him to death only because they decided his face no longer fitted.

Ted McQuaid was the next casualty of their hate for Catholics. He was with his wife waiting for a taxi to take them home from a party in the Cliftonville Road area of Belfast at 2 am on 10 January 1976. A black taxi drove towards them, passed, did a U-turn, came back and stopped. A man bearing a gun jumped out and opened fire, seriously wounding McQuaid, a Catholic civil servant, who died later in hospital.

On 7 February they struck again. This time their victim was

Thomas Quinn, a middle-aged road-sweeper, wandering home after a night out drinking. His beaten body, again with the throat cut, was found at Forthriver Way after a caller to a local newspaper gave directions. The caller said that Quinn had been killed in retaliation for RUC Sergeant James Blakely, who had been shot a day earlier.

For a time some members of the gang had been tailing a lorry belonging to a timber company as it made a regular morning run collecting both Protestant and Catholic workers from West Belfast. They decided to strike on the morning of 9 February when it made its routine stop at a newsagent's shop in Cambrai Street. As the lorry pulled to a halt, three of the gang, armed with automatic rifles, opened up on the seven men on board, four Protestants and three Catholics. But the two men who died, Archie Hanna and Raymond Carlisle, were both Protestants. On 22 February the killers struck again. This time Francis Rice was abducted, beaten with a wheel brace and then dumped in an alley at Mayo Street, with his throat cut.

By now there was a full-scale police hunt for the gang, reflecting the widespread fear the reckless killings had engendered throughout the Catholic community. The police operation was being run from the divisional headquarters at Tennent Street by Chief Inspector Jimmy Nesbitt, one of the most experienced and painstaking of the RUC's detectives, with twenty-two years' service and forty-eight commendations for his crime-fighting activities. His patch, C Division, covered the tough Republican areas of Ardoyne and the Bone as well as the Loyalist heartland of the Shankill Road, where they had the impressive track record of having solved 101 of the 132 murders since 1974. But despite their detailed knowledge of the likely 'players' in the tightly knit web of hardline Loyalists, Nesbitt and his principal aides, Inspector Jack Fitzsimmons and Sergeant Cecil Chambers, could not get a firm lead on who the 'Butchers' were.

The breakthrough came from a fortunate contact. At 2.53 am on 11 March a gunman opened fire from a car on two Catholic women in another car driving through North Belfast. There was a military patrol nearby and, alerted by the shots, they gave chase to the gunman's car. Although they lost it, the police were satisfied that a car found burning a short time later was the one used in the attack. The next day, a lady in a street off the Shankill Road dialled 999 when she saw a man acting suspiciously. He was going from house to house shaking and pushing the hedges, she reported. The police patrol were quick off the mark and arrested him. In a follow-up search they discovered what he had been looking for, a gun concealed in the hedges.

The arrested man, Lennie Murphy, was well known to Nesbitt and his team as one of the toughest men in the UVF. (Although he was born in the Catholic Falls area, Murphy's Catholic mother died when he was young and he was brought up by his Protestant father.) From subsequent police work the RUC established that it was Murphy who had fired on the women in the car, and then abandoned and burned the stolen car after the soldiers gave chase. During his flight home on foot he had dumped the gun in the hedge and it was when he had come back the next morning to retrieve it that he was arrested. As a result he was charged with the attempted murder of the two women and remanded in custody to Crumlin Road prison in Belfast.

It was not the first time Murphy had been in prison. In September 1972 Ted Pavis, a Loyalist gun smuggler who had just been released from prison was shot dead at his home in east Belfast. Murphy and an accomplice, Mervyn Connor, were subsequently charged with murdering Pavis. While they were remanded in Crumlin Road awaiting trial, Connor agreed to turn Queen's Evidence and implicate Murphy. However, on 24 April 1973 Connor was found dead in his cell, together with a 'suicide' note clearing Murphy of any involvement in the Pavis murder. The post-mortem report showed that Connor had died from cyanide poisoning. 'The dose would have been sufficient to kill twenty horses,' according to one of the detectives involved. The police obtained information and then formal statements from two other prisoners that only twenty minutes before his death they had seen Murphy put an armlock on Connor and force him to write the 'suicide note'.

The two prisoners were quickly transferred to the Maze prison for their own protection until a further murder charge could be laid against Murphy with their evidence but within a few days they withdrew their statements after being viciously assaulted by fellow prisoners. 'Virtually every bone in their bodies was broken,' reported one detective. The following June, Murphy was acquitted of the Pavis murder and released when identification evidence by prosecution witnesses was disallowed.

Murphy was totally feared throughout the Loyalist community. On 30 November 1975 after he tied Noel Shaw (the man who killed Waller) to a chair, publicly pistol-whipped and then shot him dead before a crowd in a UVF drinking club in the Shankill, no one dared even talk about it. 'Let that be a lesson to you all,' he said. The body was thrown into a laundry basket and abandoned on the rear seat of a taxi in Nixon Street, Belfast, by some of his frightened associates.

Now back in the Crumlin Road again, Murphy once more tried to protect himself. Fearing that Nesbitt would correctly deduce he was the Shankill Butcher, because the cut-throat killings had stopped, he passed a message from the prison to other members of his UVF gang to carry on with identical murders. The men who received and accepted his orders were William 'Basher' Bates, a twenty-eight-year-old shipyard stager, and Billy Moore, a taxi-man aged twenty-nine. So even after Murphy, who denied the attempted murder charges, was given a twelve-year sentence for firearms offences, his evil influence continued over the men outside.

On 5 June 1976, in a reprisal for the bombing of a Protestant bar a couple of hours earlier, Bates was one of the five gunmen who burst into the Chlorane Bar in Gresham Street on the northern fringe of Belfast city centre. The sixteen people inside were held at gunpoint as the Catholics among them were singled out. The gunmen then opened fire, killing the bar owner and three of his customers. A fifth man who was seriously wounded died later in hospital.

The next victim, Cornelius Neeson, an inoffensive man who called the bingo numbers in his local social club, was overpowered by two of the gang just before midnight on 1 August at Manor Street. He was kicked all over and suffered repeated hatchet blows which killed him. His two assailants then escaped in the black taxi in which they had been touring in search of a victim.

Late on 29 October, Stephen McCann, a university student, and his girlfriend were walking along Millfield on the edge of Belfast city centre when they attracted the attention of the new Butcher. One gang member pinned the girl to the ground and as she screamed in terror, her boyfriend was stunned with a wheel brace, bundled into a car and driven off. His body, with a gunshot wound in the head and the throat cut, was found at the rear of a community centre in Glencairn soon after 3 am the next morning.

Shortly before Christmas 1976 there was further trouble within Loyalist ranks. One of the Butchers, 'Big Sam' McAllister, a foul-mouthed man who swaggered around the Loyalist drinking dens with a pistol stuck in his portly waistband, clashed with Thomas Easton, a member of the rival UDA who told him he was unwelcome in the Glencairn club. Easton's friends ejected McAllister, who hung around outside waiting for Easton to come out. When he did there was a further clash between them and a fight developed. McAllister beat Easton to death by repeatedly hitting him on the head with an empty metal beer keg and then dragged his body to a nearby church-yard.

Another UDA man, Jim 'The Nigger' Moorehead, so called because of his dark complexion, fell foul of the Butchers a month later, again for simply entering a pub where he was not welcome. Bates was drinking in the Windsor Bar on a Saturday night and watching a football game on the popular television programme 'Match of the Day', when Moorehead, who had a tough reputation for being able to handle himself, came in and went to the lavatory. Bates followed and hit him over the head with a large spanner. As he slumped to the ground others joined in the fatal beating.

Throughout that Saturday night and all day Sunday Moorehead's battered body lay where it fell on the floor. The gang were unable to move it because of heavy security forces' activity in the immediate area. As they waited for the coast to clear they stayed in the bar drinking, stepping over the corpse from time to time as they visited the lavatory. Eventually in the early hours of Monday 31 January it was taken to waste ground at Adela Street, where it was dumped between two lorries.

The Butchers claimed their next sectarian victim on 3 February 1977. Joseph Morrisey was unable to get a taxi after spending an evening drinking with friends in Belfast city centre so he decided to walk home. While he was making his way to Antrim Road he was assaulted with a hatchet and abducted. After beating and killing him, the gang dumped his body in a car park at Glencairn, where it was discovered three hours later. He was unrecognizable. His teeth had been torn out, his fingers were broken, probably as he tried to protect himself from repeated hatchet blows, and his face had been repeatedly smashed with the tool. Among the forty wounds were multiple slash marks caused by a sharp blade. His throat had also been cut so savagely that his head was almost severed from his body. The detectives called to the scene had never seen anything like it.

Almost two months later, on 30 March, Frank Cassidy suffered the same fate. His body, with the same grisly trademarks, was found dumped at Highfern Drive in North Belfast.

The Butchers changed tactics for their next operation, enlisting the expertise of Jim 'Tonto' Watt, a UVF bomb-maker. Another man, Edward Leckey, who played the guitar in a country and western style band which entertained in the Loyalist drinking clubs, was press-ganged into driving the bombers. About 3 am on the morning of 10 April, they concealed a gas cylinder containing 5 lb of explosive inside one of a line of barrels placed as a security cordon outside a bakery at Beechmount in the Lower Falls area. It was Easter Sunday and that afternoon Republican parades, commemorating the 1916 Easter Rising, were due to form up at that spot for a march to Milltown Cemetery.

The bomb exploded without warning at 2.47 pm, killing ten-year-old Kevin McMenamin and injuring five other people, one of whom lost a leg. The incident provoked trouble between rival Republican factions and there were exchanges of gunfire at the cemetery. Later in the evening, John Shortt, the uncle of the dead boy, was shot dead by the Provos.

Nesbitt and his fifteen-strong overworked team of detectives had by now been reinforced by men from the Belfast Regional Crime Squad and 'The Ants' undercover surveillance team in a determined attempt to find the Butchers. Discreet enquiries had been made at butchers' shops and in the meat-processing trade to see if they could trace someone with hardline Loyalist views as a likely suspect. Checks were made on the owners and drivers of the black taxis, who operated the alternative bus service in the Protestant areas of North and West Belfast, but without turning up any significant clue. Known UVF members were regularly arrested for questioning and some were even put under surveillance but again the operations drew a blank. Ironically some of those involved were indeed members of the Butchers gang.

The fence of fear that Murphy, beginning his twelve-year sentence for possessing firearms, and his cruel associates had erected around their activities was so high that Nesbitt's network of informers in the Loyalist community could not even come up with any hard tips about who the police should be looking for. For a time they tried to lure the gang into a trap. Detectives, often posing as drunks, and closely watched by colleagues in vehicles nearby, went on to the streets where the Butchers usually picked up their victims, but without contact.

Early on 11 May a woman who could not sleep was out walking when she heard moans from a young man lying at the foot of a lamp post at Carnan Street in the Shankill area. He had been badly beaten and suffered slash wounds and there was a trail of blood where he had crawled from a nearby alley into the street. As he was rushed to hospital Nesbitt was told that what was almost certainly another Butcher victim had turned up – this time alive, although critically ill in a hospital intensive care unit.

The victim was identified as Gerard McLaverty, a twenty-four-year-old Catholic, and for five days detectives, with their fingers crossed that he would survive, waited anxiously by his bedside before he regained consciousness and was well enough to talk to them. Still in pain from his multiple injuries, he recounted how men had got out of a parked yellow Cortina car on the Cliftonville Road as he was walking home from a disco. They said they were detectives and asked him for identification. He produced his diary with his name and address in it, sufficient to reveal his religion. Satisfied that they had intercepted a Catholic, one of the gang produced a gun and ordered McLaverty into the car. They said they were taking him to Tennent Street police station to check him out.

Instead they headed for a disused doctor's surgery at Emerson Street in the Shankill area, which had been the UVF headquarters during the recent Paisley-led constitutional stoppage. Once inside, the four abductors produced long sticks, one with a nail embedded at the end, and took it in turn to beat their victim. While they were beating him about the head, Moore was boiling a kettle to make tea. 'I was squealing with fear and pain,' McLaverty told the detectives. When the tea was ready, the beating temporarily stopped. McLaverty declined the offer of a cup because, he told the police, he feared they might poison him.

After the tea-break, the beating resumed. When McLaverty fell to the floor they propped him up again in the chair. Two of the abductors became bored with the situation after a few hours and left him in the hands of Moore and McAllister. They untied one of his bootlaces and half-strangled him. He was bundled into a car and taken some distance away. There they tried again to strangle him with his own bootlaces but before he slipped into an unconscious state he remembered the big fat man producing a knife with a six-inch blade and slashing his wrists and forearms.

When McLaverty had finished his horrifying story Nesbitt knew that at last he had the first firm information that could lead to the capture of the notorious Butchers. From his own thorough knowledge of the Shankill hard-men, he already had a good idea of the men McLaverty had been talking about but if he was to put them behind bars he needed positive identifications.

On 19 May, only eight days after his terrifying ordeal when he had been left for dead, a very fearful McLaverty, thinly disguised under a detective's cap, found himself being driven up and down the Shankill Road in a police car to see if he could spot any of his attackers. It was the day of the local government elections and more people than usual would be on the streets but Nesbitt was backing a longer bet. If the culprits were the men he thought they were, they would be standing around outside one or other of the seedy pubs and drinking clubs they frequented.

Nesbitt's hunch succeeded beyond his wildest dreams. Standing in a group of men outside the Berlin Arms, a notorious haunt of UVF men, he picked out 'the big fat man', Sam McAllister. The unmarked police car did a U-turn at the city end of Shankill Road and during this second pass along the road McLaverty pointed out Ben 'Pretty Boy' Edwards. At the end of this unusual identity parade Nesbitt decided to arrest the two men at 6 am next morning. McLaverty's description of the yellow Cortina used in the abduction and the involvement of McAllister convinced Nesbitt that Moore might also be involved, so he ordered his arrest as well.

In the event Edwards was not at home but Moore and McAllister were taken to Castlereagh, where they were deliberately kept apart. At first they brazened out their innocence but over the next three days, as relays of detectives interrogated them, they slowly broke down and the whole grim story began to emerge. Finally, in tears, they made full confessions. 'My head is away with it. Do you think I'm wise?' asked Moore when he had unburdened himself.

The other members of the gang were rounded up and their instruments of death recovered, including two knives and a sharpening steel from under the floorboards in McAllister's house. A cleaver used in the killings was found at the home of William Townsley, who was only fifteen when he participated in the murder of Stephen McCann. Their seventeen-month reign of terror which claimed nineteen lives was over.

On 20 February 1979 at the Crumlin Road courthouse in Belfast, as the eleven men stood silently in the dock, Mr Justice O'Donnell passed forty-two life sentences and terms of imprisonment totalling 2,000 years on the eleven killers before him. The judge ordered that

Moore, guilty of eleven murders, and Bates, guilty of ten, should spend the rest of their natural lives in jail as medical reports available to him showed they suffered from 'no mental disease or illness'. 'I have resisted the temptation to cast myself in the role of public avenger,' said the judge. 'I have dealt with these men dispassionately. The facts speak for themselves and will remain for ever a memorial to blind sectarian bigotry.'

But Lennie Murphy, the man now known to detectives as the Master Butcher, was not in the dock. He was still serving his twelve-year sentence for possessing a gun with intent to endanger life. Throughout the trial there were frequent references to him, although he was only referred to as Mr X. Try as they may, the police could not overcome the fear the gang members had of testifying against Murphy.

Murphy was eventually released from prison in August 1981, having earned full remission. Within days Brian Smyth, a UVF member from Bangor, was found shot dead at Crimea Street in the Shankill area. The killing had all the hallmarks of a Murphy operation. On October 24 Murphy was arrested and questioned by the police after the body of a middle-aged Catholic, Joseph Donegan, who was abducted from outside a drinking club in the Falls area, was found beaten to death adjacent to a house owned by Murphy at Battenburg Street. Inside the house police found traces of the victim's blood and his false teeth.

Barely three weeks later, on 16 November, three gunmen firing from the back of a van ambushed and killed Murphy as he arrived by car to visit a girlfriend at Forthriver Park. Next day the Provisional IRA claimed the killing and produced sufficient inside details of the incident to persuade the police that they were indeed responsible. However, by the end of 1988 nobody had been charged with the murder.

The Provisionals, who are most comfortable portraying themselves as defenders of the Catholic community, had very good reason to kill Murphy. But in a macabre twist to the last episode of this grisly tale, several RUC detectives, with good sources in both communities, have obtained credible information that Murphy was actually betrayed by people in his own community who passed information about his plans across the sectarian divide to his eventual killers.

A few days later masked UVF men fired shots as Murphy's coffin, led by a piper playing 'Abide with Me', was being taken from his home for burial. Among the wreaths at the graveside was one from Moore, Bates, McAllister and McClay which said that they deeply regretted the death of their good friend Lennie.

# 6

# 'Wall-to-Wall Interrogation'

Throughout his first two years as chief, Newman was able to point to the growing effectiveness of his reformed Criminal Investigation Department in getting to grips with the terrorists. In 1976 the Headquarters and Regional Crime Squads, backing up the detectives in the divisions, had charged 708 suspected terrorists during the year, an increase of 121 per cent over the 1975 figure. Murder and attempted murder charges were up 7 per cent, explosives charges by 115 per cent and those for a miscellaneous catalogue of other terrorist-type offences by 187 per cent. Many of the crimes being cleared up dated back to the early days of the troubles. There was an even better trend in 1977.

The use of the corrugated-iron-walled compound inside the army's Palace Barracks, Holywood, a few miles away, had ended with internment. The system was now firmly to be seen as one of the police dealing with criminals through the courts. Processing them through a heavily fortified army barracks presented altogether the wrong impression. The powerhouse for the police operation consequently became a group of prefabricated huts at the back of the Belfast regional headquarters in Ladas Drive, Castlereagh, formerly occupied by the army. It eventually expanded to a complex of thirty-eight cells and twenty-one interview rooms. Later, on 1 November 1977, another holding centre was opened at Gough Barracks in Armagh where there were twenty-four cells and nine interview rooms. The cells were sparsely furnished, windowless rooms, with just a chair and a bed. The interview rooms were equally austere, with a table or desk and three or four chairs in each. The only accessory was an ashtray.

The amendment of the emergency laws to allow the courts to convict on a statement of admission, provided there had been no torture, or inhuman or degrading treatment, enabled the police to place a suspect under heavy pressure during interrogation. Suspects could be detained either for up to three days under the Emergency Provisions Act or seven days under the Prevention of Terrorism Act, although the latter required written authorization from the Northern Ireland Secretary of State. During these periods the suspects were held incommunicado and denied access to visitors or solicitors. The only concession they could demand was a medical examination by an independent doctor.

Solicitors said that in about nine out of ten cases the subsequent charges relied only on statements of admission made by the accused persons while under questioning. There was little, or more often nothing, in the way of independent corroborative evidence. Newman, who took personal charge of the police operation and outlined his objectives in force orders and at a number of gatherings where he addressed the detectives, felt that they were at last beginning to make an impact on the terrorist situation but, as he secretly feared, the IRA soon found a way of denting it.

Before long serious rumbles of disquiet began to circulate among sections of the legal and medical professions, who feared that the police were ill-treating or even torturing prisoners to force them to make self-incriminating statements. Several doctors reported cases of prisoners apparently being injured during their time in police custody. They cynically described the police tactics as 'wall-to-wall interrogation'. Of the 1,797 suspects interviewed in 1975, official complaints against the police were made by 184. In 1976, out of 3,042 people interviewed, 322 made a complaint afterwards. In particular, complaints specifically alleging assault during interview jumped from 180 in 1975 to 384 in 1976.

There was little public comment about the situation, except in the Republican press, until early 1977. Then the broadcaster Keith Kyle, who was researching a programme on political affairs in County Fermanagh, was approached by an SDLP councillor about the case of Bernard O'Connor, who alleged ill-treatment while being questioned at Castlereagh. Kyle followed up the allegations and his lengthy assessment of the Castlereagh situation, broadcast on BBC television's 'Tonight' programme on 2 March 1977, catapulted the issue into national prominence.

O'Connor, aged thirty-four, a father of seven, who was a school teacher and part-time driving instructor, told how he had been arrested about 5.30 am on 20 January and taken by car to Castle-reagh for questioning about his alleged involvement in terrorist activities. Over the next five days, until his release, without any charges being preferred, on the evening of 24 January, he claimed he had been subjected to brutal interrogation methods. During the first three- or four-hour interview he claimed he was made to stand on his toes with his knees bent and arms outstretched. Every time he moved from that position or refused to answer questions he said he was slapped in the face.

In subsequent interviews, which he estimated to have lasted until the early hours of the morning, he said he had been punched, knocked about the room, made to run the gauntlet of officers trying to trip him, hooded and smothered to the point where he fainted. In other interviews he told of being ordered to run on the spot for fifteen minutes, strip naked, pick a cigarette butt off the floor with his mouth and lick drops of water from a spilled glass. He said there were threats that he would be killed by the police or even the UVF. 'I got myself into a frame of mind where I was resigned to the fact that I might be killed,' he said.

Michael Lavelle, who was also questioned, told a similar story. He said one policeman had pulled a gun and clicked it around at the back of his head. 'Quite honestly, I was terrified.'

The BBC was widely attacked for broadcasting the allegations. Roy Mason said the programme was 'one-sided' and that the police were fully justified in questioning the two men on the information available to them. The RUC said it could not comment until the official complaints made by the two men were fully investigated.

But the depth of growing, responsible concern about what was going on in Castlereagh was reflected in a *Belfast Telegraph* editorial the day after the programme. 'This was not an unbalanced hatchet job on the RUC,' the paper said. 'The techniques described by the Enniskillen teacher were frankly shocking. Gross physical brutality and mental cruelty of this kind could never be justified. If there is a shred of truth in the claims, they degrade everyone living in Northern Ireland – police and citizens alike.'

'Of course prisoners are put under pressure during interviews,' said one senior detective. 'They are not going to confess to serious crimes during a cosy chat over a cup of tea. But they are emphatically not being beaten into making confessions.'

By the end of 1977 official complaints against the RUC had swollen to more than 2,000. Those alleging assault during interview had risen from 384 to 671. SDLP politician, Joe Hendron, who as a doctor had direct knowledge of several cases, said by his estimate about one in three prisoners were being ill-treated. The most common symptoms he encountered were tenderness due to thumps or punches; wrist bending; slaps to the face and head; and hair pulling. Few of the prisoners had marks. Despite this persuasive evidence he said: 'I didn't want to have policemen shot dead and on my conscience or to give the Provos propaganda, so I did not go public.' Instead he made strenuous protests to both RUC headquarters and Stormont Castle. 'The majority of the police were doing a good job under difficult and dangerous circumstances. What was going on in Castlereagh was actually undermining them.'

The volume of concern from similarly responsible sources, politicians, doctors, solicitors and churchmen, increased steadily. Jack Hermon, one of the two deputy chief constables, who had been making strong efforts to build bridges between the RUC and the same sections of the community, gave several people the direct line numbers to his desk and his home with an invitation to phone at any time if they had cause for urgent concern. He took the view that greater supervision was the answer to the problem and there was some tightening up in the monitoring system, partly to isolate any detectives who were involved in ill-treatment and partly to prevent a growing trend of prisoners injuring themselves.

This led to the introduction of more safeguards for prisoners in custody in Northern Ireland than anywhere else in the United Kingdom. A detailed, timed account was kept of the prisoner's movements from cell to interview room and back. Every medical examination, visit to the toilet, meal provided, the amount eaten, even a request for a glass of water, was carefully noted. The names of officers handling him or her at any given time were recorded.

The object was to protect the police as much as the prisoner for there was a developing trend of prisoners inflicting injuries on themselves to discredit both the police and any confession they might make. One man was found trying to cut his wrists with the broken glass from his spectacles; another was discovered butting his head on the floor; there was a case of a prisoner beating himself with his boots; another banged the metal foot of the bed up and down on his feet to bruise them.

Each case led to a modification of the custody rules or the physical features of the accommodation. After the bed incident the legs were chained to the floor to prevent them being lifted. Any object that could be used to inflict self-injury was taken away. Crockery plates and metal utensils were replaced by paper and plastic. After a prisoner hanged himself in a cell, the bed sheets were changed to paper and the cell ventilators were redesigned to prevent anything being passed through them.

A new fleet of cellular prison vans had to be introduced when there were cases of prisoners assaulting and marking each other in transit between prisons and courts. (There was contributory efficiency from this decision, for in open-plan vehicles Loyalists and Republicans could rarely be transported together without coming to blows.)

When a man jumped from the window of an upstairs room in Springfield Road station there was a hue and cry. Allegations were made that detectives had thrown him out. However, they subsided when it became clear the prisoner had landed on the roof of a car owned by one of the detectives. 'I was hardly likely to throw him on top of my own car,' he protested.

Although the RUC felt inhibited in responding to specific complaints within the virtual propaganda whirlwind that engulfed it, Newman did hit back in general terms in a lengthy public statement on 24 June. He said that the volume and nature of the allegations should be interpreted not as a worrying indication of police misconduct but as a barometer of growing police success. 'It is the objective of all terrorist organizations to discredit and destroy the police and in Northern Ireland that objective is pursued ruthlessly. Aside from this basic purpose the fabrication of malicious complaints provides terrorists with a number of benefits.'

Newman said that by pleading brutality, an arrested terrorist could hope to nullify his confession in court. The legal onus was on the police to prove beyond reasonable doubt that such brutality did not occur. In relation to what he described as the 'kangaroo inquisitions' conducted by terrorist masters, Newman said that the accused terrorist could protect himself by pleading torture. It was a valid point. UDA members, for instance, were warned not to talk during police questioning. According to a captured training document: 'If arrested during or after an operation make no statement no matter if someone else does. The organization will not accept any reason even should you only involve yourself, 48% planning + 1% operating + 1% escape and evasion + 50% silence = 100% success.'

Finally, Newman pinned his own reputation on the integrity of the RUC. 'No police force in the world is infallible. In any organization human frailty may lead an individual to fall short of the high standards laid down. In the RUC I have personally set about creating a system which as far as humanly possible is designed to prevent any potential police abuse of persons in custody – or any other misconduct – and to detect it if it occurs. The police officer who ill-treats any members of the public will receive no mercy from me, nor will he deserve it.'

As a measure of his serious intent, Newman disclosed that there were now more officers engaged in the investigation of complaints and disciplinary offences than there were in any other operational team.

The detectives at Castlereagh, where the bulk of the complaints arose, and who were the subject of them, joked with each other that they were not doing their job properly unless they had received a 17/2 – the official form notifying them of an allegation. One enterprising detective had a tie made with the figures discreetly embossed as XVII/II, but senior officers banned it. The propagandists had enough to go on without the RUC handing them a bonus.

It was in the courtrooms at Crumlin Road in Belfast that the real propaganda battle was fought, however. Every trial involved what became known as the 'statement fight' – a trial within a trial of the admissibility of the accused's statement or statements. Some of the contests lasted for weeks and involved every officer who had been in contact with the prisoner going into the witness box to be quizzed by barristers in exhaustive, sometimes hostile, detail about the period the prisoner had spent in custody. Senior and junior detectives alike were confronted in open court with allegations that they had ill-treated the prisoner during interview. The proceedings were far from a formality and the police did not have it all their own way from the judiciary, as a typical case heard in May and June 1977 illustrates.

Francis Bannon, a nineteen-year-old student, and Colm Caughey, eighteen, were jointly accused of the murder of nineteen-year-old John Mario Kelly, who was gunned down on 9 November 1975, the sixth victim of a feud between rival factions of the IRA. Bannon pleaded not guilty to the charges, which included possessing guns and ammunition with intent to endanger life. Caughey refused to recognize the court.

Crown counsel said that they would prove that Bannon and

Caughey were the two masked gunmen who had walked up behind Kelly in Ponsonby Avenue, gunned him down and then fired into his head again as he lay on the ground. The case relied principally on statements of admission made by the two youths after their arrest but the police also claimed they could link hairs found on a stocking mask with Caughey and that Bannon had lead traces on his hands when his grey mini-van was stopped shortly after the murder.

Bannon told the court that he had been punched, slapped and spreadeagled against a wall by the police who interviewed him. His head had been pushed against the wall and several times he wet himself. Two doctors testified that they had found bruises on Bannon and one said that the blows could have caused him to wet himself, although he did say an infection could also have been responsible. Caughey told a similar tale.

Lord Justice Jones decided on the medical evidence that he would not allow the two statements admitting the murder, although he stressed that in doing so he exonerated the police from any suggestion of torture or inhuman conduct. Five days later, on 22 June, Bannon was released from custody when the Crown dropped nine other charges of possessing guns and explosives and IRA membership. Caughey was later given a fourteen-year sentence for other offences, including IRA membership.

There was fresh public controversy in October when the Thames Television programme 'TV Eye' produced ten cases of what it called 'inhuman and degrading treatment'. For the first time Protestant organizations began to join in. The UDA said it had a 'thick file' of statements from its members.

For the RUC there were more ominous signs of discontent. In November about thirty solicitors held a meeting to discuss withdrawal from the Diplock courts to underline their concern about police conduct. In the event they set up a three-man steering group to collect cases of apparent police brutality and a stiff note of protest was despatched to the Secretary of State.

Before the end of the year the chorus of concern had been publicly joined by the leaders of the four main churches and there were reports that the Association of Police Surgeons had held an extraordinary meeting to discuss their worries. One of the doctors was now so anxious about the situation that he began to make spot checks on the way detectives behaved. Other doctors had approached the Northern Ireland Police Authority with their concerns. It had a statutory responsibility to oversee the conduct of the force and ensure complaints were properly dealt with. Although this led to the establishment of a joint working party with the police to monitor the situation, several members of the authority believed they were being given a comprehensive run-around by the chief constable. For months the authority tried to settle the worries in private, with the threat of resignations by sceptical authority members always present.

Between 28 November and 6 December an Amnesty International investigative team visited Northern Ireland to assess the widening allegations. It consisted of a senior Amnesty official, a Dutch lawyer and two Danish doctors. They met a series of interested parties, including the chief constable, interviewed fifty-two persons who claimed ill-treatment and visited Castlereagh to see conditions for themselves.

Sorting out the facts from the propaganda at this time was immensely difficult. One case where I was able to interview a suspect and detectives working in Castlereagh demonstrates the problem. The prisoner concerned was a Protestant labourer from North Belfast who was arrested in October for questioning about an attempted murder. After being taken from his home on a Monday morning at 5 am he was conveyed to Castlereagh where questioning about the incident began. Before he was released from custody at 11 pm on the following Wednesday, he was examined by both the police doctor and an independent doctor.

When I interviewed him, eighteen hours after his release, the suspect was clearly distressed and nearly hysterical despite being given tranquillizers by the doctor. 'I am ready to commit suicide rather than go back in there,' he said. He claimed that detectives forced him to do press-ups and lean on tiptoe and fingertips against a wall to the point of exhaustion. One 'hefty' detective, he said, had put his fingertips in the hollows behind his ears and lifted him off the ground. He had been interrogated five times on Monday and four times on Tuesday. He was only released, he claimed, because the doctor had ordered it after a detective had tried to suffocate him during an interview on Wednesday. Things had got so bad that another partner detective had actually gone for the doctor to save him.

The independent medical report stated:

On examination tender area left occiput [side of head], no marks ...

very tender both mastoids [behind ears], no marks. Difficulty removing shirt and unable to remove vest because of painful arms, other arms muscles tender, no marks. Very tender in the umbilical area and abdominal muscles sore.

He said he very rarely had a stammer but had marked stammer during examination ... he said he was hurt enough and not able to take any more. He is extremely nervous and afraid and says in a hysterical fashion: 'I can't take much more of this.'

Mr ... is slow at reading and arithmetic, and is in a very marked anxiety state and, although little marked, he was physically and psychologically abused as he described. He needs urgent psychiatric opinion.

Later, during conversation with detectives, the suffocation case was raised. Unaware that I had already heard the suspect's account of events, they said that an accomplice in the attempted murder had made a statement on Tuesday confessing his own role and implicating his partner in the crime.

Next morning, Wednesday, when the suspect was confronted with this statement, he broke down and suffered a fit, shaking and trembling. The detectives were afraid the prisoner might mark or even injure himself falling from the chair or striking the table in front of him. So one grabbed him to steady him while the other detective left the room to alert the doctor. In the interval the detective had great difficulty restraining the suspect and was forced to adopt a tight 'bear-hug' hold on him to keep him in the chair.

When the doctor arrived the prisoner was removed to the medical room, sedated and then declared unfit for interview. He was released, without charge, after the independent medical examination. The detectives, who said the prisoner had not been ill-treated or assaulted, were of the opinion that he reacted the way he did out of panic at his plight. He knew that once his accomplice had confessed he faced a lengthy term of imprisonment.

Police intelligence on the man indicated involvement with the UVF in other serious crimes and it was a matter of concern to the detectives that he would now escape justice. When I disclosed that I had interviewed the same man, they said the medical report indicated the serious mental disturbance of the suspect.

They said that recently one of their colleagues had refused to interview a suspect for the murder of an RUC man who was a close friend. The detective feared that if he had admitted the murder he might have thumped him, which would have allowed him to beat the charge. So he declared his interest and was kept off the case.

'I couldn't put my hand on my heart and say I've never thumped a prisoner,' one of the detectives admitted. 'God, we're only flesh and blood ourselves but you have to control yourself, learn to take it in your stride, whatever the provocation. Otherwise the prisoner gets off the hook. Then it's a professional and personal failure.'

The completed Amnesty report was sent to the government on 2 May. It accused the RUC of ill-treating prisoners with sufficient frequency to justify a public impartial inquiry taking place. Amnesty exonerated the uniformed officers of the RUC and concluded that legal provisions under the emergency legislation had eroded the rights of terrorist suspects and helped create circumstances in which maltreatment had taken place.

Mason wrote asking for Amnesty to give the authorities details of the seventy-eight cases they had examined so that they could take criminal proceedings, if appropriate, but the organization refused. Its policy, it stated, was not to seek such prosecutions. Mason also asked for Amnesty to delay publication of the report but the organization refused and it was issued on 13 June. Five days earlier, in the course of a parliamentary statement pre-empting the publication of the report, Mason announced that he would establish a formal enquiry.

For his part, Newman said that the Amnesty conclusions were premature and would not be justified, if at all, until they had been subjected to more comprehensive investigation. 'Rather than continue the cycle of charge and counter-charge,' he said in a statement, 'I have asked the Secretary of State to set up an independent committee of enquiry to review the present practices and procedures in relation to the interrogation of suspected terrorists.'

Newman was concerned to allay public concern about the effectiveness of the systems of police accountability. More immediately, he was worried about the morale of the force in general and the detectives in particular. He considered they were under intolerable strain from frequent internal investigation, constant hostile cross-examination in court and terrorist attacks – both on and off duty – not to mention the long hours they worked.

Judge Harry Bennett, QC, was appointed to head the enquiry and with him the Northern Ireland Office appointed John Marshall, Professor of Clinical Neurology at the University of London, and Sir James Haughton, the former chief constable of Liverpool who had recently retired as the Chief Inspector of Constabulary, attached to the Home Office.

Senior officers from the Special Branch and CID were perturbed after giving evidence to the team, which worked in private. They reported their fears to Newman, who sent them back to the enquiry to underline the RUC analysis. If the force was unreasonably hand-cuffed, they warned, its operations against terrorists which had achieved a marked reduction in the level of violence could be neutralized or rendered ineffective.

'You are dealing with some of the most violent and hardened terrorists in Europe, many of whom have had anti-interrogation training,' one officer told the enquiry. 'They have taken life without compunction and committed other bestial crimes. They are not going to admit that and face the rest of their lifetime in prison by being given tea and buns.'

But even before the Bennett report was published, the RUC's image took another serious battering when Dr Robert Irwin, interviewed on the London Weekend Television programme, 'Weekend World', on 11 March, said that he had examined more than 150 prisoners who had been ill-treated at Castlereagh during the previous three years. He dismissed the chief constable's claim that the injuries sustained by the prisoners had in the main been self-inflicted. The doctor said that joint injuries and ruptured ear-drums, which were among the cases he had seen, could not possibly have been self-inflicted. Dr Irwin alleged that some twenty detectives were responsible for the ill-treat-ment.

A few days later the Bennett report itself was published and concluded that a small number of RUC men had resorted to brutality in order to obtain confessions from terrorist suspects. Altogether the report contained sixty-four conclusions and recommendations, the most significant of which suggested that there should be a code of conduct for interrogating officers; uniformed and more senior officers should spend more time supervising interrogations; closed circuit television should be installed to monitor interviews; suspects should have access to a lawyer after forty-eight hours in custody and they should be able to have a medical examination after each individual interview with detectives.

The controversial, hard-hitting report was, however, overshadowed by what was described in the House of Commons as 'a vicious smear' by Gerry Fitt, the West Belfast MP. He was referring to news reports that Dr Irwin was anti-police because they had failed to bring to justice a soldier who had raped his wife three years earlier. In what was clearly a painful ordeal for them, the Irwins moved quickly to get the facts straight. Mrs Elizabeth Irwin had indeed been raped, they confirmed. The armed, masked culprit was an undercover soldier, traced by the police to the army base at the Grand Central Hotel in Belfast, who was quietly transferred to Germany for lack of conclusive evidence to mount a prosecution. The Irwins actually praised the RUC for their handling of the case.

Dr Denis Elliott, a former doctor in the prison service, caused further concern when he announced on 22 March that he was resigning as a police doctor in support of Dr Irwin. Dr Elliott had been in charge of the medical supervision of prisoners at Gough Barracks in Armagh since it opened. There he had taken a tough line with the detectives, often insisting that interviews be terminated just because voices were raised. He had even pre-empted one of the Bennett recommendations by forcing the police to put spy-holes in the interview room doors so that supervisory officers could oversee interrogations without interrupting them. His concern for the prisoners, which included having late-night coffee and biscuits introduced, had helped Gough avoid the same stigma as Castlereagh among the increasingly vociferous Catholic critics of the RUC's criminal investigation methods.

By July, about four months after the Bennett criticisms, the chief constable was able to report that the thirty-five recommendations he made were in hand. Perhaps the most revolutionary was the spending of more than £100,000 installing closed circuit television cameras, two in each interview room, at Castlereagh as well as at Gough and RUC Strand Road in Londonderry, which was also being used as a holding centre to interview suspects. At Castlereagh the uniformed supervisory officer had forty-two twelve-inch screens to monitor, and some senior officers in the nearby Belfast regional headquarters could also tune in and check what was going on in each of the twenty-one interview rooms.

But senior detectives, who accepted the new regime with resignation, said that hardened terrorists could not be induced to confess by office hours interrogation and they predicted, quite correctly, that the conviction rate of some 90 per cent could not be sustained. The whole affair was a victory for the IRA, they said.

In Northern Ireland's highly charged atmosphere, the legacy of the

Castlereagh controversy hung over the force like a cloud for several years more. In April 1980 there was a fresh storm of controversy when self-confessed IRA activist, thirty-nine-year-old Edward Brophy, was acquitted on forty-eight of forty-nine charges, including the La Mon restaurant massacre, because Mr Justice Kelly, trying him at Belfast Crown Court, refused to admit statements made during questioning at Castlereagh in September 1978. Brophy was, however, sentenced to five years for IRA membership, on the basis of an admission during the 'trial within a trial' on the validity of the statements. The Northern Ireland Court of Appeal quashed the conviction on the grounds that the admission could not be used in the full trial but the Crown appealed the conviction to the House of Lords. In June 1981, five Law Lords ruled unanimously that the conviction should be quashed and Brophy was released, having served one year of the sentence.

Bernard O'Connor, the man whose television interview triggered the storm of controversy, sued the chief constable, Sir Kenneth Newman, for damages after his interrogation in Castlereagh. The case was heard in May 1980 but Mr Justice Murray reserved judgement until July when he announced that he had awarded O'Connor £5,000 exemplary damages for ill-treatment.

During the trial O'Connor, said the judge, had been 'evasive and devious' when asked about about a public remark during a civil rights rally that 'the only good policeman is a dead one'. The judge also dismissed his claim that he had suffered 'organic brain damage'. But Mr Justice Murray said that it was unsatisfactory that a friend of a murdered policeman should have been among the detectives who questioned O'Connor about the murder, and he concluded that O'Connor had been ill-treated by two of the detectives who dealt with him during the twenty interviews conducted throughout the five-day interrogation.

Bennett identified fifteen cases where the injuries sustained by suspects had been 'inflicted by someone other than the prisoner himself'. Investigation of them dragged on until November 1981. One complaint was withdrawn and in the other fourteen cases the Director of Public Prosecutions decided that there were no grounds for prosecution, the deputy chief constable decided that there were no disciplinary offences to be accounted for and the Police Complaints Board ratified the decisions in all cases. That left perhaps the most notorious of all the cases to be finally wound up – the Rafferty case.

Encapsulating every complex ingredient of the Castlereagh wrangling, this neatly illustrated the difficulties in making an accurately objective judgement on the controversy or, as one senior RUC man put it, 'sorting out the molehills of facts from the mountains of fabrication'.

James Rafferty, from Cappagh, County Tyrone, was arrested on 11 November 1976 and taken to Omagh police station where he was questioned over the next three days about his alleged involvement in serious IRA crimes. But on the third day, when two doctors examined him, they ordered him to be taken by police car to the local hospital where he was detained for several days and treated for minor injuries which the hospital doctor reported he could not have inflicted on himself.

After his release, Rafferty's case was taken up by Jack Hassard, a member of the Police Authority. He became steadily disenchanted at what he regarded as RUC stalling on tackling the complaint and he pressed unsuccessfully for the Authority to use its power to set up a tribunal to investigate the conduct of Rafferty's interrogation. Hassard resigned from the Authority in July 1978, followed soon afterwards by the Catholic solicitor, Donal Murphy, who shared his frustration at the lack of action over police abuses. He accused the chief constable of preventing Authority members from gaining access to the details of complaints to which they were entitled.

In October 1978 the next protracted stage of the case began, when the Authority ordered the chief constable to refer Rafferty's case to a public tribunal set up under Section 13 of the 1970 Police Act, its first use of the provision. The Lord Chief Justice appointed Peter Gibson, QC, to head the tribunal and with him the chief constable nominated as assessors James Brownlow, the chief constable of South Yorkshire, and Alan Petrie, an assistant chief constable with the Strathclyde police force. The tribunal did not meet until 9 April 1979 and then adjourned indefinitely because a key witness, who had been convicted of possessing explosives and jailed for twenty years, had successfully applied for a re-trial. In the meantime, in June, twelve RUC officers involved in the case failed to persuade the High Court to wind up the tribunal because, they argued, evidence given there might incriminate them and prejudice any future criminal proceedings.

The tribunal did not reconvene again until December 1980 when it ran into more trouble. First the barrister representing the RUC walked out with the officers concerned when Rafferty's counsel advised him not to answer questions about whether he had been a unit commander in the Provisional IRA involved in a number of murders and explosions. Then Gibson ordered twenty-nine subpoenas to be issued, compelling the RUC officers to give evidence, but they were set aside by the High Court a few days later. Lord Justice Gibson (no relation to the tribunal chairman) ruled that the tribunal had no power to force the police or any witnesses to testify.

However, after the tribunal report was submitted to the chief constable and considered by the DPP in January 1981, four RUC officers, Detective Chief Inspector Harold Colgan and Detective Constables Michael O'Neill, Kenneth Hassan and Robert McAdorey, were charged with assaulting Rafferty during questioning. But before the detectives came to trial Rafferty was involved in more controversy. Two independent witnesses implicated him in the murder by landmine of Constables Mark Evans and John Montgomery, who were killed near Cappagh on 7 September.

Rafferty was arrested and on 30 September murder charges were laid against him and another man. During subsequent proceedings after Rafferty applied for bail, his lawyer stated that the charges had been trumped up to keep him in custody during the trial of the four detectives. The murder charges were eventually withdrawn on 6 November, shortly before the assault trial began, when a lawyer for the DPP said that the two witnesses who had implicated Rafferty in the murders had withdrawn their statements after threats from persons they would not identify.

After a four-day hearing later in November, Lord Lowry, the Lord Chief Justice, halted the proceedings and ruled that the four detectives had no case to answer. As a mark of his opinion he took the unprecedented step of ordering the Crown to meet the £23,000 costs of the defence. Rafferty, said the Lord Chief Justice, was an entirely unsatisfactory witness offering one unsatisfactory explanation after another. 'The manner in which the evidence was given condemns the giver of that evidence as unworthy of belief.' He commented that it was a pity the four detectives should have been submitted to the ordeal of a trial but it was perhaps the only way in which the affair could be brought to light.

Rafferty was still not finished. In June 1982 his civil action for damages against the RUC came to trial and lasted eight days. In a reserved judgement on 29 June, Mr Justice Kelly said it was not a 'black and white case'. However, he ruled that as Rafferty had not proved his case beyond the balance of probabilities there could be no award for damages. Listing seven instances where Rafferty's evidence had differed markedly from earlier accounts, the judge said he was left with serious doubts as to his credibility and reliability. By contrast, he noted, the police witnesses had given their evidence firmly and confidently and they gave no indication that they were lying.

A postscript to the controversy came about when a Belfastman, apprehended in Liverpool, boasted to Merseyside police how he had scarred himself with the bristles of a lavatory brush by asking repeatedly to visit the toilet while in police custody. The detectives wrote down his boasts, contacted the RUC, and in due course he was returned to Belfast, where he was found guilty of reinstated charges.

Constable Charles Simpson was a member of a mobile patrol returning to RUC Strand Road in Londonderry on 28 February 1978. Travelling along Clarendon Street, the patrol was ambushed by gunmen and he died from his wounds. On 15 April Reserve Constable John Moore, who was driving away from his home near Armoy, County Antrim, died instantly when a landmine concealed in the laneway exploded under his car.

About lunchtime on Saturday 22 April two men called at the home of Constable Millar McAllister on the outskirts of Lisburn and expressed an interested in his pigeons. He escorted them to the loft at the rear of his house where he was gunned down at point-blank range and killed. Late in the afternoon of 16 June Reserve Constable Robert Struthers was at his civilian employment in an electrical shop at Lorne Street, Londonderry, when terrorist gunmen entered and shot him dead.

The next afternoon gunmen, lying in wait at a crossroads between Camlough and Crossmaglen in South Armagh, opened fire on an RUC patrol. Constable Hugh McConnell died instantly but another officer, Constable William Turbitt, was abducted by the terrorists. Although he was almost certainly dead, the Provisional IRA issued a statement saying he was being interrogated.

The following morning at 7.30 am Father Hugh Murphy, the Catholic priest at Ahoghill, County Antrim, was roused in the parochial house by two armed, masked men, Clad in a dressing gown and slippers he was frogmarched from the house, tied, blindfolded and taken away in a car. After a drive he was taken into a shed and a coal bag was put over his head and body. A short time later in telephone calls to news organizations, the abductors said they were from the Ulster Freedom Fighters and that the priest would be released in the same condition as the missing policeman.

Of all the priests in Northern Ireland who might have been kidnapped for real or even imagined Republican sympathies, Father Murphy would have been bottom of every list, for he had fractured many of the features on the usual Catholic mould. During his thirty years as a priest he had been a chaplain to the Royal Navy, religious affairs adviser to Ulster Television and held the OBE, which he had received at Buckingham Palace in 1974. His reputation as an active ecumenist, community-minded churchman and humane pastor had won him affection and respect throughout both sections of the community. He was particularly admired for running the gauntlet of Free Presbyterian bigotry to take part in the Remembrance Sunday ceremony at Ballymena.

In the overwhelmingly Protestant village of Ahoghill that Sunday morning, people of all religions prayed for the kindly priest. Those who knew him well feared for his safety on health grounds for he was blind in one eye and suffered from a heart condition. Throughout the day, despite her own anguish, the wife of the missing policeman, Mrs Margaret Turbitt, and the Rev. Ian Paisley made constant radio pleas for Father Murphy's freedom. As the hours passed the pleading wore the kidnappers down and in the evening about 9 pm they released him near the home of one of his parishioners. At first the man did not recognize him because he was covered in coal dust from the bag used to hood him.

Constable Turbitt's body eventually turned up at Cullyhanna on 9 July. The post-mortem revealed that he had died at the time of the ambush. At first detectives assumed that Loyalist paramilitaries had indeed been responsible for the retaliatory kidnapping but, in December, after an anonymous telephone call from a woman, they launched a secret investigation into a group of police officers who had served in South Armagh. The ring-leader of the group was serving Constable Billy McCaughey, then aged twenty-nine, a former member of the Free Presbyterian Church, who was known as the 'Protestant Boy' around his native Ahoghill. His shameful exploits were recounted in a series of court cases in the summer of 1980.

In April 1977, the day after gunmen attacked RUC Ahoghill and an officer received a bullet wound on the ankle, McCaughey suggested to Sergeant John Weir, during a heavy drinking session in an

Armagh pub, that there should be a reprisal. Although Weir was doubtful, he went along with the plot. McCaughey obtained a 'clean Colt .45' he had in his house and in the early hours of 19 April the gang set out for Ahoghill. Apart from the two police officers there were two men McCaughey described as 'top UVF' from Lurgan.

Their victim was the village grocer, William Strathearn, a thirty-nine-year-old Catholic and father of seven children aged between one and eleven, who had lived in Ahoghill for thirteen years. McCaughey had singled him out because of local talk that he had looked after the rifle used in the wounding of the policeman. Village gossip also had it that burn marks on Mr Strathearn's face had been caused in an IRA bomb-making operation that went wrong. Both items were inaccurate. The burns had been caused some years earlier in a fire tragedy at a garage in which his brother had been killed.

Shortly after 2 am William Strathearn was awakened by the men knocking at his door. When he looked out of the upstairs window, one of the gang said: 'Willie, get me a packet of Aspros for the child. It is sick.' As he opened the front door he was shot twice in the head and killed. After the shooting the gun was buried at the McCaughey family home just outside the village. A senior police officer later said in open court that the dead man had been 'a very law-abiding citizen'.

It was not the first time that McCaughey had been involved in unofficial reprisals. Angered by IRA attacks on UDR members and Protestants in the South Armagh area in 1976, he was a prime mover in a gun and bomb attack on the Rock Bar, near Keady, on 5 June that year. A stolen car was used to transport the attackers to their target. When they got there a 10 lb gelignite bomb was placed at the pub door and shots were fired through the window. McCaughey fired at a man leaving the bar and wounded him in the stomach, but not seriously. Damage to the bar was also slight, for only the detonator went off. The attackers burned the stolen car and one of the pistols used in the shooting before another member of the conspiracy drove them back to the RUC station at Armagh in an unmarked police car.

Altogether six members of the RUC were involved in the offences, which were dealt with by the Lord Chief Justice, Lord Lowry, sitting at Belfast Crown Court in June 1980. He paid tribute to the detectives who 'without flinching and without fear or favour' had carried out the 'unwelcome task' of bringing their former comrades to trial.

Desmond Boal, QC, in mitigation, said that all the accused had served in the notorious South Armagh area. 'Their ordinary day-to-day activity involved them in driving over roads which from time to time were mined. Frequently they came under direct gunfire. They knew any minute might be their last on this earth. They came to see it as a struggle for personal survival and they began to see the IRA as men lurking in the darkness intent on killing them.'

The Lord Chief Justice remarked that it was 'mercifully rare' for members of the RUC to resort to such conduct. 'It is a matter of admiration that the RUC has resisted the temptation to resort to violence when friends, colleagues and neighbours have been killed.' He said he recognized that what had happened in this case sprang from a feeling of frustration by 'misguided and wrong-headed' officers that ordinary police methods had proved relatively ineffective.

William McCaughey, commended five times for bravery during his eight years in the RUC, pleaded guilty to murder, kidnapping and the pub bombing, and was sentenced to life imprisonment and concurrent terms for his range of offences, which included the armed robbery of £3,000 life savings from an elderly man. Gary Armstrong, who won promotion to sergeant during his eight years in the police and was awarded the Queen's Gallantry medal for rescuing a soldier injured in a terrorist ambush, was given a two-year suspended sentence after pleading guilty to the kidnapping and other offences.

John Weir, also a sergeant, was sentenced to life imprisonment for the murder of the village grocer. He had unsuccessfully challenged the confessions made in custody, accusing his former colleagues of ill-treating him. Being confined in Castlereagh, he said, began to drive him mad. 'I felt the walls were closing in on me. I couldn't breathe and I felt sick. I was cracking up,' he told the court. Ian Mitchell and Laurence McClure were given two-year suspended sentences for taking part in the pub bombing. David Wilson, who had declined to drive the pub bombers but kept quiet about the plot, was given a one-year suspended sentence for failing to give information.

McCaughey's sixty-year-old father, Alex, a Presbyterian elder and pillar of respectability in Ahoghill, was also given a one-year suspended sentence for failing to give information and obstruction of the police. He had spent the Sunday of the priest's kidnap in prayer and distress, knowing that Father Murphy was being held in an outhouse at his home.

Gary Armstrong, who said he found Jesus Christ in prison after his arrest, became an evangelist and founded an organization called Prison Challenge to work with prisoners and their families. McCaughey, the 'Protestant boy', also claimed to have found comfort from the Bible but he became the focus of an unhealthy cult among some members of the Apprentice Boys of Derry, who defied the leadership of the organization in parading with a standard presented by him. In April 1987, when the Northern Ireland Secretary, Tom King, visited the Maze prison, McCaughey called him a traitor and led jeering prisoners in chants of 'Ulster Says No'.

In a less publicized case involving rogue RUC officers in 1979, Derek Gilliland was jailed for eight years, Wilfred Kelly for six, John Elliott for three and William Arnold, who had only recently joined the RUC, was given two years suspended. As a response to the killing of friends and relatives they had carried out three shooting incidents in which a young man was wounded.

The RUC received widespread acclaim for digging the 'bad apples' out of its own barrel and the Gilliland and McCaughey cases were seen by senior officers as marking significant milestones along the road to making the RUC evidently impartial and professional, and therefore acceptable to both sections of the community. Nobody expected they would change attitudes dramatically but they hoped that fair-minded people would recognize the achievement and credit the force for it.

There were three more police deaths in 1978. Reserve Constable Jacob Rankin was fired on and killed when leaving RUC Castlereagh, County Tyrone, on 4 July. Reserve Constable John Lamont was walking the beat in George Street, Ballymena, on 2 August when he was killed by gunmen in a car who pulled up beside him. Reserve Constable Howard Donaghy was building a house for himself at Loughmacrory near Omagh, County Tyrone; as he was working there on 11 September he was ambushed by terrorist gunmen and shot dead.

The Castlereagh controversy understandably attracted international attention. The *Morning Star*, the voice of British communism, gave prominence to the allegations and Eastern bloc countries who were harassed by Britain about their record on human rights began using the situation in Northern Ireland as counter-propaganda. The issue also attracted much attention in the United States of America, where it was whipped up by IRA sympathizers who were both raising money and exploiting the US gun laws to obtain and smuggle arms to the IRA in Ireland. They were opposed by the British and Irish governments which had been pressuring key figures in both President Carter's White House and Congress to tighten up checks on arms purchasers and discourage misguided sympathizers from supporting violence in Ulster.

The Irish government had enlisted the influence of the most powerful Irish-American politicians in the administration to get the US to pressure Britain over policy in Northern Ireland. It was a measure of their leverage that in August 1977 they persuaded the President to promise aid to Ulster if there was a political settlement. But the British were dismayed when the Carter administration later responded to lobbying over the conduct in Castlereagh by blocking a consignment of about 3,000 US-made Ruger revolvers and M1 Carbine rifles, destined for the RUC. Ironically, on the day the embargo was announced, 2 August 1979, the IRA killed the three-hundredth soldier to die since 1969.

The decision caused some resentment in London and Belfast among security chiefs, who were only too well aware of the volume of the illegal traffic in arms across the Atlantic to the troubled streets of Northern Ireland. The decision also caused some embarrassment among the law enforcement agencies in Washington which were, for the first time, putting together a co-ordinated operation to sever the Provisional IRA's transatlantic umbilical cord.

A contemporary US government memorandum said: 'The Irish situation has become a serious problem and source of embarrassment to the United States.' The memo urged the State Department to set up a committee to co-ordinate the political implications and the activities of the investigative and law enforcement agencies, the FBI, the US Customs and the Bureau of Alcohol, Tobacco and Firearms. The decision reflected the growing volume of hard evidence from the RUC being passed to Washington through security liaison officers at the US Embassy in London.

On the afternoon of 11 April 1976 Gunner John Conaty of the Royal Horse Artillery was in a Landrover on duty in the Ardoyne area of North Belfast when he became suspicious of a girl, dressed in a green coat and slacks, apparently limping along the street. He kept her under observation and noticed the material on her right trouser leg remained taut with something protruding at her right foot. He climbed out of the vehicle and stopped her. When she opened her coat the butt of a rifle was sticking out of the waistband of her trousers. She was arrested and later at the police station in North Queen Street, where she was searched by a military policewoman, a magazine and twenty-one rounds of ammunition were discovered, concealed in her pants. A round in the breech of the rifle was unloaded and it was made safe. The courier was Ann Loughlin, a seventeen-year-old civil servant.

The gun was identified as a Finnish-made semi-automatic 7.62 Valmet and bore the serial number 146325. After forensic examination it was given to the RUC's Data Research Centre, where it was test fired. Unusually, it had no previous history and the firearms experts concluded that it had probably only recently arrived in Ireland. Nearly half the weapons being seized from terrorists at this time proved to be of US origin.

The serial number was passed to the United States Bureau of Alcohol, Tobacco and Firearms, the Federal agency charged with enforcing US firearms legislation. Under both federal and state gun laws, licensed firearms dealers must record all transactions and purchases. To prevent their lines being traced back, the gun-runners to Ireland normally cut out the section of the weapon with the embossed serial number or ground it down. Advances in forensic science techniques, using infra-red, magnets or certain acids, have, however, enabled the authorities to trace the origin of guns, even with obliterated numbers. So Rifle 146325 was quickly traced back through a New York gun dealer called George De Meo, all the way to a small shop called B & B Guns in the sleepy town of Wilson, North Carolina.

De Meo, who masqueraded as an antiques dealer, was well known to the Federal investigators. He already had a US criminal record 'as long as your arm', in the words of a US Customs investigator who strongly suspected he had Mafia connections. It was not the first time he had come to notice for supplying instruments of death to the IRA. Their favourite US-supplied weapon was the Armalite, a civilian version of the M16, the standard US Army combat rifle, which the IRA men in Ulster had quickly dubbed 'the widow-maker'.

An Armalite AR 180, serial number 12641, which had belonged to the IRA gang captured at the end of the Balcombe Street siege in London in December 1975, had been sourced to De Meo and B & B Guns, as had a Gewehr G-43 rifle, serial number 8357, seized by the Garda Siochana at Buncrana, County Donegal, 15 January 1976.

Perhaps his most deadly acquisition for the IRA were seven M60 rapid-fire heavy machine guns, stolen from a US National Guard armoury at Danvers, near Boston, Massachusetts, in August 1976. In the four years they were in the hands of the IRA, until the last one was captured in Londonderry in August 1982, they were responsible for causing ten deaths and nineteen serious woundings.

De Meo and his partners came to trial in Raleigh, North Carolina, early in 1980 as a result of the initial information furnished by the RUC. The court heard how he specialized in buying what he called 'offies' – off the record firearms. One of his main suppliers was B & B, where Howard Bruton, the proprietor, is estimated to have sold more than a hundred rifles and one million rounds of ammunition in three years.

During the trial a senior US army officer testified that soldiers on exercise at the live firing ranges at nearby Camp Lejeune retained and sold rounds of ammunition for 4 cents each to B & B. De Meo paid 8 cents a round and smuggled the ammunition to Ireland. Once the suppliers asked De Meo where the guns and ammunition were going. 'Oh, some place cool and green,' he replied.

Twice a month De Meo and his accomplice, Robert Ferraro, drove the 1,000-mile round trip from New York to Wilson to collect the hardware. The boot of their Cadillac limousine was loaded up on the main street outside the gunshop with what the Federal prosecutor described as 'high power, rapid fire, highly destructive, military weapons'. So that De Meo could reach New York safely, he had a fall-back arrangement with B & B: if he was stopped, the hardware would be retrospectively entered in B & B's records in the name of Mrs De Meo, who held a firearms dealer's permit.

De Meo was given a £9,000 fine and sentenced to ten years imprisonment. Ferraro was fined £2,000 and given two years. The corrupt gun dealer, Bruton, was fined £9,000 and jailed for five years. But De Meo offered to give the FBI the inside story of the rest of the IRA's gun-running activities in return for leniency. Over the next few years the US law enforcement organizations traced the origins of 703 firearms, mostly seized in Ulster by the RUC and army, and with De Meo's inside information they dealt repeated body blows to the IRA's efforts to obtain arms and ammunition.

In December 1977 detectives from the Garda Siochana raided a flat at Royal Terrace, Dun Laoghaire, best known as the ferry terminal south of Dublin. Inside the flat, occupied by the former Belfast IRA leader Seamus Twomey, they discovered a tightly rolled up document hidden in a pencil case. The document contained details of the regrouping of the IRA into small cells in a bid to thwart the increasing pressure from the police forces north and south of the Irish border. But more significantly it laid down a blueprint for Sinn Fein, the IRA's political puppet organization, to open a second front by becoming involved in community politics:

> Sinn Fein should come under army organizers at all levels. Sinn Fein should employ full-time organizers in big Republican areas. Sinn Fein should be radicalized (under army direction) and should agitate about social and economic issues which attack the welfare of the people. Sinn Fein should be directed to infiltrate other organizations to win support for and sympathy to the movement. Sinn Fein should be re-educated and have a big role to play in publicity and propaganda, complaints and problems (making no room for RUC opportunism).

It was compelling documentary evidence that smashed the polite fiction that the IRA only shared a common objective with the political party. A copy of the document was quickly passed to the RUC where the unfolding IRA strategy was already the subject of searching investigation.

The previous spring, Newman had set up a special detective squad, commanded by Chief Inspector George Caskey, to probe the polite fiction. He was outraged that a legal political party could promote the objects of a proscribed terrorist organization with apparent legal immunity and attempt the subversion of civil government in several areas. In particular Caskey was ordered to examine the way telex messages to the local and national media acknowledging IRA responsibility for terrorist attacks originated inside the organization. The speed with which such messages were published from the Republican Press Centre at Falls Road, the police suspected, must sometimes have involved a degree of foreknowledge. Caskey was also to examine the activities of Sinn Fein who were increasingly involving themselves in alternative policing operations in Catholic areas.

Newman was hopeful that the common law offence of conspiracy would provide a legal vehicle to enmesh the frontmen with the gunmen and bombers for the first time. Unlike their counterparts on the UK mainland, the RUC had never used the conspiracy laws against terrorist suspects, largely because the Irish legal establishment had a traditional aversion to them. Because of a recent practice direction on conspiracy by the Lord Chief Justice, Lord Widgery, Newman, however, believed that the time was ripe for a change in this attitude. To help the Caskey team assemble a prima facie case, he persuaded the Metropolitan Police to second Commander James Nevill, head of the Anti-Terrorist Squad at Scotland Yard, to Belfast. The Commander had considerable experience in bringing conspiracy charges against terrorist groups which had committed offences throughout Britain.

Caskey had a small group of officers permanently working with him but in December 1977 they were temporarily reinforced to carry out a major search operation of five Sinn Fein premises and the houses of twenty-nine activists. In April 1978, 300 officers took part in a similar operation, raiding the two headquarters offices at Falls Road, Belfast, used by Sinn Fein, local party offices in other areas, the homes of party activists and a printing works at Lurgan where the 13,500 copies of the IRA's weekly newspaper *An Phoblacht/Republican News* were produced.

The raids produced an interesting insight into the administrative workings of the terrorist organization. It was squatting rent-free in premises owned by the Northern Ireland Housing Executive and services like electricity were signed for in the name of Sean O'Neill, the fictional pseudonym used to sign IRA statements. The Provisionals were clearly concerned that future historians would give a good account of them. Sinn Fein had even appointed an archivist and they had lodged nineteen boxes of material with the Public Record Office in Belfast.

Altogether, the Caskey team assembled 8,000 potential exhibits to support the conspiracy case, including filing cabinets, typewriters, telex machines, minute books, assorted documents, notes, pamphlets, posters, card index records, letters and printing plates. The profile they were able to put together of the IRA/Sinn Fein strategy was both startling and sinister.

The detailed blueprint for the political rise of Sinn Fein, they discovered, was actually written by inmates at the Maze Prison during 1976. A 5,000-word document, headed 'Peoples Assembly' and signed 'Battalion Education Officer', analysed the shortcomings of the Provisionals to build on the failure of successive British political initiatives in Ulster. 'As each attempt failed, however, we were always given a second chance because the Brit was never able to fill the vacuum.'

The vacuum was to be filled, the document outlined, by introducing community politics 'as a broadening of the war machine'. The Provisionals were to become involved in agitation in three areas: co-operative trading to bypass the existing capitalist system; to take the credit for housing improvements and area clean-ups by undermining existing pressure groups; and policing through the establishment of a 'Peoples Police' closely linked to the Provisional IRA. The membership of this force was to be 'volunteers not directly involved with military operations, Sinn Fein personnel and sympathetic groups in the areas'.

The move into community politics was not to be by the rules of democracy. According to the document: 'Sympathetic groups will be an asset and groups with "other" leanings can be excluded or undermined.' The document concluded that 'in this set-up the war, properly guided, will never be divorced from the people or the IRA will never be isolated from them'.

The proposals for alternative policing contained in the seized documents were of supreme interest to the RUC, given its responsibility to uphold law and order and its ongoing efforts to improve relations with the Catholic community. Any challenge to the authority of the RUC would have very serious implications. The document stated: 'The aim of the policing policy other than that existing in nationalist areas at the present time is to provide the Republican alternative to the RUC reformed or otherwise. This could take the form of a Peoples' Militia which would be a body having the respect and support of the community and which would be acceptable to the IRA.'

The IRA proposals further envisaged a system of 'Peoples' Courts'. 'This would put the responsibility for law and order with the people of the area, the IRA could continue to influence the situation but would not be seen to be in control.' In another document the background to the system of Peoples' Courts was set out. Between 1919 and 1924, when they were abolished by Dail Eireann, the Republican movement operated a system of 900 'Parish Courts' and 70 'District Courts'. 'The operation of these courts,' the paper said, 'was a manifestation of Republican control and an illustration of a practical and realistic undermining of the British State on the one hand and a form of political consolidation on the other.' The document recalled that the system of courts was backed up by a Republican police force and it said that such a force would have to be created at some future date.

Through detailed examination of the haul, the RUC detectives were astonished to find the strides the IRA had in fact taken to set up its own system of law and order in West Belfast. The police found detailed records of crimes reported to the IRA through the various Sinn Fein Advice Centres and lists of suspected offenders. The offences alleged against them ranged from petty crime, defined as vandalism, through to burglary, rape and robbery.

In an attempt to understand why there was such a wave of petty crime, Sinn Fein analysed 544 complaints received at its centres between May and August 1977. Most involved boys and girls in the ten to seventeen age group, although there were eighteen- to twenty-one-year-olds involved in hooliganism 'due to alcohol and devilment'.

> The children of these areas are deprived of other outlets for their energies, their education at school leaves a lot to be desired. There are no sports stadiums, no community centres to any great extent, no play areas.
>
> It is many years since we have seen the children's street games played in these areas (hopscotch, skipping and jumping, kick the tin, ball games, rounders, etc.). Hence children's attentions have been focused on other outlets.
>
> They have experienced a degree of independence, have learned the feel and uses of money so ... derelict properties were stripped for saleable scrap, homes were broken into, meters smashed and robbed. Even the RUC are unable to cope with the problem in areas where they can move about freely [Loyalist].

Complaint forms were completed in triplicate at the Sinn Fein centres and one copy was sent to 170 Falls Road, the party headquarters, where they were listed in a dossier. The IRA ran an arbitrary system of warnings and punishments. Sometimes names of offenders were circulated locally in leaflets published by Sinn Fein or the offenders were abducted to be given a violent warning to behave better – a process one IRA document described as 'informal persuasion'.

Sometimes more direct action was taken. Three youths who stole more than £150 rent money from an old age pensioner and cleared off to Butlin's Holiday Camp were pursued and forced to return to

Belfast, where they handed back the remaining £78. More usually, however, the IRA resorted to violence. In just one month, September 1977, the RUC found that twenty-five people named on the list had been subjected to typical IRA punishments, such as beatings with pickaxe handles or hurley sticks, tar and featherings, knee-cappings or having concrete blocks dropped on their limbs.

In April 1978 the Caskey team charged six men and two women with conspiracy to prevent and defeat the course of public justice and with membership of the Provisional IRA. But the entire operation received a fatal setback on 6 September when Gerry Adams, one of the principal targets, who faced IRA membership charges, appeared before the Lord Chief Justice, unusually presiding at a preliminary enquiry. Lord Lowry said that speculation could not take the place of evidence in a court of law and that the Crown case only proved that Adams had Republican sympathies and leanings. 'There is no evidence to persuade a logical man that by parading in a prison compound on quasi-military lines a man can be accused of identifying himself as a member of the IRA.' The Lord Chief Justice accordingly refused to send him for trial and ordered his release. As a result of the decision, in February 1979 the DPP ordered the chief constable to drop all the cases brought by the Caskey team, and the charges were withdrawn.

The Lowry decision was a landmark and in retrospect can be seen as a vital development in the process that paved the way for the later emergence of the Provisionals as a serious political force. To the frustration of many senior RUC men, the organization was thus enabled to deepen and strengthen its hold in the Catholic areas, although the detailed plans for an overt alternative policy force never materialized.

The IRA maintained its interest in 'regulating anti-social behaviour' and what have become known as punishment shootings and beatings, inflicted by both Republican and Loyalist organizations, remain a depressingly regular occurrence. Such attacks peaked in 1975 with 189 and although there were only an average 70 reported incidents each year since, there was an upsurge in 1987 when 184 victims came to police notice.

The beatings meted our are far from superficial. An RUC dossier lists a number of examples of uniquely brutal conduct: a man who had his hand nailed to a floor; a nineteen-year-old who bled to death after being shot in both knees; a husband and wife being beaten by men wielding hammers; several cases of amputation following kneecapping by gunshot, and permanent disfigurement and injury, such as limping, resulting from multiple fractures or the effects of assault. Long-term hospital treatment is usually involved.

The armoury of the self-appointed punishers is frequently as simple as it is brutal. Some of the most appalling injuries have been meted out with sticks, pickaxe handles, concrete blocks, baseball bats, hammers and iron bars, as well as the more obviously lethal electric drills, shotguns or revolvers that have been used. In one notorious case a victim was kneecapped by his own brother.

In July 1984 Danny Morrison, for Sinn Fein, said there was no political kudos in taking such action. 'The IRA does it out of a moral responsibility towards the oppressed sections of the community. It is an imperfect form of justice but it is inevitable that it takes place.'

The RUC views the practice as a threat to the hope of civilizing living in Northern Ireland. In a detailed policy statement in June 1987, the force said: 'Sometimes these people, in inflicting punishment on others, will pose as "protectors" of the community in dealing with petty criminals. That is hyprocrisy. The fact is they are determined to have a monopoly on crime for themselves.' Pointing out that when caught by the police they cried for justice for themselves, the RUC said that 'in dealing with people who incur their disfavour for whatever reason they dispense appalling injustice through force and violence with no trial, no appeal and no mercy'.

The degree of community control that both the IRA and similar Loyalist groups achieved through pseudo-policing created the conditions for running other operations such as the black taxi transport service, drinking clubs and dictating who would work on building sites. These not only gave them localized political influence but allowed them to undermine official agencies, assume control of community services and build a flourishing web of rackets and extortion that enriched the paramilitary leaders and organizations and turned Belfast into the Chicago of the eighties.

Pouring resources into the undercover war was another major development sponsored by Newman. These operations were initially centred on the border but the Special Support Unit, modelled on the SAS, soon began to operate throughout the province when the Special Branch undercover surveillance teams and informers came up with tip-offs for them to act upon. The strategy was founded on Newman's belief that if the RUC was successfully to replace the army, then the 'gap' in its capabilities for this type of work must be closed. That involved not only developing a capability to deal with public order situations but also acquiring the means to handle sieges, cover surveillance operations and other similar types of incident.

In the meantime there were a number of joint operations involving the SAS. On 21 June 1978 they successfully intercepted and killed a three-man bombing team at a telephone installation in North Belfast, although a passer-by also died in the hail of gunfire. But the results of another SAS undercover operation in July were tragically imprecise. Seventeen-year-old farmer's son John Boyle went prowling about in a graveyard while his father was working in an adjacent field and he found concealed under a disturbed tombstone rifles and ammunition wrapped in plastic. At the end of the day's work his father reported the matter to the local police at Dunloy, County Antrim.

Overnight the police called in the SAS to lie in wait in the graveyard for whoever night come back to claim the guns. They suspected they might have been dumped there for use in a planned terrorist attack within the next few days. Next morning, through an oversight, the local police did not warn the Boyles to stay away from the scene and, as his father started another day's work, the son went back to the grave to see if the rifles had been removed. As soon as he reached the grave he was shot dead. The army promptly claimed he was a gunman but the RUC swiftly corrected their mistake and in due course charged the two members of the SAS with his murder. A year later in the Belfast Crown Court the Lord Chief Justice, Lord Lowry, acquitted the two soldiers.

In the early months of 1979 the undercover units of the RUC launched a major co-ordinated surveillance drive against a number of prominent IRA supporters and suspects. The province-wide operation was code-named 'Hawk'. Every suspect was given the name of a bird, every location the name of an English league football ground. The operation was to highlight the intensity of the war being fought across the invisible front line between undercover policing and covert terrorist operations, and to expose how modern technology was increasingly being harnessed by the Provos to enhance the constant threat they posed to the security forces.

At the beginning of March, acting on high-grade intelligence information, the undercover units watched as a massive 420 lb cache of explosives was slipped into Northern Ireland across the border, driven into Belfast, and in the Markets area, near the city centre, handed over to a Provisional IRA team. On the night of 6 March 1979 the Provos planned that ten two-man teams would scale the fences and plant forty-two bombs through the oil refinery and petrol tank farm at Sydenham in the heart of the Belfast docks. The spectacular had been inspired by a television news report from Salisbury, Rhodesia, where guerrillas had caused a huge fire that burned for days by attacking petrol storage tanks.

That night the SAS were deployed in the Belfast refinery but the bombers never came. The RUC were mystified and had to content themselves with the large haul of explosives which were packed in kitbags at a yard in the Short Strand area. The word that came back from the informers was that the operation had suddenly been called off late at night, shortly before it was due to get under way.

Two weeks later, on 20 March, two cars, a brown Honda Civic and a yellow Toyota, were stopped by police near Banbridge, County Down. They were travelling north from the border on the main Dublin–Belfast road. The occupants of the cars, three men and a woman, who were held for questioning included a prize catch. Brian Keenan, as the so-called director of operations of the Provisional IRA, was the man responsible for the refinery plan as well as the IRA's bombing campaign in Britain. Within two days he was taken to London by Scotland Yard detectives and after a trial at the Old Bailey in June 1980 he was sentenced to eighteen years for conspiracy to cause a three-month wave of bombings and shootings in which nine people died and 113 were injured.

Although the RUC had handed Keenan over to Scotland Yard, the ongoing Operation Hawk back in Northern Ireland received a major boost from the capture. It was to help the RUC to uncover one of the most serious breaches of government security ever to take place. In fact its true significance to the future conduct of security operations has never been fully revealed.

The key lay hidden in coded diaries, which were among many intriguing items in Keenan's possession; they included half a Lebanese bank note with a signature written on it. Special Branch detectives believed this was a vital piece of identification for a sensitive contact. Scotland Yard called in cryptologists to crack the coded diaries and it became clear from the telephone numbers, addresses and contacts that Keenan was a major link between the Provisionals and sympathizers overseas. But some of his contacts nearer home in Belfast were of more immediate interest to the RUC, especially in the context of Operation Hawk.

As a result of the decoded information passed back from London, the scope of the Hawk surveillance operation was widened to include three private houses, one at Coolnasilla Park, Andersonstown, another at Dunmurry and a third on the outskirts of Lisburn. In the early hours of 15 June, a force of 300 police backed up by 100 soldiers swooped on the three houses. What they found was described as 'a hugely significant hoard of important intelligence information'. But privately the authorities were staggered by the enormous sophistication of the Provisional IRA operation that they uncovered, with evidence that it had been operating undetected for almost six years.

Concealed in the roof space of one of the houses they found a virtual command post, with radios and unscrambling equipment tuned into the frequencies used by undercover police and soldiers. There were military-style transmitters and monitors and position-fixing devices, as well as telephone taps routed through the British Telecom network by people with the know-how to break into the systems. One of the intercepted lines was an unlisted number for the Dunmurry residence of the GOC commanding the army garrison. They now knew that the IRA had called off the refinery bombing because they had eavesdropped on radio traffic between the various units involved, including the SAS.

One of the houses, which belonged to a telephone engineer, was a virtual electronics laboratory devoted to making bombs which harnessed the most up-to-date techniques in electronic micro-circuitry. Components in the house were eventually traced back to the Ulster Polytechnic and the Grundig and Strathearn Audio factories, both of which were equipped with the sort of equipment necessary to produce the electronic and radio detonation devices then being introduced to set off bombs.

One of the eleven people arrested was found to have connections with a sub-aqua club and although there was evidence he had been to Mullaghmore, County Sligo, nobody made the connection until a few months later when Lord Mountbatten was assassinated there with a radio-controlled explosive device.

There were also many documents in the houses, including target lists and details of the houses, cars, lifestyles and movements of judges, civil servants, members of the security forces and others, some of whom had already lost their lives. But the most worrying discovery was bundles of transcripts of hours and hours of secret security forces transmissions, including those relating to Operation Hawk itself. Although the people under surveillance were always referred to by the names of birds and the locations they visited by the names of football grounds, the Provisionals had found an ingenious way of cracking the code.

One day they had arranged for their top leaders to arrive for a meeting at ten-minute intervals. By monitoring the radio traffic and comparing it with the arrival time of each person, they were able to work out the 'bird' name each represented. One terrorist who regarded himself as a bit of a hard man was quite annoyed when he discovered he had been dubbed 'Chicken' and another did not like being called 'Budgie'. By asking each member to recall his movements at particular times, they were able to decode the address each football ground referred to. In this way they were able to monitor and evade one of the most comprehensive and sophisticated surveillance operations ever mounted by the RUC.

There was to be a final and, for Keenan, an ironic postscript to the haul, for some of the material referred to operations on the British mainland that he had set up before his capture. It was a measure of his importance to the IRA that before he had even come to trial, four hardened Belfast IRA men were sent over to carry out an elaborate plan to lift Keenan from the exercise yard at Brixton prison in south London in a hijacked helicopter.

The police got wind of the operation from the documents they captured in the Hawk raids and when one of the Belfast IRA team was spotted boarding a ferry to Liverpool, using a crowd of football supporters as cover, he was put under surveillance. During the latter months of 1979 a major joint operation, involving police throughout Britain and Ireland, monitored every detail of the unfolding plot. At one point the operation was nearly compromised by an unwitting West London detective. One of the IRA team regularly visited an Irish woman friend during his time in London but she was also seeing the detective with some frequency. The undercover police could only keep their fingers crossed that the two would never meet and perhaps provoke the team into leaving London.

Finally, in December 1979, before Keenan had even come to trial, the four Belfast IRA men were arrested in a rented luxury flat in Holland Park, London, a short time before the helicopter plan was put into effect. All were later tried at the Old Bailey.

In June 1980 the last detail of Operation Hawk was completed when a thirty-nine-year-old woman, described as the unwitting courier, was given a two-year suspended sentence at Belfast Crown Court. The other ten people arrested with her, who had played a more prominent role in the affair, had jumped bail and gone to the Irish Republic.

About 11.35 am on 17 April 1979 an RUC Landrover was travelling from Newry to Bessbrook. As it passed a blue Transit van, abandoned at the side of the road, watching terrorists detonated a large bomb which blew both vehicles to pieces. The four RUC officers caught in the blast died instantly. They were Constable Paul Gray, Constable Richard Baird, Constable Noel Webb and Reserve Constable Robert Lockhard.

A few weeks later, on Sunday 6 May, a Special Branch officer, Detective Constable Norman Prue, was travelling through Lisnaskea with an army sergeant, Robert Maughan. They drew up outside the local Catholic church to buy a Republican newspaper. As they did so, four gunmen, waiting in a parked van, confronted them and opened fire. As the two members of the security forces lay on the ground they were fired on again.

Exactly two days later, on 20 May, Reserve Constable David Wray pulled up outside the Claremont Presbyterian Church in Londonderry to attend morning service. As he climbed out of his car, shots were fired at him from behind and he died instantly. His sixteen-year-old son and nineteen-year-old daughter who were in the car with him witnessed the murder of their father.

On 2 June Reserve Constable David Dunn was standing outside his home in Armagh talking to a friend, David Stinson. Gunmen in a passing car opened fire, killing them both. Next day, Superintendent Stanley Hanna, who had recently been transferred from headquarters in Belfast, was walking along a laneway near a community centre in Crossmaglen with Constable Kevin Thompson when a large bomb exploded, killing them both instantly.

Reserve Constable John Scott was a creamery collection driver in civilian life. On 22 June, as he was driving his tanker near Ardboe, he was ambushed by gunmen and murdered. Constable George Walsh died in a police car parked outside the courthouse in Armagh on 31 July when a gunman in a car pulled up alongside him and opened fire.

Constable Derek Davidson was a member of a police party fired on while investigating a burglary in the Falls Road area of Belfast. He was dead on arrival at hospital. Constable John Davidson was shot by gunmen as a Landrover he was travelling in emerged from RUC Springfield Road in Belfast. He was seriously wounded and died from his injuries nine hours later in hospital on 18 November. Three days before Christmas, Reserve Constable Stanley Hazelton crossed the border to Annacatty, County Monaghan, to collect turkeys. Gunmen ambushed him on his way back and killed him.

The closing months of Newman's command in Belfast were, however, dominated by the implications of 27 August 1979, the day Lord Mountbatten was assassinated in County Sligo and eighteen soldiers were killed in a double explosion at Narrow Water, near Warrenpoint, County Down. It was indeed what the tabloid press dubbed 'Black Monday' – the worst casualty rate suffered by the army in a single incident and the most costly day of the violence in terms of human life, with a total of twenty-three people dead.

Lord Mountbatten of Burma, the man who negotiated the British out of India, and uncle of the Queen, was holidaying as he had done for most of the previous thirty years at Mullaghmore. That morning, as his fishing boat chugged across the tiny harbour, a bomb concealed aboard swallowed the vessel in a ball of flame, killing not only Mountbatten but his fourteen-year-old grandson Nicholas and the boatman, seventeen-year-old Paul Maxwell. The Dowager Lady Brabourne, who was critically injured, died later in hospital. Seriously injured were Nicholas's twin, Timothy, who lost an eye, and Lord and Lady Brabourne.

The attack, promptly acknowledged by the Provisional IRA, shocked public opinion in Britain, which had become immune to the almost daily catalogue of atrocity reported from Belfast. It was the second time in only six months that a major public figure had been assassinated in the cause of Irish unity. In March, on the eve of the general election that brought Margaret Thatcher to power, the Irish National Liberation Army had penetrated the House of Commons and planted a bomb under the parked car of shadow Northern Ireland Secretary, Airey Neave, Mrs Thatcher's closest political adviser, who had masterminded her accession to leadership of the Conservative Party. The bomb had exploded, killing him, almost at the base of Big Ben as he drove out.

But late that August afternoon, as the horrific detail of the events in County Sligo was still unfolding, the Provisional IRA struck again. A huge bomb, concealed in a hay trailer at the roadside, was exploded as a three-vehicle convoy of members of the Parachute Regiment passed. Six soldiers died instantly, several more were badly injured.

A short time later a Wessex helicopter, carrying more paratroopers and men from the Queen's Own Highlands, descended by the gate lodge of Narrow Water Castle, at a spot some 400 yards from the scene of the blast. Some of the most seriously wounded had just been loaded aboard when there was a second huge explosion as the helicopter took off. Despite the force of the blast the pilot succeeded in keeping control and lifting above the cloud of swirling smoke and dust. Below it another twelve soldiers lay dead by the granite-walled castle entrance. At the subsequent inquest in July 1980 it was stated the bodies were so badly mutilated that some of the soldiers had only been identified by their socks and boots.

The shock waves hit Downing Street, where the prime minister, experiencing her first Ulster crisis, decided to go over to see for herself. The army, commanded by Lt-Gen. Sir Timothy Creasey, had concealed its mounting reservations about being taken out of the Ulster driving seat and now felt that the circumstances were right to vent their reservations about police primacy and the inadequacy of the RUC. Mrs Thatcher was first cornered in the tiny, map-walled operations room at the beleaguered post in Crossmaglen, where the only safe access was by helicopter. 'This is all that's left of one of my bravest officers,' said the local army brigade commander, throwing down the metal epaulettes that had belonged to Lt-Col. David Blair, the most senior victim of the double-ambush at Warrenpoint. There was further emotion as the Brigadier explained that the pins on the maps represented the toll of security forces casualties in the border area that Merlyn Rees had branded 'bandit country'.

The local police commanders had been elbowed out of this briefing by the army, which provided a second dose of detailed anti-RUC propaganda when they entertained the prime minister to a buffet lunch at the brigade headquarters in Mahon Barracks, Portadown. Later in the day, by the time she met the chief constable at Gough Barracks in Armagh, they had planted serious doubts about the security policy and the ability of the police to lead it.

Sir Kenneth was at his best in this sort of situation. According to senior RUC officers, he sat quietly listening to the prime minister and then began a forceful dissertation of defence. Appointing a director of operations, a security supremo, as the army were demanding, would be a drastic step back, he pointed out. The object of the policy was to return the army to barracks, not suck them further into the situation. The only sane way forward was to continue the planned build-up in the RUC's strength and capabilities. There was no quick or easy solution.

Back in London the prime minister decided on a compromise to settle the conflicting advice she was getting. At the beginning of October she sent the retired spymaster, Sir Maurice Oldfield, to Northern Ireland as security co-ordinator. His role was presented as that of a referee between the police and the army. Setting up shop in Stormont Castle, he was given the services of Assistant Chief Constable John Whiteside and Brigadier Robert Pascoe as expert assessors to help him examine the areas of conflict and suggest solutions. But the prime minister made it clear that she backed the policy of police primacy. Sir Kenneth was given the go-ahead to recruit the extra thousand men he had asked for.

Oldfield, who was already in poor health suffering from stomach cancer, left the province hurriedly less than six months later, after an unsavoury incident in a public house which caused his positive vetting security clearance to be withdrawn. He died in March 1981. In April 1987 the prime minister told the House of Commons that Sir Maurice's security clearance had been withdrawn after he admitted a life of compulsive homosexuality, although she did say there was no evidence that he had ever been compromised into any act of betrayal.

Sir Kenneth Newman, who was knighted in 1977, did not allow the constant criticism or regular setbacks to demoralize either himself or the force. He took great comfort from the steady reduction in the level of violence throughout his term of command as vindication of his policies and strategy. He put in long, sometimes punishing, hours. His typical day would begin about 8 am with what was called 'morning prayers'. With his most senior operational and intelligence officers and the civilian press spokesman, he would discuss the overnight reports, anything relevant in the newspapers, radio or television, the upcoming day and its likely dilemmas. Once a week he would attend a meeting with the Secretary of State and the GOC to discuss wider policy matters. Other agencies such as the security service and the prison department would be involved at this level.

Some days the chief would be at his office in Belfast receiving a stream of callers – officers visiting from other forces, journalists from all over the world, his own departmental heads, local politicians. Although he had a reputation as a police intellectual and skilled manager, he did not remain desk-bound. At least one day a week he would go out and visit stations in the front line and tackle their problems with them from first-hand knowledge. It was not uncommon for him to turn up in places like West Belfast and go out in the armoured Landrovers, sitting cheek by jowl with the men and women, sharing their dangers and listening to their troubles. He enjoyed the characteristic, frank Ulster comments and found the experience valuable in making decisions. His accessibility earned him respect from those on the ground. The chief's typical day would end with evening engagements and then as long as two hours at his desk, often past midnight, dealing with the endless succession of forms, files and letters.

One of the most notable engagements of 1979 was the emotional visit of Princess Alexandra of Kent to force headquarters at Brooklyn. On 29 June Sir Kenneth presided as she unveiled a memorial to the members of the force who had lost their lives since 1922 and dedicated two books of remembrance, one commemorating the sixty-nine members who lost their lives before 1961, the second those since 1969. The books are now on permanent display in a polished glass case in the entrance hall at RUC headquarters. Each day the page is turned to highlight one of the entries naming the dead officer and the circumstances in which death took place. During the visit Princess Alexandra said that the books of remembrance recorded only too vividly the inescapable fact that the RUC has suffered more casualties in peacetime than any other force in the United Kingdom.

During November and December the RUC began a round of emotional farewell functions for the 'Wee man'. For the first time in three and a half years Newman's steel reserve and emotions broke. As he was driven away from his last passing-out parade at Enniskillen, there were tears in his eyes as the RUC band played 'Auld Lang Syne'. In 'B' Division, which covered the Provisional IRA heartland of the Falls and Andersonstown, the presentation of an engraved replica of the Hotspur armoured Landrover left him briefly speechless with emotion and there were more tears in his eyes when his detectives unveiled a painting of Carnalea on the shores of Belfast Lough where Sir

Kenneth and Lady Newman frequently walked their dogs under the watchful eyes of their armed bodyguards.

On the morning he left Belfast, a week before Christmas, a large number of officers lined the drive at Brooklyn and applauded and cheered as he drove out. It was a rare tribute from Ulster people to an Englishman who had won their confidence and affection. Sir Kenneth reciprocated the respect. During the rest of his distinguished police career, first as Commandant of the Police Staff College at Bramshill, then as Commissioner of the Metropolitan Police, the mementoes of his Ulster command were prominently displayed in his office and he spoke with warmth of the exceptionally courageous body of men and women that made up the RUC.

He left the RUC a more confident organization than he found it. He had forced it to live down some of the old criticisms and adopt a posture of impartiality. The foundations had been laid to transform it from a small, backward-looking provincial force into the modern, efficient organization it became, setting professional and tactical standards for other police forces throughout the United Kingdom. But he had failed to break the historical Catholic opposition and to attract more young Catholics into its ranks. 'He may be the brightest boss we have ever had,' one detective said. 'But he cannot rewrite history.'

# 7

# Drinks, Dames and Debts

When the Northern Ireland Police Authority met in October 1979 to appoint Newman's replacement, there were three candidates short-listed for interview: Maurice Buck, the deputy chief constable of the West Midlands police, who had commanded operations against Provisional IRA bombers in Birmingham and become one of Britain's best-known policemen through frequent television appearances, and the two deputy chief constables of the RUC, Harry Baillie and Jack Hermon.

Although Hermon, fifty years old with thirty years' experience in the RUC, had not served the requisite two years at a senior level in another British police force, as laid down in the 1970 Police Act, there were no raised eyebrows when he was appointed. By reason of his strong, forthright personality and ability he was the clear favourite and the decision had long been regarded as a foregone conclusion within the RUC, especially since the beginning of the year when he had been posted to the Metropolitan police in London, on secondment. During his time there Hermon went on a grand tour of the capital's force. Many of the departmental visits ended with Hermon and his hosts discussing the latest developments in policing over glasses of whisky, frequently Bushmills from Ulster, provided by Hermon himself. But he was not impressed by what he saw and heard. On his return to Belfast, he was heard to say, with typical bluntness: 'You can always tell a Met man – but not much.'

He assumed command of the RUC officially on 1 January 1980 and was sworn in by Sir Robert Lowry, the Lord Chief Justice of Northern Ireland, at the Law Courts in Belfast a few days later. Born at Islandmagee, in East Antrim, Hermon had studied accountancy for three years after leaving Larne Grammar School, before deciding on an RUC career and joining up. After passing out from Enniskillen, his first posting, as a junior constable, was to the small village of Eglinton, County Londonderry. With his boundless energy and enthusiasm he enjoyed walking ten-mile beats across the mountains to places inaccessible by vehicle or bicycle. The old hands chided him for his zeal but that stopped when they were forced to walk the same beats to serve his summonses for the absence of dog licences and the like.

Hermon's life-long concept and vision of the police intimately involved with the population was acquired in that close-knit rural community where they patrolled without weapons and protective equipment and knew everyone on their 'patch' personally. There was early evidence of Hermon's self-confidence when he put a ticket for obstruction on the car of the local magistrate after several warnings went unheeded.

In 1957 he was promoted sergeant and posted to Coalisland, County Tyrone, to replace Sergeant Ovens, the booby-trap bomb victim. It was in this period that Hermon's instincts for impartiality and even-handed application of the law were honed. In difficult circumstances he sought and made what were to prove lasting friendships with members of both the Protestant and Catholic communities. His political antennae, which were to be more crucial than anyone could then have imagined, were also finely tuned there. One Sunday he was called to a football ground where rival groups of supporters were slugging it out. An official remonstrated with him because he declined to get involved in breaking up the fight. 'If I go in there they will forget their own differences and pick on me,' said Hermon. But the law was enforced. He later arrested the exhausted combatants.

There were early signs too of impetuosity leading to an embarrassing climb-down. One evening he raided a packed public house and lectured all present on respect for the licensing laws. But when he had finished, the publican pointed out to him that there was almost an hour until closing time because the clocks had changed the previous day. 'Anybody want to buy a cheap watch,' grinned a chastened Hermon, unbuckling it from his wrist.

Hermon was clearly marked out as a high-flyer in 1963 when he was sent to the Bramshill Police College, the first RUC officer ever to attend. On his return he was promoted to head constable and posted to Hastings Street police station on the western fringe of Belfast city centre. There he was known as 'Blue Streak', the name of a guided missile, because of his stern, disciplinarian approach. He would suddenly dash out of the station and pedal vigorously around the area, checking up on his men. When he later bought a car, with the registration number BSN 10, the men used to say 'Blue Streak – now in orbit'.

The 1964 Divis Street riots dominated his period there. It was the first time he encountered Ian Paisley, who was to become a long-running critic and opponent, and the handling of the affair left an indelible impression on Hermon of the bounds of political manipulation of a police force. From that point he was no longer in the mould of the traditional RUC officer class. But, demonstrating his skills for in-house politicking, he skilfully concealed his real views and did not allow them to damage his prospects.

From Belfast, Hermon returned to Tyrone, this time to Cookstown, on further promotion as district inspector. He is remembered there as being 'tough, stern, unbending and inflexible'. After a year he moved to Enniskillen as deputy commandant of the Training Centre, later taking charge in 1969. A policewoman recalls his attention to detail. She was berated because her lipstick did not match the flash of red in the RUC badge on her hat.

In late 1970, after the Hunt report, he was made chief superintendent and became the RUC's first training officer, charged with implementing the Hunt reforms. It was an awesome task to develop training schemes for the force while it was simultaneously trying to expand and cope with the worsening civil disorder and terrorist violence. Hermon's dedication to endless hours of work became almost a legend. Now based at headquarters, he divided his time between there and the depot. Once he had to be knocked up in the middle of the night by two apprehensive, apologetic officers. 'Don't worry,' said Hermon. 'The job must come first.'

He performed well, masterminding the huge recruiting intake as the RUC rapidly expanded and laying the foundations for the modern RUC and Reserve, although he formed judgements about many of the raw young men that passed through his hands then that were either to haunt their future careers or enhance their promotion prospects. Those like-minded officers, talent-spotted then, who passed his high acceptance standards, became known as the 'Hermonites'. They were to prosper under him, later moving into key jobs, implementing his ideas and acting 'as his eyes and ears', in the words of one. But given his forceful personality, it betrayed a surprising insecurity that he felt he needed the constant reassurance of being surrounded by his placemen.

In April 1974 he was appointed assistant chief constable and as well as supervising the training function he became involved in community relations work, building up a large branch with the twin aims of bridging the Protestant–Catholic community divide and bringing the force into close contact with both communities. He played a personal part, opening up lines of communication with church leaders, businessmen and other groups to create a two-way dialogue on the future of the RUC at a time when its role and shape was being widely debated. His conversation began to be dominated by sociological jargon and was peppered with words like integrity, perception and professionalism.

Merlyn Rees was mesmerized by him the first time they met. Rees was a man for thinking out loud and developing policy through discussions with his advisers. One of his favourite techniques was to hold dinner parties at Stormont House and then 'chew the fat', as he put it, over the brandy and port. Hermon was invited to one of these dinners at this time when Rees was preoccupied with policing and the future of the RUC. When the decanters began to go round the table, Hermon, whose political instincts were probably sharper than anyone else present, began to expound a lengthy dissertation on the philosophy of policing, penal policy, the political future of Ireland and the role of the RUC therein. It was a bid for the top job and an exposition of the Hermon agenda, and it worked. When he had gone, Rees remarked to one of his officials: 'Well, at least we've got a future chief constable.'

Soon after Newman became chief constable in 1976, Hermon was appointed as one of his two deputies and was assigned control of RUC operations. He sat on the Bourne committee, the only RUC member, and played a significant role in writing 'The Way Ahead', the blueprint that 'Ulsterized' security policy by reasserting the RUC's prime responsibility for maintaining law and order by beginning the process of withdrawing the army to barracks.

Just as Hermon's isolation in training had protected him from criticism for events in 1968 and 1969, similarly in the late 1970s his operational responsibility sheltered him from any apparent culpability for events in Castlereagh. Shrewdly, he took conscious steps to clear the problem up without publicly damaging the RUC. Several prominent Catholic clergymen and politicians were given a private hotline telephone number to contact him night and day about their concern over interrogation techniques and he made his disapproval known inside the force. When the Bennett report was published, he was safely out of the way in London. A clean pair of hands was essential, Hermon realized, if he was going to make any impact in the top job and achieve the goals he had defined, especially building enough trust with the Catholic community to obtain support for the RUC and attract Catholic recruits.

His vision for the future of the RUC was spelled out in his first major pronouncement as chief on 13 February 1980 when he inspected fifty-seven newly trained officers passing out from Enniskillen. 'Unlike the recruits here today and most of their colleagues throughout the force, I have been fortunate enough during my career to know what it is to walk down a street on my own, meeting and talking with people, without a flak jacket, without a gun. I want to see the day when you too can do the same. It will be a good day for you and it will be a good day for Northern Ireland.'

Although Hermon mellowed slightly in his first months in office and was praised for listening and taking advice, especially from the detective branches where he lacked personal experience, the change was only tactical. He had set his real opening agenda in widely reported remarks in the Enniskillen speech when he said that conduct which brought the RUC into disrepute would not be tolerated and that he would insist on the highest professional and personal standards. He felt that standards of discipline and behaviour had been allowed to lapse dangerously in previous years, especially in the detective branches, which he regarded as a force within a force. In his stern view, supervisory slackness had aggravated the Castlereagh problem.

He was not popular with the detectives in the Special Branch and the CID, who had borne the brunt of the campaign for terrorist convictions and the propaganda. Because he had always been involved in uniform work, training and community relations, and had never served as a detective, they felt he did not understand their problems. Many resented what they saw as his interference in the Castlereagh problem and when he attended the CID's boisterous Christmas party at headquarters, shortly before assuming command, he was greeted coolly by one senior detective. 'If you're here to enjoy yourself, Sir, you're welcome. If you're here to spy on us, you're not.'

Hermon had a reputation as a teetotal, born-again Christian which was not entirely accurate, but although he was a moderate drinker there was a strong puritan streak in him which was offended by what he saw as excessive drinking and promiscuity. So began what was called 'the purge of the three Ds' – drink, dames and debt.

Married officers involved in relationships with policewomen found themselves posted to one side of the province, their partner to the other. Anyone caught drunk, on or off duty, faced stern measures, including money fines, demotion or even a return to uniform for detectives. So too did those in financial trouble, a not uncommon situation now that the high overtime earnings of the peak years of the troubles had passed, leaving many young policemen with families to support, big mortgages and hire purchase commitments on flashy cars and other goods. The discipline was handed out by senior officers who presided over tribunals, which quickly became known as the Knock Petty Sessions. Nobody was spared in the purge. After a young policewoman, confronted with her own behaviour, made allegations about a senior officer being involved with a female civil servant, the officer, a close personal friend of Hermon, resigned shortly afterwards. The civil servant was transferred.

The 'three Ds' were not the only grounds for discipline or dismissal. On 29 May, when a group of councillors from Dublin visited Craigavon, a crowd of Loyalist protestors gathered outside the Town Hall in Portadown while they were having lunch. One of the placard-holders was Sergeant Robert Dodds, an RUC officer with twenty-eight years' service. When other officers called to keep order recognized him, a disciplinary investigation was begun but in November, before it was even concluded, Dodds was suspended from duty after taking part in illegal vigilante patrols.

At his disciplinary hearing, Dodds, who had become involved with Paisley's Free Presbyterian Church and Democratic Unionist Party, was demoted to constable and transferred, but he described the penalty as 'savage' and resigned from the force. By the time the demotion was confirmed after an appeal to the Northern Ireland Secretary of State, Dodds had won a seat on the council. The case was important because it was meant as a clear signal from Hermon that the RUC was to be strictly impartial between the two political traditions and that even the faintest vestiges of any special relationship with the Protestant community would not be tolerated.

The discipline drive electrified the force and before long virtually every station was buzzing with rumours that Hermon had made dawn raids on front-line stations and found entire watches asleep on duty. He was reputed, in stories that lost nothing in the retelling, to have found car drivers drunk, sentries asleep and to have torn strips off senior officers during unannounced day and night inspections all over Northern Ireland, 'I'd rather face the IRA any day than Hermon on an inspection,' said one officer. A persistent story in this vein, traced back by one of his staff officers, turned out to be impossible, for the chief had been at a conference in Scotland at the alleged time. When he went into hospital for a minor operation at the end of 1980, the force wags put it about that Hermon had been for a walk on Lough Neagh, when a speedboat hit him.

As one of the principal architects of 'The Way Ahead', Hermon followed the main trail he had marked out and helped blaze with Newman. Although they were colleagues who exchanged mutual public respect, the two men were never close, professionally or personally, and as soon as Newman departed Hermon moved swiftly to reshape the force as he wanted it. In his first year he put in hand a review of virtually every area of the force's activities 'with the aim of achieving more effective prevention and detection of crime'. Many felt at the time that some of this activity was unnecessary, that he was merely trying to 'de-Newmanize' the RUC and stamp his own personal mark reflecting his detached relationship with Newman, but time showed that Hermon was actually shaping his resources for the battles he had already planned.

A major study on public order tactics and organization was set up and the Special Patrol Group was disbanded in favour of Divisional Mobile Support Units which would rove province-wide and become the backbone of the RUC's capability. Most significantly, Hermon set about breaking up the force within a force that he believed the CID and Special Branch constituted. Under a policy of what was called 'cross-fertilization' some detectives returned to uniform operational duties, while CID men without Speical Branch experience moved into key jobs there. Officers considered to be 'Hermonites' were slipped into key areas. The veteran head of the Special Branch was moved to handle the Complaints and Discipline department when he explained his failure to keep Hermon informed about a sensitive security operation by saying: 'Need to know goes up as well as down, Sir.'

There was a new policy in dealing with the media, another area where Hermon had his own ideas. Unlike Newman, who was at ease with journalists and adept at steering them, Hermon suspected the way that radio, television and newspapers worked. He was particularly wary of pre-recorded radio and television interviews for he feared comments could be edited and broadcast out of the intended context. One night, during a social encounter, he astonished a group of newsmen by suggesting to a radio journalist that instead of reporting the routine round of incidents, he should instead broadcast bulletins describing how normal life was. He therefore declined most requests for interviews and preferred to see as few police spokesmen on television as possible.

His first order was to forbid police from disclosing the religion of terrorist victims, ostensibly because this was fuelling tit-for-tat retaliations. The decision was unrealistic, given that that most Ulster citizens can be safely labelled by religion because of their name or address, given the rigid sectarian geography. The policy also underestimated the competence of journalists.

Later the Press Office was incorporated into the Force Control and Information Centre at Knock and carefully prepared formal statements became the main avenue of communication. Sometimes these were delivered to camera by a uniformed chief superintendent who had been designated the official police spokesman. Although there was the minimum of disclosure, usually for compelling security or legal reasons, the RUC retained a high degree of credibility and there was none of the 'black propaganda' activity that had disfigured the army's reputation. But as a result of this policy of news management, the journalists quickly renamed it the 'force control *of* information centre'.

In the early days of his period as chief, the obsession with the media was a constant theme. In 1981 he brought in Joe Mounsey, an assistant chief constable from the Lancashire constabulary, to look at how unauthorized stories about the campaign against the terrorists were reaching the newspapers and to advise on ways to stop the leaks. Mounsey, the detective credited with originally solving the notorious Moors murders in Manchester twenty years earlier, spent nine months on the task, finally preparing confidential guidelines for keeping the media at arm's length. But the morning after they were circulated to each officer throughout the RUC, they were published almost verbatim as a front-page splash in one of the Belfast newspapers.

Hermon's honeymoon period effectively ended in December when a simmering dispute at the Maze prison which had flared into a Provisional IRA hunger strike threatened to provoke serious violence. About the same time a historic new era in Anglo-Irish relations began when Margaret Thatcher flew into Dublin for a top-level meeting with the leader of the Irish government, Charles Haughey. The repercussions of both these events were the twin themes of the rest of Hermon's time as chief constable and tested the men and women of the RUC as never before.

On 8 December Margaret Thatcher, her Foreign Secretary Lord Carrington, Chancellor of the Exchequer Geoffrey Howe and Northern Ireland Secretary Humphrey Atkins, together with a group of senior officials, flew into the Irish Republic. It was the highest-powered British delegation to travel there in the fifty-eight years since the Irish state was established. In Dublin Castle, where the irony that it was once the seat of British power in Ireland was not lost on either side, there were five hours of talks with Charles Haughey and two of his senior ministers, Brian Lenihan and Michael O'Kennedy. For an eighty-minute session the two prime ministers talked alone, with only their official note-takers present.

At an earlier meeting, on 21 May, in Downing Street, Haughey had presented Thatcher with a Georgian silver teapot and told her that politicians are remembered by history for solving the long-running historical problems, like Ireland, not for reducing the rate of inflation or bringing down the numbers of unemployment. It was an effort to stir her imagination and capture her interest to tackle what he saw as overdue unfinished business between the two nations.

The ploy seemed to have worked, for at the end of the Dublin Castle meeting both sides endorsed a communique which Haughey immediately hailed as 'an historic breakthrough'. It spoke of the economic, social and political interests of Britain and Ireland being 'inextricably linked' and revealed that the two leaders had commissioned a series of joint studies to review 'the totality of relationships within these islands'.

The new, constructive Anglo-Irish atmosphere was further boosted ten days later, on the evening of 18 December, when seven Provisional IRA prisoners at the Maze called off a hunger strike after fifty-three days, with one of them at the point of death. The strike had been pushing up tension in both parts of Ireland and Haughey had pressed Thatcher on the issue. The Dublin Castle communique had spoken of their joint hopes of resolving it.

The Maze prison occupies 133 acres on a wartime aerodrome ten miles west of Belfast. Its two-mile-long concrete perimeter wall with watchtowers and searchlights encloses eight, single-storey, H-shaped cell blocks and a group of Second World War prisoner-of-war style compounds with Nissen huts, which house a group of arguably the most ruthless, remorseless and experienced terrorists in the world.

On a typical day in 1980 there were 2,200 inmates: 365 of them had been convicted of murder; 215 of attempted murder or manslaughter; 125 had wounded or assaulted someone; 502 had been captured in possession of firearms or explosives; 2 had committed violence against the person; 58 were sexual offenders; 234 burglars; 305 robbers; 148 had carried out frauds or theft; 101 malicious damage; 41 motoring offences; and the other 100-odd a variety of other crimes. By affiliation they were almost equally Republican or Loyalist in number, testimony to the impartiality of the RUC, which had been responsible for arresting them and providing the evidence to convict them in the courts. All claimed they had carried out their crimes for political reasons.

The hunger strike had its origins in the 1976 decision by Merlyn Rees to end the distinction between those convicted of serious terrorist offences, who claimed political motivation, and what Northern Ireland Office officials called the 'ordinary decent criminals' or 'ODCs'. The distinction, known as special category status, had been conceded by William Whitelaw four years earlier in the face of a similar hunger strike, while he was angling for the bigger prize of a Provisional ceasefire.

Rees was implementing advice in Lord Gardiner's 1975 report, which said that special category prisoners were more likely to emerge with an increased commitment to terrorism than as reformed citizens. The RUC shared his concern, for senior officers regarded the Maze as 'a university of terrorism'. Rees himself said that the aimless existence followed by the prisoners, who lived in the guarded communal compounds, where they wore their own clothes (often pseudo-military uniform) and did no work, was an inadequate preparation for a return to normal living. So prisoners convicted of an offence committed after 1 March 1976 were denied special category status when they were imprisoned.

The first person affected by the new penal policy was Kieran Pius Nugent, an unemployed eighteen-year-old from the Lower Falls in Belfast, who was chased and captured by soldiers after hijacking a plumber's van on 12 March. He came up for trial in September and was sentenced to three years. When he reached the new H-blocks in the Maze prison and refused to wear prison uniform, the blanket protest was born. But outside the Maze it attracted only indifference from all but the prisoners' families and the most committed Provisional supporters.

In 1978, in an escalation of their campaign, the prisoners began what became known as the dirty protest. Instead of using their chamber pots, they urinated and excreted on the floors of their cells, using cubes of sponge torn free from their mattresses or strips of blanket to smear the mixture on the walls. The prison officers called the 300 or so prisoners involved 'the shitters'.

This development engendered widespread disgust among even some Provo sympathizers and with all their propaganda efforts failing to make the issue a major one, the prisoners' morale hit rock-bottom. They turned their frustrations on their comrades outside. Inspired by Irish history – twelve hunger strikers had died this century demanding political status – and the 1972 example, the prisoners' demand to start an all-out hunger strike became strident. The new, young, northern-dominated leadership of the Provisional IRA, who would have to back it, were distinctly uneasy. They wanted a way out, a face-saver, for they calculated that Margaret Thatcher, the iron lady, would not easily cave in. They were sensitive to the prevailing mood at Westminster where even Whitelaw had since disowned the concept of political status, telling the House of Commons how bitterly he regretted the mistake of his 1972 concession.

But then, just when the Provos needed him most, a lifeboatman bobbed up. In August 1978, with their morale at its lowest, the recently appointed Cardinal, Tomas O'Fiaich, the Catholic Primate of all Ireland, a South Armagh man of sturdy Republican views, visited the H-blocks at the Maze to see conditions for himself. He was nauseated and afterwards, ignoring the fact that the conditions were self-inflicted, described them as being like the slums of Calcutta. His widely publicized remarks caused the British government international embarrassment and when he suggested opening talks to try to resolve the deadlock, the British ministers at Stormont Castle discreetly welcomed the approach.

O'Fiaich enlisted the Bishop of Derry, Dr Edward Daly, to join him and by September 1980, acting on humanitarian and pastoral grounds, there had been five main meetings about the problem, but no progress. The Provisional leadership urged the prisoners to give the churchmen time but various concessions, such as easier compassionate parole and more letters, parcels and visits, offered through them were rejected, one by one.

The British government line hardened, bolstered by a European Human Rights Commission decision that there was no basis for the political status demand. While they were prepared to ease the regime inside the prison, there would be no movement on the central issue that crime was somehow different because the criminal claimed political motivation. Attacks on prison staff, including the murder of Albert Myles, deputy governor of the prison, in November 1978 and the deaths of five prison officers in little over four weeks in November–December 1979, contributed to the deadlock. In all, the Provos murdered eighteen prison staff, including one woman.

By the early autumn of 1980 the Provisional leadership decided that it could not resist the prisoners' pressure any longer and reluctantly it sanctioned a hunger strike to begin from breakfast time on 27 October. The churchmen decided on a final effort to avert the strike and on 23 October they met Humphrey Atkins in London. He made a new offer. The prisoners would be allowed to wear their own clothes, rather than prison uniform. It was not enough. That Sunday night the seven prisoners dined on steak and onion pie, baked beans, fruit, tea, bread and margarine, and the following morning refused breakfast. The hunger strike was on.

The Provisionals' increasingly effective international propaganda machine was trundled out in their support. Former 'blanketmen', veterans of the protest in the H-blocks, who had served their sentences, were despatched to London, Paris, Amsterdam and the United States to whip up support. A *Pravda* correspondent was briefed and wrote a sympathetic article. The Catholic newspapers were filled with solidarity advertisements. Every night in Belfast and throughout Ulster there were torchlight processions, car cavalcades and prayer vigils. (The RUC put the figure at more than 500 in the period.) It was the biggest groundswell of support the Provisionals had ever mustered. But the marches were not without their embarrassments. One chilly night a symbolic blanketman was being warmed with frequent nips of whiskey. But they were clearly too stimulating, for after a time he began flashing at some of the marching ladies and had to be hustled away by Provo stewards.

The RUC and the British government were privately dismayed by the level of Catholic support and apprehensive about the reaction to the death of one of the terrorists. Despite the overall reduction in the level of violence the situation was still far from normal. Shortly after the start of the strike a woman UDR member, out shopping in Strabane, was shot in the back and seriously wounded. A soldier was shot dead in the grounds of Altnagelvin hospital in Londonderry while waiting for a colleague who was visiting his wife and newborn baby. Three undercover soldiers operating in South Armagh slowed down and waved a following car past them. A few hundred yards further on the car was blown to pieces in a 600 lb explosion which blew a six-feet-deep crater in the road. The driver, an innocent local business-man, died instantly. Another civilian died by mistake, this time in Belfast, when he was gunned down outside the bank where he worked: he was driving a new car that had previously belonged to a member of the police reserve.

Intelligence indicated that Provisional IRA activity was continuing. In the preceding months a series of large explosives hauls by the Garda, from hiding places across the border, indicated to the RUC preparations for what would be an inevitable attempt at reprisals if any of the hunger strikers died. 'We could have a dozen policemen dead by Christmas,' said one worried senior officer, reflecting the common judgement at that time.

One Special Branch threat assessment, recognizing the ever present potential for widespread tit-for-tat killings, even discussed what it called semi-civil war. There was plenty of evidence of Loyalist terrorism. In the previous months Loyalist terrorists had killed four people closely associated with the prison protest: John Turnley, Miriam Daly, Ronnie Bunting and Noel Lyttle; and two Loyalist bombers had blown themselves up in premature explosions, one at a club in north Belfast, the other at a garage in the east of the city. The RUC also wanted to capture a gang suspected of petrol-bombing a Catholic home in the city where four sleeping children had been lucky to survive although they were severely burned.

Everyone in the RUC, from Hermon down, knew that it was the first serious test of the 'Ulsterization' policy and how high the stakes were. If the RUC failed it would be a setback of incalculable propor-tions for government policy, the force and the community. But whatever his private worries or doubts, the public Hermon was cool-headed, calm and reassuring. 'The only time my pulse rate goes up is when I ride my exercise bike every morning,' he told one visitor.

Nevertheless, in mid-December, as the climax of the strike drew near, the RUC began to prepare for the anticipated onslaught. The round of Christmas parties was cancelled and traffic police were issued with riot kit and reassigned from the planned breathalyser blitz on drunken drivers.

In the event Hermon's pulse rate remained untested. Suddenly on the afternoon of 18 December there was a serious deterioration in the condition of Sean McKenna, serving twenty-five years for two attempted murders and other offences. At 4.30 pm a senior medical consultant decided to move him to the heavily guarded military hospital at Musgrave Park. By 6 pm he was on his way down the M1 motorway to Belfast in an ambulance escorted by a single police Landrover. When he left, the other prisoners held a fifty-six minute meeting to discuss a document outlining the government's proposals for a new prison regime which had been submitted to them. After the meeting, their spokesman, Brendan Hughes, serving twenty-one years for a series of offences including possession of firearms and explosives, asked to see the prison governor. 'As far as we're concerned the hunger strike is over,' he said. It was recorded in the prison log at 7.46 pm on day 53 and within an hour McKenna was receiving medical treatment and the others had been served scrambled eggs and tea. As the news was flashed from the prison, the tension in the community rapidly reduced.

Meanwhile, the new London–Dublin intimacy aroused Unionist opinion in Northern Ireland and there were widespread suspicions that Haughey, who was regarded as an active fellow-traveller despite the improved security co-operation with the RUC that he delivered, had been able to engineer a settlement of the hunger strike on unpublicized terms favourable to the Provisionals. As ever, the loudest protests were made by Paisley, who interpreted the new accord to mean that Thatcher and Haughey had secretly agreed to hand Northern Ireland over to the Irish Republic. He ranted about the beginning of British disengagement and the dire consequences that would ensue. On 19 December, the morning after the end of the hunger strike, he met Thatcher at her room in the House of Commons. Still elated by the settlement of the Maze issue on her own terms, she interrupted his lengthy harangue with an angry rejection of all his accusations of sell-out. The scheduled one-hour meeting was cut short after half that time.

By the end of the year, despite the potential for setback, the

'Ulsterization' policy, with Hermon's added flourishes, was well on target. Hermon and the new GOC, Lt-Gen. Sir Richard Lawson, who held the DSO for heroism in the Congo and had set himself the private goal of getting the troops off the streets and into their barracks, had forged a close personal relationship and developed police-army relations to a new high. One fine day during the summer they had been seen at Portrush, County Antrim, walking along the beach together, eating ice-cream cones.

Throughout the year army khaki had been progressively replaced by RUC green in all but the province's hardest areas of Belfast, Londonderry, South Armagh, East Tyrone and the Fermanagh border. Two thousand soldiers had been withdrawn from Northern Ireland to resume their NATO commitment in West Germany, reducing the army force level to 11,000, half what it was at its 1972 peak, and it was the locally recruited Ulster Defence Regiment which now, increasingly, provided military support when the RUC asked for it.

In August, for the first time since 1969, the RUC had tackled rioters in Belfast, Londonderry, Dungannon and Newry, during the internment anniversary disturbances, and had not needed to call on the army back-up. It was a clear affirmation of the RUC's increasing capacity to cope with the task of maintaining law and order and notably boosted confidence inside the force, banishing the unease Newman had to counter earlier.

In two other significant steps that autumn the RUC relieved the RAF regiment of its duties at the passenger checkpoint at Belfast's Aldergrove airport and one of the army's three brigade headquarters was withdrawn from Portadown, achieving another significant reduction in the army's role. Shortly before Christmas a company of the Royal Scots Dragoon Guards, comprising a hundred men, abandoned the most symbolic of the army's Belfast bases, the former Grand Central Hotel, and handed responsibility for security in the centre of Belfast over to the RUC. At one time two battalions, more than 1,000 men, had been based there to patrol and protect the heart of the city.

Although the death toll since 1969 reached the 2,000 mark in January 1980, when three UDR soldiers were killed in a landmine explosion near Castlewellan, County Down, the total deaths attributable to terrorist violence in 1980 amounted to 76, a decrease of 37 on the previous year. Bombings went down from 422 to 280 and there were fewer shooting incidents, 642 compared to 728.

There were nine RUC casualties. Only three days after Hermon took control, Reserve Constable Robert Crilly was gunned down in the garage he operated in the border village of Newtownbutler, County Fermanagh. Nine days later Reserve Constable William Purse was shot dead while he was on duty outside Seaview football ground in Belfast. On 11 February two officers, Constable Winston Howe and Constable Joseph Rose, died when a landmine blew up under their Landrover while they were patrolling near Lisnaskea, County Fermanagh.

Reserve Constable Bernard Montgomery was at his civilian workplace, a factory in Ligoniel, North Belfast, when he was approached by two men who shot him dead. Constable William Magill, a member of a patrol investigating a burglary at a library in Stewartstown Road, West Belfast, died instantly when ambushed by gunmen armed with an M60 heavy automatic machine gun.

On 11 April Reserve Constable Frederick Wilson, an employee of the Northern Ireland Housing Executive, was shot dead while walking to work in central Belfast by a gunman who was the pillion passenger on a motorcycle. Reserve Constable William Allen disappeared on 31 August while operating his milk round near Newtownhamilton, County Armagh. Although he was murdered soon afterwards, his body was not discovered for twelve days. The ninth victim was also a Reserve Constable. On 23 September Thomas Johnston had come off duty at 11 pm and returned home from the RUC station in Rosslea, County Fermanagh, when he was ambushed as he opened his garage door. He died from multiple gunshot wounds.

It was only by the cruel standards of Northern Ireland that there was any comfort in the analysis that it was the least violent year for a decade. At its end, one of the mandarins in Stormont Castle, who advised the government on security policy, summed up the situation: 'I don't want to fall into the trap of saying we're winning but there is good reason to be pleased at what the police and army have achieved. However, you can't tell a widow that statistically violence is reducing. She's only got one husband and she's lost him.'

Over New Year 1981 Eugene Simons and his wife were invited to a party at Castlewellan, County Down. As arranged, they stayed the night. Early next morning he went out, allegedly to get some milk, and was never seen alive again. A priest received anonymous telephone calls that his body had been dumped in a reservoir in the Mourne Mountains but his decomposed body was not actually found until over three years later, in May 1984. He had been buried in an unmarked grave, some fifty miles away, in a bog near Dundalk, in the Irish Republic, with a bullet wound in his skull. He was conclusively identified only by dental records and a family heirloom, a small engraved crucifix.

Although Simons had been murdered by the Provisional IRA as an informer soon after his disappearance, they had kept unusually quiet about it. There was not the standard statement cataloguing the details of his apparent betrayal as a warning to others; no details of internal police arrangements about how he kept in touch, to embarrass them. Instead he vanished without trace, as if to close the book on a sensitive chapter best forgotten.

Two months earlier Peter Valente had been murdered in similarly confusing circumstances. He disappeared on the afternoon of 14 November. Early the next morning his body was found sprawled in an alleyway at the Highfield Estate in North Belfast, a favourite dumping ground for Loyalist sectarian assassins. The Provos made great public play of the likely culpability of Loyalists. Valente was portrayed as an H-block sympathizer and activist, with a brother in the Maze 'on the blanket'. 'The UDA are opposed to political status and believe that by killing Catholics they can prevent the political prisoners' struggle from succeeding,' said an official statement from Sinn Fein, the Provisional IRA's political mouthpiece.

The RUC issued a cautious, factual statement which was largely overlooked. In their view, it said, Valente had not been shot by Loyalists. They believed he had been murdered elsewhere and dumped. They did not disclose all they knew, especially that when the body was found there was a crisp £20 note carefully folded up in his shirt pocket. In the unwritten protocol of IRA–RUC relationships, the money – 'thirty pieces of silver' one detective called it – was an unmistakable pointer to the true motive for his death. Valente too was an informer.

There were two more killings in the sequence. On 21 January the hooded, bound body of Maurice Gilvary was dumped on a border road in South Armagh. The IRA said that although it was 'extremely reluctant', it had killed him for 'endangering the Republican Army and undermining the struggle'. Twenty-four-year-old Gilvary came from the Ardoyne area of north Belfast. A month afterwards Patrick Trainor, another informer, suffered the same fate. On the evening of 24 February he was pushed out of a London-type black taxi on the

Glen Road in West Belfast and shot dead from a second car which pulled alongside him. Later, a statement from the Provisional IRA claimed he had been an informer for five years, earning between £10 and £70 a time, depending on the value of his information to the security forces.

Although all four men died from Provisional IRA bullets, they were in fact the victims of what a senior RUC officer described as 'an extraordinary and unique piece of treachery' by a member of the RUC Reserve. The officer concerned, who lived in Carrickfergus, was attached to the elite Bronze section of the Special Patrol Group, based at Musgrave Street station in the centre of Belfast. It played a crucial role in anti-terrorist work, backing up undercover officers on dangerous surveillance duties, making dawn swoops to arrest suspects or seize arms dumps and lying in wait for terrorists when informers provided tip-offs about planned attacks.

The officer was captivated by the danger and intrigue, and nurtured an ambition to join the Special Branch. He was advised repeatedly that he was not eligible: only full-time members of the force could join and then only by invitation after an exhaustive security check and selection procedure. But the officer, ignoring this reality, set out to persuade his superiors that they were wrong, that he was able to do this difficult job. He thought that if he associated with Sinn Fein members, through them he would get to know IRA men who would provide him with information that would impress his authorities, who would then realize his value to the Special Branch.

During the spring and summer of 1979 he made repeatedly clumsy efforts to cultivate Provisional IRA sources. However, his associations brought him to the notice of the Special Branch, who photographed him with known IRA men at several locations. He was arrested on 26 October 1979. In his possession the RUC found a list of police addresses and private car numbers, including those of several senior Special Branch officers. During interrogation he admitted that the Provisionals had turned him and that he had received substantial sums of money for his information. The list was for handing over that very day. On 7 December 1979, after pressure from senior RUC officers, the Attorney General consented to no prosecution being mounted. The trial would have disclosed too many sensitive and embarrassing details of the war of the informers. The officer was dismissed from the RUC and ordered to leave Northern Ireland, largely for his own safety from the Provos. The police managed to salvage something from the wreckage. One of the policeman's contacts was Peter Valente and the Special Branch managed to 'turn' him to work for them, and for nearly a year he provided a stream of information.

On the night of 20 October 1980 RUC officers with sledgehammers broke down the door of a house in West Belfast and led an armed assault because they believed terrorists had taken it over to mount an attack on the security forces. Whether they were too early or the attack had been aborted is not clear. But there were no terrorists inside, only a very frightened family. The Provisional IRA began investigations into the obvious leak and Peter Valente came under suspicion. He was followed by the Provos to check on his activities. During this time they observed him at a hotel on the outskirts of Belfast meeting two men, one of whom wore a poppy. To the watching IRA that was the give-away which sealed his fate. Republicans like Valente did not mark Remembrance Sunday. Policemen did.

During his subsequent interrogation Valente filled in the missing pieces of the Provisionals' jigsaw and triggered off a chain reaction that had its origins in the policeman's treachery. Maurice Gilvary was identified as the source of the leak that had led to the SAS killing three IRA bombers in 1978 as they planted bombs in a telephone engineering complex at Ballysillan. Simons had given away explosives dumps in County Down which led to the arrest of several bomb teams as the explosives were collected and ferried into Belfast for use against targets there. Trainor had been another link in the police chain which allowed them to monitor Provisional IRA activities in the city. But for both sides in the remorseless war the affair was only a temporary setback.

On the evening of 9 January 1981 a group of INLA terrorists gathered at a house in the Markets area of Belfast and collected three guns. One of them hijacked a car in which they cruised at random around parts of south Belfast and the city centre, looking for members of the security forces to attack. In Bradbury Place they spotted two policemen on patrol but before they could get into a suitable position to ambush them, the officers crossed the road. A short time later they spotted another two RUC men on a routine beat along Great Victoria Street. One of the gunmen got out of the car, walked up behind Reserve Constable Lindsay McDougall and shot him in the head at close quarters. He died in hospital five days later, the first police casualty of 1981.

At breakfast time in 16 January, as the former MP and prominent Republican sympathizer, Mrs Bernadette (Devlin) McAliskey, her husband and three children were getting ready for the day in their home near Coalisland, County Tyrone, a gang of Loyalist gunmen burst in. The parents were gunned down in front of their children and left for dead. But the prompt arrival of a nearby patrol of soldiers from the Parachute Regiment, which had been alerted by the gunfire, undoubtedly saved their lives when medical help was quickly summoned.

In a swift reprisal twelve days later, up to a dozen heavily armed and masked members of the Provisional IRA slipped over an unapproved border crossing from County Monaghan and took members of two families hostage in their homes near the village of Tynan, County Armagh. They commandeered two cars and shortly before 9 pm about eight members of the gang drove up to Tynan Abbey, an eighteenth-century mansion set in the middle of a 900-acre estate. It was the home of Sir Norman Stronge, the former Speaker of the Northern Ireland Parliament, and his son James, a retired Grenadier guardsman, who was a member of the RUC Reserve.

The terrorists blew in the front door of the house with an explosive device and as some of the gang planted incendiary bombs around the building, others shot the two men dead where they had been sitting in the library. The initial explosion was heard throughout the area and as the first of the incendiaries exploded, starting a huge fire which destroyed the house, police officers from the village station arrived at the Abbey in an armoured police car which they pulled across the main gate to block the get-away cars.

Two gunmen then approached the police car and fired repeated bursts from high velocity rifles against it at point-blank range. When they found the bullets would not penetrate the metal or glass, they tried firing into the cracks around the door. The terrifying ordeal of the officers in the car lasted for ten minutes until reinforcements arrived, but during the ensuing gun battle the terrorists escaped across the border.

Despite satisfaction about the effectiveness of the protective measures to the RUC car, subsequent forensic examination showed that the officers inside had had a fortunate escape. As a result an urgent programme was begun to reinforce police cars even more strongly against bullets.

The Stronge killings rekindled the fears of the Protestant border communities and provoked yet another row about the failure of security policy. In an unprecedented snub, Humphrey Atkins was told he would not be welcome at the funerals and he stayed away. Once more cross-border Provisional IRA murder became an issue for the Unionists to deploy against having closer co-operation with the Irish government.

Paisley's response to the killings and the Thatcher-Haughey initiative did not come immediately but when it did, unannounced in the early hours of 9 February, it was a 'show of strength' typical of his flamboyance. Five invited journalists, taken by a circuitous route in cars and then a blacked-out van, found themselves on a cold, dark, windswept County Antrim hillside, from where the yellow lights of Ballymena and Antrim could be seen. Formed up in ranks were 500 men, many clad in balaclava helmets or pseudo-military uniform. One held a union flag, picked out in torchlight. At a whistle blast they came to attention and waved pieces of paper in the air. According to Paisley, these were gun licences.

The men, he claimed, were members of a 'Third Force', which included members of the RUC Reserve and UDR, who would stop at nothing if an attempt was made to hand the Loyalists of Northern Ireland over to those whom they believed to be the enemies of their country. 'Blandishments will not fascinate us, nor will threats intimidate us, for under God are we determined that wheresoever, whensoever and howsoever we shall be called upon to make our exit we shall die as free men,' he orated. When the story broke at breakfast time, Belfast's humourists promptly branded it as the 'Third Farce' and the predictable political slanging match began.

However, as he received first reports of the stunt, Hermon was acutely embarrassed. One of the first questions was how 500 men were able to mobilize at dead of night without the security forces finding out. Paisley's circus had moved in, performed and struck camp without anything untoward being reported to the police headquarters' control, which closely monitors events twenty-four hours a day. Hermon's first enquiry concerned Paisley's two regular armed RUC bodyguards who were supposed to escort him night and day. What had they been doing? That morning they were travelling with Paisley, so two other bodyguards were despatched to replace them. A roadside rendezvous for the transfer was arranged by radio as they were recalled urgently for questioning by their superiors.

As a result of the incident, the regular police bodyguards for VIPs, who frequently became friendly with their charges, were reorganized into a pool to inhibit too close a relationship between the guard and the guarded. They were also given direct instructions to report back any future activity that was clearly as illegal as these midnight manoeuvres.

Paisley's claim that members of the security forces had participated struck right at the heart of Hermon's mission to make the RUC politically impartial and acceptable to the minority community. So, unknown to all but a handful of his most senior colleagues, Hermon ordered a top secret, counter-intelligence operation, reporting directly to him, to monitor and investigate links between members of the force and political and terrorist organizations. The operation was later to become permanent.

Three days before Paisley's demonstration, at 8 am on 6 February, Reserve Constable William Lewis and a colleague, who were on their way to take up guard duty at the RUC sports ground, Newforge, stopped to buy newspapers at a shop in Balmoral Avenue, Belfast. As they came out, gunmen opened fire from behind a hedge. Lewis died instantly. The other officer was seriously wounded. (On the fifth anniversary of the attack Mrs Sandra Lewis with her teenage son and daughter went to the scene and laid a wreath. 'The last five years have been sheer hell,' she said.) Two days later another Reserve Constable, Alexander Scott, was shot dead outside his wife's grocery shop at My Lady's Road in East Belfast.

Within days of his mountainside manoeuvres Paisley was embarrassing the security forces again. In the House of Commons on 12 February he made allegations that on the night of the Stronge killings an army helicopter had been unable to pursue the terrorists for lack of fuel and that an army patrol, which should have been guarding Tynan Abbey, was instead being wined and dined at a nearby house. Humphrey Atkins, at the despatch box, vehemently denied the charges and Paisley called him a 'liar', earning a five-day suspension from the chamber.

The next evening at Omagh, County Tyrone, Paisley set out on the 'Carson trail', a series of eleven rallies around the province, modelled on a similar campaign by Sir Edward (later Lord) Carson during the Home Rule crisis, when he had toured in an open landau with an escort of farmers on horses. But despite all his efforts to whip up a reaction, Paisley's trail was marked by small crowds even at the final demonstration beside Lord Carson's statue in front of the Parliament Buildings at Stormont on 28 March.

The growing Loyalist frustration with Hermon and the RUC spilled into violence on 3 April during renewed midnight manoeuvres by 1,000 men in three locations. When a police patrol went to the scene of one demonstration in Omagh, they were attacked and forced to fire warning shots in the air after one Landrover was overturned and another pushed into a ditch. It was a grim omen of worse to come, but there was a more immediate crisis already at boiling point.

When the prisoners in the Maze studied the document they had been given at the climax of the December hunger strike, there was general agreement that it did not come anywhere near the central demand for political status. Their leader, twenty-seven-year-old Bobby Sands, serving fourteen years after being caught with a firearm in October 1976 during a bombing attack on a Belfast furniture warehouse, was highly critical of the previous hunger strikers, who caved in, he believed, at the very moment when they had the best chance of winning their demands.

The first sign of trouble came on 24 January 1981 when the prisoners accused the government of reneging on the December agreement and issued a threat to resume the death fast. Three days later ninety-six prisoners smashed up the new furniture that had been placed in their cells and resumed the dirty protest. Danny Morrison, one of the emerging breed of young, streetwise Provo leaders, said: 'The Brits had the prisoners on the floor where they wanted them, but then they insisted on putting the boot in as well.'

Sands renounced his position as leader and decided to front the new hunger strike himself, with other prisoners following at weekly intervals so that as they reached the point of death in rotation they could keep the pressure on for concessions. When it was announced on 5 February, the British government maintained its position and from the outset it was clear that at least Sands would have to die before either side moved. When he began fasting on 1 March, he wrote in his diary: 'I am standing on the threshold of another trembling world. May God have mercy on my soul.'

The diary and his writings were quickly rushed out in pamphlet form by the increasingly professional and prolific Sinn Fein publicity department. 'I am but another of those wretched Irishmen born of a risen generation with a deeply rooted and unquenchable desire for freedom,' wrote Sands. He was not a criminal, as the British government insisted. Instead, he was assiduously promoted as being in the image of the great Irish patriots, philosophers and poets, and, as it turned out, politicians.

On the third day of his fast the news was dominated by Mrs Thatcher's visit to Belfast to get a first-hand account of the rising tension in both communities and to reassure the Unionists about their position in the United Kingdon. The new-found rapport with Dublin had significantly cooled after some rash talk by Haughey and one of his ministers about the imminence of a united Ireland. She went nowhere near the hardline Republican areas, where graffiti and elaborate murals, urging support for the hunger strikers, covered every available wall and gable but as her helicopter dropped low over East Belfast on its way into Stormont, two angry Loyalists in a hotel car park stood shaking their fists at it, shouting 'No surrender'.

Thus the sudden death of Frank Maguire, the nationalist MP for Fermanagh–South Tyrone, was largely overshadowed. It was, however, to have important, long-lasting implications. The constituency, centred on Enniskillen, is a deceptive battleground, for surrounding the fish-rich waters of Lough Erne is some of the most picturesque scenery in Ulster. But along the border, which criss-crosses the rolling green hills, the Provisional IRA's terrorist campaign had been waged at its fiercest, consolidating the traditional sectarian divide.

The constant murder of part-time security force members from the UDR and RUC Reserve had forced many of their neighbours to abandon their isolated family farms on the border and flee to the relative safety of Enniskillen. Others stubbornly stayed living in their vulnerable houses, prey for the gunman or booby-trap bomber as they carried out their daily routine, protected only by a handgun and an emergency warning rocket on the house roof. Many of those stalked and killed were only sons, the heirs to the farms that had been in their families for several generations. Some of them were gunned down in terrifying circumstances, driving school buses or milk lorries; a postman was lured to his death with a bogus letter; a schoolteacher was shot in front of his class. The Protestants accused the Provos of genocide.

Although there was a Catholic majority in the seat, it was only winnable if the vote was not split between the various anti-Unionist factions. Noel Maguire, a brother of the former MP, emerged as the agreed candidate after a round of talks. However, the Provisionals suddenly realized what a powerful coup it would be if the agreed candidate was Sands and he won the seat. On the day nominations closed, they put Sands up and then, when it was too late for anyone else to oppose him, they forced Maguire to withdraw his nomination, giving Sands a clear run. Morrison said later that Maguire was subjected to 'intense pressure and moral blackmail'. In fact the Provisionals threatened to smear him publicly as a homosexual.

The various anti-Unionist factions, united mainly by emotion, voted Sands in as their new MP when polling took place on 9 April. At the count next day, on the forty-first day of his fast, he was declared the winner by 1,446 votes over Harry West, his Unionist opponent. Now the Provos did not even have to whip up the story. News teams from all over the world flew into Belfast for the death watch. 'Rt. Hon. Bobby Sands, MP' was hastily painted over the earlier graffiti.

In the Vatican the Pope became interested and called for reports from the Church in Ireland. Three Irish members of the European parliament were allowed to visit Sands, by now holding court in a ward in the Maze prison hospital, but they were unable to find any formula for breaking the deadlock. For three days at the end of April, Ulster-born Father John Magee, one of the Pope's closest aides, shuttled between the prison hospital and Stormont Castle in another vain mediation effort.

Both sides were unbending. Sands would settle for nothing less than full political status. The British government, clearly more sensitive now that they were dealing with an elected MP, stood its ground that political status was not on but that the reforms to the prison regime outlined in the December document remained on the table. They took steps to rush a bill through parliament preventing convicted prisoners from standing for election. The prospect of a succession of hunger strikers fighting by-elections had to be ruled out. So, in the early days of May, with all hopes of compromise exhausted and tension steadily rising in the community, both sides waited for the life in Sands' wasting body to expire. The end came at 1.17 am on 5 May, the sixty-sixth day of the hunger strike. An army chef at the Maze prison won £500 in a sweepstake for correctly predicting the time.

A few minutes later the duty-officer at police headquarters telephoned Hermon, who was asleep in his flat on the first floor. 'Well, you know what to do,' he said. 'I'm going back to sleep.' As ever, Hermon was being deliberately cool under pressure to mask his very real fears of serious sectarian violence.

April had been a discouraging month. While he had been assessing the security implications of the hunger strike and laying plans, nine more people had died. Constable Kenneth Acheson from RUC Bessbrook was among them. On 2 April, soon after 11 pm, as he was driving home after completing his shift, a booby-trapped device attached to his car exploded. Five days later the Provisional IRA claimed responsibility for shooting dead Mrs Joanna Mathers while she was acting as a census enumerator in Londonderry. On 20 April rioting in the city intensified after two youths were killed by a speeding army Landrover.

On 25 April Hermon's fears were all too evident from a hard-hitting statement aimed at the law-abiding majority and the hard men on both sides. Accusing the Loyalist leaders of 'sabre-rattling', he said that paramilitary leaders on the Catholic side were 'deliberately stirring up Roman Catholic fears in an effort to orchestrate tension. We must say, beware, don't fall for this. I say keep it cool and leave this to the extremists who are trying to foster violence. We'll deal with them.'

Two days later another policeman died. A group of officers were clearing roads in West Belfast after a spate of hijacking. As they approached one abandoned lorry, an explosive device went off, killing Constable Gary Martin.

As the violence and tension increased in the final stages of the fast, the entire RUC had been placed on a twelve-hours on, twelve off shift pattern, with all but essential desk-bound officers deployed on the streets. Within minutes of Sands' death the news was flashed under a prearranged code to the fleets of grey Hotspur Landrovers containing the twenty-two Divisional Mobile Support Units, the new cutting edge of the RUC's public order tactics. These units, equipped, armed and trained to deal, often at short notice, with riot and counter-terrorist operations throughout Northern Ireland, deployed to planned locations, particularly along the miles of concrete and corrugated iron 'peace lines' in Belfast that divided the Protestant and Catholic areas – the interfaces as they were called in police jargon.

The situation was the first test of the expanded DMSUs and their new public order strategy, drawn up by a working party of riot-toughened RUC officers, whose manual would later be copied by every British police force. The key to the strategy was distance, to keep rioters at bay and prevent their missiles injuring officers. The armoured Landrovers would be used in waves to break up rioting crowds into smaller groups; they would also push hijacked vehicles aside; the smaller crowds would be further thinned out by officers using Federal riot guns and plastic baton rounds; when the groups were well dispersed, then arrests might be possible. The emphasis was on avoiding standing confrontations, keeping the riots fluid, avoiding injury to officers by keeping them protected in their vehicles and identifying ringleaders for later arrest by photographic and video evidence. Sophisticated cameras, with a capacity for night photography, were introduced and became the basis for subsequent successful prosecutions.

The hunger strikers' funerals, with their inevitable emotional overtones and the Provisionals' desire to use them as armed propaganda, which would rouse Protestant feelings, presented particular policing problems. Careful plans were made for the RUC to take custody of the bodies after death, supervise the completion of formalities, such as identification and post mortems, and prevent funeral processions in mixed areas where trouble was likely.

The army would be in the background to support the police if needed with more men, armoured bulldozers and cranes to clear obstacles and, if necessary in an extreme situation, heavier firepower. The Spearhead battalion had been flown into the province the day before Sands' death, when an army officer had offered an interesting redefinition of the threshold of military aid to the civil power: 'Our job is to deal with the gunmen when hooliganism turns to terrorism.' But Hermon was privately determined that as much as possible the RUC would contain the situation on its own as further proof of its capability and professionalism.

The timing of Sands' death after the last Downtown Radio bulletin of the day at 1 am led police commanders on the ground to hope that it would be 6 am, when the radio came on the air again, before news of the death would spread. But soon after 2 am their hopes were dashed when loudspeaker announcements were made from cars in the hardline Republican areas. The bin-lid bashing began immediately and then the violence erupted. Within twenty-four hours four people had died: a milkman and his son, making their deliveries in Belfast, after rioters stoned their lorry and caused it to crash; an

RUC officer, Constable Philip Ellis, who was shot dead by a sniper while on duty at one of the sectarian interfaces in North Belfast; and a terrorist who blew himself up in a premature explosion.

With only a brief lull for Sands' large funeral to wend its way through West Belfast on 7 May, the violence continued, receiving fresh impetus on 12 May when twenty-five-year-old Francis Hughes, serving life for murder, died after fifty-nine days' fasting. After his body was handed over to the family there was an undignified chase across South Belfast as the police moved to stop a procession through West Belfast and insisted the hearse go directly to Bellaghy, the dead man's home village.

Two days later Constable Samuel Vallely died in hospital after a rocket attack on his Landrover while it was on patrol in West Belfast. On 19 May five British soldiers were killed in a landmine attack on their vehicle near Newry. On 21 May two more hunger strikers died in quick succession: Raymond McCreesh, twenty-four, serving fourteen years for attempted murder, and Patsy O'Hara, twenty-three, serving eight years for possessing a hand grenade, had both been fasting for sixty-one days. The post-mortem report on McCreesh said that his weight had fallen from ten stones to seven; the cause of death was formally stated as 'self-starvation with terminal bronchopneumonia'.

The cycle of violence continued, flaring to renewed intensity as each hunger striker died. The RUC bore the brunt of the trouble, coming under sustained attack from so many petrol, nail and acid bombs that they lost count. The death toll continued to rise. On 27 May Constable Mervyn Robinson was ambushed and shot dead by terrorists while leaving a public house at Whitecross in South Armagh. Four days later Reserve Constable Colin Dunlop was on security duty at the intensive care unit inside Belfast's famous Royal Victoria Hospital when a gunman killed him. Reserve Constable Christopher Kyle was ambushed and seriously wounded in the laneway leading to his home at Mullaghslin, near Omagh, on 17 June and died shortly afterwards in hospital.

Three days later Constable Neal Quinn was off duty, enjoying a lunchtime drink in the Bridge Bar at North Street, Newry, where he had been stationed for many years. He had just put his arm around the shoulder of a companion when two young men wearing motorcycle helmets burst in. One of them held the door ajar while the other opened fire with a silenced revolver. As Quinn ran towards a back door crying: 'No boys, not me, not me,' both fired at him several times. When he fell, the killers rode off on a stolen motorcycle. He was buried a few days later, on the day he was due to have retired from the RUC. His killing marked yet another mournful milestone, for he was the hundredth RUC victim of the troubles.

The hunger strike meanwhile remained deadlocked. Two prisoners had been elected to the Irish parliament earlier in the month when a new government, led by Dr Garrett FitzGerald, had taken office in Dublin. Efforts to break the deadlock over prison conditions continued, with various secret and semi-public initiatives from several quarters amidst growing signs of disillusionment among the families of those queueing up to die. The prisoners themselves were on a moving conveyor and could not see any honourable way off it, for only total victory would vindicate the deaths that had already taken place. When Humphrey Atkins restated the concessions on offer if the strike ended, they dismissed his statement as 'arrogant', and the death of hunger striker Joe McDonnell on 8 July hardened attitudes again and temporarily halted any further moves. There was more vicious rioting when police and troops stormed his funeral in Andersonstown and arrested the Provos' armed and masked 'colour party'.

The sixth hunger striker, twenty-six-year-old Martin Hurson, serving twenty years for possessing explosives, died suddenly on 13 July, after only forty-six days' fast. Moves to break the impasse continued and after high-level inter-governmental contacts between Dublin, Washington and London, the International Red Cross sent a team into the prison. The prisoners called instead for direct negotiations with the British government. Atkins refused.

The families of the hunger strikers were now bitterly divided about the next steps. Some said that the IRA should 'order' the men to halt their death fast and they held a series of angry meetings, often lasting long into the night. One anguished mother brandished a knife at an IRA leader and insisted he call an end to the fast.

Matters took a decisive turn on 31 July when another mother took the situation firmly into her own hands. When Paddy Quinn lapsed into a coma after forty-seven days, she authorized immediate medical intervention to save him. But the deaths went on. A day later twenty-five-year-old Kevin Lynch, serving ten years for firearms offences, died on his seventy-first day without food. Two days later the eighth prisoner, Kieran Doherty, also twenty-five years old, and serving twenty-two years for possessing firearms and explosives, who had earlier won a seat in the Irish parliament, died on the seventy-third day of his fast.

Shortly before lunchtime the same day, two RUC vehicles were patrolling the road from Fecarry to Loughmacrory, near Omagh, when terrorists detonated a landmine under the second vehicle. Constable John Smyth and Constable Andrew Woods lost their lives.

Despite the now open divisions among the families and intensive activity by mediators, the stalemate at the Maze prison continued and there were two more deaths. Tom McElwee, twenty-three, serving twenty years for manslaughter, died on 8 August; he had lasted sixty-two days. Mickey Devine twenty-seven, serving twelve years for firearms offences, died twelve days later after a sixty-day hunger strike. He was the tenth, and as it turned out the last, to die.

On 7 September two police vehicles were patrolling near Cappagh, County Tyrone, the home village of dead hunger striker Martin Hurson. In a carbon copy of the Omagh attack, the second vehicle, an armoured Cortina, was wrecked in a huge explosion which blew the car seventy yards away, killing the two constables inside and leaving a fifty-foot wide, fifteen-foot deep crater in the road. Constables William Evans and Stuart Montgomery were so badly mutilated that they could only be identified by their fingerprints. Evans, twenty years old, had been posted to his station, RUC Pomeroy, a week earlier. Eighteen-year-old Montgomery had only taken up duty an hour earlier and was on his first patrol. Detectives later found a command wire leading to the firing point on high ground 400 yards away but they later had to withdraw murder charges against two men. It was a familiar problem. Two witnesses to the outrage refused to give evidence in court.

A week later James Prior, a successful businessman and farmer, who had held several senior cabinet posts, replaced Humphrey Atkins as Secretary of State. On the evening Prior arrived in Ulster, Reserve Constable John Proctor was visiting his wife and new baby at the Mid-Ulster hospital in Magherafelt. As he returned to his car in the park outside, he was confronted and died instantly from gunshot wounds.

Prior and his new ministerial team, Lord Gowrie and Nicholas Scott, urgently set about ending the hunger strike. The disillusionment among the families was now the critical factor and the futility of further deaths was bravely pointed out to them by Father Denis Faul, who played a key role in having the fast ended on 3 October. In the final deal, the prisoners received not a single concession beyond what was already on offer in the December document.

It was ironic, therefore, that the real beneficiaries of the terrible and unique sacrifice would turn out not to be the prisoners, but the leadership outside the prison, who had for so long opposed the hunger strike. Sands' election victory had in fact laid the foundations for the Provisionals to move into politics. Morrison later defined their strategy in the chilling phrase: 'Going forward to take power with an Armalite in one hand and a ballot paper in the other.' The policy would dominate the rest of the decade.

The RUC had lost three more officers before the strike was ended. On 18 September Reserve Constable Silas Lyttle was walking the short distance between his home and his drapery shop in the village of Ballygawley, County Tyrone, when he was gunned down. He was rushed to hospital, seriously wounded, where he died on 17 November. At 11 pm on 26 September, Constable George Stewart was off duty, having a drink in a public house at Killough, County Down, when two hooded gunmen entered the bar and opened fire, fatally wounding him. Two days later Constable Alexander Beck was killed in a Landrover which came under rocket attack in West Belfast.

Apart from ten of the twenty-three hunger strikers, another sixty-seven people died in the associated violence: fifteen policemen, fifteen soldiers and thirty-seven civilians. More than 750 people were injured. The RUC dealt with 1,205 Republican demonstrations attended by an estimated 355,000 people. The whole episode entailed some two million hours of police duty at a cost of £9 million. But the end of the hunger strike brought only a temporary respite for the RUC. Within a few weeks the IRA plunged Northern Ireland into fresh turmoil.

Early in 1981 Paisley visited Hermon at police headquarters. Their relationship had been one of increasing mutual distrust since the events at Ballymena in May 1977. In February, preaching at his Martyrs' Memorial Church in Belfast, the week after the mountain parade, he had criticized the chief constable for giving orders 'to take senior policemen off investigations into IRA crimes and putting them to the business of calling to decent Protestant homes. I know an inspector – it is my business to know these things – who was taken off the investigation into the murder of his colleague, shot in the back a few days ago – that dear man, who so often sat in this church rejoicing in the Gospel – and was ordered to take part in the harassment of Protestants.'

More recently, in March, Paisley had publicly abused the chief for boarding a bus to apologize to the Lord Mayors of Belfast and Dublin and a group of councillors on a goodwill visit, after a mob led by Paisley attacked them in the foyer of the Europa hotel. In Paisley's current demonology Hermon was ranked third behind the prime minister and Northern Ireland Secretary as 'an enemy of Ulster'. During the meeting Paisley spoke of his position as leader of one million Protestants, 'the majority', as he was fond of calling them. He told Hermon that at the end of the day he would have to do what the Protestants told him. 'My majority is the people who abide by the law,' snapped Hermon.

Throughout his Carson trail and the hunger strikes, Paisley kept up a barrage of criticism of security policy in general and Hermon in particular. He called him a 'paid puppet' and a 'petty little Fuhrer'. There were regular manoeuvres too by the 'Third Force'. At Sixmile-cross, County Tyrone, on 2 July Paisley led a march of 1,000 men, formed up in ranks who responded to military-style commands. 'Shall we allow ourselves to be murdered by the IRA or shall we go out and kill the killers?' he thundered. The presence at his side of Percy Kyle, the father of Reserve Constable Christopher Kyle, who had recently been murdered by the IRA, helped fuel Paisley's claim that members of the UDR and RUC Reserve were involved with his illegal militia. Such allegations were strenuously denied by an angry Hermon, whose secret counter-intelligence operation was now a permanent one. In September Paisley even wrote to the prime minister offering his force to back up the security forces. 'I can assure you that vast numbers of men are now ready and able to come forward to take on this task.'

Paisley's antics deeply embarrassed the Official Unionist Party, who were just as concerned about the violence but confined themselves to uttering what they saw as helpful suggestions to the RUC: shooting petrol bombers, forming an air corps and setting up a network of citizens with CB radios to alert the police to crimes. Their restraint at such a difficult time was crucial in denying Paisley widespread support.

But the Official Unionists' mood suddenly and swiftly changed. On the morning of 14 November three gunmen arrived at the Finaghy community centre in South Belfast. Inside, the Rev. Robert Bradford, the local MP, was holding his regular Saturday morning constituency surgery. His RUC bodyguard and the caretaker were standing outside talking, to escape the noise from a junior disco, when two men in paint-spattered overalls approached. They pulled guns and ordered them to kneel down on the path. The caretaker, Ken Campbell, was then shot dead while other gunmen burst in on the MP. He was hit seven times and died instantly, slumped at his desk. The bodyguard, for whom the caretaker was mistaken, managed to fire three times at the getaway car, but without effect. In a short time a telex message claiming responsibility for the killing was transmitted from the Provisional IRA's Falls Road offices.

The reaction was immediate and angry. Several of the dead politician's colleagues were meeting in Belfast when they heard of the assassination and critical statements were quickly issued. Attacks on two Catholic youths – one died immediately, the other a week later – renewed the ever-present fears of all-out sectarian clashes. With talk of civil war springing from even the most moderate lips, a serious crisis atmosphere quickly developed.

The assassination of one of their own shocked the House of Commons and there was a sombre mood on 16 November as Prior made a formal statement. Paisley interrupted and shouted 'Nonsense', and with two other Democratic Unionist Party MPs began barracking Prior. After shouts of 'Get them out' from now horrified British members, Paisley was ordered to leave. As he did so, he shouted 'Amen'.

The strength of Protestant anger was dangerously evident at Bradford's funeral. When Prior arrived at the church, his police bodyguards had to fight off a crowd shouting 'murderer'. Inside the church he was hissed by the congregation and despite waiting thirty minutes after the service, his bodyguards and other RUC men had to fight to clear a path to get him into his car and away.

Both Unionist parties called a work stoppage on 23 November to protest about the assassination and the level of violence. They held two rival rallies at Belfast City Hall but apart from some scuffling at Paisley's, there was no trouble. That evening, however, Paisley resumed centre-stage when he presided over another 'Third Force' show of strength at Newtownards, County Down, this time with some 6,000 men on parade.

The police were still at full stretch dealing with sporadic street disturbances. On 28 November a group of police officers were on duty at Unity Flats, a notorious sectarian flashpoint. At 12.10, in a carefully planned attack, terrorists detonated a bomb that had been concealed behind a corrugated iron fence. Constable William Coulter took the full force of the blast and was killed. None of the residents in the nearby flats suffered as much as a scratch and detectives concluded they had been tipped off to stay out of range. The local Catholic bishop, Dr William Philbin, said that they shared the murderers' guilt.

The political air was thick with threat and controversy, and both Prior and Hermon realized the dangerous implications of what was increasingly a challenge to the authority of the government and police. Prior had laid down the law a few days earlier when he accused extremists on both sides of fostering a crisis of confidence in Ulster. Reaffirming that 'the rule of law must prevail', Prior said: 'The government understands the anxieties of Protestants and Catholics who are at risk from murdering gunmen. The government shares their anger. The government seeks no confrontation either with the majority or the minority community. But it will respond to any challenge to its authority.'

The police then revealed that after extensive investigations into the activities of the 'Third Force', files on certain people had been sent to the Director of Public Prosecutions and further police enquiries were taking place into Paisley's utterances and his rallies. Hermon even went on television, only his second interview, to ram home the point that no organization would be allowed to usurp the functions of the police or army.

Paisley quickly backed down. In a series of speeches peppered with fresh insults to Hermon, he carefully distanced himself from anything faintly illegal and in a verbose 'Declaration of Intent' couched in archaic, biblical language, he offered the government the use of his private army. Needless to say the offer was not accepted and by the end of the most difficult and dangerous year since 1972, having foiled a pre-Christmas IRA bombing blitz, there was once again such an encouraging measure of public tranquillity that the RUC felt confident enough to throw open the gates each evening and allow cars into Belfast city centre's heavily guarded control zone for the first time in seven years. Given the turmoil of November, it was scarcely believable that December was the first month for ten years in which no violent death occurred.

Looking back on the year, Hermon attributed the avoidance of serious conflict to two factors: the professional skill, courage and dedication of both the police and army; and the good sense of the overwhelming majority of decent people, Catholic and Protestant, who did not become involved in violence nor take the law into their own hands. But, calling for more support from the community to use its eyes and ears to help the police and harry the terrorists, he said: 'The whole fabric of society is threatened by self-appointed armies whose object is to seize power and dictate to the people not only what they should do or not do but whether they should live or die.'

During a question and answer session with the Central Committee of the Police Federation on 18 November, in the tense aftermath of the Bradford assassination, Hermon had been exceedingly frank. He admitted that the RUC was not 'scoring' against the hard-core terrorists. Although almost 918 people had been charged with offences in 1981, it was a significant drop from the 1,308 charged five years earlier. The drop was most noticeable for the most serious offences. Murder charges were down from 131 to 48; of the 95 murders recorded in 1981 only 26 had been cleared. The main reason was a familiar one – lack of evidence.

As a result of intensive, sophisticated undercover surveillance of suspected terrorists and the cultivation of informers, all too often detectives knew the perpetrators of the most vicious crimes. Increasingly they were able to use their information to inhibit or foil planned outrages. But through trained resistance to interrogation or the fear of witnesses, they were frustratingly unable to convert the intelligence into evidence and thus bring charges. The fear among witnesses was now so well established that it was only rarely that offenders even needed to take the extra risk of resorting to open intimidation. When a prison officer was murdered on the steps of a Catholic church, after attending Mass, none of the 600 people in the congregation was even prepared to make statements to the police.

But things were to change. Three nights after the Federation meeting, a water inspector was driving his mini-van through Ardoyne, one of the Provisional IRA strongholds in North Belfast, when he was flagged down by three masked men dressed in khaki-coloured Parka jackets and blue jeans. Ordered out of the van, he was asked for his driving licence and told to keep his eyes down while the van was searched. Moments later he was cleared. 'This is an IRA road block. We know you're a Protestant but we're letting you go on.' The road block was an IRA propaganda stunt, being photographed for the organization's weekly newspaper, *Republican News*.

Nearly an hour later the three men caught the eye of an RUC sergeant in charge of a six-man unit patrolling the hostile area in an armoured Landrover. He ordered his driver to pull in front of them and two were immediately apprehended. The third man, twenty-seven-year-old Christopher Black, ran off down a nearby alley but was quickly captured. In the immediate vicinity the police found three woollen balaclavas, with eye holes in them, dropped in haste. The three men were put into the police Landrover and after a brief stop at the local RUC station, they were taken across the city to Castlereagh. An hour later a scenes of crime officer requested samples of head hair but all three men refused. Next day, Sunday, at lunchtime, after they had refused again, the samples were taken forcibly.

Although Black brazened out his position, that afternoon he was in a state. He had been out of prison only eleven months after serving five years of a ten-year sentence for armed robbery. Now here he was in custody again, faced with serving the five-year balance of his first sentence, under the conditional release provisions, as well as another term for his most recent activities. Even before his arrest there had been growing disenchantment with the Provos and the cause; he had shot to miss during at least one terrorist operation. But he was afraid of some of the more ruthless men in the Provos who would stop at nothing. Only a month earlier Anthony Braniff, another member of his group, had been tortured with lighted cigarettes and then murdered for allegedly giving information to the police. Even families were not safe from them. Hard men, who turned up at a darts match and dance organized to raise money for Braniff's wife and three children, ordered the band not to play and turned guests away.

Black decided that the only way out of his predicament was to do a deal with the police. But that Sunday evening, when he made an offer to turn Queen's evidence in exchange for his own freedom, he was only faintly encouraged. It was the oldest trick in the book and the hard-nosed RUC men, like detectives everywhere, wanted to see how far he was prepared to go. So he made a lengthy statement but, as he later admitted in court, he told the police some lies, as an insurance against a deal falling through. The statement would be used, if he ended up back in the Maze, to prove to his IRA colleagues that he had not squealed. But the policemen evaluating Black's proposition were encouraged and when he refused to see a solicitor, sent by the IRA leaders outside, the prospect of a deal increased.

Next morning there was an urgent conference about the case in both Castlereagh and RUC headquarters. The legal principle of turning Queen's evidence was a well-established one. In suitable circumstances the RUC had used it to good effect in the past and detectives from RUC Tennent Street, who suspected many of Black's known associates of a catalogue of serious terrorist crime, were more than enthusiastic. So senior officers gave the go-ahead for a swift, secret operation. Later that day Black was allowed a meeting with his wife. In the evening after dark, as Black was making a sixty-two-page statement about his IRA career, implicating his former accomplices, an extraordinary convoy stopped outside the Black home in Ballyclare Street. As soldiers and policemen kept watch, everything they owned, except the blinds on the windows, was piled into a furniture van, crewed by a team of police and soldiers, and his wife and four young children were taken into protective custody. They were given temporary accommodation in the married quarters at one of the heavily guarded army barracks on the outskirts of Belfast.

Over the next few days an IRA training camp, over the border in County Donegal, was exposed and the RUC arrested more than forty people on Black's information. The IRA leadership quickly realized that the police had real information. The arrest raids did not take place at dawn, as was almost a tradition; instead they were timed for 10 am. Black disclosed that those on the run, who had slept in safe houses to avoid the dawn swoops, returned home for breakfast at their own firesides. The era of the 'supergrass' had begun.

In the early hours of 4 January 1982, Hermon, newly knighted in the New Year's Honours list, published a letter of rebuke that he had written to Constable Alan Wright, the chairman of the Northern Ireland Police Federation. It was a pre-emptive strike against yet another episode of Paisley mischief-making scheduled to be unveiled at a news conference that morning. The affair had its origins in the meeting of the Federation's central committee on 18 November after Hermon's departure. One of the twenty-two strong committee, all Protestants, one a woman, remembers: 'It was an emotional meeting, feelings were running high. There was concern whether we, as policemen, were doing enough.'

The meeting, in the Federation's newly completed £350,000 office block in the RUC complex at Garnerville in East Belfast, had begun at 10.30 am. After general discussion for an hour, one of the committee proposed a vote of no confidence in the chief constable. Another promptly seconded it but before the vote was taken two members indicated that they would abstain because they had no mandate from the officers they represented. The motion was defeated 10–9. Wright, who had been elected full-time chairman six years earlier, abstained.

At that point, knowing that the chief constable himself was outside the room, waiting to address the meeti..g, another vote on whether or not they should meet him was defeated 14–5. Three of those who had expressed no confidence in him then walked out, refusing to listen to what he had to say. When Hermon came in and sat down, the first person to speak was the man who had proposed the motion, but he did not tell the chief of the vote or its outcome. 'There was a full and frank discussion,' according to one of the committee. 'We were concerned about the recent wave of deaths and trouble. It was questions and answers. There was a lot of soul-searching on both sides.' The session ended after an hour and the meeting broke for lunch.

In the afternoon during a further two-hour discussion, the subject of the 'Third Force' came up at the end. The thrust of the argument was that the B Specials should be reformed under the aegis of the RUC. But only eleven members voted on the issue, throwing the proposal out 9–2. However, before the meeting had even ended, news of the Hermon vote had leaked. During the afternoon a member of the force, widely regarded as having Paisley's ear, had telephoned the Federation office enquiring about the vote. He was told only that it had been defeated.

The call rang alarm bells among some committee members, who realized the serious implications of the way the meeting had developed. They knew their remit embraced only matters of 'welfare and efficiency' and that it was not legitimate to interfere with operational policy. With their customary discretion, however, there was no public disclosure of the proceedings or doubts.

Paisley clearly obtained a full account of the meeting within hours. At the news conference announcing his 'day of action', he made an oblique reference to what he knew. Interpreting the vote to suit his own ends, he said that half the force wanted rid of Hermon because they had lost confidence in him.

There the matter rested until Hermon's letter. He said that the discussion about an additional force was 'manifestly improper and highly damaging to the standing of the RUC'. He criticized what he called 'a defeatist attitude' which 'could only have the effect of undermining morale and giving encouragement to the terrorist objective of de-stabilizing the economy'.

Hermon had been tipped off that Paisley was planning to leak the minutes of the meeting and represent them as further evidence of a lack of confidence in him. So at the same time as Paisley was holding his press conference on 4 January, the Federation committee began what was to be a tense, day-long meeting. It ended in the late afternoon when Alan Wright, the intensely loyal chairman, resigned. He resented what he regarded as disloyalty to the chief, the force and the Federation among some of his colleagues and those who leaked the minutes to Paisley, allowing him to exploit the situation for political advantage. He went on immediate leave and spent the next few days at home saying nothing.

The crisis provoked the rank and file of the force into an appraisal of its role and standing with the community. There was no doubt of its dedication to defeating terrorism, its courage and its increasingly evident impartiality between Catholic and Protestant in protecting and serving the community. A clear consensus emerged that members of the force whose sentiments and criticisms matched word for word those of Paisley were an unrepresentative minority, compromising the reputation and integrity of the RUC. 'It's a fact that those who cry loudest for tough security measures are those with the cushiest jobs,' one constable said at the time. 'The men at the frontline rarely complain.'

By the end of the week two of the seven regions had passed formal motions calling on Wright to reconsider his resignation, and many other officers, jointly and singly, sent similar messages. The Central Committee met again on 9 January to consider Wright's resignation. At the end of another day-long session, Wright withdrew his resignation and then a unanimous vote of confidence was passed.

It was a crucial episode for the RUC and the future of Northern Ireland. 'We faced a stark choice,' recalls one source. 'We had to stand behind Alan Wright and the concept of an impartial force. If Paisley had been able to get us, then next it would have been Sir Jack's skull on a plate and we would have become nothing but a tool of extreme Loyalism.'

The outcome was a clear victory for Hermon but instead of savouring the fact that the Federation had seen off its own extremists, the affair sowed seeds of resentment that were to sprout and flower for years. A few months later, when the subject came up at a dinner for visiting MPs in the GOC's residence at Lisburn, Hermon poured out his scorn. Lawson tried to calm him. 'There's three useless things in this world,' he said. 'A man's nipples, the Pope's balls and a vote of confidence from the Northern Ireland Police Federation.' But Hermon refused to take the point. Within a year he had transferred five of those who voted against him, for 'operational reasons'. He also ordered the Federation to abandon plans to buy and open a social and recreational centre for its members but backed down after pressure from Prior and the threat of court action by the Federation.

There was further public embarrassment for the RUC in a remarkable murder trial that opened in Belfast on 23 February. The judge, Mr Justice Murray, said later that by any standards it was 'a most extraordinary, if not a unique, case'. For the prisoner in the dock was Charlie McCormick, a forty-four-year-old Special Branch detective-sergeant, who denied murdering a fellow police officer and twenty-six other charges, including armed robberies and illegal possession of firearms and explosives. The police officer was Sergeant Joe Campbell, who was shot dead at the gates of the RUC station at Cushendall, County Antrim, on 25 February 1977.

The principal witness was Anthony O'Doherty, a one-time police informer, who had earlier been sentenced to eighteen years for a series of offences. His evidence shed unprecedented public light on that most dangerous area of anti-terrorist police work, the secret transactions between a detective and an informer. McCormick, dressed in a green blazer and grey slacks, sat in the dock, head bowed, taking copious notes, as O'Doherty, a tall, gangly man, dressed in denim jacket and jeans, spent almost five days in the witness box telling his story.

According to O'Doherty, the two men first met in 1969, when he was selling the Republican newspaper, *United Irishman*, during the Sir Roger Casement memorial rally at Murlough Bay, County Antrim. 'I twigged he was a Branch man,' said O'Doherty. 'I noticed my picture being taken by another man.' Two years later he was arrested among the first wave of internees but released a few days later when, he said, he agreed to ring McCormick at Ballymena police station to give him information about terrorist activity.

However, after a wages snatch at a shirt factory he was arrested again and detained, this time for six months, first on the prison ship, *Maidstone*, in Belfast harbour, then at the Maze. McCormick and other

Special Branch officers visited him four or five times during this period, he claimed, seeking what information he had picked up from other inmates. He was released in June 1972. 'Nobody told me to join the Provies but I was told to get in on the Provies scene,' he told the court.

O'Doherty, assigned the designation Agent 294 to protect his identity, then described how he became a professional informer, meeting McCormick, his 'handler', three or four times a week. 'I gave him information about eight or ten landmines, who's who and billets in the Provies. We destroyed billets and gathered up a lot of weapons and explosives.' 'Who do you mean by we?' asked the judge. 'Me and the police,' replied O'Doherty, who disclosed he had been given 'fivers and tenners' for his information, which saved the lives of many soldiers and policemen.

In December 1973 the Provisional IRA kidnapped Ivan Johnston, a Special Branch officer who had recently left the RUC, as he drove a lorry across the border. He was interrogated and tortured, by being manhandled into a bath of scalding hot water, before he was shot and his body dumped close to the border two days later. Under torture, before he was murdered, he named O'Doherty as a police informer.

This led to O'Doherty being 'court-martialled' and sentenced to death by the Provisionals. He told the court of two lucky escapes from their murder squads. At the Four Seasons hotel in Monaghan, in the Irish Republic, he fought off potential abductors and gave himself up to the Irish police, who returned him safely across the border. The second time he was taken away from a public house by armed men, who neglected to search him. 'I knew I wasn't coming back. They took me away for interrogation and then I would say to shoot me. But I was wearing cowboy boots with a gun down them. I got the gun to the driver's ear, then I got away.'

After these episodes he alleged that senior Special Branch officers, including McCormick, provided him with guns for his own protection. The first gun they gave him was a .38 revolver but as they had no suitable bullets he was told not to fire it. 'I told them the gun was no use to me. It would do me more damage than the Provies.' Later he was given a .32 Harrington Richardson, then a .45 revolver, and the police allowed him to keep a hidden Provisional IRA sten gun that he had turned up during an arms search. McCormick then encouraged him to use the guns in fake attacks on a police station, a policeman's house, and police and UDR patrols as a way of 'getting me back into the swing of things with the Provies'.

During this time O'Doherty said that he was on the run, living rough, sleeping in fields and haysheds and different houses to keep ahead of the Provisional IRA hitmen. 'Sergeant McCormick was more sympathetic to me than the rest of the Special Branch. He gave me money, fed me, gave me clothes, anoraks he got from the army.' He even took him home for Christmas. 'We were like brothers at that stage. I was dependent on him and, up to a point, he was dependent on me. He didn't seem to have any other agents working for him.'

Soon after, according to O'Doherty, their relationship took a different turn. 'Charlie had money difficulties. He was living high, he had a mortgage and was parted from his wife.' He allegedly suggested that they carry out a robbery in Cushendall, County Antrim. To steal a car, McCormick provided keys from a master bunch, held at Ballymena police station and gave the informer a wig, a hand grenade, a pistol and a pillowcase for the money, the court was told. It was the first of a series and not all were a success. Once a postmistress and her husband chased them off with a hail of apples and oranges during a raid. At a furniture shop the owner dropped a wad of money on the floor. 'But we both ran out without it. Charlie thought I had lifted the money. I thought he had.'

O'Doherty said the robberies were planned after McCormick milked information from fellow police officers about the movement of money. A favourite target was post offices in Catholic areas because, with the larger families, they could expect a better haul from the family allowance money. After McCormick had shown him an uncomfortably close likeness on a police photo-fit picture of a suspect for the robberies, he began to wear two nylon stockings as face masks. 'They showed I had a prominent nose. I thought if I wore two masks it would push it down a bit and change things.'

But in 1977, said O'Doherty, things began to go seriously wrong. He was questioned by police officers who had become suspicious of McCormick. One officer who had become extremely suspicious, in McCormick's view, O'Doherty said, was Sergeant Joe Campbell, the village policeman in Cushendall, who had reportedly seen them carrying out a robbery. McCormick allegedly said: 'Campbell has twigged on to us. He will have to go.'

O'Doherty then said that he was driven by McCormick to Cushendall where he was induced to shoot Campbell, but he refused. The court then heard that McCormick, a recognized Special Branch marksman who had helped guard the Queen and Prince Philip during their 1977 Ulster visit, took a mask and a rifle with a telescopic sight from the car and went off to shoot Campbell himself. When he arrived back, fifteen or twenty minutes later, panting and out of breath, O'Doherty said that McCormick remarked: 'That is the end of the trouble or the start of the trouble.' O'Doherty said he replied: 'That is definitely the start of it.' Later, in a bid to shift suspicion from McCormick, O'Doherty said they made a bomb to plant under his car to give the impression he was an IRA target.

Under close and persistent cross-examination by Desmond Boal, QC, for McCormick, O'Doherty agreed that he had lived a life of deception and had become a practised liar. 'The nature of my work entails that I have more lying to do than a normal human being. I had to lead a double life. I didn't tell anybody the truth for I wasn't going to last twenty-four hours.' When McCormick gave evidence, he admitted O'Doherty and he were friends. 'You don't like to give informers the impression you're using them.' He said the Provisional IRA was 'light years ahead of the Special Branch in intelligence and methods'. O'Doherty was a double-agent being used to 'put down me and the Branch,' he said. 'The case is the biggest frame-up ever.'

In his judgement on 2 April, Mr Justice Murray recalled that Boal had denounced O'Doherty as a killer, a liar, a hypocrite, a play actor, a devious and plausible villain, a maker of bargains with the police and a person of considerable intellectual dexterity which he frequently used to attribute to other people's crimes which he himself had committed or in which he had been involved. 'At the end of the long day,' said the judge, 'my firm conclusion is that it would be highly dangerous and wrong to convict the accused of any of the crimes charged against him on the evidence of O'Doherty unless that evidence is supported by clear and compelling corroboration.'

McCormick was consequently acquitted of twenty-three of the charges, including murder, and convicted only of a £3,000 bank robbery, hijacking a vehicle and the possession of a rifle in suspicious circumstances where, the judge decided, there was evidence to support O'Doherty's account. He was sentenced to twenty years' imprisonment.

However, in January 1984, McCormick was released from prison after his conviction and sentence were quashed on appeal. The three judges decided that Mr Justice Murray 'had lacked the cogent and compelling corroboration which he had declared to be indispensable to a finding of guilty'. McCormick remained suspended from duty as an RUC officer and was discharged from the force in June 1985. A month later O'Doherty was quietly released from prison after serving only four years, half the time he was sentenced to.

Mrs Rosemary Campbell, the widow of the dead police officer, who had been in court with various of her eight children throughout the case, said of the verdict: 'I can accept it – I only hope the children are strong enough to accept it.'

The entire affair caused shockwaves within the RUC. After the main trial, the Special Branch Superintendent, who had been McCormick's immediate boss, abruptly resigned from the RUC. Other officers were transferred and stricter supervision of the activities of the Special Branch was introduced. The case marked the virtual end of the Branch's golden days as a law unto itself, a force within a force, and enabled Hermon to achieve one of his main goals. But it was still a vital cog in the anti-terrorist campaign and it was not the last time it was a centre of controversy.

On Sunday 28 March Inspector Norman Duddy and his two teenage sons, David and Mark, attended morning service at Strand Road Presbyterian Church in Londonderry. They had just returned to their car to go home when a motorcycle, with two men on board, pulled up beside them. The pillion passenger, whose face was covered by a scarf, pulled out a handgun and fired several shots at close range into the policeman's body. He was pronounced dead on arrival at hospital.

Two mornings later, a woman cleaner at a Belfast police station was waiting outside her home for Constable David Brown, who regularly gave her a lift to work. As he turned his car in the narrow street she heard three bangs and thought he had driven over a bottle and burst a tyre. Then she realized it was shots. When she reached the car he was slumped over the steering wheel. 'If I get to hospital quickly, I might live,' he said. But he died in hospital on 16 April after bronchopneumonia developed as a result of the gunshot wounds. Before he died he was promoted to the rank of sergeant.

During the morning rush hour in Londonderry on 4 May, Constable Samuel Caskey and a colleague were on patrol in The Diamond in the centre of the city. As they passed a parked van, the rear doors swung open and terrorist gunmen fired on them. Caskey died from his wounds.

Later that month, after a debate stimulated by Irish members and some British Labour supporters, the European Parliament in Strasbourg called for a ban on the use of plastic bullets throughout the EEC. The bullets had become the centre of controversy following the deaths of seven people, three aged under fifteen, from injuries attributed to them, during the hunger strike period. The official account, that the deaths took place during rioting, was locally disputed in nearly all the cases and led to controversy during the subsequent inquests.

In one case a juror objected to a lawyer's tough questioning of a soldier who had fired a baton round which killed a man. In another case there was uproar from relatives in court when a coroner found that a twelve-year-old girl had been killed during a 'technical' riot, although that verdict was later overturned after further legal proceedings. In at least one other case there was disagreement among a jury over the circumstances of a death and evidence from a senior police officer was rejected by a jury after it had seen a sequence of Canadian television news film which contradicted him. Later, in a series of civil actions, which were generally settled out of court without any admission of liability, substantial sums of compensation were paid by the authorities. The family of one victim settled for £68,000. A youth who lost an eye received £32,500.

The plastic bullets were introduced by the army in 1973 as a safer alternative to rubber bullets after the authorities failed to suppress a controversial survey by two Belfast surgeons which claimed that they were dangerous and inaccurate. But by the early part of 1982, after thirteen deaths and many hundreds of injuries had been blamed on them, the same surgeons concluded the plastic bullets were even more lethal and called for modifications. Separate official figures showed that there was an average of one death for every 18,500 rubber bullets discharged but the rate of death from the newer plastic variety had increased to about one in 4,000.

Plastic baton rounds, or 'pbr's' as the security forces prefer to call them, are cylinder-shaped, hard pvc projectiles, four inches long, with a diameter of one and a half inches, fired with a muzzle velocity of 160 mph from Federal riot guns. It is intended that they should be fired at the lower parts of rioters' bodies. There are two sorts of pbr – a 25-grain explosive-charged round for short range and a stronger 45-grain round for longer distances. The RUC, who first acquired the weapon in 1978, only use the short-range rounds.

The Northern Ireland Secretary and the RUC had vigorously defended the weapon throughout 1981, when 29,601 rounds had been fired. Between March, when the RUC began to record injuries, and July that year, 203 people received hospital treatment as a result of being hit by a baton round. At the height of the rioting after Sands' death, the RUC had put on display the array of lethal missiles that had been thrown at them. In a typically hard-hitting outburst Hermon had said: 'The critics demand – ban the plastic bullet – or – hold an inquiry into the plastic bullet. But do they demand – ban the petrol bomb – or – hold an inquiry into the nail bomb or rocket?' Hermon insisted that in his 'considered professional judgement' the weapon was a 'reasonable response to the violence with which the security forces are contronted'. In many cases, where they would have been justified in using real bullets, they had not done so, he said.

At the time the government was especially sensitive about the subject. After serious rioting in several of Britain's rundown inner-city areas in 1981, which exposed the inability of the police to cope, a high-powered team of senior officers visited the RUC for a crash course in riot control. As a result of their study, 3,000 plastic baton rounds had been issued to the British police as they urgently developed riot capability on the RUC model. The issue sparked off political rows with councillors and community groups in several cities, forcing the Home Office to publish guidelines for using them. In effect they were only to be used on the direct order of the local chief constable when all other means to control any trouble has been exhausted.

Although it maintained a bullish public line on the use of pbr's and announced technical modifications to reduce the risk of casualties, the government was so fearful that moves to have the weapon declared in breach of the European Convention on Human Rights would succeed that a senior officer from Scotland Yard was tasked to evaluate the alternatives. His path had already been well trodden by both the army and RUC, who were inundated by approaches from all over the world offering ideas and equipment. Nevertheless, he looked again at water-canon-based alternatives spraying irritants, dye, gas, stench or even electrified jets of water. Other devices included a 'tennis ball', a hard plastic ball, rocket-fired nets to trap rioters, bean bags or softer plastic bullets. One system involved smothering trouble-makers with foam, another was a banana-peel-based substance fired along the street, which caused them to slip. But on grounds of effectiveness or medical danger, the plastic bullet, despite its imperfections, emerged as the only practical solution.

In the event the legal moves against the plastic bullet foundered and they remained in the police armoury. By the end of 1987 none had been fired in anger on the British mainland and their reduced use in Ulster reflected the reduction in street confrontation. In 1981, the year of the hunger strike, there were 29,601 rounds discharged. In the following year only 489 were fired. As one RUC man remarked: 'If there's no rioting, there's no need to fire them.'

# 8

# 'Popularity Is Not My Business'

The RUC celebrated its Diamond Jubilee in June 1982 with a variety of functions. The most solemn was an inter-denominational service of thanksgiving at St Anne's Cathedral in Belfast. Among the clergymen who participated was Father Hugh Murphy, the survivor of the 1978 police kidnapping, again courageously recognizing by his presence that in a civilized society the police have to be supported by all. On parade was a new standard, incorporating the RUC's harp and crown insignia, presented to the force by the Northern Ireland Police Authority. As part of the celebrations an RUC Service Medal was announced, recognition of the special courage required to be a police officer in Ulster. At headquarters the 100 surviving founder members of the RUC were entertained by senior officers; a book of nostalgic pictures, neatly titled 'Arresting Memories', was published; and 25,000 copies of a commemorative postage cover were issued.

On accepting the new standard from Sir Myles Humphreys, chairman of the Police Authority, Hermon said: 'We look to the future with realism and with hope. Difficulties and dangers there are certainly, but I do not doubt the ability of the men and women of the force to rise to and surmount the challenges which lie ahead.' After more than two testing years in the job, the challenges faced by both Hermon and the RUC remained essentially the same. The Provisional IRA threat was as potent as ever, bolstered by the emotional impact of the hunger strike and the consequent Sinn Fein political gains in the local councils. The Loyalist hardmen were still active and required police attention.

Nevertheless the policy of police primacy and 'Ulsterization' quietly progressed. About 2,500 soldiers had been withdrawn since Hermon took over, and the army presence and profile was being steadily lowered. In the same period more than 1,000 police officers had been recruited and trained, bringing the strength of the force up to 12,500, four times the pre-troubles establishment. The level of RUC activity on the ground, especially in Catholic areas, had increased.

Everyone concerned knew that they faced a long haul, that there was no magic overnight stroke to restore normality and, despite the threat of continued violence and death on and off duty, police morale remained high, for it was clear that the tide had been decisively turned against the terrorists. They could no longer operate at will. Their heartlands in Belfast and Londonderry were well opened up to intensive patrolling and surveillance, and the flow of arms and explosives was harder to maintain. Although there would inevitably be setbacks and further tragedy, inch by inch, progress was being made. Hermon summed it up: 'We're into long days and short nights.'

Hermon himself had become a uniquely controversial figure, certainly by comparison with all the previous Ulster police chiefs. After his repeated brushes with Paisley, he closed his door on politicians, scarcely bothering to disguise his contempt for the way they exploited the RUC for their own ends and hijacked the newspaper headlines to parade their self-importance. Unionist leaders, unsurprisingly, had little good to say of him and some even claimed he was a secret Paisleyite who would throw his weight behind him in a declaration of independence. Paisley, on the other hand, conducted an unremitting 'Hermon must go' campaign and always drew loud applause from his audiences and congregations when he bracketed the prime minister, 'Mrs Traitor', and her 'puppet' Hermon conspiring 'to sell Ulster out into a united Ireland'.

More than any other factor Hermon valued his operational independence from political direction and his accountability only to the law and the courts. He deplored the Unionist call for 'control of security', for it really meant a return to the bad old days of Stormont when the force was run by the Unionist Party. He knew that any such control would involve one-sided application of new anti-IRA laws, which would in effect be anti-Catholic. The strong Unionist reaction to Hermon was rooted in this, for the Unionists resented the fact that Hermon was so vigorously his own man and would not be told what to do.

On the Catholic side, Hermon's image was equally controversial. A number of influential Catholic politicians and churchmen, who had unpublicized access to him, gave discreet, private support to the force, and regarded him as the best, most sensitive police chief the province had ever had. But he was more widely regarded as the latest in a line of repressive police bigots prepared to tackle the Catholics and pussyfoot with the Protestants.

Inside the force he attracted the same extreme reaction; his officers respected him but either liked or hated him. All but a few feared him to the point where they kept their private views to themselves. Many believed that he saw himself as the first all-Ireland police chief, others that he was destined for a career in politics. He was not popular, either, among the security mandarins at the Northern Ireland Office for his straight-talking, often passionate approach. Several times during the hunger strike saga his blunt criticisms of the way it was being handled were taken with less than good grace, and behind his back in Stormont Castle there were murmurs about his inability to see where policing stopped and politics began.

In the context of divided Northern Ireland such diverse and contradictory perceptions of the man suggested that his policies were probably right. By positioning himself in the centre of the whirlpool and taking criticism from all sides, a case for his impartiality and fairness could be argued. 'He was paying the price of policing such a divided society,' recalled one of his colleagues. 'The best he could hope for was a grudging respect.'

Hermon remained aloof and unmoved by the stir he caused. Like all visionaries, he was imbued with a tangible sense of confidence, which often bordered on the arrogant. He was, anyway, privately convinced of the rightness of his policies and the need to force them through, whatever his critics or the faint-hearts said. 'Popularity is not my business. Command is,' he said frequently as he singlemindedly pursued his carefully planned course. He placed his faith in the 'good sense of the overwhelming majority of the community', a concept he trusted implicitly. Colleagues, who remember their own nervousness at certain points, talk now about Hermon's instinctive understanding of the Ulster character and his shrewd judgement, through good contacts in both communities. 'There were dangerous times when I did not share his faith or judgement,' admits one colleague. 'But I have to say he was proved right. Every time we approached the abyss, it moved.'

But the force of violent events since 1980 and the low calibre of most of those in politics were such that Hermon could not achieve his real aim – to restore law and order to the point where reasonable political discussion, leading to a political solution, would become possible. Undeterred, he bided his time. Security policy, and his command, remained the most popular targets for political exploitation, while the police continued as prime terrorist targets. The most regular commitment in his diary was still making painful sympathy visits to the families of murdered officers and following the funeral slow-step behind their coffins as the RUC band, with black shrouded drums and instruments, played the all too familiar death marches.

During the rest of 1982 eight more RUC officers lost their lives. On 11 June Detective Constable David Reeves was killed when a booby-trapped television set exploded in a Londonderry house. On 1 October Reserve Constable John Eagleson was shot dead while riding his motorcycle to his civilian job in Cookstown. Four days later another Reserve Constable, Charles Crothers, was shot dead while opening the gates at his civilian workplace, a Department of the Environment depot in Londonderry.

Three officers, Sergeant John Quinn, Constable Allan McCloy and Constable Paul Hamilton, died on 27 October when terrorists detonated a large bomb under their armoured Cortina at Kinnego Embankment, Lurgan. (This incident figured later in the Stalker/Sampson controversy.) Detective Constable Gary Ewing and a civilian friend were killed on 9 November by a booby-trapped explosive device attached to their car outside the Lakeland Forum in Enniskillen. A week later two Reserve Constables, Ronald Irwin and Samuel Corkey, were shot dead at the security barrier in Markethill, County Armagh.

The year ended with a major atrocity when eleven soldiers, including eight members of the Cheshire Regiment, and six civilians – five women and a teenage boy – died in a no-warning explosion at the Droppin' Well in Ballykelly, a disco adjacent to the army base there. The 5 lb gelignite bomb had been smuggled into the disco in a small hold-all and was abandoned under a table. (Four years later, two sisters and two men, self-confessed INLA members from Londonderry, were jailed for life for the seventeen killings, and the daughter of one of the women, who had helped in the reconnaissance of the disco, was jailed for ten years for manslaughter.)

The ninety-seven-name-long terrorist casualty list for 1982 could well have included members of the RUC band. On 9 July, when they were playing at a graduation ceremony at Queen's University, Belfast, undercover detectives watched as terrorists planted a car bomb, to ambush their two mini-buses afterwards. The band drivers were alerted and told to take a different route, while a follow-up operation was mounted to capture the bombers. Later at Belfast Crown Court three Provisional IRA members received sentences between thirteen and eighteen years for conspiracy to murder the band. They were part of a seven-strong IRA gang convicted of sixty terrorist offences, including a mortar bomb attack on a police station and several car bombings in which civilians were injured and property extensively damaged.

The year was also marked by what senior RUC officers felt was the long overdue imprisonment of Bobby Storey, a dangerous terrorist known as the 'legal Houdini' because of the number of times he had been acquitted by the courts through lack of evidence or legal technicalities. The Storey case contains intimidation of witnesses, resistance to interrogation and uncertain identifications, all the ingredients that make it so difficult for the police to lay charges, and is a compelling example of the difficulty for a society in conflict of maintaining the balance between civil liberty and providing the police and courts with adequate powers to protect the community from the crimes of ruthless terrorists.

Storey, one of a family of three, born on 11 April 1956, was in his teens when the troubles began in 1969. Two years later, during a search of the family house at Riverdale in West Belfast by the security forces, guns were discovered under a bed and his older brother Seamus was arrested and charged. One day playing football, while on remand in Belfast prison, Seamus was one of nine prisoners who escaped when rope-ladders were slung over the prison wall from outside. A year later, after his recapture, he refused to recognize the court, insisted on wearing a black beret and announced he was a member of the Provisional IRA. He was sentenced to three years.

Bobby too had 'come under notice', as the Special Branch put it, but as a schoolboy suspect there was nothing they could do. However, on 11 April 1973, his seventeenth birthday, he was arrested, and detained without trial in the Maze prison until May 1975, when detention was being phased out. After his release, police and soldiers kept a wary eye on his activities, frequently screening him and monitoring his movements. But he next came to specific police attention on 31 January 1976 after a huge explosion and fire destroyed the Skyways Hotel at Belfast's Aldergrove Airport.

From witnesses' descriptions of 'a tall fellow with a spotty face', the police suspected Storey was the man, accompanied by a girl, who had left the bomb in a hold-all in the bar. He was arrested and told he was to be put on an identification parade. At 6 ft 4 in he was exceptionally tall and when the parade took place, he exercised his right to be seated while the witnesses inspected the line-up. Both picked him out. But when the case came to trial the judge said that although he regarded the witnesses as 'honest', he found the evidence 'unsatisfactory and unsafe', so Storey was acquitted. He did not go free, however, for by then he faced a murder charge.

On 11 March 1976 a man parked his car on the Andersontown Road in Belfast, leaving his two teenage children in the back, while he called in a shop. On his return he found the car gone and the two children standing on the footpath. They said it had been hijacked by a tall man and a girl. A short time later the car stopped at a house in Dunmurry and two men got out. They asked for Henry Scott and were told by his grandson that he had gone to the Farmers Inn public house, which he owned. The men then pulled guns on the grandson and forced him to accompany them to the pub. When they got there the grandson was sent inside to get Mr Scott, who was gunned down by the taller of the terrorists, and killed. The tall man told the second man: 'Finish him off.' Then they drove off in the stolen car.

Storey was identified as the tall hijacker and gunman at identity parades in Belfast prison and charged with murder. After the committal hearing when the evidence had been heard and the documents served on the accused, the two teenage witnesses received bullets in envelopes at their home. Understandably, their father refused to let them give evidence at the trial. But the grandson of the murder victim did and again identified Storey, this time from the witness box. 'I could not forget the face of the killer,' he told the court.

The trial judge, Mr Justice Kelly, convicted Storey's teenage companion of the murder, because the weapon and ammunition had been recovered from his house, but he refused to convict Storey because the absence of any other evidence besides identification raised doubts about whether or not he had been the gunman. The trial, in March 1977, coincided with the public controversy over Peter Hain being accused of a London bank robbery solely on identification evidence.

The verdict caused dismay to the police officers in charge of the case. Storey was now known as the 'Brain Surgeon' inside the Provisional IRA, because he did 'head jobs', and the police had information, but not evidence, of his involvement in a number of vicious murders, including an attempted mass killing at the Homestead Inn, a public house near Belfast, in which only one person died. A senior detective involved in the case was so angry at the acquittal that he could not resist mentioning it to the judge when they met socially a short time later. 'That was a wrong decision. It may cost somebody his life,' he said.

Three months later Storey was arrested again. This time he was charged with the attempted murder of members of the security forces in Turf Lodge but in December 1977 the charges were dropped by the prosecution. His solicitor protested vigorously to the court that his client had spent four needless months in prison awaiting police forensic evidence which did not materialize.

Almost immediately Storey faced a further attempted murder charge, this time in connection with the shooting and wounding of a soldier by gunmen firing from a flat at Lenadoon in West Belfast. But at the trial in May 1979, the judge refused to convict when he heard the police had tricked him into making a verbal admission of the crime. The detectives interviewing him had said his fingerprint had been discovered at the firing point in the flat. 'If it's my fingerprint I must have been there,' said Storey. In reality his fingerprint had been discovered in the getaway car, but the judge refused to convict on this evidence because the car could not be connected to the attempted murder. Storey once again walked free from the court.

But within months he was in custody again. In the early hours of 14 December 1979 officers from the Anti-Terrorist Squad at Scotland Yard swooped on a luxury flat in London's exclusive Holland Park area and arrested four Irishmen. Among them was Bobby Storey. The gang had actually been under surveillance by both the RUC and Scotland Yard for several months and the swoop came hours before a daring plan, using a hijacked helicopter, to rescue an important Provisional IRA leader from Brixton prison, where he was awaiting trial. When the four escape planners came to trial at the Old Bailey in March 1981, Storey pleaded 'not guilty'. He claimed to have come over from Belfast simply to look for work and was lodging with friends. He insisted he did not know of their IRA connections or that there were firearms in the flat. The jury convicted his three co-accused but failed to agree on Storey. They, of course, knew nothing of his history. The judge ordered him to be retried.

The second jury, which also knew nothing of his record, accepted his explanation that he had met one of the other plotters on the Liverpool ferry and had simply been offered a place to stay in London. But when he left the Old Bailey in April 1981, the Home Secretary signed an order under the Prevention of Terrorism Act excluding him from mainland Britain, and he was promptly returned to Ulster.

One afternoon, three months later in August, when the hunger strike violence was at its height, the observer in an RUC Landrover, who had just heard over his radio that a soldier had been wounded in a shooting incident, spotted Storey and two others in a car speeding through Andersonstown. The Landrover gave chase and rammed the car without managing to stop it, but a few minutes later, when it was cornered in a petrol station, the three occupants ran away, after an exchange of shots. The police, now reinforced after a radio alert, pursued the men on foot and captured them. 'Hands up, Bobby,' said the arresting officer who confronted him at the rear of the petrol station. 'We've got you this time.' In the car they found two rifles.

Storey, this time caught red-handed, was convicted of possessing the firearms with intent and sentenced to eighteen years' imprisonment. He was, however, acquitted on an attempted murder charge, for wounding the soldier, because there was no firm evidence to link the speeding car to the shooting.

The conviction was widely celebrated inside the RUC, for Storey was regarded with some awe as 'one of the toughest nuts we ever had to crack'. Detectives remember how he once resisted sixteen hours' interrogation a day for seven days, by relays of their most experienced interrogators, without even giving his name. He simply sat staring at the wall, resisting all attempts to draw him into even casual conversation. In his cell, between interrogations, he shadow-boxed and did press-ups to keep alert. He also demonstrated an uncanny understanding of the psychology of the interrogation process. Once a detective, considerably shorter than Storey, told him to sit down. 'If I sit down you will only stand to dominate me. You sit down and I will stand and dominate you,' he replied, looking defiantly down on the detective.

Even behind bars Storey remained a danger. In September 1983 he was one of the eight prime movers in the mass escape of thirty-eight dangerous terrorists from the Maze prison. When one of the overpowered guards in cell block H7, where the escape originated, tried to sound the alarm, another prisoner had to restrain Storey from killing him with one of the small revolvers smuggled into the prison to arm the escapers. Save the bullets, he was told, they might be needed to get out the main gate. Although Storey did get out of the prison, he was one of the nineteen escapees quickly recaptured. In fact he had been free for only an hour when an RUC patrol spotted him, less than a mile from the prison, trying to avoid the cordon of checkpoints by wading across the River Lagan.

The mass escape was only one of a number of serious outrages in 1983. In January Judge William Doyle was murdered outside a Catholic church in south Belfast after attending Sunday Mass. Towards the end of the year, in November and December, there was a concentration of serious incidents.

On 4 November seventeen RUC inspectors and sergeants were attending a lecture on 'The police in the community' at the polytechnic at Jordanstown, on the northern outskirts of Belfast, when an explosion took place without warning. Inspector John Martin and Sergeant Stephen Fyffe died instantly and Sergeant William McDonald died on 12 August 1984 from his serious injuries. The bomb, which had been concealed in the false ceiling of the lecture room, injured thirty-three people, including non-police students in an adjacent room.

Charles Armstrong, a member of Armagh council and also a UDR part-timer, was blown up and killed outside the council offices on 6 November. Two weeks later three people were killed and seven injured when breakaway INLA members, using the name 'Catholic Reaction Force', burst in and opened fire on the congregation of nearly seventy men, women and children in the Mountain Lodge Pentecostal Gospel Hall at Darkley, near the South Armagh border, during the Sunday evening meeting. One of the congregation had been tape-recording the hymn-singing when the gunmen struck, and captured the 'crack-crack' of the fatal shots interrupting the singing and organ accompaniment. Edgar Graham, a law lecturer, was gunned down on the street outside Queen's University on 6 December. He was an Official Unionist member of the Assembly, elected a year earlier, and was outspoken in calling for tougher anti-terrorist legal and security measures.

Altogether seventy-seven people died in terrorist attacks in 1983, twenty less than in the previous year, but the RUC death toll increased from twelve to eighteen, including the victims at the polytechnic. The first casualties of the year were Sergeant Eric Brown and Reserve Constable Bernard Quinn, who were shot dead by gunmen at The Square, Rostrevor, County Down. Reserve Constable John Olphert was serving in his shop and post office in Londonderry on 18 January when masked men came to the door. He slammed it shut but was wounded when they fired a shot through. Then the gunmen burst in and killed him. A month later, on 20 February, Reserve Constable William Magill slipped out of the RUC station at Warrenpoint to a nearby shop; while returning, he died in a hail of gunfire. The next day in Armagh, Sergeant William Wilson was covering a patrol in Lower English Street. He died when a bomb in the building beside him exploded without warning.

Shortly before 3 pm on 2 March Constable Lindsay McCormick, a neighbourhood policeman, was on his rounds in Serpentine Road in north Belfast. He was a familiar sight at that time, when the children were due to come out of the local schools. His job and his presence were evidence of the growing recognition that whatever the terrorist problems, the RUC had to be community-based, seeing the children across the road, chatting to their mothers, offering a protective hand. So none of the waiting parents took undue notice as he stood with two young men talking. But then suddenly there was a scuffle and what one eyewitness described as the sound of a vehicle backfiring. The policeman fell to the ground. One of the young men walked over to him and emptied his revolver, five shots, into the policeman's head. Then the two unmasked killers walked to their waiting getaway car.

Two weeks later, on 15 March, another policeman died. Reserve Constable Frederick Morton was driving his bread van along the Portadown Road out of Newry when he was fired on by gunmen in an overtaking car. His vehicle ran off the road out of control and crashed. He was dead at the wheel. Constable Gerald Cathcart had just reached home at Malone, Belfast, on 16 May after a day's work in RUC headquarters when he was shot after getting out of his car and died shortly afterwards in hospital. On 26 May Reserve Constable Colin Carson was manning the checkpoint outside RUC Cookstown when a van pulled up. As he came forward to check it, the side door opened and terrorist gunmen inside cut him down with gunfire.

Late in the evening of 6 September a family was watching 'The Godfather' on television when three armed men commandeered their house in the Catholic housing estate at Cathedral Road, Armagh.

Shortly after midnight when a neighbour drove up, they ran out and fired several bursts of gunfire into his car. The driver died instantly. He was Constable John Wasson, aged sixty-one, a member of the RUC for forty-two years and its second longest serving member, who was within a month of retirement. He had refused to move from the area, which the police regarded as dangerous for him, and believed he was a community policeman helping the community. He also refused to carry a gun. A year later, when a man with INLA connections was being charged with the murder, he simply whistled.

Two patrolling officers died on 6 October when gunmen approached them on foot while they were on duty in Downpatrick, County Down. The dead officers, both Reserve Constables, were James Ferguson and William Finlay. Constable John Hallawell was a member of the community relations branch. On 28 October he called at a house in the strongly Republican Shantallow area of Londonderry. As he was leaving, terrorist gunmen closed in on his car and opened fire at close range, killing him. Reserve Constable John McFadden finished duty at RUC Ballymoney after midnight on 5 November. As he pulled into the drive of his home at Rasharkin he was ambushed by gunmen. He died a short time later in hospital.

Reserve Constable William Fitzpatrick was finishing the renovation of a new house near Kilkeel, County Down, on 10 November. As he was inside working, terrorist gunmen fired through a window, killing him. Two days later RUC Carrickmore, County Tyrone, came under heavy mortar attack just after 6 pm. Constable Paul Clarke, one of the forty policemen in the post, was caught in the blast and killed. Six other officers were injured. As always with such indiscriminate weaponry, there was a hair's breadth margin between minor and multiple casualties.

Within eighteen months, Christopher Black's path, turning Queen's evidence against his former terrorist accomplices, had been followed by thirty others, twenty from the Republican camp and ten Loyalists. What had begun as an opportune attempt by one disillusioned terrorist to save himself from a long spell in prison quickly developed into a conscious new tactic and became the main thrust of the constant campaign to convict terrorists. At its peak about 500 people were arrested and charged with almost 1,500 serious offences, including murders, shootings and explosions, dealing the terrorist organizations their most damaging blows ever.

The effect on the level of violence was swift and noticeable. In North Belfast alone, overall terrorist activity showed a sixty-one per cent reduction in the six months after the arrest of Black and his accomplices compared with the previous half-year. In the same period murders dropped from eleven to three, bombings from twenty-six to one and shootings from ninety-eight to forty-two. This dramatic pattern was repeated elsewhere. The INLA became virtually dormant, as did the UFF and UVF. The Provos were badly affected in Belfast and Londonderry but not as much in the rural areas. 'There are people alive who would otherwise not have been,' said a detective justifying the new phenomenon.

There was conflict about what the terrorists turned informers should be called. The Provos initially preferred 'supertouts', then later 'paid perjurers'. The RUC described them as 'converted terrorists', but the newspaper headline writers preferred the existing Fleet Street sobriquet 'supergrass' and that stuck. The years 1982–84 thus became the 'years of the supergrasses'.

The concept was nothing new. Turning Queen's evidence was a well-established legal principle and the 'supergrass' extension of it had been instrumental, for nearly twenty years, in ridding London of some of its worst gangsters and criminals. Until now the RUC had used the tactic sparingly; the UVF's East Antrim gang had been largely convicted on accomplice evidence; the Provisional's M60 gang was broken by inside information.

But it was indeed a new phenomenon that key members of a virtual terrorist generation should be almost queuing up to betray their former comrades in crime and save themselves. Black was a typical example. Like him, the other supergrasses found the glamour of terrorism tarnished, the constant fear of the dawn arrest knock debilitating and where they faced lengthy terms of imprisonment they badly wanted to salvage some sort of life with their wives and children. Hermon said that the development of 'converted terrorists' reflected a fundamental change of attitude in a community tired of murder and violence, and terrified of intimidation and racketeering.

Some observers were sceptical that all the supergrasses had such high motives. Father Denis Faul believed that many of them were already under pressure inside their own organizations. 'They are terrified as they are caught between two ruthless groups of people. They know their own people are after them and the police can offer protection but there is always the fear that if they do not co-operate they will be released to the mercy of the terrorists.' Events showed that some of them were indeed already compromised informers, running for their lives, or petty criminals acting out of naked self-interest.

In exchange for their testimony, most of the supergrass prosecution witnesses were promised immunity for their own crimes, a new start abroad with their immediate families and a false identity, to prevent reprisals. Others who had confessed to serious offences, notably murders, did not get immunity but were given private assurances that they would get more lenient sentences in exchange for their testimony and then a new, safe life abroad.

Talk of vast rewards – sums of £50,000 upwards were mentioned – was largely inaccurate. The supergrasses generally received just board and lodgings and spartan pocket money from the authorities, about £5 a day, usually in line with social security rates. But some extras, like an odd night out drinking, were provided from the personal funds of the RUC detectives assigned to them as minders, who invariably developed close relations, sometimes even verging on friendship, with their charges.

Those who were given immunity from prosecution were taken mainly to Britain to await their spell in the Belfast witness box. They were given homes in the married quarters of police and army establishments, where they lived with their armed RUC minders. Those still in prison were housed in a special supergrass annexe at Crumlin Road prison in Belfast, to protect them from the revenge of their former partners in crime. There they enjoyed a softer regime, with perks like television and films on video tape. Some were even allowed excursions outside the prison with their minders, to have a few drinks or even to visit a wife or girlfriend.

Where the RUC did permit visits, it was in carefully controlled circumstances. One set of parents were allowed to see their daughter but not their supergrass son-in-law. The wives, in these cases, were either the strength or weakness. If they were behind their husband, like Mrs Christopher Black, then it contributed to his confidence but if the wife was unsettled, then so too was the husband.

There is no doubt that the advent of the supergrasses created a most serious crisis of confidence within the terrorist groups. 'Every time they had a meeting to plan something they just did not know if the other guy was going to go through with it or if he would end up implicating them,' said one detective at the time. 'They did not know who to trust.' The effect was most profound on the terrorist frontmen, who masqueraded as political sympathizers and took great trouble to keep themselves at arm's length from the actual handling of weapons or explosives. These planners and controllers, the godfathers or untouchables, who were the longstanding targets of police intelligence gathered, now faced the real possibility of serious criminal charges against them. Some went on the run to avoid arrest, others predicted their imminent arrest and proclaimed in advance their innocence of what they said would be trumped up charges.

The first counter-measure the PIRA announced was a conciliatory one, an amnesty for informers and supergrasses. Anyone who confessed to them would have nothing to fear. Then they tried a few manoeuvres through the courts, with relatives seeking orders against the chief constable requiring him to produce either the supergrass or his wife. Black's in-laws tried to force the RUC to produce his wife but the courts refused to make any order.

Inevitably when the soft tactics failed to break the supergrass system, the terrorists resorted to type. The wife of one supergass was kidnapped, then the father of another, although in the end they were both released unharmed. Neither of the grasses affected retracted after the kipnaps but several others could not stand the threat and the pressure, and did so. They were feted at PIRA press conferences after their releases, clearly to encourage the others, but the central strategy was not upset. In several cases, almost immediately another defector stepped forward to save his own skin by volunteering evidence, so most of the suspects remained in custody.

The most spectacular retractor, however, was Robert Lean, reputed to be the second-in-command of the PIRA leadership in Belfast. In 1981 and again in 1982 he had been arrested on the word of other supergrasses and then released when they withdrew their evidence. He claimed that while he was in custody the RUC had offered up to £80,000 for his co-operation in breaking the IRA command structure in Belfast. But in September 1983, after he was re-arrested, his wife and five children were quickly taken into what the police called 'protective care'. As some of the biggest names in the Provo's command structure in the city were then arrested on the basis of his statements, the RUC hailed him as the most important supergrass of all. Twenty-seven people were charged with offences ranging from murder to membership of the PIRA and there was undisguised rejoicing at the alleged high calibre of the Lean catch.

But at the beginning of October 1983 Lean's wife and children returned home from their temporary sanctuary at an army base outside Belfast and she made a public plea for him to retract his evidence. 'I have spent the last twenty-four days trying to persuade my husband Bobby to leave the custody of the RUC. I am heartbroken for the families and kids of the innocent men he has implicated. I am just hoping Bobby will come home to his wife and family.'

Soon after midnight on 19 October he did. That night he was staying in quarters at Palace Barracks, Holywood, on the eastern outskirts of Belfast. During the previous evening his police minder had left car keys on the mantelpiece. Lean says he lifted the keys, waited until his minder had gone to bed, shaved off his moustache to disguise himself and drove out of the heavily guarded army base in the policeman's car. Later that day at a Sinn Fein-organized news conference he retracted his evidence and a few days later those charged were released from custody. 'Lean comes clean,' screamed the headline on that week's *Republican News*, celebrating a propaganda coup against the supergrass system that, with hindsight, many senior RUC officers now believed to have been a carefully planned operation by the PIRA to discredit it.

The first supergrass actually to give evidence in court was Clifford McKeown, a twenty-three-year-old Loyalist, who had implicated twenty-nine men from Portadown in UVF activities, including murder and armed robbery. McKeown told the court in July 1982, during a preliminary hearing to take depositions, that he had been sentenced to death by the UVF for giving information to the police. During the five days he was in the box there was almost constant heckling and jeering and shouts of 'liar', and more than once the magistrate had to call for order or threaten to suspend the hearing. On the afternoon of the fifth day there were more catcalls and jeers when McKeown suddenly announced he was withdrawing, 'I refuse to give further evidence and any evidence I have already given will be withdrawn from the court.'

At subsequent trials, McKeown was sentenced to ten years for an £800 armed robbery at a post office and eighteen of those people he had named were imprisoned for up to twelve years each after eventually pleading guilty to a catalogue of attempted murders, conspiracies to murder, armed robberies and membership of the UVF. McKeown later appealed but the Lord Chief Justice, sitting with two other judges, dismissed it. 'We are dealing with offences committed by a habitual criminal,' he said. 'We consider the sentence quite appropriate.'

To avoid further unruly scenes the DPP dealt with other cases by bills of indictment, a rarely used legal ploy to commit accused persons directly for trial, bypassing the preliminary hearing. This had the beneficial side effect of speeding up the start of trials, which were taking up more and more of the resources of both the police and the courts' service. During exchanges at a remand hearing about the delay in starting the Black trial, it was disclosed by the Crown that 150 police officers were involved in preparing the case, that ten typists were doing the paperwork and that the case papers ran to a total of 1,500 pages. Altogether 70,000 pages had to be photocopied for all involved in the proceedings.

The Christopher Black case finally began in December 1982 and he spent sixteen days in the witness box in January and February 1983 giving evidence against the thirty-eight people he had implicated. In all there were 550 witnesses. The trial finally ended in August after 120 days, the longest and, at £1.3 million, the costliest criminal trial ever held in Britain or Ireland. It had taken place in bizarre circumstances, with the most dangerous of the accused, in the prison officers' judgement, in the dock and the rest spilled out on adjacent seating, surrounded by police and prison officers. More police sat in the public gallery and from time to time armed police, with rifles, even sat on the bench adjacent to the judge. When Black was present, his minders guarded him closely and stood by the witness box as he spoke. The lawyers, twenty-five for the defence alone, staggered into court each day with their bundles of documents, which towered over them as they sat in the well of the court. The supergrass era provided a £4.6 million legal aid bonaza and several senior members of the small Northern Ireland bar were reputed to have earned annual salaries of at least £250,000 during it.

Mr Justice Kelly, who, singlehanded, had the unenviable task of keeping track of the evidence, described Black as 'one of the best witnesses I have ever heard' at the end of the trial when it took him eight and a half hours over three days to deliver his judgement and hand down the sentences. Altogether thirty-five people were convicted, four getting life sentences for the murder of a part-time member of the UDR and the deputy governor of the Maze prison. In all sentences totalling more than 4,000 years were passed. As Black, his wife and four children began a new life away from the threat of reprisal in Northern Ireland. Mrs Margaret Black, his sixty-two-year-old mother said: 'Now Chris is as good as dead.'

The strain such a long trial imposed on the court system, the judge, the police and the legal profession intensified the growing opposition to the supergrass tactic. Members of the judiciary were far from happy that increasingly people named by one informer and charged were promptly re-charged on the evidence of another super-grass and kept in custody when the original grass reneged or retracted his evidence. One extreme case involved INLA member Thomas 'Ta' Power, who was remanded in custody for four years on the word of five successive supergrasses before receiving a life sentence for murder, which was later quashed on appeal. He is reputed to have been the longest serving remand prisoner in either British or Irish legal history, having completed the equivalent of an eight-year sentence before facing trial.

Such injustices, the bills of indictment and the ever lengthening delays provoked what was to be a long, sustained campaign against the supergrass evidence and trials. Prisoners and relatives jeered and disrupted bail and remand hearings. Courts were picketed and MPs lobbied at Westminster. Lawyers, and not only those of left-wing views or sympathetic to the Republican or Loyalist causes, became openly concerned for the purity of the legal process. Their misgivings were given ample justification by two trials in 1983 when the potential flaws in the supergrass system were most graphically exposed to public view. The first trial involved a former UVF activist, Joe Bennett. In the second an INLA defector was the star witness.

The events that led to Bennett becoming a supergrass began on 5 May 1982 in Balloo, County Down. Shortly before 11 pm that night, sixty-nine-year-old Hubert McCann was reading in his sitting room. He was the local sub-postmaster and the dwelling was part of his post office and grocery shop situated at the crossroads of the normally tranquil hamlet. His two elderly, unmarried sisters, who lived with him and shared the running of the business and the home, were in the kitchen. Suddenly Hubert heard loud screams from his sisters. When he reached the kitchen he saw a tall man, in dark clothes and with a tight-fitting black hood, with eye holes, over his head. Behind him there were two more masked men, also in dark clothes. The three old people jointly tackled the raiders. Hubert remembers seeing a knife and hearing the muffled bang of a gun shot. During the scuffle, he dislodged the mask of one of the men. As he pursued him into the yard he pulled on the sleeve of the man's jacket and he ran off leaving Hubert holding a black leather jacket. He locked the back yard gate and returned to the kitchen. There he found his sister Maureen, slumped, moaning in a chair. He laid her gently on the floor and, as he dialled 999, she died from a deep stab wound in her heart.

The brutal murder of the old woman shocked even the hard men of East Belfast and caused a great deal of resentment. Before long the finger was being pointed at Joe Bennett and with his abundance of enemies it was not long before the police heard too. They turned over his flat at Park Avenue and the house of a former girlfriend. 'Tell Joe that if we don't get him first the UVF will,' the detectives said. Bennett had first sought refuge with a woman friend, whom he persuaded to dye his hair, then went on the run again. The police finally traced him fifteen days after the murder and lodged him in Castlereagh for questioning.

Bennett, aged thirty-five, was no stranger to the RUC. Ironically, the son of a police officer, he had been in trouble for years. At eleven he had a juvenile conviction for larceny; at fifteen he was convicted for misusing an air gun; and at eighteen he notched up a second firearms conviction, this time for possessing a weapon in suspicious circumstances. Early in 1972, after being recruited by a workmate in a bookmaker's shop, he was sworn into the outlawed UVF at a clandestine meeting in West Belfast Orange Hall. Bennett, by now married with two young children, made an effortless transition from Belfast's criminal underworld to the twilight world of the city's terrorism and racketeering. He even used his dead father's police uniform to carry out robberies and other operations.

When the army seized UVF weapons, ammunition and explosives that he had been keeping at his home, Bennett was arrested and remanded in custody to await trial. However, he was given compassionate bail because his wife was suffering from cancer. Four months later, after her death, he jumped bail and went on the run from the security forces, rising to become second-in-charge of UVF explosives. When the number one killed himself in a premature explosion, Bennett replaced him. During this time there is evidence of his involvement in several bombings in which two people died. Although they were carried out by the UVF, Bennett often chose the targets to settle his own scores. UVF activists remember him as a hard-drinking man, downing pints and vodka, with an equally voracious taste for gambling, but usually losing, on slot-machines, dogs and horses.

At this time he was living with a married woman, separated from her husband, and using her house as a bomb factory. In March 1974 the army uncovered his cache and sealed off the street while Bennett was forced to carry all his explosives outside and neutralize them. He was later sentenced to twelve years' imprisonment for explosives offences and, having earned full remission, was released in March 1980. He moved in with another married woman and, through a UVF contact, found a job at the King's Inn in East Belfast. He resumed his drinking, gambling and UVF activities.

A few months later he found another job, this time acting as bouncer in another East Belfast bar plagued with brawls. Bennett cut a formidable figure, tall, solidly built, with a thin pencil moustache and a penchant for flashy suits. He soon restored order, giving the trouble-makers merciless kickings with his hand-sewn, elastic-sided, heavy-rimmed boots. But he lost the job within months after his taste for the good life got the better of him again. The UVF were pressing' for the repayment of a £600 loan to buy a car and the bar owners had discovered £1,350 missing from their till, most of which they suspected had been spent in an adjacent bookmakers. To relieve his mounting financial pressures, and maintain his fast women and slow horses lifestyle, Bennett resorted once again to a series of armed robberies in the early months of 1982. In one of them he broke into the bar he had just been sacked from and opened the safe with the key he had earlier stolen. Another of them was the robbery at Balloo post office, which led to the death of Miss McCann.

When the cell door at Castlereagh clicked shut behind Bennett, he had every reason therefore to believe he was going behind bars for a life sentence with a lengthy minimum imposed, given his record and the murder of the old lady. As far as Bennett knew, she had died from the single gunshot he fired during the scuffle, not the knife wound to her heart. Bennett also knew that he faced a certain and unpleasant death from the UVF if he ever got out. But he was aware that the police had been granting immunities to people like himself. Turning supergrass, he realized, would free him from his twin predicament, a long term in prison or a UVF bullet. When his interrogation began, Bennett asked for and eventually got a deal. In return he made a forty-seven-page statement about the UVF, revealing gun-running missions to the United States and Amsterdam, contacts with neo-Nazi groups who wanted the Ulster terrorists to attack Jews in Britain and a catalogue of murder, robbery and bombing in Belfast. When Bennett formally identified one of his former accomplices in the interview room at Castlereagh, the man quoted Kipling to him: 'Before a nation's eyes, a traitor claims his prize, what need for further lies, we are the sacrifice.'

After a twenty-one-day hearing at Belfast Crown Court in March and April 1983 Mr Justice Murray spelled out, in a three-and-a-quarter-hour judgement, why he believed Bennett's evidence against the fourteen accused before him. Then he handed down sentences totalling 200 years. They were stunned, for they were so confident that Bennett had been convincingly discredited during seven days of cross-examination that a celebration party at an East Belfast hotel and Spanish holidays had been arranged. All had to be hastily cancelled.

The decision provoked widespread disquiet in both political and legal circles. Bennett, described by the defence barrister as 'a monster wanting in all the human virtues', was accused of perjury by not admitting to some of his earlier operations, especially those in which people had died. The RUC said, in his defence, that he had not been shaken on his denials in rigorous cross-examination. The judge was impressed by this point in testing his credibility and deciding to accept Bennett's evidence.

But Mr Justice Murray was himself publicly criticized for the apparent conflict between his judgements in this case and the McCormick/O'Doherty case where he decided not to accept O'Doherty's evidence against McCormick without independent corroboration. The judge was clearly aware of the disparity for he discussed the case law on informer and supergrass evidence at length and noted: 'It seems to me . . . there is undoubtedly some conflict amongst the judges and law lords who have dealt with the topic.' Mr Justice Murray shared the misgivings on the third point of disquiet – the question of the scope and terms of Bennett's immunity. The judge had commented on the Crown's 'most undesirable attitude in not producing a witness in authority' to give evidence on the policy of immunity. There was growing public concern that self-confessed killers should not benefit from immunity arrangements.

The controversial concept of supergrass evidence was dragged into near total disrepute at the end of the year in the fourth 'show trial', when John Patrick Grimley was called to give his evidence against eighteen members of the INLA who faced seventy-six terrorist charges. Forty-year-old Grimley was the self-confessed founder and leader of the INLA in Craigavon, a hybrid new town twenty-five miles from Belfast. Although his name had been widely published in court reports and was freely bandied about the court, he insisted on being referred to as 'Witness A' when he entered the box and sat, at an uncomfortable angle, his back pointedly turned to the prisoners in the dock. Two smart-suited bodyguards, with arms folded, stood at all times beside him.

Grimley confidently trotted out his evidence-in-chief but when Desmond Boal, QC, began to cross-examine him on his personal life, motives and attitudes, his composure swiftly evaporated. In a week-long cross-examination that had all the ingredients of court room farce and drama, Boal, probably the toughest questioner at the Ulster bar, broke Grimley down. Amidst many denials and evasions Grimley confessed to a life of crime, with forty criminal convictions, since the age of thirteen. He told of three successive spells with regiments of the British Army, twice joining under false pretences, twice faking suicide attempts to gain discharge. Then it was back to more crime, assaults and robbery. He had a job for a time but when he lost it he drank the £2,000 redundancy money in eight weeks. The court then heard of his drift from crime to terrorism, burning down a block of flats causing damage of £100,000, leading IRA flag parties and how he flaunted himself in pubs as an IRA man, running up drinking bills he had no intention of paying. But the IRA cracked down on him after a drunken escapade in a pub when he grabbed the microphone and, dressed in a mask and hood, abused the patrons with swear words.

During most of this time he was also acting as a police informer, getting between £25 and £250 a time for his information. He said he had agreed to inform to avoid being prosecuted for sexual assault. When he was forced out of the IRA, he said that the police, who turned a blind eye to his continuing freelance criminal activities, encouraged him to become involved with the Irish Republican Socialist Party so that he could continue to provide them with information. From that he drifted into the INLA, where he eventually became the leader of a cell involved in gun smuggling and plotting acts of terrorism (immediately made known to the police), including a plan to kill the MP, Harold McCusker. However, he lost his position as leader for accidentally wounding another member of his unit after a drunken night out. Inevitably he came under suspicion as an informer and was threatened by other members of the INLA. However, rather than shoot him, they told him to go to a priest, to use his case to publicly discredit the police, but Grimley instead gave himself up to his Special Branch handlers and decided to turn Queen's evidence.

After Boal had piled on the pressure for a week Grimley asked the trial judge, Lord Justice Gibson, for an adjournment, as he was 'very tired both physically and mentally'. But he did not reappear as scheduled a few days later and after a further adjournment of a week the judge suddenly halted the trial after twenty-seven days. Grimley was a liar, he said, who 'lived in a sort of half-world between reality and charade'. Seven of the accused were acquitted because of the lack of subsidiary evidence but three were given suspended prison sentences and eight others custodial sentences totalling fifty-one years.

The Grimley case marked a significant turning of the tide against the RUC's use of supergrasses. The judiciary became sensitive that it was being pushed to the point where it was seen as rubber-stamping police tactics by convicting people on the uncorroborated word of supergrasses in a court already emasculated by the absence of a jury. Precisely what terms and inducements were on offer to 'converted terrorists' had been kept a rigorously guarded secret by the authorities, who did little more than deny that lump sums were being paid. The judiciary indeed became so sticky on this point that senior police officers gave formal evidence in later cases to persuade them that inducements were not on offer, only practical benefits to protect the supergrass and his family and set them up in new, safe surroundings.

In the seven years to mid-1985, looking after the safety of informers and supergrasses had cost £1.3 million, according to a parliamentary answer by the Northern Ireland Secretary. Some of those who benefited were among the sixteen retractors who had either withdrawn their evidence or refused to testify in court. But to keep faith with future informers or supergrasses, the authorities had to honour the undertakings and immunities already granted.

Many politicians were seriously concerned about the issues raised by the supergrass cases. Peter Archer, the Labour opposition spokesman on Ulster and a former government law officer, was actively opposed to the principle. But while the trials in the pipeline continued, attention shifted to the outcome of the appeals that had been lodged.

All persons convicted in the non-jury courts under the anti-terrorist legislation had an unfettered right to have their case reconsidered on both evidential and legal grounds by three judges in the appeal court.

Although Bennett's accomplices were released on appeal in December 1984 and other supergrass convictions were overturned, the Black case decision was the one regarded as setting the benchmark. Again, the sheer scale and complexity of the case caused a lengthy delay. This time the judges had also to read the transcripts of the 120-day trial as well as the voluminous case papers. The appeal hearing itself lasted sixty days and the verdict did not come until July 1986 when many of those on lesser sentences had already completed their terms. Eighteen of those convicted had their sentences quashed but in four cases, where there was independent evidence – usually statements of admission – the convictions were upheld. The appeal panel, headed by Sir Robert Lowry, the Lord Chief Justice, decided that the trial judge, despite his great experience and care, had overestimated the honesty of Black. Most significantly, the appeal judges were careful to defend the principle of an informer giving evidence and it being accepted uncorroborated, where its weight and credibility satisfied the trial judge. In this case it was not safe to accept; in others, in the future, it might well be, was the thrust of the decision.

The Attorney-General, Sir Michael Havers, had already mapped out the same ground. In a speech at a legal function in Belfast the previous March, he had said that corroborative evidence was not essential but he reminded his audience that the judge had to warn the jury, or in their absence himself, of the inherent dangers in accepting accomplice evidence. He said that sixty-seven people had been found guilty on such evidence in 1984 and 1985, while eighty-seven were acquitted, an indication that the Northern Ireland judiciary were scrupulous in convicting only on proof beyond reasonable doubt.

What is now regarded as the final blow to the supergrass system came on 23 December 1986 when twenty-four INLA men convicted on the word of Harry Kirkpatrick were released by the appeal court. Kirkpatrick, a self-confessed five times' killer, had received a life sentence with no minimum term for his testimony. One of those released was the previously mentioned Thomas 'Ta' Power, who had by then spent five years less a month in prison and who was to die less than a month later in a bloody internal INLA power struggle.

The Lord Chief Justice made it clear that he was under no illusions about the calibre of the men he was releasing. In all probability, he said, they were important members of the INLA who had carried out the serious crimes Kirkpatrick attributed to them.

Of all the people charged in the supergrass era on accomplice evidence, the only ones whose convictions stuck had other evidence against them. It was ironic that a number had made confessions after being confronted by the supergrass and consequently went to prison, while those who had remained silent walked free. The untouchables remained immune, although their enforced imprisonment, albeit temporary, had undoubtedly resulted in a marked reduction in violence. However, the price paid for the respite was considerable when measured in loss of confidence and respect for the judicial system.

By the late 1980s the RUC were thus forced back on conventional measures, with all their shortcomings, to stem the terrorist tide. The bitter INLA power struggle and feuding, which had developed within the prisons when the factions were locked up, erupted almost immediately after the end of the Kirkpatrick proceedings and sixteen died before it was resolved. The rise in Provisional IRA violence since 1987 and the resumption of commercial target bombing, like pubs and hotels, was not coincidental in the judgement of the RUC.

Many lawyers and politicians felt that it would have been more honest, whatever the political difficulties, to have adopted a policy of detention without trial rather than tinker with and further devalue the conventional legal and court process. With one judge trying to grasp the complex case against as many as thirty-eight defendants, there was a high risk of unsafe verdicts. Abuses of process like endless remands and bills of indictment also brought the courts into disrepute. Indeed the supergrass policy fuelled and largely justified the case for three judge courts where there was no jury.

In the final analysis, the supergrass concept collapsed because the RUC, understandably, overplayed their hand. In previous cases where Queen's evidence was turned, the cases were more thoroughly prepared and considered on the merits. The sheer volume of work in this instance, and the temptation to strike a telling blow at the highest terrorist echelons, permitted disreputable characters like Grimley and Bennett to slip through. The RUC gain was thus only a temporary one, although as one detective said, if it was your life saved, then you at least would think it worthwhile.

The dozen or so supergrasses promised a new life were shipped out of Northern Ireland in strict secrecy and resettled. One of the detectives involved in the delicate operation had an unscheduled encounter at London Heathrow one hot summer day while seeing one of his charges off to his new life abroad. He was carrying a substantial sum of cash, the packets of banknotes distributed around his clothing, including his overcoat. By chance he met a Northern Ireland MP and his bodyguards, who insisted he join them for a drink. They would not take 'no' for an answer so he suffered an embarassing session with them, in a crowded bar in sweltering heat, constantly refusing to take off his overcoat and unable to explain why.

Back in Belfast the ever belligerent terrorist organizations had sworn to find and kill the traitors. But with one notable exception the supergrasses have vanished without trace. The exception is Joe Bennett, who, as predicted by RUC men who knew him, reverted to type, robbing and womanizing. In July 1986, under his new name of John Graham, he appeared at Nottingham Crown Court and was jailed for ten years. He had pleaded guilty to the armed robbery of £10,250 from a bookmaker in Derby and conspiracy to rob a bank in the city the previous January. As he was sent down, he blew a kiss at an attractive divorcee whom he had wooed and won with tales of his daring undercover work in Ulster.

Much of the political opposition to the supergrass policy had been voiced in the Assembly, elected to Stormont in autumn 1982. It was James Prior's chosen vehicle for yet another attempt to steer Ulster's warring politicians into some form of political agreement for the future government of the province. Prior adopted an idea from Dr Brian Mawhinney, the Belfast-born MP for Peterborough, for a concept called rolling devolution. It envisaged devolving power in stages as agreement between the two sides was reached. Working together, in the first instance on areas of common interest, like agriculture and the economy, would hopefully develop enough trust between the politicians on both sides for them to forge a deal on the more difficult problems.

But Prior's hopes were stillborn when the moderate Catholic SDLP opted out and said that while it would contest the election, it would not take its seats in Stormont. Instead it had persuaded all the main parties in the Irish Republic to set up the New Ireland Forum, to draw up a blueprint for the political future of the island. The SDLP had been shaken by the political support for the Provisionals triggered off during the hunger strike and the harder mood within the Catholic community, and could not risk being portrayed as soft in comparison with the Provisionals. So although both groups on the Catholic side won seats in the Assembly, it was doomed from the start to be no more than a Protestant talking shop, with only the two Unionst parties and the small, middle of the road Alliance participating.

Nevertheless the Assembly did some good work. In its advisory role scrutinizing new legislation, ministers were surprised and impressed at the amount of constructive work and thoughtful reports it produced. It also provided a valuable safety valve for the anger in the Unionist community, especially in the tense, violent days of 1983, when Paisley convened a midnight session immediately after the Darkley Gospel Hall incident to express the revulsion everyone shared.

Recognizing that the security issue was such a central one in securing any political advance, Prior had initially signalled that a new, beefed up Police Authority, with Assembly members being given seats, was on offer as part of the rolling devolution process. Although this idea foundered early, because of the boycott by Catholic politicians, Prior and his advisers welcomed the Assembly's proper interest in security matters. In May 1983 there was a debate on the chief constable's report for the previous year enlivened by Paisley revealing yet another internal RUC document, of which he said: 'This is dynamite.' It was in fact an operational instruction on dealing with band parades.

Later in 1983, in October, following the reorganization of the RUC's territorial divisions from sixteen to twelve to take account of the shifts in population, especially in the greater Belfast area, there was another Assembly discussion on the RUC. The level of debate was low and poorly informed, apparently being based on little more information than that in the RUC press release. There were parochial gripes about men being redeployed from one station to another. Only the MP Ken Maginnis, clearly drawing on his first-hand experience as a former major in the UDR, sounded anything like knowledgeable. One Democratic Unionist Party member said that he disagreed with security policy but supported the RUC. The members were as one in voicing their support for the force. One said that many owed their lives to its dedication. As in May, when Paisley claimed Hermon had snubbed the Assembly, there were repeated attacks on him and cries for him to go. He was personally criticized for imposing overtime cuts to thwart the anti-terrorist campaign and for carrying through such a major reorganization without consulting MPs and other elected representatives.

The consultation sentiment was shared by Prior and his most senior security advisers. He had encouraged his junior ministers and senior officials to subject themselves to public examination by the specialist subcommittees of the Assembly. Giving them a taste of power was a deliberate part of his strategy. Hermon, however, whom Paisley had continued to bait inside and outside the Assembly, resisted public and private invitations to meet Assembly members or address them. In his place he invariably nominated one of his assistant chief constables.

Although nothing was ever said in public, Hermon's attitude exasperated Prior and the Northern Ireland Office, which regarded his refusal to deal with the Assembly and its members as stubborn and high-handed. They considered there was no threat to his operational independence and much to be gained from a demonstration of police accountability to elected representatives of the community. Every other chief constable in the country maintained elaborate links with his local MPs and councillors. Some of his mainland colleagues did not relish having to deal with the 'loony left' or openly left-wing police monitoring groups, but accepted it as part of a necessary dialogue.

The issue came to a head in the immediate aftermath of the Darkley Gospel Hall shootings. Prior invited the leaders of the four main parties to meet him, the chief constable and the GOC, to discuss security. The encounter was consciously intended to break the ice between Hermon and the politicians, and, through them, to reassure the community that even more vigilant security measures had been adopted. There was a particular fear of a church door reprisal, for crowds entering or leaving a church were an easy target for travelling gunmen or car bombers. But despite the fears and turmoil in the community, the joint invitation merely triggered off a bout of political manoeuvring between the party leaders, with only the moderate Alliance party being willing to attend. Prior cancelled the meeting, saying that their behaviour was 'frankly incredible'. Later he described the incident as 'a dreadful reflection on our political life and a lost opportunity'.

The problem of police contact with the politicians was finally resolved early in 1984 when the Police Authority hosted a series of meetings with the political parties at which Hermon was present. They were low-key affairs. Paisley led a delegation to one of the meetings on 1 February and, predictably, said afterwards that he had no confidence in the chief constable. The feeling was mutual, for both the police and the Northern Ireland Office felt let down by the politicians. After Edgar Graham was murdered, more than forty Assembly members had expensive security measures installed in their homes at considerable public expense. These included bullet-proof glass and doors, outside security lighting and secure 'panic button' links to local police stations. Some were also supplied with remote-controlled garage doors so that they could drive in under cover before getting out of their cars and others even had closed-circuit television surveillance cameras installed.

The arrangements offered in the Assembly had been an attempt to give the politicians real input to security policy but none of them seemed prepared to move the debate to higher ground. On the Catholic side there were politicians condemning violence, often cour-ageously, but all too often protecting their backs by criticizing the security forces. Every incident would be followed by spokesmen and personalities voicing complaints about security policy on the tele-vision and radio bulletins and in the papers, blaming the British and Irish governments for every death and injury. Paisley's great catch-cry, echoed by his followers, was for the government to 'go on the offensive to root out terrorism'.

A typical outburst followed the playing of the Irish national anthem during a Catholic band parade in two overwhelmingly Catholic villages in North Antrim in August 1983. The local DUP Assembly-man wrote to Prior complaining about RUC inaction. Prior replied that as the selection of music was unlikely to cause a breach of the peace, no action had been taken; such matters were best left to the discretion of the police on the spot and he reiterated his confidence in their judgement. The Assemblyman was unmollified. ' "The Soldier's Song" is the national anthem of a foreign country and stands for murder, anarchy and the destruction of Northern Ireland,' he said.

When the critics were pinned down to detail, their solutions proved unworkable. Early in 1984 a group of Paisley's bright young DUP lieutenants, 'the Duppies', who had been notably critical of security tactics, spent five days in Israel studying security. When they came back to Ulster they presented a plan for a 300-mile-long barbed wire fence along the border with the Irish Republic; it would be fitted with sensors controlled by computer, so sensitive that they would be able to distinguish between a cow brushing the fence and somebody cutting it. Apart from cost – their estimate for erecting the fence was £13 million with free army labour – the scheme ignored the number of men who would be required to guard and repair it, and the practical difficulties for farmers and others with interests on both sides. A look at the Berlin Wall or Iron Curtain across Europe might have been more instructive than the Israel inspection trip.

However, narrow prejudice, rather than practicality, was a regular hallmark of DUP thinking on law and order. During an Assembly discussion on sexual morality, one of Paisley's zealots called for adultery to be made a criminal offence, with what he called an 'adequate punishment' but not stoning or burning at the stake. When the suggestion reached the RUC, one senior officer winced: 'As if we hadn't got enough problems.'

Sex, or to be more accurate, homosexuality, was quite coincidentally at the heart of yet another controversial matter involving both the RUC and DUP. The scandal, which took its name from Kincora, a spartan, publicly run boys' home located in a large detached villa in East Belfast, first came to public attention in a notable scoop by Peter McKenna in the *Irish Independent* on 24 January 1980. McKenna reported that teenage boys in care at the home had been recruited for homosexual prostitution; that a member of the staff was involved with a Loyalist paramilitary group; and that there had been a longstanding 'cover-up' by the Social Services department, the police and the Director of Public Prosecutions.

The RUC moved swiftly after publication and later the same day announced that it had initiated a formal investigation. The officer appointed to lead it was Detective Chief Inspector George Caskey, a tall man with a taste for smart suits and a passion for golf, who had distinguished himself in earlier anti-terrorist investigations. In December 1981, after an exhaustive investigation by Caskey and a small team of detectives, the Kincora case, and charges of sexual abuse at other homes, spanning almost twenty years, came before Belfast Crown Court. To assemble the evidence they had traced and interviewed 300 of the 400 Kincora inmates, all over the United Kingdom and as far afield as Europe and North America. It was an enquiry that required unusual discretion, for many of them, settled in jobs, married and with children, had put their unhappy memories behind them. But some thirty-three made formal complaints, enough to ground a prosecution.

At the end of the hearing, Sir Robert Lowry, the Lord Chief Justice, condemning what he called 'unpleasant and disgusting' offences, imprisoned three men, who had pleaded guilty to multiple homosexual assaults at Kincora. They were Joseph Mains, the former warden, who got six years, Raymond Semple, deputy warden, five years and William McGrath, the former housemaster, four years.

Instead of settling the matter, the court case gave rise to a series of sensational newspaper allegations that Kincora was the centre of a top people's vice-ring, which included senior members of the British administration in Northern Ireland. They were said to have orchestrated an official cover-up to protect themselves because the alleged homosexual high-jinks were used by the British security services to blackmail prominent politicians for intelligence purposes.

For a time the scandal even seemed to threaten the credibility of the Rev. Ian Paisley, who was simultaneously involved in a 'Save Ulster from Sodomy' campaign to prevent homosexuality between consenting males being legalized in Ulster, as it was in the rest of the United Kingdom. (The wags promised to 'Save Ulster from Sodomy – and have a better Gommorah'.) The names of other prominent Unionists, several members of the RUC and even Britian's legendary spymaster, Sir Maurice Oldfield, were also circumstantially dragged into the controversy. The rumours were not without some substance, but despite them being assiduously fostered for more than nine years, conclusive evidence to justify the most sensational of them has still not emerged.

The link that fuelled the rumours connecting what the Lord Chief Justice called 'loathsome and perverted behaviour' at the boys' home and the world of Protestant politics was William McGrath, who became known to the Caskey team as the 'Beast of Kincora' when they heard about his sometimes brutal homosexual behaviour. Dr Donald Soper once described Belfast as 'a city of religious nightclubs' – its God-fearing population was able to worship at a large number of establishments, some grand brick-built edifices, others corrugated-iron sheds in dingy back streets with exotic names like the Iron Clad Temple and the Mustard Seed Mission. McGrath was a well-known figure on this religious circuit but even in the late 1940s, as one clergyman remembers, he had already a certain notoriety. 'Young Christian people were warned about him.'

The course of events that led to Kincora began in the 1950s when McGrath was running Faith House in South Belfast. Bible students were whipped up into an emotional state by McGrath, who would then sexually assault them as 'an act of love'. One former student remembers that McGrath used any excuse or pretence for such contact and justified it by referring to David and Jonathan and Jesus and John, the beloved disciple. Close relationships between men, he believed, were part of God's plan. Another person who knew McGrath at this time says that it was a case of 'Praise the Lord and drop your trousers'. One young man, who came under the influence of McGrath at this time, although he strenuously denies any homosexual relationship, was Roy Garland, who was later, as the Mr X of the Kincora scandal, to become McGrath's principal critic. Throughout the 1960s, after Garland had inherited the prosperous family business producing firelighters, bleach and disinfectant, he provided McGrath with substantial sums of money for both his own use and 'the Lord's work'.

When the troubles began in the late 1960s, McGrath had become increasingly obsessed with the idea that he was the leader of a chosen people, Ulster Israelites. He began to translate his fantasies into political terms, forming a group called 'Tara' which gradually developed from an anti-Catholic, anti-communist pressure group into what McGrath presented as a pseudo-military group by the early 1970s. Its slogan then was: 'The hard core of Protestant resistance. We hold Ulster that Ireland might be saved and that Britian be reborn.'

McGrath, who had also founded an Orange Lodge and become prominent in the Order, undoubtedly had some influence or hold over important Unionist figures at this time. He was once a member of a delegation, led by Paisley, which met James Chichester-Clark, then prime minister, to protest about the security situation, and among those who flocked to meetings in his East Belfast home were prominent members of the Stormont government and parliament. 'The atmosphere at them was bizarre,' one former MP remembers. 'It opened with prayers. It was more like a séance than a political meeting and there were very heavy religious undertones. McGrath was like Walter Mitty making long, mumbling recitations. At one point he went into a trance and said he could see guns for the IRA being loaded into dock warehouses.'

Roy Garland, who had himself risen to some political prominence in the Unionist Party, was one of McGrath's closest associates at this time. But he developed growing reservations about his activities, which came to a head on 1 March 1971 when he refused to read an 'Act of Dedication', written by McGrath, at a Unionist rally in Belfast's Ulster Hall. McGrath threatened to denounce him as a traitor. Shortly afterwards Garland sued him to recover about £2,000, loaned for the 'Lord's work' and for goods delivered to McGrath, ignoring the advice of a cleric not to 'take a brother to law before the unbelievers'. At the same time he decided to expose McGrath's homosexual tendencies, which in Northern Ireland at that time were illegal. He confided in Miss Valerie Shaw, a missionary in Paisley's Free Presbyterian Church, to whom he also showed letters from McGrath with homosexual undertones.

About the same time McGrath, who had taken to describing himself as a welfare officer, had applied for the vacant job of house-father at the Kincora boys' hostel, a few minutes walk from his own house in East Belfast. The hostel, in a house that once belonged to a doctor, was opened by the Belfast Welfare Authority in 1958 with accommodation for between ten and twelve teenage boys in need of care or, ironically as things turned out, thought to be in moral danger. McGrath, who had no formal qualifications, wrote in his application that he had a lifetime involvement in church and social work and was looking for 'a deeper sense of vocation'. He was appointed and began work at the home in August 1971.

It was some time before Garland and Shaw found out, but when they did they were horrified. What happened after that, during the early 1970s, is still a matter of dispute. They claim that they made repeated attempts to warn first Paisley, then Martin Smyth, leader of the Orange Order, and the RUC, all of whom neglected to take any decisive action to have McGrath either investigated or removed. Paisley claims that although Shaw and Garland raised the matter with him, they produced no evidence with which he could confront McGrath and that no mention was made of his employment at Kincora. However, Paisley did ban McGrath from the pulpits of his church. Smyth recollects that he raised the matter 'within the collar' – that is, in the secrecy of the Orange Order – and later with the welfare authorities, but nothing further was done. There was a feeling that it was a smear concocted by British Intelligence to discredit the Unionist cause.

It is beyond dispute that in 1975, Colin Wallace, a civilian press officer at the army headquarters in Lisburn, told several journalists about McGrath's homosexuality, his employment at Kincora and his connection with Tara, although the laws of libel and healthy suspicion of the source, who was later sacked in disgrace, deterred any of them from printing the information.

By now a whole series of internal allegations about Kincora had piled up from social workers and inmates, which dated back as far as 1967 when two boys had gone into the Belfast Welfare Department to complain about their treatment. Although their complaints were investigated, and considered to be malicious, each reported incident was singly insufficient to ring alarms bells. Crucially, supervision and accountability were so disparate that the various suspicions and inconclusive allegations were not brought together in a way that would have caused alarm and revealed the consistent pattern of accusations that homosexual assaults were taking place.

The first recorded police contact with the Kincora allegations was in May 1973 after an anonymous telephone call about Tara, McGrath and his conduct. A routine police report was made through the local station but was dismissed as malicious and no further action was taken. A similar call in January 1974 was not even reported to the police. However, by then an RUC investigation, best described as unorthodox, was under way. In November 1973 an RUC Drugs Squad officer, Detective Constable James Cullen, was approached by Valerie Shaw on behalf of Roy Garland. Because he was going on a training course in England, it was several months before the detective actually met the two complainants but when he did, on 1 March 1974, he promptly bypassed the entire RUC criminal investigation system and made an appointment to see the Assistant Chief Constable, Bill Meharg, then in charge of RUC Criminal Investigations.

Meharg, a survivor of the dying breed of old school RUC officers, who was steadily losing the fight against an overwhelming workload and was too proud to admit it, told Cullen to make further enquiries, maintain an official log of them and keep him informed. Cullen maintains that at this time he was more concerned about the paramilitary dimension to McGrath and his homosexual activities rather than the welfare of the boys in the home. Meharg recalls that when he received a further detailed report from Cullen later in the month, with the McGrath/Garland letters for his information, he did not initiate a formal crime investigation because no actual incidents of assault or indecency were alleged. In his view the letters were ambiguous rather than overtly homosexual. Their lack of knowledge of the parallel allegations was clearly crucial, for the Cullen dossier, in isolation, was as insufficient as the others within the system at the time.

Colleagues say now that Meharg would have been shocked by the report, for despite his long service as a police officer he retained strong religious views and was relatively unworldly. In the prevailing circumstances, they say, it is therefore not surprising no action was taken. 'At that time there was daily murder and mayhem and you had rooky detective constables here handling murders that in England would have involved a Chief Superintendent and a hundred officers. Against that background a few queers was hardly as high priority,' says one officer.

Two years after this first Cullen/Meharg contact, Garland got in touch with Cullen again and expressed concern that McGrath was still at Kincora. After renewed consultation with Meharg, Cullen contacted the welfare authorities and the first discussion between them took place. But although Cullen was advised of the 1967 allegations against Mains and given a copy of the report, the co-ordination, on both sides, was so faulty that a full picture of the various episodes of unease and allegation still did not emerge.

In yet another episode that subsequently accelerated the cover-up theory, Cullen's report to Meharg was 'lost' in the RUC's internal mail between the police station at Donegall Pass in Belfast and Meharg's office at headquarters. As far as the RUC was concerned, the situation at Kincora did not become a live matter again until the Caskey investigation was begun and Mains, Semple and McGrath were imprisoned. The key questions that remained afterwards were whether or not there had been a high-powered cover-up, involving the RUC, army or security services, and if the welfare authorities over the years had been negligent in not detecting the homosexual abuses.

The RUC responded to the wave of newspaper interest by extending the Caskey investigation to take account of the further allegations. At the same time, in January 1982, the Department of Health and Social Services set up an independent tribunal to review the past management of Kincora and other children's homes. But when it met for the first time on 11 February there was more controversy. The members had sought and received assurances from the Department that the police investigation was complete and allegations of an official 'cover-up' had been resolved. When they discovered that criminal aspects of the matter were still under investigation, three of the five members and one of the legal representatives immediately resigned.

By this time the RUC was directly embroiled in the Kincora scandal with a wave of allegations that it had turned a blind eye while a top people's vice ring was run from the home, with British intelligence operatives using the inmates as homosexual prostitutes. The tide of innuendo and gossip reached such proportions that Hermon asked Her Majesty's Inspector of Constabulary to send in an outside officer. So, in February, Sir George Terry, then chief constable of Sussex, arrived in Belfast with instructions to oversee the continuing Caskey enquiry and, more importantly, to review independently the role of the RUC in handling the earlier complaints about the home.

Meanwhile, a murder and a suicide stoked the fires of speculation further. On 29 January a gunman walked into John McKeague's East Belfast stationery shop and shot him dead. McKeague, a well-known homosexual and a leading figure in Loyalist paramilitary activity, had a penchant for surrounding himself with smartly uniformed young boys and men. There were immediate but conflicting claims of responsibility made by telephone to news organizations. The first, from the Loyalist Red Hand Commandos, was dismissed by the RUC, who believed that the other, from the INLA, was genuine, despite the fact that only one of the two words in the recognized code was accurate. The rumour machines reached full capacity when it was revealed that McKeague had been named as a homosexual contact by former Kincora inmates, had been interviewed by the Caskey team and was formally warned that a file on the allegations against him was being considered by the DPP. McKeague, an embittered man, who had been frozen out of Loyalist politics, had often threatened to destroy some of those who passed him on the way up and these remarks were recalled as evidence that he had been killed to silence him and protect the secrets of Kincora.

Another well-known East Belfast political figure linked with Kincora and mentioned during the Caskey investigation was former Stormont MP and Belfast councillor, Alderman Joss Cardwell, a seventy-year-old bachelor, who was found dead in the front seat of his car in the garage at his home on 25 April. Two months earlier several city councillors, who had pledged to support Cardwell's nomination for Lord Mayor, suddenly withdrew when his name was linked with the scandal and the police interviewed him. At the inquest the coroner said that his death from carbon monoxide car exhaust fumes was 'inexplicable' but the conspiracy theorists reckoned that Cardwell shared the dark secrets of Kincora from his days as chairman of the council welfare committee, once responsible for operating the home.

As the tide of innuendo and unsubstantiated rumour grew more lurid by the day it was, ironically, William McGrath who injected an overdue note of reality. On 2 March he drew up a statement in prison, which his lawyers published a few days later. He challenged his detractors to prove that he was involved in a vice ring at Kincora or elsewhere; that he recruited young people for prostitution; that he was in contact with politicians or businessmen for this purpose; and that he received payment or reward for such services.

To this day, although the rumours continue unabated, no firm evidence has been produced to prove them and nobody has come forward to answer McGrath's challenge. In October 1983 Sir George Terry reported on his investigation. He said that no evidence of a top people's vice ring had been uncovered; that there were no grounds for any further prosecutions; and that the RUC had handled the earlier complaints satisfactorily.

In February 1986 the last official chapter on Kincora was published by the Northern Ireland Office. This was the report by Judge William Hughes and a committee of inquiry into the welfare aspects and management deficiencies of what had been revealed by the Kincora scandal. It made fifty-six recommendations to improve management techniques, screen and train staff, record complaints and liaise formally with the police so that nothing similar could ever happen again. In their concluding remarks the tribunal noted that the participants over the years resembled 'a tableau vivant of people wandering lost in a maze of their own creating'. It was an appropriate footnote, but there is still a body of opinion in the British parliament and elsewhere which still believes that the full story has yet to be told.

# 9

# In the Eye of the Storm

The constant haemorrhage of RUC life continued throughout 1984. In the late afternoon of 10 January Reserve Constable William Fullerton was driving home after completing a spell of duty at RUC Warrenpoint. Just outside Newry, as he negotiated a roundabout, gunmen opened fire from a vehicle which pulled alongside and he received fatal gunshot wounds. Two officers, Sergeant William Savage and Constable Thomas Bingham, died instantly on 31 January when a landmine exploded under their police vehicle near the village of Meigh as it patrolled the road between Newry and Forkhill.

In the early hours of 12 April a suspicious hold-all was reported in the front garden of a house at University Street in Belfast. Constable Michael Dawson was a member of a police patrol tasked to investigate and as he stood talking to the householder the device exploded without warning. He was declared dead shortly after arrival at the nearby City Hospital. A breakfast-time landmine explosion claimed two more RUC lives on 18 May. Constable William Gray and Reserve Constable Trevor Elliott were in a police vehicle travelling between Camlough and Crossmaglen when the 1,000 lb device went off, killing them instantly. A third officer in the unmarked armoured police car, which was blown fifteen yards into a field, survived.

Constable Michael Todd was taking part in a planned search and arrest operation in Lenadoon, the IRA stronghold in West Belfast, at 3 am on 15 June when he was shot and killed by terrorist gunfire. On 11 August Sergeant Malcolm White and another officer were patrolling between Gortin and Greencastle in County Tyrone when a landmine exploded underneath their police vehicle. The Sergeant was seriously injured and died the next day in hospital.

In his annual report for 1984, the chief constable noted that in all major respects the number of terrorist incidents was the lowest for thirteen years but he also commented on 'the horrifying fact' that since 1969 a total of 200 police officers had been killed and 4,800 injured, some disabled for the rest of their lives. 'How can one adequately acknowledge this grief and suffering by so many individuals and families in the service of the community? It says much for the men and women of the RUC that against this background of sustained physical attack and constant danger they remain imbued with the commitment to give of their best to the whole community,' he wrote.

At 05.40 am on 20 February 1985 Robert Gillespie returned to his home in Armagh after working a night shift. As he entered the kitchen three armed and masked men overpowered him. The keys of his van were taken, a towel was put over his head, his boots were removed and the laces used to tie his hands. He was then led to the bedroom, made to lie face down and his ankles were also tied. One of the gunmen regularly checked to see he had not struggled free. Some time later he heard them leave the house. After an interval there was the sound of gunfire, his van being driven away at fast speed and more firing.

The victim of this Provisional IRA attack was Sergeant John Murphy, a community relations officer. He was driving a police minibus out of a primary school, fifty yards from the Gillespie house, after dropping a group of schoolchildren who had been participating in an inter-schools' quiz, organized by the police to foster better community and police relations among young people. At the subsequent inquest the coroner, who heard that thirty-six shots had been fired at the officer from three points, described the murder as 'an atrocious act of barbarity'.

The RUC's steadfastness in the teeth of this unremitting violence was nowhere stronger than in the border town of Newry, a market town with an overwhelmingly Catholic population, thirty-eight miles from Belfast. The main police station in the town, at Edward Street, had been progressively fortified over the years as the threat and attacks intensified. The original red-brick building could hardly be seen behind a twenty-feet-high wall of concrete and corrugated iron which was constantly monitored by remotely controlled closed-circuit television cameras.

Life for the police was so dangerous that none of the officers was able to live or socialize locally. They commuted to their high risk jobs from safer areas twenty to thirty miles away. Despite the opening of a second base at Downshire Road, accommodation in the station was at a premium as the RUC shouldered the main security burden from the army and strength in the area increased, so the station canteen was moved to a portable building erected in the yard.

The Police Federation had long protested about the standard of accommodation in the division. Many stations had been unpainted for years and were riddled with damp and other structural weaknesses, aggravated by the effect of bomb blasts and gunfire. Space was so limited at Forkhill that officers on call had to sleep in the cells. Newry in particular was considered an unsafe and uncomfortable station but officers reluctantly accepted the risk and conditions because of advanced plans for a purpose-built less vulnerable station on a greenfield site outside the town.

At 06.32 pm on 28 February 1985 about ten officers were in the canteen. Two of them, from the Drugs Squad in Belfast, had called in for tea while making enquiries in the area. Another, from the Complaints and Discipline branch, was in the town to meet a priest to hear allegations of police misconduct. He was dining with Chief Inspector Errol McDowell, the local police commander. Chief Superintendent Bill Stewart, the divisional commander, should have been there too, but he was called away. Some sixty yards away, Monaghan Street was crowded with late-night shoppers, when suddenly there were the thuds of a series of explosions followed by the thump of larger blasts. McDowell recognized them as the distinctive sounds of a mortar attack and shouted for people to move. As he ran from the canteen he remembers debris falling around him.

Eight of the other nine officers in the canteen died instantly in the attack. The ninth, a woman officer, was pulled from the debris by frantic colleagues but her legs and one arm had been blown off and she died before reaching hospital. It was the worst death toll in a single incident suffered by the force. The bodies were retrieved from the debris and placed in the station garage. Some were so badly mutilated that fingerprints, taken from personal items in their lockers, had to be used to identify them. Those who died were: Chief Inspector Alexander Donaldson, from the Complaints and Discipline branch; Sergeant John Dowd and Woman Constable Ivy Kelly from the Drugs Squad; Constable David Topping, Woman Constable Rosemary McGookin and Reserve Constables Sean McHenry, Denis Price, Paul McFerron and Geoffrey Campbell.

The mortars were fired from tubes attached to a steel frame welded on to the back of a stolen lorry. Wooden pallets were used to build the load up and it was covered with tarpaulins until it was parked in the firing position in a disused creamery yard, lined up in the direction of the station by the tall radio mast. In all, nine devices were fired, each containing 45 lb of explosive designed to go off on impact. These mortars were known as Mark Tens by the bomb disposal men and were an improvised terrorist weapon which had been used eighteen times since first appearing in 1979. The launching tube is formed from steel piping, and gas cylinders, with stabilizing fins welded on the rear, are filled with the explosive. The weapon is notoriously inaccurate and therefore indiscriminate. In this attack only one device scored a direct hit; the other eight fell in the general area and not all exploded. Some actually overshot the station but if they had fallen short they might have devastated a shop or a restaurant which were within the trajectory path.

The Newry mortar attack, described by the Northern Ireland Secreaty, Douglas Hurd, as 'a squalid act of multiple murder staged as an international spectacle', demonstrated the hair's breadth between luck and disaster but it also prompted a review of the vulnerability of security force bases. An urgent work programme was begun to clad similar portable buildings with concrete walls, and roof fortifications were also strengthened. But despite the sense of shock that chilled the entire RUC, there were no recriminations, only determination to carry on with their work.

Within days detectives had arrested a number of suspects for questioning about the attack. On 5 March, as Loyalist demonstrators with the Union flag and a hangman's noose demonstrated outside Banbridge court house, seventeen-year-old Lawrence O'Keefe wept as he was charged with murder. When he came to trial in June 1986 Lord Justice Gibson, in sentencing him to five years for manslaughter, accepted that he had no inside knowledge of the attack and merely acted as lookout for the terrorists who planned it and put the lorry into position. By the end of 1987, almost two years after the incident, no other person had been charged, although the names of those involved are well known around the Newry area and to detectives.

The mortar attack was, however, not the only police tragedy in Newry in early 1985. On 13 April an armoured Hotspur Landrover pulled up outside the courthouse at 09.39 am and Reserve Constable

Michael Kay got out to cover the other members of the patrol. As he took up position, a bomb in a parked vehicle exploded without warning, killing him and a passing civilian. The protection afforded by the armoured vehicle saved the lives of the other police officers. In a follow-up operation the RUC established that the bombers had taken over a house with a view of the area and, having placed the bomb in a stolen vehicle adjacent to the courthouse, lay in wait for their victim.

Just over a month later, on 20 May, the dangers of policing in the Newry area were once more tragically illustrated. Shortly before 10 am two armoured Cortina patrol cars took up position on the northern side of the border at the Killeen crossing point on the main Dublin-Belfast road. They were there to rendezvous with a security van, carrying a £2 million-value load of cash and bullion from the Irish Republic, and escort it. As one of the RUC cars pulled out in front of the heavy armoured truck, which had just left its Irish police and army escort and crossed the border 100 yards behind, there was a huge explosion. The police car disintegrated in the blast and the four officers inside died instantly. They were Inspector William Wilson, Constable David Baird, Woman Constable Tracy Doak and Reserve Constable Stephen Rodgers.

The four police officers in the other car were uninjured, as were the four security guards, who remained locked inside their vehicle for seven hours after the incident until keys were brought to release them and the bomb disposal team cleared the area. The bomb, estimated by the army experts at 1,000 lb of explosive, had been concealed in a large cattle trailer parked at the side of the road, which had earlier been hijacked by armed men.

At the ceremonial police funeral of WPC Doak, a few days later, the former Moderator of the Presbyterian Church, the Very Rev. Ronald Craig, neatly articulated the frustration of the police and the community at the continued slaughter. 'Surely,' he asked, 'the industrious, warm-hearted, peace-loving in this land far outnumber the heinous murderers who are hell-bent on the destruction of our beloved country and we can work together to bring an end to this era of tragedy and heartbreak.'

But the killing continued. Sergeant Hugh McCormac was attending Sunday Mass with his family at a monastery near Enniskillen on 3 March 1985 when he was gunned down. Reserve Constable John Bell was working in his garage at Rathfriland on 29 March when he was shot; he died later in hospital. Another Reserve Constable, William Agnew, died from gunshot wounds when he was ambushed at Kilrea on 16 June. Two days later Constable William Gilliland was killed in an explosion at Kinawley. On 31 August Inspector Patrick Vance was shot dead in the driveway of his home at Crossgar.

During the summer months of 1985 the British and Irish governments were working more closely together than ever before to try to end the tragedy and heartbreak. The inter-governmental talks had their immediate origins in the report of the New Ireland Forum published in May 1984. The Forum, the brainchild of SDLP Leader John Hume, who persuaded the Irish government to set it up, was the Irish nationalist response to Prior's rolling devolution scheme which the SDLP had boycotted. More importantly, it was seeking a new definition of constitutional nationalism as a rejection of the PIRA's armalite and ballot box strategy in order to head off the growing political support for PIRA frontmen among the Catholic minority. Hume, and Dublin, feared that the PIRA, through the political wing of Sinn Fein, might eventually eclipse the SDLP. Sinn Fein was therefore excluded. Apart from the SDLP, the Forum comprised the three main parliamentary parties in the Irish Republic.

Dublin feared the rise of the Provisional IRA as a political force because ministers and officials there knew well that once the PIRA had become established in the north, they would export their revolutionary socialism to the south, bringing the risk of ultimately destabilizing the country and possibly turning it into Europe's Cuba. After the Provisionals bombed Harrod's, the famous London department store, shortly before Christmas 1983, Garrett FitzGerald had denounced them more forcefully than any Irish leader before. He described them as 'the common enemy' of the British and Irish people.

The New Ireland Forum began work at Dublin Castle in May 1983 in both private and public session, trying to produce an agreed blueprint for the future of the island which would enable Catholic and Protestant in the north to live together and amicably share the island with the south under a mutually agreed relationship or form of government. In the year of its existence it stimulated some of the most searching thinking and analysis of the Irish situation since partition.

Although they had been invited to participate, the Ulster Unionist parties declined, even refusing to make a submission of their views. Predictably they rejected the three constitutional options outlined in the final report: a unitary state governed from Dublin; joint sovereignty over the north between London and Dublin; or a federal arrangement between Dublin and Belfast. The report also contained some of the most telling commentary on the scale of the Irish tragedy, measured in detail by a series of special studies. One, entitled 'The cost of violence', poignantly spelled out the human and financial balance sheet: more than 2,300 deaths and 24,000 injured and maimed in 43,000 episodes of shootings, bombings and arson. The cost of security operations in north and south between 1969 and 1982 topped £4.2 billion; compensation for personal injury and damage to property in the same period exceeded £1 billion.

The lost opportunity costs for both parts of the island are virtually incalculable but employment and prosperity arising from inward investment and tourism suffered. Even the price of electricity was affected because IRA terrorists repeatedly severed the cross-border inter-connector, with serious knock-on implications for costs for both ordinary consumers and industry. The report estimated the total direct and indirect cost of the violence between 1969 and 1982 to be well in excess of £11 billion, a savage financial blow to both parts of the far from prosperous island.

At first the British government dismissed the Forum report and its list of options. Prior preferred to keep the emphasis on his rolling devolution efforts in Belfast. The bombing at the Grand Hotel in Brighton on 12 October, when two people died in an IRA bomb attack from which the prime minister and most of her cabinet had a near escape, hardened British opposition. Although Mrs Thatcher had been personally affected by her close brush with assassination – 'This was a day I was not supposed to see,' she said emotionally after church the following Sunday – the aftermath of such an atrocity, the British government judged, was not the time for any sign of weakness. That would only give further encouragement to the IRA which believed that sufficient violence would in the end force the British out of Ireland. In November, at the end of a summit meeting in London with Garrett FitzGerald, during which the Irish side had been pressing the merits of the Forum report, Margaret Thatcher dismissed the three options with a ringing 'Out, Out, Out'. Although the Irish were crestfallen, they took great care not to publicly damage their lines to the British. Instead they turned for help to the United States.

A month later in Washington, President Reagan, who had visited Ireland the previous summer, where he and his aides had been emphatically lobbied about the merits of the Forum report, privately pressured Thatcher. At the same time senior Irish and British officials co-operated to engage her interest. They succeeded. By the time she was back in Washington, the following February, serious Anglo-Irish talks were under way and, addressing the United States Congress, she was able to speak of her joint commitment with FitzGerald 'in the quest for peace and stability in Northern Ireland'.

The talking between British and Irish officials continued through the spring, summer and early autumn. From time to time the prime ministers themselves, or their most senior colleagues – Sir Geoffrey Howe and Douglas Hurd for Britian, and Peter Barry and Dick Spring for Ireland – intervened to keep things moving and avoid deadlock. The Irish pressed vigorously, against initial British opposition, to be given a consultative 'say' in the running of Northern Ireland, short of a breach of existing British sovereignty, so that they could more effectively drive the wedge between the Catholic community and the IRA. In return they offered a more vigorous security policy along the border and closer co-operation with the Royal Ulster Constabulary to thwart IRA terrorism. Most significantly, they offered to turn recent Irish history on its head by recognizing the existence of Northern Ireland as a separate political entity as long as the Protestant majority wished that to be the case.

As the negotiations proceeded throughout 1985, the British government tried to involve the reluctant Unionists in constructive political dialogue, but without success. They seriously misread the situation and underestimated Mrs Thatcher's willingness to adopt a radical course in Ireland. She had, after all, they reminded themselves, once described Ulster as being 'as British as Finchley'. And she had gone to war over the Falklands to prevent Argentinian infringment of British sovereignty. But for the first time in British-Irish history the Orange card was trumped and the uncompromising Unionists were ignored as the two governments pressed forward. Their alliance culminated in a prime ministerial summit at Hillsborough on 15 November where Thatcher and FitzGerald signed the Anglo-Irish Agreement.

At lunchtime that day, as the two prime ministers prepared to sign the agreement in Government House, Hillsborough, which was sealed off by a heavy security cordon of police, three miles away in Lisburn, retired Reserve Constable William Hanson and his wife returned home from a shopping trip to Belfast and switched on the television news. The bulletin was dominated by the summit but there was also news that a police officer had been killed in an expolsion at Crossmaglen. The Hansons were immediately concerned about their son David, who was stationed there and, as they had no telephone at home, William set out to ring Lisburn police station. As he left the house three policemen and a policewoman arrived. 'I just said to myself, "This is it." I knew then,' he recalled afterwards.

Earlier that morning Constable David Hanson and another RUC officer, with a military escort, were taken by helicopter from Crossmaglen to the border. They were to patrol along the Castleblayney road, back to the village, while the six soldiers would be deployed in the fields at each side of the road to give them cover. At 10.20 am, seconds after the policemen waved on a car, a massive 200 lb bomb concealed at the side of the road exploded without warning. The blast blew other members of the patrol off their feet but although Constable Hanson, who took the full force of the explosion, was rushed to hospital by helicopter, he was found to be dead from multiple injuries. The incident, reported to the political leaders gathered in Hillsborough, was a sombre reminder of the evil they were trying to remove.

The new agreement's most historic provision enabled the Irish to station officials in Belfast at a joint secretariat with the British to monitor the implementation of the agreement and allow the Irish government to act as advisory advocate for the Catholic minority. A new inter-governmental conference, chaired by the Northern Ireland Secretary and the Irish Foreign Minister, would give political impetus to a comprehensive programme of legal, social and economic reforms.

The agreement, which was soon ratified by overwhelming majorities in both the British and Irish parliaments, was acclaimed internationally. Both the United States government and the EEC Commission promised financial aid to underpin it. There was also support and a promise of help from Canada and Australia. 'The agreement is a fresh start for Ireland,' said Dr Garrett FitzGerald.

The Anglo-Irish agreement had major implications for the RUC. It sucked the force into the eye of the Northern Ireland political storm as never before and provoked a crisis of confidence among the members and their families on a scale that the IRA could only hope for. Unionist politicians actually attempted public subversion of the force and faced it with the most serious test ever of its professionalism, integrity and impartiality.

What turned out to be the RUC's most searching ordeal, worse than even 1969, had actually begun in the summer of 1985, while Unionist suspicions about the Anglo-Irish talks were rising. Coincidentally the force tackled the vexed question of provocation and trouble arising from the traditional Ulster summer marching season. Unionists promptly accused Hurd and Hermon of dancing to Dublin's tune in seeking to regulate some of the traditional marches and the issue was exploited out of all proportion, originating serious Protestant disaffection with the RUC for the first time in its history.

Hermon had in fact long signalled his intentions to deal with the effects of provocative marches but the timing of the move, with speculation about the emerging Anglo-Irish agreement stoking Protestant fears, was unfortunate. When Hermon began planning, several years earlier, he had no idea that when he made his move the historic sensitivity would be acutely aggravated by unforeseen political developments.

The first sign of his reservations about the provocative aspects of marching, which turned into a constant, indeed conditioning, theme, came in the annual report for 1980. Reviewing his first year in charge, he pointed out the frequent requirement for large numbers of police to be deployed to combat the public order threat from politically inspired marches and demonstrations. 'It is unfortunate, after the experience of more than a decade of violence and civil disturbance, that such activities have not been abandoned in favour of less inflamatory forms of political expression,' he wrote.

In 1981, the year of the hunger strikes, Hermon reported that the cost of policing the parades and ensuing disorder was £12 million – resources that 'could more productively be deployed for the benefit of all'. A year later there were congratulations and thanks for those who exercised 'maturity and responsibility' which led to a drop in the number of parades.

There was no direct reference to the problem in 1983 but the 1984 report, published in early 1985, put the subject very firmly on the public agenda for that year's marching season:

I feel bound to say that the objective of community reconciliation is not helped by the defiant insistence of some sections of the community on parades and routes regardless of circumstances, and by some insensitive, provocative bands and demonstrations and the tensions they cause. The insistence on parading in circumstances which made undue demands on the security forces and pose a threat to public order, is a grave and increasing cause for concern.

A timely parliamentary question arising out of the report elicited the information that it had cost £2 million and required the equivalent of 39,000 police officers to control 2,400 demonstrations during a six-week period that year.

Given the scale of the marching season in Ulster – 1,450 Loyalist and 450 Republican parades were scheduled in 1985 – the number of flashpoint parades at less than fifty was pretty small. But such was the emotional and political background that the real danger for the RUC lay in the possibility of hardliners resisting re-routing, tempers rising and trouble spreading throughout the community. Thus great store was laid in secret talks with leaders of the Orange Order and other march organizers to achieve agreed compromise. While the divisional commanders had pursued this line, Hermon had been building up alternative resources for what he had decided would be a decisive summer, preferably by agreement but, if necessary, by confrontation.

The force could now muster 3,500 men, deployed in DMSU formations, highly trained in public order tactics, with the equipment and mobility necessary to operate, at short notice, anywhere in the force area. Their worth had been proved during the traumatic days of the hunger strikes and their skills had since been honed further in both training and operational roles. Among senior RUC men there was confidence that if they had to fight with provocative marchers they would win.

It was regarded as vital to the future of both the RUC and the province that tackling the running sore of provocative marches would be seen as an RUC achievement. But so fundamental was the principle at stake that Douglas Hurd emphasized that Hermon could call on as many soldiers as he needed. There was by no means unanimity in the senior echelons of the force either about the policy or the strategy. Some senior men feared being caught in province-wide confrontations with the majority Unionist population while the IRA exploited the overstretch. Hermon soothed their fears and placed his faith in what he invariably called 'the good sense of the law-abiding majority'. As the marching season approached, several senior men, who did not share his faith, crossed their fingers.

As tension and threats of defiance were made, there was constant police contact at local level in a bid to bypass the inevitable hotheads and secure support for the limited re-routing from Hermon's law-abiding majority. It worked in nearly all the fifty target locations where population movement, redevelopment and other physical changes, such as the repositioning of roads, had changed the religious mix of an area and made previously welcome parades unwelcome. In some cases, like Lurgan, where the bands and marchers were asked to shift five feet by walking on one side of a traffic island rather than the other, the required change was remarkably symbolic.

In other places, however, the traditional 'not an inch' Unionist mentality persisted and the police were forced into compulsory legal action. The first encounter came at the overwhelmingly Catholic village of Castlewellan, County Down, on 27 June when a parade through the village was banned. Marchers were halted at a cordon of Landrovers and minor skirmishes developed during which twenty-two police and two civilians suffered injuries. Prominent among the protesters were local Paisley supporters, including a woman councillor who climbed up on a police vehicle and screamed abuse. Next morning their leader addressed himself to the situation at a news conference in Stormont. Returning to his familiar anti-Hermon theme, he said that he had been approached by officers who were 'sickened' by what they were being asked to do. He claimed that many had refused to enforce the Castlewellan ban and that hand-picked teams of Catholic police officers had been formed to do what he called 'Dublin's dirty work'. According to Paisley, there had been a Garda observer present as well 'to take stock'. Then, in a significant outburst, studded with typical belligerence and exaggeration, Paisley mapped out the ground on which the battle for the hearts and minds of the RUC was to be fought over the next eighteen months or so:

> If the RUC are going to push the tricolour and Dublin down our necks and be used as the stooges of Dublin, then the whole might of Protestant resistance will be brought against them. If they are going to put us into the Free State in a clandestine way, and the RUC is going to be the weapon, then the RUC and anyone who stands in our way is going to be opposed. It's going to be a battle to the death. The time has come for the police to choose whether to be for Northern Ireland or against it.

That evening there was more trouble when police prevented a crowd of 4,000 from parading through Gortalowry, a Catholic estate on the outskirts of Cookstown, County Tyrone. An angry Protestant woman spat 'black bastards' at the policemen holding the line and said: 'I never thought I'd say it but I wish the IRA would shoot them all dead tomorrow.'

Next day in the town's Protestant Monrush estate a crowd of stone-throwing Loyalists attacked a house occupied by two young policewomen and damaged the nearby residence and car of a part-time reservist. On 11 July a crowd of thirty broke away from a bonfire party and attacked the home of a retired RUC man. He had settled there after the IRA had bombed his home in Coagh eleven years earlier. It was a grim omen of worse to come but for the time being the immediate attention switched to Portadown, a town described by one police officer as the 'Vatican of Ulster Protestantism'.

The Orange Order was founded in 1795 a few miles from the town at The Diamond, near Loughgall, and in upholding its uncompromising doctrines the worst of Portadown's extreme Protestants are as bitter and twisted as their Catholic counterparts in Londonderry. They had long regarded it as their inalienable right to march triumphantly through the Catholic-populated Tunnel area each summer, led by bands playing as loudly and provocatively as they could.

In July 1873 the *Belfast Newsletter* had reported how 100 police with fixed bayonets confronted an Orange mob. When a Sub-Inspector struck a horse with his sword to stop it breaking the police lines, the air was black with stones thrown at the police. They were ordered to charge and in repeated clashes several people were injured and one killed by the police bayonets. The Sub-Inspector was felled by a brick on the head and given a severe kicking by a section of the mob as he lay on the ground. Only the intervention of a crowd from a public house, who dragged him inside for safety, prevented him from further injury. The entire clash appears to have been futile for, according to the report, the Orangemen formed up and marched through the Tunnel 'without either giving or receiving the slightest offence' as the riot raged.

The Tunnel had therefore been a flashpoint for as long as most people in the town could remember. Older residents recalled that the RIC had always drafted large numbers of reinforcements into the town for the Twelfth marches and there were vivid memories on both sides of even earlier confrontations between British cavalry and the Orangemen. In those days the Tunnel from the town centre along Obins Street was the main route out of the town to the west, so despite the hostility of the local Catholic population, the political and geographical climate provided little option but to push the marches through.

Today the Tunnel is a dreary place, a ghetto shared by some seventy families, its walls scarred by IRA graffiti, with a dirty scrapyard, a pork and a furniture factory, blocks of badly kept modern flats and several rows of terrace houses, many bricked up. The Republican graffiti confirm the allegiance of the residents. Moreover, with the advent of the motorway network, a new internal ring road and the pedestrianization of the bridge under the main Belfast-Dublin railway, it was simply 'coat trailing' for the marchers to insist on the traditional route. The access under the bridge, now confined to pedestrians, was so low and narrow that the parades had to lower their flags and banners, walk through in almost single file and re-form on the other side.

Throughout their entire consideration of strategy to reform the Ulster marching season, the RUC knew that Portadown would be the seminal battle. In the early days of July the leadership of the Orange Order frantically tried to distance itself from Paisley and the troublemakers who fuelled the tension by spreading a tide of unfounded rumours through the Loyalist community. A typical scare began with a newspaper story that RUC volunteers were being sought to learn the Irish language. The claim was true. However, it did not reflect preparations for integration with the Garda Siochana, as the scaremongers shrieked. Instead it was for the very solid operational reason that as IRA activists made more and more use of the Irish language, the RUC needed officers fluent enough to deal with them. But a militant faction within the Orange Order in Portadown would not be placated. As tension mounted over what action the RUC would take, they organized a monster Orange Rally on 3 July to protest at 'the denial of our civil rights to walk the Queen's highway'. The rally passed off without incident but tension remained high.

Three days later the RUC announced its policy. Urging people not to play into the hands of either the PIRA or UVF, who were manoeuvring to exploit the situation, the RUC said that a church parade would be allowed through the Tunnel next day, Sunday, but that the other parades on 12 and 13 July would not. The church parade passed off with minor scuffles between the police and local Catholic protesters. The clashes were for the record. Everyone knew that the real test would come on the Friday morning, the Twelfth.

The previous evening, as the traditional bonfires blazed, nearly 1,000 police were drafted into Portadown. A battalion of the Queen's Own Highlanders set up tents in the public park adjacent to Obins Street and commandeered the local parish hall. At dawn, as the RUC blockaded the area with their Landrovers, the Orangemen began to gather at their halls and soon the sound of bagpipes being inflated and tuned and drums being beaten and stretched contributed to the rising tension. The Orangemen had no clear strategy. The moderate minority wanted to recognize change and go on with their celebrations. Others wanted to converge on Portadown as a protest. The minority of hotheads wanted to storm the police barricades and march through.

Shortly before 8 am the police took up positions by their vehicles as the bands and marchers began to form up. Then, to the strain of their stirring anthem 'The sash my father wore', Loyal Orange Lodge 7, the appropriately named Breagh Leading Heroes, a cadre of craggy-faced, middle-aged men in black bowler hats and their Sunday-best suits, walked up to the police line and stood marking time as a senior police officer affirmed that they would not be allowed to march through. The confrontation lasted two days and there were sporadic clashes with the police during which plastic bullets were fired. On the Twelfth evening in the town centre, there was more concentrated rioting for two hours as the police held back a stone-throwing mob from the Tunnel area. Inside, the Catholics briefly abandoned their hostility to the security forces and women poured out of their houses with cups of tea and platefuls of sandwiches for the soldiers waiting in reserve. At the end of the two days, there were twenty-eight policemen injured but no marchers had broken the ban. More importantly, the soldiers had not been involved. The RUC had coped on its own.

It was a signal step for Northern Ireland and by the beginning of September, as the marchers traditionally put away their sashes and bowler hats until the spring, the RUC was quietly satisfied. The marching issue had been joined without serious conflict and even the most diehard Orangeman knew that things would never be the same again. The final count confirmed Hermon's confidence in the good sense of the majority of the community. Out of a total of 1,897 Loyalist and 223 Republican parades, only 3 were banned and 22 re-routed. However, the achievement was not without cost, for 260 members of the force sustained injuries. Their impartiality was underlined by the arrest figures – between 27 June and 9 August. 468 Loyalists and 427 Republicans were charged with offences connected with public disorder.

In Dublin, Dr Garrett FitzGerald praised the RUC for the even-handed way that they had handled the marches. Although his words marked a distinct change in Dublin's traditional attitude to the force, they played into the hands of those angry Protestants who had by then firmly smeared the force as 'tools of Dublin'. That winter, the usual respite from marching did not take place. Instead, the political temperature soared as the Anglo-Irish talks entered their final phase.

Recognizing their increasingly vital role in events, Paisley continued his campaign against the RUC with another of his spurious 'revelations' in August. This time he claimed 'on very good authority' that a secret Home Office document proposed that the reference to the Queen should be removed from the RUC's oath of allegiance. It was followed a short time later by an equally spurious claim from another Loyalist politician that the RUC's green uniform was to be changed to blue. This canard originated inside the RUC stores at Sprucefield, ten miles from Belfast. The department there responsible for acquiring items of uniform had indeed received a small number of blue garments, samples of a new summer lightweight tunic sent for evaluation to the RUC. They were of course made up in blue, for the mainland police forces, but later, when the RUC eventually placed an order, the garments were supplied in the distinctive green.

The net effect of mischievous stories like this was to increase disaffection between the Protestant community and the RUC, and draw the force into political controversy. As the speculation and rumour-mongering increased through the autumn, there was some anxiety at the top and in Stormont Castle about how the force would react if there was a 'backlash' against the imminent agreement. However, experience of the summer situation, which the Northern Ireland Office had regarded as an opportune test of the RUC's impartiality pedigree, tended to indicate that the force would remain true to its policing role despite the growing pressures. There was nevertheless concern when the attacks on police homes spread from Cookstown to Portadown during the tension there. In August five police families had to be moved from their homes in Portadown after petrol bomb attacks and threats. A jeering crowd gathered as police vehicles were used for the operation.

After the Anglo-Irish agreement was signed and published, Hermon called together his senior officers for an explanation of its implications. On 29 November he issued a message to the entire force dispelling some of the misunderstandings being fostered by mischievous politicians. 'Politics is not the business of the RUC, our business is policing,' the statement said. The chief constable 'cleared the air', as he put it, stating that the RUC would remain the RUC with its dark-green uniforms and existing badges. He pledged that the force would remain free of political interference and explained how he would work, under the terms of the new agreement, to improve co-operation across the border with the Irish police. In conclusion he recalled the 'heavy burden carried by the RUC' for the previous sixteen years, the 'grievous sacrifices' made by the force and his pride in how it had remained 'steadfast and unshaken':

> That pride is shared by many others outside the RUC. I believe that the people of Northern Ireland can rightly repose confidence in our commitment to them. We for our part must do all within our power to enhance that confidence . . . I believe that our future lies in our abiding dedication to serving all the people of Northern Ireland impartially and justly, without fear or favour, without regard to religon, class or creed.

The Unionist community reacted angrily against the 'Dublin diktat', as some called it. They pledged to bring it down by withdrawing from the district councils, boycotting public bodies and severing contacts with government ministers. There was an ugly incident at Belfast City Hall when Secretary of State Tom King was attacked as he left after an engagement and police had to defend him from a mob. All over Ulster eye-catching red, white and blue posters appeared, proclaiming 'Ulster says No'. Once again Ian Paisley proclaimed 'resistance to death'.

The force passed its first significant test on 23 November when a vast crowd, approaching 300,000 strong, gathered at Belfast City Hall to protest at the agreement. It was certainly the largest gathering in Ulster since the disturbances began in 1968 and may have been the largest ever. Apart from the obvious organizational problems associated with a demonstration on that scale, like traffic diversion, the RUC had to be on its guard for trouble. With emotions running so high and the ever present possibility of sectarian attack, it was much to its credit that apart from the hooligan activities of a handful of youths, the event passed off without serious incident.

Fraying Protestant tempers snapped, however, on 11 December when the first meeting of the new Anglo-Irish conference took place in Belfast. The sight of an Irish Foreign Minister and officials being helicoptered into Stormont was too much for the crowds who had assembled to protest and several arrests were made as the police defended new barbed wire cordons erected by the army around the Castle. A couple of miles away thousands of workers from the aircraft factory and shipyard had stopped work and marched on Maryfield, the headquarters of the new Anglo-Irish secretariat. There they wrestled the gates of the complex to the ground and were only prevented from attacking the building by the police, who fired plastic baton rounds. During several hours of violent clashes, thirty-eight police officers were injured.

There was more trouble on 4 January. A crowd of protesters had spent the week marching from Londonderry to Belfast and that Saturday afternoon they converged on Maryfield for a protest rally. As the speeches ended, an unmarked police car was overturned and set on fire, triggering off clashes in which another twenty-three RUC officers were injured.

On 23 January the RUC were at the heart of a major security operation when by-elections were held in the fifteen Northern Ireland seats held by Unionists, who had resigned from parliament in December as part of their protest. They set themselves a target of 500,000 'No' votes to demonstrate to Thatcher the opposition to her initiative. But it was a costly gesture for they lost one of the seats and failed to reach the target.

A month later, on 25 February, when the Unionist leaders Ian Paisley and James Molyneaux returned to Belfast after a Downing Street meeting with Margaret Thatcher, the Unionist hardmen, who had been pacing restlessly in the background, vetoed further talks and forced the two politicians to take the protest on to the streets. Two days later, dredging up the memory of 1974 and the UWC, a 'Day of Action' was called for 3 March as the beginning of a concerted campaign to bring down the agreement. Paisley and Molyneaux announced that the action would be peaceful and within the law, and that the protests would be co-ordinated in each constituency by the MP. The police were told there would be seventy-five caval-cades of vehicles.

However, by dawn that morning oil and nails had been strewn, closing the M1 motorway, and roadblocks, usually consisting of farm machinery, trailors and tractors, were in position across Northern Ireland, bringing traffic to a halt. In Belfast hijacked vehicles were used to block roads and crowds of masked pickets manned the barricades intimidating those who wished to pass. Hermon had announced that the RUC would endeavour to keep the main roads open but the strategy was applied more robustly by some of his officers than others. In Londonderry, for instance, vigorous action was taken to keep the Foyle Bridge clear but on the main Belfast–Dublin road, near Dromore, County Down, a succession of RUC officers were content to keep a massive obstruction under observation for more then seven hours without interference.

The government was angered at the widespread disruption and lawlessness, especially in Belfast city centre where a rampaging mob caused considerable damage. Ministers regarded it as a serious failure by the police. Hermon later claimed that the police had removed 425 out of 687 obstructions and defended what he called the 'stupendous police effort'. He accused some politicians of conspiring with what he called 'sinister elements' to ensure maximum chaos. 'We did not get this 100 per cent right but we did get it very right indeed.' Whatever the claims and counter-claims, the general perception was that the police had not done a good job and although blame for the extent of the lawlessness rebounded on the politicians, the day's events illus-trated the growing tensions being caused within the RUC by the Anglo-Irish protests.

These were embarassingly demonstrated three days later when the Rev. Ivan Foster, one of Paisley's closest associates, played a tape-recording at a news conference. The clandestine recording had been made on 24 February during a routine meeting of about 400 rank and file policemen in the Police Federation's social club at Carrick-fergus. The agenda contained the usual mundane items discussed by trade unions, including rent allowances and police pay, and only part of the meeting dealt with the policing implications of the agreement. Foster highlighted speeches by two sergeants which were greeted by whistles, applause and feet stamping. One of them, direct-ing his remarks to the Federation Chairman, Alan Wright, said: 'I would ask you as a final point, are you prepared to convey from this meeting tonight the complete disgust which the members of the Police Federation have both in the Police Authority and their political masters and the Chief Constable for their recent collaboration in the system which has rendered the RUC a political puppet in the eyes of the people of this country?'

The Federation and the Authority both moved swiftly to limit the damage to the RUC's reputation. An angry Wright denounced the recording and its author as 'an irresponsible betrayal of trust' and the Authority said the views expressed in no way reflected the attitude of the majority of RUC officers. The Northern Ireland Office recognized the right of people in a democratic society to express dissenting views. 'What is important is that members of the RUC continue to do their duty. They have proved themselves ready and willing to do so.'

But inside Stormont Castle, as it became ever more clear that the RUC was the cement that would either bind the Anglo-Irish agreement or cause it to crumble, there was a dangerous complacency among some ministers and their officials about feelings within the RUC. In his typically forthright way Hermon had promised that his police force would do as it was told. But as politicians plotted to subvert it, the integrity of the force was recklessly taken for granted and the strength of emotional turmoil inside the ranks was dangerously underestimated.

Certainly the vast majority of police men and women, whatever their private political views, did not for a moment question their duty or the laws they were expected to uphold. But there was within the force a minority whose vociferousness was out of proportion to their strength. Three of them, masked to prevent recognition, were interviewed on television voicing opposition to the agreement. By such tactics and their presence, combined with the relentless goading of politicians, they imposed serious pressures inside the RUC.

In the aftermath of the Day of Action these became critical when the sporadic attacks on police houses that had earlier taken place in Cookstown and Portadown started again. That evening fifteen police homes were attacked, eight in Portadown. The attacks reached epidemic proportions at the end of the month after the Secretary of State banned an Apprentice Boys march through Portadown on Easter Monday on the advice of the Chief Constable. In ensuing rioting 100 plastic baton rounds were fired at Loyalists by the police, wounding one rioter, who died later.

Within days there had been forty-five attacks on police homes and families. On 4 April in Lurgan, where Lady Jean Hermon, the chief constable's wife, called on families who had been intimidated, a crowd gathered and threw eggs and tomatoes at her. In Lisburn on 11 April shortly before dawn several members of the Gracey family escaped from their petrol-bombed home only after a Catholic neighbour raised the alarm. Fred Gracey, the head of the family, had once served in the force, a path followed by no less than four of his sons. After looking at the wreckage of their home, one of them said he was certainly not leaving the police. 'I'm very proud of my job and I don't want to leave the force.'

Many police officers and their families had narrow escapes. One family group was watching television when petrol bombs were hurled into their living room; a part-time woman reservist and her mother escaped from their home with their clothes on fire after their door had been battered down and petrol bombs thrown, only to be greeted by a jeering crowd. Another reservist was shot in the hallway of his North Belfast home. Other officers woke to find their homes ablaze or full of smoke and had to run for their lives. One father devised a game to see which of their three young children could get out of the house first when mammy or daddy ordered it. But the youngest child was not fooled. She always insisted on bringing her Teddy. 'I can't leave him to burn.' The intimidation was even more subtly carried out by the graffiti writers. 'Join the RUC and come home to a real fire,' they wrote on the gables. 'Buy and die,' was daubed on homes abandoned by police families.

The vulnerability of the police community, which had for years lived under the ever present reality of IRA violence, created shock waves through the force. The absence of fathers on duty at night created more strains, for that was usually when the intimidators struck. The way the issue became linked with the RUC's so-called enforcing of the agreement was spelled out in a letter to *The Times* on 30 April from the British MP, Sir Eldon Griffiths, who was parliamentary adviser to the Police Federation. Conceding that it was 'not the business of the RUC to be for or against the Anglo-Irish accord,' Sir Eldon said: 'I adhere to the view that it is impossible in a free society for a civilian police force to police for long against the majority.'

To placate the fears of the force, the chief constable set up an emergency housing unit at the Belfast headquarters. Where it was necessary, officers were provided with extinguishers, blankets and firefighting advice. Those who wished to move were accommodated in police quarters and helped to safeguard their belongings until a new dwelling was obtained. The camaraderie of the RUC was the most telling tactic as the police family rallied to protect those at risk.

By June the attacks began to peter out after sustained condemnation from Protestant church leaders and other responsible opinion. By the end of the year there had been 564 incidents and 120 police families had had to abandon their homes. As many as 111 families were attacked or threatened more than once. The weapons used against them ranged from daubed slogans to bricks, petrol bombs and shots. 'It is only by an act of God that we did not sustain fatal casualties,' one senior man remarked.

The onset of the marching season meant there was to be little respite for the RUC. Once again the Tunnel proved to be a flashpoint and there were clashes with an agreed parade going to Drumcree parish church for a service on 6 July when undertakings to the police that there would only be local participants were broken by the organizers. Four days later Molyneaux and Paisley placed carefully worded newspaper advertisements which stopped short of an outright call to mutiny. Calling on them to stage a 'Curragh style revolt', the advertisments and interviews were the most serious attempts ever at public subversion of the force. They were also an admission of weakness that the steam was beginning to run out of the anti-agreement protests.

Although there were ugly scenes in Portadown again on the evening of 12 July, when an RUC Landrover was overturned and set on fire, the defiance had begun to melt and the beginning of a sullen acceptance that the agreement was not to be overturned set in. The police banned a march from going through the Catholic part of Keady on 8 August and easily contained the rioting that resulted, aggravated as it was by the return of Peter Robinson MP, who had earlier been arrested while across the border in nearby Clontibret at the head of a mob of cudgel-carrying, masked men.

At the end of the year Hermon was able to report that although greater manpower than ever before had been deployed to police the year's 1,950 marches (170 down from the previous year), all but 67 had gone off without incident or disorder. One of those where serious trouble was only contained by firm police action was the first anniversary of the agreement rally in Belfast on 15 November. Gangs of youths on their way to the rally began breaking windows and looting liquor stores in the city centre. When police moved to intercept them, rioting developed on the fringe of the vast crowd, within sight of the platform party outside the City Hall. The windows of a jewellery shop and a sports outfitter next door were broken and as police fired plastic baton rounds they were pelted with golf balls and other looted missiles. When MP Ken Maginnis courageously moved in front of the crowd waving his umbrella to try to disperse the rioters, he was jeered and jostled.

This clash effectively marked the end of major street protests against the agreement. After a march-free winter a new Public Order regulation came into effect on 1 April. Based on a similar new act, recently effective in the rest of the United Kingdom, it gave the police tougher powers to control and direct processions. Formal notification had to be given of all events, except funerals, and the Flags and Emblems Act, which banned the display of the Irish tricolour, was repealed. In future the test would be whether flying the flag would cause a breach of the peace.

Paisley and other Unionists thundered that the new Order was 'a recipe for civil war'. They called a 'Day of Defiance' to mark its introduction but it proved to be an embarrassing flop. Even in his Ballymena stronghold he could only muster a handful of protesters and it was clear that the sting had gone out of the Unionist opposition. On Easter Monday hundreds of vigilant but relaxed Royal Ulster Constabulary officers kept a friendly eye on the Marathon as it wended its twenty-six mile neutral way back and forwards through the Berlin-style 'peace-walls' in defiance of Belfast's rigid sectarian geography. It was the sort of normal public order task for the RUC that is all too rare in Ulster.

The marching season was the most peaceful for years, with disorder at only 26 of the 1,976 demonstrations. The Orange marches were not allowed through the Tunnel and the introduction of a new band contract by the Orange Order helped to curb the excesses of the 'Kick the Pope' or 'blood and thunder' bands. Henceforth they were to be subjected to tighter control by parade organizers, their repertoire of provocative tunes and behaviour was to be curbed and they were banned from drinking in transit to demonstrations and at them.

There were other signs of crumbling Protestant protest. The possibility of being surcharged personally for huge legal costs and a £25,000 contempt fine injected a fresh note of reality into Belfast

City councillors, who had been continuously adjourning meetings and refusing to conduct business. Other protesting councils were under similar pressure. There was too a distinctly unfavourable public response to calls for civil disobedience by withholding rates, television licences and road tax. In fact on all sides churchmen and businessmen, who still did not welcome the agreement, were pressuring the politicians to talk not protest. The loss of more than 1,000 jobs in the mainly Protestant East Antrim area over the summer and the announcement that the Industrial Development Board only attracted half the new jobs that it had hoped to during the previous year provided a timely reminder of the consequences of further political and community instability and served to concentrate minds.

Although Northern Ireland generally remained in a high state of turmoil, by November 1987, Unionist apathy was so widespread that the leaders decided not to risk the humiliation of a badly attended City Hall rally to mark the second anniversary of the Anglo-Irish accord. Instead they called a demonstration at Hillsborough. The police planned for a vast assembly by closing off one of the carriageways on the Hillsborough by-pass to provide car parking and deployed a large force, backed up by soldiers, in the countryside around the picturesque village. But only a few thousand people turned up, scarcely enough to pack the square and main street.

Reviewing the year at Christmas, one senior RUC man, who had been intimately involved in the public order strategy, expressed cautious confidence that the province had entered a new era as far as marching and demonstrating was concerned. He believed that a combination of police tactics, responsible behaviour by organizers, and the provisions and penalties contained in the new Order had worked.

A few days later Cecil Walker, the North Belfast MP, became the first martyr when he was arrested and taken to Belfast prison after refusing to pay a £50 fine for a breach of the new Public Order legislation. He was one of a procession of MPs and prominent politicians fined or bound over for public order offences who voluntarily ended up in prison. During January 1988, as a succession of cases were dealt with throughout the province, several magistrates warned that there would be stiffer penalties and custodial sentences for continued breaches of the act. Public opinion, however, remained tranquil despite the imprisonments and the police were confident that at least in the sector of controversial marches they had made real and lasting gains.

Reviewing the situation over the preceding years, late in 1987, Hermon openly blamed the politicians for much of the trouble and accused them of 'irresponsibility and narrowness of view'. He said that far too much was expected of the police force in effecting political and community reconciliation. 'I believe that politicians, community leaders generally and certainly the churches have all got the capacity to do more than they are doing. Many of them are doing a great deal but not sufficient of them and they cannot expect the RUC to solve the problems.'

Such outspokenness and his public willingness to implement the policing provisions of the Hillsborough agreement had more and more drawn Hermon into the political firing line. Sir Eldon Griffiths, called him a 'tin god'. Nevertheless, the greater stability and political realism that took frail root in all but the most closed minds during the Anglo-Irish agreement aftermath were in no small way attributable to Hermon's confrontational style. In the words of one of his closest colleagues, he was very much the man for the moment, Hermon bluntly stated:

> We will maintain the rule of law, we will restore it if broken, we will apply the law impartially. We will pay a sacrifice which I do not believe any police force has been asked to pay. But more and more not only the people of Northern Ireland but their professed leaders must come to their senses and realize we need more support than we are getting.

Throughout the crisis one senior man at Knock had described the RUC as a big tree with lots of branches. As the strains on police loyalty and community tension developed, he expected that at least some branches would fall off – 'but the trunk would remain intact'. When it was all over he looked back with some relief. 'Thanks to Hermon, we never even lost a twig.'

Meanwhile the RUC's sacrifice at the hands of the Provisional IRA continued unabated. On the evening of 7 December 1985 Constable George Gilliland and Reserve Constable William Clements were killed in sustained bursts of gunfire outside the RUC station at Ballygawley, County Tyrone. As their bodies lay at the station gates, terrorists planted a bomb outside the main door. Before it exploded, demolishing the station, the other officers on duty were forced to run for their lives. Two more officers died on 1 January in Armagh. At one minute past midnight, as the echo of the bells ringing in the new year still hung in the air, Constable Andrew McCandless and Reserve Constable Michael Williams, who were both on patrol in Ogle Street, took the full force of a bomb placed in a litter-bin which was detonated by remote control as they passed.

On 11 February Detective Constable Derek Breen was off duty, drinking in a public house at Maguiresbridge, County Fermanagh, when gunmen burst in and opened fire, killing both him and a barman. On 23 April in Newcastle, Inspector James Hazlett, taking his dog out for a late-night stroll, was shot down on the porch of his home by gunmen who had lain in wait. As he lay wounded they approached him and fired again, killing him. The Inspector had been awarded the British Empire Medal in 1973 for throwing himself on top of a civilian when a bomb went off in Belfast. He had been commended seven times for exceptional police work and had survived several earlier terrorist attacks.

A landmine explosion on 22 May in South Armagh fatally injured Constable David McBride and Constable Lawrence Smith together with Major Andrew French of the British Army. On the evening of 8 July Constable John McVitty and his twelve-year-old son were working on their farm near Roslea, County Fermanagh, when gunmen crossed the nearby border and murdered him. Later that month, during the hot, sunny Saturday afternoon of 26 July, three RUC officers were sitting among shoppers in Margaret Square, Newry, with the doors of their armoured Cortina car open. Three men dressed in butcher's aprons approached and before the officers could react they opened fire at close range, killing them. They were Sergeant Peter Kilpatrick, Constable Charles Allen and Constable Karl Blackbourne, who had only passed out of the new RUC Training Centre at Garnerville in East Belfast a few weeks earlier.

The joint police/army post at New Barnsley in West Belfast came under mortar attack on 11 October. Reserve Constable Desmond Dobbin was killed by shrapnel from one of the bombs which exploded in mid-air as he was running to take cover. He was a talented amateur painter and his scenes of police life hang in several stations as a memorial. On 10 November Constable Derek Patterson called to visit a friend at Fitzroy Avenue, Belfast. As he left he was shot and killed.

Although she was not a member of the RUC, the death of the chief constable's wife, Lady Jean Hermon, on 18 November after a short illness was widely mourned inside the force. As president of the RUC Widows Association, she had always taken a sincere interest in the welfare of bereaved families and those of disabled and injured officers.

Attacks on the bases used by the security forces had long been a constant feature of the IRA campaign but in the summer of 1985, as the force was preoccupied with the marching crisis, they entered an evil new phase. Towards the end of June the Provisionals in Londonderry warned contractors building a new police station at Lisnagelvin that they were 'legitimate targets' and would be shot. Within a few days construction ground to a halt when the workmen left the site and before long the tall cranes were dismantled and removed.

On 19 August Seamus McAvoy pulled up outside his bungalow in the south Dublin suburb of Donnybrook. He was apprehended by armed men, taken inside and shot dead. McAvoy was a successful businessman from Coalisland in Northern Ireland, where he employed thirty people in a firm making portable buildings. Many of them were supplied to the security forces to provide extra, or often after IRA attacks, emergency accommodation. The Provisional IRA admitted that it had been responsible for the carefully planned murder and claimed to have repeatedly warned the dead man to stop trading with the security forces.

Three days later armed men burst into a pub in Strabane and shot Daniel Mallon dead. He was not the intended victim. The Provisional IRA gunmen had been looking for a building contractor who carried out work for the security forces. When they called out his name in the crowded pub, Mr Mallon, a retired shopkeeper, looked round and was promptly shot by mistake. A few weeks later, on 21 November, German-born Kurt Koenig, a former catering manager for the RUC, was shot dead outside his home in Londonderry.

During the period to the end of the year there were a succession of complementary devastating attacks on police and army stations. RUC Plumbridge was destroyed by a 500 lb bomb. Extensive damage was caused to RUC Ballinamallard by a bomb in a van. Constables undergoing initial training had a narrow escape when their dormitory in the RUC depot at Enniskillen was so badly damaged in a mortar attack that it had to be vacated. RUC Toomebridge was the target of an 800 lb bomb. Two RUC men died in the gunfire and explosion which devastated RUC Ballygawley. Mortar attacks damaged RUC stations at Tynan, Castlederg, Carrickmore and the army post at the Camel's Hump in Strabane.

As a result of PIRA threats, building work also stopped on RUC stations at Strabane and Larne, and a new high security prison at Maghaberry in County Antrim. The authorities found too that the usual contractors declined to accept the repair work on the seriously damaged stations. At the beginning of January they were forced to deploy Royal Engineers from the British army to carry out urgent restoration and fly in the Spearhead battalion, 550 members of the Royal Anglian Regiment, to give them cover. Michael McAtamney, the deputy chief constable, affirmed that whatever the IRA did, the RUC would never be driven from its barracks like the RIC in the 1920s. A few days after he spoke RUC Carrickmore was bombed again, the second time in less than a month.

The campaign of threats, murders and attacks continued throughout 1986. A 400 lb bomb in a van wrecked RUC Coalisland and in May bombs were thrown over the fence at builders repairing the damage. RUC Cloughmills was bombed and builders withdrew from RUC Omagh after threats. In June, Michael Murphy, a prominent Catholic educationalist, who was a member of the Police Authority, resigned after a public threat against its members. The Provos said that the Authority was an integral part of the 'apparatus of repression' in that it 'bought the weapons for the RUC and had oversight of the building contracts for new and damaged barracks. Its members could expect no leniency.' Although the Northern Ireland Office publicly 'regretted' the resignation, it was privately greeted with dismay and provided the IRA with a considerable propaganda coup.

Within a week another contractor was murdered. The body of Terence McKeever, a Catholic electrical contractor from Armagh, was dumped near the border in South Armagh. His hands were bound behind his back and he had been shot in the head. In a statement, the IRA said that his firm had carried out extensive contracts for the security forces and that, before he was killed, Mr McKeever had given them information about other contractors and security forces. The statement did not warn of the 150 lb booby-trapped device planted near the body, which was detected and successfully defused.

The usual round of condemnation followed the incident but the Provisionals gave a defiant response. Speaking at Bodenstown in the Irish Republic on 22 June, Martin McGuinness, one of the hardliners in the movement, said: 'All the resources and technology and weaponry available to the British government have not been sufficient to defeat our struggle.' Killing contractors 'posed serious problems for the British government,' he said. 'The lifeline that sustains British forces in Ireland includes those people who build interrogation centres and who service British Army camps and barracks which depend on protection and security.' McGuinness claimed that the IRA 'had now shattered that sense of protection'.

Businessman John Kyle, who operated a quarry and sand and cement works, was shot dead in a bar at Greencastle, near Omagh, on 30 July and next day the Provisionals renewed their threat against building workers and contractors. On 4 August they notched the threat up several degrees when it was widened to include anyone working for or supplying the security forces. The statement was the most explicit ever naming several contractors and companies, like British Telecom.

Ten days later a prominent advertisement was placed in the *Irish News* headed 'To whom it may concern. I, Francis O'Kane of Garvagh Co. Derry, have stopped working for the security forces. I and men employed by me have not done any work for the security forces for the past three months. Signed – Francis O'Kane.' A tide of similar announcements followed. Petrol stations, bakeries, shops and other suppliers publicly declared that they had severed their contracts with the security forces. The large breweries, oil and petrol companies and taxi firms were all caught in a dilemma. Many said nothing and quietly continued trading. Others stopped. John Laing, the national construction company, pulled out of a contract at RAF Aldergrove. The climate of fear was so persuasive that binmen in the predominantly Catholic towns of Strabane and Newry refused to collect rubbish from the local police stations.

The outlawed Ulster Freedom Fighters provoked serious sectarian tension when armed and masked men made counter-threats against the Provisionals in a video-recording delivered to the BBC in Belfast for broadcast. It was the first time the medium had been used in Ulster for propaganda purposes.

The IRA attacks continued throughout August. A bomb was defused outside RUC Mountpottinger in Belfast and the Camel's Hump checkpoint in Stabane was attacked again and demolished. Raiders drove a JCB excavator with a bomb in the bucket into the RUC station at The Birches, near Portadown, and after it exploded, devastating the unmanned building, they strafed it with gunfire. In the centre of Londonderry, Melvyn Bell was shot dead as he sat in his car. The Provos said he was an electrician who had worked for the security forces.

At the beginning of September the authorities, who had been playing down the scale of the problem they faced, were forced to admit that only one of the sixteen RUC bases attacked in the previous twenty months had been repaired. In addition they conceded that the £150 million building programme for new police stations had virtually stopped.

Another murder took place in Magherafelt on 24 October. Kenneth Johnston, a shop manager for Jim Henry and Co., was sitting in a car with a commercial traveller discussing business when a motorcycle pulled up and the pillion passenger dismounted, approached the car and shot him four times at close range in the head. The traveller was wounded in the head and chest but survived. The Provisional IRA said the firm carried out work for the security forces as justification of the killing.

On 27 November there was nearly a repeat of the carnage at RUC Newry. In an almost carbon copy attack, mortar bombs were aimed at the station but they overshot, demolishing nearby houses and injuring thirty-six civilians. However, the campaign against the security forces' suppliers and bases began to taper off with the bombing of RUC Lisburn Road in Belfast a few days before Christmas 1986, when the driver of a hijacked school bus was made to park it outside the station while his family was held hostage at their home. Twenty minutes after he did so and raised the alarm, the huge bomb exploded with a bang that was heard up to ten miles away. Seven hundred homes in the closely built-up streets around the station were damaged in the blast but thanks to frantic and brave efforts by the police from the station and local residents, everyone in the vicinity was roused and shepherded to safety before the explosion. The debris of the station, ignited by a gas main, actually burned for two days while firemen and demolition workers fought to control the blaze.

In another murder in Magherafelt associated with that of Kenneth Johnston, Harry Henry, brother of the proprietor of Jim Henry and Co., was dragged out of his home and murdered by the Provisionals in April 1987. The same justification was claimed. At the beginning of May, in the sixth attack on an RUC station in Belfast in less than a week, Finbarr McKenna, an active IRA terrorist, killed himself when a device he was preparing to lob at RUC Springfield Road exploded prematurely.

Barely a week later, on 8 May, the Provos suffered a shattering blow. That Friday afternoon, in a carbon copy of the attack on RUC The Birches, IRA men hijacked a blue van in Dungannon and a mechanical digger from a farm. In the early evening, eight heavily armed terrorists, dressed in overalls, converged on RUC Loughgall with a large bomb in the bucket of the digger. The driver rammed it through the perimeter fencing at the station but after it exploded a force of highly trained SAS soldiers, who had been lying in wait, sprang into action.

In a swift and violent operation, during which an estimated 1,200 rounds were fired, the SAS killed eight terrorists. A ninth man, in a car near the scene, was also killed, while another man, his brother, survived, although badly wounded. They were later found to have been innocent victims of the operation. Another man, a keg beer technician who was on his way to repair the pumps at a local drinking club, was pulled from his vehicle by heavily armed soldiers during the attack. He was later released.

It was the worst casualty toll suffered by the terrorist organization in a single incident: their Newry in RUC terms or Warrenpoint in those of the army. The dead men were all hardened terrorists well known to the security forces. One of them was an escapee from the Maze in the big 1983 break-out, others were important leaders and activists, with track records of terrorist involvement.

Eight guns were recovered from the dead men at the scene: three Heckler and Koch 7.62; two FNC .223 rifles; one Belgian FN 7.62 rifle; a Spaz 12-bore shotgun and a .357 Ruger revolver. One or more of these weapons had been used in thirty-three terrorist incidents. The Ruger revolver was actually a police weapon which had been stolen from the body of Reserve Constable Clements, one of the two officers gunned down in the raid on RUC Ballygawley in December 1985. It was later used in the murder of a part-time UDR soldier at a sewage works near Omagh and in the killings of contractors John Kyle at Greencastle and Kenneth Johnston in Magherafelt. It was also fired in two attempted murders.

Three of the weapons were used in the killing of Harry Henry. Another three murders, all of members of the UDR, were attributable to them, as well as a series of ambushes on members of the security forces both on and off duty over a wide area of West Ulster. Although possession of a gun is not conclusive evidence, it is reasonably certain that the terrorists killed at Loughgall were implicated in the other crimes. The history of the weapons provided an authoritative profile of the way an IRA gang operates and the extent of their activities.

Seven of the terrorist funerals were to take place in Northern Ireland and the eighth, that of Jim Lynagh, in his native Monaghan across the border. Police attempts to discuss the arrangements with the relatives were angrily rebuffed and when the Provisionals fired a salute over Lynagh's coffin and there were scuffles once the cortege had crossed the border, the RUC determined that there would be no paramilitary displays at any of the burials in the north. In the event they passed off without incident but at that time the conduct of terrorist funerals was a particularly volatile issue.

Ever since the first IRA casualties in the early 1970s, the sight of tricolour-covered coffins, masked men with guns firing salutes, lines of slow-marching mourners and other pseudo-military trappings had been regarded as an affront by the law-abiding majority. Loyalists soon aped the format when they had victims to bury and the resulting outcry from both sides stirred major political exchanges. The terrorists attempted to portray themselves as legitimate 'soldiers' and they claimed it was appropriate to fire salutes over the coffins of their dead comrades. The propaganda value it afforded meant that funerals often became battlegrounds between the security forces and mourners. During the earlier years of the 1980s, as the RUC public order capacity increased, they had adopted a progressively tougher approach to the prevention of such funerals. During the 1981 hunger strikes, for instance, stringent precautions were taken to foil paramilitary displays and there were several ugly clashes when police and troops moved in after shots had been fired over coffins.

This long-running sore came to an unexpected head on 13 March 1987 during the funeral of Reserve Constable Peter Nesbitt. On 10 March he was a member of a mobile patrol lured to investigate a robbery at a shop in Ardoyne. When he dismounted from the vehicle, he took the full force of a terrorist bomb concealed in a shop doorway. As his funeral cortege was travelling to Roselawn Cemetery on the eastern outskirts of Belfast a no-warning 100 lb car bomb exploded at the gatehouse, injuring four policemen on duty there. The city was then tied up for hours with forty bomb scares. The IRA issued a warning to what it called the 'RUC ghouls' – 'if you want to bury your dead in peace then keep a dignified distance from the funerals of nationalist and republicans.' Nicholas Scott, the British minister responsible for law and order matters, accused them of 'plumbing new depths of depravity' by defiling the sanctity of a funeral.

On 24 March, in the grounds of a Catholic church in Londonderry, two masked men fired shots over the coffin of IRA gunman Gerard Logue, who had killed himself with an accidental firearm discharge. The church authorities were outraged that gunmen who had desecrated church property should be applauded. Edward Daly, the Bishop of Derry, responded firmly by banning requiem Mass at any future terrorist funerals.

A few weeks later, IRA activist Larry Marley was shot dead at his home in the Ardoyne area of North Belfast by the UVF. With the Provos spoiling for a showdown, the funeral posed an impossible dilemma for the RUC. If it backed off and the Provos exploited the gap with a provocative display, like that in Londonderry, they would face serious criticism. On the other hand, if they went in too rigorously they would play into the hands of the ever able propagandists. 'It was a no-win situation from the outset,' said one senior officer.

On the morning of 6 April, just as the funeral was scheduled to get under way, the family objected to the strength of the RUC presence in the vicinity of the house. After some hours of negotiations by priests, when the police refused to withdraw, the family, at the prompting of several IRA leaders who were clearly orchestrating events, postponed the funeral for twenty-four hours. The stalemate continued when the mourners gathered again the next morning and the funeral was once more postponed on the grounds that the police presence was oppressive. By now the issue had blown up into a major crisis and the politicians were swopping accusations with each other. On the third morning, as a result of overnight consultations between police commanders and the family, through Catholic churchmen, the police had deployed further away from the house, although they were still there in strength. The funeral procession then got under way but its progress to the local church and then to Milltown Cemetery was marred several times by violent clashes between police and mourners, who had swollen to 5,000-strong over the three days:

The situation created a substantial outcry, even from Catholic quarters usually hostile to the Provisionals' cause. Sir John Hermon conceded that the situation had been 'disastrous' for the RUC in terms of its relations with the Catholic community but he reiterated that control of the funeral had been taken from the family by elements of the IRA leadership with the full intent of making it 'a paramilitary showcase'.

However, corroboration that the Provos would continue to exploit funerals if given a free hand by the RUC came later in the year when two IRA terrorists died in a premature explosion while transporting a bomb through Londonderry. In defiance of the Bishop's earlier order, the Provisionals announced a requiem Mass for the two dead men and turned up at the church with the coffins, where they were allowed reluctant entry only in the interests of dignity. Once more there were delays in getting the funeral procession under way after the service because of protests about the proximity of police escorting the cortege. After a time the police withdrew some distance, a concession that was rapidly exploited by the appearance of an armed, masked man who fired a number of shots in the air from a handgun. As police moved in to restore order there were angry clashes and plastic baton rounds had to be fired.

The attack on the Nesbitt funeral forced the RUC to mount elaborate security operations to prevent any attacks on other sensitive funeral processions. However, early in 1988 the Provisionals announced that they would no longer fire salutes over coffins in order to prevent mourners being endangered. Nevertheless the entire question of policing funerals is one of those issues that will be a running sore as long as the violence continues.

The first victim of violence of 1987 was Constable Ivan Crawford. On 9 January, as he was patrolling through the centre of Enniskillen, terrorists watching from a parked car detonated a bomb placed in a litter-bin as he walked past. On 23 March a booby-trapped device exploded in a car outside Magee College in Londonderry, killing Leslie Jarvis, an instructor in the prison service. A short time later, Detective Chief Inspector Austin Wilson and Detective Sergeant John Bennison, who had been called to the scene, were killed when a secondary device in the car exploded. Reserve Constable George Shaw was driving out of RUC Ballynahinch on 3 April when gunmen concealed across the road from the station opened fire, killing him. Another officer closing the station gates was wounded.

On Saturday 11 April two Reserve Constables, Frederick Armstrong and Robert McLean, were keeping an eye on late-night revellers in the seaside town of Portrush. They both died instantly when they were shot from behind at close range. Nine days later Inspector David Ead was walking alone through Easter holiday crowds in Newcastle when he was approached from behind and shot dead. The gun had earlier been used in the triple Newry killing by men dressed as butchers. Three days later in Londonderry Sergeant Tom Cooke had just left his golf club to go home when he was intercepted by gunmen in the car park and murdered.

Constable Samuel McClean, who was stationed at RUC Coalisland, was doing some work on his parents' farm across the border near Ballybofey in County Donegal, on 2 June, when he was ambushed by gunmen. He attempted to fight them off with a shovel but he was overpowered and shot dead. Three days later, in an impressive display of police solidarity, the Garda Siochana mounted a major security operation as an RUC delegation of 100 men crossed the border to attend the funeral.

# 10

# A Most Damaging Episode

Sir John Hermon and his wife planned to spend the month of November 1982 in the United States, visiting their daughter who had recently married and settled there. It had been a bad year and Sir John had taken no leave so he was looking forward to the break and seeing his daughter's new home. What happened in County Armagh during the time he was away was, however, to overshadow the rest of his police career, provide a rare insight into the usually invisible front line of undercover intelligence work and create a recurring crisis that shook Anglo-Irish relations to their very foundations. Ironically, the series of events have become known as the Stalker affair but they could equally be described as the Hermon affair, for his is the largest role.

In the latter months of the year there had been a serious upsurge in violence throughout Northern Ireland. The final three months saw forty-seven murders, almost as many as in the preceding nine months. The violence was especially acute in the Armagh area, where Dominic McGlinchey, a thirty-time killer (by a conservative police estimate), was the leader of a bunch of renegade Republicans whose activities were even more bestial than those of the Provisional IRA. With a high degree of fear and tension in the community there, and intelligence indicating that further murders were being planned, the RUC drafted in its E4A undercover surveillance unit and the uniformed Special Support Unit, an anti-terrorist team trained in 'firepower, speed and aggression', according to the subsequent court testimony of a senior police officer. They had in fact been trained by the SAS.

On 11 November, acting on intelligence that a part-time soldier was to be murdered, they mounted a day-long operation, watching three men they suspected would carry out the killing. The day's events were directed over secure radio channels by the Tasking and

Co-ordination Group at Gough Barracks in Armagh. Late that night, after the men crashed through a police road block in their car, they were shot dead in a hail of police gunfire. Hermon was just going to bed when he was told of the incident and he went off to America the next morning untroubled. Later that day the police announced that they had not recovered any firearms from the car. The three dead men, Gervaise McKerr, Eugene Toman and Sean Burns, were, however, all given IRA-style funerals and few people, except the most committed Republicans, protested.

In a second incident, on 24 November, Michael Tighe was shot dead and Martin McCauley seriously injured after a shooting at a hayshed in Ballyneery, near Lurgan; three pre-war rifles, not capable of being fired, were recovered from the shed. The day after Hermon returned from his holiday, on 12 December, a third incident took place. Seamus Grew and Roddy Carroll were shot dead at a housing estate on the outskirts of Armagh. Again, no firearms were recovered from the car.

The accounts that the RUC put out concerning all three incidents were partly untrue. They later justified this on the grounds of a 'critical and completely proper need to protect operational methods and police sources of information'. The officers concerned in the operations were also sworn to secrecy, under the Official Secrets Act. The CID detectives investigating the three cases were not even told the whole story. There was a serious political outcry about the three incidents and even moderate Catholic politicians were concerned about what was already being called the RUC's 'shoot-to-kill' policy. The force strenuously denied the claim but memories were still fresh about another case in which a man had been shot dead by police in Belfast. The 'gun' he was holding turned out to be a paintbrush, with which he was painting slogans on a wall.

In an affair that has since become a highly personalized slanging match between Hermon and Stalker, the unsung man who more than anyone else ensured that the discrepancies came to light was the Director of Public Prosecutions for Northern Ireland, Sir Barry Shaw. From the outset he took a robustly independent line on the matter. When reports on two of the incidents were first drawn up within the RUC's Criminal Investigation Department, charges were said to be justified in only one of the two cases. Hermon, who had decided to back his men vigorously, did not however agree with this conclusion and when the reports were submitted in due course to the

DPP, they recommended that no charges should be brought against any of the police officers involved. Hermon then sent two senior Special Branch officers to reinforce the reports by giving the officials and lawyers at the DPP's office a verbal briefing on what is described by RUC sources as the 'secret background' to the incidents.

The Director ignored the RUC's conclusions and this indirect pressure and ordered the Deputy Chief Constable Michael McAtamney to re-investigate the incidents, and waiving the Official Secrets Act, with the consent of the Attorney-General. Eventually he ordered four police officers to be charged with murder, a constable for the death of Grew, and a sergeant and two constables in connection with the shooting of Toman. Although all were subsequently acquitted, the disclosures at their trials, during 1984, about the RUC's abuse of the Official Secrets Act to publish a false cover-up story, police witnesses being ordered to lie and change their evidence, illegal incursions across the Irish border and the existence of the SAS-trained anti-terrorist squad, caused a major political and diplomatic row. The British ambassador was called in by the Dublin government and given a formal ticking-off about the border incursion.

The judge at one of the trials, Lord Justice Maurice Gibson, congratulated the police on despatching the terrorists to what he called 'the final court of justice'. His remarks provoked the IRA to stake him out for assassination, which they carried out in April 1987, killing both Gibson and his wife in a carefully laid ambush at the border.

Later there was more controversy when one coroner refused to open the inquests and resigned because of 'grave irregularities' in the police files. A second coroner also refused to take the cases because he was the son of a former senior police officer who had been in command at the time of the shootings.

As a result of the row the government announced that it was bringing in an outside police officer to carry out an independent enquiry into the whole sequence of events. The man who was appointed, by the Inspector of Constabulary, Philip Myers, was John Stalker, the deputy chief constable of Greater Manchester, who had spent most of his twenty-eight years in the police as a detective. Hermon said that the investigation would be conducted in a way which would command 'the greatest public confidence'.

Stalker arrived in Belfast in May 1984 but he claims that from the beginning of his enquiry he encountered RUC obstruction, alleging that the chief constable refused to suspend two officers nominated by him (which is denied by Hermon), that officers were unavailable for interview and files were sometimes found to be 'out'. More than once Stalker had to go to Hermon because members of the eight-strong team were being given the run around by the RUC. Stalker made himself even more unpopular with the RUC when, in August 1984, he offered to take over the investigation into the death of Sean Downes, who was killed by a police baton round, fired at close range, during disturbances in West Belfast when the RUC tried to arrest an American IRA sympathizer who had entered Northern Ireland illegally.

When Stalker delivered his interim report, with a bill for £300,000 – the cost of his work – in September 1985, it was described, dismissively, by Hermon as 'voluminous', and it was four months before the section directed to the DPP was even forwarded. However, within four weeks the law officers had directed Stalker to make further enquiries and arranged for him to get access to material held by MI5, the security service, including a tape-recording of the shooting incident in which the police killed Michael Tighe at the hayshed.

Stalker discovered that the shed had actually been under surveillance for months, after a lorry load of explosives, first detected in Banbridge on 29 August 1982, had been trailed there. However, on 27 October, shortly before the first 'shoot-to-kill' incident, IRA bombers managed to evade the watchers and remove the explosives, which were used to kill three policemen nearby with a massive landmine. Despite the botched operation, the surveillance on the shed continued until Tighe and McCauley stumbled into the trap.

MI5 and Hermon opposed Stalker's return to the province for some months. Hermon even returned letters to him unopened. In private conversations both men were vigorously bad-mouthing the other. Then, on 29 May, three days before a private ultimatum that he would resign from the enquiry and go public expired, Stalker was stood down from his post in Manchester because of unspecified disciplinary offences. It was then disclosed that the security services' tape had been 'wiped' for security reasons.

The decision about Stalker was taken at a meeting in Scarborough, nearly two weeks earlier, during the Police Federation's annual conference. Sir Lawrence Byford, Her Majesty's chief inspector of constabulary, who was attending the conference, chaired the meeting between Sir Philip Myers, the regional inspector of constabulary responsible for both the RUC and Greater Manchester Police, James Anderton, chief constable of Greater Manchester, and Colin Sampson, chief constable of the West Yorkshire police force, who was called in to handle the case. Later that week Myers and Sampson travelled to Belfast for discussions with the chief constable of the RUC.

The answer to whether the Stalker affair was a conspiracy or a coincidence lies in the Scarborough meeting. If it was a coincidence that Stalker should be stood down at this point in the Ulster enquiry, then why did the police chiefs make such a monumental blunder in putting Sampson in charge of both the ongoing Ulster case and the new investigation into Stalker, thus creating a linkage in the public mind that was to fuel all sorts of stories? But if it was a conspiracy to get rid of him and discredit him, then they would have needed the linkage to fulfil their plan. Whichever version is the right one, however, the whole saga did not end there.

Stalker, who was on leave, was called into the Manchester police headquarters on Thursday, 29 May, a week after the Scarborough meeting, and asked to stay on extended leave until Sampson had carried out an investigation to see if he had committed a disciplinary offence. In a situation without police precedent, Stalker was not formally suspended under police regulations, told of the allegations against him or where they had originated. He only learnt what they were when he met Sampson after more than a week of speculation and rumour and a public plea at a press conference.

Senior colleagues of Stalker in the Greater Manchester Police were angry at the way he was treated and caused such visible distress. 'If we treated a suspect like that there would be a hue and cry,' one colleague said. Two nights before he was stood down from his post, Stalker and his wife Stella had dined with the Andertons and the forthcoming allegations, which Anderton already knew about, were not mentioned, even privately.

The precise nature of the allegations against Stalker and who made them have never been clearly established. At first colleagues thought that an officer either disciplined by Stalker or turned down for promotion may have complained about him. There was even talk that he may have been the victim of rivalry between freemasons and non-masons within the Manchester force. There are indications he was fingered by a police informer. But a good deal of the suspicion centred on his association with and alleged acceptance of hospitality from local property developer and Conservative Association chairman

20 Sir Kenneth Newman, second from left, with other senior RUC officials and army officers attending the funeral of murdered constable Hugh McConnell, 1978.

21 Sir Jamie Flanagan (*below left*) and 22 RUC policewomen searching shoppers in Belfast city centre.

**23** An RUC
casualty of the
Londonderry Civil
Rights
disturbances,
1978.

**24** Victim of a
rocket attack,
Constable Michael
Paterson, in
hospital, 1981.

**25** RUC Birches
station, County
Armagh, after the
bomb attack in
1985.

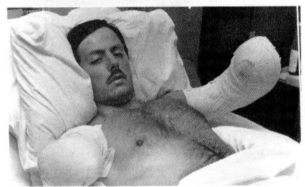

**26** The RUC using plastic bullets during rioting in Londonderry, 1981.
**27** Rioting in Belfast, 1984, when Sean Downes was fatally injured by a plastic bullet.

**28** Searching around Dunloy in County Antrim after shooting between the SAS and terrorists, 1984.

**29** An RUC officer on border guard duty.

30  The RUC removing barricades on the Loyalist Day of Action, Shankill Road, 1985.

31  The RUC, in armoured Landrovers, and the army on the street after rioting in Belfast, 1986.

32 The still smouldering wreckage of Lisburn Road RUC station, Belfast, 1986.

33 Heavily protected Andersonstown station in West Belfast.

34 In riot gear at the funeral of IRA man Laurence Marley, Belfast, 1987.

35 The funeral of Constable Clive Graham, murdered by a sniper in 1988.

36 Sir John Hermon, with GOC Lt.-Gen. Lawson, in the police control room at RUC headquarters.

37 An RUC constable on joint patrol with a member of the Royal Irish Rangers, County Fermanagh, 1988.

Kevin Taylor. Both men admitted to being friends after meeting seventeen years earlier when their daughters attended the same convent school in Northenden and said that although they went on a nine-day holiday to Miami together in 1981, Stalker paid for his own travel and accommodation.

Taylor was, however, already under police investigation and the discipline probe into Stalker was partly based on photographs taken at a lavish birthday party four years earlier at Taylor's home. The photographs, some said to have been taken with an instant camera, were among a substantial quantity of material seized by the Greater Manchester Police from the luxury home at Summerseat, Bury, to the north of Manchester. A police source said that nearly thirty boxes of papers and documents were removed with the approval of Taylor and his solicitor.

Sampson's report on Stalker turned out to be mere tittle-tattle. The most substantive charge was that he misused his official police car by giving friends lifts to and from social functions. Stalker was fully reinstated by the Manchester Police Authority in August, without charge or penalty, and after an uneasy period he resigned in March 1987.

By then relations between the Royal Ulster Constabulary and the government's law officers in Northern Ireland were seriously strained because the latter were actively resisting pressure to shelve the 'Stalker report' and drop the criminal proceedings against up to a dozen RUC officers which were under consideration. Senior RUC officers argued that any charges would seriously damage morale and that court cases, inevitably held in public, could endanger police lives by revealing details of the way intelligence from informers and other sources was gathered and handled. They also feared that hitherto secret operational tactics would be revealed to terrorists during court proceedings and that the workings of the RUC Special Branch would be exposed to unprecedented public scrutiny.

The arguments failed to impress the Attorney-General and the Northern Ireland DPP, who ordered the chief constable of West Yorkshire, Colin Sampson, urgently to complete the 'shoot-to-kill' investigation into the activities of the RUC units. They were being increasingly embarrassed by the continued twists and turns of the Stalker affair and wanted to avoid any insinuation that they were party to any smear campaign or cover-up which would give further ammunition to critics of the administration of justice in Ulster. They were particularly sensitive at this time because the Irish government, under the terms of the Anglo-Irish agreement, was pressing for major legal reform to increase Catholic confidence in the police and courts. The Stalker scandal, with its mushrooming allegations, became for Dublin a symbol of the problem and every development was closely scrutinized there.

It was against this background that the DPP overruled what Stalker claims was Hermon's earlier decision and, in consultation with Sampson and Myers, insisted on the suspension from duty of two RUC superintendents involved in the affair, who were being recommended to face charges of conspiracy to pervert the course of justice. The decision was announced late on 12 July 1986.

By now police informers involved in the episode and many secret intelligence operations in Ulster had been compromised by disclosures arising from the Stalker affair, according to sources within the Royal Ulster Constabulary. 'There is no doubt that the IRA learned a lot about our most sensitive tactics and we had to suspend virtually all of our most valuable technical surveillance operations,' one officer admitted. RUC sources said that the IRA mounted internal investigations and reopened dormant suspicions about some members as a result of the unprecedented public disclosure of how the undercover security campaign was conducted. 'This has been a most damaging and costly episode which goes far beyond the boundaries of the Stalker investigation and the full price may never be calculated,' the RUC officer said. 'I fear many lives being lost.'

One informer who died was David McVeigh, a forty-year-old married man with four children from Lurgan. Soon after dawn on Wednesday, 10 September 1986, a passer-by contacted the RUC station in Newry to report that a body was lying on the Flagstaff Road outside the town, about 100 yards inside the Northern Ireland border. The man, who had been shot in the head, was dumped face down in a ditch with his legs left on the road. About the same time an anonymous caller telephoned a priest in Lurgan and said that the body was McVeigh, who had been executed by the IRA as an informer. Nobody had missed him until then. He had told close friends in Lurgan he was going off to an IRA training camp in County Donegal for a few days, an obvious ploy by his killers to lure him away without suspicion.

According to an IRA statement, justifying the murder, McVeigh was 'confronted with the evidence of his activities' – an IRA euphemism for what an RUC source said was a violent interrogation over several days. The IRA statement said that the organization made 'exhaustive enquiries' to identify the source of information concerning IRA operations in Lurgan. McVeigh, it was claimed, admitted receiving £20 every three weeks when he met two RUC Special Branch 'handlers' called George and Jim at locations such as the local golf club, a school and a boating marina. From time to time he received bonuses of up to £200 when his information led to the arrests of IRA terrorists or the capture of arms and explosives.

For two years it had been official RUC policy never to confirm or deny if a murder victim was in fact a police informer but Special Branch sources and local people who knew him admit that McVeigh, a digger driver, was once the leader of the Provisional IRA unit in Lurgan. In January 1982 he began to work for the police after he was questioned about a bomb attack on Lurgan golf club. Since then he had hung around more active IRA members in the town, drinking with them to pick up information for passing on to the RUC. He had an unlisted telephone number to get in touch with his Special Branch contacts. For a long time he did not come under any suspicion himself. With two brothers serving long prison sentences for their part in IRA operations which killed two policemen and a member of the Ulster Defence Regiment, his Republican credentials were impeccable. But in an internal IRA purge after the Stalker disclosures he was accused of betraying the location of the load of explosives smuggled into the hayshed at Ballyneery, and was subsequently murdered.

The disclosure of the involvement of MI5 in 'bugging' the hayshed, and the discovery of a radio transmitting device concealed in the car of a prominent Sinn Fein member about the same time, alerted the IRA to the sophisticated methods of technical surveillance increasingly being used by the security forces. Consequently they began adopting what the RUC describe as 'counter measures', which means carrying out minute examination of vehicles and premises to ensure no listening or tracing devices have been installed. As a result the police had virtually to abandon all technical surveillance operations for a considerable time.

On 25 January 1987 a major Anglo-Irish row developed after the Attorney-General announced that there would be no further prosecutions arising out of the Stalker/Sampson investigations. The timing of the announcement was forced by the imminent publication of

Stalker's book, giving his side of the story. Stalker, who had said nothing about the affair since his retirement, broke his silence at the beginning of February on publication of his book. Most importantly he concluded that there was no 'shoot-to-kill' policy and that further prosecutions would not be appropriate but he was scathing about the way Hermon and the RUC had conducted the affair. A few days after publication the RUC issued a short reply to Stalker, denying that he was obstructed or that they conspired to have him removed from investigation. The detailed rebuttal of his case has yet to be given.

The affair threw a further dark cloud over Anglo-Irish relations. Stalker was lionized in Dublin when he went to sign copies of his book, with queues stretching for the length of Dawson Street on both sides. He was hailed as the hero who had done his honest best to sort out the perennnially big, bad RUC. On 12 February, when prime ministers Margaret Thatcher and Charles Haughey met in Brussels, Haughey said that Anglo-Irish relations were at an impasse and the quality of security co-operation must be affected. Talks between the police forces were temporarily halted.

Five days after the Brussels summit, Northern Ireland Secretary Tom King announced that, arising from the Sampson report on the RUC, Charles Kelly, the chief constable of Staffordshire, would carry out a disciplinary investigation into RUC officers up to the rank of chief superintendent, while the Police Authority would consider if more senior officers, including Hermon himself, had committed disciplinary offences.

The tide of police opinion was now running firmly against Stalker, for breaking rank and telling all he knew. The Association of Chief Officers, of which he was a member, were critical and on 23 February the six Manchester police officers from the Stalker investigation team still serving dissociated themselves publicly with the book.

On 29 June the Police Authority in Belfast cleared three senior officers, Hermon, McAtemney and Assistant Chief Constable Trevor Forbes, head of the Special Branch, of any disciplinary case to answer arising from the Stalker/Sampson investigation, but the decision was only by a single vote. In July it was disclosed that the two suspended officers had been allowed to resign but the chief constable stated that twenty officers were to be disciplined as a result of the Kelly report into the Stalker/Sampson investigation. At a tribunal in March 1989, all but one were reprimanded or cautioned. Earlier, in November 1988, almost exactly six years after the controversial deaths, the abnormally delayed inquests were finally opened, but relatives of McKerr, Toman and Burns walked out almost at once when the coroner ruled that, in line with the law, he would admit unsworn statements by the police officers who carried out the killings and would not compel them to give evidence or face cross-examination. Legal challenges and further attempts to hold the inquests dragged on for another six years until September 1994, when a coroner in Belfast decided to abandon the effort after the High Court in Belfast backed Annesley's refusal to hand over the Stalker report. During the years in between, Stalker's friend, Kevin Taylor, sued the Greater Manchester Police for wrongful arrest and, with the case only part-heard in court, accepted undisclosed damages in an out-of-court settlement, adding yet another layer of suspicion to the way the affair was handled.

At a police function in Londonderry just before Christmas 1985 Hermon had produced his new, freshly tailored, replacement uniform, cut from the distinctive green cloth worn by the RUC and embellished with the usual emblems of rank and the red-flashed RUC harp crest. It was not an act of vanity but a calculated gesture to spell out quite clearly that not only was the RUC uniform going to remain green (contrary to wildly unfounded rumours about the provisions of the Anglo-Irish Agreement) but that Hermon, who was just starting his seventh year as chief, intended to stay put in the post for some time longer.

The signal was received with mixed feelings in high places in the force and the government. There was a discreet 'Hermon must go' lobby building up among ministers and some senior officials but the lack of an heir apparent and Hermon's political antennae kept him out of controversy until the turmoil over the Anglo-Irish Agreement became the major preoccupation. Those who were closest to events, however, knew the force was unsettled, especially at the middle command level.

There was a recent worrying sympton when forty-two officers from the middle and senior ranks applied for the £20,000 a year (and car) post as chief security officer at the Northern Ireland Electricity Service. Signs of a potential mass exodus of highly experienced officers seriously worried the Northern Ireland Office, where senior people felt that Hermon was biting off more than he could chew and becoming involved in a lot of unnecessary quarrels. They would have preferred to see him acting more cautiously, especially with the Northern Ireland Police Federation. James Prior, the Northern Ireland Secretary, had early despaired of Hermon's turbulent relations with the Federation when Lord Plowden had gone back to Britain in defeat, having failed to find a formula to bring the Federation into line with Britain where members could attend Police Authority meetings as observers. Hermon, the only British police chief who opposed such attendance, stood by his original opposition and refused to negotiate.

Early in 1986 Hermon failed to call the triennial elections for Federation representatives in time, a breach of his responsibility under the 1971 Police Association Regulations. According to the rules, approved by Parliament, the chief constable has to give a month's notice of the election date, set another for nominations to close and appoint divisional commanders as returning officers to oversee the polling. The formal force order was only issued on 16 January, after complaints to the Northern Ireland Office and chief constable by the Federation's secretary, John Elder. The Federation accepted legal advice to let the poll go ahead rather than cause a vacuum but it was open to any RUC officer up to the rank of chief inspector, the senior federated rank, to make a formal complaint. In the event the elections went smoothly but left a legacy of further distrust. This failure to call the elections was, Hermon has stated, an administrative oversight in his department.

For months Hermon had been trying to force the Northern Ireland Office to impose a tighter rein on the Federation. He had tangled with them over a new constitution and redrawing their branch board boundaries to match the new RUC divisions introduced nearly two years earlier. Security advisers at the Northern Ireland Office who were reviewing the workings of the 1970 Police Act, which governs the operation of the RUC, and making the most fundamental study of the force since Lord Hunt in 1969, had even been persuaded to include in it the role and responsibilities of the Federation, at Hermon's insistence.

It was the latest in a line of clashes with the Federation, most of which Hermon lost. He opposed their Carrickfergus social club project but climbed down when they threatened court action. When Alan Wright, the Federation Chairman, voiced a few general thoughts in a radio interview about the way the police were increasingly having to carry out duties more appropriate to soldiers, Hermon ordered the Federation not to talk to the news media without his permission.

(The Federation is supposed to confine its public utterances to matters affecting the 'welfare and efficiency' of its members but this public row reflected a long-held view by Hermon that the Federation made a far too elastic interpretation of its rights, to the point where they ended up commenting, sometimes critically, on matters of force or government policy, for which they had no responsibility.) Wright ignored Hermon, called a very public news conference and then went to court when Hermon instituted disciplinary proceedings. A judge told the two parties to go away and settle their differences. The charges were dropped.

There had been other rows about the Federation magazine, *Police Beat*, restating their wish to be a civilian-type police force. A year earlier Hermon had forced the Federation to remove a critical editorial about the breakdown in relations with the Garda Siochana. Trouble was brewing too over Hermon's apparent use of the transfer procedure as a punishment and the way he handled some disciplinary matters. In one case the Federation successfully applied for a judicial review of the way Hermon had handled a disciplinary matter at the 'Knock Petty Sessions' – the RUC name for the internal discipline proceedings at which he presided.

Why Hermon involved himself in this feuding was a source of bewilderment to ministers, officials and even many of his most senior colleagues especially at a time when the force's morale was under pressure from both the Provisionals and the Protestant community. There was complete support for him maintaining disciplinary standards, and respect for the way he often dealt compassionately with offending officers, but complete dismay at the excessive zeal with which he pursued often trivial matters. They believed that what rankled with Hermon was the narrowly defeated vote of no confidence five years earlier.

Hermon also seemed to have a bee in his bonnet about women police officers. Under national sex equality legislation, which came into effect in Northern Ireland in 1976, men and women had to be treated equally in the workplace. The government appointed a watchdog to see that they were: the Equal Opportunities Commission. Although the armed forces were given exemption from the legislation, the police service was not and theoretically every police job was therefore open to men and women.

Hermon, however, took the old-fashioned view that front-line policing was no work for women, especially in Northern Ireland. As a matter of force policy, he instructed the recruiting branch to apply rigorous yardsticks to female applicants. At the same time he set about weeding out many of the women in the Reserve, especially full-timers. The height requirement was changed to make it more difficult for them to qualify, the hours of duty they were allowed to work were drastically reduced and women were even bussed into troubled areas on Friday and Saturday nights in the hope that such dangerous duties would induce them to resign voluntarily. An internal force memorandum said that the policy was 'to outwardly accede to the discrimination law while continuing to apply certain discriminatory practices'.

In November 1980, Mrs Marguerite Johnson was told that her contract as a member of the full-time Reserve was not being renewed, on the grounds that because it was necessary to arm police officers and it was policy not to allow women to carry guns, a man would have to be employed to do her job. With the help of the Equal Opportunities Commission she began proceedings against the RUC in an industrial tribunal, alleging sexual discrimination. A few days before the case was due to be heard in May 1981, the Secretary of State issued a certificate to prevent any review of the case, in order to safeguard national security and protect public safety and order.

The industrial tribunal decided, after hearing complex arguments from both sides, that there was a case to answer: if Mrs Johnson had been a man, her contract would not have been terminated. She continued serving in the police, on a part-time basis, as her case began what was to be a lengthy journey through the courts. After several skirmishes in the High and Appeal Courts in Belfast, mainly over whether the attempted gag was valid or not, the case went to the European Court of Justice in Luxembourg. The chief constable argued that the discrimination against women in relation to firearms was because they would be more likely to become terrorist targets or have their weapons stolen; their ability to do welfare work would be compromised; and arming women would be a more serious departure from the principle of an unarmed police force. The Court ruled in May 1986 that while the chief constable had the right to bar women members of the force from carrying guns, he could otherwise not treat them less favourably than men. Mrs Johnstone had therefore established her case of sexual discrimination and went back to the industrial tribunal in Belfast.

The case was heard in January 1987 and by now thirty other

women who had been similarly treated were also making claims for compensation. During the hearing it was disclosed that the Northern Ireland Office had refused to allow the RUC a blanket exemption from the legislation. After seven days, during which Hermon repeatedly clashed with Anthony Lester, QC, the barrister for the women, the case was suddenly halted and negotiations for a financial settlement began. A month later it was announced that the thirty-one women would share an award of £250,000. The decision prompted claims from nearly 300 other women Reservists who had also been dismissed. At first they were told they could not claim because of a time limit but in the end they too shared a £1 million financial settlement announced in November 1988. One of the former policewomen spent much of her award on decorating her dining room and buying a splendid table and chairs which she now calls the 'Hermon suite'.

The first of the policemen murdered in the latter half of 1987 was Sergeant Robert Guthrie, shot dead in an ambush outside RUC Antrum Road, Belfast, on 23 June. Four days afterwards Constable Norman Kennedy was shot dead by an IRA gang who broke into his home in Ballymena with sledgehammers. He had only moved there a few months earlier, having been driven out of his previous residence by Loyalist intimidation.

On 26 August, Detective Constables Stanley Carson and Philip Malone, both Special Branch ports officers, were shot dead by gunmen while drinking in the Liverpool Bar at Belfast docks. A third officer was wounded but survived. Five days later Reserve Constable Winston Finlay was shot dead outside his home at Ballyronan near Cookstown by gunmen who lay in wait for him. On Remembrance Sunday, 8 November, eleven people died when a bomb went off without warning as the crowd was gathering around the cenotaph in Enniskillen, County Fermanagh. Two of the victims had RUC associations, Reserve Constable Edward Armstrong and ex-Sergeant Samuel Gault.

The callousness of the Enniskillen bombing shocked people into a renewed sense of outrage at the endless toll of death and destruction in Northern Ireland. The feeling in the highest echelons of government that something must be done to end the violence once and for all was soon strengthened by perhaps the most worrying intelligence assessments ever presented to the government by security chiefs.

On 1 November, a battered old freighter named the *Eksund* was intercepted off the French coast. When the ship was boarded by French customs officials it was found to be a floating arsenal, carrying 150 tons of arms, ammunition and explosives, from Libya to Ireland, for the Provisional IRA. Over the years the erratic Libyan leader, Colonel Gaddafi, had flirted with the IRA but this unprecedented measure of aid was seen as a way of using the IRA as surrogates to get back at Britain for allowing the United States aircraft that bombed Libya on 14 April 1986 to operate from British bases.

The relief, shared in London, Dublin and Belfast, that such a deadly consignment had been denied the terrorists was short-lived, for when the French interrogated the irishmen on board the *Eksund* they discovered that it was probably the fifth and largest such consignment to have been supplied to the IRA. The French intelligence authorities advised the British and Irish governments that the IRA had probably already received more than 150 tons of hardware, including SAM7 ground-to-air missiles and several tons of Czechoslovakian-made Semtex, a lethal, odourless, military plastic explosive that was twice as powerful and destructive as anything the IRA had ever obtained before. The authorities in Ireland were anyway becoming increasingly aware of Semtex, which had first turned up in an unexploded IRA mortar bomb fired at a British army observation post at Drumackavall in South Armagh on 28 October 1986, but the scale of the shipments that had been run ashore sent shock waves through both governments.

About a week after the haul, it was discussed on 9 November at a cabinet meeting in Dublin. Afterwards the new Garda commissioner, Eamonn Doherty, who had only just been appointed, was instructed to go north urgently and to meet Hermon. Next day in Belfast the two police chiefs came up with the idea of a joint nationwide search for the arsenal and on 16 November the Anglo-Irish conference met in Dublin to approve and finalize the search details.

A week later, on 23 November, the search for arms and hiding places on both sides of the border began, but the results were disappointing. Nothing of substance turned up, only a network of storage places, like the concrete underground bunkers linked by a tunnel found at Gort, County Galway. The Irish government ordered the searches to continue. In parliament in Dublin, Gerry Collins, the Justice Minister, said: 'All the signs are that this cargo was intended to raise the campaign of violence on to a new plane, a plane not hitherto reached in the history of this state since the early 1920s.'

On New Year's Eve Hermon disclosed that the IRA already had SAM7 missiles, although they had not been used, and predicted a major IRA offensive in 1989. Eight days later the security forces' worries increased considerably when they discovered that the Loyalists too had obtained a new supply of arms. On 8 January three UDA men were arrested in Portadown after police stopped two cars containing 61 AK47 rifles, 30 Browning/FN 9mm automatic pistols, 11,500 rounds of ammunition, 150 anti-personnel fragmentation grenades and grenade launchers for AK47s, making it the largest ever Loyalist arms haul.

Hard evidence that the IRA had indeed obtained more equipment came on 26 January when a major arms cache was found buried in bunkers under the beach at Five Fingers Strand, Malin Head, County Donegal. Soon afterwards, on 3 February, another major IRA arms haul was seized from an ice-cream lorry stopped by police at the M1 Sprucefield roundabout near Belfast. It contained 2 RPG7 rocket launchers, 13 warheads, 20 hand grenades, 15 Kalashnikov rifles, 32 magazines, 12 Webley .38 revolvers, one 7.62 GPMG and 10,000 rounds of assorted ammunition. Next day the RUC captured another large Loyalist arms cache in North Belfast, which comprised an RPG7 rocket launcher, rockets and boosters, 38 Kalashnikov rifles, 15 handguns, 100 grenades and 40,000 rounds of ammunition. Three weeks later the Garda uncovered another cashe at Old Portmarnock, North Dublin: 12 RPG7 rockets, 91 × 7 lb blocks of Semtex, 3 GPMG tripods, 30 rifles, 64 hand grenades and 32,000 rounds of assorted ammunition, some said to have Libyan markings.

By the end of March, Tom King was able to tell the House of Commons that to date the security forces in Northern Ireland had seized 250 weapons, 65,000 rounds of ammunition and 2,700 lb of explosive. The Gardai, he said, had captured 250 weapons, 100,000 rounds of ammunition and 600 lb of commercial explosive. By the end of 1988 both governments estimated that they had captured or the terrorists had used just five tons of the estimated arsenal. The searches continued throughout the year. In one five-week period before Christmas the RUC searched 700,000 vehicles and 1,100 buildings, and seized another 3,500 lb of explosives.

During the year the IRA attracted considerable criticism for killing a number of civilians in mistake for security force and other targets. In July three members of the Hanna family were killed by a large bomb intended for a judge. A young woman was shot in the mistaken belief she was a member of the Ulster Defence Regiment. Two passers-by perished in another bomb directed at army or police patrols, and in Londonderry two 'good neighbours' were murdered when they went to check on a man living alone. He had been abducted and his flat booby-trapped in the expectation the police would arrive to check on him. Gerry Adams had retorted after one of the incidents that 'the IRA must get its house in order'.

Two other IRA attacks, which between them killed a large number of soldiers, were to have far-reaching political consequences. After the Enniskillen bombing, Downing Street had ordered a review of security policy: the prime minister was not impressed by what she thought were limp reasons for merely 'soldiering on' in Ulster. Behind the backs of the ministers and commanders there, the Ministry of Defence was asked to come up with new ideas for action. The request was passed to one of the military academies in the Home Counties and before long a joint study by a group of army, navy and air force officers had devised the idea of an army brigade, specifically responsible for sealing the border with the Irish Republic. The idea appealed to Mrs Thatcher, who had long believed that solving the border question was the key to pacifying Ulster.

Against the advice and wishes of the outgoing army commander, Lt-Gen. Sir Robert Pascoe, and Hermon, the new formation, designated 3 Brigade, was put into position. It quickly assumed responsibility for a strip, up to twenty miles wide in parts, along the 280-mile border. the Police were pulled back from the zone, allowing the army to 'lurk' about seeking terrorists, as the gung-ho new brigadier put it.

By then a new army commander had arrived, Lt-Gen. Sir John Waters, called 'Muddy' by his staff, whose enthusiasm for the new brigade, which he had helped midwife before his arrival in Belfast, quickly soured army-police relations. Waters, however, received a shattering blow in June, only a couple of days after arriving at Lisburn. Five soldiers, who had left their minibus unattended while they took part in a fun run, were killed less than a mile from the army headquarters by a Semtex bomb attached to the bus.

The prime minister, very concerned about the fate of her 'boys', called again for reports and action. Her concern was heightened by the chain of events after three terrorists were shot dead by the SAS while setting up a bomb outrage in the British colony of Gibraltar on 6 March. When the three terrorists were being buried in Belfast just over a week later a Loyalist called Michael Stone infiltrated the mourners and threw home-made hand grenades among them before running away, firing shots which killed three people, before he was overpowered and arrested by the police.

At the funeral of one of Stone's three victims a few days later, two corporals from the Royal Corps of Signals strayed into the path of the funeral. The tense crowd of mourners, many of them IRA supporters, feared a repetition of the Stone affair and the corporals' car was attacked by a mob. After a violent struggle, the two soldiers were dragged from the car, stripped and beaten senseless before being shot dead with their own weapons. One was a new boy to Belfast, the other an old hand, and it is clear there was nothing more sinister to their journey than having a look round, albeit a foolhardy one. Their restraint in not opening fire from the car before they were overpowered was noteworthy, although they clearly underestimated the serious danger they were in.

The incident, seen in all its horror on television, struck a further chord of frustration in Downing Street and the prime minister went to RAF Northolt, just outside London, when the two bodies arrived back in Britain for burial. It was an unprecedented gesture for two ordinary soldiers and illustrated the growing pressure from the top of the government for something to be done.

The introduction of genetic fingerprinting was announced as a measure to help the police win the battle against terrorists but in the summer, as a sign of the prime minister's unhappiness with policy, the security minister, John Stanley, was abruptly axed. The police and army were at least in agreement on their relief at seeing his back. His behaviour was showing signs of stress and was rendering him increasingly ineffective.

The real storm did not erupt until the end of August when, just after midnight on 20 August, a large Semtex bomb planted at the side of the Omagh-Ballygawley road ripped a civilianized army coach apart. Eight soldiers among a party just returning from leave in England were killed and many others injured. At first the army tried to conceal the truth from the Northern Ireland Office and Downing Street but as the debriefing progressed it revealed an appalling trail of security lapses by the army. The coach, which was not armoured to protect it against blast damage, had taken the short route to the Omagh barracks that night despite the fact it was blacked for security reasons; it was the twentieth time in a month that the blacking was ignored. Also, the arrangements for handling soldiers in the public terminal at Aldergrove airport were so primitively insecure that the IRA had no difficulty in targeting the arriving and departing military personnel. From the successive incidents of the fun run bombing, the death of the two signallers, and the coach ambush, it was clear that a dangerous complacency had set in.

When she was told of the Ballygawley atrocity the prime minister, holidaying in Cornwall, flew to London and that night at Downing Street, she dined with King, Hermon and Waters, who had been summoned to see her. There was some tough talking and the General in particular was told he had better sharpen up the army's attitudes. The mood was not improved by an IRA boast that they were stepping up attacks on soldiers to stimulate the 'Troops Out' cause in time for the army's twentieth anniversary in the province in August 1989.

The clamour for a reintroduction of internment without trial grew to a deafening level in the hours after the bombing but, despite many soldiers and police being in favour of it, the commanders and politicians decided against it. The prime minister made it clear, however, that she wanted other effective action forthwith, and over the next few months there followed a succession of 'get tough' measures which were promoted from the prime minister's own desk in London. Despite growing pressure to intern the terrorist suspects without trial, that option was consistently rejected. Instead a series of measures was introduced to isolate the political frontmen for the terrorists and to make it easier to convict the terrorists themselves through the courts.

The right to silence was abolished first. In future a judge would infer guilt from the unwillingness of a suspect to make a statement to the police or go into the witness box and give evidence. Persons standing for election would have to sign a declaration against the use of violence for political ends. A ban was introduced preventing spokespersons for Republican and Loyalists groups from being directly interviewed on radio and television. A new Prevention of Terrorism Act came into force giving the police tough new powers to investigate the financial umbilical cords that supported terrorism. The rate of remission of prison sentences for convicted terrorists was reduced from one-half to one-third.

The programme reflected a growing frustration in government that it could not get to grips with the Provisional IRA nor achieve any political breakthrough that would lead to a new era of peace.

The only progress achieved had been the Anglo-Irish Agreement but it too had failed to deliver the elusive settlement. Privately ministers and officials began to talk of 'bolting the lid on the Ulster cauldron' for fifteen or twenty years to see if the IRA's drift towards politics might cause it to split, isolating the hard-core of 'violence or nothing' men, in the hope that a new generation of more pragmatic politicians might emerge. The more perceptive began to talk of the 'Vietnam syndrome', with the army locked in endless conflict. The military coined their own phrase for the situation. They were, they said, on the 'plateau of violence', which they forecast would stay indefinitely at around 100 deaths a year unless there was a political settlement or impossibly draconian security measures were introduced. It was little comfort to be told that, statistically, the average Ulster citizen was twice as likely to meet his death in a road accident than as the result of an act of terrorism.

The tougher measures were, however, welcomed by the rank and file in the police as an overdue sign of firm government intent. 'Terrorism in Northern Ireland is an evil vocation followed by professionally trained and dedicated criminals who cannot be recovered by society and who should be put behind bars for life,' said Alan Wright of the Police Federation. 'Unless the government, courts and security forces upgrade their security policy, police funerals will become an even more frequent sight in Northern Ireland.' Wright knew what he was talking about from bitter first-hand experience. He had followed the coffins of too many colleagues not to. His own niece had been killed in the 1985 Newry rocket attack.

Throughout 1988 and into 1989 the funerals went on. On 25 January 1988 Constable Colin Gilmore was killed when an improvised impact grenade, known as a drogue bomb, was thrown at his Landrover, while on patrol in the Falls Road, Belfast. On 21 March Constable Clive Graham died in hospital after being shot by a sniper while he was part of a patrol operating a road check in the Creggan area of Londonderry.

Detective Constable John Warnock was killed while driving through Lisburn on 2 August when a bomb attached to his car exploded. Constable John Larmour was shot dead while working in his brother's ice-cream parlour at Lisburn Road, Belfast, on 11 October. He became the 2,700th victim of the violence since 1969. Fifteen days later Constable Hugh McCrone was killed when gunmen ambushed his unmarked police car two miles from Kinawley, County

Fermanagh. On 21 November Reserve Constable William Monteith was shot dead at close range while manning a security barrier in Castlederg. Another Reserve constable, his nephew, was slightly wounded.

In the early hours of 28 January 1989 Constable Stephen Montgomery and a colleague were parked in a police car outside a pub at Sion Mills watching a crowd disperse from a disco. A drogue bomb was dropped on the roof of their car from the roof of the pub and it exploded killing him and seriously injuring the other officer. As the two men were being tended by soldiers and police who rushed to the scene, the crowd jeered, cheered and threw glasses and bottles at them from the pub. After the incident the local police commander, Superintendent Joseph McKeever, said: 'During the last twenty years of violence, brutal killings by terrorists have evoked an ever increasing sense of revulsion as one atrocity seems to supercede another in the degree of depravity shown by the killers.'

Hermon announced in October 1988 that he would retire at the end of May, 1989. He had been deeply hurt by several newspaper attempts to smear him in connection with the purchase of a yacht from a man who turned out to be an international swindler. Since the death of his wife he had found the regular attendance at police funerals a growing ordeal and had withdrawn into himself for a time. However, early in 1988 a new spring was evident in his step and when he announced his engagement soon after the news of his retirement it was no surprise. He married Miss Sylvia Paisley, a thirty-five-year-old law lecturer, on New Year's Eve 1988.

For all the controversy that hovered around him, and despite the strong reactions he generated, Hermon will go down in history as one of the giants in Ireland's public life. When civilized political behaviour becomes the norm, his influence in establishing it will be seen to have been crucial. Although not a politician, his political impact was considerable in setting boundaries of tolerance and conduct for politicians to operate within. The lessons of Divis Street were indeed properly applied.

He also played a vital role in holding the community and RUC together during traumatic times like the hunger strikes and in the aftermath of the Anglo-Irish Agreement. The community owes him a notable debt for that. The age-old sore of provocation from sectarian marches was also tackled decisively for the first time and new limits of behaviour imposed. Shillington and Flanagan, it could be said, fought and saved the RUC from extinction; Newman transformed it into a professional police machine. But perhaps Hermon's greatest achievement was to give the RUC a new pride, instilling values of professionalism and impartiality that will benefit the RUC and the Northern Ireland community for a long time to come.

Whatever their faults, the RUC is a body of men and women of unrivalled courage and dedication to the community they police. The divided people of Ulster are fortunate that they have as community guardians people of such calibre. The police themselves recognize that they are a breed apart and that even if they can attract more general community support, they will never be popular. One police analyst has likened their role to that of a public toilet: no one likes toilets intruding all over the place, but when people want either a toilet or a policeman, they want one in a hurry.

The interviews for the new man to head such a remarkable force took place in Belfast over the two days at the end of February 1989, when four of Britain's top policemen, the final candidates to replace Hermon, were each subjected to a searching personal and professional half-day interview by eight members of the Northern Ireland Police Authority. There was predictable political acrimony that none of the three RUC candidates among the thirteen applicants was even short-listed.

The front-runner for the post was clearly Geoffrey Dear, the fifty-two-year-old chief constable of the West Midlands, with thirty-two years of police service behind him. His career, with its blend of hands-on policing and academic achievement – a mould he helped to design – is now the stylized one for any high-flying British policeman and equipped him admirably for the challenges of Ulster. From walking the beat as a constable in Peterborough he had progressed to mid-Anglia, where, having taken a law degree at University College, London, he was in command of police in Cambridge during student riots in the early 1970s. In 1972 he was appointed assistant chief constable in Nottinghamshire before moving three years later to become Director of Command Training at Bramshill, the police staff college in Hampshire, where Britain's top policemen are groomed.

After returning to Nottingham for a time, where he won the Queen's Commendation for brave conduct after breaking a siege and arresting an armed hostage-taker, he was promoted to deputy assistant commissioner at Scotland Yard. There he was closely involved in the reorganization masterminded by Sir Kenneth Newman and in tackling the investigations after the 1981 Brixton riots and the mistaken shooting of Stephen Waldorf two years later. This role as a skilled trouble-shooter singled him out in 1985 when the troubled West Midlands force, which had also been involved in several unhappy firearms episodes, needed a new chief constable.

Dear's main rival was Brian Hayes, a Londoner, aged forty-nine, who knew Ulster well from his dangerous days at the Special Branch officer who had guarded William Whitelaw when he was Northern Ireland Secretary in the early 1970s. A keen sportsman with thirty years' police service, Hayes was a well-qualified challenger, having worked his way from the beat in South London, through the CID to the Special Branch and then A10, at the time the department charged with tackling the widespread allegations of corruption at Scotland Yard. From there he moved to Surrey as assistant chief, then Wiltshire as deputy, before returning to Surrey as chief constable in 1982. Like Dear, he had academic achievements and had travelled widely as a policeman, studying problems and alternatives throughout the world.

The two other contenders were Hugh Annesley and John Smith, both assistant commissioners at Scotland Yard. Annesley, a fifty-year-old, Dublin-born Protestant, who joined the Met thirty years earlier, had wide policing experience, mainly in London where he served in West End Central, Brixton and at Heathrow Airport, but with a spell in Sussex at the rank of assistant chief constable. Back with the Metropolitan force as assistant commissioner, he commanded most of the front-line branches at Scotland Yard, including the CID, Special Branch, Anti-Terrorist Branch, Drugs, Fraud and Murder Squads as well as the Royalty and Diplomatic Protection Groups.

Smith, also aged fifty, joined the Met in 1962 after three years with the Irish Guards. He rose swiftly through the ranks, serving successively with the Vice, Anti-Corruption and Drugs Squads. In 1981 he moved to Surrey, as an assistant chief constable and then deputy, before returning to Scotland Yard as the assistant commissioner for management support, overseeing much of the administration that keeps the Met in operation.

At the end of the interview process on 22 February the Authority surprised everybody by selecting Smith, considered the least likely of the four candidates. The decision was far from unanimous, for there was friction over the choice between the sub-committee who made the decision and the full Authority board. In the end, however, it was Smith's name which was submitted to the Northern Ireland Secretary, Tom King, for final approval.

Dear had been ruled out for a number of reasons. Above all, the Authority was sensitive to political accusations that all they could go was to rubber stamp the apparent Northern Ireland Office nominee. For months past there had been stories in both the British and Irish newspapers forecasting that Dear would replace Hermon. Despite his impressive police record, the hotly tipped Dear was out, primarily the innocent victim of Authority/Northern Ireland Office internal politics.

Smith had impressed the committee most because he laid down no conditions. After eight years of the autocratic, frequently dictatorial Hermon, the Authority had their own ideas about the way the new chief would operate and Smith impressed them as a policeman who would actively take account of their views. But the security advisers at the Northern Ireland Office refused to advise Tom King to approve his appointment and a day-long tussle began. Annesley had returned to London after the interviews convinced he was out of the running, according to friends at the Yard, but late in the afternoon of 22 February he emerged as the compromise candidate. He had interviewed well, impressing the committee with his knowledge of the problem and scored significantly, as events turned out, with his willingness to move to Belfast. The Authority submitted his name to Stormont Castle at 6.30 pm that evening. Next morning at 10 am the appointment was approved and four hours later announced at a press conference in a Policy Authority office block at Carrickfergus. Annesley thus became chief constable, with a salary and allowances worth some £60,000, taking command of the 12,880 men and women of Britain's second largest police force on 1 June 1989. He is, said Authority chairman Tom Rainey, 'the best man for the job'.

In making the appointment the Northern Ireland Police Authority wanted a man with a certain combination of skills. He had to have a proven track record of managing a big police force. The RUC budget had grown to more than £1 million a day. He had to oversee a programme of civilianization to free more trained police officers for police work and involve himself, with the Authority, in pushing forward a £20 million a year building programme for the next five years, providing more 'hardened' stations to protect police from terrorist attacks and improving accommodation to increase police efficiency. A wish-list, were the money to be made available, was headed by a new force headquarters and training centre.

The new chief was also expected to undertake a high profile community relations programme. At the end of 1988 the Authority had created a network of local liaison committees based on the district councils. They envisaged this being expanded to bring the public more into contact with the policing process at every level. In particular they wanted the new man to lead a determined lobby on Catholic politicans and churchmen to win more overt approval for the force and pave the way for a substantial growth in the number of Catholic recruits. A Catholic assistant chief constable, Cathal Ramsey, had said that membership of the force was 'an honourable calling' but minority hostility remained and Catholic membership, which had stuck stubbornly at around the ten per cent level, was to fall to seven per cent.

When Hugh Annesley flew into Belfast to face the news media the morning after his surprise appointment, no one realized more than the new chief himself that if he was to make any impression on this daunting agenda, the tone he set and the first impression he created would be crucial. After the white smoke, announcing the appointment, had cleared, the RUC, still stung that none of its own candidates had even made the shortlist, wanted to see the calibre of this southern Irish-born Protestant – 'neither one thing or the other', in the words of one RUC man, reflecting the usual Orange or Green stereotyping in Northern Ireland. Annesley was faced with simultaneously selling himself to the force, the community and the political leaders, not an easy assignment in divided Ulster, where remarks to reassure one constituency all too easily alienate the others. 'It's a bit like going blindfold into a minefield,' said one RUC well-wisher that morning.

Annesley passed the first test with flying colours. Faced with the loaded question of whether he was British or Irish, he replied with superior sensitivity that he was a senior British police officer of Irish background. While agreeing that his new job was 'probably a bed of nails', he said 'I feel culturally comfortable'. Being Irish, understanding the history and background, was an advantage, he thought. 'This is an outstanding senior appointment where I feel I have something to offer professionally and culturally because of my commitment to the RUC and Northern Ireland. I will not become a cult figure,' he insisted. 'I believe I am and will continue to be even-handed, and will continue to deal with all with whom I come into contact in a fair manner irrespective of colour, race, creed or code.'

On the question of developing and improving relations between the RUC and both sections of the community, he said: 'I would expect to meet a large number of people once I'm in post. I would want a dialogue between the RUC and the represnetatives of the community.'

In a diplomatic but assertive way he put down several important markers. He would be living with his Scots-born wife over the shop in Belfast, and his young adult son and daughter would be coming over when their careers and studies permitted. He envisaged serving at least five years with the RUC. His first priority would be to 'sit, listen and learn. I have no preconceived ideas, the situation is too complex for that.' Change would only come after careful consideration when it was necessary, he said, but he emphasized that any organization which wanted to remain vibrant needed change. Perhaps the strongest signal concerned his management style. Command would be delegated to the lowest effective level. 'I believe that terrorists, whether in Northern Ireland or elsewhere, indulge in criminal activities and that's the bottom line.'

With the favourable impressions of him already fostered on the police 'bush telegraph' between London and Belfast, and the positive reaction to the way he set out his agenda and attitudes, the largely unknown Annesley thus blew into the RUC on 1 June with a fair wind. Senior officers had already made clear their ungrudging support, while the force at large braced itself, with some relief, for a swing back to the quieter, discursive management style of Sir Keneth Newman.

Recognizing the importance of cross-border co-operation with the Garda Siochana in tackling terrorism, Annesley said he knew the Dublin team well and looked forward to working with them. His sensitivity was similarly welcomed in Dublin where the *Irish Times* splashed on the fact that the new chief was locally born.

Developing the relationship with the Irish police to unprecedented levels of intimacy was seen as a high political and security priority by both governments and forces. The perception of the IRA as a common enemy was stronger in the Irish Republic then than ever before and the futility of the continued 'armed struggle' widely recognized. Despite his reputation as a 'wild Republican', the Irish prime minister, Charles Haughey, was no supporter of the Provisional IRA and, consistent with the political realities affecting the more volatile of his supporters, he cooperated to move the parameters of security co-operation to make them more effective. Concessions on overflights by British military helicopters, arrangements for British bomb disposal teams to cross the border for a short distance when necessary and tougher laws to ensure extradition of terrorist suspects to Britain and Northern Ireland were quietly conceded. Other secret technical assistance was given to the Irish security forces to help them detect IRA arms and explosives dumps.

In this context, Hermon's departure was welcomed with relief in Dublin, where he always generated more political suspicion than respect. His relations with Dublin reached their all-time low in the early 1980s as a result of what has been called the Dowra affair. In September 1982 the RUC arrested James McGovern at his home in Northern Ireland and detained him under anti-terrorist legislation. The same morning McGovern was due in court at Dowra, across the border, to give evidence in a case where he alleged an Irish police officer, Garda Thomas Nangle, had assaulted him in a public house. When McGovern did not turn up, the case against the policeman was dismissed.

It was later alleged that the RUC had arrested McGovern, at the request of a senior police office in Dublin, to prevent him turning up. When it was revealed that Nangle was the brother-in-law of the then Irish justice minister, Sean Doherty, the affair, together with other episodes of political interference in the activities of the Irish police, developed into a major political scandal in Dublin. The Dowra case caused a lengthy rift between the Garda and the RUC, and the Commissioner, Larry Wrenn, had no contact with Hermon for more than three years until the signing of the Anglo-Irish Agreement, when both governments told their police chiefs to operate its pro-visions for closer police co-operation.

In the meantime Hermon irritated Dublin and caused serious political crises on several occasions by criticizing the Garda and their effectiveness on the border. After the bombing at Killeen in 1985, in which four RUC members died, he ignored the opinion of the army's chief bomb disposal officer and stated that the device was detonated from a firing point in the Irish Republic. Later he returned to the attack against the inadequacies of the Garda at an international police conference in Texas, his remarks causing another diplomatic storm between the two governments.

Although he thre himself wholeheartedly into the new post-

Agreement era of co-operation, Hermon maintained a certain lofti-ness and distance. Soon after the accord came into force he stalled on developing a new code of conduct for the RUC because Irish government sources and Catholic politicians claimed it was one of the fruits of the accord. Hermon rightly judged that if the code was seen to have Dublin's fingerprints on it, there could be great difficulty in having it accepted because of the volatile atmosphere at the time. It was anyway a piece of political opportunism by the nationalists, for the drafting of the code was already well advanced.

Similarly Hermon resented efforts from the same quarter to present the tough line on provocative Orange marches and the new public order legislation as the result of Dublin pressure when he had already decided to confront the problem himself. He was also angry at the pressure from Dublin to bring what they saw as the 'culprits' of the Stalker affair to book.

Much of the problem lay in the different relationships between the forces and their respective governments. In the south, they had no concept of the operational independence of a chief constable. There, the minister of justice and his officials called a large number of the tunes to which the police, even in the most senior ranks, danced. Promotions were subject to political approval and this ensured ready compliance with the wishes of government in the higher echelons of the police. Senior officers were in fact openly talked about as owing allegiance to one party or another.

This attitude made it difficult for Irish ministers and officials to understand how Hermon could all too frequently run amok, as they saw it, with the government's wishes. Northern Ireland Secretaries, like their Home Office counterparts, had learned to take their senior policemen with them as a way to bypass the chief's right to invoke his independence from political direction, although there were many instances of patience running out with Hermon.

Despite these tensions, cross-border understanding and co-operation steadily improved and reached new levels of rapport. When Lord Justice Gibson and his wife were murdered there were none of the routine recriminations; both governments reiterated that they were at one in getting to grips with the killers. The RUC accepted the shortcomings of the Garda in resources and skills with resignation and took comfort from the clear commitment of the force, with Irish defence forces' support, to tackle the IRA to the best of their ability.

The strength of this historic new north-south rapport was clearly seen on 20 March 1989, when two senior RUC officers returning from a meeting with their counterparts in Dundalk were ambushed and murdered by the Provisional IRA. Chief Superintendent Harry Breen, commander of the 'H' division which covered Down and Armagh, was being driven by Superintendent Bob Buchanan, the officer responsible for border liaison, when the heavily armed gunmen ambushed their car just after it had re-entered Northern Ireland, near Jonesborough. Hermon promptly stifled idle speculation that they had been betrayed by the Irish police and, together with Garda Commissioner, Eugene Crowley, said the incident would not halt the developing police relationship and affirmed the commitment of both forces to find the killers. The murders were a blow to the RUC. Harry Breen was the most senior man to become a terrorist victim.

A few weeks earlier, on 27 February, Gabriel Mullaly, a former inspector who had been retired from the RUC for two years, died when a booby-trapped device blew up under his car at a traffic junction in East Belfast, a reminder that even a former policeman was still a target for the terrorists. These most recent deaths underlined for Annesley the terrible price regularly exacted from the RUC.

Each of his predecessors was in his own way – by personality, experience or profile – a man for his hour, in that his particular qualities proved vital to the RUC at crucial moments. By this measurement it was hoped that Annesley, with his unique Irish Protestant background and British policing expertise, would in turn prove to be the man of his hour to the lasting benefit of the RUC and the troubled community in Northern Ireland.

# 11

# 'A Bright Future'

There was a profound change in the atmosphere at RUC headquarters throughout the summer of 1989 as Hugh Annesley eased himself into his new job. Keeping a low public profile, he set about listening, looking and learning, as he said he would. The ground was not completely new to him. As Assistant Commissioner at New Scotland Yard with responsibility for specialist operations – overseeing the Special Branch, Anti-Terrorist Unit, as well as the Drugs and Fraud Squads and International crime teams – he had become acquainted with Irish policing affairs and visited both the RUC and Gardai, gaining some first-hand experience of the problems and pressures they faced.

The contrast with Hermon's autocratic style could not have been greater. For the first time in years command was vigorously delegated, senior officers were encouraged to express their views and there was a range of advice discussed at the regular COG meetings – the Chief Officers Group. Annesley asked questions, listened and coaxed out the consensus. 'I think that if the decision emerges quietly and at a lower level, it will give a greater sense of job satisfaction to those who have had ownership of it on the way up than if it appears always to be imposed,' he said later, explaining his brand of command philosophy. Before long COG had become a fortnightly discussion rather than a weekly agenda-setting event. One of the mandarins at Stormont Castle colourfully characterized the differences between the two chiefs. 'Hermon was a rock with waves crashing round him. Annesley prefers to ride with the tide,' he said.

As the summer marching season got into full swing, Annesley, kitted out in his new RUC uniform and regulation flak jacket, went out on the streets to see things for himself. On 12 July he watched several of the Orange parades as part of a busy familiarization programme, visiting RUC stations throughout Northern Ireland, introducing himself to the men and women under his command and studying the rigid sectarian geography that dictated the way they could do their testing job. In public he said very little, an omission that was widely accepted as a wise one, until he found his feet.

In private he was full of admiration for the force, commenting favourably on its extraordinary resilience. He was impressed by how even-handed and fair-minded he found it to be and appreciative of the support from police families, prepared to live in the wearing circumstances of constant threat. 'I think this force stands alone anywhere in the world in its capacity to take so much for so long,' he said.

The IRA had promised a long, hot summer to mark the twentieth anniversary of the deployment of troops in Ulster and tension soared as the mid-August anniversary season approached. The security forces mounted intensive surveillance, searching and traffic-checking operations to inhibit terrorist activity. The strategy worked and a number of major terrorist attacks were deterred and pre-empted although one big bomb did get through, devastating the courts complex in central Belfast, where only a few weeks earlier Annesley had been sworn in by the Lord Chief Justice of Northern Ireland, Sir Brian Hutton.

Annesley, and not the terrorists, scored the propaganda coup of the summer when he walked the Falls Road, at the front of the IRA supporters' main march in August. It was a convincing demonstration that west Belfast was most certainly not a 'no-go' area for the RUC and showed that the new chief was not short of personal courage. That evening on television and next day, in the newspapers, his picture dominated the coverage and he was even given credit for having the police relax their cordon to prevent demonstrators being crushed during the rally and speeches at the end of the march.

The highly favourable impact within the force was however blunted by a surprising internal message circulated to all ranks the next day. Annesley wanted it to be known that he had not directly talked to Sinn Fein or interfered in the operational decisions on the ground and had left them to the officers responsible. His reaction caused raised eyebrows throughout the force which questioned the need to defend, albeit disown, such a winning gesture.

As ever in Ulster, the relative calm was soon overtaken by fresh controversy. In the early hours of Friday 25 August 1989, Laughlin

'Locky' Maginn, aged 28, was sitting watching television with his wife, Maureen, 29, in the downstairs front room of their house at Lissize Avenue, Rathfriland, a small County Down market town. Their four children, Grace, 11 months, Ryan, 6, Laughlin, 9, and Jenny, 10, were all asleep upstairs. Just after 1 am, the glass in the window was suddenly broken, and a burst of shots directed into the room. As Maginn, already wounded, ran for the stairs, the gunmen threw a piece of carpet over shards of glass left in the window frame, climbed in and pursued him. Slowed by his injuries, he was cornered on the landing and shot in the hand, arm and chest. As the gunmen escaped in a stolen car, later found burned out a mile away, a neighbour reached Maginn, who was covered in blood and choking. With his wife and children screaming in terror, he died a few minutes later.

During the night a member of the outlawed 'Ulster Freedom Fighters,' a nom de guerre frequently employed by the UDA, telephoned a Belfast newsroom and said Maginn had been killed because he was a 'liaison officer' for the Provisional IRA.

It is highly probable that matters could have rested there. Maginn, the 2,754th victim of the troubles, might merely have joined the long list of unsolved sectarian murders, forgotten by all but his family and close friends. Perhaps sooner or later, the RUC might have picked up somebody involved in the murder, and, in due course secured a scarcely noticed conviction. The question of his alleged IRA activity may never have been satisfactorily resolved, either way. This time however, in a propaganda stunt of Pyrrhic proportions, the UFF decided to confront its critics, including Protestant politicians and churchmen, who said that it merely killed Catholics at random for reasons of pure bigotry. In attempting to justify the Maginn murder, however, the UFF triggered off a series of far-reaching events that fractured the grip of the UDA in its Shankill and East Belfast heartlands and provoked the imprisonment or overthrow of many of its longstanding leaders. More significantly, they called into serious question the integrity and reputation of the RUC and the UDR.

Over the weekend after the shooting, Chris Moore, an energetic young reporter with the BBC in Belfast, received a phone call from a contact within the UFF. On the Sunday night, when he turned up at the rendezvous in a car park, he says he was taken at gunpoint by masked men to a house near Ballynahinch, Co. Down. There he was given a photocopy of an intelligence document and shown others as well as a video tape, apparently shot inside a security base. All the material, compiled by the security forces and classified 'confidential' or 'restricted', related to the identities and movements of alleged IRA suspects. Among them was Locky Maginn – 'heavily traced as an IRA suspect', according to the intelligence document compiled by the police.

The Maginn family, through their solicitor, Rory McShane, had already vigorously denied the UFF claim. Moreover, in the aftermath of Moore's report, broadcast on 29 August, they now revealed that Locky had been systematically harassed by the security forces and had even been threatened. At police headquarters in Knock where these facts were well established among senior officers, the alarm bells were ringing loudly. The Irish authorities in Dublin were also interested. For months they had been pressing their concern about the harassment of suspects by the security forces. Over a hundred specific complaints had been made ranging from petty taunting at road checks or during house searches through to serious threats against individuals or their families. After the SAS killing of three IRA terrorists planning an atrocity in Gibraltar there were reports of security force personnel shouting 'SAS – 3, Provos – nil', in the streets. Now minority confidence in the police and army was further threatened by these serious disclosures, which appeared to confirm allegations of collusion with the Loyalist murder gangs.

Inaccurately, as events turned out, the culprits at first appeared to be from the RUC. The document, which identified Maginn as an IRA suspect, was said to have been circulated to some three or four hundred police, operating in the south Down area. Finding the one that went astray was considered to be a tall order. What had not been publicly disclosed at that time, but what was known to police chiefs and ministers, was that a display cabinet inside the RUC station at Dunmurry, on the outskirts of Belfast, had been forced open earlier in August and other documents, relating to twenty-nine IRA suspects, were also missing. Initial suspicion pointed to the police officers in the station.

Annesley was now plunged into the first real test of his mettle since becoming chief constable a few months earlier. He decided to be open about the problem and to demonstrate that the RUC would not tolerate such behaviour. The decision was therefore taken to bring in a senior police officer, from another British force, to lead the investigation. On the surface it was a straightforward option. The principle of an apparently independent officer coming in to sort out wrongdoing in another force was well-established within the British police service but the RUC still suffered open wounds as a result of the recent outside investigation by John Stalker, then the Deputy Chief Constable of Greater Manchester, who had been appointed in 1984 to look into the background of three cases where an RUC anti-terrorist unit had shot six men dead in three incidents. Two years later he was controversially removed from the investigation, alleging that he had been obstructed by the RUC, at the same time as what turned out to be unfounded allegations were made about his relationship with criminals in Manchester, known as the 'Quality Street Gang'. The RUC have always denied obstructing Stalker and say his removal was not connected with his investigation.

The legacy of the Stalker affair was therefore a major factor in choosing the outside officer who would be brought in this time. The issue struck right at the heart of public confidence in police discretion and confidentiality for the RUC's many critics had to be convinced that the investigation would be meticulous and thorough, not a cover-up. Annesley started phoning fellow chief officers in Britain looking for a senior, experienced candidate above the rank of Assistant Chief Constable. Most of all the officer needed to be a detective with a good track record. With his third call to Cambridgeshire, Annesley found someone he knew from his days in London who fitted the bill. John Stevens, the recently appointed Deputy Chief Constable of the Cambridgeshire force, based at Huntingdon, had come up through the ranks of the Metropolitan Police in London, including a spell with the legendary Flying Squad. After consultations between Annesley and the chief constable of Cambridgeshire, Stevens was appointed. He had a reputation as a shrewd, unflappable and tough detective, precisely the qualities needed for what was going to be a demanding assignment which, if it went wrong, could well wreck his reputation and even end his police career.

So, having recruited his own CID commander, Superintendent Laurence Sherwood, also ex-Flying Squad, as the first member of his team and leaving his wife to cope alone with the bare floorboards and the carpet fitters in his new home, they flew into Belfast for the first time on the evening of Friday 15 September. During a meeting at the RUC headquarters at Knock, Annesley and other RUC officers briefed the two English detectives about their task well into the early hours of Saturday morning.

Stevens had quickly grasped the political essentials of his brief, and during a lunchtime photocall at the RUC's front gate, he pledged a thorough and independent investigation. Fears that his work would degenerate into another war of nerves and obstruction between outside investigators and the RUC were quickly dispelled. The Police Federation and the Superintendents Association, who between them represented virtually the entire force, said their members would be giving full cooperation to the Stevens team. Annesley underlined the point in a tough statement shortly afterwards. 'The RUC will not tolerate wrong-doing should it be uncovered within its own ranks or flinch from tackling it in any other branch of the security forces or elsewhere in society. Criminality will be dealt with without fear or favour, as has been evidenced by the bringing to justice of a substantial number of both loyalist and republican terrorists over many years,' he said. To ensure that his message would reach the widest possible audience, it was published as a sizeable paid-for advertisement in the Belfast newspapers on 21 September. Significantly it was also inserted into the Dublin-published *Irish Times*, where the chattering classes in the south, who still maintained an immoral ambivalence between the RUC and the IRA, would see it.

Over the next few days, installed in offices on new police premises at Carrickfergus which once served as a cigarette factory, Stevens set about building his team. Altogether it reached twenty-two at its peak, detectives of all ranks, handpicked from four forces: Cambridgeshire, Surrey, Hampshire and the Metropolitan police. Two were women. Later a member of the Royal Military Police Special Investigation Branch, joined them. Within a short time they had established a computerized incident room at Carrickfergus and another at Huntingdon. Both were fully computerized and linked by secure data transmission lines, utilizing HOLMES, the Home Office Linked Major Enquiry System, state-of-the-art software developed to meet police needs in major criminal investigations as a result of serious shortcomings identified during the Yorkshire Ripper case some years earlier. Security at both locations was paramount. Access to the incident rooms was confined to the members of the Stevens team and entry to the computer system was only possible through the use of special passwords.

By the time the team started work they had been given three major lines of enquiry to follow: the leak of the security documents identifying Maginn; the theft of other material from the police station

at Dunmurry; and the disappearance of a further document from the
3UDR base at Ballykinler. But over the next month they were
engulfed and sidelined by an avalanche of further leaks. Classified
security documents appeared confetti-like as far apart as the *Sun*
newspaper, the Darlington *Northern Echo* and the *Daily Record* in
Scotland. Seamus Mallon, the SDLP MP, also produced some, sent
through the post he said. Altogether details and photographs of
almost a thousand male and female terrorist suspects surfaced. What
was turning up were known officially as 'terrorist recognition aids' –
usually photo-montages containing mug-shots of terrorist suspects
and a brief description about them or why they were wanted. The
documents, usually of the lowest 'Restricted' security classification
under the Official Secrets Act, had been compiled by the RUC's
Criminal Intelligence Unit and passed out in their thousands over the
years of the troubles to police and soldiers operating on the streets.

They were sometimes known as 'bingo lists' and the people
featured were often called 'players'. Without such documents there
would have been little point in deploying patrols and carrying out
checks for terrorist suspects as the security forces would have had no
idea who they were looking for. However, instead of the documents
being handed back, as they should have been, some were kept for
undoubtedly sinister purposes but most were retained as no more
than souvenirs by soldiers, at the end of tours of service in Northern
Ireland. In this regard the Stevens team scored an early success. The
document published in the *Sun* on 21 September was seized by the
police and subjected to forensic examination. Indentations and other
marks on it enabled them to trace the origin of the document and its
distribution. Within a week, a twenty-one-year-old private, Shaun
Cunliffe, serving with the Royal Artillery in West Germany, had been
questioned, arrested and brought back to Northern Ireland where,
later in March 1990, he was fined £500 for providing the montages
to the *Sun*.

In a bid to stem the rising tide of montage-leaks some 153,000
members of the Army, Royal Navy and Royal Air Force, were given a
short amnesty, until the end of October 1989, to hand in any
unauthorized documents in their possession. From that date a new
disciplinary offence of obtaining or having unauthorized possession
of security documents was introduced. The amnesty did not apply to
the RUC, whose regulations already covered the situation.

With the heat now firmly on them, Loyalists made two distinct efforts to lay confusing trails for the Stevens investigators and discredit the RUC, who had carried out a two-hour search of the UDA headquarters in East Belfast on 3 September and removed videos and other documents for examination. In the first, photomontages of some twenty-five suspects, provided by the Irish police, the Garda Siochana, to the RUC, were pushed through the letterbox at the Belfast home of David McKittrick, the correspondent for the London *Independent*. This was a deliberate attempt to embarrass the Irish authorities but Dublin did not rise to the bait and said that it would not be allowed to prejudice cross-border security cooperation. The second episode was a much more elaborate plot. Terry McLaughlin of the *Irish News*, the Belfast morning newspaper mainly read by Catholics, was lured to a city hotel. There he was shown, but not given, sixty-four 'documents' containing the names of 233 people, said to be Republican activists living across the border in Bundoran, Dundalk and Drogheda. McLaughlin was told that the material had been compiled by the 'Inner Circle', a clandestine group widely organized within the RUC with the twin aims of 'eradicating Republican terrorism' and 'doing all in its power to bring down the Anglo-Irish Agreement'. The spokesman said there was no way the Stevens enquiry would stop the flow of information they had access to. The paper devoted the top half of its front page to the hoax on 2 October creating further controversy and concern.

The RUC sent detectives to officially interview McLaughlin, but the chief constable had been assured from the outset by the Special Branch that the claims were groundless and the very next day he publicly and unambiguously dismissed them as 'arrant nonsense'. He was able to do so with such confidence thanks to the work of a secret counter-intelligence unit within the RUC. It had been set up by Sir John Hermon in 1981 after the Central Committee of the Northern Ireland Police Federation had discussed reforming the B Specials and failed to pass a confidence motion in his leadership by one vote. Since then the 'watchers' had become a permanent team who monitored the behaviour of any police officers suspected of being security risks or Loyalist sympathisers.

At a later stage of the investigation, in January 1990, a fire seriously damaged the office complex being used by the team at Carrickfergus. At first there were fears that the blaze was an arson attack, another attempt to discredit or disrupt the investigation. The Irish Foreign minister even supported this version of events. It seems however that a member of the team had caused the fire by carelessly stubbing out a cigarette in the wastebin close by a desk. The RUC said that forensic tests had clearly established this accidental cause of the fire. When an embarrassed Stevens failed to endorse this, the conspiracy theorists emjoyed a field day. RUC officers were said to have worn out a juke-box playing the Billy Joel song, 'We didn't start the fire', in the presence of members of the Stevens team sharing secure RUC living accommodation when working in Northern Ireland.

These other matters, as they were clearly designed to do, succeeded in diverting attention away from by far the most sinister events to be examined: those surrounding the Maginn murder. Even before the Stevens team had been formed, the RUC had made some progress with the murder investigation. They had established that some weeks before the killing, a man on a motorcycle had been in the locality asking neighbours about Maginn's movements. From their own intelligence, gained through effective penetration of Loyalist groupings, the RUC had already picked up whispers of a UDR link to the case. Indeed the Special Branch were already following up reports of rogue UDR members residing in the Lisburn area. On 8 September a number of suspects from there were arrested and taken to Gough Barracks, Armagh for questioning. Among them were two UDR soldiers, Private Andrew Smith, 29, and Andrew Brown, 25. On 10 September both were charged in connnection with Maginn's murder and, in March 1992, were jailed for life for providing information to the UDA. Lord Justice Kelly said that those who passed on information about the homes, cars or movements of victims were equally guilty of murder as the gunman who fired the fatal shot. Meanwhile both soldiers were then re-interviewed by members of the Stevens team who were armed with the dossier on the harassment of Maginn, provided to them by Rory McShane, his solicitor. Even in death Maginn had not been allowed to rest in peace. On 21 November 1989, his grave was dug up and the coffin damaged. The name plate was ripped off as well as a crucifix and efforts had been made to smash it and prise off the lid, probably with spades.

Maginn worked with his father, running a poultry business, and travelled extensively through south Down and Armagh every day delivering chickens to shops and restaurants. According to those who knew him, he was 'a big, strong, strapping country fella'. They say he was straight-talking, head-strong, undiplomatic and not easily cowed. He was more than prepared to defend his corner. These friends deny he was involved with the IRA but say that, because of some of the company he kept, they can well understand why the police should think he was.

According to his mother, speaking on the BBC Panorama programme in February 1990, the cycle of harassment which culminated in Locky Maginn's death began when he was arrested in September 1981, aged twenty. After his release, she said: 'He was very pale and very quiet and I asked him what was the matter. He told me that the police had blackmailed him – what they called blackmailed – offered him money, for him to infiltrate, to get into the IRA and become an informer. He was very, very frightened, very frightened, scared, very scared.' In fact Maginn made his wife write down his account of what the police said to him. 'If I did not not do it [become an informer] they said that the UDR and police would harass me all the time. They said that they would put the word around that I was in the IRA. They said that there are plenty of good loyalist protestants who would like to take a shot at me if they thought I was involved in the IRA.'

Events in the last two years of his life seem to sustain Maginn's version of the threats that were made against him. According to the record kept by Rory McShane, Maginn was constantly being stopped and prosecuted for a variety of offences. On 20 May 1986 he was stopped at Rostrevor and subsequently prosecuted for having no Public Service Vehicle certificate and failing to produce his driving licence and insurance certificate. The next month he was in trouble again, this time for failing to notify the change of ownership of a car. In May 1987, after he disturbed three men interfering with his car outside his house, a row developed. Maginn was eventually charged and the men produced as crown witnesses against him. The list continues with a series of traffic offences. Often he was prosecuted for failing to report at the police station with his documents after being stopped at checkpoints or booked for having no road tax. He stopped going to the station because he was only delayed or further harassed when he did so, said McShane. More than once they made him empty the contents of his vehicle, including his poultry, and then left him standing by the side of the road to re-load as they drove away. Once, in June 1987, he was even stopped and searched three times in the length of three hundred yards, by two patrols of Royal Marines. In August 1989, two days before his death, he was disqualified from driving for three years after being convicted of further offences, including failure to produce his driving licence and insurance certificate. Only a few days earlier, on the way back from a day out to Butlin's holiday camp with the children, his wife had finally persuaded him to move over the border to the south and settle there, to get away from the mounting trouble he faced in the north.

During all of this time, and before, he was never questioned, charged or convicted in connection with any terrorist-type offence. Only once, in August 1988, had he been taken into custody. Held at Gough Barracks, Armagh for two days, his clothes were taken away for examination but he was released without charge and they were later returned.

It was a few months after this that the incident took place which frightened Maginn the most. On 9 November at about 1.30 pm he was stopped by a UDR patrol at the Cove Bar, between Hilltown and Newry. During the encounter, one of the soldiers said to him: 'I have a wee word of warning. I will stiff you when I get the chance.' In the argot of the Northern Ireland troubles, the word 'stiff' has become a verb, meaning to kill. McShane recalls that the incident caused Maginn great concern and distress. 'He was very nervous, very agitated, very concerned and he asked us to write in specific terms outlining the exact words of the threat that had been made against him.' So on 14 November, five days after the incident, McShane wrote a formal letter of complaint to the UDR, drawing attention to the incident and the unwarranted frequency with which his client was being stopped and checked by the regiment. The UDR replied on 18 January 1989 admitting that Maginn had indeed been stopped, that he was searched and had his identity checked. They denied that he was threatened and said he had been treated courteously at all times. The Stevens team set about tracing the official record of how Maginn had been treated. The papers concerning the prosecutions yielded some details of the dates, times and locations where he had been stopped. Patrol records and reports provided further information. Most detailed of all were the print-outs from 'Vengeful', the sophisticated computer system used to monitor the movements of suspect and stolen vehicles, which contains the registrations of every vehicle in Northern Ireland. Within seven seconds a security patrol anywhere in Ulster can verify any vehicle. The computer also records details of each time any vehicle passes through certain fixed points like Belfast airport and the permanent border checkpoints or is stopped and checked by a patrol.

While this work was going on, another section of the Stevens team was following up the Dunmurry police station thefts. It had been established that the two display cabinets in the station had been forced open and the montages removed between 11 and 14 August 1989. This period coincided with the twentieth anniversary of the British Army being deployed to help keep the peace in Northern Ireland. Accordingly, with many demonstrations planned and the threat of a major IRA atrocity to mark the anniversary, the security forces were on full alert. Dunmurry, located as it is on the fringe of the IRA's west Belfast heartland, provided an ideal location to hold reserve units. So, during the days in question, far more than the usual number of personnel had been in the station, making it highly difficult for the Stevens team to narrow the scope of their suspect list. Undeterred, they traced the identities of detachments of police present during the period and began the arduous process of interviewing each one. Several hundred RUC officers were involved and every statement was filed in the Holmes system and cross-referenced.

Before long the Stevens collators recognized a clear pattern developing in their investigation. The Ballykinler document incident was soon seen to be an isolated red herring – it had been removed from a drawer to get a soldier into trouble. To their surprise, however, the lines of enquiry from both the Maginn and Dunmurry investigations had begun to converge and point in the same direction, towards one company of 7/10UDR, based at Palace Barracks, Holywood, just outside Belfast. At first the Stevens team were suspicious and feared they were being sidetracked deliberately, just like they had been over the 'Inner Circle'. At that time, it was still the conventional wisdom that rogue policemen rather than UDR soldiers were to blame for the most sinister leaks. Every shred of evidence was therefore re-examined and re-evaluated but the more the work progressed the more positive the grounds for suspicion of the UDR. Stevens was so sure of his ground that he took the kind step of ringing one of the RUC men based at Dunmurry to tell him that he was in the clear. The officer concerned had been a prime suspect from the outset of the investigation.

The RUC Special Branch already harboured their own suspicions about the UDR unit, the same one from which a Colour-Sergeant, John Fletcher, had absconded and sold eighteen weapons to the UDA in August 1986, some of which were later used in sectarian killings. Accordingly the decision was taken that every soldier currently serving in it would be subjected to intensive vetting. What was turned up was later described by one senior police officer as 'a can of worms'.

As a result of the screening of the soldiers an arrest list was drawn up. The Stevens team had anyway no powers of arrest in Northern Ireland so a major swoop was planned with the RUC to carry it out. Some sources say the team wanted to lift a hundred UDR soldiers, the entire company concerned, and were pressed to scale it down. Authorizing the operation and maintaining security caused some angst within the RUC but, in the event, in the early hours of 8 October, the top secret swoops took place. Twenty-eight UDR soldiers were taken into custody and their homes were searched. John Cope, the Northern Ireland security minister, later estimated in a parliamentary answer that the operation, involving 334 RUC officers, had cost £45,000.

The operation provoked strong anger from Unionist politicians. Ken Maginnis, once again the champion of the UDR, criticized the way the personal security of the officers had been compromised. Until the swoops, even their neighbours did not know that some of the men were in the UDR. As a result of their exposure, ten of them, who were released without charge after being questioned, subsequently moved home, with financial help from the funds provided by the government to assist members of the security forces compromised by the terrorist threat.

There was criticism, too, of the extent of the apparently trivial UDR wrongdoing exposed by the Stevens investigation as a result of their comprehensive operation. Of the twenty-eight suspects, eight were released without charge. Of a further nine, reported to the Director of Public Prosecutions for a variety of firearms and ammunition irregularities, no further action was taken. Three other soldiers were found guilty of similar offences and given absolute discharges. Four more were fined £50 and another £100 for breaches of the Firearms (Northern Ireland) Order, 1981 while only three faced serious charges and were imprisoned. Stephen Harris and Wallace Andrews were each given twelve months for the theft of the montages from RUC Dunmurry. In the most serious case, Edward Stewart was given ten years. He turned out to be an armourer, supplying and servicing weapons for the UDA.

The Stevens team shrugged off the criticism and, in so doing, were vigorously supported by the RUC. There was no way they could achieve the necessary element of surprise by giving any warning of their intentions or inviting the soldiers to attend for interview. Even if they had been apprehended, coming or going for duty, to protect their security as the critics suggested, it would still have been necessary to search their homes. Despite the recriminations of some UDR people, the RUC has not demurred in its support for the operation. Indeed, the Army itself recognized that if there was a UDR 'boil', the sooner it was lanced the better. For that reason, there was no criticism from the headquarters at Lisburn, who cooperated thoroughly as the saga unfolded.

Eight months after beginning work, the Stevens team finally submitted their report to Annesley. Alongside the results of their criminal investigation, the weighty volume contained eighty-three specific recommendations, some general, some applying to the RUC, others to the Army and a number exclusively to the UDR. The full, worrying, report was not published, but in May 1990 a security-sanitized summary was. Reading between the lines it painted a far from flattering picture of the conduct and accountability of the UDR, clearly reflecting what Stevens judged to be a highly unsatisfactory state of affairs. The authorities have so far managed to conceal the full extent of the scandalous irregularities exposed by Stevens but they played a major part in the decision to merge the regiment with the Royal Irish Rangers, creating the Royal Irish Regiment with effect from 1 July 1992.

Among the most important recommendations by Stevens were those designed to improve the calibre of soldier being accepted into the regiment by giving the RUC a more formal and effective role in the procedure. The report said the vetting and screening system employed to monitor UDR membership was deficient and understaffed and called for higher recruitment and monitoring standards for the UDR, comparable with those applying to the RUC. It suggested there should also be far greater police involvement in the process. In particular Stevens said there needed to be a review of the screening and vetting specifications and for senior police and army officers to discuss cases where adverse police vetting reports are received about UDR members and recruits. Referees nominated by applicants were to be interviewed while all applicants should be subjected to a security interview. While the Army would have the final say on who was recruited into the UDR, the RUC was to be more fully and formally integrated into the selection process.

Widening out beyond that part of the report which focused exclusively on the UDR, its most important recommendation was that, in future, all intelligence material relating to terrorist suspects should be subject to rigorous audit and accountability. Its most startling admission was that applicants for the Ulster Defence Regiment, who received adverse police vetting reports, were nevertheless recruited into the Regiment and went on to commit terrorist-related and criminal offences while in service. The report also confirmed that some members of the security forces did pass classified intelligence information to Loyalists and criticized the serious lack of controls and adequate accounting procedures to protect sensitive documents. However Stevens reported that while there was a degree of collusion, 'it is restricted to a small number of individuals, who have gravely abused their positions of trust', and he stressed that the abuse was 'not widespread or institutionalized'. Stevens defined the dilemma for the security forces as being to find a way to satisfy the need for them to be properly informed and operationally effective without compromising restricted information. 'It must be acknowledged in the present climate that leakages of information from the security forces may never be completely eliminated,' he said. 'However, if the measures recommended in respect of the police, the army and other organizations are introduced, then there is every hope that future collusion between the security forces and paramilitary groups will be eradicated.'

The Stevens enquiry took written statements from 1,900 witnesses, followed 2,000 lines of investigation and expended 2,000 man hours interviewing detained persons. They recovered 2,600 documents, most of them having originated in the security forces. 'A complex network of intelligence of all types was uncovered, involving the supply and exchange of information between Loyalist paramilitary groups, with the Ulster Defence Association at the centre,' the report said. The security force documents were all of the lowest security classification, 'Restricted', and dated from the 1970s. The most recent document recovered was prepared in June 1988. All the material gathered during the enquiry and recorded by Holmes totalled 96,000 cross-referenced entries.

During its course, the report said, ninety-four people were arrested, with fifty-nine subsequently being charged with offences under the Prevention of Terrorism, Official Secrets and Firearms Acts. No RUC officers were charged although a report concerning two of them was rejected by the DPP due to lack of evidence.

While Annesley pledged to implement those sections of the report applying to the RUC, one of the main suggestions affecting the force was quickly discounted. Annesley said that the formation of a special Anti-Terrorist detective unit was impracticable in the Northern Ireland context. He pointed out that in 1989, on the British mainland, there had been twenty-three terrorist incidents requiring detailed scenes of crime examination lasting from three days to three weeks. In the same period in Ulster there were 1,655 similar terrorist incidents. Annesley said that in terms of logistics, personnel and containment, the same intensive approach was just not viable for the RUC. Work was already in hand on another Stevens suggestion, to set up a Serious Crimes Squad, pulling together the range of scientific support services, fingerprints, forensic science and photography for the RUC into a single expert unit. A major shake-up of the RUC's fingerprint bureau was also foreshadowed with more staff and advanced training to make the most of the computer-based technology that was to be acquired.

Stevens called for better accounting and supervision of intelligence systems and new procedures to restrict the production of intelligence documentation. He also suggested there should be strict controls over the dissemination and handling of documents, recommendations which would ensure that those responsible for passing confidential information could easily be traced and held criminally responsible. He was highly critical of the ease with which a small number of individuals were able to avoid discovery while illegally trafficking security force documents because of inadequate security procedures. Annesley revealed that all intelligence documents are now numbered so that they can be readily checked and accounted for. He also demonstrated how police collator's bulletins, containing information about terrorist suspects to brief police and troops on security duties, are now printed on sensitized paper which produces only a black sheet if it is photocopied.

Tighter controls over the use of photocopiers, access to computer systems, especially the central vehicle index, and more secure storage methods for sensitive documents were put in hand as a result of the report and have since been introduced. Intelligence bulletins were also given more limited circulation within the security forces with nominated officers being made responsible for keeping records safe.

Annesley reacted strongly to criticism that the Stevens investigation was flawed because it had not uncovered evidence of wrongdoing within the RUC itself. Describing that as a 'regretful and unjustified innuendo', he said that 'the RUC is entitled to the same standard of justice as anyone else. Unless there is evidence, as opposed to speculation, of wrong doing, then my officers are entitled to the virtue of innocence.'

In a bid to bind the ill-feeling and rifts between the police and UDR arising from the effects of the Stevens investigation, the Chief Constable also paid tribute to the UDR who, he said, 'have been subjected to a level of wholesale denigration that is simply not justified. I think the UDR does an exceptional job in this province and the RUC simply could not operate effectively without them. It is, I think, particularly poignant that whilst the whole Regiment is being criticized in a catch-all way, their members, like my own officers, are being murdered by terrorists as they perform their duty on behalf of the whole population of Northern Ireland.'

Meanwhile, through autumn 1991 and into early 1992, the concluding acts of the Stevens enquiry reached the courts in Northern Ireland. During a major trial in October, Crown Counsel told Mr Justice Carswell that a house in Londonderry was 'the focal point' for twelve members of an Ulster Loyalist 'intelligence gathering cell' who were using documents compiled by the security forces to target people for assassination. When police raided the house at Sperrin Park in November 1989 they uncovered a 'multiplicity of documents' and Counsel said the house was being used as a base where the documents could be 'obtained, detailed, collated and classified'. When the occupant, Robert Alexander Allen, 34, was arrested, he told police the documents were to be used by the Ulster Clubs in a civil war situation but the Crown alleged Allen was the leader of the cell and the documents were being used for 'targetting people, meaning to prepare them for, or setting them up for assassination.' Allen was one of twelve people, including a former prison officer, who faced a total of thirty-six charges ranging from conspiracy to murder, intimidation and recording and collecting information useful to terrorists. A detective, who gave evidence about the police raid on Allen's house, said that the documents found there contained information about IRA, INLA and Sinn Fein members from the Londonderry area and throughout Ireland. The documents included photo-montages of suspects and the court was told that beside the photograph of one particular suspect someone had written in blue ink: 'dead as a door nail'.

A year earlier Stevens had been forced to defend his team against 'unjustified and unwarranted comments' about his work in Northern Ireland after the withdrawal of charges against five prominent Loyalists at Belfast Magistrates' Court in October 1990. He said it would be improper for him to enter into public discussion of these matters. 'I hope the public will understand that I am restricted in what I may say because many matters which are the subject of my investigation are still to be decided by the courts.' The measured tone of the statement concealed a fair degree of resentment, not only by Stevens, but in the RUC as well, at the storm of criticism that broke around them after five men, leading members of the Ulster Defence Association, were released when charges concerned with the illegal possession of confidential police documents were withdrawn. The row reflected the continued core problem in fighting terrorism in Northern Ireland which is that the police all too often cannot substantiate charges brought against suspects because of insufficient evidence. Witnesses are regularly threatened, corroborative evidence is rarely available, suspects refuse to make statements and forensic evidence is often inconclusive or inadequate to secure conviction.

Stevens was forced to learn, like the unfortunate John Stalker before him, that it is the supreme test of the professionalism of any mainland police officer to work in Northern Ireland and emerge unscathed from the all-engulfing maelstrom of political controversy. Nevertheless Stevens emerged with his reputation not only intact but enhanced, earning promotion to chief constable of the Northumbrian force, a post he took up in October 1991. Through its support for the Stevens investigation, the RUC convincingly showed that it is the enemy of all those who break the law and that there is no special dispensation for anyone, least of all those in the security forces who, through a sense of misguided patriotism, take the law into their own hands.

During the course of the Stevens enquiry the IRA continued to target the RUC for murder. Annesley was in office less than a month when he attended his first RUC funeral, that of Constable David Black, who was killed on 24 June by a bomb attached to his car in Strabane. On 1 July, Constable Norman Annett, who was a month short of retirement after thirty-four years' service in the RUC, was gunned down and killed while visiting his elderly mother at Garvagh, Co. Londonderry. Reserve Constable Alexander Bell died on 24 July, seventeen days after his patrol car was devastated by a landmine in an ambush near Cushendall, Co. Antrim. Superintendent Alwyn

Harris was driving to church from his home in Lisburn on 8 October when a booby-trap device attached to his car exploded, killing him. Twelve days later Constable Michael Marshall died when his car came under a hail of fire from an anti-aircraft gun and burst into flames at Belleeks, near Newry. On 9 November, Constable Ian Johnston was shot dead while taking part in an anti-terrorist operation in north Belfast. A colleague fired on him by mistake.

The accidental killing of Constable Johnston triggered the unmasking of a man who was probably the RUC's most successful agent ever inside the Provisional IRA and led to the imprisonment of Danny Morrison, one of the movement's most influential and outspoken figures. Within the enclosed circles of the IRA, Danny Morrison, 37, was known as the 'Lord Chief Justice'. He earned the nickname because he was called in to preside over 'kangaroo courts', after someone, usually a suspected police informer, had fallen foul of the organization. In many cases he was, according to security sources, the senior member of the terrorist leadership who played judge and jury and decided if they should live or die.

The affable Morrison kept this side of his Republicanism well concealed and as publicity director of Sinn Fein and editor of the IRA newspaper *An Phoblacht/Republican News*, used his considerable talents as a communicator and his authority as an elected representative, to promote and justify, at home and abroad, even the IRA's most brutal activities over the previous ten years. He was, in fact, the classic example of the day-time politician and night-time terrorist. 'A man,' in the words of his defence counsel, Desmond Boal, QC, 'accustomed to walking a minefield on the verge of unlawfulness.'

But in May 1991, after a nineteen-day trial at Belfast Crown Court, in what is unquestionably one of the landmark cases of the campaign against terrorism in Northern Ireland, Morrison faced the real Lord Chief Justice, Sir Brian Hutton, and lost. His bragadoccio performance in the witness box, when he tried to weld the incompatible elements of his defence with loyalty to the Republican cause, was over-shadowed by his intellectual arrogance and inability not to attempt to score propaganda points against the police and the courts, a contest he resoundingly lost.

The origins of the Morrison case went back sixteen months to the beginning of January 1990, when the RUC dramatically rescued their star informer from the clutches of the IRA just before he was to be murdered. Its outcome, with Morrison and several of the most important IRA activists in Belfast consigned to long terms of imprisonment, was highly significant on a number of grounds. Putting a 'godfather', like Morrison, behind bars convincingly exposed the fiction that Sinn Fein and the IRA are, as he had long claimed, no more than independent fellow-travellers sharing the same journey. This exposure is all the more telling because it was Morrison who, in 1981, coined the vivid phrase about the IRA taking power in Ireland 'with a ballot paper in this hand and an Armalite (rifle) in this hand,' certainly the most revealing expression of IRA strategy ever made in public.

The case also demonstrated, for the first time, the value of the 'right to silence' restrictions in helping bring terrorists to justice. Morrison was forced to go into the witness box in a final, vain bid to extricate himself from what Crown counsel, John Creaney, QC, described as his part in a 'deep conspiracy' to murder Alexander Lynch, 33. Lynch, by his own admission, was a one-time IRA member who admitted to being a police informer, after being abducted and interrogated by a self-styled IRA 'security' unit.

The trial provided a rare and revealing insight into the crucial role of the police informer in security strategy in Northern Ireland. For over six years, until the IRA unmasked him, Lynch, now said to be the most valuable IRA informer ever to have been recruited by the RUC, manoeuvred dangerously back and forth across the invisible front line of the secret intelligence war. His tip-offs to his Special Branch handlers about imminent terrorist attacks are credited, by the police, with having directly saved at least a dozen lives and prevented damage to property from bomb attacks running into millions of pounds.

Lynch had been steeped in terrorism since the age of fourteen, for nigh on twenty years. By the time he was recruited as a police informer in 1983, he had sustained gunshot wounds in a clash with soldiers and served two terms in prison. He agreed to work for the police to avoid another prison sentence for the theft of a shotgun. As a driver for the outlawed Irish National Liberation Army he obtained valuable information about members, safe houses and potential targets, all of which was passed on to the Special Branch, using his codename, Mr Turner.

In January 1985 he was given three handguns in a plastic bag and told to transport them across Belfast, for use in a terrorist attack. After handing over the guns in a flat, Lynch said he was slipping out to a takeaway restaurant for hamburger and chips. Instead he rang the police to tip them off about the pending terrorist attack. His usual handler was not available to protect him and when the police raided the flat a short time later, Lynch was still there, and was arrested. To protect his cover he made a statement minimizing his part in the affair and later pleaded guilty in court, receiving a four-year prison term for possessing firearms. On his release in January 1987, he resumed his work as a police informer, this time moving in on the Provisional IRA operating in the tough Ardoyne, Bone and Oldpark areas of north Belfast. He was attached to a so-called 'intelligence cell' giving him access to the reconnaissance and planning of attacks.

Over the next few years, Lynch's consistently high-grade information foiled an IRA plot to machine-gun five police officers in a minibus on their way to Belfast prison and, during a bomb attack on the Short Bros aircraft factory, he actually disrupted bombs he was helping plant to ensure they would not explode. He also helped foil a plot to attach boobytrap explosive devices to an armoured police car being used to transport the Ulster Unionist MP, Cecil Walker, and his bodyguards, undoubtedly saving their lives. On another occasion he warned police in north Belfast to move a police community relations officer for his own safety. Gunmen had stalked him for weeks and once refrained from opening fire to kill him because of the proximity of civilians outside a church. For this work, saving lives and millions of pounds in potential compensation claims for the consequences of commercial bomb attacks, he received regular sums of between £30 and £400 from his police contacts as well as substantial bonuses, totalling, it was reputed, some £50,000 over an eighteen-month period.

The IRA has admitted that Lynch's double role led to the imprisonment of many individuals and the seizure of large quantities of weapons and explosives and, in a clear bid to discredit him, they claim that he took part in terrorist attacks, in which members of the security forces were killed and injured, to gain credibility with the organization and protect his cover. From the witness box Lynch said: 'I have done a lot of bad things in the past but I have made amends by what I was doing for the police.'

His downfall began on the night of 9 November 1989 when undercover RUC officers, from the élite anti-terrorist unit known as the Headquarters Mobile Support Unit, raided a house in the New Lodge Road area of Belfast. Acting on information from Lynch that weapons had been moved there in preparation for an attack, the police moved in from the front and rear. During the operation Constable Ian Johnston, 31, was accidentally shot by a colleague and killed.

The IRA, as ever paranoid about informers within its ranks, deployed a high-level 'security' unit, specifically charged with hunting them down. Lynch was one of those investigated soon afterwards. Clearly he did not satisfy his questioners, who decided he was to face abduction and interrogation. This was planned for the weekend of 5–7 January 1990 in the upstairs bedroom of a nondescript terrace house at 124 Carrigart Avenue, in the Lenadoon area of west Belfast. The Martin family, who lived there, were Sinn Fein supporters, and at least once before they had allowed the IRA to use their house. Almost a year earlier, between 25–26 February 1989, a local estate agent, James Fenton, who had come under IRA suspicion, was held and interrogated in one of the Martins' bedrooms. A ten minute, tape-recorded confession which ends with an emotional plea for mercy, later played to Fenton's father to justify his killing as a police informer, was extracted before he was taken out and shot dead at the edge of a nearby school playground.

Mrs Veronica Martin, 44, who lived with her husband, James, 55, told the police she was in the bath that Sunday night when she heard shots, shortly after Fenton had been taken from the house. She said: 'I'm sorry it ever happened. I even got rid of the furniture in the back room, I was so disgusted.' Nevertheless when the Martins were approached again for the use of the house they agreed.

On the Friday evening, 5 January, Lynch was lured there and overpowered. Ushered upstairs, where he was spreadeagled on a bed in a darkened room, he was minutely searched by four or five people, who even parted his toes. A metal detector was passed over his body. Blindfolded with cotton wool and bandages kept in the house since the Fenton interrogration, his hands were tied and he was positioned on a chair. With an anti-bugging device operating in the background, the interrogation began. Lynch was told by a man, who said he was trained in Libya, that he would be deprived of food and sleep until he broke and confessed. If he did not, the interrogator said, he would get 'a jab in the arse and wake up in South Armagh.' He was told he would be hung upside down in a cattleshed, beaten up and nobody would hear the screaming.

Over the Friday night and into Saturday morning two teams

quizzed Lynch. At one point an interrogator tapped him on the side of the temple and said: 'You'll get it right there.' Lynch said in court: 'I was very frightened. I knew that if I admitted being an informer I would be shot dead. I knew that if I didn't I would be shot dead anyway. The only place you go from the IRA interrogation is to the grave.' Confronted with this situation Lynch made first a written, and then, in a shaking voice, a tape-recorded confession. He was given no food while he was held although his captors were given meals of stew and a fry-up, made by Mrs Martin, which they ate in the bedroom in front of him.

Armed with the Saturday morning confession, Lynch's captors discussed his fate throughout the rest of the day and through Sunday. That afternoon Morrison was contacted by Anton Murray, regarded by the police as one of the most senior and ruthless IRA leaders in Belfast. On Sunday evening, together with Murray, he went to Carrigart Avenue. Morrison insists he 'smelt a good story' and was going to make plans for Lynch to appear at a press conference to discredit the RUC by saying they wanted him to set up two IRA leaders for the police to shoot them. The police believe, but the court did not accept, that Morrison was there to approve the immediate murder of Lynch. Moments after he arrived at the Martin house, the police, backed up by soldiers, swooped. As they knocked, there was panic inside. Morrison ran out the back and into the house next door where he was later arrested. He told the family to say he was visiting. They testified in court that he was not.

As the police continued to knock outside, Lynch, who says he was resigned to death, was brought downstairs and told to watch television and keep his mouth shut. At the same time, Murray broke open the cassette tape holder and unravelled the tape recording of Lynch's confession. It was later reconstituted by forensic experts and proved to be vital evidence. One of the police officers, who rescued Lynch, said later that he was 'in an emotional state, clammy to touch, tears welled up in his eyes.' Police later recovered fingerprints on a tape recorder, the anti-bugging device and other items, including tea mugs, newspapers and a bottle of tomato sauce, as well as evidence gleaned by matching fibres from various other articles, to link those arrested in the Martin house to the murder conspiracy.

Morrison, brazen and arrogant to the end, laughed at the police who arrested him and refused to give any account of his movements. From the witness box he said the IRA had a right to kill informers and he accepted a share of moral responsibility for its campaign. But the able Morrison, a novelist (West Belfast published in 1989), propagandist and elected politician (NI Assembly 1982–86), whose prominence and fluency in the Republican cause could well have guaranteed him an influential political career, was instead consigned to the oblivion of a prison cell. As he said, wryly, in court, he now recognized he had made 'a big mistake'. Morrison, dressed in a cream shirt, tie and slacks, stood grim faced in the dock as the Judge told him he was not taking into account Morrison's activities on behalf of Sinn Fein or his criminal record of motoring and public order offences, in assessing the sentence.

Jailing him for eight years after he was acquitted of conspiracy to murder, the Judge said that he may well have been at the house to arrange for the murder of the informer and may have played a more sinister role in the case than the prosecution could prove beyond reasonable doubt. 'You may well have played a much more sinister part than the Crown was able to prove by evidence admissable in court and I sentence you only on the basis of the evidence and my findings in relation to the evidence,' he said.

James Martin, 54, who twice allowed his house in the Lenadoon area of Belfast to be used by the IRA to hold and interrogate suspected informers, was imprisoned for a total of twelve years. His Southampton-born wife, Veronica, 45, who made meals and tea for the terrorists holding the informer in an upstairs bedroom, was given sentences totalling three-and-a-half years. Their son, Liam, 26, embraced his parents in the dock when he was freed with a six-month sentence suspended for two years. The Judge said he had pleaded guilty and was put into the situation by his father. Although he took a meal up to the terrorists, he disapproved and told his father so, said the judge. 'Everyone in Northern Ireland knows that interrogation by terrorist organizations will almost certainly involve brutality, ill-treatment, threats, putting someone in fear and may end in murder,' said the judge. Recalling that another informer, James Fenton, had been held in the Martin home in January 1989, before suffering the 'savage and cruel fate inflicted on so many by the IRA – being shot in the head at close range,' the Lord Chief Justice said that when Martin made his house available a second time he 'must have known there was a definite prospect the other man would have been shot and murdered as well. That conduct was deeply evil,' the Judge told Martin.

Three other men, who held Lynch prisoner while the IRA pondered his fate, were also imprisoned. Daniel Caldwell, 35, and James O'Carroll, 29, were each given ten years while Gerard Hodgins, who once worked in the Republican Press Centre in Belfast, was given twelve years. The Judge said he had been given a longer sentence because of his earlier record of terrorist activity when he served a fourteen-year prison sentence for firearms and explosives offences. Anton Murray, 41, who destroyed the tape recording of Lynch's confession when the police surrounded the house, had, the judge said, played a dominant role in the holding of the prisoner, and was sentenced to eight years. Erin Corbett, 29, a mother of three, who had allowed her home to be used on five occasions for terrorist planning meetings, was given concurrent sentences of five years each suspended for five years. The judge said that but for the fact her husband was in prison for terrorist offences, and she had a young family, she would have been given a sentence in custody. Michael Maguire, 23, who pleaded guilty to making his car available for the purposes of terrorism, was freed after receiving a suspended twelve-month sentence.

But while the case was a major victory for the RUC and underlined the increasingly hostile Catholic attitude to the IRA, as evidenced by the willingness of some of the witnesses from west Belfast to give evidence and defy kidnap, threats and intimidation, it was only a symptom of an all too slowly changing pattern.

The seemingly perpetual shortcomings in the relationship between the force and the minority were most graphically illustrated by the case of the so-called Newry hostages which blew up when two young Catholic men who defied an IRA ultimatum to leave Ireland after being branded as 'criminals', took refuge in the sanctuary of the Roman Catholic Cathedral in Newry, Co. Down. They moved in at lunchtime on Saturday 17 August 1991, soon after the IRA deadline for taking 'direct military action' against them passed. Their parents, families and other supporters, who supplied sleeping bags and flasks of hot drinks and sandwiches, shared their vigil. On the first morning, as priests celebrated the cycle of Sunday morning masses, the two, Liam Kearns and David Madigan, unshaven and visibly tense and nervous, sat behind the iron-barred window of a small ante-room at the side of the church. Both proclaimed their innocence and said they would be staying put until the IRA lifted the death threats. Cardinal Cahal Daly, the head of the Catholic Church in Ireland, personally authorized the indefinite sanctuary because 'it is a question of protecting the sanctity of human life.'

But the Cardinal and those closest to the two young men knew well that it was only the force of public opinion, not any moral scruples about infringing holy ground, that kept the IRA gunmen at bay. Three years earlier, IRA terrorists dressed in white butchers' uniforms had used the Cathedral as cover while they murdered three RUC officers, sitting in a police car a few yards away.

Ignoring the IRA ultimatum and running to the Cathedral was a rare act of public defiance of the IRA and exposed one of the most serious underlying problems in Northern Ireland – the deficiency of ordinary policing in the so-called 'hard' areas where the police faced the greatest difficulties. It is dangerous to put men on patrol in such areas because of the risk of attack. All too often the terrorists have lured police into ambushes with bogus emergency calls to incidents. Thus the police response times are not as rapid as they, and the community, would like and there is little real chance of police contact with the community. People are either hostile or afraid to relate to them. The lack of conventional law and order is aggravated by high levels of unemployment and other social problems.

One area where this combination is clearly evident is in the Dromalane and Fathom housing estate in Newry, where the course of events that prompted the IRA ultimatum began. According to Sinn Fein, in the early hours of Sunday 11 August, two men, one a party member, the other a teenager who sold the IRA newspaper *Republican News*, were beaten with iron bars by intruders who pulled them from their beds. Twenty-four hours later, in the early hours of the morning, the IRA acted. According to its own grandiose account, after a number of 'Volunteers' armed with impact grenades and rifles were deployed to give cover on routes leading into the area, a twelve-strong 'Active Service Unit' moved in 'to carry out a punishment action against a number of identified individuals.' Fortunately for them, none of those targetted was at home when the IRA gang smashed its way into houses and ransacked them but later that day a local priest was given the six names and told to pass on the ultimatum: Be out of Ireland by noon Saturday or face unspecified 'direct military action.' Later in a statement the IRA, accusing them of being a 'criminal gang operating an intimidation campaign', named the six men: brothers Hugo and Sean Brown, Liam Kearns, David Madigan, Gervas Henry and Noel McClory, whose ages range from 17 to 23. Three of them reportedly left Newry for England at once.

Kearns and Madigan remained in the spartan room in the Cathedral for eleven days before leaving for another, less public hiding place within Northern Ireland, still protesting their innocence. They said pressure from the Catholic clergy in Newry had driven them to leave. One priest even asked them to negotiate with Sinn Fein, the IRA's political wing, and then commented: 'What's a bullet? You'll only get knee-capped.' Both remained adamant they would not be seeking any accommodation with the IRA other than the lifting of the threat against them. At Christmas the IRA said they could return home at the end of March 1992. It was not the first time the issue had arisen. For years a major pre-occupation of the IRA had been 'policing' the Catholic communities which it claims to defend. People who fall foul of the organization are regularly intimidated or attacked, sometimes for being involved in petty crime, often for simply standing up to the terrorists. The Loyalists are at it too, but, in both cases, 'policing' is merely a euphemism for thugs protecting their own interests acting as judge, jury and, all too frequently, executioner.

In 1990 alone there were 106 such shootings and 69 assaults, many of the people subjected to them having been 'jointed', that is being shot through the kneecaps, ankles or elbows, or indeed all three joints. There have been other instances where victims have had heavy concrete blocks dropped on their limbs or have been beaten with iron bars and even hammers. During the preceding year a Londonderry man was driven out of the city when he phoned the police to investigate what was happening at a neighbour's house. The police arrived and thwarted a terrorist operation for which the house had been taken over.

There had been an increasing backlash against the unspeakable brutality of alternative IRA policing in many areas and a woman whose own son was kneecapped formed a pressure group, Families Against Intimidation and Terror (FAIT). There are other signs of the community increasingly crying out for conventional policing.

Despite the clear and disgraceful efforts of some of the Newry clergy to concede a policing role to the IRA, some reconciliation and religious groups provide protective sanctuary and an escape line out of Northern Ireland for people under terrorist threat. Such networks are jealously guarded by their sponsors and the utmost discretion is maintained about any activity or actions they take, but it is an open secret that many young men and a few women have been spirited out of Ulster away from the clutches of the pseudo-military godfathers on both sides.

Sometimes public pressure can be applied successfully. In one case, a campaign, led by Father Denis Faul, was credited with obtaining the release and saving the life of a man abducted by the IRA for interrogation as an informer. Father Faul has said that people threatened by terrorist organizations should go public and seek to have the weight of community opinion against the IRA focused on the threatened victim.

Rooting these signs of change and helping them to grow and flourish in a Northern Ireland divided by history, prejudice and fear is however a slow and wearing process, as illustrated by the Newry affair. Optimism, pragmatism and courage are rare and fragile commodities, which, as the RUC now knows to its cost, all too easily evaporate when the going gets rough.

This became evident yet again in the latter half of 1991, when political deadlock combined with a fresh bout of violence pushed the total death toll since 1969 over the 2,900 mark and showed no sign of stopping. Any sense that terrorism had been crippled or that peace was possible was replaced by renewed frustration and hopelessness. Throughout the summer, with the terrorists in the throes of a vicious tit-for-tat sectarian campaign that had prompted Archbishop Robin Eames and Cardinal Cahal Daly to voice fears of impending civil war, family after family of the victims pleaded for no retaliation, for others to be spared their grief and anguish. At the year end the death toll had reached 94, the highest total since 1982, and the cost of damage caused by an intensified wave of vehicle and incendiary bombings in the weeks before Christmas soared to almost double the budgeted £20m. Massive traffic disruption caused by bomb scares and increased security checks, gun and bomb attacks on public houses, sectarian killers stalking the streets for victims and a wave of firebomb attacks on shopping centres and other targets helped recreate the despair and anxiety of the early 1970s which most of the people had struggled to overcome. After the glimpses of normality and sunshine in previous years, the threat of the clouds of violence closing over again was all the sharper.

The politicians were significantly to blame for this change of mood. After months of patient negotiation, Mr Peter Brooke, the Northern Ireland Secretary since 1989, finally coaxed the main political parties to the conference table for a planned negotiation between them to create a new political institution to govern Northern Ireland. The next stage of his scheme provided for talks with the Irish government to forge a new cross-border political arrangement, to transcend the 1985 Anglo-Irish Agreement.

Although the Northern Ireland parties did meet face to face for the first time in sixteen years, at Stormont in May and June, procedural wrangling and longstanding distrust caused the process to stall before the Irish government became involved and any substantial progress was made. The single major gain consolidated by Mr Brooke was the winning of Unionist recognition that there had to be dialogue with Dublin in any future talks.

In the ensuing vacuum, with the level of violence soaring, and politicians blandly resuming their deadlocked postures, Ken Maginnis, the Ulster Unionist MP, called on the government to appoint a security supremo for Northern Ireland answerable to the Cabinet in London. He said that a retired military officer or civil servant should fill the post with a brief to bypass the Northern Ireland Secretary and direct the battle against terrorism. The call reflected the sense of frustration increasingly evident in the community but also among some sections of the army and police, a feeling heavily aggravated by pessimism due to the stalling of the talks. The MP, who had served for twelve years as a Major in the Ulster Defence Regiment, accused successive Northern Ireland Office ministers of failing to understand the security situation and get to grips with it. In particular, he said businessmen were being 'bled white' by terrorists and racketeers and that something must be done 'because they are reaching the end of the road.' Maginnis pointed to the way economic strategy had been thought out and directed throughout the 1980s, leading to the success achieved in generating £1bn investment in Belfast, Londonderry and other towns, as evidence that his idea would work.

In floating the idea of a dedicated security supremo, Maginnis was reflecting widespread criticism of not only his warring political peers but Brooke and Annesley, who correctly forecast the surge of violence but seemed unsure about the appropiate response. Annesley even suggested that bringing back internment without trial might have to be considered, an option of last resort that only served to raise the temperature further. Brooke's remark that there could be no protection for every person, all the time, was also heavily resented. Although he was only stating the obvious limitations on the reach of the security forces, many people felt that his assurances about the governments' commitment to eradicating terrorism had become ritual affirmations of a policy that was long on rhetoric and short on action. Attention was drawn to the lengthy delay in meeting the request from the RUC for more officers as evidence of government complacency at a time when responsible church and community leaders feared the onset of the worst communal violence since the early 1970s.

But despite the fears and the criticisms, and the cautious public response by Brooke and Annesley, the atmosphere in Stormont Castle remained calm. The seasoned politicians who had weathered similar bad patches in the past, knew there was no quick fix for the problems of Northern Ireland, only a hard and remorseless grind. Government policy remained firmly that there is anyway no exclusive security solution to the Northern Ireland problem and that progress can only come about through coordinated political, economic and security improvements, all of which must be addressed as a joint agenda. It was well understood, for instance, that the re-introduction of internment, to lock up terrorist suspects without trial, would have greater moral and legal force if it was applied by a new locally agreed and elected political body in office at Stormont. Any British government that did so, especially if the Irish did not follow suit, would be pilloried in the US and Europe and by every human rights organization in the world. There is also a strong recognition that a locally mandated, political body could invoke far greater pressure on the Irish government to step up the political and operational commitment to clamping down on the IRA activitists who use the south for preparing and planning much of their equipment and many of the attacks that eventually take place in the north.

As the political process and the levels of violence ebbed and flowed, RUC officers continued to be prime targets for the IRA with another twelve losing their lives in 1990. On 22 January Inspector Derek Monteith was murdered in the kitchen of his Armagh home by gunmen who fired through the window. Reserve Constable George Starrett, who also resided in Armagh, was killed in identical circumstances on 28 March. Constable Harold Beckett and Constable Gary Meyer were shot dead at close quarters by two gunmen who crept up behind them while patrolling in Belfast city centre on 30 June. Three officers, Constables David Sterritt, Joshua Willis and William Hanson, were travelling in a police car on the Armagh–Caledon road on 24

July when a huge landmine was detonated as they passed. A Catholic nun, travelling in the opposite direction, was also killed. Detective Constable Louis Robinson was abducted at the border, south of Newry, on 16 September while returning from a fishing trip to the Irish Republic. Two days later his body, with gunshot wounds to the head, was found dumped on a country lane nearby. Constable Samuel Todd, a dog handler, was shot dead when two masked men fired into his van as he pulled to a halt at the security gates in High Street, Belfast on 15 October. A month later, on 10 November, terrorist gunmen ambushed four duck shooters on the shores of Lough Neagh, near Lurgan, and killed them. Two of the victims were police officers, Inspector David Murphy and Reserve Constable Thomas Taylor. In another incident near Lurgan, on 20 December, Reserve Constable Wilfred Wethers was murdered as he arrived home after a spell of duty.

In the first nine months of 1991 another six members of the RUC were murdered. Detective Constable John McGarry was killed on 6 April when an under-car booby-trap exploded while he was visiting relatives at Ballycastle, Co. Antrim. Sergeant Samuel McCrum, aged 62, who died a week later, had served in the force for 36 years. He was found with gunshot wounds, lying in the antique shop run by his wife at Lisburn. Another Sergeant, Stephen Gillespie, also a well-known athlete, died when his Land Rover was hit by a rocket at Springfield Road, Belfast on 2 May. Fifteen days later, Reserve Constable Douglas Carrothers was murdered when a bomb went off under his car outside his home at Lisbellaw, Co. Fermanagh. In another fatality on 25 May, Constable Edward Spence lost his life when confronted by gunmen while on patrol at Lower Crescent, Belfast. English-born Constable Erik Clarke, who was serving with the RUC after sixteen years in the Royal Artillery, was killed in a mortar attack on a joint army-police patrol at Swatragh, Co. Londonderry on 17 September.

So as 1991, the twenty-fourth consecutive year of violence, ended, with the overall death toll relentlessly going on for 3,000, it provided a suitable moment to assess the prospects for both the chief constable, at the mid-point of his projected five-year command of the RUC, and for the force itself, as it prepared to mark its seventieth anniversary in June 1992.

Perhaps the most notable feature of Annesley's stewardship was his low public profile which, inside some sections of the force, made him the victim of a certain amount of lighthearted banter, but it nevertheless mirrored conflicting views about the man and a mixed verdict on his performance. Some regarded him as a disappointment, a remote, distant and insecure figure who never really got to grips with the RUC. Others saw him as a consummate professional, delegating, thinking strategically to effectively equip and position the RUC for the uncertain future. In taking on such a testing job, Annesley could not help but be compared with his towering predecessors, Hermon and Newman. Although both had little in common, especially their differing heights and personalities, they dominated the force during their time in charge. Hermon, largely through his forcefulness, and Newman, through his studious professionalism, stamped their authority on the RUC in a way that Annesley failed to achieve. He did much that was expected of him: visited police widows, slow marched in funeral processions, inspected a passing out parade and made the rounds of the force divisions and specialist departments. With the RUC having been used to strong men, who led from the front, the impact of Annesley's quiet effectiveness was blunted by his formality and desire to be seen to delegate and defer to his line management. 'If he would even prowl the corridors at headquarters and stop for the odd informal chat and drink he would be better thought of,' said one colleague. 'The word would soon get around that he is an impressive guy.'

Despite publishing annual reports and strategy documents and giving a few fleeting interviews and news conferences, Annesley did not help his reputation through his failure to initiate and develop a major public debate about the RUC and its future role at a time when the community needed not only reassurance but a lead. There were sufficient public platforms readily available to him for a series of major speeches that would have stamped his own indelible mark on the force at a watershed time but he'd largely failed to avail of them. Part of this omission is accounted for by his conscious decision not to constantly pop up in the public arena believing that, when he chose to say something, it would be treated all the more seriously because of its rarity. In his favour, he did mount a vigorous public defence of the RUC when it was necessary, especially in the run-up to the initiation of the Stevens enquiry and then after the Channel Four 'Dispatches' documentary which seriously concerned the RUC in October 1991 by recycling, in a most unconvincing fashion, the so-called 'Inner Circle' story to a national audience. His handling of the critical aftermath of a controversial fatal shooting by one of his officers in Cookstown in October 1991 was also notable for its frankness and sensitivity. Once it became clear that the victim, Kevin McGovern, 19, a student, was not involved in an ongoing terrorist operation, Annesley immediately admitted the fact and issued public condolences to the family. From the outset he called in the Independent Commission for Police Complaints to supervise the investigation and then robustly insisted there would be no cover-up with the DPP and the Commission ultimately deciding whether the officer should face criminal or disciplinary charges.

But because he and his views did not become better known and admired through greater exposure, Annesley, like his predecessors a skilled and visionary professional with his own personality and style, continued to be heavily misunderstood. Despite the mixed reaction he generated, his time in Belfast was not barren. From the time he took over, relations with the GOC and the Army were elevated to a new level of intimacy. 'Things have not always been so harmonious at the top,' one insider admitted. The benefits of this relationship have trickled down through the ranks of both organizations, a process helped by a major reorganization of military and police operational boundaries so that for the first time in over twenty years of joint operations, all are now common.

Annesley also concerned himself with the command structure at headquarters, a long-term plan to abolish the three posts at the rank of Senior Assistant Chief Constable, reverting to the system of two Deputy Chief Constables with Assistant Chief Constables responsiblee for each of the major departments and main operational regions. Recognizing one of the most serious management weaknesses, the lack of a pool of RUC officers fully qualified to compete for these top posts, Annesley despatched relays of middle and upper rank officers to the Police Staff College at Bramshill and other establishments. He also set up secondment and exchange schemes with a number of mainland forces so that in the future, senior RUC commanders will have benefited from experience gained in other forces and will meet this long-overlooked criterion in the selection process and career development of the most senior officers.

While the government continued to insist that fighting terrorism in Northern Ireland remained its first priority, growing evidence emerged that, for the first time since the outbreak of the terrorist campaign, financial considerations were being applied to the security effort. This was well illustrated by Annesley's determined eighteen-month battle to get an extra 400 officers which increased the RUC strength up to an all-time high of 13,250. In pressing his case however, Annesley found officials envisaged a trade-off whereby the manpower increase would be offset by a cut in the money allocated for overtime. Senior RUC officers calculated that would leave them with a gain equivalent to only 200 extra officers. At the same time they complained that rigidly applied overtime allocations had become so tight that their efforts to fight terrorism were being hampered. Commanders on the ground were being forced to count the cost of operations and only mount those which prevented them overshooting their closely monitored budgets. 'The plain fact is that there are not enough men on the ground to do what the public expects of them,' one police source said.

The huge increase in administrative and supervisory duties, such as those required under the Police and Criminal Evidence Act, coupled with the overtime restrictions, imposed such a burden on the force that fewer and fewer officers were available for duty on the ground. Middle-ranking officers, in particular, had become increasingly desk-bound and unable to get out to supervise their men and women. The RUC calculated that by the Home Office yardstick, used to assess the number of extra officers each police force is entitled to, there was a case for another 600 officers. The force bid for an extra 400, after what one senior man described as some 'good housekeeping', so there was much dismay when the wrangling started.

The major upsurge in violence in the latter half of 1991 (after the stalling of the political talks), brought discontent abut these restrictions to a head. Commanders wanted to deploy a large number of patrols for reassurance and deterrence and Annesley gave the go-ahead, defying the financial limits that had been set. Shortly before Christmas, after the IRA had resumed devastating parts of central Belfast with large vehicle bombs for the first time in years, the overtime restrictions were virtually abandoned. When the compensation bill rapidly exceeded the budgeted £20m for the year and looked like doubling, the government was forced to freeze some public spending, the first time ever the price of terrorism had been exacted from plans to build roads and other amenities.

Looking to the future, Annesley had a clear vision of the RUC role and the sort of force it should be flexible enough to become when the conditions were right. 'We did not create the position that we're in. My officers do not want to go around in armoured vehicles. They don't want to wear heavy flak jackets. They don't want to go round with Heckler and Koch sub-machine guns. They would like to go back to the sort of policing that was known in this province twenty-five years ago.' Annesley believed that the cause of law and order and peace could best be advanced by the police maintaining a firm operational thrust. 'That we will do. We will not back off from terrorism. We will not back off from riotous demonstrations. We will not back off from any aspects of public order which cause injury or difficulty to the community in general. But the force must be sufficiently flexible to change with the times,' he said. That meant, he believed, having first class management, a capacity for reviewing and learning from events around the globe and a willingness to innovate not stagnate, thinking that this is Northern Ireland, it will not work here.' At the moment we are doing what is essential. We'd really like to move on and do what is desirable and that means more people patrolling, more on community relations, more neighbourhood policing, more visible police preventative patrolling,' he said. 'We must be willing to ensure that the organization is structured and flexible and able to move with the times. We must move to a position whereby we can eventually get out of those armoured Land Rovers, put down those flak jackets and long and short firearms and work towards a general community-based policing service.'

With Catholic membership of the force still stubbornly well below the ten per cent mark, and the legacy of Castlereagh, Shoot-to-kill and other controversies having still to be lived down in many Catholic eyes, Annesley was under no illusions about the long and arduous road ahead in winning the consent of the Catholic community. These factors and the inordinate risk faced by young men and women from Catholic backgrounds coming forward to join the force, also made it more difficult to build an RUC more representative of the community. In spite of its continuing trials and tribulations and the consistent efforts to disrupt its work, kill or maim its members and undermine its integrity, the RUC maintained its impartial stance in the divided community. Its goals were clearly shared by many of the best and brightest of the young people in Northern Ireland, including many university graduates, with fifteen candidates competing vigorously for each vacancy that arose in the force. Those serving continue to meet outstanding standards of efficiency, compassion and bravery. If they had not, with the help of the Army, recovered 1.5m bullets, 10,500 firearms, 100 tons of explosives and charged 15,000 people with terrorist offences over two violent decades the ravages of terrorism on the community they protect would have been even greater.

Even those members of the force maimed and forced to leave by the effects of terrorism continued to provide inspiration and demonstrate a different sort of courage rebuilding or carving out new lives for themselves. At the forefront of this category is Michael Paterson, a former Constable, who lost both arms in a terrorist rocket attack. Ten years later, in July 1991, he was awarded a PhD in Applied Psychology at Queen's University, Belfast.

Just before noon on 28 September 1981, then aged 24, he was sitting in the passenger seat of an armoured Land Rover patrolling in west Belfast, the heartland of the Provisional URA. The driver was Constable Alexander Beck, 37, married with a son and a daughter, aged 12 and 10. As the vehicle slowed to negotiate a ramp on the road a rocket slammed into the bodywork just behind the driver's door. It exploded inside the vehicle creating a fireball full of swirling shrapnel from the armour plating. The roof buckled and blew off. Those moments of terror are now frozen in Michael Paterson's memory. 'I can recall hearing an explosion off to the left. Then I felt the pain. I saw my right arm was off and the left was hanging. There was shrapnel in my right thigh and I knew the other leg was broken because of the shape of my foot. I looked over at Alex. He was slumped over and I knew he was dead.' Michael remained conscious and recalls a colleague coming from the second vehicle in the patrol to turn off the two-tone horns which had bee knocked on by his severed hand. Then an army medic bandaged his arms and helped remove him from the damaged Land Rover.

That evening Michael had planned to take his wife, Hazel, of only twenty-three days to a champagne dinner to celebrate her twenty-fifth birthday. Instead he was in a bed at the Royal Victoria Hospital in Belfast coming to terms with the fact that he was permanently disabled and that his career in the RUC was inevitably at an end. Two years earlier, he had defied his mother's fears and joined the force. 'The possibility of being attacked always crossed your mind. I was in a blast bomb attack and had been shot at but it did not worry me at all.' He remembers the sinking feeling when he had to hand in his warrange card, finally ending his links with the force.' I was down in the mouth but I knew I had to look to the future.' Almost as soon as he left hospital, three months after the attack, he was making plans which included the objective of proving that he could do more than simply conquer his physical disabilities. The first step was to acquire artificial arms and learn to use them. Then he enrolled at the University of Ulster, where, after four years' study, he obtained a degree in psychology.

Work on his PhD started immediately. This three-year study involved writing a thesis on the social and psychological adaption of individuals and their families to prolonged disability. Working across the political and social divide in Northern Ireland, Michael researched forty-seven affected families, measuring their problems against an equal number of 'control' families with no history of disability or chronic illness. Although none of his subjects were affected by terrorism Michael believes that his own experience put him in a strong position to evaluate the problems.

Michael manages to do his work with the aid of a harness, artificial arms and a variety of prongs and hooks which allow him to hold a pen and tap a computer keyboard. He has mastered the use of a knife and fork but finds things like toast a problem to deal with. He gives much of the credit for the success of his new life to his wife, their two daughters, aged 16 months and three and a half years, and the support from former colleagues in the RUC and the Disabled Police Officers Association. He has since begun work on another research project into disability and is looking for a suitable long term job to exploit his new skills. 'At one stage when my first career was up in smoke, as it were, I wondered what else I could do. I thought I would enjoy the academic world and could cope but I have exceeded all my own expectations,' he said.

As former chairman of the Police Federation, Alan Wright knows first hand that stories like this are the tip of the iceberg, typical of the largely selfless men and women prepared to give their all for the RUC and the benefit of the people of both communities in Northern Ireland. While conceding that the future is uncertain and depends on a lot of outside influences and people, such as politicians, he is certain of one thing. 'The RUC will continue to do the job whatever the laws laid down for them to administer. And they'll just go on doing it. New men and women will come in. New ideas will be formulated. And if the politicians, I believe, can help in any way, and I'm sure they're willing to do this, then I always think there is a bright future here. There has to be. Really all the sacrifices the RUC made and the deaths of their colleagues – it can't go for nothing. It shouldn't.'

# 12

# 'The Silence of the Guns'

As Northern Ireland moved into the 1990s and a third decade of violence, optimism about a bright future seemed hopelessly premature. In the early hours of 25 May 1991, a cadre of Loyalist gunmen from Londonderry slipped a few miles across the Irish border to the tranquil seaside village of Buncrana. They forced entry into a house at Cockhill Cottages, shot the occupant dead and escaped. They have never been brought to justice. Their victim was Councillor Eddie Fullerton, 56, a Sinn Fein member of Donegal County Council, who for years had been an influential, and very active, member of the Provisional IRA.

This raid, audacious by previous Loyalist standards, mirrored many such murderous cross-border forays in the opposite direction by the IRA, and marked the extension of a cycle of tit-for-tat slaughter of an intensity not seen since the early 1970s. The Fullerton killing underlined the emergence of a new breed of ruthless Loyalist terrorists, prepared to 'terrorise the terrorists' by targeting IRA and Sinn Fein personalities directly. Over the next few years they consistently attacked homes and offices occupied by people from Republican organisations, and took the lives of twenty-three members and associates. All too often there was not even the pretence of branding the victims Republicans. Many were singled out and gunned down for no more reason than that they were Catholic: a chilling policy articulated in paint in the Loyalist areas of Belfast by the initials ATD – Any *taig* (*Catholic*) will do.

For years RUC detectives had talked disparagingly of 'Prod jobs': jammed guns, missed victims, getaway cars that failed to start, drunken escapades and petty robberies which enabled the perpetrators to be easily rounded up. In one case, a team planning to bomb a Catholic public house arrived without a match to light their crude device; on another, a Loyalist gunman sent to murder the Sinn Fein leader, Gerry Adams, failed, shot himself and was caught by passers-by. But the new cells of young Loyalist killers had skilfully analysed and copied the way the IRA operated and targeted its victims. The Byzantine rivalries between the UVF, UFF and a host of other Loyalist militias were forgotten and a new Combined Loyalist Military Command was set up to co-ordinate their terrorist (and eventually political) activities. Their small cells thwarted police efforts to infiltrate; arms were smuggled in under the noses of the security services and, although many were seized, sufficient got through to pose a serious threat, and they learned to destroy forensic evidence which would betray or convict them in court.

'We have decided to take the war to the IRA. We have the willpower, the manpower and the firepower,' a Loyalist terrorist leader boasted, at the time. That these young hardliners were unleashed as fresh petrol on the flames of Northern Ireland was, ironically, a by-product of the otherwise effective work of the Stevens investigation, revealed in a dramatic court case early in 1992. This exposed the front line of the undercover war at the heart of the Northern Ireland conflict; and the emergence of the new generation of Loyalist activists. It also highlighted the frustration felt by front-line operators in the security forces and the damaging rivalries between the RUC and British Army, as they struggled to combat terrorism within tight legal constraints, especially in running and justifying the activities of informers.

In a carefully choreographed hearing which began on 22 January 1992, Brian Nelson, 43, pleaded guilty to twenty terrorist charges at Belfast Crown Court. He was an ex-soldier who had continued to work for the British Army as a double-agent after being inserted into the Ulster Defence Association as chief of intelligence, until his arrest by the Stevens team. He admitted his part in five conspiracies to murder people allegedly connected with the IRA, including the Belfast Sinn Fein councillor Alex Maskey, and a series of offences arising from the collection and possession of information useful to terrorists. Brian Kerr QC, appearing for the Crown, said that Nelson had played a 'vital, indispensable and pivotal role' in targeting the victims and plotting their murders. At the same time, according to Mr Kerr, Nelson was giving information about UDA activity and personalities to his British Army 'handlers', intelligence officers working on anti-terrorist duties. In one case, Nelson warned the Army five times that a particular man was being targeted for murder, but no action was taken and the UDA gunmen ended up killing the innocent brother of their intended victim. His information, the Crown prosecutor said, was often passed on after the event and sometimes 'was not as complete as it could or ought to have been'.

Nelson, a short, slight man with thick-lensed glasses, wearing a grey pin-stripe suit, white shirt and striped tie, stood in the dock between two tall prison officers for over thirty minutes as the thirty-five charges were read to him. He replied 'guilty' or 'not guilty' in a soft Scottish accent after each charge, but Crown lawyers asked Lord Justice Kelly not to proceed with fifteen of the charges, including the murders of two Catholics, to which Nelson pleaded not guilty. The judge was advised that the charges to which Nelson had pleaded guilty properly reflected his criminal responsibility and the interests of justice would best be served by leaving the others on file. The Crown, he was told, had reached its decision 'after scrupulous assessment of possible evidential difficulties for the prosecution' if the charges went ahead.

Mr Kerr outlined how Nelson had joined the UDA in 1972. By 1983 he had become an 'intelligence officer', but had left Northern Ireland two years later and gone to work in Germany. The British Army, to whom he had offered his services as an 'agent' in 1983, contacted him and asked him to return to Belfast and work for them inside the UDA. He was appointed Senior Intelligence Officer and given access to what Kerr described as 'a considerable volume of information obtained by UDA intelligence, information which Nelson built upon and supplemented by his own activities.' He created P Cards, an index listing those the UDA considered legitimate targets because of their apparent connections with Irish Republican terror groups: the IRA, INLA and IPLO. Nelson, said Kerr, was 'an active and willing participant in murder plans', providing pictures and details of potential victims, carrying out sightings and surveillance, using electoral rolls to verify addresses and reconnoitring and drawing maps of their homes for the gunmen. The court was told how, in July 1988, Nelson had gone to a restaurant in north Belfast after the Sinn Fein Councillor, Alex Maskey, had been sighted there. Afterwards he toured various drinking clubs rounding up members of the UDA and trying to obtain a weapon to attack Maskey, who had gone by the time the gang turned up.

The hearing was adjourned to enable a vital witness to be brought to Belfast. When it resumed a few days later, the former head of the British military intelligence unit in Northern Ireland gave evidence that Nelson was 'an important agent of some standing whose product was passed throughout the intelligence community in Northern Ireland at the highest level'. He said that in a three-year period, 730 intelligence reports of high value had been generated from the agent's information and he had disclosed threats to the lives of 217 people. Of these, five had later died. One was shot dead by the SAS in Gibraltar, another died of natural causes and three had been murdered by Loyalist terrorists. The intelligence officer, a lieutenant-colonel, whose name was written down for Lord Justice Kelly and not disclosed, was clearly annoyed that a prize intelligence asset was on trial, and said that Nelson was a 'very courageous man' who had become 'a victim of the system'. He said he was personally embarrassed that 'the system has been unable to recognise the real difficulties of running agents within terrorist organisations. I was in the business of running agents to bring down and disrupt terrorist organisations. I feel a personal, moral responsibility. He wouldn't have done it if I hadn't ordered him to infiltrate, but the real moral responsibility lies with the system that has not been able to come to terms with the realities and difficulties.' He said there were no formal guidelines for using agents to infiltrate terrorist organisations and added that Home Office guidelines about the use of informers were 'more appropriate for dealing with the criminal fraternity in the East End of London rather than terrorists in Northern Ireland. Agents by their very nature are committing criminal acts just by membership of terrorist organisations. It is well-nigh impossible for them to avoid some criminal involvement.'

Admitting that Nelson had not always got it right, the lieutenant-colonel said he had been reprimanded on occasions for allowing himself to be drawn into active participation in terrorist activity. But Nelson had been in a particularly vulnerable position and faced interrogation and a brutal death if there was the slightest suspicion that he was an agent. In 1988 he had been subjected to a violent interrogation including electric shocks with a cattle prod, an ordeal he 'survived through his courage'. Nelson's health had suffered from his 'schizophrenic existence between satisfying his handlers and the demands of the terrorist organisation. We had to get him into a position where he had the confidence and trust of his terrorist associates. We really tried to get him to a position where any targets for assassination were going to be discussed with him but we could never guarantee that he would be party to potential lifesaving information all the time.' In his opinion, Nelson, who gave up a £500-a-week job in Germany and returned to Belfast where the Army paid him just £200 a week, was not loyal to the UDA. He was a team player, loyal to the Army, who wanted to make up for past misdemeanours, save lives and help bring down the terrorist organisations.

Mr Desmond Boal QC called for Nelson to be treated leniently, and said that the case was 'wholly exceptional. He helped save the lives of people who, ironically enough, are now screaming about his activities.' Lord Justice Kelly jailed Nelson for ten years for conspiracy to murder and imposed concurrent prison sentences totalling 101 years. At the request of the Crown a series of other charges, including two of murder, which Nelson denies, were set aside to be proceeded with only by leave of the court. Before pronouncing sentence, the judge acknowledged that using undercover agents was 'long recognised as a legitimate device to secure convictions', especially in the case of terrorists and drug traffickers, but he added that if an agent committed a crime he could not expect to be immune: 'There is no half-way house from criminal culpability in these circumstances . . . He was tasked by Army intelligence to learn the workings of the UDA, to pass on information about the murderous activities of the UDA but not to get involved with the murder gangs.' The judge then referred to the five conspiracies to murder to which Nelson had pleaded guilty. 'In each case he took steps of his own accord to confirm the addresses and habits of his victims and in one case he transported a machine-gun.' He had 'crossed the dividing line between criminal activity and intelligence gathering by conforming to UDA requirements rather than instructions from Army intelligence'.

As a result of the Army evidence the Director of Public Prosecutions set up a review to determine whether Nelson's military handlers withheld information about Loyalist murder plots from the RUC and failed to take action to prevent attacks taking place so as to protect Nelson. In particular the DPP ordered an examination of the records concerning the murder of a Belfast solicitor, Patrick Finucane, shot dead at his home in Belfast on 12 February 1989. RUC sources have always insisted that Nelson told his Army handlers that Finucane, who came from a Republican family and frequently represented IRA suspects, was being targeted and that the information was not passed to the police as quickly as it should have been. The BBC's *Panorama* programme, which covered the Nelson case, claimed that an abortive plot to kill another solicitor, Paddy McGrory, who represented the three terrorists shot by the SAS in Gibraltar in 1988, was also concealed from both McGrory and the police.

The legal authorities finally decided to take no action, although comprehensive written guidelines about recruiting and handling informers were introduced. Stevens, whose lengthy investigation had triggered the Nelson case, was awarded the Queen's Police Medal for work which led to prison sentences totalling 550 years being imposed on 44 people. Summing up the investigation, he said he had put forward a substantial number of recommendations intended to prevent, as far as is possible, a recurrence of the circumstances which gave rise to his enquiry: 'These measures will undoubtedly benefit the security forces and the community in the years ahead.'

Whatever the gains for the integrity of the intelligence-gathering system, the Stevens investigation and the conviction of Nelson made it more difficult for the RUC to obtain reliable information about the new Loyalist power structure. Cleaning up the spaghetti-like complexities of the undercover intelligence war in Northern Ireland and rounding up the ageing and longstanding leaders of the Loyalist groupings was costly in the short term. The leaders who were detained were more concerned with feathering their own nests from the webs of racketeering and extortion they controlled. More importantly, they curbed the militancy of reckless young recruits, and their demise cleared the way for a take-over. The result was a ruthless tit-for-tat campaign fought with increasing savagery by Loyalists and Republicans. At the end of 1991 deaths from terrorism were the greatest since 1982, but the most worrying aspect was the switch in targets from security force to civilians. Seventy-five civilians were murdered, the highest number for fifteen years. Another feature of the upsurge in sectarian murder was multiple killings. Republicans and Loyalists slaughtered between two and eight people in thirteen attacks in 1991, a reflection of the ruthlessness and recklessness among a fresh generation of killers. On both sides, these young men – and increasingly women – had been born into Ulster's enduring violence and sterile hatreds and were prepared to resort to the gun and bomb to perpetuate them. The resulting levels of fear and hatred on both sides were unprecedented and calls for reconciliation appeared to go unheeded.

The worsening security situation did not hinder the Chief Constable,

Sir Hugh Annesley, from issuing an optimistic three-year strategy statement at the beginning of 1992. He said that the key aim of the RUC was to defeat terrorism and achieve peace in Northern Ireland. 'There can be little doubt that support for the police is the wedge that will increasingly isolate the terrorist from our society. We will therefore reinforce this and seek to increase our existing high level of community support,' he said. Working from hard-won intelligence, obtained in difficult and dangerous circumstances, the counter-terrorism offensive led by the RUC had succeeded in preventing many intended outrages by republican and loyalist terrorist groups, Sir Hugh added. He stressed that foreknowledge of terrorist intentions was vital to prevent atrocities: 'Penetrating their structures and successfully pre-empting their activities instils fear in the terrorist and strikes at the very roots of their organisations. Public co-operation and understanding in this task is crucial if we are to succeed.'

Sir Hugh also identified the need to frustrate the movement of terrorists and their weapons and explosives, as well as cutting off finance, 'the lifeblood of all terrorist organisations'. He set the RUC six goals to achieve over the three years: it should reduce the incidence of terrorism, enhance its relationship with the community by working to increase public confidence and support and detect more non-terrorist crime. Road accidents should be reduced and public order maintained; the force should also enhance organisational effectiveness and give the Northern Ireland community a quality service.

Financial pressures were now bearing down on the RUC and security policy in Northern Ireland, but Sir Hugh argued that it was better to spend £3m protecting town centres from the bombers than £30m rebuilding them, a view which finally prevailed in Stormont Castle, where the emphasis of Treasury demands to curb public spending was focused. There was growing concern about the cost of providing the full range of public services in Northern Ireland to standards often exceeding those in England, Scotland and Wales. Annual public spending per head of the population was running at £4594, one third more than the national average expenditure of £3411. At around £1 billion a year, maintaining law and order took a considerable slice of the £7.4 billion Northern Ireland budget. By the early 1990s the cost of the police service alone had soared to over £600m. The courts cost £13.5m and criminal legal aid (much of it for those charged with terrorist offences) was £7.5m. Apart from the 13,000 police officers at the sharp end, the criminal justice system had swollen to support about another 8000 jobs: 4752 at the Northern Ireland Office, including the prison service; 667 in the courts; 300 probation workers and 445 in training schools for young offenders; fifty-five judges and seventy part-time or deputy members of the judiciary, as well as 1400 solicitors and some 300 barristers, who derived a good part of their living from both criminal and civil work arising from the troubles and their effects.

The year 1992 was three days old when Kevin McKearney became the third of four brothers to die violently. Married with four children, he was shot dead by the Loyalist UVF as he served in the family butcher shop in the County Tyrone Village of Moy. His death was generally regarded as being in retaliation for that of Robin Farmer, a nineteen-year-old Protestant student, murdered by the IRA four days before Christmas in his family's shop in the same village. The intended victim had been the dead man's father, a former member of the RUC Reserve, who had been pushed out of the line of fire by his brave son.

As the killings continued, August brought Northern Ireland to a grim milestone when the death toll from twenty-three years of unremitting violence reached 3000. At first Hugh McKibben, a twenty-one-year-old from the Grosvenor Road area of Belfast, shot dead during a feud between rival factions of the Republican INLA, was thought to be the 3000th victim. However, after a police investigation concluded that a fifteen-year-old youth had not been the victim of a sectarian encounter, the body count was recalculated and the dubious distinction fell to Private Paul Turner, an eighteen-year-old soldier serving with the Light Infantry, who died instantly when a single-shot sniper opened fire on his patrol in Crossmaglen. Turner was not even born when the Army was first deployed in Ulster in August 1969. When John Gallagher, a Catholic, was shot by B Specials during a night of rioting in Armagh at that time, nobody conceived that the victims would be so numerous and would include people from every section of the Northern Ireland community, as well as soldiers from every part of the British Isles. On average, over those twenty-three years from 1969 to 1992, there was a death every third day. There were only three months when no lives were taken: July 1985; February 1990; and June 1992. The carnage in Northern Ireland means that in virtually every cemetery there is a victim's grave. Had there been slaughter on the same scale among the population of mainland Britain, the death toll would have reached 111,000.

With no apparent end to the conflict in sight, the Chief Constable spoke of the Republican and Loyalist gangs who continued to outdo each other in fanatical hatred, blind bigotry and sectarian savagery. The cumulative effects of more than two decades of violence had imposed an even more rigid sectarian geography. Constant population movement in Belfast, for instance, had created a network of ghettoes: the population in thirty-five of the city's fifty-one electoral wards was more than ninety per cent Protestant or Catholic. Such was the fear and hostility between them that at thirteen interface locations high, concrete 'peace walls' divided the communities on both sides at their own request. In rural areas, the sectarian boundaries, though not so visibly delineated, were equally rigid, with Catholics and Protestants mainly living separate, segregated lives. There were a few oases of reconciliation and tolerance, but the ancient hatreds ruled.

Policing and protecting such divided and partisan communities tested the professionalism and effectiveness of the RUC to the limit, and the 3000 deaths – each officially classified as murder – imposed an incredible workload on the 600 detectives and support staff. Each fatal incident had to be meticulously investigated, witnesses questioned and statements taken; every scene had to be photographed and mapped, and extensive fingerprint and forensic examinations conducted. Eighteen hundred of the murders were still formally unsolved by the end of 1996, but the clear-up rate of 40 per cent represents a creditable performance by the criminal investigation units. There will never be a complete clear-up: many of the killers became victims themselves and some multiple convicted killers did not face charges for all their victims. The clear-up rate might have been higher had the mechanics of criminal investigation been harnessed to computers as they are today. 'We had to maintain thousands of card indexes of suspects, witness statements and background material on each murder,' says a retired senior detective. 'Sifting manually . . . for links and leads depended on hours and hours of methodical work, exceptional memory and often luck. Now the computers can accurately compare all that material in a very short time and analyse it with total precision. If we had had that sort of equipment we would undoubtedly have solved many more of those murders.'

Some of the most startling technological advances have been made in fingerprint identification. Given the general background of intimidation in Northern Ireland, where witnesses are generally unwilling to assist the police and suspects are trained to resist police interrogation, there is a strong reliance on forensic and fingerprint evidence. Undoubtedly, the most decisive way to nail an offender is by matching a fingerprint from the scene of a crime. This science, known as dactyloscopy, has been in active use in Britain for over a hundred years and its value is undiminished. The first recorded instance of a fingerprint securing a conviction in Northern Ireland was in 1924, one year after the RUC Fingerprint Bureau was set up, when a Belfast shopbreaker was traced and apprehended. In Northern Ireland now, where it is difficult to secure convictions against hardened criminals rarely caught red-handed, seldom prepared to confess their guilt during questioning and regularly freed because frightened witnesses will not testify against them, fingerprints have been a vital factor in putting many in prison. They are used extensively to verify the identity of people arrested, charged and convicted and the identities of people admitted to and detained in prison, and can eliminate suspects from police investigations.

The Police Authority and the RUC therefore invested in building the capability of the RUC to utilise the science more effectively. A computerised automatic fingerprint recognition system which could search through the 1.3m images in the collection became fully operational in 1993, and can do in four minutes what would have taken a fingerprint officer three weeks, working manually. As a result, in the first year of operation the number of positive identifications increased by 43 per cent. However, the new computer only speeds up the time-consuming process of matching fingerprints. Once this is done, the experts must identify sixteen points of similarity between any two prints, the minimum standard of proof accepted by the courts for the guilt of an offender. Increasingly, this skilled work is being done by civilians to free police officers for other duties.

Although the RUC was slower than other British police forces in adapting to the use of information technology, from the early 1990s the productive use of computers contributed increasingly to its detection rate, which hovers around 35 per cent each year and is consistently among the highest of any United Kingdom constabulary. Indeed, despite terrorism, according to the 1992 figures the number of recorded crimes in Northern Ireland (67,532) was lower than any of the forty-two police force areas in England and Wales. Nevertheless, 'these encouraging statistics are no comfort to the wife and children or the parents of the latest sectarian murder victim from whatever side he or she might come,' as a senior RUC officer remarked.

There have been frequent criticisms of the apparent impotence of the police in the face of terrorist campaigns, and calls for draconian security action, including the reintroduction of internment without trial. However, over many years, the police and government had honed a security policy which was designed to withstand the politics of individual atrocities by providing constant attrition and deterrence to the terrorists, whatever the ebb and flow of their crimes. Research had shown that the typical ·terrorist was a nineteen-year-old, poorly educated male from a deprived, working-class background. The government had therefore instituted programmes to 'target social need' on both sides of the sectarian divide, especially in the areas where violence was most effectively incubated. They hoped to lure the most vulnerable youngsters into a more constructive life-style. At the same time, the government insisted that no short cuts could be taken in security policy. Terrorists were criminals who had to be brought to justice within the law. There would be no shoot-to-kill policy, internment or heavy-handed policing.

The environment in which the police and army had to operate continued to be volatile, however, and the continuing high level of sectarian tension was exacerbated throughout the early 1990s by specific events. One such was the proscription of the Ulster Defence Association on 10 August 1992. Announcing the ban, the Northern Ireland Secretary, Sir Patrick Mayhew, said, 'I have taken this action because I am satisfied that the UDA is actively and primarily engaged in the commission of criminal, terrorist acts and so merits proscription under the provisions of the Emergency Provisions Act.' The ban was more cosmetic than meaningful, and came at a time when there were signs that the organisation was engaged in a major internal feud. Ned McCreery had been killed at his home in East Belfast as part of the running purge against the old guard leadership, trying to hold on to their profits from racketeering and extortion and the ownership of public houses. The split between rival factions was emphasised when a prominent member of the leadership was arrested and charged with the sexual abuse of two under-age girls in the UDA headquarters in Belfast.

The proscription and notably tougher policing by the RUC in Loyalist areas, in response to the increase in sectarian attacks, brought the RUC into conflict with a large section of the Loyalist community. Robin McLaughlin, the Assistant Chief Constable responsible for policing the city, who had once had a coffin and hearse sent to his home when he was investigating sectarian murders in east Antrim, made no apology for discharging the RUC's obligation to the whole community. 'Lives have undoubtedly been saved as a result of recent police actions,' he insisted. During extensive overt and covert operations the RUC seized a number of weapons, including a missing police revolver, and some of the guns were ballistically linked to attacks and killings by the UVF and UFF over previous years. But the police tactics, including searches of houses and premises, caused a wave of resentment in the Protestant community, especially in the Shankill and other parts of north Belfast, the heartland of the UDA and UVF, and the traditionally supportive relationship between the RUC and the Protestant community came under strain. There were noisy demonstrations outside Tennent Street police station and Belfast Prison, where Loyalist suspects were being held on remand. On one occasion police had to evict protesters from court after two Protestant men, accused of attempted murder, were refused bail, and there were reports that shopkeepers in the Shankill area had refused to serve members of the RUC. In a worrying incident, a mobile police patrol was fired on by a Loyalist gunman. Although nobody was injured, the attack raised fears that hardline Loyalists might turn their guns on the police, compounding the problems of dealing with the constant threat of ambush by the IRA.

Loyalist hostility sprang from a general and growing insecurity among Protestants who felt that Britain was steadily loosening the bonds of the union with Northern Ireland. They also believed that government social and economic policy favoured disadvantaged Catholic areas and that the police were discriminating against Loyalists: despite the intensity of the IRA campaign, the arrest rate for Loyalists was roughly twice that for Republicans. This figure, of course, reflected the fact that the police were able to penetrate the Loyalist gangs more easily than those of the IRA.

During the early 1990s, the activities of the newly militant Loyalists and the revitalised Republicans dominated the agenda at the regular liaison meetings between the RUC and Garda Siochana. The RUC was, naturally, primarily concerned about the continued IRA threat to Northern Ireland while Gardai anxieties focused on the growing frequency of Loyalist outrages in the south of Ireland, notably incendiary attacks on shopping centres in Dublin and elsewhere in the Republic. Security co-operation across the border, which had once been a source of friction between the British and Irish governments, had settled into a comfortable, but guarded, intimacy since the signing of the Anglo-Irish Agreement in 1985; by the early 1990s police and troops on both sides of the border regularly mounted joint search operations to disrupt IRA activity, seize stocks of arms and explosives and inhibit Loyalist cross-border incursions. In the recent past the British and Irish security forces had discovered a trawler with a false deck, container lorries with hidden compartments and an array of specially constructed hiding places under farm buildings in the countryside and in or under houses in the Belfast area and various places south of the border.

A series of these co-ordinated operations in 1992 coincided with the most visible escalation of security measures in the greater Belfast area since the start of the troubles. The city was almost permanently ringed by a network of mobile checkpoints which caused delays and disruption to traffic. In outlying towns, control zones were reintroduced and security gates re-erected so that the centres could be closed off at night to prevent vehicle bombs from being detonated. The RUC said that the operations were mounted in response to intelligence reports that the IRA had stockpiled large quantities of explosives. After a 2000lb explosion devastated the Forensic Science Laboratory and nearly 800 homes in south Belfast, police pickets were placed at other potential targets. The force headquarters at Knock in east Belfast and Government House at Hillsborough, where the Northern Ireland Secretary and members of his ministerial team reside, received notably increased levels of security attention. Advanced equipment and sniffer dogs were brought in to help the special search teams, who were central to preventing bombs being placed and were briefed on IRA techniques which were becoming ever more sophisticated.

The IRA underlined its activities with a fine-tuned sense of propaganda. In the south Armagh village of Meigh, early one evening, an estimated fifteen men with weapons and military-style uniforms mounted an illegal checkpoint, visited two local men accused of being involved in drugs dealing and ordered them to leave the area. Such displays were a direct challenge to the authority of the RUC and designed to portray the IRA as protectors of the Catholic community. They were also a show of strength: the terrorists were reported to have flaunted several new high-velocity guns, powerful enough to penetrate the bullet-proof jackets of police and troops in Northern Ireland. Such devastating weaponry underlined the threat posed by the revitalised reign of IRA terror begun in the late 1980s after the arrival of massive shipments of arms, ammunition and explosives from Libya.

There were other sources of supply. In September 1992, for instance, four IRA members from Londonderry were apprehended by the Garda Siochana at St Johnston on the Donegal border. They were in possession of a large cache of weapons which included an MG3 heavy machine-gun, capable of a range of 2000 metres when mounted on a tripod. The German-made weapon was stolen from the Norwegian army in 1984. The IRA also demonstrated evil ingenuity in developing improvised weapons and adapting everyday items such as fertiliser, gas cylinders, electronic timers and the like for purposes of terrorism. These home-made weapons posed just as serious a threat to life and limb as standard ordnance. The most powerful menace came from HME (home-made explosive), which was basically standard agricultural fertiliser reprocessed to improve its explosive capabilities. HME enabled the IRA to deliver its most punishing punches, the vehicle bombs, often loaded with several thousand pounds of mix, which devastated whole streets or the centres of small country towns. Ireland, both north and south, is heavily dependent on agriculture, and the cost and inconvenience of preventing access to fertiliser meant the terrorists continued to obtain it in large quantities. However, thanks to the experience gained in Northern Ireland, the Army's bomb disposal experts had developed what the soldiers called a 'pig-stick', a cylindrical metal disrupter which fired a jet of pressurised water at very high speed into a bomb, halting the timer and breaking the link between detonator and explosive before one could set the other off. When the IRA realised that this new measure could neutralise their bombs, they gave shorter and shorter warnings to stop the bomb disposal teams reaching the scene in time.

Among the most lethal home-made devices the IRA devised and introduced was the coffee-jar bomb, an improvised hand grenade which they tossed at police and military patrols. Several soldiers were killed by the devices, which contained up to two pounds of Semtex and an impact detonator designed to explode when the glass jar broke. The weapon was totally indiscriminate, and nineteen civilians were injured by one thrown at police officers outside the Queen Street station in June 1991. Only the skill of the surgeons prevented a policeman from losing his leg, and the threat to public safety was so serious that the police took the unusual step of warning coffee-jar bombers that they were liable to be shot on sight. Another serious problem was the use of ordinary heavy-duty magnets, used to attach sophisticated under-vehicle booby-trap devices. Security bases were festooned with warning posters reminding personnel to check their vehicles carefully. How easily electronic technology and equipment could be adapted to detonate explosive devices was graphically illustrated by the use the IRA made of photo-flash slave units. These American-made, cordless, remote-controlled devices are legitimately used in the photographic industry to initiate flashlighting units. The IRA incorporated them in elaborate bomb traps: the headlights of a vehicle or even the blue lamp on a police car could set off an explosion from as far away as 800 yards.

The PRIG (Projected Recoilless Improvised Grenade) was another deadly weapon. Its components included innocuous items such as a baked-beans tin, a packet of biscuits and a length of piping. The pipe was attached to a handgrip and firing mechanism. The food tin contained the Semtex charge fired from the mouth of the pipe. Two packets of biscuits were inserted in the back of the pipe to counterbalance the shoulder-launched projectile and prevent recoil. The weapon was simple to construct, easy to conceal, easily portable and fatally effective. After the deaths of both policemen and soldiers from direct hits on their vehicles, extra armour had to be fitted for better protection. In time, the RUC introduced new marks of its basic Land Rover patrol vehicle with more effective protection for those travelling inside. The Army brought in a new, less vulnerable, Land Rover and replaced the ageing Pigs (one-ton Humber armoured cars) with the Saxon, a wheeled APC specially developed to operate in Northern Ireland.

The IRA's 'engineers' presented another serious challenge to police stations and Army bases with what they called the 'barrack-buster', a massive mortar, fired either singly or from a bank of linked tubes of commercial piping welded onto special steel launching frames. A small charge of explosive is placed at the base of each tube and linked to others by wires which connect them to the electronic detonating mechanism and timer. Stolen vehicles are generally adapted to act as a base-plate; the roof is cut away and the frame welded into position. Four-wheel-drive jeeps, vans, farm vehicles and flat-bed or quarry lorries have all been stolen and used for this purpose. The mortars, of which at least sixteen models and modifications have been identified, vary from a one-pounder packed with Semtex to barrack-busters which can contain up to several hundred pounds of home-made explosive. The weapons are generally constructed in workshops on both sides of the Irish border, where industrial gas cylinders, normally used for heating, medical purposes or even to pump draught beer, have been adapted to hold explosives and firing mechanisms. Engineering factories have been used to produce some components, while farm buildings have been commandeered to convert vehicles into a firing platform. The devices are designed to explode on impact, and threaten not only security force bases but the surrounding area, which frequently includes schools, shops and domestic or business premises, for the IRA has never refined the detonation technique or aiming of the weapons. Many have fallen off target and failed to explode or, in some cases, have caused death to passers-by and extensive damage to property.

As well as weaponry, the IRA engaged in tactical development, always seeking to catch the police and Army off-guard. The 'human bomb' attacks on 24 October 1990 undoubtedly rank among the most savage outrages ever mounted by the IRA. In the early hours of that morning, Patsy Gillespie, a Catholic who lived in the Shantallow area of Londonderry and worked as a chef in the local Fort George Army base, was forced into a vehicle loaded with explosives and ordered to drive it to the border checkpoint at Buncrana Road on the outskirts of the city. When the vehicle arrived at the checkpoint, the bomb was electronically detonated by terrorists travelling behind in another vehicle. Gillespie and five soldiers from the King's Regiment, who were manning the post, died instantly. In a simultaneous attack at the Cloghogue checkpoint near Newry, Ranger Cyril Smith, a twenty-one-year-old Catholic serving with the Royal Irish Rangers, helped free a male civilian tethered to a similar vehicle bomb and get him to safety, but Smith died when the bomb went off while he was ensuring nobody else was in the firing line. He was decorated posthumously.

Lieutenant-General Sir John Wilsey, Army commander in Northern Ireland, was deeply affected by the incidents and initiated a major review of operations and security at the border outposts. Even before his staff officers had completed their studies, however, the vulnerability of the posts and the difficulty of protecting police and Army occupants was again underlined when the IRA deployed its biggest ever bomb – 8000lbs of HME – at the Annaghmartin checkpoint in County Fermanagh on 4 September 1991. If the overloaded farm trailer, being towed by a tractor, had not become bogged down in a wet field, the Army estimates it would have wiped out the post and the score of soldiers in it, as well as causing extensive damage to houses, farms and buildings over a wide area on both sides of the border.

Fresh fears about the safety of security force personnel manning permanent checkpoints along the border were raised after another soldier was killed in a huge explosion at the Cloghogue checkpoint on 1 May 1992. This time the IRA used a railway line to deliver the bomb. The checkpoint, jointly manned by soldiers and police, is adjacent to the Cloghogue railway bridge, a mile south of Newry, where the main road and railway line between Belfast and Dublin run parallel for a stretch. Vehicles crossing the border, three miles farther south, were checked and sometimes searched as they passed in both directions, but there was no routine halt check of the fourteen freight and passenger trains which passed each day. Two hours before the bombing a man and his wife were held hostage by four armed terrorists in their home beside the main road, about half-way between the checkpoint and the border. The terrorists used a tracked hydraulic digger, stolen from their hostages, to hoist the heavy bomb and the railway bogey onto the line before they were rolled into position beside the corrugated iron wall of the checkpoint and detonated, probably by remote control. The huge explosion was heard over a radius of several miles, and injured many in the vicinity. The Northern Ireland security minister, Michael Mates, a former soldier, said that Fusilier Andrew Grundy, the twenty-two-year-old single man who died in the blast, had shown 'courage of the highest order' by staying at his post after spotting the maintenance bogey being used by the terrorists to deliver the 1000lb bomb. It exploded before he could finish shouting his warning through the intercom to the base control point. The attack came as rebuilding work was being completed at the Newry post after the October 1990 strike, and as the Army completed a £25m building scheme, involving the redesigning and further fortifying of all the border checkpoints – a result of the Wilsey review.

The task of guarding the 280-mile border is daunting, for there are 291 crossing-points capable of being used by vehicles and thousands of others passable on foot. With some roads cratered and closed by the Army, traffic was funnelled through checkpoints in a bid to control the movement of suspects and deter the passage of guns and explosives. The patrol bases checked about 2000 to 3000 vehicles a day, although one of the busiest main road checkpoints, on the Buncrana road from Londonderry, once counted almost 10,000 vehicles in a single day. On top of the risk to police officers and soldiers manning the posts, the local communities faced danger and disruption. Farmers whose fields straddled the border often had to make detours of miles to feed animals or cut crops; local businesses and services suffered great inconvenience. School buses in the rural border areas, for instance, often had to make roundabout journeys to collect and return young pupils.

When the border building project was being studied, the Irish government rejected British approaches to establish joint manned posts on the frontier line, a bid to make the posts safer for the RUC and British Army personnel and minimise local disruption. The IRA would not have dared to attack them because of the risk of killing or injuring Irish policemen or soldiers, and their establishment would have been a powerful symbol of co-operation between the security forces against a common enemy. But the bid was politically compromising for the Dublin government. While the IRA was regarded as a threat to the security of the Irish state, such operational intimacy would have been too controversial. A hue and cry arose, followed by tongue-in-cheek diplomatic protests, whenever British Army helicopters or ground patrols strayed across the meandering border. As a result of these sensitivities and the lack of Irish enthusiasm, the idea was dropped and the Army were forced to locate the checkpoints some distance from the border for better protection.

There were sharply differing opinions within the police and Army about maintaining the posts because of the limited intelligence they produced and the numbers of personnel exposed to great risk of attack in manning and guarding them. One military officer spoke disparagingly of the millions spent 'so that RUC officers could safely do point duty at the border', but ministers supported the project because of the reassurance it gave to Unionists, especially those living along the border. The new chain of posts, now described by the police and Army as patrol bases, were built within a triangular fort, a military principle dating from Roman times. This meant that two sentries could observe all three perimeter walls from two watchtowers. The central building – known as the 'submarine' – was a hardened structure designed to withstand the IRA mortars then in use. Most bases were serviced entirely by air because of the dangers of land-mines on the roads. When foot patrols (police officers protected by soldiers) left the base, they fanned out across the countryside along varied routes, avoiding woods and hedges and other points where ambushes might have been set. Helicopters ferried personnel in and out, and brought in all supplies, removing rubbish in slings under the craft.

After the 'human bomb' attacks had been analysed, sections of eight-feet diameter concrete pipes, on their sides, were placed next to the checkpoints so that the soldiers could leap into them for cover. Sandbagged observation and machine-gun posts were dug into the side of the roads. Surveillance cameras and intercoms reduced the need for personnel to be in the open, and observation towers up to forty feet high were built on nearby hills and vantage points as additional cover for the checkpoints. Soldiers and policemen manning these towers had to climb up a series of steep ladders to reach the top, so waste pipes were installed for the sentries to relieve themselves while on watch. With the Berlin Wall down, the Irish border construction project caused one senior soldier to comment in despair on the Irish conflict. 'From our bases in Germany we can now drive peacefully all the way to Warsaw or Moscow yet, here, from Londonderry, I can see the beautiful hills of Donegal only a few miles away but I cannot go and visit them.'

The collective Republican and Loyalist threats in the early 1990s were greater than at any previous stage of the troubles and – quite apart from the difficulties of policing and monitoring the border – caused the security forces to make constant changes to the way counter-terrorist activities were conducted, both operationally and logistically. This involved improvements in protection of buildings and fixed locations, repeated upgrading of armoured protection in vehicles and new ways for patrols to operate on the ground. Helicopters began to cling to the treetops when flying across the countryside and sometimes operated in groups with one higher, a machine gunner at the open door, providing top cover. This was due to the fear of attack from heat-seeking ground-to-air missiles (which never happened) and the risk of being fired on by heavy calibre, automatic anti-aircraft guns, which on several occasions contributed to bringing down helicopters, although the IRA never made a direct hit. Among visiting VIPs astonished by the high-speed, low-level flights were the Queen Mother and ministerial aides, who described how the clattering helicopters scattered sheep and cattle in the fields below.

*

Technology and techniques evolved to provide greater protection for police stations in all parts of Northern Ireland. At the outset of the terrorist campaign – when rioting crowds attacked them with petrol bombs, stones and occasional gunshots – floodlights, window shutters, sandbags and barbed wire were more than adequate to give protection to the police. However, as the terrorists developed mortars and acquired RPG7 rockets and launchers, chain-link fences around buildings and fuel stores were essential to prevent direct hits and roofs were strengthened to deflect devices or cause detonation. The development of vehicle bombs, packed with home-made explosive and incendiary material, led to the building of blast walls and the creation of stand-off areas around many police stations. The advent of the 'proxy' bomb – where a hostage is held to ensure the vehicle is delivered to the intended target, required further reinforcement: chicanes, barriers and control zones to prevent hijacked vehicles being abandoned or driven into police premises.

The threat faced by police stations was highlighted on 28 February 1985 when the RUC station at Corry Square, Newry was attacked with improvised mortars; nine officers (seven men and two women) were killed. A subsequent court case, brought by the Police Federation, established that the Police Authority and the RUC had a duty of care to police officers. This set off yet another programme to upgrade the often outdated facilities and ineffective levels of protection at police locations. Research into developing more effective mortar protection measures was urgently accelerated in military scientific and weapons establishments throughout Britain. Before this time vulnerable buildings had been covered with a steel-mesh umbrella for protection from mortar blast. In many cases these makeshift measures were unsightly. New prefabricated, hardened structures were developed which provided greater resistance and met higher design standards. Their effectiveness was confirmed in 1993 when they withstood attack by the Mark 15 Mortar.

The Buildings Division of the Police Authority, working with senior RUC officers, directed the campaign to repair and protect RUC premises, but they had also to devise and manage a programme to maintain and modernise an expanding police estate which, by 1996, numbered 200 properties. The Authority and the RUC were determined that, unlike the unfortunate Royal Irish Constabulary in the 1919–22 period, the force would not be driven from any location by attack or intimidation. Despite 2778 serious attacks on police stations between 1969 and 1995, the Authority and RUC drove forward a massive construction programme by mustering a civilian force of officials, professional advisers, contractors, tradesmen, labourers and others which, at its peak in the early 1990s, had a strength of 7000. Between 1985 and 1995 they completed 229 building projects for the RUC at a cost of £129m.

The operation was not without its casualties: twenty-four civilians involved in construction work were targeted and murdered. The first was a prominent Catholic businessman, Seamus McEvoy, murdered in Dublin in August 1985, whose construction company was engaged in police and Army building projects. About the same time another firm was forced to halt work on a new station at Lisnagelvin, Londonderry, after sustained intimidation of the workforce. These incidents marked the beginning of a concerted terrorist effort to thwart the programme. The Police Authority launched a major counter-initiative. With the help of a number of contractors and suppliers, who had indicated their willingness to continue working for the Authority, the work went on. Specialised Army units were involved in a huge secret operation, set up to carry out construction work in the most dangerous locations, particularly along the border. After months of pre-planning, hundreds of police and soldiers were deployed to run in convoys of workers, equipment and materials and guard the sites while the construction work was carried out. Nothing was ever revealed about the existence or activities of the Northern Ireland Works Organisation (NIWO), which a police officer described as a 'cloak and concrete' operation.

While the police were firmly in control of security policy on the ground, they still depended heavily on the muscle and expertise of the Army, whose support, particularly in the area of bomb-disposal, was vital. The bomb-disposal unit, 321 Explosive Ordnance Disposal Company, recorded the twenty-first anniversary of its involvement in the Northern Ireland campaign on 21 November 1992, and received many congratulatory messages. Sir Patrick Mayhew, said their work 'has undoubtedly saved many from the misery of unemployment, from the shock and trauma of destroyed homes and, most importantly of all, from shattered lives.' Sir John Wilsey, the Army Commander, said; 'The contribution our bomb disposal men have made to the safety of the public goes far beyond these shores. The skills and knowledge they have accumulated have been used to benefit people all over the world.' But it was business as usual on the day with a 100lb bomb having to be defused in the New Lodge district of Belfast early in the morning. During those twenty-one years the teams had dealt with 41,300 incidents including almost 9000 explosions. They had defused 5000 bombs and made safe or captured more than 200 tons of explosive. 'Our job is to put ourselves between a bomb and the public to protect life and property,' said the commanding officer of the unit, which protects the identity of its members as rigorously as the SAS and the Intelligence Corps. Twenty of its officers have lost their lives, and a further twenty-three have been injured while dealing with terrorist devices.

Bomb disposal techniques in Northern Ireland have come a long way from the early 1970s, when the 'operator' as he is known, had little more to work with than a Stanley knife, hooks, rope and a pair of pliers. 'We had to get in close to the device, cut it apart and take it to pieces. The terrorists watched us and changed the way they constructed the bombs to defeat us,' he recalled. Anti-handling devices and multiple wiring circuits were incorporated into bombs to confuse or injure the disposal men. 'It was a step by step escalation, with the terrorists and ourselves travelling along different sides of the same road,' he said. Today, with the IRA using state-of-the-art electronics to arm and detonate their bombs, the teams have an array of high technology equipment to help them disrupt and defuse what are called 'improvised explosive devices'. The basic tool is the £50,000 Wheelbarrow, the tracked platform vehicle operated by remote control which can be equipped with a range of devices, many top secret, enabling the operator to tackle a bomb from a distance with the aid of high-definition television. From time to time Wheelbarrows, which have been copied all over the world, are blown to pieces as a bomb-disposal team loses the race to defuse a bomb. The operator works closely with another member of the four-man team known as the 'bleep', who controls an electronic counter-measures van loaded with equipment designed to detect and deflect electronic and radio emissions.

What has not changed over the years is the need for outstanding qualities of concentration and courage from members of the teams. 'Even though we have many technical aids to assist us, at the end of the day someone has to take the long walk along the cleared street to make absolutely sure things are safe,' said the commander of the unit, whose radio callsign and mascot is Felix, the cartoon cat with nine lives. The unit is widely known as '321', and has won more awards in peacetime than any other unit in the British Army: 2 George

Crosses, 16 OBEs, 21 MBEs, 19 BEMs, 33 George Medals, 65 Queen's Gallantry Medals and well over 100 commendations and mentions in dispatches. The Explosive Ordnance Disposal operators play down their role. 'Most of the time we're in a lot less danger than the infantrymen out on patrol,' said one disposal officer. The commander explained that fear comes after the event. 'At the time you don't know what you're dealing with. You expect the worst and you're never disappointed.' He said the members of the unit, who serve six-month tours of duty, watched each other for tell-tale signs of stress, and remarked that without the support of their wives and families in the UK and Germany the soldiers would not be able to cope. 'They are the real heroes, the unsung heroes, who keep the guys going.'

The high reputation the Army enjoyed for its work in Northern Ireland was earned by units like 321 but, as the Nelson case illustrated, relations between the RUC and the Army could often be difficult. Apart from damage to the police–army working ties, there was the potential to upset fundamentally their joint efforts to maintain law and order and develop a better relationship with the Catholic community. In an effort to underline the lead role of the RUC and minimise contact between troops and the local community, especially in those predominantly Catholic areas where tensions were likely to be greatest, by 1992 every Army patrol was accompanied by at least one police officer. The police officer led the patrol to the point where an attack took place, then the soldiers were deployed to protect the officer. Since the introduction of this system in the mid 1980s there has been a noticeable decrease in reports of military excess or bad behaviour. The Independent Assessor of Military Complaints Procedures reported in 1992 that on an average day there are 2350 soldiers on the ground throughout Northern Ireland, each interacting with five members of the public. Each of these 4.3 million encounters is a potential complaint, yet in an average year only 200 formal and 400 informal complaints have been made to the Army about the conduct of troops. Although misconduct is rare, it can speedily neutralise the long periods of good work and confidence building.

One such incident involving members of the Parachute Regiment took place in Coalisland, County Tyrone in May 1992 after a member of the regiment had suffered multiple injuries, including the loss of both legs, in a bomb attack by the IRA. About twenty soldiers from the Third Battalion of the Regiment were involved in verbal exchanges and fist fights in a public house and on the street in the centre of the village, whose population of 5000 is virtually all Catholic and includes many Republican sympathisers. Local political leaders accused the soldiers of going on a rampage of revenge. The commander of the patrol was immediately suspended from duty and, in an unprecedented move, the Army Brigadier, in whose area the regiment had been operating, was relieved of his post, the first time a senior officer had been so treated. During the same period two soldiers were charged and convicted of murder after a youth was shot dead in Belfast and, after other fatal Army shootings, members of the Royal Marines and the Parachute Regiment went on trial. The marines were acquitted, but a paratrooper was jailed for murder after the deaths of two joy-riders in Belfast. The cases showed that the Chief Constable meant to keep security policy stringently within the law, and that there would be no immunity for those who flouted it.

The Republican and Loyalist killing continued throughout 1993 and into 1994. The terror and tragedy it caused was encapsulated in the first of eighty-four violent deaths during 1993.

Three days into the new year, UVF gunmen burst into a combined shop and dwelling at Lisnageer, near Dungannon, County Tyrone. Diarmuid Shields, 19, was shot first and the gunmen then murdered his fifty-one-year-old father, Patrick, in his bed. Among the mourners at the funeral was Julie Statham, the student girlfriend of Diarmuid. Barely a month later she took her own life. Friends said that she died of a broken heart. Tragedies like this, caused by killers on both sides, had condemned Northern Ireland to a scale of conflict teetering constantly on the brink of civil war. For a terrible week in October 1993 – certainly one of the worst periods in the troubles – it seemed as if the community would go over that brink.

The spark ignited at 1.11 p.m. on Saturday 23 October when two young IRA terrorists, dressed as delivery men, entered Frizell's crowded fish shop on the Shankill Road, Belfast and planted a bomb. Before they were able to leave, it exploded, killing one of the bombers, Thomas Begley, and seriously injured the other, Sean Kelly. Ten others perished in the attack, aimed at the leaders of the Loyalist terrorist organisations, who the IRA claimed had been meeting in a room above the shop. Not so; the victims were the owners of the shop and customers, and their deaths caused a wave of fury among the Protestant community. The Catholic sector was swept by fear of inevitable retaliation. Later that evening, after an anonymous call to a radio station, the police found the body of a Catholic, Sean Fox, 70, with a gunshot wound to his head, lying in the living room of his house at Glengormley. The next day two Catholic workmen were shot dead and another five injured when Loyalist gunmen opened fire at a council cleaning depot in a Catholic area of west Belfast. Two more Catholic brothers died at the hands of Loyalists forty-eight hours later, when gunmen entered their house in Craigavon and opened fire. Seven more died when Loyalist gunmen burst into the Rising Sun bar at Greysteel, near Londonderry and opened fire indiscriminately. Such attacks have spawned a new phase in the jargon of the troubles: 'a spray job'. The week's violence brought Northern Ireland to utter despair.

By the end of 1993 the death toll had reached eighty-four and for the first time since 1975 Loyalists had killed more people than Republicans, forty-eight to thirty-six. Despite the calls on all sides for a ceasefire, an end to violence and political talks to forge a lasting settlement, there was no public sign of remorse on the part of the killers or a respite from murder. In his annual report for 1993, Annesley summed up the frustration of the RUC and the law-abiding majority of the community:

> The genuine desire for peace within a majority of both communities is not in itself enough. The reality is that terrorists reside and operate within each community. Each community has, therefore, a responsibility to ensure that there is no hiding place for murderers in its midst, that terrorism is utterly rejected and will not be tolerated. Each community should see itself as the protector of the other and that the well-being of both is inextricably bound together. What, after all, have Republican and Loyalist terrorists done for their respective communities other than to destroy life and the quality of life?
>
> The mutuality of concern which communities must have for each other, and their joint concern for the well-being of the security forces who are protecting them is, I believe, a crucial part of the process towards peace. To the extent that either community falls short in its practical and moral rejection of terrorism or withholds whole-hearted support for the police, the regrettable outcome can only be that death and destruction will be unnecessarily prolonged.

The same pattern of tit-for-tat violence and killings of security force personnel continued into 1994. On 18 June there was another mass killing: six men were murdered in a UVF attack at O'Toole's bar at Loughinisland, County Down, on customers watching a televised World Cup football match.

The attack came as security forces were reeling from a major catastrophe, which wiped out almost the entire top echelon of the intelligence community in Northern Ireland. In the early evening of 2 June, a twin-rotored Chinook helicopter, flying from Aldergrove to Inverness in thick, low mist, plunged into a hillside on the Mull of Kintyre. Sabotage has been ruled out, but the precise cause of the accident has not been established. An RAF investigation blamed pilot error but this verdict was overturned by a civil investigation. All on board died instantly: four RAF aircrew and twenty-five passengers – ten RUC officers; nine Army officers, all working for military intelligence; and six members of the security services. All were senior controllers of the intelligence war in Northern Ireland, crucial to analysis of the information which flowed into RUC headquarters and Stormont Castle, and to the shaping of the government's security and political policies.

The victims included John Deverell, a high-ranking MI5 officer, who was the Director and Co-ordinator of Intelligence at the Northern Ireland Office, and one of the most influential advisers to the Secretary of State and his ministers. The loss to the RUC Special Branch of ten long-serving and experienced members was grievous. Assistant Chief Constable Brian Fitzsimons, 52, who had only days earlier announced his pending retirement, was the most senior officer to die. He had served twenty-one of his thirty-one years' RUC service in the Branch and was an unrivalled expert on the workings of the Republican and Loyalist organisations of Northern Ireland. The other RUC victims were Detective Chief Superintendent Maurice Neilly, 45; Detective Chief Superintendent Desmond Conroy, 55; Detective Superintendent Robert Foster, 41; Detective Superintendent Ian Phoenix, 51; Detective Superintendent William Gwilliam, 50; Detective Superintendent Philip Davidson, 45; Detective Chief Inspector Dennis Bunting, 39; Detective Inspector Kevin Magee, 44, and Detective Inspector Andrew Davidson, 39.

Delivering a eulogy at a ceremony of reception at RAF Aldergrove, when their bodies were returned to Northern Ireland on 7 June, the Chief Constable said:

> Time and time again they prevented horrific outrages which Republican and Loyalist terrorists intended to inflict on this community. Time and time again they saved lives and averted destruction. It is not possible, even now, to reveal the extent to which they so outstandingly served the well-being of the people of Northern Ireland and the nation as a whole.

The crash would have been a devastating, if not terminal, set-back to the counter-terrorist campaign but, as those aboard the doomed helicopter knew, the terrorist campaigns were about to come to a halt: the government had long been engaged in unpublicised peace talks with leaders of the IRA.

When Peter Brooke became Northern Ireland Secretary in July 1989, he was widely assumed to be a caretaker until after the British general election, a safe pair of hands, keeping the lid on a conflict that had endured for two decades without any sign of a solution. Some thought he had been banished to Belfast, as James Prior before him, after a lacklustre stint as Conservative Party chairman. It was some time before informed Ulster watchers realised that this was far from the truth, that he was a highly skilled political operator working to a carefully planned agenda. In the year before Brooke arrived, Tom King and Brian Mawhinney had begun to woo the Unionists in from the self-imposed political cold, where they had sulked since the signing of the Anglo-Irish Agreement in 1985. Brooke extended this work and launched a twin-track, highly secret initiative, sending emissaries to talk directly to the IRA for the first time in fifteen years. He was after a more fundamental answer than the return of a symbolic devolved administration at Stormont, playing for one of the most elusive prizes in British politics: a durable solution to the Irish question.

As a man of Irish stock, Brooke had a fine-tuned sense of Ireland's historical sensitivities and knew that the confluence of events and public opinion which he had inherited was the most promising since 1973, when William Whitelaw achieved the short-lived power-sharing settlement. Brooke judged that a 'window of opportunity' was open. As the province marked the twentieth anniversary of troops being deployed to keep the peace, there was a groundswell of opinion that the next two decades must not be as bad as the last two. Above all, the violence had to be halted. Local politicians had to be forced to do something apart from wringing their hands and blaming Britain. Brooke also wanted to end the intolerable financial burden of peace-keeping in Northern Ireland. He judged that there were the most realistic hopes for conclusive inter-governmental and inter-party agreement on the political future of Ireland since partition in the early 1920s. If he could succeed in forging with Nationalists, Unionists and the Irish government new relations between Britain and the two parts of Ireland, it would be one of the great political triumphs of the century.

In an interview with the Press Association to mark his first hundred days at Stormont, Brooke drew parallels with the intractable Cyprus problem of the 1960s and promised that the British government would be 'imaginative and flexible' in responding to a ceasefire and an end to violence. The remarks caused political outrage; Brooke was dismissed as a loose-tongued fool by many Unionist politicians, but he refused to be provoked. He knew that the analogy with Cyprus would stir deep interest in the IRA's most influential councils. Their strategists had studied the history of British involvement and withdrawal from the divided Mediterranean island and the problems of its subsequent partition. They regarded it as a model for the solution in Ireland. One IRA leader even carried in his wallet a series of creased and yellowing cuttings and cartoons from British newspapers which demonised Archbishop Makarios and then hailed him as a statesman on the steps of 10 Downing Street. 'That will be us one day,' he would say.

Moving stealthily on several fronts, Brooke tried to steer the politicians and the terrorists towards the 'window of opportunity' – the politicians in public, the terrorists in secret. Private messages were reinforced by coded public signals encouraging the IRA to renounce violence. The SDLP leader, John Hume, who did not at first know of the British government's secret initiative, had been engaged in his own efforts to win an end to violence. Shocked by the Remembrance Sunday bombing in Enniskillen in November 1987, Hume had opened a dialogue with the Sinn Fein leader, Gerry Adams, who was campaigning within the Republican movement for a peace strategy based on a lasting ceasefire. Hume had repeatedly urged Brooke to clarify and spell out Britain's long-term policy in Ireland. In November 1990, Brooke responded with what was a break-through pronouncement: 'The British government', he declared, in a speech in his City of London and Westminster constituency, 'has no selfish strategic or economic interest in Northern Ireland: our role is to help, enable and encourage. Britain's purpose . . . is not to occupy, oppress or exploit, but to ensure democratic debate and free democratic choice.' If there could be agreement, Brooke was saying, Britain would be no obstacle. It was a powerful incentive to the band of pragmatic thinkers in the Republican movement and marked a landmark in the development of British policy.

By the time Brooke handed over to Sir Patrick Mayhew in April 1992, he had triggered intensive internal debate about future policy within the IRA, drawn all the political parties into a first round of exploratory round-table talks at Stormont and stimulated several contacts between Republicans and Loyalists and even between Loyalists and the Irish government. The ensuing peace process was long and difficult, potholed with setbacks, evasions and procrastination. The debate within the IRA, obsessed about betraying those killed or imprisoned, was particularly laboured. The intensified IRA violence which accompanied the internal strategy debate amounted to a violent show of strength so that, in the event of a ceasefire, they could say, 'We stopped. We were not defeated.'

The fragile seeds that Brooke had so painstakingly nurtured eventually sprouted in the Downing Street Declaration of December 1993. This document, fashioned from original drafts by John Hume, was hammered into its final form by officials from the British and Irish governments. It was designed to create a basis for a ceasefire and subsequent negotiations, within the framework outlined by Brooke.

The Provisional IRA announced an open-ended ceasefire with effect from 31 August 1994. Unlike the preliminaries to earlier ceasefires, when the IRA mounted attacks right up to the deadline to demonstrate its strength, the campaign of violence ground to an unspectacular halt. On 30 August shots were fired at the RUC station on the Fermanagh border at Belleek; a joint RUC/Army patrol came under fire in Belfast; warning shots were fired at Swatragh, County Londonderry, when three suspects in a car failed to stop for the police; and two home-made machine guns were recovered in a raid in Belfast. Loyalist violence spluttered on for another six weeks and included a car-bomb attack which caused damage to the Sinn Fein headquarters at Falls Road, Belfast. On 13 October 1994 the Combined Loyalist Military Command, which included the UDA and UVF, confirmed that it would observe an open-ended ceasefire. Billy Hutchinson, one of their emerging leaders, was asked what mandate he had to move into politics. 'Our mandate is the silence of the guns,' he said.

When the violence stopped, the death toll since 1969 had reached 3171, which included twelve RUC casualties over the preceding two years. Constable Colleen McMurray, 34, the wife of a police officer, was the first RUC victim of 1992 when she was killed in Newry on 28 March by a horizontally fired mortar which hit the police car in which she was travelling. Constable Jim Douglas, the father of a teenage son and daughter, was shot dead on 10 October, unarmed and off-duty, by gunmen in the Monico bar in Belfast city centre, where he was drinking with a group of friends. Alan Corbett, 25, a full-time member of the RUC Reserve from Banbridge, County Down, was killed by a one-shot sniper while conducting a vehicle check in the border village of Belcoo on 15 November. On 23 January 1993, Constable Michael Ferguson, a Catholic and the son of a policeman, was shot dead at point-blank range by gunmen while he was on patrol outside a shopping centre in Londonderry. Reggie Williamson, who had served in the RUC Reserve for eighteen years, died on 24 February when a booby-trap device exploded underneath his car near Loughgall, County Armagh. The next day a sniper claimed the life of Constable John Reid, 30, on patrol with soldiers at Castleblayney Road, in Crossmaglen, and 2 November a sniper murdered Reserve Constable Brian Woods in the centre of Newry. Two RUC members, Constable Andrew Beacom and Reserve Constable Ernest Smith, perished when gunmen attacked them as they slowed down at a road junction in County Fermanagh on 12 December. Constable Johnston Beacom, 30, was killed on 17 February 1994 when a mortar was fired at his Land Rover in the Markets area adjacent to central Belfast. Constable Jackie Haggan, 33, was off-duty and enjoying a night out at the Dunmore Park greyhound racing stadium, Belfast, on 10 March when a gunman walked into the bar and shot him dead. The killing was witnessed by his wife, Kim, who was pregnant with their third child. On 20 April, Constable Gregory Pollock, 23, was killed by a mortar fired at his patrol vehicle in Spencer Road, Londonderry. He was the 296th RUC victim since 1969 and there were hopes that he would be the last. The new situation, the first peace for over twenty-five years, was to have a profound effect on the people of Northern Ireland and the RUC.

# 13

# Days like This

As faith in a 'troubles-free' future bloomed in the aftermath of the 1994 ceasefires, Belfast-born Van Morrison's song 'Days like This' was adopted as the anthem of the new peace. The lyrics articulated the general relief that violence had been halted and that people could go to work, shop or to a pub or restaurant without fear of attack. For those under thirty years of age, it was their first experience of what was locally termed as 'normality'. However cautiously some judged the long-term situation, everybody wanted to believe that after a quarter of a century of conflict the Northern Ireland community stood on the threshold of an era free from violence and division. With the guns and bombs silenced, the way was clear for political negotiations toward an enduring settlement.

Within hours of the ceasefires, the government, the Royal Ulster Constabulary and the Army inaugurated a cautiously progressive response to the absence of violence and low levels of threat to the community. The moves had been fore-shadowed in a top secret, fifty-four-point document, drawn up by the Army in 1992, with the knowledge of the police, and passed to the IRA through intermediaries as part of the secret process to encourage a ceasefire. Over the following months, much of the security framework which had impeded ordinary life for so long was dismantled. The Army's heavy armoured Saxon vehicles stopped patrolling the streets and were withdrawn to barracks. Soldiers replaced their protective helmets with regimental berets and discarded their bullet-proof jackets. Rifles were no longer carried in the ready-to-fire position. As the response plan had promised, female soldiers ceased to wear combat trousers and wore skirts. In many areas soldiers were taken off the streets altogether and remained inside police stations as a 'quick reaction force' or were returned to their barracks to be plunged into training and sport to keep them occupied. At first, each step taken was easily reversible, but the longer the ceasefire held and confidence grew, the more sweeping were the changes, and by the first anniversary the security profile had been transformed.

Army support for the police had been reduced by three quarters and in many places, including Belfast, withdrawn altogether. Several units had returned to their barracks in Britain and Germany. Around the 200-mile border with the Irish Republic, routine vehicle checks had been discontinued, a number of border bases were removed and 104 crossing-points were opened. A three-year plan to restore all the cratered roads and rebuild the bridges was in place – significant for border-based communities. At Aughnacloy, for instance, Army engineers constructed a footbridge across a border stream so that a football team could once again use its playing field and changing rooms, separated by the frontier, without a detour before and after every game. Throughout Northern Ireland traffic control zones were lifted, checkpoints and barriers around town centres reopened or removed. In Downpatrick, the massive steel cages over the streets around the police station, to frustrate mortar attack, were dismantled, and in Londonderry the observation tower which dominated the sky-line above RUC Rosemount was taken down. In Belfast, the Civilian Search Unit, which searched pedestrians and traffic was stood down and disbanded. At the city's international airport the perimeter approach roads, closed for twenty years, were reopened and the checkpoint controlling access was closed. In March 1995, the Queen was able to visit Belfast and travel across the new road and rail bridges in Belfast, close to the Republican Markets and Short Strand areas, without protest or incident. The process of demilitarisation was widely welcomed, except by a dog in Newtownbutler, County Fermanagh, shot dead by a soldier after it attacked members of a joint police/Army patrol who, in the new spirit of goodwill, had stopped to talk to its owner.

The ceasefires had a dramatic effect on the way the 13,500-strong RUC did its job. Fortifications around most police stations were dismantled and, in many areas, gates and front doors were opened, at least during the hours of daylight, to make access less forbidding. Several police stations held open days, letting local people in to see their work, something unthinkable a short time before. RUC officers rapidly moved into a conventional community role, walking the beat and responding to calls for assistance. Ever more confidently, they patrolled the streets without heavy weapons and bullet-proof jackets and without the military. Those who had long endured the physical effort and back pain from wearing cumbersome protective jackets found the new freedom a relief. Unshackled from the threat of attack, they could idle and talk to people without taking up defensive postures. The sight of uniformed police officers dancing with crowds in Bangor in summer 1995, celebrating the fiftieth anniversary of VE-Day, symbolised the relaxed policing environment.

More significantly, there was a marked improvement in relations between the police and the minority community. Local shopkeepers now willingly served the police, where before they would have feared intimidation or attack for doing so, and in one village the local bakery resumed dawn deliveries of hot scones and soda bread to the local station. On New Year's Eve 1994, at a recently besieged border station in County Fermanagh, the locals gathered outside just before midnight and insisted the police join them in the nearby bar for a midnight drink. Incident books quickly filled up as people once more resorted to the police to resolve disputes, enforce the law and regulate their lives. Increasingly the armoured, unmarked patrol cars were fitted with illuminated signs and revolving blue lights. A new fleet of white, police-liveried cars was procured and deployed to carry out conventional patrolling, with a particular emphasis on traffic policing.

As the death toll from violence subsided, the police were able to give priority to reducing the carnage on the roads, where twice as many people died as were victims of terrorism. A cadre of liveried motorcycles was deployed for traffic enforcement and to provide a visible police presence in the community. Opinion surveys showed that the public wanted a constant, visible police presence on the streets. For the police officers concerned, 90 per cent of whom had joined since the troubles began, peace was, in the words of one superintendent, 'a learning process. We are trying to get away from the "Land Rover syndrome" of policing in strength and instead encourage a more approachable type of individual policing. But much work needs to be done.' Most officers responded positively to the prospect of conventional community policing and in some stations demanded training in inter-personal skills so that they could work more effectively with the public.

Of all the participants in the Northern Ireland peace process, none was more central than the Royal Ulster Constabulary. Police incompetence had played a major part in the outbreak of the troubles twenty-five years earlier and their competence and sensitivity, it was clear, would be a crucial factor in making the ceasefires work and in holding the ring for a new political settlement to emerge. Nobody wanted to see the peace process founder, so the need to exercise discretion in policing the peace was well understood from the outset. The RUC made it clear that there would be no let-up in its efforts to solve unsolved crimes and bring offenders to justice, but commanders warned their subordinates that how they handled arrests, patrolled and generally fulfilled their responsibilities might determine the success of the ceasefire. Any hasty response could upset the fragile calm and lead to the RUC being blamed for a breakdown.

The RUC which emerged from the conflict was a very different force from that driven into fortified police stations and armoured vehicles in the early 1970s. Its numbers had grown from 3000 to 13,000 with another 2000 civilians in support. There were 2000 vehicles, including patrol cars, armoured Land Rovers, mobile canteens and even a clinic on wheels for the Occupational Health Unit. Collectively they covered 31 million miles a year. In addition, the force had a flotilla of 11 boats and 90 highly trained dogs – 52 German Shepherds, 31 Labradors and 7 Springer Spaniels – who could chase suspects or sniff explosives or drugs. Since 1969 the RUC had become a confident, efficient, well-trained organisation commanded by well-educated officers, many with a strong sense of vocation and a clear vision of the role of policing in a turbulent society. True, it was still overwhelmingly Protestant in character and some appalling hardline sectarianism and bias was to be found in its ranks, but, given visionary and courageous leadership, it was possible to remedy the shortcomings and remould it to win the co-operation of the deeply divided community. The ceasefires prompted a substantial increase in young Catholics applying to join the force, reflecting a more supportive attitude among the minority community.

Policing in Northern Ireland had, of course, long been a volatile and controversial issue. Almost as soon as the ceasefires were called, the British and Irish governments – as well as local politicians – served notice that the RUC's future would be one of the most prominent topics when they began to hammer out a political settlement. With his government's policy proposals on the table for discussion, the British prime minister promised a return to exclusively civilian policing for Northern Ireland. The Irish prime minister called for the

RUC to be restructured as part of the emerging peace process.

On the night the IRA ceasefire took effect, Republicans underlined that doing away with the RUC was their highest priority when they triumphantly painted out the letters 'RUC' outside several Belfast police stations and daubed the word 'Garda' instead. A few days later they served an 'eviction notice' on the officer in charge of the Woodbourne station in west Belfast. This coincided with the launch of a concerted campaign calling for the 'unacceptable' RUC to be disbanded; a clever poster, showing a silhouetted police officer with an orange sash, was extensively fly-posted throughout the Catholic areas. In some housing estates road signs were erected to indicate no-go areas for the police. This reflected the IRA's long-standing ambition to have a role in policing its heartland areas, which would underpin its community influence. The epidemic of brutal punishment beatings after the ceasefires, in both Republican and Loyalist areas, for what was called 'anti-social behaviour', was a direct illustration of this strand of IRA policy and showed that the Loyalists too wanted a stake in future policing arrangements. Alienation between the police and many Protestant communities continued to be a problem.

The ceasefires also gave rise to calls for a 'peace dividend' – money formerly expended on law and order to be diverted to boost neglected social and community need. This prompted speculation about the future role and size of the RUC, causing a great sense of hurt within the force and raising fears about job security. Sir Patrick Mayhew tried to calm these fears in September 1994 when he said that the government would proceed with caution and that any changes would 'be put in train, carefully, sympathetically and gradually. We are not going to turn our backs upon those to whom I have already paid tribute for having held the line for so long.' However, Sir Patrick seemed to overturn those assurances in a newspaper interview in London on 21 December, when he said, 'There will certainly be a need for far fewer police and I am told that the ordinary policing needs of the public in ordinary times might be in the order of 3500.' Reverting to an RUC of that size, the pre-troubles strength, would entail wholesale job losses, and the remarks had a deeply unsettling effect.

Having sustained 296 deaths by the time of the ceasefires, and many thousands of injuries, these remarks (and others about downsizing and police reform) caused a significant drop in morale among the 13,000 members of the RUC and their families and created a greater sense of isolation from the community. A feeling of resentment also developed that their courage and sacrifices was being written off. A reminder of what the RUC had endured came on 2 March 1995, when Constable James Seymour, who had been in a coma after being shot on 4 May 1973 at the RUC station in Coalisland, finally died. The RUC's collective hurt and frustrations, and deep-seated police scepticism about the durability of the ceasefires, became more and more evident. 'Leopards don't change their spots,' said one officer when asked his opinion of the ceasefires. 'It's all too good to be true. When will it break out again?' Such feelings were more bitterly articulated by the chairman, Les Rodgers, at the Police Federation's annual conference on 5 June 1995.

> For the terrorists it may be a matter of discarding the guns and dining with the diplomats but this new style of self-presentation does not fool the members of my Federation. There may be no life-threatening terrorist violence at the moment. But the terrorism goes on. Police officers are still being targeted and, since the ceasefires, several have moved home because of explicit or implicit threat.
>
> There are enough guns and explosives in caches still available to the IRA to mobilise a small guerrilla army. These weapons will not rust in the thatch as they did in times past. They are well protected against the elements and concealed deep enough to prevent detection. While they remain available to those who aspire to sit at the conference table, democracy will still be under threat.
>
> Not that the hostility and threat against this force comes entirely from the terrorist organisations and their apologists. They are also lionised by a whole gaggle of commentators, ranging from an often insufficiently critical media to parasitic and irrelevant academics. Those who stand on the touchline of politics and terrorism and who shout the loudest from the stand always believe they understand and can play the game better. They are no friends of law and order, for their aim is to undermine trust in this force.

Over the years of conflict the police had come almost to represent a third community in divided Northern Ireland. Working from armoured vehicles, fortified police stations and to a large extent protected by soldiers when they patrolled, they had little contact or intimacy with the community they policed. They maintained dialogue with community representatives and gathered intelligence about the dynamics of the communities they served, but there was a distance, reinforced by their own lifestyles.

By Northern Ireland standards, the police earned large amounts of money. In 1994–5, for instance, the average salary for a constable was £33,500 including an overtime payment of £7000. Some officers working long hours earned even more: one member of the close protection unit, who clocked up 120 hours a month overtime guarding a public figure, was paid about £50,000 that year. Their prosperity, and the need for tight personal security, enabled the police to live in clusters of safe, comfortable, middle-class ghettoes, largely in the greater Belfast area. Aided by generous rent allowances, they bought exclusive houses, often lavishly furnished and equipped, and two holidays abroad a year were not uncommon, providing opportunities to relax away from the threat of violence. They were able to afford good cars in which they travelled, frequently some distance, to their stations and thus became detached by not living among the community they policed. Because of the unremitting terrorist threat, both on and off duty, their private lives were lived with great caution. Police children were taught, from their earliest days, not to open the door to callers, or to answer the telephone; above all, never to touch daddy's gun, which in police homes was as familiar as the television in the corner or the kettle on the worktop. When asked at school or work what their daddy did, police children invariably lied: 'He's in the civil service,' they would say.

Police families understandably chose their friends and associates with great care and the dictates of security meant that, to a marked extent, they socialised only with other police, prison officers or civil servants in the same position, to whom they could talk about their work and problems in a sympathetic environment. Apart from dangers, the police were under unique pressures. At the scene of every atrocity, they came face to face with the bloody and messy consequences. One young officer, straight from the Training Centre, was posted to RUC Andersonstown to replace another who had been shot and seriously injured. On his first night's duty he was at the scenes of four terrorist murders. Another told of returning home from a landmine explosion in which four of his colleagues had been killed to find that his dog recoiled from his smell.

The overwhelming number of police officers and their families coped well with the long hours, trauma and dangers, but for a significant minority it caused great personal difficulties. Marital problems were common and the private behaviour of many officers was sometimes extreme. Two officers were accused of multiple murders of members of their families and convicted at their trials. Alan Anderson was charged with murdering his wife, Judith, 36, and his father-in-law, the Reverend Eric Davidson, 74, a retired cleric, in Cookstown in December 1992. Although he was acquitted on appeal, and freed, he was dismissed from the RUC and awarded compensation. John Torney denied killing his wife Linda and their children, at their Cookstown home in September 1994. He was convicted of murder and the conviction was later confirmed on appeal. Given the high disposable income, particularly among young, single officers, drinking problems were common. One young constable, who had been awarded the Queen's Commendation for Brave Conduct, after coming under gun or bomb attack on eleven occasions, began drinking heavily, accumulated debts and ended up committing robbery.

An internal survey, carried out by the RUC's Occupational Health Unit in 1988, estimated that one in ten officers were being treated for stress-related complaints, including extreme anxiety and ulcers. In 1996 the RUC disclosed that fifty-five police officers had committed suicide since 1970, forty-seven of them with handguns issued by the force for their personal protection. The tip of this iceberg of stress, and its often tragic consequences, was glimpsed in public from time to time. In October 1984, Constable Gary Dickson, 22, who was upset by the recent suicide of a close friend in the Ulster Defence Regiment, shot dead the mother of a girlfriend during an argument. He then embarked on a 100-mile journey across Northern Ireland for nearly sixteen hours, hijacking cars and taking hostages, including a pregnant woman, before he shot himself as police were closing in. Another young constable, Neil Gillis, 23, killed himself in 1986 while playing Russian roulette with his loaded revolver in the police station at Pomeroy. In April 1990, a twenty-five-year old reserve constable, Paul Craig, shot himself in the head with his police revolver because he could not come to terms with the break-up of his relationship with a woman.

Suicide was also the culmination of an extraordinary chain of events early in 1992. On 3 February, Constable Allen Moore, 24, from Ballymena, County Antrim, attended the funeral of his friend, Constable Norman Spratt. He had been shot dead, with his personal gun, by his wife during a violent drinking bout. (She was cleared of murder after the jury accepted that the gun had gone off accidentally.) Late in the evening after the funeral, Moore, who had been drinking heavily, returned to Spratt's grave in Comber cemetery and fired a number of shots in salute. A woman living nearby saw a red BMW car parked close to the cemetery with its hazard lights flashing. After hearing a single shot and then, after a pause, six more shots she dialled 999 and called the police. By then the red car had been driven off towards Newtownards but the police gave chase, took the driver into custody and discovered he was an RUC officer and very drunk. After being disarmed, he was given into the custody of another officer who took him to his home to sleep it off. Arrangements were made for him to attend a medical examination the next day so that the RUC's comprehensive support mechanism could be employed. But when he woke, Moore gave his police host the slip and went to his home in Bangor, where he collected his legally held, pump-action, semi-automatic shotgun, and drove to Belfast. At the time he should have been seeing the doctor, he bluffed his way into the Sinn Fein Centre at Falls Road, posing as a journalist. Taking the shotgun from a hold-all, he opened fire and killed three people in the waiting room. Over the next three hours Moore visited a number of public houses and made telephone calls to the police admitting the shootings. Before the police could track him down, he went to a lonely spot on the Lough Neagh shore, where he turned the shotgun on himself and committed suicide.

The case focused unprecedented attention on the stress and strain suffered by the RUC, and highlighted the difficulties of spotting officers who could not stand the pressure. On the surface Moore had been a model officer during his six years in the force. He had served with distinction in several tough areas and earned the Queen's Commendation for Gallantry when he arrested a terrorist who had thrown an explosive device at his patrol vehicle. Moore was typical of the prosperous police officer, living in a bungalow at Bangor, County Down, dressing well and driving a BMW. Behind this façade of level-headed normality he was an increasingly disturbed man. He was infatuated with a married woman colleague and was drinking heavily on a regular basis. During one binge he broke both ankles jumping off a wall and was off work for six months. More seriously he made bombs which were sent through the post to three people associated with Sinn Fein, although none of them suffered injury. He was also obsessed with a novel, *Summary Justice*, about a rogue RUC officer who conducts a single-handed war of revenge against the IRA. These danger signs were not recognised or discovered until after Moore's death when his horrified friends and colleagues realised the extent of his mental disturbance. At the inquest into his death the Belfast Coroner, Mr John Leckey, described him as 'a time-bomb waiting to explode'.

*

Although the RUC had recognised the damaging effects of stress on its officers and was involved in pioneering work to deal with it, spotting and handling the symptoms was uncharted territory. 'We are all human beings,' said Deputy Chief Constable Blair Wallace. 'Some cope with stress better than others.'

Until a few years earlier, in the aftermath of an horrific shooting or explosion, senior officers would call their men into the office and put a couple of bottles on the table. Any officer who couldn't drink and forget his ordeal was judged to have a weakness; the stiff upper lip was all. Weakness couldn't be admitted either to oneself or, worse, to a colleague. Any hint of being unable to cope was a black mark and could, and did, prejudice reputation and promotion prospects for many. As it became increasingly clear that the by then legendary RUC drinking bouts were aggravating the problems, in the teeth of opposition from the command hierarchy, the Northern Ireland Police Federation persuaded the Police Authority and RUC to blaze a trail ahead of any other police force and set up a special unit to study and tackle the stress problem. This resulted in the formation of the Occupational Health Unit, the recognition of post-traumatic stress as a legitimate and debilitating condition and a new, sympathetic attitude within the force. Confidential counselling was provided, supervisory officers were trained to recognise the symptoms, and victims no longer had their careers blighted. Colleagues were encouraged to report anyone exhibiting signs of stress: 'Better to blow the whistle on him than attend his funeral,' said a senior officer.

The ceasefires did not remove the strains experienced by Northern Ireland police officers. Although they were freed from the threat of terrorist attack, many found it difficult to come to terms with the lessening of tension. Others, whose workloads had decreased or who spent more time at home, became involved in friction with their wives and families. Many who had been engaged in sensitive or controversial operations dreaded that one day, as in Bosnia or South Africa, there would be war crimes tribunals or truth commissions and they would face retribution for their actions. Some were so worried they kept diaries and copies of papers to use in their defence.

Many families experienced financial worries for the first time as the substantial reduction in overtime working caused salaries to drop significantly. During the 1994–5 financial year, from April to March, RUC officers worked 5.7 million hours overtime, a decrease of 13 per cent on the previous year. In the six months before the IRA ceasefire on 31 August 1994 officers worked a daily average of 17,200 hours overtime. Over the next six months the average came down to 12,900 hours. During the pre-ceasefires period, officers in some areas were working between 50 and 60 hours extra each month, with a force average of 45 hours. By June 1995 this was 24 hours. This meant a decrease in individual pay packets, but the reductions led to considerable savings in the police budget, 70 per cent of which was wages and salaries. In the six months before the ceasefires the overtime allocation had been overspent by £2.3m but by the end of the financial year the reduction in overtime activity meant an overall saving of £6.1m for the year. These savings continued in the first quarter of 1995–6, with every 1000 hours reduction in the daily hours level representing a saving of £5m in the cost of policing.

In a bid to monitor the impact of these changes, and the implications of the changing security situation, the Chief Constable set up a Health and Welfare Advisory Group in September 1994. Reporting directly to him, it was given the task of ensuring that stress/debt counselling was readily available: the group was also a conduit between command and the staff associations to discuss the post-ceasefire demands for reform and restructuring. While the need for change and eventual down-sizing was conceded by the RUC, the force was concerned that the process should be handled sensitively and cautiously. Above all, their capacity to maintain law and order should not be compromised by hasty reductions in manpower or role. Despite the hope and optimism still widely invested in the belief that the ceasefires were for good and would lead to a political deal, they sensed that the situation ahead was volatile and uncertain.

So that full consideration could be given to future changes, the Northern Ireland Office, the Police Authority and the RUC jointly established the Fundamental Review of Policing in April 1995. Headed by Ronnie Flanagan, an up-and-coming assistant chief constable with outstanding leadership potential, its brief was to define the nature and level of policing Northern Ireland would need in the years ahead, quantify the organisation and structures that would be necessary to deliver it, and cost the financial implications. Although Flanagan recognised that there were budgetary imperatives, with the Treasury in London looking for an early reduction in the disproportionate costs of policing Northern Ireland, he insisted his work would not be handcuffed to financial considerations only.

The core team to carry out the review consisted of a superintendent, a chief inspector, three inspectors and one official each from the Authority and the Northern Ireland Office. Their first task was to define what the community would expect of the police in the years ahead. Extensive use was made of questionnaires to selected target groups, and they visited nine other British police forces, as well as the Garda Siochana, to collect examples of best practice and new ideas which could be adapted for use in Northern Ireland. Other public sector organisations and some large commercial firms were also visited to gather material and expertise. An occupational psychologist and other academics were consulted. Studies of crime and traffic patterns, police activity analyses and social and economic profiles in six representative areas were carried out to produce a new manpower allocation formula so that policing could be effectively wedded to the needs of the community. At every stage the staff was consulted and informed about the developing study. A video was made, outlining the scope and purpose of the review so that everybody knew what was intended, and regular bulletins and news sheets were produced and circulated. 'The more the peace developed, the more insecurity there was about jobs and the future. We wanted to make sure everybody knew precisely what was going on,' Flanagan explained.

Towards the end of 1995 a radical blueprint for future policing was taking shape. It proposed the most sweeping policy and organisational shake-up in the history of the RUC which would turn the pyramid of command upside-down. The central police headquarters in Belfast would lose its day-to-day control over policing the community and an entire tier of command – the 16 operational divisions – would be stripped away, with a substantial saving in terms of manpower and administration. Under the new structure, the 38 subdivisions covering Northern Ireland would be recast into 28 new police 'areas'. These would broadly correspond to the 26 local council districts, with Belfast being split into two or three areas. The local police superintendent (chief superintendent rank was abolished in 1994) would be the pivotal figure in the policing structure, having direct responsibility for personnel, budgets, resources, operations, crime and traffic policing and relationships with the local community. Inspectors under his command would have a broader management role in implementing these responsibilities and ensuring their delivery through sergeants and constables.

The new-style police service headquarters (the words 'police force' now being proscribed) would provide central services such as recruitment, training, inspectorate, discipline and specialised support and would essentially become a policy and resource centre, defining strategy and allocating manpower and resources, all of which would be devolved to the new areas. In the long term the full-time Reserve would disappear but the part-time Reserve would continue to have a strong local focus and to encourage community-minded people to serve. The new plan, devolving real power and command to the area superintendents is intended to be flexible enough to be tailored to the needs of the local community. Rural and inner city areas have different problems and each needs to be individually policed. A key element would be reorganising the network of Community Police Liaison Committees to form one in each area, with a broadly based membership of elected and community representatives to work with their local police officers in setting priorities and targets.

The review also grappled with the sensitive question of future police strength. By normal British standards, Northern Ireland was significantly over-policed. Not including up to 19,000 service personnel in support, there was one officer for every 135 of the population compared to 1 for 256 in London and 1 for 446 in England and Wales. Sussex, Kent and Surrey, with populations similar to the 1.6m in Northern Ireland, managed with police strengths of between 3500 and 4000. On the more generous London ratio, the future size of the Northern Ireland police would be about 6250. The review refrained from putting a figure on the future strength, but defined a number of key assumptions and sketched out three situations which would dictate the pace and limits of any downsizing. The key assumptions were that the RUC remained an entity, the single police organisation responsible for Northern Ireland, with a brief to maintain the manpower, training and equipment necessary for the task without routine military support. Also taken into account was the propensity to serious public disorder inherent in the divided community and the underlying risk of a return to politically motivated violence at some time in the future. Another key factor was the lack of police 'mutual aid' available to the RUC. In the event of an emergency or unforeseen public order problem developing on the British mainland, there are standing arrangements for trained reinforcements to be supplied at a moment's notice. If a sudden situation developed in Northern Ireland, the RUC could not rely on speedy support, so it needed what was described as a 'surge capability'.

Against this background, the review said that while territorial and policy reorganisation should take place, manpower levels should be dictated by developments in the political and security situations. If there was a return to full-scale terrorism then, clearly, there could be no reduction in numbers and an increase might be needed to compensate for the lack of military support. By the mid 1990s the end of the Cold War had led to major reductions in the strength of the Army and the disbanding or amalgamation of many front-line regiments. New commitments, notably in former Yugoslavia, meant that the Army was finding it harder to maintain its 12,000 Northern Ireland garrison and keep 'Spearhead' battalions on stand-by for emergency reinforcement. On the other hand, if there was a convincing and permanent renunciation of violence by the terrorist groupings, with weapons and explosives surrendered, the peacetime establishment could be reached. This, informed estimates said, would see the RUC shrink to a rock-bottom 5000 over a period of up to ten years. The most likely situation was the middle one, where the force strength would be cut to between 7500 and 8500, where there were *de facto* ceasefires but the terrorist organisations had not disarmed and continued to pose a threat.

By the time the first drafts of the review had been completed at the end of 1995, it seemed that the whole process might be academic, for major cracks were developing in the IRA ceasefire, causing collateral pressure on the restraint of Loyalist groups. On the back of the initial euphoria which greeted the ceasefires, the two governments were pushing ahead urgently to exploit the unprecedented political opportunity created. Building on the Downing Street Declaration of December 1993, the British and Irish governments published, in February 1995, a far-reaching discussion document outlining a political framework for the future of the island of Ireland. The proposals were subject to negotiation and agreement by all the parties in Northern Ireland; referenda in both the north and the south; legislation approved by both the British and Irish parliaments. They were designed to meet the conflicting demands of Unionists and Nationalists within a democratic framework based on consent. They aimed to restore local democracy in Northern Ireland and to promote all-Ireland agreement and reconciliation in a lasting political settlement. John Major said, 'The unimaginable of two years ago has been achieved, the unimaginable of two years ahead must now be begun.'

*

Despite the political risks it had taken in talking secretly to the IRA and encouraging the 1994 ceasefire, the British government accepted it only grudgingly and with poor grace. Key advisers harboured grave private doubts about the IRA's political vision and skills, its sincerity and the ability of the pragmatists to carry the organisation forward in one piece. A split would mean a bloody feud and power struggle and cause a more violent rump to emerge to maintain the campaign for a united Ireland. 'History shows that IRA pragmatism always ends in a violent scattering match,' said one senior British source.

With this in mind, the British government was uncompromising in insisting on the early decommissioning of terrorist weaponry. Their doubts were reinforced by constant reports from the RUC Special Branch that the IRA continued to gather information about potential targets and carry out some dummy-run attacks. At least twelve police officers were forced to move house during the ceasefire period because of this. 'Any group which is wholly committed to constitutional and democratic methods can have no need for illegal arms and explosives, surface-to-air missiles and mortars. The challenge of democracy is to persuade others by force of argument, not by force of arms,' said Michael Ancram, the British minister leading the exploratory political dialogue. While the Irish government, and virtually everyone else, agreed that decommissioning was an essential element of a credible peace and political process, Republicans and Loyalists maintained it could be addressed only in the context of the formal negotiations to follow the ceasefires. There were also formidable practical and legal problems. What about weapons that had been used in serious offences? Should they be forensically tested? What would happen to those who handed over such weapons? What were the legal implications of an amnesty? How would it affect the feelings of relatives of victims of unsolved murders? How, indeed, could the terrorists be trusted, and how could it be proved that all arms had been handed over? The British government was therefore reluctant to authorise face-to-face contact with the IRA's political representatives; this soured the Republican attitude given that there had been secret talks for years. British doubts strengthened about the IRA's sincerity and its willingness to recognise the *Realpolitik* of the situation: that even the Irish government did not want and could not afford a united Ireland.

The first serious threat to the credibility of the ceasefire came in November 1994 when IRA activists shot dead Frank Kerr, a postal official, at the Newry sorting office during a raid in which £130,000 was stolen. After assurances that it was an unauthorised renegade enterprise, both governments extended benefit of the doubt and dropped their protests. During ensuing talks with British officials there was nothing but gloom when Sinn Fein expounded an agenda unchanged since the early 1920s, which had little relevance to the political realities of the late 1990s. By the time Ancram finally met Sinn Fein at Stormont in May 1995 (the first official talks between the government and Sinn Fein for seventy-three years and the first direct ministerial contact since 1972), the Republicans were becoming more and more cynical about British good faith in the peace process. By the autumn of 1995 the hardliners and doubters were gaining the upper hand in the internal strategy debate still going on inside the IRA. Despite the steady dismantling of security in response to the ceasefires, they complained about the slow progress being made towards the promised political negotiations.

In November, on the eve of the first-ever visit of a United States president to Northern Ireland, the British and Irish prime ministers cobbled a deal for an international commission to study the de-commissioning problem and come up with a plan, thus clearing the way for political negotiations. But even as President Clinton's motor-cade detoured through Belfast for a prearranged handshake with Sinn Fein leader Gerry Adams, a public endorsement of his role as peace-maker, IRA hardliners had decided that the ceasefire should be ended. At the same time, in a secret workshop in South Armagh, a lorry was being fitted with false panels to ferry a deadly cargo of explosive across the Irish Sea. Over the Christmas and New Year period, as the inter-national commission worked against the clock to formulate de-commissioning proposals, the IRA was putting its intention to end the 'total' ceasefire into action. Even a late-January Washington meeting between Clinton and Adams failed to convince them that they had more to gain from the political process, however sluggish it was, than a return to violence.

The international commission members were George Mitchell, former US Senator, General John de Chastelain, from Canada, and Harry Holkeri, a former prime minister of Finland. Its findings were published on 24 January 1996. A set of principles was supplied to govern entry to the planned political talks and the commission recom-mended 'that the parties to such negotiations affirm their total and absolute commitment'

(a) to democratic and exclusively peaceful means of resolving political issues;

(b) to the total disarmament of all paramilitary organisations;

(c) to agree that such disarmament must be verifiable to the satisfaction of an independent commission;

(d) to renounce for themselves, and to oppose any effort by others, to use force, or threaten to use force, to influence the course or the outcome of all-party negotiations;

(e) to agree to abide by the terms of any agreement reached in all-party negotiations and to resort to democratic and exclusively peaceful methods in trying to alter any aspect of that outcome with which they may disagree; and

(f) to urge that 'punishment' killings and beatings stop and to take effective steps to prevent such actions.

The report was welcomed on all sides. John Major then announced plans for elections in Northern Ireland as 'a gateway' to the talks. Adams said Sinn Fein was implacably opposed to elections, which he said would lead to a return of Stormont rule. It was the final straw for the IRA. On 2 February, the home of a reserve policeman at Moy, County Tyrone, was raked with fifty-seven shots, signalling a return to violence. A week later, in the early evening of Friday 9 February, the lorry, prepared in South Armagh and loaded with a cargo of explosives, was trundled into position outside an office complex called South Quay Plaza, in the former Docklands area of east London.

Acting on a warning call to the *Irish News* in Belfast, Metropolitan police were still clearing people from the nearby office complexes when the bomb went off at 7.01 p.m., killing two shop workers. Shortly before the detonation, Radio Telefis Eireann newsroom in Dublin received a telephone call indicating that the ceasefire was over. When the message had not been broadcast a short time later, the caller rang again to confirm. The news, underlining a remarkable intelligence failure by both the British and Irish security forces, took the government machines in Belfast, London and Dublin by surprise. Less than a week earlier, Annesley, the chief constable, had said there were no grounds for believing that the IRA was planning to break the ceasefire but that it was keeping its mainland machine 'oiled'. At RUC headquarters in east Belfast, Deputy Chief Constable Blair Wallace, in charge in Annesley's absence, summoned senior colleagues to a crisis meeting; throughout Northern Ireland local police commanders were called back to their posts. Their first priority was to ensure the safety of police personnel and their stations, so body armour, machine-guns and rifles were immediately reissued to those going out on patrol, security gates at police stations once more clanged shut and sentries were again posted. There was no immediate return of Army patrolling nor were the border checkpoints reimposed. Responses were prepared depending on events.

Two days later, Adams, the principal architect of the ceasefire strategy, said that the absence of negotiations made the collapse of the ceasefire inevitable. It was a message he had first articulated in December, but which was only now taken seriously. The IRA, unmoved as ever by the international criticism that greeted its decision, maintained a *de facto* ceasefire in Northern Ireland but unleashed more terror on the streets of London. Within a week, another device was discovered and defused in a telephone kiosk in London's West End. Three days later, Edward O'Brien died when a bomb he was transporting by bus exploded prematurely, also in the West End. On 9 March a bomb exploded in a dustbin in Fulham, and on 17 April another went off in a large house in Kensington. On 24 April, a powerful Semtex bomb failed to explode underneath Hammersmith Bridge.

By then both governments had moved into overdrive in a frantic bid to halt the violence and induce restoration of the ceasefire. They were concerned that the provocation would cause the Loyalists to reignite the sectarian conflict. Within twenty days of the first London bomb, a prime ministerial summit in Downing Street announced that all-party talks on the future of Northern Ireland would start 'directly and without preconditions' on 10 June. With elections set for 30 May, the IRA was put under intense pressure from London, Dublin and Washington to restore the ceasefire, fight the elections and enter the talks. Without the ceasefire, Britain made clear that Sinn Fein would not get into the talks. The IRA refused to budge. When the election votes were counted, Sinn Fein exceeded all expectations by increasing its share of the total from 12 to a record 15 per cent. The Loyalist paramilitaries too, through the Ulster Democratic Party (linked to the UDA), and the Progressive Unionist Party (close to the UVF position), attracted sufficient support to win places at the talks. When the negotiations got underway at Stormont on 10 June 1995, the Loyalists, whose ceasefires remained intact, were admitted; Sinn Fein were left to protest outside that their mandate had been ignored.

\*

Throughout 1995, as London, Dublin and Washington energetically urged Sinn Fein and the IRA to reinstate the ceasefires, there was an inexorable drift back to conflict. Even before the talks began, there were signs that IRA hardliners had gained the upper hand in the argument about strategy and were actively planning a return to war. On 7 June Detective Garda Jerry McCabe was shot dead and a colleague injured during an armed robbery attempt at a post office in Adare, County Limerick. Eight days later, 206 people were injured when a large bomb, concealed in a van, exploded without warning outside the Arndale shopping centre in Manchester.

Meanwhile, in the Irish Republic, follow-up security sweeps to apprehend McCabe's killers uncovered a sophisticated bomb factory and storage bunker in remote farm buildings, near Clonaslee, County Laois. Sixteen mortars, containing Semtex, timer/power units and other devices were being made ready for use. This, and another attack on a British Army base at Osnabruck in Germany, underlined the deterioration in the peace process. Whatever lingering optimism there had been about its credibility and the IRA's sincerity was extinguished with the exposure of a remarkable instance of political duplicity.

According to an internal Republican document, leaked early in the seventeen-month ceasefire period, their strategy was based on the acronym TUAS, which, although it was not fully spelled out, peacemakers were told stood for 'Total Unarmed Strategy'. However, after the Manchester bomb, IRA sources revealed that the peace process was built on a mirage, for TUAS was sold to doubting IRA activists as 'Tactical use of unarmed strategy', a temporary concept and not a final renunciation of violence, to which the IRA was understood to be committed.

The uneasy peace in Northern Ireland was shattered on 7 October, when two large car bombs went off inside the British Army's headquarters at Thiepval Barracks, Lisburn, seven miles from Belfast. The blasts were consecutive, and many of the thirty-one people injured were seriously hurt in both, including an Army officer who died three days later. As Sinn Fein/IRA came under further pressure to restore the ceasefire, there was consistent evidence of further preparation for conflict. In London two major IRA operations were foiled by the security services. Plans for a wave of attacks on installations providing power and water to the city were foiled and ten tonnes of HME and a number of 'safe houses' were uncovered in a second successful operation, during which an IRA member was shot dead by the Metropolitan police.

More ominously there were tangible signs of a split in the Republican movement with the emergence of the Continuity Army Council, thought to comprise disenchanted hardline terrorists. It was linked to a well-planned bombing which devastated the Killyhevlin Hotel at Enniskillen in July and a large car-bomb, planted in central Belfast in September and defused by the Army. In November, the Irish police discovered five separate lots of weapons and explosives close to the border at Hackballscross, County Louth. Three armed and masked men rifled fifty-five units at a storage facility in west London and retrieved a cache of terrorist material, and a number of men were apprehended in north Donegal making preparations for a mortar attack. Shortly afterwards, on 18 November, after a three-day police/Army search operation, the firing point for a mortar attack was discovered on the outskirts of Londonderry. The Continuity Army Council emerged again, placing a 600lb car bomb outside the RUC station at Strand Road, Londonderry, which was neutralised before it exploded. This attack caused the RUC to review security at all stations and at Strand Road barriers were replaced, prohibiting through traffic past the station.

Undeterred by these events, John Hume, the SDLP leader, who had played a major part in nurturing the 1994 ceasefire, continued to work for a renewal but his optimism was not widely shared. Police fears that the situation was deteriorating were confirmed by the discovery and defusing of a 2500lb bomb being trundled into position near an Army base at Armagh on 28 November. A week later the RUC scored again when three mortars, thirty incendiary devices and a quantity of ammunition were captured from a house at Whiterock, west Belfast, where it had been concealed behind a false wall. As Christmas 1996 approached, a police officer guarding a Loyalist politician was wounded inside a Belfast hospital in an attack claimed by the IRA. A cloud of fear gathered once more over the people of Northern Ireland. They knew that renewed IRA violence would shatter the Loyalist ceasefires, which had become increasingly fragile since the summer, partly because of the resumption of IRA activity, but more directly as a result of the upsurge of sectarian tension which plunged relations between the Unionist and Nationalist communities to a new low.

*

The reason for the increased tension was all too familiar: marching. The 'marching season' imposes a heavy burden on the police and on inter-community relations. The police do not give permission for parades to take place nor do they issue any form of licence or certificate. The RUC has repeatedly pointed out that a parade may be unwise, offensive or insensitive but these are not sufficient reason for the police to exercise their powers under the principal legislation, the Public Order (NI) Order 1987. They can intervene and impose conditions on marches only to prevent serious public disorder, serious damage to property or disruption to the life of the community. Their decision has to be justified in law.

The right to march is, of course, a cherished freedom in a democratic society and a legitimate expression of political opinion or religious or cultural tradition but, as with all rights, it should be exercised responsibly. Some may wonder why up to 3500 marches a year are necessary in Northern Ireland, and more than half of them in July and August. In Strathclyde, where there are many cultural affinities with the Ulster situation, the community gets by with 1118 parades. In Merseyside, which also shares Irish traditions, there are about 425 parades a year. The exercise of the right to march in Northern Ireland seems to be about six times that elsewhere in the United Kingdom.

The great majority of people taking part in parades present no problem but some participants intend them to be triumphalist and antagonistic to the opposite culture, or community, or tradition. In some cases they set out to make difficulties for the police, putting them in the impossible position of keeping rival factions apart and trying to reconcile differences between hostile parties. Over the years the police have made great efforts to encourage agreement between the communities over controversial parades. Population changes, redevelopment and new roads have all contributed to tensions over routes and many 'traditional routes' were modified by discreet local agreements brokered by the RUC. Ever since the traumatic period of the Anglo-Irish Agreement in 1985 the marching season has, however, been relatively peaceful, despite a one-third increase in the number of parades. In 1995, there were 3500 – of which 2581 were Loyalist and 302 Nationalist – with 1619 happening in July and August. There was disorder at thirteen parades, most seriously at three flashpoints: Garvaghy Road, Portadown; Ormeau Road, Belfast; and Londonderry.

There were residual tensions in Portadown, the so-called 'Vatican of

Loyalism', caused by the routing of a traditional July march through the Garvaghy Road, which had become a strong Catholic area. Following sustained protest from local residents, in July 1995 the police decided to re-route the pre-Twelfth church parade and blocked the road adjacent to Drumcree parish church. A three-day stand-off developed before a deal was done under duress with the local Catholic residents to allow the parade through. This was celebrated as a victory by Orange leaders, which set the scene for further trouble at the Ormeau Road a few days later. This had become a flashpoint in 1992 when, in the aftermath of a sectarian shooting at a bookmaker's in which five Catholics were murdered, local Orangemen marched past the shop in highly offensive fashion, waving five fingers in the air and shouting slogans such as 'five nil'. According to Sir Patrick Mayhew, this action 'would have disgraced a tribe of cannibals'. The police had tried to broker an accommodation with both sides by limiting the number of parades passing along the road. But, buoyed by their success at Drumcree, the Orangemen threatened that if they were not allowed to march through on the Twelfth morning, the entire Belfast demonstration (up to 100,000 marchers) would abandon its planned route and lay siege to the Ormeau Road. Faced with this ultimatum, the police decided to force the march through, and bruising clashes with the Catholic residents followed.

There was similar trouble there when the Apprentice Boys marched on 12 August and even more serious clashes in Londonderry later that day when police cleared Nationalist demonstrators off the old city walls to enable the march to pass. Ironically, these were provoked because the walls, closed for years for security reasons, had been reopened as part of the post-ceasefire relaxation. Old hatreds were inflamed and, over the marching months, there was an epidemic of more than 100 sectarian arson attacks. Among the targets were 61 Orange halls and 25 Catholic churches. The RUC was relieved to reach the calmer autumn period, especially as it had contained the situation without bringing soldiers back on the streets. Thus, although the events of the first summer of peace were worrying, there was hope that a way could be found to resolve the differences between the marchers and the affected communities. For the first time professional mediators worked with both sides and despite the fact that there were vast reservoirs of antagonism and distrust to be drained, they played a role in defusing the crisis at Portadown and came within an ace of getting a written agreement signed and implemented on the Ormeau

Road question. When these events were reviewed at the end of the summer, grants were made available from the government's community relations funds to enable the mediators to work more actively with the parties throughout the winter, so that workable agreements could be achieved to avoid confrontation in 1996. At the same time the RUC prudently began planning to deal with disorder, by forming and training seventy-five Divisional Mobile Support Units in case the initiative failed.

By Easter 1996 it was clear that the Loyal Orders were in uncompromising mood. The collapse of the IRA ceasefire in February and the government's efforts to restore it and draw Sinn Fein into the political talks caused uncertainty and resentment. The high profile role of the Irish government in the political process in Northern Ireland exacerbated anxieties that a political initiative would sweep away partition and leave the northern Protestants abandoned by Britain and at the mercy of the Irish Republic.

There was a growing feeling that a stand had to be taken against concessions, appeasement and weakness. This was not confined to the members of the marching orders; it was shared by some of the influential business and middle-classes. In the autumn of 1995 this mood had propelled David Trimble, the Ulster Unionist MP whose Upper Bann constituency includes Drumcree, into the party leadership. When the police decided to halt the first of the season's marches along the Ormeau Road, a stand-off developed and there were ugly clashes. The mediators, working in Belfast, Portadown and Londonderry were unable to make progress. In most cases the Loyalists refused to meet the mediators, claiming that the IRA was orchestrating the discontent and that residents' groups were phoney front organisations. There was indeed some unease among the more moderate residents in the affected areas that they were having to stand shoulder to shoulder with the Republicans, but opposition to the parades was unanimous and uncompromising. In Portadown, there was extreme resentment at the triumphalist behaviour of the local Orangemen, who had struck a 'Siege of Drumcree' medal for those who had taken part in the stand-off. 'In their mythology they had elevated Drumcree to the same level as the Battle of Boyne,' said a Portadown resident. 'That was deeply offensive.'

Given the atmosphere of political discontent and rising frustration on the Protestant side, the scene was set for serious trouble. As the marching season got underway in the spring, prominent figures on the Orange and Unionist side said their civil rights and religious liberties were being compromised to appease the IRA. They made no secret of their intention to use force of numbers to overstretch the police and create a crisis if they did not get their way over the marches. The trigger would, of course, again be Drumcree, and what happened would depend on how resolutely and effectively the police handled it.

There was a general feeling throughout Stormont Castle, the RUC and the Nationalist community that the marching tensions and the resulting communal upheaval would not be extinguished until the business of the Garvaghy Road routing was settled. Ideally, this would have been treated as a local problem and kept low-key but in the current political circumstances that was not possible. The Unionist community saw the situation as a matter of principle and decided on what amounted to a last stand.

Annesley and his most senior advisers were faced with an impossible dilemma. Pushing the march through would attract criticism from the entire Catholic community and cause great damage to police relationships with them. According to police intelligence reports, there was a likelihood of wider communal conflict and disorder in other Nationalist areas throughout Northern Ireland. Halting the march would protect the RUC's growing reputation for even-handedness, but would be a confrontation with the massed ranks of the Protestant community on the scale of 1974, when the Ulster Workers Council general strike succeeded because of police impotence, or of 1977, when a strike attempt led by Ian Paisley was vigorously opposed and put down.

Efforts to avert the looming confrontation by initiating dialogue and working at a local accommodation continued until the eve of the march, but without success. The Orange side were unyielding in refusing to meet the residents, who were rigidly opposed to the march going through. Annesley and his aides had engaged in talks with both sides and monitored every move for weeks in a bid to work out a compromise. A large map of the area had been prepared, and police officers shuttled between the sides marking changing combinations of routes in coloured ink, but reached no agreement. The RUC's senior commanders gathered in Belfast on Friday 5 July to take a decision whether or not the march should go through and to finalise their strategy, knowing that their decision would have far-reaching consequences for the RUC and the Northern Ireland community. The Superintendents Association and the Police Federation were both consulted, and were the first to be advised that Annesley had decided to halt the march. As instructions went out to every police station to muster the newly trained force of Divisional Mobile Support Units to enforce the decision, a news conference to announce it was called for the following morning.

When the Orange march left Drumcree Parish Church on the Sunday afternoon and headed for Garvaghy Road, its way was blocked by a phalanx of police with Land Rovers. The Army had erected a barbed-wire cordon along the fields on either side of the confrontation point. The first cadre of Orangemen, ruddy-faced countrymen in their best suits, clad in Orange sashes, white gloves and bowler hats, some carrying swords, marched up to the police lines and stopped inches from the grim-faced officers. Over the next few days, as the stand-off continued, Orange sympathisers blocked roads throughout Northern Ireland by hijacking and burning vehicles. Violent clashes took place and naked sectarian hatred on a scale not seen since 1969 was unleashed. A large number of schools, churches and houses were attacked and burned. Belfast's international airport was sealed off at one point and an undertaker collecting a body had to remove a crucifix from a coffin to get it through; the priest escorting the funeral party was so frightened of being attacked that he removed his clerical collar. At Lurgan, a Catholic taxi driver was abducted and shot dead, a killing with all the signs of a sectarian motive, which raised fears that the strained Loyalist ceasefires were finally crumbling. In parts of Belfast, Catholic and Protestant families who had moved into mixed areas in the relaxed atmosphere of the ceasefires found themselves under threat; the sight of refugees fleeing from their homes, their belongings piled in vans and lorries, once more became commonplace.

As night followed violent night, crowds of Orangemen flocked to Drumcree in solidarity, and the destruction continued throughout Northern Ireland, with the police caught between rampaging mobs. Sometimes they struggled to confront the lawlessness, but there were many instances where they stood by as spectators. Despite the most extensive Army support on the streets since the ceasefires, it was clear by the Wednesday night that the RUC was overstretched and exhausted and that there was insufficient military support to keep the roads open, protect the community and disperse the mobs. Over the loudspeakers at Drumcree, the police were subjected to a relentless cycle of intimidation. According to RUC sources, individual officers were named and offensive personal remarks called out; one woman officer was taunted about a recent miscarriage; married officers were heckled or jeered at about the safety of their wives and families. One officer was confronted at the barbed wire by a fellow elder from his church and informed that he and his family would no longer be welcome to worship there. Elsewhere, police families came under attack in their homes in many Protestant areas: in one seaside village a mob stormed the house and armed police had to take the officer, his wife and two-year-old son to safety. Other police families had to flee their homes as mobs threw bricks, rocks and petrol bombs.

As the Drumcree crisis entered its fifth day, and with the traditional drinking and drunkenness around the bonfires due that night, July 11, it was apparent that the intensity of the disturbances had taken the Northern Ireland Office by surprise. Sir Patrick Mayhew came under fire for complacency and misjudging the seriousness of the crisis when he rounded on a television interviewer and said, 'I say, cheer up for heaven's sake. Why always gloom away and take the most extreme view? Cheer up.' As the gravity of the situation dawned at Stormont Castle, there was frantic overnight activity from Wednesday into Thursday – the deadline for action. Loyalists were warning that there would be a bloodbath if the police or Army tried to disperse them. The police had been concerned during Wednesday by the appearance of a heavy excavator and reports that others, and a slurry tanker (to spray police and soldiers with a mix of petrol and sugar) would spearhead an assault on the barbed-wire cordon and the police lines.

Late on the Wednesday evening, crack military reinforcements, in the shape of the First Battalion of the Parachute Regiment, arrived at RAF Aldergrove, and a reconnaissance party hurried to Drumcree to assess the scene, reporting back that the Paras could stop the Orangemen only by firing on them. This was the regiment involved in the Bloody Sunday massacre of Catholic civil-rights marchers in Londonderry in 1972, so the prospect of a repeat against the Protestants was unthinkable. With no real option and increasing fears that the Orangemen were preparing to rush the lines and invade the Garvaghy Road, Annesley was forced into a major climbdown. The decisive factor was when staff association representatives advised him that police morale was at breaking point and they were demanding greater protection for their wives and families. Annesley also doubted that an ongoing initiative by the leaders of the four main churches would break the impasse in time. Early on the Thursday morning he issued orders for the stand-off to be lifted and for the Orange march to be pushed through the Garvaghy Road.

The effect of this extraordinary about-turn on the Catholic community throughout Northern Ireland was compounded by the aggressive way the police cleared the road for the marchers. Catholic opinion was shocked by the forceful police action, which contrasted starkly with their failure to take action against the Loyalist mobs.

Later in the day, while the impact of this decision and its violent implementation were still sinking in, further fatal damage was done to the RUC relationship with the Catholic community when the Ormeau Road was flooded with police and vehicles and the area sealed overnight so that sympathisers could not obstruct the route of the Orange march on the twelfth. This march was being allowed because the Belfast Orangemen were again threatening to abandon their usual route and lay siege to the Ormeau Road. The decisions to permit the marches were bad enough in Catholic eyes, but the way they were enforced was worse. The result was to provoke further nights of serious disorder, mainly in the Catholic areas. The disturbances were at their worst in Londonderry, where the rioting was as prolonged and intense as anything seen in the early 1970s. For two consecutive nights the police were under sustained petrol-bomb attack in the city; each night, they estimated, 2000 had been thrown.

As the violence subsided on 16 July, its terrible extent and implications became clear. The police logged 8000 incidents and calculated that up to 24,000 petrol bombs had been thrown. They had fired 6000 plastic baton rounds, the most intensive use of the weapon since the week following the death of Bobby Sands in May 1981, when 4000 had been discharged. One man died in the disturbances – a Catholic crushed by a military vehicle in Londonderry; 149 police officers and 192 civilians were injured; 39 police homes were attacked and 28 officers and their families forced to move permanently. As in 1985–6 the personal allegiance of policemen and women was brought close to breaking-point. Some officers were indeed members of the Orange Order and others had close family or relatives as members. 'During the stand-off there were people on both sides of that confrontation who were blood relatives,' one senior officer said, and not all RUC officers demonstrated the impartiality that they should have.

During July and August six were suspended from duty and a seventh reported for taking part in Orange parades or protest demonstrations. (Some subsequently left the force and others were dealt with by internal discipline.)

The Police Authority calculated that the disturbances had cost the RUC well over £10m. The housing authorities faced a £1m bill to resettle 251 civilians driven from their homes, and public transport executives said it would cost £5m to replace buses destroyed in the violence. Education authorities estimated damage to schools of at least £3m and the roads service said that repairs would cost £1m. Tourism, which had flourished during the summer of peace, was in ruins; hotels and boarding houses reported floods of cancellations.

But what was incalculable was the damage done to the prospects for community stability and a lasting peace. The government's security and political policy lay in ruins. The disturbances had unleashed sectarian hatred that everyone hoped had been buried for good. The prospects for prosperity and inward investment evaporated as businesses, horrified by the destruction, pocketed their chequebooks and cancelled plans to provide jobs. Anglo-Irish relations plunged when prime minister Bruton accused the British government of reneging on its responsibility to protect all citizens and maintain the rule of law. As people talked openly of the violence being as bad as 1969, when the troops had to come in, the extent of the setback was summed up by a velvet-voiced US news correspondent who stepped from behind a burning vehicle in Londonderry and said to camera: 'Ulster is back to square one.'

When the political implications began to be evaluated, Annesley was in the firing line and had to mount a robust defence of his actions, but his pending retirement, announced well before the crisis, insulated him from serious pressure to resign. He blamed the Portadown Orange Lodge and the Garvaghy Road residents for what had happened, saying that over the preceding year they had failed to sort out the problem because of paramilitary manipulation on both sides: 'If you get two groups who will not give an inch then the RUC haven't got a magic wand.' He explained the decision to permit the march in a BBC interview on 14 July:

> I was faced with a serious and deteriorating public order situation, not only in Drumcree, where we might have anticipated some protest, but across the province. This was a potentially violent and disorderly crowd who were intent on making their protest and we did not and could not, even with 3000 policemen and soldiers, have contained that. I have not

and would not and never contemplated issuing the order to fire on a crowd in the United Kingdom. It had to be a back-off situation. If the rule of law had to be turned back in the short term, so be it. I made an honest, professional and proper decision with the entire support of my two deputy chief constables and the overwhelming number of my assistant chief constables. When we got to the position that it could not be sustained, I changed it.

Having first decided to take a stand, Sir Hugh owed it to the RUC and the community at large to ensure that he had the contingency planning, the resources and the will to carry his decision through as his predecessor, Sir Kenneth Newman, had done in 1977 when faced with an equally vicious Loyalist threat.

In explaining the extraordinary climbdown after the nights of destruction and disorder, Sir Patrick Mayhew and RUC sources made much of the fear that at least 50,000 Orangemen might overrun the police lines at Drumcree and rampage through the Garvaghy Road estates causing extensive loss of life. The scenario was entirely foreseeable, but there appears to have been no planning for it. The Orange supporters could have been prevented from travelling to Portadown by deploying cadres of police and soldiers to prevent trains and buses run by the public utilities from being used to transport demonstrators. In the same way that the demonstrators paralysed the road network, security forces could have been deployed to prevent Orange supporters reaching Portadown by car by mounting checkpoints all over the north. As in 1977, adequate troop reinforcements to back the original decision should have been flown in ahead of the crisis, not when the situation was out of control. (To be fair to Annesley, it later transpired that large-scale military reinforcements were not available. With 11,000 soldiers committed to peacekeeping duties in former Yugoslavia, post-Cold War manpower cuts and a serious shortage of recruits, the Army was suffering from serious overstretch.)

With the battle of Drumcree, Northern Ireland again navigated one of those decisive turning-points which determine the course of events. Its mishandling imposed a terrible legacy on the RUC and exacerbated the problem of policing. At a single stroke, it sundered twenty-five years of painful and increasingly tangible progress in transforming the relationship between the RUC and the Catholic minority community. The scale of the damage done to the RUC–Catholic relationship was coldly articulated on Sunday, 14 July, by Cardinal Cahal Daly, primate of all-Ireland. Speaking at mass in Portadown, he accused the British government of an abdication of responsibility:

> When will the RUC, which many unionists see as exclusively 'their' police force, be seen by Nationalists as being equally concerned to safeguard their rights too and to respect their feelings too, so that Nationalists could some day call it 'their' police force too? There is . . . a huge crisis of confidence in the police among the Nationalist community at large. In my own modest way I have tried for years to urge both the police and the Catholic public to work to build up mutual trust and confidence. For the present that confidence has been totally shattered. Restoration of confidence will require immense and prolonged efforts on the part of the RUC. Sadly, their whole process of confidence building has now to be built all over again, virtually from zero.
>
> That process must now be recommenced and it must be vigorously pursued and it should be conducted on the part of the RUC, as far as Nationalists are concerned, in a genuine spirit of humility, regret for what has happened and readiness for real change. Radical measures will be needed, both as regards the RUC and the Police Authority and the Police Complaints Commission, but changes are essential. Every society needs a police force in whose integrity and impartiality all political communities and all social strata can have confidence. Northern Ireland needs this more than most societies do.

A public opinion survey for the Police Authority, published in December 1996, underlined the accuracy of the Cardinal's words: 82 per cent of Catholic respondents thought the RUC should be reformed, replaced or disbanded, compared with 70 per cent a year earlier. The proportion of Protestants supporting the same proposition had increased from 23 per cent to 32 per cent in the same period.

Annesley retired quietly on 3 November. His last public act as a police officer earned him applause from the passengers on a Belfast-bound aircraft when he subdued a drunk man who tried to open the door in mid-air. As Annesley retired to his Surrey home, to immerse himself in do-it-yourself activities, there was general consensus in Belfast that he had been no more than a competent pair of hands, and that, Drumcree apart, he had avoided being sucked into any debilitating controversies. His management style left two camps in Belfast: those who admired him and those who felt bruised. He stayed at the helm of the RUC much longer than the five years he had first promised; his hopes for bigger police jobs – leading the Metropolitan Police, running Interpol or heading a new national anti-terrorist unit in Britain – all failed to materialise. In his resignation statement he spoke of his 'considerable pride and pleasure at the development and progress of the RUC; the enhancement of its operational effectiveness and quality of service.' As achievements, he cited a number of internal management and operational innovations which, while important, amounted to an unremarkable record given the challenges facing the RUC.

His statement underscored Annesley's unwillingness and failure to get to grips with the controversial and difficult issues that had to be resolved if the force was to win the consent, co-operation and participation of the whole community. It is indeed arguable that in his relentless application of British policing philosophy and standards, he never really understood the implications of policing a society as complex and divided as Northern Ireland. Although he paid public lip service to the need for improving Catholic relationships and co-operation with the RUC, his insensitivity to the minority community was evident from the opening passage of his annual report for 1994: 'The powerful symbolism of the Queen opening the futuristic new bridge across the Lagan and the practical demonstration of people coming together during the historic visit of President Clinton were vivid and powerful images of the aspirations of so many for a better future.'

There is no mention of the equally powerful symbolism of repeated visits by the Irish head of state, President Mary Robinson and only a single picture of her is included in the report, contrasted with four pictures of the Queen, one of the Prince of Wales, another of the Princess of Wales, two of the Duke of York and one each of the Duke and Duchess of Kent. As a Dublin-born Protestant, a professional police officer, head of the RUC for seven years and a senior public figure in Northern Ireland, Annesley should have been aware of the need for balance and the negative signal such imbalance sends about his attitude and that of the RUC, which has to be accountable, even-handed and serve the entire community.

The Police Authority set up a nine-strong panel of members to choose the new chief constable. On 29 August, the three candidates short-listed for the £100,000-a-year post, trooped into the conference room on the sixth floor of River House, in central Belfast, for interview. There was one applicant from outside the RUC, Scotsman Bill Taylor, 49, the commissioner of the 900-strong City of London police, who had experience of Irish terrorism from his days in the Metropolitan Police. The other two candidates were the RUC's deputy chief constables: Blair Wallace, 59, and Ronnie Flanagan, 46. During forty years in the RUC, Wallace had worked in virtually every part of Northern Ireland and served in nearly every department. He was well known throughout the force and popular with those under his command. However, from the outset, the front-runner was Flanagan and there was little surprise when his appointment was announced.

On 4 November 1996, the day he officially took over from Annesley, Flanagan received a mass of congratulatory messages but the one he valued most was a card and bouquet sent by an elderly woman neighbour who was present when he was born on 25 March 1949, in a modest, redbrick terrace house at 31 Ballymoney Street, in the religiously mixed, working-class Oldpark area of north Belfast. His grandfather, a former sergeant-major in the British Army, had a small claim to fame, having (so the family's verbal history records) involuntarily given his name to a young London-Jewish conscript named Winthrop, who became a star as Bud Flanagan of the Crazy Gang, adopting the name as revenge on his formidable old sergeant-major. Flanagan remembers his grandfather as an unpaid community leader, working for the Northern Ireland Labour Party, writing letters and dispensing advice to people in the Docks area, where he lived. His father was a painter in the Belfast shipyard, a dirty, dangerous, semi-skilled job. He was a voracious reader and encouraged his children to get and use their maximum number of library tickets: 'Although he had no formal education whatever, I never knew anyone with such a formidable general knowledge. I remember him watching television programmes like University Challenge and answering the questions.' With his father's encouragement, Ronnie read widely and developed a love for Dickens. His mother worked as an assistant in Ferguson's fruit and vegetable shop in the Oldpark Road. The family needed every penny to make ends meet, for Ronnie was the youngest of six children: a first-born sister and four brothers.

Although he was raised as a Protestant, attending Donegall Street Congregational Church every Sunday, he mixed freely with Catholic contemporaries. 'Everybody gathered wood for the eleventh of July bonfire in the street and everybody watched the bands and the lodges the next day.' He started school at the local Finniston primary and then moved to Belfast High. He was already a keen sportsman as a member of the Manor Street Boys Club so the senior school immediately drafted him into their rugby team as a hooker, not least because one of his older brothers had played in that position with some skill.

There was no family involvement with the police, but he wanted to join the RUC after completing grammar school. His parents insisted, however, that he should finish his education, so he enrolled at Queen's University, Belfast to study physics. Soon afterwards, he ran into a friend in the Students' Union who had joined the RUC and was being helped to take a law degree. This was a recent innovation and arose from the Hunt report recommendations to improve the calibre of RUC officers. His friend encouraged Flanagan to contact the newly established recruiting department and before long he had joined the RUC on the understanding that his university studies would continue.

After basic training at Enniskillen, in the university vacations, he was posted to the Queen Street station, in downtown Belfast, so that he would be close to the university. The RUC demanded, however, that he should study a subject more appropriate to a police career than physics and he was instructed to work for a degree in psychology. Flanagan says he joined the RUC because 'there was genuinely a desire on my part to do something about it and the police seemed to me a very attractive vehicle to be of some service, to make a contribution to the well-being of the community. I love this wee place,' he laughs. The young Constable Flanagan was soon in the thick of events. His first night on duty, 15 August 1970, was spent guarding the Royal Navy recruiting office in Belfast, which had been bombed earlier in the day. Another day he was on the beat in Wellington Place when colleagues patrolling in a Land Rover halted a suspicious van and apprehended the occupants. Flanagan arrested one of them and took him to the nearby station where he admitted there was a bomb in the van. When the bomb disposal officer arrived, the terrorist offered to help clear the device so, with a rope tethered round his ankle, the police and soldiers watched as he lifted the bags of explosive from the van onto the street. Flanagan recalls 'being blown on to my backside' more than once by the force of explosions and making regular arrests. 'One day I was in Marlborough Street when I caught a guy running away from an abandoned car which later exploded. He eventually got fifteen years.'

As the IRA bombing campaign increased, he was present at the scenes of multiple deaths. He vividly remembers Bloody Friday in July 1972, when 26 bombs went off in 90 minutes, killing 11 and injuring more than 130 people. His belief that the troubles would soon be over was shattered by then. In fact, pressure on the police was so intense after the introduction of internment in August 1971 that

Constable Flanagan was posted to the Criminal Investigation Department for a time as a relief detective. The work was so intensive that he could not attend university lectures, so his studies lapsed. (Eventually he graduated from the University of Ulster with a HNC in Police Studies and a BA and Masters in Public Sector Studies.) In 1973 he was promoted and moved to the busy Castlereagh station in east Belfast as Station Sergeant. There he came under the influence of a wise old Sergeant, who taught him that good policing depended on common sense, treating people decently and having a sense of humour. Three years later he moved to the Waterside station in Londonderry on promotion to Inspector and from there back to the Personnel Department at Headquarters in Belfast. In 1978 he went to Castlereagh again, as duty inspector responsible for running the controversial Holding Centre, where terrorist suspects were detained for interrogation. Flanagan's next move came after the publication of the Bennett report, which introduced a comprehensive set of rules for the treatment of suspects, following an international propaganda campaign. He was required to help implement the new guidelines, including the installation of closed circuit television monitoring of the interview rooms. In 1981 he moved to his native north Belfast, after joining the Special Branch as a detective inspector, and soon afterwards became detective chief inspector in command of the Headquarters Mobile Support Units, the élite anti-terrorist units who carried out some of the most difficult and dangerous work against the killers and bombers. In the aftermath of the shoot-to-kill controversy, Flanagan was charged with introducing tighter command and control of the units and new selection and training standards for their members. In 1987, having been promoted to Detective Superintendent, he was given another sensitive Special Branch command, running the Tasking and Co-ordinating Group from Gough Barracks, Armagh, which directed police and soldiers involved in the undercover war along the border from south Down to west Fermanagh. His next job brought him back to force headquarters in Belfast where he ran the Special Branch operations department, responsible for surveillance and intelligence work throughout Northern Ireland, and monitoring the links of both Republican and Loyalist terrorists further afield.

During this period, in the summer of 1989, Flanagan spent three months at Police Staff College at Bramshill, Hampshire, completing the Intermediate Command Course, to qualify him for promotion to the rank of Chief Superintendent but after only a few months back in

Belfast he returned to Bramshill as a member of the directing staff, this time as a Chief Superintendent running the course. In 1991 he became a student again for six months, successfully completing the Senior Command Course, which qualified him for chief officer rank. By the end of 1991 he was back in Belfast. Soon afterwards he was appointed assistant chief constable and early in 1992 made responsible for policing throughout the Greater Belfast area. It was at this point that Flanagan moved into the public eye. His willingness to go on radio and television and discuss policing matters singled him out as a good communicator and articulate proponent of the RUC's case. At a time when the majority of his colleagues had no public profile, his open-door policies created contacts and opportunities for a wide range of community groups to engage in dialogue with the police, often for the first time.

In the aftermath of the Chinook disaster, Flanagan reluctantly left Castlereagh again to repair the terrible gap left in the Special Branch, but he maintained his reputation for openness and accountability by becoming the first head of the department to take part in a live, simultaneous radio and television phone-in on BBC Northern Ireland shortly afterwards. From that point in 1994 he rose swiftly to the top of the command pyramid, moving from acting deputy chief constable, to deputy and then chief constable in under two years. He and his wife, Lorraine (they married in 1970), have three sons, one of whom is a constable in the RUC. Flanagan these days has little time for leisure but he formerly played rugby for Ulster and still takes an active interest in the sport. He is also keen on boxing and enjoys the rivalry of the annual match between the Garda Siochana and the RUC.

Even before Flanagan moved into his new office at police headquarters on 4 November, he signalled that his was going to be a radical and pro-active period. With carefully chosen words, he committed himself and the RUC to a process of internal reform and police-community reconciliation and signalled an end to the neglected opportunities which had characterised the Annesley era. In a deft move, to bolster his impartiality, he admitted publicly that he was not a member of any of the Protestant Loyal Orders, and that he had once been a Freemason but had resigned.

He inherited a police force whose morale was worse than at any time since the traumatic events of August 1969. Hostility and alienation from both sides of the community had never been greater and the existence and role of the RUC was under threat from various political factions.

The conflicting range of ideas and opinions already on public record indicated how difficult it would be to find accommodation. Some were predictably hardline and unyielding, others far-seeing and pragmatic. It was no surprise that David Trimble, the Ulster Unionist Party leader, described changing the name of the RUC as 'damn silly and offensive. I don't know that the term "royal" is that much of a problem. It's part of the things that identify us as living in the United Kingdom.' The SDLP published a paper calling for a new 'Northern Ireland Police Service', with a change of uniform to signify 'a sense of a new departure and a new identification'. Sinn Fein initiated a call for the RUC to be disbanded but, in a surprising and constructive intervention, the Sinn Fein leader, Martin McGuinness, also said there could be a role for some RUC officers in future policing. 'All of us have to recognise – as was the case in . . . other parts of the world – that there will be people, even in a policing service which we absolutely reject at this moment . . . who may have a role to play in the future.' The Ulster Unionist MP, Ken Maginnis, generously suggested that fair employment legislation be suspended so that recruiting for the RUC could be conducted on a 50-50 basis for ten years to build up the proportion of Catholics to 25 per cent. A number of academics also pronounced, among them Professor Mike Brogden, who suggested that IRA and Loyalist 'kneecapping squads' should be recruited and trained by the RUC to keep order in their communities.

Reconciling these conflicting views and finding an acceptable accommodation would test even Flanagan's well-honed skills as a communicator and visionary thinker, noted for his outstanding professionalism and deep commitment to the RUC and the community. The turbulent convulsions of the 1996 marching season had demonstrated once again that while the police could all too easily exacerbate the situation by excessive or insensitive policing, they could not solve it. Flanagan had already grasped this and constantly sought consensus and agreement to the many problems which beset both his force and its relations with the community. He also knew that if he was to safeguard the RUC in its existing form much beyond its seventy-fifth birthday on 1 June 1997, he had little time to act and needed to move swiftly and decisively to prove good faith, establish credibility and head off both his own voluble detractors and those of the RUC.

At the end of 1996, as Northern Ireland hovered at a blind bend, he knew that all the potential security and political scenarios were fraught with combinations of difficulty and danger for the RUC and that there were no obvious or easy solutions available. He admitted as much on his appointment when he said that there was no point moving to reduce alienation on the Catholic side only to replace it with alienation among Protestants – or indeed within the force.

Flanagan was well aware of the sensitivities and raw feelings among his officers but by admitting the need to change the RUC's Protestant-dominated culture to accommodate women and Catholics, unlike Annesley, he signalled an essential willingness to take on entrenched attitudes and initiate long overdue internal reform. RUC canteen culture was still stubbornly male-dominated, Protestant, British and Unionist and there remained a hard-core allegiance to values and practices that compromised the concept of an even-handed impartial police service. Orange and Masonic membership was wide-spread; only one in fourteen officers was a Catholic; members were required to swear an oath of office pledging to 'well and truly serve our sovereign lady, the Queen'; and symbols of 'Britishness' abounded. What, for instance, was the justification for flying the Union flag over police stations of the twelfth of July, a day that so unambiguously represents Unionist triumphalism? By failing to create a neutral working environment, the RUC was in breach of Northern Ireland's fair employment legislation, designed to stamp out religious discrimination.

The centrality of policing reform in any settlement of the troubles was emphasised in the Mitchell Commission report of January 1996:

> We share the hope, expressed by many on all sides, that policing in Northern Ireland can be normalised as soon as the security situation permits. A review of the situation, with respect to legally registered weapons and the use of plastic bullets, and continued progress toward more balanced representation in the police force would contribute to the building of trust.

Making the RUC acceptable to the minority without arousing hostility from the majority had long been one of the most difficult issues in reforming policing. The admission, by Sir Patrick Mayhew, in August 1996, that he could not guarantee the RUC's ability to hold the line in any future confrontations had damaged the credibility of the force. By the end of 1996 the RUC was facing the most uncertain situation in its difficult history. With the IRA ceasefire ended and provocative Republican violence again escalating, despite high-powered calls for peace from Washington, London and Dublin, there were doubts about how long the Loyalist paramilitaries could maintain their restraint. The prospect of another troubled marching season threatened further instability. As the RUC faced its seventy-fifth anniversary, in June 1997, the role, size and responsibilities of the organisation, even its very existence, were issues of fundamental dispute and the final outcome of the debate was unpredictable.

# 14

# Waiting for Patten

The RUC marked its seventy-fifth anniversary with a series of events throughout 1997. There was a service of thanksgiving at St Anne's Cathedral, a concert in the Waterfront Hall, Belfast, which symbolically featured the combined choirs of the RUC and An Garda Siochana, and a poorly attended three-day tattoo at the Ballymena showgrounds which ran up a loss of some £20,000. To underline its commitment to the community, the entire force, through a series of anniversary year fund-raising events, was able to present a cheque for £240,000 to the Northern Ireland branch of Mencap, a charity which cares for mentally handicapped people. The anniversary was, however, a fairly solemn affair. As the chief constable wrote in his annual report for the year: 'Change is very much in the air. It pervades the very atmosphere, not just within the police service, but the very structure and ethos of relationships within Northern Ireland itself and these islands. I make no apology for saying that the evolving situation in which we now find ourselves has a very great deal to do with the selfless dedication of the men and women of the RUC supported by the British Army and the Garda Siochana.' He went on to say that the year's momentous political developments were 'to do with changing attitudes within the wider community, but not least because of the RUC's success in creating the relative calm which enabled the public and their elected representatives to even countenance discussing their age old fears and mistrust with those of often diametrically opposed views'.

Events had indeed moved swiftly throughout 1997. During a Christmas 1996 visit to Belfast, the weary-looking prime minister, John Major, had struck a particularly uncompromising stance: 'The government will never yield to the IRA campaign even if it lasts another fifty years.' Although the multi-party, British–Irish intergovernment political talks at Stormont, under the chairmanship of former United States Senator George Mitchell, had been in sporadic session for months there was no real work being done. The participants largely occupied themselves by rehearsing, yet again, their historically intransigent positions with interludes when they indulged in circular arguments about rules and procedures. It is a remarkable tribute to the patience and tenacity of Mitchell, and his fellow peace-brokers, the retired Chief of Staff of the Canadian armed forces, General John de Chastelain, and the former Finnish prime minister, Harry Holkeri, that they persisted in the teeth of such political rudeness and immaturity.

Sinn Fein had, of course, been excluded from the negotiations when the IRA ceasefire was ended with the London Docklands bombing early in 1996 and remained deaf to widespread pleas to restore the ceasefire and resume talking. Like the other political parties, it was waiting for the outcome of general elections, due in both Britain and the Irish Republic in 1997. A sea change in Britain after eighteen years of Conservative rule was keenly anticipated. The future Labour government was already signalling in private, through intermediaries, that, once safely in office, it would be altogether more pragmatic.

In the meantime, the IRA remained highly active. In January alone, Belfast was disrupted for a day by twenty hoax bombs; two RUC stations were attacked; horizontal mortars were fired at mobile patrols in Shantallow (Londonderry), Kennedy Way and Springfield Road (Belfast), Downpatrick and Toomebridge; and an RUC sentry was injured in the leg when a rocket was fired at the main courts complex in central Belfast. On 12 February, Lance Bombardier Stephen Restorick was shot dead by a sniper while deployed at a checkpoint in Bessbrook, near Newry, the 655th soldier to perish in the Ulster conflict since 1970. The casualty toll was not entirely one-sided. On 26 March, undercover soldiers opened fire and wounded a man they said was in the act of throwing an explosive device at the RUC station in Coalisland.

Republicans were keen to demonstrate that they were participating in what had come to be called the 'peace process' from a position of strength. It was their case that they could continue their campaign indefinitely and that they were most certainly not being forced into any sort of surrender. The message was primarily aimed at Downing Street and the potential new Labour government but there was a less explicit agenda. The IRA leadership was continuing carefully to prepare its troops for the big political compromises that lay ahead in order to minimize any split or breakaway that would inevitably develop when the hard political choices came to be made.

Although the Loyalist ceasefires remained nominally intact at this time, UVF activists were blamed for planting a bomb containing a substantial charge of commercial explosive outside a Sinn Fein office in the border town of Monaghan. The bomb was defused by the Irish Army before it could explode. Firebomb attacks on tourist information offices at Banbridge and Newcastle were attributed to hardline Loyalists opposed to an international, all-Ireland tourist marketing campaign, which had just been launched. In March, the RUC arrested a man during a post office robbery and, after discovering a list in his possession, warned twenty IRA sympathizers that they had been targeted.

The British general election date was finally set for 1 May and the campaign was formally declared underway on 17 March, ironically, given its importance to the Irish peace process, St Patrick's Day. Within a week, the IRA launched its own campaign, one of disruption, that was to last until polling day. Over the next few weeks, it successively halted the national rail, motorway and air networks throughout the British mainland, bringing the country to a standstill on several days. The most notable occurrence was the disruption of the world-famous Grand National horse race at Aintree, Liverpool, on 5 April. A bomb hoax forced the race to be abandoned and to be run again forty-eight hours later amid unprecedented security measures. Five days later, in Londonderry, Reserve Constable Alice Collins was shot in the back and seriously wounded while on duty outside the courthouse. Although she is not counted among the official list of RUC casualties, her injuries did contribute to her death a year later at the age of forty-seven.

As expected, Britain routed the Conservative government at the beginning of May and elected a new administration, headed by the charismatic Tony Blair, who was given a landslide majority of 147 seats in the House of Commons. The new prime minister confirmed Dr Mo Mowlam, who had shadowed the Northern Ireland portfolio in opposition, as the new Secretary of State and she flew into Belfast on 3 May to take up the post. Speaking to a cluster of journalists and camera crews in the city centre, she said it was 'a great honour and a great challenge' to be given the job. She then called on the IRA for an unequivocal restoration of the ceasefire – 'demonstrated in words and deeds' – so that Sinn Fein could join the political talks, scheduled to restart on 3 June. Significantly for the RUC, she also signalled that 'policing reform' would be among her priorities.

These two themes were reinforced two weeks later when Blair himself flew to Belfast. Speaking at the city's annual agricultural show at Balmoral, he said: 'It is no accident that this is my first official visit outside London.' In a wide-ranging address he condemned the 'pathetic futility' of the IRA's pre-election activity and revealed that he had authorized officials to explore with Sinn Fein the prospects for renewing the IRA ceasefire. 'You cannot hold the process to ransom any longer. So end the violence. Now.'

In the context of policing, Blair added: 'We want to increase public confidence in policing through measured reform based on the [Dr Maurice] Hayes report on the complaints system and last year's [Labour Party] consultation paper on structural change.' He concluded: 'I am convinced that the time is right finally to put the past behind us and meet the deep thirst of the people of Northern Ireland for peace, normality and prosperity.'

Violent Republicans had already given their verdict on revitalizing the peace process. A week earlier, during the evening of 9 May, an unarmed, off-duty police officer was murdered in a gay bar in downtown Belfast. Darren Bradshaw, twenty-four, who had been formally warned by his superiors that he was compromising his personal security by frequenting the Parliament Bar, was drinking inside with a number of friends when, at about 10 pm, a red Toyota car pulled up outside. The vehicle had been stolen the night before and was fitted with false number plates. Two gunmen got out, one from the rear, the other from the passenger seat. One held up the bouncers at the door while the other entered the bar, singled out the policeman and shot him three times in the neck and body. The gunmen were then driven off in the car, which was later found burned out in a side street off the Falls Road. The dead officer was the first RUC terrorist casualty for some three years.

Despite the attack, Sinn Fein delegates met British officials in Belfast on 21 May to explore the grounds for renewing the ceasefire. Communal tension was escalating, with both Republicans and Loyalists engaging in violence and confrontation in the run-up to the annual trials of the summer marching season. The RUC's unenviable position as 'piggy in the middle' was again tragically underlined in the early hours of Sunday 1 June when another off-duty police officer lost his life, this time at the hand of violent Loyalists. Late on the Saturday evening, Constable Greg Taylor, forty-one, married with three children and a policeman for twenty-three years, a police colleague and a friend went into a crowded bar in Ballymoney, Co. Antrim, for a drink. The police officers were recognized by some of the one hundred or so customers, who included Loyalists, and there was some angry jostling and jeering about the RUC's role in upholding a ban on a Loyalist parade in the nearby village of Dunloy. When the officers and their companion left the bar at about 2 am on the Sunday morning, a crowd was lying in wait for them outside. Taylor made a frantic call from his portable telephone to the local police station seeking help but none was available: there was only a single constable on duty and the nearest patrol car, with two officers on board, was eight miles away. The crowd closed in on Taylor and he was so savagely kicked and beaten that he died almost immediately. His two companions managed to escape the mob. Eight men went on trial for the murder and two were jailed for life. Another two, who denied murder but admitted manslaughter, were imprisoned for four years. The others were acquitted. The day of the murder coincided with the seventy-fifth anniversary of the RUC's formation and it cast a dark shadow over the memorial service at St Anne's Cathedral in Belfast that afternoon. The Church of Ireland primate, Archbishop Lord Eames, told the congregation there were too many 'peace-lovers in Northern Ireland but not enough peacemakers. Society must find its way to peace. Society must find the means of addressing division. A police service cannot produce a peace society has not been able to find for itself.'

For several years the peace process, with its associated and ever more rancorous talk of police reform and RUC downsizing, had been generating uncertainty and even anger within police ranks. There now smouldered a deep sense of hurt that their great sacrifice was being ignored and a growing sense of insecurity that, come the peace, they would be paid off and cast into an uncertain future, where they would find themselves unemployable, their reputations smeared and their personal safety compromised. Some officers involved in the most controversial episodes of the troubles so feared being called before future 'war crimes' or 'truth' commissions that they unofficially retained files and photographs to defend themselves. The Police Federation, quite properly reflecting the anxieties of its members, warned of premature optimism over the end of terrorism and railed against calls for RUC reform. The word reform, the Federation felt, implied that what had gone before, the danger and the commitment and the courage, was to be disowned. It did, however, concede that change was necessary. In a bid to quantify what the future held for its members and the practical assistance they would need, the Federation secured funding from the European Union programme for peace and reconciliation in Northern Ireland and the Police Authority to carry out an extensive internal survey. The survey confirmed that there was widespread concern about job security and future healthcare among the 12,750 Federation members in the force. Although nine out of ten officers said they would not be financially independent if they left the RUC and would need to seek new jobs, few had taken any active steps to explore alternative career options should they be made redundant. The survey also revealed that as police work largely consisted of processing paperwork and dealing with the public, nine out of ten officers did not believe they were qualified for any other job. With only 6 per cent of officers having had advanced education to degree level or higher, the research indicated a strong demand for external work experience schemes and academic courses to equip them to find new careers or start small businesses. 'Our study identified two main areas of concern,' said David McClurg, the Federation secretary. 'One concerned how we could prepare officers to change into alternative careers from the police. The other is what long-term assistance we should be providing for the officers who have been maimed and injured during the years of violence.'

The sense of hurt, anxiety and frustration, which was intensified by Mowlam and Blair giving the topic of police reform such initial priority, finally spilled out in public during the annual conference of the Police Federation at Newcastle, Co. Down, on 3 June. Les Rodgers, the chairman, did not mince his words.

> Secretary of State, you had hardly time to warm your new seat at Stormont Castle when you were quoted as saying that reform of the RUC would be a priority. Let me be plain speaking here. This word 'reform' is seized upon by everyone as if it were the open sesame to a comprehensive and enduring agreement on the future governance of Northern Ireland. That, if the police were reformed, all our troubles would be over and, magically, everyone would be content.
>
> [...] We want to become the police service capable of commanding province-wide community support well into the twenty-first century. If that is your definition of reform then it is one shared by every one of the officers I represent. But our critics do not mean what we mean by reform.

Their idea of reform is abolition of the RUC.

I am sure, Secretary of State, you will understand that in the face of such provocative and gutless remarks and attacks my members are the ones who are heading towards zero tolerance when it comes to listening to criticism which calls for reform of this Force. Over the years the RUC has held this community together when at times it would almost have disintegrated under the pressures of civil disorder. We have stood firm in an unenviable and isolated position doing our best to keep communities from each other's throats. At all times we have worked to bring communities together in support of the rule of law. We are now being portrayed by our enemies as part of the problem of Northern Ireland rather than its essential protective binding.

At the end of his speech he was given a massive ovation.

Mowlam, attending the conference for the first time, followed him to the rostrum and launched into a justification of her plans. 'Even the best police service must acknowledge and evolve in response to changes in technology, in society and in public expectations of the police service. I therefore intend to bring forward legislation which will clarify the roles of the Government, the Police Authority and the Chief Constable in policing Northern Ireland and introduce a number of measures to increase police accountability and public confidence. These are not changes introduced for the sake of change; they are a carefully crafted package of measures as proposed in our paper – 'A Police Service for All People' – which we produced in May 1996.'

Being the feisty political figure she is, Mowlam then singled out one of the chairman's remarks for reply: 'And if I just may say so, without being unduly critical, when Les talked in his speech about the situation of zero tolerance, I just don't think that is helpful. I understand the frustrations. I understand the anger people feel when they are caught stuck in the middle, but I don't think zero tolerance is acceptable for anybody. And I think if we are going to get anywhere in the weeks and months ahead we've all got to make that extra effort and not turn inwards or turn backwards.'

The clash was a significant indication of the poor morale inside the RUC and the growing belief within the organization that, despite all its courage and resilience over the years, a hostile new Labour administration was, in fact, preparing to make it a pragmatic political sacrifice. Some were very angry. The majority accepted it with resignation. 'That's politics for you,' said one officer.

Behind the scenes, at this point, the new government was working frantically to persuade the IRA to renew the ceasefire and clear the way for Sinn Fein to participate in the Mitchell talks, which had reconvened that very day. At the end of the week Sinn Fein's political prospects were boosted when it won a seat in the Irish parliament for the first time, at the conclusion of an Irish general election which brought a Fianna Fáil-led coalition and a new prime minister, Bertie Ahern, into power. With Mitchell at the talks helm in Belfast and new leaders in London and Dublin with fresh mandates, the expectation was that there would now be the most determined and co-ordinated push for peace ever attempted in Northern Ireland. It soon became clear, however, that at least some hardline Republicans were far from enthusiastic about facilitating it.

On the morning of Monday 16 June, Constable John Graham, thirty-four, and Reserve Constable David Johnston, thirty, were patrolling along Church Walk, Lurgan, a short distance from the town's police station when they were both shot at close quarters. Eye-witnesses said the attackers approached, fired at the officers and then shot them again after they fell to the ground. The incident took place outside a doctor's surgery and medical staff immediately rushed to their assistance. 'We heard the shots from inside the surgery and we were by their sides within thirty seconds. But it was too late – they were already dead,' one of the doctors recalled. The cold-blooded double murder sent shock waves through the efforts to restore the IRA ceasefire and was widely condemned. At the White House in Washington the official spokesman pronounced President Bill Clinton's 'outrage'. Nevertheless, efforts to make peace continued. On 25 June, the British and Irish governments issued a five-week ultimatum to the IRA to call a ceasefire and stated that after a further six weeks, on 15 September, Sinn Fein could join the Mitchell talks, which had now been given a deadline of May 1998 to come up with a comprehensive political deal.

In the meantime, Northern Ireland suffered another violent convulsion as, for the third successive year, the Drumcree church parade prompted widespread disorder. Tension had been mounting for months before the parade and, soon after taking office, Mowlam had launched an initiative to search for an accommodation. She met all the protagonists but, faced with complete deadlock, had to leave the chief constable to decide how to handle the situation. The intelligence at his disposal indicated that violent Loyalists intended to launch a campaign of protest and disruption if the march was halted. This would bring the entire region to a halt and undoubtedly trigger off serious and widespread sectarian conflict. Yet he was also aware that if the march was pushed through it would have to be done forcefully and that serious collateral disorder would be triggered off in Catholic neighbourhoods. He calculated that pushing the Orange march through the disputed section of the Garvaghy road was the lesser of two evils, as he put it, and his officers did so on Sunday 6 July. Over the next four violent days, sixty RUC officers and fifty-six civilians were injured and 117 arrests were made. The security forces fired 2,500 plastic baton rounds in answer to 402 hijackings, the throwing of 1,506 petrol bombs and another 815 attacks on them. Despite this bloodletting and the sectarian murder of a young Catholic girl in her Protestant boyfriend's home, the IRA then finally succumbed to the months of sustained private political pressure and reinstated its ceasefire, ordering another cessation of military operations from midnight on 20 July. As indicated earlier by the two governments, Sinn Fein was then invited to the political talks, which got underway on 15 September. The main Unionist parties boycotted the negotiations for a few days but then turned up despite the provocation of dissident IRA terrorists who exploded a 400lb bomb in the centre of Markethill, Co. Armagh, in an unsuccessful bid to embarrass Sinn Fein. By 24 September, despite continuing deadlock over the when and how of terrorists giving up – decommissioning – their explosives and weapons, the parties had brought an end to sixteen months of procedural wrangling and agreed ground rules for the conduct of the negotiations. Within another fortnight they were dealing face to face. It was the first time in over seventy years that Unionists and Republicans had come into such close proximity. But by the time the talks adjourned for Christmas on 17 December there was more acrimony than agreement in the air, for they had still failed to settle the list of issues to be discussed.

Over the turn of the year into 1998, hardliners on both sides combined to give the process a potentially fatal jolt. On 27 December, the notorious Loyalist leader Billy Wright, who headed the hardline Loyalist Volunteer Force, was shot dead inside the Maze prison by members of the equally extreme Republican splinter group, the Irish National Liberation Army. Over the next four weeks seven Catholics and one Protestant were shot dead. Most of the murders were attributed to Wright's allies but the credibility of the Loyalist ceasefires was called into serious question when the chief constable revealed the involvement of the outlawed Ulster Freedom Fighters. The UFF's political frontmen, the Ulster Democratic Party, were consequently temporarily suspended from the talks when they moved to London for a week at the end of January.

Nevertheless, more violence followed with the killing of a drugs dealer and two Loyalists, this time the blame clearly lying with the IRA. The police quickly charged three people with known IRA connections and, when the talks moved to Dublin for a week, Sinn Fein was temporarily suspended from the proceedings. Hours later a car bomb which devastated the picturesque village of Moira, Co. Down, was blamed on the Continuity IRA, a breakaway Republican group opposed to the ceasefire. Over the next few weeks the same group caused more destruction with a car bomb, abandoned adjacent to the RUC station in Portadown, and mortar attacks at the stations in Armagh and Forkhill. Further attacks were foiled when the Irish police captured a 1,000lb car bomb in the border town of Dundalk and another bound for England, possibly for an atrocity at the Grand National, was intercepted at an Irish ferry port. At the end of March, Cyril Stewart, fifty-two, a retired member of the RUC Reserve, was ambushed and murdered by INLA gunmen as he packed shopping into his car after a trip to a supermarket in Armagh.

Senator Mitchell decided the time had come to concentrate the minds of Northern Ireland's disputatious politicians, so he set a deadline of 9 April for agreement of proposals for a settlement in Northern Ireland and announced that until then negotiations would take place at Stormont virtually round the clock. The British and Irish prime ministers flew in for the concluding marathon and in the late afternoon of Good Friday, 10 April, after a continuous thirty-hour session of petulance, brinkmanship and real negotiation, what has become known as the Belfast Agreement was finalized.

It is unarguably the most comprehensive, detailed and far-reaching treaty so far conceived in a bid to resolve the Irish question. It provided for a redefinition of the constitutional relationship between the two parts of Ireland, a power-sharing administration in Belfast, a series of north–south bodies jointly to administer key functions, such as health, tourism and agriculture, and a new set of east–west co-operation groups, to include England, Wales, Scotland and the offshore islands, such as the Isle of Man. In addition, there were provisions to enable the early release of prisoners convicted of terrorist offences, to integrate human rights legislation into the Northern

Ireland system and to promote greater equality and mutual recognition of the cultural heritage and traditions of the entire community.

On 22 May, the Agreement was overwhelmingly endorsed in simultaneous referenda: in Northern Ireland by 676,966 (71.12 per cent of those who voted); and in the Irish Republic by 1,442,583 (94.39 per cent). On the back of this mandate, Northern Ireland voters elected a 'shadow' Assembly on 22 June which met soon afterwards and, before adjourning for the summer holidays, put a programme of work in hand to prepare for the assumption of power.

From the RUC's point of view the most important section of the Belfast Agreement was the one headed 'Policing and Justice', for within it was a mandate for the most basic reappraisal of policing and criminal justice since partition.

The participants recognize that policing is a central issue in any society. They equally recognize that Northern Ireland's history of deep divisions has made it highly emotive, with great hurt suffered and sacrifices made by many individuals and their families, including those in the RUC and other public servants. They believe that the Agreement provides the opportunity for a new beginning to policing in Northern Ireland with a police service capable of attracting and sustaining support from the community as a whole. They also believe that this Agreement offers a unique opportunity to bring about a new political dispensation which will recognize the full and equal legitimacy and worth of the identities, senses of allegiance and ethos of all sections of the community in Northern Ireland. They consider that this opportunity should inform and underpin the development of a police service representative in terms of the make-up of the community as a whole and which, in a peaceful environment, should be routinely unarmed.

The participants believe it essential that policing structures and arrangements are such that the police service is professional, effective and efficient, fair and impartial, free from partisan political control; accountable, both under the law for its actions and to the community it serves; representative of the society it polices, and operates within a coherent and co-operative criminal justice system, which conforms with human rights norms. The participants also believe that those structures and arrangements must be capable of maintaining law and order including responding effectively to crime and to any terrorist threat and to public order problems. A police service which cannot do so will fail to win public confidence and acceptance. They believe that any such structures and arrangements should be capable of delivering a policing service, in constructive and inclusive partnerships with the community at all levels, and with the maximum delegation of authority and responsibility, consistent with the foregoing principles. These arrangements should be based on principles of protection of human rights and professional integrity and should be unambiguously accepted and actively supported by the entire community.

Policing was always going to be one of the most contentious issues at the Stormont negotiations. Inside the talks, the Unionist side adopted its customary proprietorial 'hands off the RUC' stance, denouncing even the most perfunctory change as unnecessary and amounting to nothing more than IRA appeasement. The prospect of the RUC being replaced by cadres of locally recruited community constabularies – 'putting the knee-cappers into uniform', as one delegate articulated it – caused apoplexy to Ulster Unionist defenders of the RUC. On the other side of the argument stood Sinn Fein, demanding the total disbandment of what Martin McGuinness called 'the most discredited police force in western Europe' and the SDLP, marginally less hawkish, but still determined to achieve root and branch reform. The idea of remitting consideration of the future of policing to an independent commission was born early in 1998 in a bid to postpone facing up to the long-standing problem which some of the participants recognized had all the potential to cause the entire talks process to founder. The scope of the text was therefore all the more remarkable for the diversity of the political parties who had endorsed it.

The daunting task of bridging the political gulf and articulating an agreed new beginning for policing was given to an independent commission to be chaired by Chris Patten, the former Governor of Hong Kong, who had most recently presided over the colony's return to China. He was no stranger to Northern Ireland having served there as a minister from 1983 to 1985 and was best remembered as the man who forced the Londonderry City Council to be renamed the Derry City Council, a change which infuriated Unionists and pleased Nationalists. So, from the very outset, clear battle-lines were drawn, for both sides anticipated that Patten would apply the same logic and come out for the renaming of the RUC.

On 3 June, Mowlam announced the other seven members of the Commission, who would each contribute a different perspective and expertise. They were Sir John Smith, a former Deputy Commissioner in the Metropolitan Police, who also has previous experience as one of

Her Majesty's Inspectors of Constabulary; Kathleen O'Toole, a former Boston police officer who was then Secretary for Public Safety in Massachusetts and who had already worked with the RUC as a consultant on training; Peter Smith, a QC with over twenty years' experience who came from a Unionist background; Dr Maurice Hayes, a prominent Catholic, former senior civil servant and subsequently ombudsman, who had more recently produced a review of the police complaints system; Professor Clifford Shearing, Director of the Centre of Criminology at the University of Toronto; Dr Gerald Lynch, President of John Jay College, New York; and Lucy Woods, the Chief Executive of British Telecom in Northern Ireland. When they held their first meeting in Belfast shortly afterwards, they were given a substantial bundle of background reading material, including an earlier edition of this book, which, they were advised, they should read first as an introduction.

The Chief Constable, Ronnie Flanagan, decided to put any further implementation of the 189 recommendations of his own fundamental review of policing on hold on the grounds that he might be accused of pre-empting the Commission's findings. He also set up a small team of officers, located in a portable building in the grounds of RUC head-quarters, to support and facilitate the Commission. Their brief was to make a professional policing case on every issue and to provide the Commission with all the material they required. The strategy of frankness was so unlimited that Flanagan even allowed the Commission to examine the secret and sensitive files on the Stalker affair and other equally controversial episodes. Patten had been allocated one of the small flats in the Hillsborough Castle complex for the duration of his work and, as he was getting to grips with his terms of reference, the two men had several lengthy discussions there. Flanagan was uneasy about the Commission from the start. He was, of course, a totally hard-headed professional leader and well ahead of even his most senior colleagues in seeing the case for change. But he was also emotionally attached to the RUC and its traditions, and, given his working-class origins in north Belfast, deeply proud to have become its leader. On several occasions he publicly defended the 'Royal' prefix and condemned the possibility of a change as 'tokenism'. Before any change was sanctioned he said that there should be 'rigorous research' to determine what the people of Northern Ireland felt about the idea. 'It's not just a name. It's a title conferred by royal charter. There are very few policing organizations in the world that enjoy that privilege. It makes us proud.' He warned repeatedly that ill-considered change might merely lead from alienation between the RUC and Nationalists to alienation between the RUC and the Unionist community and insisted that any reconstruction of the RUC should only proceed in line with a convincing reduction in the terrorist threat.

'Ronnie's problem was that on this issue his head and his heart were not always completely synchronized,' said one of his senior colleagues. Flanagan was worried that the pressure on Patten to be radical would not only emasculate the RUC but create a new policing system that would ultimately prove to be unworkable. He feared that Patten would bow to Nationalist ambitions and concede a formal policing role to the erstwhile terrorist organizations. He was in a lonely and isolated position and like the men and women under his command, he initially felt besieged. 'The RUC has been used as a political football and my officers are determined to defend themselves against the bombardment of propaganda they have faced in recent years,' he said repeatedly in a series of interviews after the setting up of the Commission. To reassure his officers, he set up a telephone hotline to deal with rumours, and the recently established force newspaper, *Call Sign*, carried regular bulletins about what was going on.

Patten was obliged to produce his report by the summer of 1999 but he decided very early on that it could not come out between Easter, when the marching season started, and the end of August, when it concluded. Given that a pre-Easter report would look over-hasty and be open to criticism for being superficial, the Commission then pencilled in Tuesday 7 September 1999 as the intended publication deadline and got down to work. The policing landscape they surveyed was a very different one from that which had prevailed until the breakthrough ceasefires of the summer of 1994. Despite the ups and downs of the uneasy peace, the RUC had steadily carried forward a programme of what could best be described as cautious normalization. They had developed an innovative Community Awareness Programme (CAP) designed to foster greater under-standing among police officers (overwhelmingly from Protestant back-grounds) of the social and cultural diversity in Northern Ireland. For the first time, the doors of the training centre at RUC Garnerville were thrown open to a wide spectrum of outsiders, including clergy from all the main denominations, writers, journalists and musicians. A ceilidh night was introduced, at which bands and groups were able to show the distinctiveness, as well as the similarity, in the music enjoyed by people from the two main traditions. The idea was that once the Community Awareness Programme had been fully fashioned, using the new recruits as guinea pigs, it would be rolled out to include every member of the RUC. Getting the course going was not without its difficulties. At first the programme was dubbed the 'campaign against the Protestants' because of its emphasis on respect for cultural diversity, but as more officers became exposed to it they called it the 'campaign against the police'. Senior officers dismissed the hostile reaction, saying it highlighted the need for just such a training programme and remained confident that it would, in time, achieve its aim of promoting more tolerance and sensitive attitudes among police officers.

Despite the shortcomings in their interpersonal communication skills, the inevitable result of thirty years of having to police from a safe distance, police interaction with the public also markedly changed. Hitherto, the public had been subject to the constant snap checkpoints and searches mounted to monitor and intercept terrorist activity. Officers were wary of answering 999 calls promptly, especially in vulnerable areas, in case they were being lured into an ambush. Similarly, they were unlikely to linger on the streets because of the danger of snipers. The new police profile was markedly different. Officers freed from sentry and security duty were redeployed on the streets, walking beats. Some specialist, highly-trained anti-terrorist units with expertise in undercover surveillance and intensive investigation were drafted into the campaign against drugs, for since the ceasefires there had been a marked increase in the abuse of recreational drugs such as cannabis and Ecstasy and the appearance, for the first time, of hard drugs such as crack cocaine, LSD and heroin. This redeployment was in line with a new policy more actively to meet community expectations of the police. The new emphasis on community policing focused officers on making contacts with and getting to know people in the areas they policed in a way that had not been possible before.

These efforts were nationally acknowledged and rewarded for the first time in January 1999 when an RUC sergeant who ran a neighbourhood policing unit in the Laganside area of Belfast won a major national award for community policing. Sergeant Stephen Jones came top of a list of candidates from thirty-nine other forces in

England, Wales and Northern Ireland to be nominated Community Police Officer of the Year. It was a considerable achievement, for his beat included some of the most prestigious business and leisure areas on Belfast's waterfront as well as the Markets district of the city, an area with a long tradition of violence and terrorist influence. The sergeant, who had been in the RUC for more than twenty years, said, 'I feel very honoured to win this award. But I certainly did not win it on my own. I've been helped by the support of my wife and family and the teamwork of the eight constables in the Laganside neighbourhood unit based at Musgrave Street RUC station. I enjoy being a police officer. The terrorist ceasefires are allowing me to do what I joined the RUC to do – to be out there on the street, in the community, meeting people and helping them. People do not want to go back to the bad old days. I am optimistic about the future, working in partnership with local people and tailoring our policing service to their needs.'

This kind of ground-breaking activity was complemented by other equally bold initiatives. In the run-up to Christmas 1998, the Belfast Chamber of Commerce and city centre traders offered the police temporary use of a unit in the large Castlecourt shopping centre to use as a reporting centre. They were keen to have a constant police presence at the height of the shopping rush. Flanagan saw this as just the sort of new thinking the RUC should be exhibiting and readily backed the project. However, when it opened for business on 8 December the initial impact was marred by an unruly Sinn Fein picket and scuffles as the police tried to prevent them from wrecking the premises. Nevertheless, at the end of the one-month trial, Flanagan (who, in the interim, was knighted in the 1999 New Year Honours) was well satisfied with the outcome. Three hundred people had called at the centre and the RUC's evaluation of its usefulness suggested the technique could be developed in certain places on a permanent basis.

The police also took a renewed interest in overcoming a range of community problems and worked closely with other public agencies. A network of specialist liaison officers was created to tackle domestic violence; and the extension of national race relations legislation to Northern Ireland caused the RUC to pay formal attention to the small ethnic minority population, mainly of Chinese and Indian origin. There was also a greatly renewed emphasis on traffic policing.

Despite this progressive internal transition to a more conventional policing environment, the pressure from outside the RUC for radical change continued to gather. Ever since the ceasefires there had been a constant flow of papers and policy statements from political parties and pressure groups, most characterized by an obvious lack of practical knowledge of even the basics of policing or so shrouded in propaganda or prejudice that they were irrelevant. In early 1997, the powerful Northern Ireland Affairs Committee of the House of Commons, consisting of thirteen MPs from all parties under the chairmanship of former Northern Ireland Secretary Peter Brooke, decided that it would hold a formal inquiry into 'The composition, recruitment and training of the RUC'. They began taking evidence in November 1997 and produced their lengthy report on 27 July 1998. The most revealing observation among the 450 pages of dense evidence and statistics they produced came from Colin Smith, the Inspector of Constabulary responsible for the RUC. Testifying to an excessive caution in introducing change within the RUC, he said: 'There is a tendency to want to set up a working party, to want to go round and check the temperature in many places and look for ideas, and a reluctance to reach the point where a decision has to be made.' As a symptom of what it considered to be the slow pace of change in the RUC the committee pointed to the continued importance of drill in the training system and questioned its significance to the skills required of modern police officers.

The committee's fundamental error was in simply reasserting that because Northern Ireland is an integral part of the United Kingdom the Union flag is the appropriate flag to fly over police stations. In so doing, it continued to place the RUC in the British/Unionist tradition. Although there was an implicit recognition of the divisions in Northern Ireland society running through the report, it under-estimated their rigidity and failed to take sufficient account of the Nationalist perspective and historic sensitivities. There was also, notably, no recognition of the growing alienation between the RUC and hostile sections of the Protestant community. By failing to grasp the essential need for neutrality between the communities and fashion it as the cornerstone of a new policing order in Northern Ireland, the Brooke committee can be said to have disappointed.

The committee of MPs wasted the opportunity to give a more radical lead and help the RUC to shed the shackles of its history. Although it generated a predictable fuss with the proposal that future RUC recruits should be banned from membership of secret, oath-bound organizations like the Orange Order, Freemasons and Ancient Order of Hibernians, and prompted angry voices with the suggestion that the Union flag should no longer fly over police stations on 12 July, the MPs were merely highlighting symptoms of the deeper problem and prescribing a minimum response. What they should have done was articulate the philosophy of a workable new policing order and lay down far more extensive guidelines for it to be achieved. Nevertheless, the impressive thoroughness with which the MPs gathered evidence and compiled background material made a significant and well-informed contribution to paving the way for the more comprehensive reform that was required.

The same cannot be said of Mowlam's contribution. As she had promised immediately after the general election, Mowlam pushed ahead with preparing a Police Bill, which was first laid before parliament in December 1997. Although the Northern Ireland Office had been tinkering with draft legislation for nearly five years, the Brooke Committee study was already underway and policing was to figure in detail in the ongoing Mitchell talks agenda, Mowlam bullishly ploughed on with her legislation which was not only premature but imperfect.

Nevertheless, there were a number of significant innovations in the Bill. It established the Northern Ireland Police Service, to consist of the Royal Ulster Constabulary, the Royal Ulster Constabulary Reserve, traffic wardens and civilian support staff, and provided for the new office of Police Ombudsman responsible for independent and rigorous investigation of complaints against the police. New administrative arrangements whereby the Chief Constable, and not the Police Authority, would be responsible for the £600m police budget and the employer of officers and civilian staff were also included. Through the concept of an annual policing plan, agreed between the Authority and the Chief Constable, a yardstick was established by which to measure how many crimes were cleared up; the effectiveness of traffic policing; and just how satisfactorily the vast sums expended on policing were being spent. In a bold and praiseworthy break with the past, the Bill abolished the form of Oath of Office sworn by constables in Northern Ireland, which originated in Section 17 of the Constabulary (Ireland) Act 1836 and included swearing allegiance to the Queen. This had read:

I (name) swear by Almighty God that I will well and truly serve our Sovereign Lady the Queen in the office of (rank) without favour or affection, malice or ill-will; that I will to the best of my power cause the peace to be kept and preserved and that I will prevent to the best of my power all offences against the same; and that, while I shall continue to hold the said office, I will faithfully, according to law, to the best of my skill and knowledge, discharge all the duties of the said office and all such duties as may be attached to such office by law and that I do not now belong to and that I will not, while I shall hold the said office, belong to any association, society, or confederacy formed for or engaged in any seditious purpose, or any purpose tending to disturb the public peace, or in any way disloyal to our Sovereign Lady the Queen and that I will not, while I shall hold the said office, engage or take part in the furthering of any such purpose, or take or administer, or assist or be present at or consent to the administering of, any oath or engagement binding myself or any other person to engage in any such purpose.

The new declaration merely required officers to state: 'I hereby do solemnly and sincerely and truly declare and affirm that I will faithfully discharge the duties of the office of constable', which were spelled out in the body of the legislation.

These topics apart, the Bill received a hostile reception during its first parliamentary outing and was roundly criticized from both sides of the House of Commons. Its most serious weakness was that it side-stepped the fundamental issue of police accountability. The central flaw in the 1970 Police Act was that it did not rigorously define the individual role and duties of the Secretary of State, the Police Authority and the Chief Constable and the interaction between them. This enabled successive Chiefs to ignore and defy the Authority and rendered the notion that the police were effectively accountable to the community nothing more than a polite fiction. Ever since the process of police reform had been heralded in a discussion paper in 1994, it had been common ground that this gap would be remedied. Instead the Bill contained what the Patten Commission later rebukingly described as 'labyrinthine provisions as to objectives, performance targets and policing plans, and the respective roles of the Secretary of State, the Police Authority and the Chief Constable. We have found these confusing, both in the text and in the oral briefings we have received from government officials (and we are mystified as to why this legislation was put through parliament in the weeks following the establishment of this Commission, given that our terms of reference required us to take a new look at the subject).' In particular the Commission expressed concern at the power given to the Secretary of State 'who appears to be able to give the Chief Constable directions over the head of the Police Authority' as to the exercise of his/her functions. 'This power is unique to Northern Ireland: for example, the Home Secretary has no such power in respect of police services in England and Wales. We have sought, but have not received, coherent explanations of the rationale for this provision. It has been suggested to us that guidance under the section would not be binding and that, therefore, it does not empower the Secretary of State to direct the police. We are not persuaded that this is so or, at any rate, that such guidance would be so perceived by recipients. We do not believe that the Secretary of State or a future minister in the Northern Ireland Executive should even appear to have the power to direct the police and recommend that this provision of the Police Act be repealed.'

By the time Mowlam had pushed her imperfect Bill through parliament before the summer recess at the end of July 1998, the waves of optimism flowing from the Belfast Agreement had already begun to recede. That month, the newly created Parades Commission (designed to relieve the RUC of decisions on troublesome marches and bring an element of cross-community oversight into the problem) had ruled that the Drumcree church parade could not proceed along the Garvaghy Road. The police enforced the decision and a major confrontation developed but when three young boys from a Catholic background perished in their beds as the result of a sectarian petrol bomb attack in Ballymoney, Co. Antrim, the tide of shock and revulsion caused wiser counsel to prevail and the Orange Order backed away from an all-out confrontation over the 12 July period. A low-key Orange vigil was maintained at Drumcree, beside the church, and throughout the rest of the summer a series of occasionally violent protest marches took place. During one clash on 5 September, Constable Frank O'Reilly, thirty, a Catholic married to a Protestant, lost an eye and sustained serious head injuries when extreme Loyalists threw a blast bomb. After fighting for his life for five weeks, he died on 6 October, the 301st RUC casualty of the conflict. He left three young children, including a baby scarcely three months old. His murder was the eighth attributable to Loyalists. The IRA was responsible for 277 deaths; Republican splinter groups, the INLA and IPLO caused another twelve and three officers were murdered by unknown groups. To this list of casualties could be added a further seventy RUC officers who had taken their own lives because of the unique pressures they faced.

# 15

# A New Beginning

The peace process was essentially in deepening trouble because of mistrust. Ulster Unionists were not prepared to trigger the legislation to bring the Belfast Agreement into full effect because Sinn Fein and the IRA would not formally begin the process of decommissioning weapons and explosives. Neither side would make the first move because they feared the other would not reciprocate. Sinn Fein accused the Unionists of not wanting them in government while the Unionists said their opponent's commitment to democratic means was in doubt because of their refusal to dispose of the means of terrorism. Although the referendum had been overwhelmingly in favour of the Agreement, opinion within the Unionist community had been more evenly divided and the more Sinn Fein prevaricated, the more the opponents of the Agreement gained ground. There was particular anger that the early release of both Republican and Loyalist terrorist prisoners was going ahead with a steady flow of the 500 or so who were eligible emerging from custody well ahead of their original release dates. All this resulted in a weakening of the position of the Ulster Unionist leader, David Trimble, who was the First Minister designate, and forced him to adopt an uncompromising 'no guns, no government' position to prevent his opponents seeking to overthrow him as party leader.

For their part, Republicans were engaged in a new war, this time one of words with each other. The pro-ceasefire faction was working to minimize the divisions within the movement and to avoid any violent breakaway, which would result in an internal feud and inevitable assassinations. They feared a return to an uncontrolled campaign of terrorism, which they knew would instantly drain the reservoir of goodwill they had built up, especially in the United States, where the Clinton administration had worked vigorously in support of the peace process. However, hardline Republicans accused the faction, led by Martin McGuinness and Gerry Adams, of compromising in the fight for the ultimate goal of a united Ireland and settling for a deal that would only prolong partition. This disillusionment was given a singularly violent expression on Saturday 15 August.

Between 2 pm and 2.30 pm that afternoon a maroon-coloured Vauxhall car was parked in front of a row of shops on Market Street, Omagh, close to the junction with Dublin Road, and two people got out and walked away. At 2.32 pm the first of two warning calls, including an authentic code word to indicate the caller was not a hoaxer, was made from one of two public telephone boxes in Forkhill, Co. Armagh, to the Ulster Television newsroom in Belfast. A short time later there was a second call followed by a third, this one to the unstaffed Omagh office of the Samaritans, which was automatically diverted to and answered in Coleraine. All three calls indicated that the bomb had been placed at the Courthouse or Main Street, causing police, who had rushed to the busy town centre, to clear people away from that area towards Market Street, into the immediate vicinity of the Vauxhall, where the bomb timer, contained in a plastic lunch box, was steadily ticking away. At 3.10 pm the device, consisting of some 500lbs of explosive, went off, killing twenty-nine people and injuring 220 others, the greatest loss of life in a single atrocity in Northern Ireland. Among the dead and injured was a group of Spanish children who had been studying English in Buncrana, Co. Donegal, and who were on a coach trip to Omagh with some local Irish children. One twelve-year-old Spanish boy died, as well as a teacher from Spain. Three young boys from Buncrana, aged eight, eleven and twelve years, were killed in the explosion. Three generations of women from one family from Augher, Co. Tyrone, also lost their lives: a sixty-five-year-old grandmother, her thirty-year-old pregnant daughter and eighteen-month-old granddaughter.

The atrocity sparked off the largest ever joint police investigation in Ireland, with the RUC and Garda Siochana combining their resources as never before to track down the bombers who were believed to belong to the Real IRA, another self-styled breakaway faction which had emerged from the rancorous debate ongoing within the Republican movement. Over the succeeding months the police on both sides of the border interviewed 6,000 potential witnesses, carried out 3,500 door-to-door enquiries and took 2,600 statements. A team of officers from the Anti-Terrorist Branch of the Metropolitan Police in

London travelled to Omagh to assist the RUC in removing sixty tons of rubble from the bomb scene for minute forensic examination. Altogether, forensic scientists looked at 400 items, including two telephone kiosks from Forkhill, Co. Armagh, from where the warning calls originated. They were able to reconstruct fragments of the bomb and tell the police the timer-power unit had been inside a plastic lunch box in the vehicle. For the first time in the UK or Europe, the police utilized the traceability features of modern telecommunications systems and sifted through the dialling records, but not the content, of some 500 million calls made on the day of the bombing to trace not only the warning calls but a series of conversations between the bombers and fellow-conspirators in a lookout car as they made their way to and from Omagh on the afternoon of the bombing. As a result of the huge investigation, seventy-eight people were arrested for questioning in a successive series of co-ordinated swoops on both sides of the border – fifty-five by the Garda and twenty-three by the RUC. However, all but one were subsequently released without charge. The remaining man was charged with conspiracy to cause explosions and membership of an illegal organization and was scheduled to stand trial in Dublin in early 2000.

Despite the pessimism that subsequently enveloped the peace process after the Omagh bombing, President Clinton decided to go ahead with his planned morale-boosting visit to Northern Ireland and so, on 3 September, Air Force One touched down at Belfast International Airport for the second time in three years. Flanagan was among the welcoming party on the tarmac. As they had previously, the RUC co-operated with the US Secret Service in putting in place the massive security screen which constantly surrounds the president and earned formal praise for their unrivalled professionalism from the globe-trotting agents. (It was later revealed that the cost to the RUC was £1.2 million.) The president's itinerary included a visit to the putative future Assembly at Stormont and a speech at the Waterfront Hall in Belfast, where he warned that difficult decisions lay ahead and that the politicians would have to rise above petty disputes in a spirit of reconciliation. He said 'courage and reconciliation must drive the Assembly to its many tasks including the decommissioning of weapons, the forming of the Executive Council, the adaptation of the RUC so that the force would have the confidence of all, ending street justice, securing early prisoner release for those who had rejected violence, and building a just society, where human rights were birth rights'. The president added that there may be more bombs and continued heated debates, but it was the way that people reacted to this which would determine the future. The determination for peace must not be broken, he said. There must be only one dividing line – between those for peace and those who want to wreck it – and not between Catholics and Protestants. 'America is with you, the entire world is with you,' he concluded. Later he visited the scene of the atrocity in Omagh.

By now Patten and his commissioners were out and about, learning the realities of policing on the ground and on the front line. In August, observing the policing of the Apprentice Boys' march through the Diamond flashpoint in Londonderry from the third-floor window of a government office building, Patten had a clear view as an officer was surrounded by a Republican mob, dragged to the ground and assaulted before another officer fired warning shots in the air and led a charge of colleagues to rescue him. In October 1998, the Commission commenced what was to be a programme of forty public meetings over the autumn, winter and spring, taking them into every part of Northern Ireland to gather evidence and impressions and listen to what people thought of and expected of their police service. Some of the meetings were predictably, and sometimes volubly, dominated by those for or against the RUC but there were many emotion-soaked moments when the commissioners heard harrowing first-hand accounts, from all perspectives, of what had gone on in Northern Ireland over the preceding thirty years. In all, some 10,000 people attended the series of meetings and about 1,000 of them spoke. The Commission's researches also took them further afield – to Britain, Canada, South Africa, Spain and the United States – as well as to the Garda Siochana and the Council of Europe in Strasbourg.

To press its case for the disbandment of the RUC during this crucial information-gathering and decision-making phase, Sinn Fein, and other like-minded critics, some of them clearly co-ordinated or manipulated, began a sustained propaganda assault to undermine and discredit the force. In Catholic areas all over Northern Ireland, a blizzard of 'Disband the RUC' and 'SS RUC' slogans and posters appeared on walls, gable ends and lamp-posts. RUC stations were regularly picketed. The police came under routine physical attack, even when carrying out what were errands of mercy. In Londonderry city centre, an officer was stabbed in the back and another injured when a stone-throwing mob gathered as they were assisting a man who had collapsed in the street. Soon afterwards, in west Belfast, police laid a line of riot shields across muddy ground on a building site to rescue two boys who had become trapped. They too came under attack. Direct intimidation was used to discourage any contact between the RUC and the Catholic community. In March 1998, Donegal Celtic, a football club based in west Belfast, was drawn against the RUC team in a round of the Irish Cup. Sinn Fein objected to the club taking part in the fixture but the officials and players – whose first team pool voted 23–1 in favour – decided they would go ahead. However, after a round of coercion, during which people associated with the club were visited in their homes, the club changed its mind and reluctantly withdrew from the competition. In the spring of 1999, pupils from two Catholic schools withdrew from outdoor pursuits events organized by the RUC. Twenty-three fourth form pupils from St Dominic's Girls School in west Belfast did not travel to the Mourne Mountains after Sinn Fein threatened to mount a picket. At Draperstown, Co. Londonderry, a Sinn Fein councillor campaigned against pupils from St Colm's High taking part in another RUC-organized event. The anti-RUC campaign even extended as far as New York, where IRA sympathizers succeeded in forcing the Police Department to cancel a boxing tournament in which both Garda and RUC fighters were due to take part.

Every incident that called the RUC's professionalism and impartiality into question was thus magnified into a series of causes célèbres. One such was the case of Robert Hamill. In the early hours of 27 April 1997, in Portadown town centre, rival crowds of Loyalist and Nationalists were taunting and attacking each other for about thirty minutes. Hamill, twenty-five, a married Catholic with three children, who was walking home with a male cousin and other relatives after a night out was brutally assaulted by about thirty of the crowd. His head and brain injuries were so severe that he died twelve days later in hospital. The incident attracted controversy after it was alleged that four RUC officers, sitting in a Land-Rover nearby, witnessed the incident and did not intervene. Six men were later accused of murder but, after some witnesses withdrew statements, charges against five of them were withdrawn. There was conflicting evidence during the trial of the sixth man, where some eye-witnesses said they had to go to the police vehicle and plead with the officers to get out and others who said they had been out on the street doing their best to handle the disturbance. Lord Justice McCollum reserved judgement on 25 February 1999 at the conclusion of the prosecution evidence when Paul Hobson, twenty-one, from Portadown, who was accused of murder, did not call witnesses and declined to give evidence himself. Later he was acquitted of murder but sentenced to four years' imprisonment for causing an affray. At the end of September 1999, the Director of Public Prosecutions decided not to bring charges, including neglect of duty, against any of the RUC officers involved.

An equally penetrating tactic was the exhumation of a series of dormant scandals and grievances which were then fully exploited by calling for reinvestigations or public inquiries into them. By far the most embarrassing of these, from the RUC's standpoint, was the murder of controversial solicitor, Patrick Finucane. On 12 February 1999, the tenth anniversary of the killing, for which nobody had been convicted, advertisements calling for a public inquiry into the case, countersigned by a large number of lawyers, appeared in a number of newspapers. The same day, the pressure group British–Irish Rights Watch delivered a confidential report to the British and Irish governments and to the United Nations-appointed Special Rapporteur on the Independence of Judges and Lawyers, Param Cumaraswamy, who was also in favour of an independent public inquiry into the case. The report largely concerned the activities of British military intelligence and its agent Brian Nelson (see Chapter 12). Much of it had already been well rehearsed in public during Nelson's trial but the report also contained previously unpublished allegations concerning the relationship between some RUC Special Branch officers and Loyalist terrorists. When the Director of Public Prosecutions asked for a report, Flanagan ordered an internal investigation and, as a result of what he was told, decided in April to recall John Stevens, by now the Deputy Commissioner of the Metropolitan Police, with a comprehensive brief to reinvestigate the murder and all associated matters. At the time of writing the investigation was continuing.

The RUC was plunged into another serious crisis of confidence on 15 March when Rosemary Nelson, Hamill's solicitor, was murdered by an under-car booby-trap bomb, placed by Loyalists. She had just driven away from her home in Lurgan when the device exploded, killing her instantly. The anti-RUC propaganda machine swiftly moved into action even before the post-mortem on her shattered body. There were immediate accusations of RUC collusion in the killing and calls for a murder investigation entirely independent of the RUC.

At the time of her death, Nelson had been embroiled with the RUC and the Independent Commission for Police Complaints (ICPC) in a dispute about the effectiveness of the RUC's investigation into a series of complaints Nelson had made alleging that police officers had insulted and threatened her. Nelson had first emerged as a controversial figure in the summer of 1997 after one of her clients had been acquitted of the murder of a former member of the Ulster Defence Regiment. Shortly afterwards she represented the same man when he was charged with the close-quarters murder of two community police officers in Lurgan and she was instrumental in having the charges dropped. During the same period she was also closely involved in the Drumcree situation as the legal adviser to the Garvaghy Road Residents Association. Arising from these events, a series of official complaints were made that summer and passed to the RUC's own Complaints and Discipline Branch, which is based at Lisnasharragh in east Belfast, for formal investigation.

As is the practice with such serious complaints, the ICPC appointed one of its members, Geralyn McNally, a barrister, to supervise the investigation. She was legally entitled to sit in on interviews with the complainants, witnesses and the police officers involved and direct the investigating officers to pursue whatever lines of inquiry she thought appropriate. Nelson co-operated fully with this RUC investigation. However, there was a major clash between the RUC and the ICPC over the conduct of the investigation. Twelve months after it had commenced, the commission formally reviewed progress and came to the conclusion that the investigation was not being conducted by the RUC at a pace and in a manner which reflected the seriousness of the allegations. The ICPC was acutely sensitive to the issue because that year it had received thirty-six complaints concerning police behaviour in relation to fifteen solicitors. Eighteen of the complaints originated from two legal practices, one of them Nelson's. This unease was communicated to the Secretary of State Mo Mowlam and to Flanagan. When he was advised of the situation he immediately offered to bring in independent officers from an outside police force. Paul Donnelly, chairman of the ICPC, regarded this as a demonstration of the chief constable's personal commitment to rigour and transparency. Accordingly, Commander Niall Mulvihill, from the Metropolitan Police in London, whose rank is the equivalent of an assistant chief constable, was interviewed and approved by the ICPC and appointed to lead a new investigation into the Nelson case in July 1998. Shortly before her death, the ICPC arranged to see Nelson and the people who had complained on her behalf to discuss the outcome of the completed investigation. They were to be told that the Mulvihill investigation had been completed to the ICPC's satisfaction and had found that while the original RUC investigations had not been conducted 'in a truly outstanding fashion they were adequate'. As a direct result of the case, Flanagan overruled years of RUC opposition and conceded that interviews with terrorist suspects should be fully recorded in sound and vision to put beyond any doubt claims about police misconduct or ill-treatment during the interrogation process.

In a country town comparable to Lurgan outside Northern Ireland, Rosemary Nelson would have been preoccupied with buying and selling farms and houses, making wills, settling estates and representing clients who have fallen foul of the law in many minor ways. But she found herself in a cauldron of political turmoil, civil disorder and sectarian hatred, with clients and a stock-in-trade of an altogether more serious nature. Her work took her well beyond the confines of the local courthouse. A few weeks before her death she had accompanied a delegation from the Garvaghy Road to Downing Street and she regularly received visitors from all over the world enquiring into the events she was handling. Such was the partisan nature of the community she served that the traditional neutrality of the legal profession had evaporated: she worked for one side and was hated by the other. Hardline Loyalists, to whom she had become as much a hate figure as the other murdered solicitor Pat Finucane, sought to justify her murder and smear her reputation by spreading malicious untruths about her. She had been having an affair with one of her clients, a notorious Armagh Republican, they said. Others claimed that her slight facial scars were the result of surgery to repair injuries caused by a premature explosion while she was making bombs for the IRA. She did have scarring but it was actually the result of an operation to remove an unsightly birthmark.

Flanagan realized that the new allegations against the RUC would gather credibility if he did not take prompt action. As a first step, on the same afternoon of the murder he telephoned Dan Crompton, one of Her Majesty's Inspectors of Constabulary, in Bristol and asked that a senior British officer be sent to provide independent oversight of the investigation. In a bid to secure some international credibility for the investigation, he also placed a call to a senior contact at the Edgar Hoover Building in Washington DC, the headquarters of the FBI.

Within forty-eight hours, the Chief Constable of Kent and a team of British detectives had arrived in Belfast together with an FBI agent. The latter's specific task was to oversee the forensic examination of evidence, a situation rich in irony for it was the RUC's world-beating explosive expertise which had helped unravel the Oklahoma bombings in the US some years earlier. Flanagan said the outsiders had been brought in 'to ensure and to demonstrate honesty of purpose, professionalism and integrity in this investigation of the murder'.

Day-to-day supervision of the investigation was delegated to another British officer, Colin Port, Deputy Chief Constable of Norfolk. He had two teams under his command, one from the RUC working side by side with British detectives on the murder inquiry, and a second consisting exclusively of non-RUC officers whose job it was to seek any evidence of RUC collusion in the murder plot. At the end of September, after six months' intensive work, the investigators had still not succeeded in bringing the killers, or any accomplices, to justice. Indeed, they were still requesting additional public assistance in tracing several people who could hold vital clues, among them two women with clipboards who were seen in the area about a month before the killing and a motorcyclist who was in the area the night before. They also wanted to speak to a woman who was dropped off by taxi near the Nelson house early on 15 March and hoped to trace several vehicles, including an old-style Vauxhall Nova and a white saloon car, both travelling nearby the night before the killing.

The furore surrounding the Nelson case convinced the majority of RUC officers that they were facing an international witch-hunt, heavily stimulated and manipulated by Sinn Fein. They saw the avalanche of claims and investigations alleging misconduct, collusion and partiality on a grand scale as part of an escalating, orchestrated campaign to discredit the RUC and force Patten to advocate its disbandment. There was therefore widespread dismay throughout the RUC in June when Flanagan, the RUC's most articulate and convincing advocate and an unerringly adroit media performer, was subjected to what the RUC saw as unfair trail by television on the BBC's *Panorama* programme, which looked at the background to the Finucane and Nelson cases and probed the allegations that the RUC had been bad-mouthing and threatening certain lawyers.

Flanagan was not long, however, in hitting back. In an interview with *The Times* he said there was a real risk of people being taken in by the cleverly constructed myth that what had been going on for the past thirty years was some sort of struggle between two sides of equal validity when what actually had been going on was a struggle between right and wrong, between good and evil. Clearly intending to influence the Patten Commission, the Chief Constable said that the RUC was being subjected to an onslaught ranging from well-meaning misunderstanding to outrageous falsehood. He told *The Times* that what hurt his officers was the deafening silence from middle Ulster; from people who listen to others using the murder of Rosemary Nelson for clear political purpose and remain silent. He insisted that he had gone to unprecedented lengths to allay genuine concerns about the investigation of the Nelson murder but added 'whatever is done doesn't seem to be enough'.

Despite the fears of another major community convulsion, Drumcree and the Twelfth of July period passed off far more peacefully than the RUC had dared hope. Indeed, apprehension had been so high that, for the first time, Flanagan had sent officers for training and had hired two water-cannon vehicles from the Belgian police for the duration of the marching season. The tactical idea took root after he had seen the dispersing effect of an Army fire hose inadvertently turned on rioters at Drumcree a year earlier. The security statistics for the period from 4 to 13 July 1998 and 1999 underline the dramatic change in the situation. Public order incidents were down from 614 to 43; arrests from 266 to 49; petrol bombings from 625 to 17; hijackings from 178 to 4; and criminal damage to homes, buildings and vehicles from 761 incidents to 70. Only 25 RUC officers were injured, compared to 76 the previous year and one plastic baton round was fired in contrast to 823 a year earlier. Although there was some violence, including arson attacks which destroyed some city centre property, the Apprentice Boys of Derry parade in August also passed off without serious incident. At one point the water cannons were actually deployed in the city centre but not used. Overnight, Assistant Chief Constable Alan McQuillan, who was in charge of the operation, had taken the unusual step of publicly revealing intelligence that Republican elements in the city were intent on drawing the RUC into a major confrontation as part of their ongoing campaign against the force. Afterwards he was satisfied the rioters had backed down once their plans had been exposed.

By this time the peace process was in utter gridlock. Three major initiatives, each presided over by the two prime ministers – at Hillsborough Castle just before Easter; at Downing Street in May; and again at Castle Buildings, Stormont, in early July – had failed to persuade either Sinn Fein or the Unionists to go first or even jump together in taking the next steps to triggering the transfer of power to Belfast and the full implementation of the Agreement. All sides settled for a review by the original peace-broker, George Mitchell, to last through September. The chasm of distrust was widened further during the summer when IRA activists were found to have been illegally importing handguns from Florida to addresses in Ireland through the mail. The murder of a number of drugs dealers in the Newry-Dundalk area over the summer bore all the hallmarks of the IRA. So too did the continuing wave of punishment shootings and beatings in Catholic neighbourhoods, which were equally brutally replicated by Loyalists. (Since the 1994 ceasefires Republicans had carried out 789 such shootings and assaults and Loyalists were responsible for 905.) The murder of Charles Bennet, an alleged police informer, in Belfast on 30 July, the 3,296th victim of thirty years of conflict, was the clinching factor for many who feared that the process was uncontrollably unravelling. Small wonder then that there was simply hollow laughter at the end of August when Mowlam pragmatically pronounced the ceasefires intact and declined to use her powers to halt the ongoing early release of terrorist prisoners. 'The peace we have now is imperfect, but better than none,' she said as cold comfort. The central sticking point remained decommissioning. Sinn Fein continued to insist it was not a pre-condition under the terms of the Agreement. The Unionists remained steadfast: no guns, no government.

New levels of political hysteria were reached after the political mis-interpretation of a number of what turned out to be pretty accurate leaks from the now imminent Patten report. Altogether it was a most inauspicious atmosphere for the publication, which was always going to be problematical given the passion stirred on both sides by the policing issue. The original target date of 7 September had been moved on two days late in July at the final Commission meeting which endorsed the completed report, so that all the members could be in attendance and demonstrate their unanimous backing for their 175 recommendations.

Sir Ronnie Flanagan was at his desk in the RUC's headquarters at Brooklyn in east Belfast on the Monday morning before publication of the Patten Commission report for a routine start to what was to be a momentous week for the force. Sitting with his jacket off and half-moon spectacles on, his first task was to put the finishing touches to a letter of reassurance about the contents of the imminent report. 'The RUC stands ready for significant change,' he wrote. 'I could not be more proud to lead you in these challenging times and to watch you succeed as you always do.'

The draft completed, he walked across the corridor, past the portraits of his predecessors, four inspector generals and six chief constables, to deliver it to his secretary for typing and distribution throughout the force. By then his deputy and eight assistant chief constables had gathered for the usual Monday morning 'prayers', a meeting during which the top commanders reviewed the events of the previous week and discussed what was on the agenda for the coming one. Ironically, although Patten was to dominate the coming week, it was not mentioned. The police commanders knew its findings were already set in stone, there was nothing more they could do to influence it and nothing they could say in public until it was published on the following Thursday morning. 'We had been waiting for Patten for so long, it was hard to believe that at last the wraps would be off and we would know what the future held for us,' said one of the officers.

Patten and his team had completed their report at the end of July and sent it off to be printed abroad in a vain bid to prevent it being prematurely leaked. Although nobody outside the Commission had formally been shown a final draft, those involved in policing were able to put together a pretty accurate forecast of what it was going to say. By then, with the fears of a violent summer arising from the Drumcree march not having materialized, Flanagan was able to give his undivided attention to preparing for the release of the report, an occasion he foresaw was fraught with potential difficulty. RUC morale was already low. The predominant feeling was one of uncertainty. Flanagan, who is noted for his common touch and close affinity with those in the ranks, was well aware of the swirling emotions and how they were being aggravated by rumour. He'd veered throughout August from being outgoing and jovial, trying to shore up morale, to appearing a lonely figure, retreating into himself as he pondered what to do. Some of his closest colleagues feared he might even resign and leave it to a successor to carry the Patten recommendations forward.

But on the Wednesday morning, twenty-four hours before the official publication, as he was driven to the Interpoint Centre in

Belfast, to the Commission's office, to receive his own copy of the report and to be officially informed of its contents, he seemed more purposeful and jaunty than he had for weeks. That night, having read the final version, Flanagan decided he could publicly endorse the report, although he knew some aspects of it would deeply offend many of his officers and that implementing some of its far-reaching and ground-breaking recommendations would take time, sensitivity and commitment.

On the Thursday morning, Patten was at the Interpoint Centre early to prepare for his news conference. Copies of the report had been made available at 8 am and, while journalists read through it, he wandered around the room surrounded by photographers and cameramen. As he began to speak at 10 am, officially launching the report entitled 'A New Beginning: Policing in Northern Ireland', four miles away, a grim-faced Les Rodgers, Chairman of the Police Federation, was sitting in his office at RUC Garnerville. He had just returned late the night before from an international policing conference in Australia and was watching Patten on television while putting the finishing touches to a statement to be read at his own news conference a short time later.

Although he was satisfied that 'thirty-nine and a half' of the Federation's forty-four suggestions to Patten had been included in the report's 175 recommendations, Rodgers was preparing to go on the warpath to prevent the name of the RUC being changed. 'We have made it clear all along that we do not believe there is any substantive argument for the name to be abandoned. Its loss amounts to a repudiation of the professionalism, courage and sacrifice of our police officers,' he wrote.

By lunchtime, Flanagan had completed a series of one-to-one radio and television interviews and was sitting in his office at RUC headquarters in Belfast, watching the BBC news bulletin on a monitor while waiting to do a live interview. At one point Patten came on screen, talking about his work on the report. 'This is by far the most difficult job I have ever done,' said the former governor of Hong Kong.

'You should try being Chief Constable of the RUC,' retorted Flanagan.

The Patten Report on the future of the Royal Ulster Constabulary instantly became one of the landmark documents of the Northern Ireland conflict and, despite the predictable controversy it immediately generated, it will, in the longer term, clearly be acclaimed by historians. By the conventional standard of official public reports it is an unusually articulate and elegantly written document. Besides citing predictable policing authorities such as Sir Robert Peel, Rowan and Mayne and the Lords Scarman and Denning, it also finds room to quote Abraham Lincoln, the episcopal father of the Northern Ireland-born poet Louis MacNeice and the Roman poet, Juvenal. More than that, it is a frank, intellectually reasoned and logically argued practical manifesto to progressively transform the seventy-seven-year-old Royal Ulster Constabulary from a police force with a paramilitary mindset into a rebranded Northern Ireland Police Service with a new philosophy as a routinely unarmed, high technology, community-based, non-aggressive, close contact constabulary working in partnership with the people it will serve and protect.

The report did not underestimate the enormity of the task or the visionary gains to be made. 'There is no perfect model for us, no example of a country that, to quote one European police officer, "has yet finalized the total transformation from force to service". The commitment to a fresh start gives Northern Ireland the opportunity to take best practice from elsewhere and to lead the way in overcoming some of the toughest challenges of modern policing.' The commissioners warned that 'it will take time and it will not be easy' and asserted that a fresh start 'is the right way, the only way, to make certain that the rule of law, not the rule of the gun and the baseball bat, prevails in every community'.

One of the most remarkable features of the report was its penetrating analysis of the failure of policing in Northern Ireland for several generations.

The identification of police and state is contrary to policing practice in the rest of the United Kingdom. It has left the police in an unenviable position. In one political language, they are the custodians of nationhood. In its rhetorical opposite, they are the symbols of oppression. Policing, therefore, goes right to the heart of the sense of security and identity of both communities and, because of the differences between them, this seriously hampers the effectiveness of the police service in Northern Ireland.

Policing cannot be fully effective when the police have to operate from fortified stations in armoured vehicles, and when police officers dare not tell their children what they do for a living for fear of attack from extremists from both sides. We have studied policing in other countries and while we can discover no model that can simply be applied to

Northern Ireland, we can find plenty of examples of police services wrestling with the same sort of challenges.

Having so succinctly defined the dilemma, the Commission went on to set authoritative parameters for the way ahead. Its most fundamental, controversial and headline-grabbing recommendation – that the Royal Ulster Constabulary should not be disbanded but should henceforth be named the Northern Ireland Police Service – was buried away at number 150 of the 175 recommendations. In this context, the Commission went on to propose that the Police Service should adopt a new badge and symbols entirely free from any association with either the British or Irish states, that the Union flag should no longer be flown from police buildings and that, on those occasions on which it is appropriate to fly a flag on police buildings, the flag flown should be that of the Northern Ireland Police Service and it, too, should be free from any similar associations. The colour of the current police uniform – rifle green – should be retained, but a new, more practical style of uniform should be provided. Recognizing the dedication and sacrifice of RUC officers, and of the continuity between the past and the future, the Commission emphasized that these proposed changes did not extend to existing memorials in police stations. It also singled out the Disabled Police Officers' Association and the Widows' Association, saying that in many cases injured officers and widows had not been treated as well as they should have been by the police and the welfare services. It noted that compensation packages awarded in the early years of the Troubles were derisory and recommended that a substantial fund should be established to provide adequate recompense and assistance to injured police officers, injured retired officers and their families, as well as police widows. The Commission recommended that the Widows Association, like its counterpart for the disabled, should be given an office in police premises, free of charge, and a regular source of finance adequate to run their organization.

The report asserted that the heart of the new policing order should be the European Convention on Human Rights and deplored the fact that in the current RUC training curriculum, there were only two sections out of 700 dedicated to human rights, compared to forty to drill and sixty-three to firearms training. Respect for and understanding of human rights had to be fully integrated into the ethos of the new police service through training, monitoring, a new code of ethics, the appointment of a specialized legal adviser and the incorporation of an undertaking to respect and uphold human rights into a revised oath of office to be taken by all officers in the police service. The envisaged oath would commit officers to acting with fairness, integrity, diligence and impartiality and to according equal respect to all individuals and to their traditions and beliefs.

The Commission also recommended that to replace the current Police Authority a new Policing Board should be created with a statutory primary function to hold the Chief Constable and the police service publicly to account. The Board's responsibilities would include setting objectives and priorities for policing over a three-to-five-year period, negotiating the annual policing budget and measuring performance against the budget and the Annual Policing Plan with particular attention to crime trends and patterns and measuring police performance in public order situations. It would also follow such things as recruitment patterns and trends, including fair employment and equal opportunities performance, and training needs. Its duties would include assessing public satisfaction with the police service and, in liaison with the Police Ombudsman, recording patterns and trends in complaints against the police. The Board would also have the responsibility for appointing all chief officers and civilian equivalents. The Board would have nineteen members, ten Assembly members drawn from the parties making up the new Northern Ireland Executive, and nine independent members selected from a range of different fields, including business, trade unions, voluntary organizations, community groups and the legal profession.

The report further supported devolving responsibility for policing (bar matters of national security) to the Northern Ireland Executive as soon as possible, and the simplification of the Police (Northern Ireland) Act 1998 so that the respective roles of the Secretary of State, the Policing Board and the Chief Constable became clear, with the Chief Constable given operational responsibility for the direction and control of police officers and civilian staff.

To further public accountability, on a district level the Commission recommended that each of the twenty-six District Councils should establish a District Policing Partnership Board (DPPB) as a committee of the Council, with a majority elected membership, the remaining independent members to be selected by the Council with the agreement of the Policing Board. At monthly meetings of the DPPB and the police District Commander, the police would be able to present reports and answer questions and the Board could in turn reflect community concerns and priorities to the police. The report advocated that the District Councils should have the power to contribute an amount initially up to the equivalent of a rate of 3p in the pound towards the improved policing of the district, which could enable the DPPB to purchase additional services from the police, other statutory agencies or from the private sector. This proposal generated intense controversy because it appeared to open the way for the paramilitary groups to become involved in the policing process through the private sector. The fear was that private security companies, who would be fronts for the terrorist groups, would be retained as security guards in parks, shopping centres and other locations to supplement the conventional police presence. There was serious alarm about the implications of this among senior RUC officers and conventional politicians who said they would closely examine the enabling legislation to ensure strict and proper safeguards.

The Commission outlined the responsibilities of the Police Ombudsman, whose appointment to bring a new independent rigour to the investigation of complaints against the police was already in the pipeline when the report came out. The Ombudsman, said the report, should take initiatives and exercise the power to initiate inquiries or investigations even if no specific complaint had been received; be responsible for compiling data on trends and patterns in complaints against the police, or accumulations of complaints against individual officers; and should work with the police to address issues emerging from this data. (In October, Nuala O'Loan, a senior law lecturer at the University of Ulster and a member of the Police Authority since 1997, was appointed to the £75,000-a-year post as Police Ombudsman-designate to set up new investigation teams, independent of the police, and to prepare formally to take over the task of dealing with allegations of police misconduct from the summer of 2000.)

According to the report, policing with the community should be the core function of the police service. Every police station and every neighbourhood (or rural area) should have a dedicated policing team with responsibility for policing its area. Each team member should clearly display his or her name on his/her uniform as well as the name of the locality for which the team member is responsible. The commission added: 'What we emphatically do not mean by "community policing" is vigilante groups policing neighbourhoods with baseball bats, or, at the other extreme, what the Philadelphia police chief, John Timoney, has described as "sitting around the trees, holding hands and singing 'Kumbaya'".'

The Commission outlined a series of views on police buildings and vehicles. New police stations should have, so far as possible, the appearance of ordinary buildings; they should have low perimeter walls, and be clearly visible from the street; but they should have security features which could be activated or reinforced as necessary. Existing police stations should – subject to the security situation in their areas and to health and safety considerations – be made less forbidding in appearance, more accessible to public callers and more congenial for those working in them. The public reception areas inside police stations should be made more welcoming and civilian receptionists could replace police officers. The question of moving towards the desired objective of a routinely unarmed police service would have to be periodically reviewed in the light of developments in the security environment. Police cars, it went on, should continue to be substituted as patrol vehicles in place of armoured Land-Rovers. The role of the army should continue to be reduced, as quickly as the security situation would allow, so that the police could eventually patrol all parts of Northern Ireland without military support.

Dealing with the use of plastic baton rounds (PBRs), which had caused so much debate over the years, the Commission said an immediate and substantial investment should be made in a research programme to find an acceptable, effective and less potentially lethal alternative. The police, it said, should be equipped with a broader range of public order equipment than the RUC currently possessed, so that a commander had a number of options at his/her disposal which might reduce reliance on, or defer resort to, the PBR. The use of PBRs should be subject to the same procedures for deployment, use and reporting as apply in the rest of the United Kingdom. Their use should be confined to the smallest necessary number of specially trained officers, who should be trained to think of the weapon in the same way as they would think of a firearm. Use of PBRs should in the first instance require the authorization of a district commander and should be justified in a report to the Policing Board, which should be copied to the Police Ombudsman. Wherever possible, video camera recordings should be made of incidents in which the use of PBRs is authorized. Officers' identification numbers should be clearly visible on their protective clothing, just as they should be on regular uniforms. The Policing Board and, as appropriate, Police Ombudsman should actively monitor police performance in public order situations, and if necessary seek reports from the Chief Constable and follow up those reports if they wish. Guidance governing the deployment and use of PBRs should be soundly based in law, clearly expressed and readily available as public documents.

Turning to the process of change facing the RUC, the Commission made some telling comments which highlighted the scale of the cultural and attitudinal revolution to come. The Commission described the RUC as an 'organization which is commanded rather than managed' and quoted an operational officer in Newry who had told them: 'Nobody comes down to discuss policy decisions – we are told.' The Commission asserted that this hierarchical and bureaucratic style of management had to change. There was also a rebuke about the vigour with which the RUC had dealt with the 'bad apples' within its ranks over the years. 'They should be dealt with. We are not persuaded that the RUC has in the past had adequate systems in place to monitor and, when necessary, act upon complaints against officers.' The new Northern Ireland police leadership team should include specialists in change management. The leadership team should produce a programme for change, to be presented to the Policing Board and reviewed periodically by the Board. The efficiency and effectiveness of each chief officer should be judged on the basis of, among other things, his or her capacity to introduce and adapt to change.

The Commission largely accepted and endorsed the plans for territorial reorganization and the streamlining and devolution of command structures first outlined in Flanagan's Fundamental Review. It confirmed that there should be one district command for each District Council area, headed by a superintendent and resourced sufficiently to be self-contained for day-to-day policing purposes and capable of marshalling strength to cope with most unexpected demands. District commanders should have fully devolved authority over the deployment of personnel (officer and civilian) within their command, devolved budgets (including salary budgets), authority to purchase a range of goods and services, and to finance local policing initiatives.

The removal of the divisional layer of command and the regional headquarters should go ahead. There should be a direct reporting line from each district commander to the appropriate assistant chief constable at central police headquarters, where there should be a slimmer structure that reflected the shift of focus towards community policing and the delegation of responsibility to district commanders. There should be no more than one deputy chief constable and the number of assistant chief constables should be reduced to six, with the rank of chief superintendent finally being phased out. Special Branch and Crime Branch should be brought together under the command of a single assistant chief constable.

Turning to the future size of the police service, the Commission said the 3,000-strong Full Time Reserve should go but that there should be an enlarged Part Time Reserve of up to 2,500 officers, the additional recruits to come from those areas in which there were currently very few reservists or none at all. Provided the peace process and the security situation were maintained, the Commission estimated the approximate size of the police service over the next ten years should be reduced to 7,500 full-time officers, with those retiring being offered generous, enhanced severance and early-retirement financial packages. Additionally, police recruiting agencies in Great Britain should take full account of the policing experience of former RUC reservists in considering applications for employment in police services in Great Britain and the government should offer former reservists the opportunity to participate in British policing contingents in United Nations peacekeeping operations.

Emphasizing the need for a police service which was fully representative of the entire community (roughly 60 per cent Protestant and 40 per cent Catholic), the Commission said that every effort should be made to ensure that the composition of the staff of the Policing Board, the NIO Police Division (or any successor body), and the office of the Police Ombudsman should be broadly reflective of the population of Northern Ireland as a whole, particularly in terms of political/religious tradition and gender. It also called for the creation of a neutral working environment in police establishments, in line with Northern Ireland's fair employment legislation, designed to outlaw all forms of discrimination.

In what is perhaps the most forthright passage in the entire report, the Commission told the minority community it was finally time for them to get off the fence and participate fully in the policing process. It called on all community leaders, including political party leaders and local councillors, bishops and priests, schoolteachers and sports authorities, to take steps to remove all discouragements to members of their communities applying to join the police, and, indeed, to make it a priority to encourage them to apply. In particular, it said the Gaelic Athletic Association, a major all-Ireland sporting organization with a decidedly Nationalist culture, should repeal its rule 21, which prohibits members of the police in Northern Ireland from being members.

The Commission suggested that the police should contract out the recruitment of both police officers and civilians into the service and that non-police interviewers should be included on recruitment panels. The recruitment agency should be encouraged to advertise imaginatively and persistently to reach groups who were under-represented in the police and should seek to identify Northern Ireland Catholic officers – particularly those in more senior ranks – in other police services, including the Garda Siochana, and encourage them to apply for positions in the Northern Ireland police. Lateral entry of experienced officers from other police services, and secondments or recruitment from non-police organizations should also be actively encouraged.

In an effort to accelerate immediately the rate of Catholic recruitment to the police, the Commission devised a novel scheme whereby an equal number of Protestants and Catholics would be drawn from the pool of qualified candidates who have satisfied the basic selection criteria. This departure from the principles of appointment on merit only, together with affirmative action, breached existing and rigidly enforced Fair Employment legislation. Accepting and implementing this plan to counter under-representation raised fundamental and difficult questions which the government and parliament would have to ponder very carefully. The drive to eradicate unfair employment practices in Northern Ireland had been steadily, but not dramatically, effective in tackling religious or gender discrimination and the government had always resisted any pleading for special treatment. If an exception were made for the police, however compelling the reason, it could undermine the credibility of the legislation in other sectors.

In order that the new police service should meet the highest standards of excellence and gain professional skills, the Commission insisted that a new purpose-built police college should be founded at the centre of a well-considered training, education and development strategy, both for recruit training and for in-service training.

The report outlined a series of proposals for a much closer relationship between the Northern Ireland police and the Garda Siochana.

Each should have written protocols covering key aspects of co-operation and there should be an annual conference, designed to drive forward action in areas of common concern. The Commission proposed posting liaison officers from each service to the central headquarters and/or border area headquarters of the other; structured co-operation in training; long-term personnel exchanges; the compilation of databases in all the main areas of cross-border criminality, such as drugs, smuggling, vehicle theft and terrorism; implementing improved radio and information technology links; joint emergency and disaster planning; and the pooling of investigative teams after major incidents with a substantial cross-border dimension, akin to the arrangements which exist between Kent and the police services of France and Belgium.

In an effort to maintain independent outside pressure on the process of police reform, the Commission said that an eminent person from a country other than the United Kingdom or Ireland should be appointed as an oversight commissioner, for five years, with responsibility for supervising the implementation of its recommendations. The government, the police service and the Policing Board (and DPPBs) should provide the oversight commissioner with objectives (with timetables) covering their own responsibilities, and should report on the progress achieved at the periodic review meetings, and account for any failures to achieve objectives. The commissioner should in turn report publicly after each review meeting on the progress achieved, together with his or her observations on the extent to which any failures or delays are the responsibility of the policing institutions themselves or due to matters beyond their control.

President Bill Clinton and prime ministers Tony Blair and Bertie Ahern promptly endorsed the report as providing for a radical new beginning for policing in Northern Ireland and called for careful reflection on the proposals. Flanagan, predictably, was less fulsome: 'Let no one underestimate the hurt that will be caused by the suggestion that the title should be changed and that the emblems and the crest of the organization should be changed. That will cause tremendously deep hurt to my serving officers, to their families, to retired colleagues, to the families who have been bereaved and to our disabled officers. I know of no organization, other than the RUC, which has sustained such hurt on behalf of others.' But he went on to say that if the police were to gain new support without alienating existing support 'then, perhaps, the pain has to be endured. My officers and I are ready for change. No organization I know has shown itself to be more adaptable down the years. The big question is: "Is society here similarly ready for change? Are they ready to play their part in full partnership with their police?" If they are, then perhaps we can truly bring about that new beginning that Mr Patten hopes to facilitate.'

The wider reaction to the report was varied. Sinn Fein was clearly unhappy that disbandment had not been suggested but it took an initially cautious 'we will study it' line and set up a party working group to do so. Almost immediately it then publicly opposed any notion of Flanagan leading the new service and continued its criticism of the RUC at every opportunity. In October, it hit out at the Garda for setting up training sessions for seventy RUC officers as part of their preparation for a year-long peacekeeping deployment as part of the United Nations contingent in Kosovo. Around the same time in Dungannon, a Sinn Fein councillor unsuccessfully opposed the installation of a closed-circuit television system in the town centre 'because it would be used by the RUC to spy on local people'. In south Down, an elected Sinn Fein Assembly representative distributed a letter to a number of Catholic schools continuing the campaign to halt RUC visits. One principal, who described the Sinn Fein letter as 'intimidating and offensive', was promptly backed up by the Catholic Council for Maintained Schools, which supported the principle of police officers visiting schools, saying they had been doing so for many years with few complaints. At first the SDLP blandly welcomed the Patten report as an 'opportunity for all' but the party then intervened in the schools controversy insisting it was quite proper for Catholic pupils to hear from the police about matters such as child protection and road safety. The party accused Sinn Fein of adopting 'a sinister agenda which, if it succeeds, would lead to telling schools what they should teach and who they should teach'. In a more significant indication of an emerging, post-Patten change in the Nationalist anti-police mindset, Fr Timothy Bartlett, who had written the Catholic Church submission to the Commission, gave the report a conditional welcome and said that the Church would encourage its members to join the police if the proposed new, politically and culturally neutral service came about. But the appearance of a painted slogan – 'Disband the NIPS' – on a wall in west Belfast, within days of the report coming out, underlined the extent of the major change in the mindset that was still necessary.

From the Unionist side there was widespread hostility ranging from the Rev. Ian Paisley's customary accusations of 'appeasement and betrayal' to the more measured, but equally hostile, 'disappointing' verdict of Ken Maginnis, the Ulster Unionist security spokesman. The depth of hostility to the Patten proposals, which rapidly developed even among moderate, pro-Belfast Agreement Unionists, was evident at the party conference in Enniskillen in early October when David Burnside, a Northern Ireland-born, London-based, public relations consultant, urged the party leadership to make the campaign to save the RUC's name and symbols 'the bottom line, because if we lose this one we have lost an essential part of the union'. Ulster Unionists, who had built up links with leading Conservatives and right-wingers in London through regular breakfasts, where specially imported Northern Ireland bacon, sausages and soda bread were served, planned to use the influence of what had become known as the 'Ulster fry' circuit to pressure the Blair government into preserving the RUC name. The *Daily Telegraph* endorsed the campaign and published coupons for its readers to sign and return as a mark of support. A 'Defend the RUC' Internet website was also established. The Conservative party hierarchy responded positively, adopting an anti-Patten line, but a proposal to parade some disabled RUC officers on the platform at the party conference in Blackpool in October was dropped after a wrangle over fears that they would be diminished 'as freaks in a circus'. Paisley, meanwhile, set about organizing his own series of 'Defend the RUC' rallies throughout the autumn of 1999, although it was clear he was as much concerned with mustering opponents of the Agreement as with the future of the force. It was a common feature of both campaigns that the Unionists persisted in claiming the RUC as 'our' police to the exclusion of the Nationalist community. This proprietorial attitude only served to highlight why policing continued to pose such an intractable political problem.

For its part, the Police Federation discreetly distanced itself from the Unionists' overt political campaigning but mounted its own equally strident and scaremongering anti-Patten crusade, heavily based on the 'royal' recognition, the 'history' of the RUC and its 'Britishness'. The centrepiece of its case was to be a petition, which stated:

We the undersigned demand that no measures be taken to weaken the Royal Ulster Constabulary's capacity to provide the first line of defence against Republican and Loyalist terrorism in these islands. Although we acknowledge and support the need for constructive change in policing in Northern Ireland, we deplore the Patten Report's dishonouring of the sacrifice, courage and professionalism of the RUC in its recommendations that the force give up its proud name, badge and other symbols.

Police forces throughout Britain were enlisted in a bid to achieve the target of one million signatures, so that the petition could be presented to the prime minister early in 2000 before parliament was asked to enact legislation to give effect to the Patten report. The Federation's blinkered and inappropriate response to the new situation played into the hands of Sinn Fein and the RUC's critics and dismayed those, including many Nationalists, who were at last prepared to come off the fence and actively work with the police. 'When I listened to Les Rodgers harking back to the past, he only proved the case for change and led me to wonder if Patten had gone far enough,' said one prominent Catholic politician.

Meanwhile, inside the Northern Ireland Office, Mowlam had ordered work on drafting the necessary new legislation to begin immediately after Patten had published. In line with the public commitment she had made after her appointment in May 1997, she wanted action without delay. Indeed, she only reluctantly agreed to a consultation period up to the end of November 1999 after heavy pressure from a range of advisers and officials. Her own game plan had been to have legislation tabled in parliament by the end of the year, with a simultaneous start on downsizing the force. With intelligence indicating dissident Republicans making plans to attack the security forces, especially along the border, and the likelihood of the mainstream IRA going back on a war-footing, with a consequent Loyalist response, Mowlam's impatience caused Flanagan to issue several public warnings that he would resign if his capacity to protect the public was compromised before there was a convincing end to the threat of terrorism.

Mowlam, whose position in Belfast had become steadily more untenable as the peace process gridlocked and her popularity plummeted throughout 1999, was finally relieved of her post in a cabinet reshuffle on 11 October. She was plainly unhappy with the decision and reluctant to go. In a valedictory article, written for the *Belfast Telegraph* two days later, she once more returned to her obsession with police reform:

A number of my predecessors have said to me once you do the job of Secretary of State for Northern Ireland you can never ever close the door and leave it behind you. It will certainly live on in me. I will watch attentively as reform of the police on the basis of the Patten Commission's work takes place. Reform made successfully will be central to peace and stability in the future.

Mowlam was replaced by the altogether more cerebral Peter Mandelson, the controversial figure who was credited with masterminding the creation of New Labour and astutely guiding Tony Blair to the party leadership and power. Forced to resign from the government ten months earlier after a scandal over his financial affairs, Mandelson, regarded as the prime minister's closest political ally and confidant, was offered the Belfast posting, at a time of great political difficulty, as the route to political rehabilitation. Significantly, the new Secretary of State did not identify policing reform as one of his immediate priorities when he arrived in Belfast, and it was notable that within forty-eight hours the security minister, Adam Ingram, was put forward to take the force out of the gathering storm over the future of the RUC. The British government was still 'in listening mode', he insisted, and the 'strength and feeling' of views expressed by groups such as the Police Federation, RUC officers and families of officers killed would be heard. Ingram added that the British government had accepted the broad thrust of the Patten Report but it remained to be seen how many of its 175 recommendations would be implemented when legislation was brought forward early in 2000.

The final verdict on the future of the RUC and a new beginning for policing will thus belong to the British parliament. It is conceivable that by the time of its seventy-eighth anniversary on 1 June, the RUC will be no more and Northern Ireland will be being policed by the new police outlined by Patten. However, with the politicians still squabbling over the implementation of the Belfast Agreement in the autumn of 1999 and the possibility that the deal could collapse altogether, there remains a lingering worry that the threat of terrorism could emerge again. In that scenario, with Northern Ireland again engulfed in violence and the police once more a force under fire, much of the Patten report, like that of Lord Hunt in 1969, could well be shelved.

Whatever happens, there will be profound changes to policing in Northern Ireland in the near future. Many of the recommendations on the RUC's composition and training, command structures and organization and community policing may still go ahead. After Patten there can be no going back for an organization which, despite professionally embracing so many concepts of modern technology, still cherishes and preserves the practices of what Flanagan has vividly described as a white, male, Protestant internal culture, in too many respects still largely unchanged since the formation of the force in 1922. Over the years, despite preserving this core culture, the RUC has shown great ingenuity and resilience in coping with the challenges of conflict. Now it has to undergo a management and cultural revolution and forge the new practices and principles, so effectively signposted by Patten, for policing in a more conventional environment. 'When a Catholic woman eventually becomes Chief Constable we will know we have succeeded,' said one senior RUC officer.

# Index

A Specials, 38, 43, 65, 66
Acheson, Constable Kenneth, 251
Adams, Gerry, 214, 360, 412, 456, 457, 458
Agnew, Reserve Constable William,314
air-raids, 74, 75
Aldergrove airport, 134, 240, 277, 362
Alexandra, Princess, of Kent, 224
Allen, Constable Charles, 334
Allen, Reserve Constable William, 241
Allied Control Commission, 79
Amnesty International, 191, 196
Anderson, Alan, 447–8
Anderson, Constable Charles, 69
Anderson, Constable Norman, 94
Anderton, James, 348
Andrews, John, 92
Anglo-Irish Agreement, 316, 317, 325, 353, 363,
    364, 370
Anglo-Irish Treaty, 35, 41, 50
Annesley, Hugh, 366, 367, 368, 369, 372, 373,
    377, 386, 387, 388, 389, 401, 402, 403, 405,
    406, 407, 417, 435, 436, 451, 457, 464, 466,
    468, 470–1
Annett, Constable Norman, 390
Apprentice Boys of Derry, 104, 110, 111, 167,
    206, 328
Arbuckle, Constable Victor, 116
Archer, Peter, 294
Arnon Street killings, 56, 61
Armour, Reserve Constable Samuel, 160
Armstrong, Reserve Constable Edward, 357
Armstrong, Reserve Constable Frederick, 342
Armstrong, Gary, 205
Army, British, 74, 90, 109, 110, 115, 123, 124,
    126, 130, 131, 156, 157, 159, 162, 167, 169,
    218, 240, 273, 334, 337
'Arresting Memories' 273
Association of Police Surgeons, 193
Atkins, Humphrey, 234, 237, 246, 247, 254, 255
Atlantic Buildings, Belfast, 48
Auxiliaries, 31, 33

BBC, 337
B Specials, 18, 39, 40, 43, 66, 71, 74, 82, 88, 90,
    91, 99, 101, 106, 107, 109, 110, 115, 116,
    119, 126 263
Baggley, Woman Reserve Constable Linda, 141
Baggley, Reserve Constable William, 131, 143

Baillie, County Inspector Harry, 117, 226
Baird, Reserve Constable Andrew, 133
Baird, Constable David, 313
Baird, Constable Richard, 220
Baldonnel panels, 133
Balbriggan, 33
Baldwin, Stanley, 70, 72
Bannon, Francis, 192, 193
barrack-buster mortar launchers 425–6
Barry, Peter, 316
Bates, Sir Dawson, 40, 42, 43, 47, 56, 57, 59, 60,
    61, 63, 66, 68, 70, 71, 80
Baxter, Samuel, 69
Beacom, Constable Andrew, 440
Beacom, Constable Johnston, 440
Beck, Constable Alexander, 256
Beckett, Constable Harold, 402
Begley, Thomas, 434
Belfast Agreement 488, 489–90
Belfast boycott, 50
Belfast City Hall, 40, 63, 258, 325, 331, 332
Belfast Telegraph, 41, 48, 59, 77, 81, 97, 189
Bell, Constable Alexander, 390
Bell, Constable Brian, 131
Bell, Inspector George, 134
Bell, Reserve Constable John, 313
Bell, Melvyn, 338
Bennett, Judge Harry, QC, 196, 197, 198, 199,
    230
Bennett, Joe, 289, 290, 291, 292, 295, 296, 297
Bennison, Detective Sergeant John, 342
Berry, Chuck, 164
Better Government of Ireland Act, 38
Bingham, Constable Thomas, 309
Black, Christopher, 261, 262, 283, 284, 285, 286,
    288, 295
Black, Constable David, 390
Black and Tans, 31, 32, 33
Blackbourne, Constable Karl, 334
Blair, Lt-Col. David, 222
Blair, Tony 481, 482
Blakely, Sergeant James, 134, 178
Bloody Friday, Belfast, 125
Bloody Sunday, Belfast, 42
Bloody Sunday, Londonderry, 123
Boal, Desmond, WC, 102, 205, 268, 293, 294, 391
Bogside, 10, 109, 110, 111, 112, 113
bomb disposal teams, 424, 432

Boundary Commission, 44, 50
Bourne, John, 140
Boyle, John, 216
Bradford, Rev. Robert, MP, 257, 258, 260
Bradley, Sam, 113, 114, 116, 142
Bramshill, Police Staff College, 225, 227, 365, 405, 474–5
Breen, Dan, 28
Breen, Constable Derek, 334
Breen, Chief Superintendent Harry, 372
*Britannia* HMY, 170, 171
British Airways, 25
Britten, County Inspector F.S., 63
Brooke, Sir Basil, later Lord Brookeborough, 71, 90, 96
Brooke, Peter, MP, 400, 401, 402, 437–8, 495
Brooklyn, 96, 224, 225
Brophy, Edward, 199
Brown, Sergeant Eric, 282
Brown, Constable William, 172
Browne, Andrew, 25
Brownlow, James, 200
Bruton, John, 468
Buchanan, Superintendent Bob, 372
Buck, Maurice, 226
Buckingham Palace, 23, 134, 167, 203
Buckley, Constable Robert, 121
Bulkies, 16, 21
Bunting, Detective Chief Inspector Dennis, 436
Burke, Thomas, 21
Burns, James 'Rocky', 79
Burns, Sean, 345, 353
Burntollet Bridge, 106
Byford, Sir Lawrence, 347

C Specials, 39, 43, 65
Cairo Gang, 33
Callaghan, James, 110, 115, 116
Carruthers, Constable Douglas, 403
Calvin, Reserve Constable Joseph, 125
Cameron, Lord, 105
Campaign for Social Justice, 102
Campbell College, Belfast, 73
Campbell, Reserve Constable Geoffrey, 311
Campbell, Sergeant Joseph, 172, 265, 267
Campbell, Ken, 258
Campbell, Lloyd, MP, 47
Campbell, Constable Norman, 160
Campbell, Mrs Rosemary, 269
Campbell, Reserve Constable William, 128
Carders, 13
Cardwell, Alderman Joss, 307, 308
Carrington, Lord, 234
Carroll, Constable Raymond, 124
Carroll, Roddy, 345
Carson, Reserve Constable Colin, 282
Carson, Sir Edward, 22, 23, 40, 41, 247, 248
Carson, Detective Constable Stanley, 357
Carson trail, 247
Carswell, Mr Justice, 389
Casement, Sir Roger, 24, 25, 265
Caskey, Chief Inspector George, 210, 211, 214, 301, 306, 307
Castlereagh, 97, 110, 113, 154, 184, 187, 188, 189, 190, 192, 194, 197, 198, 199, 200, 206, 207, 229, 230, 261, 262, 291

Cathcart, Constable Gerald, 282
Caughey, Colm, 192, 193
Cavendish, Lord Frederick, 21
ceasefire, 439, 441, 463
Central Citizens Defence Committee, 117
Chambers, Sergeant Cecil, 178
Chambers, Constable George, 125
Charmside, Special Constable William, 55
Chastelin, General John de, 456, 480
Cheshire Regiment, 276
Chichester-Clark, Major James, 108, 109, 110, 117, 121, 303
Churchill, Sir Winston, 46, 54, 55, 58, 76, 79, 80
Civil Rights Association, 102, 104, 105, 113
Clark, Reserve Constable Samuel, 133
Clarke, Constable Erik, 403
Clarke, Constable Paul, 283
Clements, Reserve Constable Joseph, 133
Clements, Reserve Constable William, 333, 339
Clinton, Bill, 456, 471, 501–2
Clones, railway station, 53, 54, 55
Cobb, Inspector James, 172
coffee-jar bombs, 424
Coleman, Detective Sergeant, 117
Coleman, Mrs Lily, 67
Colgan, Detective Chief Inspector Harold, 201
Collins, Gerry, 358
Collins, Michael, 25, 26, 28, 33, 35, 38, 43, 44, 49, 50, 54, 55, 56, 58
Colonial Office, 20, 44
Coulter, Constable William, 259
Community Relations Commission, 115
Conaty, Gunner John, 207
'Confidential Telephone', 124, 147
Connolly, James, 25
Conroy, Detective Chief Superintendent Desmond, 436
conscription, 76
Constabulary Act 1835, 16
Constabulary Act 1922, 48
Constabulary Act 1963, 97
Constabulary Code of Regulations, 19
*Constabulary Gazette*, 27
Constitutional Convention, 139, 160
Cooke, Sergeant Tom, 343
Cope, John, MP, 385
Corbett, Alan, 440
Cork County Club, 37
Corkey, Reserve Constable Samuel, 276
Corry, Detective Constable Stanley, 123
Coulter, Sergeant George, 132
Council of Ireland, 30, 36
Covenant, Ulster, 23
Craig, Sergeant Albert, 159
Craig, Sir James, 38, 40, 43, 44, 50, 54, 55, 56, 58, 59, 62, 65, 66, 70
Craig, William, 104, 105, 106
Crawford, Lt-Col. Fred, 23, 42, 60, 92
Crawford, Constable Ivan, 342
Crawford, District Inspector Malcolm, 91, 93
Creasey, John, QC, 392
Creasey, Lt-Gen. Sir Timothy, 159, 222
Crilly, Reserve Constable Robert, 241
Criminal Investigation Department, 72, 94, 117, 150, 154, 187, 197, 230, 232, 345
Croke Park, 33

Crooks, Reserve Constable William, 134
Crothers, Reserve Constable Charles, 276
Crothers, Reserve Constable Gordon, 175
Crowley, Eugene, 372
Crozier, County Inspector Thomas, 97, 98
Cullen, Detective Constable James, 305, 306
Cummings, Detective Constable Neville, 134
Cunliffe, Shaun, 379
Cunningham, Constable Cecil, 122
Cunningham, Special Constable Thomas, 55
Curragh, The, 23, 34, 40
Currie, Austin, 103
Curtis, Gunner Robert, 121
Curzon, Lord, 28, 33
Cush, Constable Thomas, 159

Dail Eireann, 26, 30, 33, 35, 43, 44, 50
*Daily Mirror*, 122
Daly, Cardinal Cahal, 397, 398, 400, 469-70
Daly, Dr Edward, 236, 341
Data research centre, 208
Davidson, Detective Sergeant David, 5
Davidson, Constable Derek, 221
Davidson, Constable John, 221
Davidson, Detective Inspector Andrew, 436
Davidson, Detective Superintendent Philip, 436
Davies, Constable Noel, 132
Davison, Constable Samuel, 172
Dawson, Constable Michael, 309
Dear, Geoffrey, 365, 367
Denham, Reserve Constable Raymond, 124
Dempsey, Head Constable Thomas, 74
Derry Journal, 64
De Valera, Eamonn, 54, 55, 76
Devenney, Samuel and family, 109, 110, 117, 118, 126
Deverell, John, 436
Devine, Mickey, 255
Devlin, Inspector Alfred, 123
Devlin, Bernadette (McAliskey), 245
Devlin, Paddy, 157
Diamond, Harry, MP, 93
Dillon, family, 14
Diplock courts, 147, 193
Diplock, Lord, 149
Disabled Police Officers Association 409
Dispatches, 404
Divis Street, 99, 100, 228
Divisional Mobile Support Unit (DMSU), 165, 232, 251, 319
Doak, Woman Constable Tracy, 313
Dobbin, Reserve Constable Desmond, 334
Docklands bomb, 457
Dodd, Sergeant Ronald, 123
Dodds, Sergeant Robert, 231
Doherty, Eamonn, 358
Doherty, Detective Constable John, 128
Doherty, Kieran, 151, 254
Doherty, Sean, 370
Donaghy, Constable Howard, 206
Donaldson, Chief Inspector Alexander, 311
Donaldson, Constable Samuel, 118
Dorsett, Sergeant David, 127
Douglas, Constable Jim, 439
Dowd, Sergeant John, 311
Downes, Sean, 347

Downing Street, 43, 44, 80, 102, 222, 234, 436, 360, 361, 362
Downing Street Declaration, 439, 454
Dowra, 370
Downtown Radio, 252
Doyle, Judge William, 281
Droppin' Well, 276
Drumcree march, 461-6, 476
Drummond, Thomas, 16, 19, 71
Drury, Chief Superintendent Kenneth, 117
Dublin Castle, 17, 18, 19, 24, 25, 26, 27, 28, 33, 37, 234, 314
Dudgeon, District Inspector, 63
Duggan, G. C., 41
Duke, Henry, 25
Dunlop, Reserve Constable Colin, 253
Dunn, Constable David, 220

Ead, Inspector David, 343
Eagleson, Reserve Constable John, 276
Eames, Robin, Archbishop of Armagh, 1, 9, 400
Easter Rising, Dublin, 1916, 24, 26, 28
Eksund, 357, 358
Elder, John, 354
Elizabeth, Queen, 89, 102, 167, 168, 169, 170, 171, 268
Elliott, Doctor Denis, 198
Elliott, Reserve Constable Trevor, 309
Elliot, Inspector William, 131
Ellis, Constable Philip, 253
El Salvador, 2
Emergency Provisions Act, 149, 188
Enniskillen, RUC Depot, 72 80, 86, 131, 224, 226, 228, 230
Equal Opportunities Commission, 355, 356
Erskine, Lord and Lady, 101
Europa Hotel, 257
European Convention for the protection of human rights, 149, 271
European Court of Human Rights, 122
European Court of Justice, 356
European Human Rights Commission, 237
European Parliament, 250, 270
Evans, Constable Mark, 201
Evans, Reserve Constable Thomas, 143
Evans, Reserve Constable William, 133, 255
Ewing, Detective Constable Gary, 276

Families Against Intimidation and Terror, 399
Faul, Father Denis, 126, 255, 284, 400
Faulkner, Brian, 93, 97, 102, 122
Fawkes, Guy, 11
Fenian bombers, 20, 21
Fenton, James, 394, 396
Ferguson, Constable Michael, 440
Ferguson, Reserve Constable James, 283
*Fife* HMS, 170, 171
fingerprints, 148
Fingerprint Bureau, 419-20
Finlay, Reserve Constable William, 283
Finlay, Reserve Constable Winston, 357
Finucane, Patrick, 415
FitzGerald, Dr Garrett, 254, 314, 315, 316, 317, 324
Fitzsimons, Assistant Chief Constable Brian, 436
Fitzsimmons, Inspector Jack, 178

Fitt, Gerry, MP, 100, 104, 197
Fitzpatrick, Commandant Matt, 54
Fitzpatrick, Reserve Constable William, 283
Flags and Emb lems Act, 1954, 82, 99
Flanagan, Sir Jamie, 129, 130, 133, 134, 365
Flanagan, Detective Inspector Peter, 131
Flanagan, Ronnie, 451, 471, 472–7
Fletcher, John, 384
Forbes, Constable Thomas, 77
Forbes, Assistant Chief Constable Trevor, 352
Forde, Constable Robert, 132
Forsyth, Constable John, 131
Forensic Science Laboratory, 148
Foster, Detective Superintendent Robert, 436
Foster, Rev. Ivan, 327
Fox, Sean, 434
Freeland, Lt-Gen. Sir Ian, 115, 120
Freeman, John, 163
Free Presbyterian Church, 99, 101, 203
Freemasonry, 27
French, Major Andrew, 334
Fullerton, Councillor Eddie, 411
Fullerton, Reserve Constable William, 309
Fyffe, Sergeant Stephen, 281

Gallagher, John, 418
Garda Siochana, 35, 133, 209, 323, 343, 355, 369, 371, 372, 380
Gardiner, Lord, 235
Garland, Roy, 303, 304, 305
Garnerville, 1, 86, 262, 334
Gault, Ex-Sergeant Samuel, 357
*Gazette* see *Constabulary Gazette*
Gelston, J. F., Deputy Inspector General, 63
George, David Lloyd, 35, 44
George V, King, 22, 23, 40, 70
Gibson, Lord Justice, 201, 294, 312, 346, 371
Gibson, Peter, QC, 200, 201
Gibson, Reserve Constable Robert, 125
Gillespie, Paddy, 426
Gilgunn, Sergeant Peter, 124
Gillespie, Sergeant Stephen, 403
Gilliland, Derek, 206
Gilliland, Constable George, 333
Gilliland, Constable William, 314
Gilmore, Constable Colin, 363
Gilvary, Maurice, 242, 244
Gladstone, William Ewart, 21, 27
Gormanston, 45
Gough Barracks, 90, 187, 198, 222, 345
Gough, Brigadier General Hubert, 34
Government of Ireland Act 1920, 33, 36, 42
Gowrie, Lord, 255
Gracey, Fred and family, 329
Graham, Constable Clive, 363
Graham, Edgar, 281, 300
Grand Hotel, Brighton, 11, 155, 315
Grant, W., MP, 72
Gray, Constable Paul (d. 1975), 132
Gray, Constable Paul (d. 1979), 220
Gray, Constable William, 309
Grew, Seamus, 345, 346
Griffiths, Sir Eldon, MP, 329, 333
Grimley, John Patrick, 292, 293, 294, 296
Greenwood, Sir Hamar, 33, 44, 47
Greer, Reserve Constable William, 172

Gregg, Constable Thomas, 91
Gresham Hotel, Dublin, 35
Griffith, Arthur, 24
Grundy, Fusilier Andrew, 427
Guthrie, Sergeant Robert, 357
Gwilliam, Detective Superintendent William, 436

H Blocks, 236, 237
Haggan, Constable Jackie, 456
Hallawell, Constable John, 283
Hamer, Constable William, 134
Hamilton, Constable Paul, 276
Hamilton, Special Constable Samuel, 78
Hanna, G. B., QC, 81, 82, 94
Hanna, Superintendent Stanley, 220
Hanson, Major David, 112
Hanson, Constable William, 402
Hanson, Reserve Constable William, 317
Harland and Wolff, 74
Harris, Supt. Alwyn, 391
Harrison, Woman Reserve Constable Mildred, 132
Harrison, Reserve Constable Robert, 172
Harron, Constable Andrew, 125
Haslett, Constable John, 122
Hassan, Constable Kenneth, 201
Hassard, Jack, 200
Haughey, Charles, 234, 239, 246, 248, 352, 370
Haughton, Sir James, 196
Havers, Sir Michael, 295
Hay, Constable Ian, 73
Hayes, Brian, 366
Hazelton, Reserve Constable Stanley, 221
Hazlett, Inspector James, 7, 334
Heaney, Constable James, 159
Henderson, Reserve Constable Arthur, 131
Hendron, Joe, 190
Henry, Harry, 338, 339
Hermon, Sir John, 2, 100, 142, 190, 226, 227, 229, 230, 232, 233, 238, 239, 240, 246, 247, 248, 251, 256, 257, 259, 260, 262, 263, 264, 265, 269, 273, 274, 275, 284, 298, 299, 300, 318, 319, 320, 323, 325, 327, 328, 333, 341, 344, 346, 347, 350, 352, 353, 354, 355, 357, 358, 359, 360, 362, 364, 367, 370, 371, 373, 380, 404
Hermon, Lady Jean, 329, 334
Holkeri, Harry, 456, 480
HOLMES Computer, 378, 384
Home Affairs, Ministry of, 59, 64, 66, 71, 89
Homeless Citizens League, 102
Home-made explosives (HME), 424
Houston, Constable Samuel, 125
Howe, Sir Geoffrey, 234, 316
Howe, Constable Winston, 241
Howth gun-running, 24
Hughes, Brendan, 239
Hughes, Francis, 253
Hughes, Judge William, 308
Hume, John, 110, 314, 460
Humphreys, Sir Myles, 273
Hunger strikes, 235, 248, 249, 250, 252, 254, 255, 256
Hunt, Lord, 115, 116, 119, 228, 354
Hunter, Sergeant James, 143
Hunter, Constable William, 94
Hurd, Douglas, 316, 319

Hurley, Sergeant Dermot, 123
Hurson, Martin, 254
Hutton, Sir Brian, 374, 391

Incident Centres, 130
Independent Commission on Policing in Northern Ireland
    (Patten Report) 497–8, 511–20
*Independent, The*, 380
India, 14
Inner Circle, 380, 384
*International Criminal Police Review*, 2
Invincibles, 21
Irish Constables Act, 16
Irish Distress Committee, 47
*Irish Independent*, 301
Irish Republican Army, 28, 30, 31, 32, 35, 36, 37,
    38, 42, 45, 46, 49, 50, 54, 55, 56, 57, 58, 73,
    74, 76, 77, 78, 79, 89, 91, 93, 97, 105, 108,
    109, 118, 125, 134, 151, 161, 262, 374, 378,
    411, 412, 413, 422, 423, 426, 427, 428, 432,
    438, 439, 455, 458, 459, 460
Irish Republican Brotherhood, 17, 20, 24, 25, 26
*Irish News*, 44, 51, 53, 134, 380
*Irish Times*, 41, 378
Irwin, Reserve Constable Ronald, 276

Johnson, Mrs Marguerite, 356
Johnston, Woman Constable Alison, 8
Johnston, Detective Constable Andrew, 132
Johnston, Constable Ian, 391, 394
Johnston, Kenneth, 338, 339
Johnston, Reserve Constable Thomas, 241
Johnston, Councillor William, 125
Johnston, Ivan, 129, 266
Jones, Lord Justice, 193

Kay, Reserve Constable Michael, 313
Kearns, Liam, 397, 398, 399
Keenan, Brian, 217, 219
Kelley, Sean, 434
Kelly, Charles, 352
Kelly, Woman Constable Ivy, 311
Kelly, John Mario, 192, 193
Kelly, Mr Justice, 199, 201, 278, 288
Kennan, John, 69
Kennedy, Sir Albert, 91, 93, 94, 97, 108, 133
Kennedy, Constable Norman, 357
Kerr, Brian, 412–3
Kerr, Frank, 455
Kettles, Reserve Constable Francis, 143
Keys, Sergeant Henry, 143
Keys, Constable Robert, 125
Kilmallock Barracks, 28
Kilpatrick, Sergeant Peter, 334
Kincora, 301, 302, 303, 304, 305, 306, 307, 308
King, General Sir Frank, 162
King, Tom, 206, 325, 352, 359, 362, 367, 437
Kingsmills massacre, 133
Kirkpatrick, Harry, 295, 296
Knock petty sessions, 231, 355
Koenig, Kurt, 335
Kyle, Reserve Constable Christopher, 253, 257
Kyle, John, 337, 339
Kyle, Keith, 188
Kyle, Percy, 257

Labour Party, Northern Ireland, 96
Lagan, District Inspector Frank, 117, 119

Laird, Constable James, 78
La Mon House, 174, 175, 199
Lamont, Reserve Constable John, 206
Larmour, Constable John, 363
Larne Harbour, 23, 42, 58
Laverty, Constable Robert, 125
Lawson, Lt-Gen. Sir Richard, 240, 265
Lean, Robert, 286, 287
Lemass, Sean, 96
Lenihan, Brian, 234
Leslie, Constable Robert, 122
Lester, Anthony, WC, 357
Levellers, 13
Lewis, Mrs Sandra, 247
Libya, 358
Light Infantry march, 20
Listowel, 28, 31, 32
Local Government (Emergency Powers) Act, 43
Lockhard, Reserve Constable Robert, 220
Logan, Constable William, 124
Logue, Constable Michael, 129
Longstone Road, 82
Loughgall, 339
Loughridge, Dr J. C., 66
Love, Detective Constable David, 133
Lowry, Lord Chief Justice, 201, 204, 214, 216,
    226, 287, 295, 296, 302
Luftwaffe, 75
Lynch, Alexander, 392, 393, 394, 395
Lynch, Constable Kenneth, 173
Lynch, Kevin, 254
Lyons, Special Constable James, 78
Lyttle, Reserve Constable Silas, 256
Lyttle, Special Constable William, 53

Macauley, Constable Ronald, 128
MacCurtain, Thomas, 31, 37
MacDermott, Mr Justice, 151, 155
Macmillan, Woman Sergeant Marion, 80
Macready, General Sir Nevil, 31
McAdam, Detective Constable Ronald, 143
McAdorey, Constable Robert, 201
McAllister, Constable Ernest, 124
McAllister, Constable Millar, 202
McAtamney, Michael, 336, 346, 352
McAteer, Hugh, 79
McAvoy, Seamus, 335
McBride, Constable David, 334
McCabe, Detective Constable Noel, 159
McCabe, Detective Garda Jerry, 459
McCall, Constable Thomas, 131
McCambridge, Constable John, 143
McCandless, Constable Andrew, 334
McCarthy, Constable Patrick, 79
McCaughey, Constable Billy, 203, 204, 205, 206
McCauley, Martin, 345, 347
McClean, Constable Samuel, 343
McClinton, Constable Thomas, 131
McCloy, Constable Allan, 276
McCluskey, Con and Patricia, 102, 103
McConkey, Ex-Sergeant Noel, 3
McConnell, Constable Hugh, 202
McCormac, Sergeant Hugh, 313
McCormick, Charlie, 172, 265, 266, 267, 268,
    269, 292
McCormick, Constable Lindsay, 282

McCreaken, Constable John, 172
McCreery, Ned, 421
McCreesh, Raymond, 253
McCrone, Constable Hugh, 363
McCusker, Harold, MP, 293
McDonald, Sergeant William, 281
McDonnell, Joe, 254
McDougall, Reserve Constable Lindsay, 244
McDowell, Chief Inspector Errol, 311
McElligot, Sergeant Thomas, 28
McElveen, Constable William, 128
McElwee, Tom, 255
McEvoy, Seamus, 431
McFadden, Reserve Constable John, 283
McFerron, Reserve Constable Paul, 311
McGarry, Detective Constable John, 403
McGlinchey, Dominic, 344
McGookin, Woman Constable Rosemary, 311
McGovern, James, 370
McGovern, Kevin, 405
McGrath, William, 302, 303, 304, 305, 306, 308
McGrory, Paddy, 416
McGuinness, Martin, 336, 337, 478
McHenry, Reserve Constable Sean, 311
McKane, Reserve Constable Samuel, 172
McKay, Reserve Constable Arthur, 159
McKeague, John, 307
McKearney, Kevin, 418
McKeever, Superintendent Joseph, 364
McKeever, Terence, 336
McKenna, Finbarr, 338
McKenna, Peter, 301
McKerr, Gervaise, 345, 353
McKeown, Constable Barney, 14
McKeown, Clifford, 287
McKibben, Hugh, 418
McKinney, Edward, 55
McKittrick, David, 380
McLaughlin, Robin, 421
McLaughlin, Terry, 380
McLean, Reserve Constable Robert, 342
McMahon, Owen and family, 55, 61, 64
McMillan, Liam, 99, 100
McMurray, Constable Colleen, 439
McNiece, Constable David, 132
McNulty, Detective Constable Patrick, 172
McPherson, Constable Robert, 132
MrShane, Rory, 376, 381, 382, 383
McVeigh, David, 350, 351
McVitty, Constable John, 334

Madigan, David, 397, 398, 399
Magee, Detective Inspector Kevin, 436
Magee, Father John, 250
Magee, Patrick, 155
Magill, Constable William, 241
Magill, Reserve Constable William, 282
Maginn, Laughlin, 375, 378, 381, 382, 383
Maginnis, Ken, MP, 298, 331, 385, 401, 478
Maguire, Frank, 249
Maguire, Noel, 250
Mains, Joseph, 302
Major, John, 454, 457, 479
Mallon, Daniel, 335
Mallon, Seamus, MP, 379
Malone, Patrick, 133
Malone, Detective Constable Philip, 357

Manchester airport, 134
Manchester bomb, 459
*Manchester Guardian*, 43
Mandelson, Peter 524
marching season, 319
Mark, Robert, 115
Marley, Larry, 341
Marshall, Professor John, 196
Marshall, Constable Michael, 391
Martin, James and Veronica, 394, 395, 396
Martin, Constable Gary, 251
Martin, Reserve Constable Hugh, 173
Martin, Inspector John, 281
Maryfield, 326
Maskey, Alex, 412–3
Mason, Roy, 158, 159, 160, 161, 162, 164, 165, 166, 168, 171, 172, 189, 196
Mates, Michael, 427
Mawhinney, Dr Brian, MP, 297, 437
Maxwell, General Sir John, 25
Maxwell, Sergeant Patrick, 133
Mayhew, Sir Patrick, 421, 431, 438, 445, 466, 478, 479
Maze prison, 147, 151, 155, 173, 179, 206, 211, 234, 235, 236, 239, 248, 250, 255, 261, 265, 280
Mee, Jeremiah, 31
Meehan, Sean, 124
Megaw, Constable Robert, 128
Meharg, Assistant Chief Constable Bill, 305, 306
Meyer, Constable Gary, 402
Metropolitan Police, Dublin, 16, 26
Metropolitan Police, London, 16, 21, 31, 80, 115, 129, 136, 137, 226, 378
Military Police, 117, 124, 127, 141, 157, 208
Millar, Constable Robert, 118
Mitchell Commission, 456, 478
Mitchell, George, 456, 480, 488
Molyneaux, James, MP, 326, 330
Monteith, Inspector Derek, 402
Monteith, Reserve Constable William, 364
Montgomery, Reserve Constable Bernard, 241
Montgomery, Constable David, 124
Montgomery, Constable John, 201
Montgomery, Constable Stephen, 364
Montgomery, Constable Stuart, 255
Mooney, Chief Superintendent Billy, 86, 153
Moore, Chris, 375
Moore, Reserve Constable John, 202
Moore, Constable Thomas, 123
Moore, County Inspector W. S., 63
*Morning Star*, 206
Morrison, Constable Charles, 127
Morrison, Danny, 391, 392, 395, 396
Morrow, Reserve Constable David, 173
Morrow, Sergeant Thomas, 124
Morton, Reserve Constable Frederick, 282
Mounsey, Joe, 233
Mountbatten, Lord, 218, 221
Mulcahy, General Richard, 35
Mullaly, Gabriel, 372
Murphy, Donal, 200
Murphy, Canon High, 9, 202, 203, 205, 273
Murphy, Sergeant John, 310
Murphy, Lenny, 179, 182, 185
Murphy, Michael, 336
Mowlam, Mo 481, 485, 496, 523

Murphy, Inspector David, 403
Murphy, Constable Patrick, 77
Murray, Anton, 395, 397
Murray, Chief Suprintendent Frank, 5, 6
Murray, Mr Justice, 199, 265, 268, 292
Murtagh, Inspector William, 134
Myers, Sir Philip, 346, 347, 348, 350
Myles, Albert, 237

National Council for Civil Liberties, 70
Neave, Alrey, 221
Neilly, Detective Chief Superintendent Maurice, 436
Nelson, Brian, 412–5
Nelson, Reserve Constable Kenneth, 143
Nelson, Rosemary 504–7
Nesbitt, Chief Inspector Jimmy, 178, 179, 180, 183
Nesbitt, Reserve Constable Peter, 340, 342
Nevill, Commander James, 211
New Ireland Forum, 297, 314, 315, 316
Newman, Sir Kenneth, 129, 136, 137, 138, 139,
  140, 141, 142, 143, 144, 145, 148, 149, 150,
  151, 157, 159, 164, 166, 167, 171, 173, 175,
  187, 188, 191, 192, 196, 197, 199, 210, 215,
  222, 223, 224, 225, 226, 229, 232, 240, 365,
  404, 469
Newry mortar attack, 312
*Newsletter*, 50, 53, 62, 125, 160, 321
Newtownards Training Camp, 59, 86, 87
Nicholl, Detective Constable Robert, 125
Nixon, Constable James, 125
Nixon, District Inspector John W., 61, 62, 63, 64
North, Reserve Constable Robert, 172
Northern Ireland Office, 129, 130, 145, 299, 308,
  328, 336, 353, 354
Northern Ireland Works Organisation (NIWO), 431
Nugent, Kieran Plus, 235

O'Brien, Edward, 458
O'Connor, Bernard, 188, 199
O'Connor, Sergeant Daniel, 131
O'Doherty, Anthony, 265, 266, 267, 268, 269,
  292
O'Donnell, Mr Justice, 184
Official Secrets Act, 345, 346, 379
O'Flaich, Cardinal Tomas, 236
O'Grady, Detective Constable Sean, 134
O'Hara, Patsy, 253
O'Kennedy, Michael, 234
Old Barneys, 14
Oldfield, Sir Maurice, 223, 302
Olphert, Reserve Constable John, 282
Omagh bomb 500–1
O'Neill, Constable Bernard, 124
O'Neill, Constable Michael, 201
O'Neill, Captain Terence, 96, 100, 102, 106, 108
Operation Harvest, 90
Operation Hawk, 216, 217, 218, 219, 220
Operation Jigsaw, 153
Operation Knife Edge, 176
Operaton Monarch, 167
Orange Lodges, 43, 59, 61, 71
Orange Marches, 70, 72, 82, 319, 371
Orange Order, 59, 60, 71, 304, 319, 321, 322,
  331
O'Sullivan, Sergeant Tobias, 28
Outdoor Relief, 67, 70
Ovens, Sergeant Arthur, 91, 227

Paisley, Rev. Ian, MP, 99, 100, 101, 102, 104,
  106, 161, 163, 165, 166, 203, 228, 231, 239,
  246, 247, 256, 257, 258, 259, 262, 263, 264,
  274, 298, 300, 320, 325, 326, 327, 330, 464
Paisley, Miss Sylvia, 364
Palace Barracks, Holywood, 110, 187, 287
Panorama, 382
Parachute Regiment, 222, 245
Parnell, Charles Stuart, 21
Pascoe, Lt-Gen. Sir Roebrt, 223, 360
Paterson, Michael, 408, 409
Patten, Chris 490; *see also* Independent Commission on
  Policing in Northern Ireland
Patterson, Detective Inspector Cecil, 121
Patterson, Constable Derek, 334
Peace, Preservation Act 1814, 15
Peace Preservation Force, 15, 16
Peacocke, Anthony, 97, 108, 109, 112, 116
Peel, Sir Robert, 13, 14, 15, 20, 71
Peel, Sir Robert Memorial LOL, 61
Peep O'Day Boys, 13
Peoples Democracy, 106
Petrie, Alan, 200
Philbin, Dr William, 259
Phoenix, Detective Seuperintendent Ian, 436
Phoenix Park, Dublin, 20, 21, 47
photo-flash slave units, 425
pig stick, 424
Pim, Sir Richard, 79, 82, 86, 91, 92, 93, 94
plastic bullets, 270, 271, 272
Plowden, Lord, 354
Police Act 1970, 226, 354
Police Authority, 115, 121, 123, 125, 129, 141,
  142, 143, 193, 200, 226, 273, 298, 328, 336,
  354, 365, 367, 368
*Police Beat*, 3, 355
Police Complaints Board,.199
Police Federation, 1, 121, 123, 139, 140, 172,
  260, 262, 263, 264, 265, 311, 327, 328, 329,
  363, 378, 380
*Police Review*, 127, 136
Pollock, Constable Gregory, 440
Poor Law Guardians, 67
Porter, Robert, QC, 111
Power, Thomas 'Ta', 289, 295
Pravda, 237
Prevention of Terrorism Act, 188, 280, 362
Price, Reserve Constable Denis, 311
Prince of Wales Own Regiment, 112
Prior, James, 255, 258, 259, 265, 297, 298, 299,
  354
Proctor, Reserve Constable John, 255
Projected Recoilless Improvised Grenade (PRIG), 425
Provisional IRA (Provos), 118, 120, 122, 130, 139,
  143, 148, 155, 156, 160, 168, 169, 173, 175,
  176, 185, 207, 212, 214, 217, 218, 219, 222,
  226, 234, 236, 237, 238, 239, 242, 243, 244,
  245, 249, 250, 254, 256, 258, 266, 267, 273,
  277, 278, 279, 284, 286, 293, 296, 298, 314,
  315, 335, 336, 337, 340, 341, 342, 344, 351,
  358
proxy bombs, 426, 430
Prue, Detective Constable Norman, 220
Public Order Act 1951, 82
Public Order Order, 331, 332
Public order, tactics and equipment, 107, 108, 138,
  141, 251, 271, 272
Public Record Office, Belfast, 18, 64, 211

Purse, Reserve Constable William, 241
Purvis, Constable David, 128

Q Cars, 97
Quality Street Gang, 377
Queen's Own Highlanders, 222, 323
Queen's University, 106, 276, 281
Quinn, Reserve Constable Bernard, 282
Quinn, Sergeant John, 276
Quinn, Constable Neal, 253
Quinn, Paddy, 254

racketeering, 126, 140, 146, 215
Radcliffe, Major-General Sir Percy, 40
Rafferty, James, 199, 200, 201, 202
Rainey, Tom, 367
Ramsey,Cathal, 368
Rankin, Reserve Constable Jacob, 206
Rees, Merlyn, 130, 142, 144, 145, 153, 158, 160,
   167, 222, 229, 235
Reeves, Detective Constable David, 276
Regan, County Inspector John, 18, 19, 49, 79
Reid, Constable John, 440
*Republican News*, 143, 211, 260, 287, 391, 398
Republican Police, 35
Republican Press Centre, 210, 397
Reserve RUC, 115, 119, 124, 141, 246, 249, 257,
   356, 357
Reserve force, RUC, 91, 95, 107
Restoration of Order in Ireland Act, 31
Ribbonmen, 13
RIC (Royal Irish Constabulary), 12, 16, 17, 18, 19,
   21, 26, 27, 28, 29, 32, 35, 36, 38, 39, 40, 42,
   43, 44, 45, 46, 47, 48, 49, 52, 54, 56, 60, 62,
   84, 85, 336
Rightboys, 13
Robertson, Sir James, 115
Robinson, Sergeant Frederick, 131
Robinson, Constable Lovis, 403
Robinson, Constable Mervyn, 253
Robinson, Peter, MP, 330
Rodgers, Reserve Constable John, 131
Rodgers, Reserve Constable Stephen, 313
Rodgers, Les, 446, 484, 511
Rolston, Detective Constable George, 128
Rose, Constable Joseph, 241
Ross, Constable Henry, 91
Ross, Constable John, 131
Royal Air Force, 75, 113, 146, 169, 170, 240,
   337, 361
Royal Corps of Signals, 361
Royal Engineers, 162, 336
Royal Horse Artillery, 207
Royal Irish Constabulary *see* RIC
Royal Irish Rangers, 386
Royal Irish Regiment, 386
Royal Marine Commandos, 170, 382
Royal Military Police, 378
Royal Scots Dragoon Guards,240
Royal Ulster Constabulary, and band, 276; boats,
   97; books of remembrance, 224; budget, 368;
   Catholics, 83, 84, 115, 368, 476; code of
   conduct, 371; ceasefire, 444; detection rate, 97,
   126; dogs, 81, 94; establishment, 97, 99, 131,
   141; force strength, 453; name, 477–8; pay, 96,
   447, 450–1; punishment shootings, 214; radio,

81, 97, 99; ranks, 119; recruiting, 9, 81, 85,
   127, 141; reorganization, 98, 298, 452; service
   medal, 273; suicides, 448–9; tear gas, 111, 112,
   113; uniform, 96, 115, 119, 353, 477; United
   States, 206–9; water-canon, 82, 110; Widows
   Association, 335; women police, 80, 132, 476
Royal Victoria Hospital, 4, 143
Royal Welsh Fusiliers, 162
rubber bullets, 270
Russell, Detective Constable William, 123
Ryan, Constable John, 69

S Plan, 73
St Anne's Cathedral, Belfast, 1, 273
Sampson, Colin, 276, 348, 349, 350, 351, 352,
   377
Sandford, Reserve Constable Henry, 127
Sands, Bobby, 248, 249, 250, 251, 256
Saor Uladh, 90
SAS *see* Special Air Service
Scally, Constable John, 90, 91
Scarman, Lord, 114, 116
Scotland Yard, 108, 115, 117, 121, 136, 138,
   148, 150, 211, 217, 271, 279, 365, 366, 367,
   373
Scots Guards, 169
Scott, Reserve Constable Alexander, 247
Scott, Reserve Constable John, 220
Scott, Reserve Constable Joseph, 160
Scott, Nicholas, 255, 341
Semtex, 358, 361
Seymour, Constable Jim, 2
Shankill Butchers, 176, 178, 180, 181, 182, 183
Shaw, Sir Barry, 345
Shaw, Reserve Constable George, 342
Shaw, Miss Valerie, 304, 305
Shea, Paddy, 29, 32
Sheehan, Constable Kenneth, 172
Sherwood, Superintendent Lawrence, 377
Shields, Diarmuid and Patrick, 434
Shillington, Sir Graham, 111, 112, 120, 121, 126,
   127, 128, 129, 365
'Shoot to kill', 345, 347
Simons, Eugene, 241, 242, 244
Simpson, Constable Charles, 202
Sinn Fein, 24, 26, 28, 30, 31, 33, 38, 51, 210,
   211, 213, 273, 351
Smith, Andrew, 381
Smith, Constable Lawrence, 334
Smith, Ranger Cyril, 426
Smyth, Lt-Col. Gerald, 31, 37
Smyth, Constable John, 255
Smyth, Martin, 304
Solly-Flood, Major General Arthur, 57, 58, 59
Soloheadbeg, 26, 28, 29
Somme, The, 24
Soper, Dr Donald, 302
Spears, District Inspector R. R., 51
Special Air Service (SAS), 215, 216, 217, 218,
   339, 344, 346, 360, 376
Special Branch, 21, 36, 73, 117, 121, 129, 131,
   150, 162, 268, 197, 215, 217, 230, 232, 238,
   243, 244, 265, 266, 267, 268, 269, 277, 294,
   346, 349, 351, 352, 384
Special Constabulary (*see also* A, B and C Specials),
   40, 42, 43, 48, 52, 54, 55, 57, 58, 59, 60, 65,

69, 75
Special Investigation Branch (Army), 127
Special Irish Branch, 21
Special Petrol Group, 152, 232, 243
Special Powers Act, 57, 58, 68, 70, 117, 162
Special Support Unit, 215, 344
Spence, Constable Edward, 403
Spender, Sir Wilfred, 39, 69
Spring, Dick, 316
Sprucefield, RUC stores, 50, 324
Staines, Michael, 35
Stalker, John, 276, 344, 345, 346, 347, 348, 349,
   350, 351, 352, 353, 371, 377, 390
Stanley, John, 361
Starrett, Constable George, 402
Sterritt, Constable David, 402
Stevens, John, 377, 378, 379, 380, 381, 383, 384,
   385, 386, 387, 388, 389, 390, 404
Stevenson, James, 47
Stewart, Chief Superintendent Bill, 311
Stewart, Constable George, 256
Stone, Michael, 360, 361
Storey, Bobby, 277, 278, 279, 280, 281
Stormont Castle, 41, 162, 164, 165, 190, 236,
   241, 250, 275, 324, 328, 367, 373, 376
Stormont, 72, 76, 81, 82, 93, 96, 97, 99, 100,
   101, 115, 116, 117, 123, 127, 129, 161, 274,
   297, 326
Stormont House, 229
Strathearn, William, 204
Stronge, Sir Norman and James, 245, 246
Struthers, Reserve Constable Robert, 202
Superintendents Association, 378
*Sun, The*, 379
supergrass, 262, 284, 292, 294, 295, 296, 297
Swanzy, District Inspector Oswald, 31, 37

Tara, 303, 305
Tasking and Co-ordination Group, 345
Taylor, Bill, 471
Taylor, Kevin, 349
Taylor, Reserve Constable Thomas, 403
'Teeth in apple case', 175
Terry, Sir George, 307, 308
Thatcher, Margaret, 222, 234, 236, 239, 249,
   316, 352, 360
Third Force, 130, 246, 257, 258, 259, 263
Thompson, Detective Constable Joe, 134
Thompson, Constable Kevin, 220
Thrashers, 13
Tighe, Michael, 345, 347
*Times, The*, 21, 171, 329
Todd, Constable Michael, 309
Todd, Constable Samuel, 403
Toman, Eugene, 345, 346, 353
'Tonight', TV programme, 188
Topping, Constable David, 311
Torney, John, 448
Traffic Branch, 72, 80, 97
Trainor, Patrick, 242
Trim, 32
Trimble, David, 463, 477
Tunnel, The, 321, 322, 330, 331
Turbitt, Mrs Margaret, 203
Turbitt, Constable William, 202, 203
TUAS ('Total Unarmed Strategy'), 459

Turner, Private Paul, 418
'TV Eye', 193
Twaddell, W. J., 58
Twomey, Seamus, 210
Tynan Abbey, 247
Tyrie, Andy, 161, 163, 164

Ulster Defence Association (UDA), 126, 153, 161,
   163, 164, 165, 166, 180, 181, 191, 193, 375,
   376, 387, 389, 390
Ulster Defence Regiment (UDR), 141, 166, 238,
   240, 246, 249, 257, 267, 281, 298, 339, 351,
   360, 379, 381, 383, 384, 384, 386, 387
Ulster Division 36th, 24, 49
Ulster Freedom Fighters, 203, 284, 337, 375
Ulster Hall, 100
Ulster Protestant Association, 51
Ulster Special Constabulary, 37
Ulster Unionist Council, 22, 23, 41
Ulster Workers' Council, 130, 133, 161, 162, 326
Ulster Volunteer Force (UVF), 23, 24, 36, 37, 39,
   42, 67, 92, 101, 102, 119, 122, 151, 152, 153,
   155, 161, 176, 179, 180, 183, 185, 195, 284,
   287, 290, 291, 341
Ulsterization, 140, 239, 240, 273
Unionist Party, 22, 274
*United Irishman, The*, 24, 265
United Unionist Action Council, 160, 161, 162
Unity Flats, 110

Valente, Peter, 212, 212
Vallely, Constable Samuel, 253
Vance, Inspector Patrick, 314
Victoria, Queen, 16
Vietnam, 11, 137
*Voices and the Sound of Drums*, 29
Volunteers, Irish, 24, 25

Walker, Cecil, MP, 332, 393
Wallace, Deputy Chief Constable Blair, 450, 457,
   471
Walsh, Constable George, 220
Wallace, Colin, 304
Warnock, Detective Constable John, 363
Wasson, Constable John, 283
Waters, Lt-Gen. Sir John, 360, 362
Webb, Constable Noel, 220
'Weekend World' TV programme, 197
Weir, Sergeant John, 203, 204, 205
West, Harry, 102, 250
Wethers, Constable Wilfred, 403
White, Harry, 83
White, Sergeant Michael, 309
Whiteboys, 13, 14
Whitelaw, William, 123, 127, 236
Whiteside, John, 223
Wickham, Sir Charles, 40, 43, 47, 48, 59, 60, 61,
   63, 68, 71, 72, 74, 76, 79
Williams, Reserve Constable Michael, 334
Williams, Tom, 77
Williamson, Reggie, 440
Willis, Constable Joshua, 402
Wilsey, Lieutenant-General Sir John, 426, 431
Wilson, Detective Chief Inspector Austin, 342
Wilson, Constable Cyril, 131
Wilson, Reserve Constable Frederick, 241

Wilson, Harold, 99, 102
Wilson, Field-Marshall Sir Henry, 23, 34, 40, 42, 57, 58
Wilson, Constable Mercyn, 127
Wilson, Inspector William, 313
Wilson, Sergeant William, 282
Wolfe Tone, 20
Wolsely, Harold, 113, 116
Woods, Constable Andrew, 255
Woods, Constable Brian, 440

Worthing-Evans, Laming, 34
Wray, Reserve Constable David, 220
Wrenn, Larry, 370
Wright, Alan, 172, 262, 263, 264, 327, 328, 354, 355, 363, 409
Wyllie, Constable William, 128

York, Duke and Duchess of, 1
Yorkshire Ripper, 378
Young, Sir Arthur, 116, 117, 119, 120

Also available from Arrow

# THE TROUBLES

## Tim Pat Coogan

Ireland's Ordeal 1966–1995 and the Search for Peace.

Tim Pat Coogan is one of the few journalists and writers who actually influences political events as well as writing about them. His study of *The IRA* and his biographies of *Michael Collins* and *De Valera* are all highly controversial and definitive. This is his most important book to date; a study of the Troubles in Ireland from 1966 to the present day and beyond. He is in a unique position to write it as the most authoritative observer of the nationalist cause, with strong political contacts on both sides of the border.

The history of what Tim Pat Coogan persuasively argues is the unfinished business in the North is in fact a much broader and deeper conflict, involving politics in Britain, Ireland and America, intractable constitutional issues, and two cultures dating back to the sixteenth century and beyond. It is the story of two conflicts, one secret, the other overt. The violence is but one aspect, although a key one. Using never before published information, Tim Pat Coogan leads us through a complex and often devious story and assesses realistically and with inside knowledge the new possibilities for a lasting peace in Ireland.

# THE GUNPOWDER PLOT

## Antonia Fraser

## BESTSELLERS FROM ARROW

| | | | |
|---|---|---|---|
| ☐ | The Six Wives of Henry VIII | Antonia Fraser | £10.00 |
| ☐ | Mary Queen of Scots | Antonia Fraser | £10.00 |
| ☐ | The Weaker Vessel | Antonia Fraser | £10.00 |
| ☐ | King Charles II | Antonia Fraser | £10.00 |
| ☐ | Cromwell: Our Chief of Men | Antonia Fraser | £12.99 |
| ☐ | The Warrior Queens | Antonia Fraser | £8.99 |
| ☐ | The Troubles | Tim Pat Coogan | £10.00 |
| ☐ | Michael Collins | Tim Pat Coogan | £10.00 |
| ☐ | De Valera | Tim Pat Coogan | £10.00 |
| ☐ | The Conservative Party from Peel to Major | | |
| | | Robert Blake | £10.00 |

Prices and other details are liable to change

---

ALL ARROW BOOKS ARE AVAILABLE THROUGH MAIL ORDER OR FROM YOUR LOCAL BOOKSHOP AND NEWSAGENT.

PLEASE SEND CHEQUE/EUROCHEQUE/POSTAL ORDER (STERLING ONLY) ACCESS, VISA, MASTERCARD, DINERS CARD, SWITCH OR AMEX.

| | | | | | | | | | | | | | | | | |
|---|---|---|---|---|---|---|---|---|---|---|---|---|---|---|---|---|

EXPIRY DATE ................ SIGNATURE ...........................................

PLEASE ALLOW 75 PENCE PER BOOK FOR POST AND PACKING U.K.

OVERSEAS CUSTOMERS PLEASE ALLOW £1.00 PER COPY FOR POST AND PACKING.

ALL ORDERS TO:

ARROW BOOKS, BOOKS BY POST, TBS LIMITED, THE BOOK SERVICE, COLCHESTER ROAD, FRATING GREEN, COLCHESTER, ESSEX CO7 7DW.

TELEPHONE: (01206) 256 000
FAX:      (01206) 255 914

NAME.........................................................................................

ADDRESS...................................................................................

..............................................................................................

Please allow 28 days for delivery. Please tick box if you do not wish to receive any additional information ☐

Prices and availability subject to change without notice.